A UNIFORM SYSTEM FOR ARCHITECTURAL WORKING DRAWING ABBREVIATIONS

SYMBOLS USED AS ABBREVIATIONS:

L	angle
ℂ	centerline
C	channel
d	penny
⊥	perpendicular
PL	plate
φ	round

ABBREVIATIONS:

ABV	above
AFF	above finished floor
ASC	above suspended ceiling
ACC	access
ACFL	access floor
AP	access panel
AC	acoustical
ACPL	acoustical plaster
ACT	acoustical tile
ACR	acrylic plastic
ADD	addendum
ADH	adhesive
ADJ	adjacent
ADJT	adjustable
AGG	aggregate
A/C	air conditioning
ALT	alternate
AL	aluminum
ANC	anchor, anchorage
AB	anchor bolt
ANOD	anodized
APX	approximate
ARCH	architect (ural)
AD	area drain
ASB	asbestos
ASPH	asphalt
AT	asphalt tile
AUTO	automatic
BP	back plaster (ed)
BSMT	basement
BRG	bearing
BPL	bearing plate
BJT	bed joint
BM	bench mark
BEL	below
BET	between
BVL	beveled
BIT	bituminous
BLK	block
BLKG	blocking
BD	board
BS	both sides
BW	both ways
BOT	bottom
BRK	brick
BRZ	bronze
BLDG	building

BUR	built up roofing
BBD	bulletin board
CAB	cabinet
CAD	cadmium
CPT	carpet (ed)
CSMT	casement
CI	cast iron
CIPC	cast-in-place concrete
CST	cast stone
CB	catch basin
CK	calk (ing) caulk (ing)
CLG	ceiling
CHT	ceiling height
CEM	cement
PCPL	cement plaster (portland)
CM	centimeter(s)
CER	ceramic
CT	ceramic tile
CMT	ceramic mosaic (tile)
CHBD	chalkboard
CHAM	chamfer
CR	chromium (plated)
CIR	circle
CIRC	circumference
CLR	clear (ance)
CLS	closure
COL	column
COMB	combination
COMPT	compartment
COMPO	composition (composite)
COMP	compress (ed), (ion), (ible)
CONC	concrete
CMU	concrete masonry unit
CX	connection
CONST	construction
CONT	continuous or continue
CONTR	contract (or)
CLL	contract limit line
CJT	control joint
CPR	copper
CG	corner guard
CORR	corrugated
CTR	counter
CFL	counterflashing
CS	countersink
CTSK	countersunk screw
CRS	course (s)
CRG	cross grain
CFT	cubic foot
CYD	cubic yard
DPR	damper
DP	dampproofing
DL	dead load
DEM	demolish, demolition
DMT	demountable
DEP	depressed
DTL	detail
DIAG	diagonal

DIAM	diameter
DIM	dimension
DPR	dispenser
DIV	division
DR	door
DA	doubleacting
DH	double hung
DTA	dovetail anchor
DTS	dovetail anchor slot
DS	downspout
D	drain
DRB	drainboard
DT	drain tile
DWR	drawer
DWG	drawing
DF	drinking fountain
DW	dumbwaiter
EF	each face
E	east
ELEC	electric (al)
EP	electrical panelboard
EWC	electric water cooler
EL	elevation
ELEV	elevator
EMER	emergency
ENC	enclose (ure)
EQ	equal
EQP	equipment
ESC	escalator
EST	estimate
EXCA	excavate
EXH	exhaust
EXG	existing
EXMP	expanded metal plate
EB	expansion bolt
EXP	exposed
EXT	exterior
EXS	extra strong
FB	face brick
FOC	face of concrete
FOF	face of finish
FOM	face of masonry
FOS	face of studs
FF	factory finish
FAS	fasten, fastener
FN	fence
FBD	fiberboard
FGL	fiberglass
FIN	finish (ed)
FFE	finished floor elevation
FFL	finished floor line
FA	fire alarm
FBRK	fire brick
FE	fire extinguisher
FEC	fire extinguisher cabinet
FHS	fire hose station
FPL	fireplace
FP	fireproof

THE PROFESSIONAL HANDBOOK
OF ARCHITECTURAL
WORKING DRAWINGS

THE PROFESSIONAL HANDBOOK OF ARCHITECTURAL WORKING DRAWINGS

Dr. Osamu A. Wakita
Professor of Architecture, Los Angeles Harbor College

Richard M. Linde
A.I.A. Architect, Richard Linde & Associates, Inc.

JOHN WILEY & SONS   New York   Chichester   Brisbane   Toronto   Singapore

Library of Congress Cataloging in Publication Data:

Wakita, Osamu, 1931-
    The professional handbook of architectural working
drawings.

    Includes index.
    1. Architecture—Working drawings.   I. Linde,
Richard M.   II. Title.
NA2713.W338 1984   720'.28'4   83-23291
ISBN 0-471-88575-4

Printed in the United States of America

10 9 8 7 6

Copyright credit list continued on page 522

PREFACE

This book is designed to present attitudes, skills, and the fundamental concepts of architectural drafting to persons who will benefit from this knowledge in their professional practice. Beyond skills and concepts, the authors hope to communicate to readers an understanding of state-of-the-art architectural drafting as a means of graphic communication. The professional architect or draftsperson needs a clear and fluent command of the language of architectural drafting.

The Professional Handbook of Architectural Working Drawings is divided into three parts. Chapters 1 to 5 are designed to build what we have called "professional foundations" and provide basic information about drafting equipment, office procedures, and fundamental skills in addition to an understanding of the evolution of construction documents and methods of construction. Chapters 6 to 14 bridge the gap between theory and practice. These chapters demonstrate the preparation of site plans, foundation plans, floor plans, elevations, building sections, and other drawings. Throughout this section the ability to communicate general design concepts through specific working drawings is emphasized and reinforced. Chapters 15 to 18 present case studies that show the evolution of working drawings from the design concept through the finished construction documents for four different buildings: a beach house, a mountain cabin, a theatre, and an office complex. The four buildings make use of different building materials and systems. Simple wood, heavy timber, masonry, and steel and wood are the materials displayed in these case studies.

Regional differences, as they affect construction methods, are one of the most difficult subjects to address. We conducted a national survey to illustrate the diverse problems faced by different regions. The results of this survey are carefully summarized and included in this book. The case studies were also selected to show extreme conditions such as wind, rain, earthquake, and snow.

Appropriately, the illustration program in this book is its outstanding feature. Over 700 illustrations including photographs were created specifically for the book by its authors.

We would like to acknowledge the contributions of several people to this book—two in particular. **Marilyn Smith**, coordinator and administrative assistant, was responsible for all phases including manuscript preparation, correspondence, and reproduction to mention just a few. Her participation was invaluable. **Louis Toledo** was coordinator of all of the drafting phases of the book, including most freehand lettering and the establishment of the various stages of drawings as developed in the case studies. His supervision proved to be a major asset.

We also thank Vince Toyama for his participation in the drafting of the office building, the condominium project, and all freehand details and freehand sketches. Gregory Haddon, along with developing the drawings for the beach house, was responsible for all corrections and additions to the various drawings. He was also instrumental in the conceptual development of many of the sequential lessons. Nancy Wakita was responsible for much of the detailed and tedious coordination of reviews, checking drawings, indexing, and typing. We are grateful for her spiritual support as well. Mark Wakita's major responsibility was organizing the research questionnaire. Also among his duties was the organization of the reproduction drawings. William Boggs was responsible for scheduling and the aerial photography of the major structures in the book. Judy Joseph, our editor at Wiley, helped bring the book from proposal to reality. We are grateful for her professional attitudes and approach. We thank Jill Mellick for her excellent editing of the original and final manuscripts and Georgia Linde for her assistance in proofreading the manuscript at various stages.

Osamu A. Wakita
Richard M. Linde

CONTENTS

CHAPTER 17
CONCEPTUAL DESIGN AND CONSTRUCTION DOCUMENTS FOR A STEEL AND MASONRY BUILDING—THEATRE   355

CHAPTER 18
CONCEPTUAL DESIGN AND CONSTRUCTION DOCUMENTS FOR AN OFFICE PARK   415

1

BASIC DRAFTING
REQUIREMENTS

Kinds of Drafting Equipment

Basic Equipment

The drafting tools needed by a beginning draftsperson and the basic uses of those tools are shown in Figure 1.1 and are as follows:

1. **T-square.** A straight edge used to draft horizontal lines and a base for the use of triangles.
2. **Triangle.** A three-sided guide used to draft vertical lines and angular lines in conjunction with a T-square. The 30°/60° and 45° triangles are basic equipment.
3. **Erasing shield.** A metal or plastic card with pre-punched slots and holes used to protect some portions of a drawing while erasing others.
4. **Eraser.** A rubber or synthetic material used to erase errors and correct drawings.
5. **Scale.** A measuring device calibrated in a variety of scales for ease of translating large objects into a small proportional drawing.
6. **Drafting tape.** Tape used to hold paper while drafting.
7. **Drafting pencil and lead holders.** Housing for drafting leads.
8. **Lead pointer.** A device used to sharpen the lead in a lead holder.
9. **Divider.** A device resembling a compass, used mainly for transferring measurements from one location to another.
10. **Compass.** A V-shaped device for drafting arcs and circles.
11. **French curve.** A pattern used to draft irregular arcs.
12. **Circle template.** A prepunched sheet of plastic punched in various sizes, for use as a pattern for circles without using a compass.
13. **Plan template.** Prepunched patterns for shapes commonly found in architectural plans.
14. **Dusting brush.** A brush used to keep drafting surfaces clean and free of debris.

Additional Equipment

In addition to the tools listed above, a number of others aid and simplify the drafting process. They are shown in Figure 1.2.

1. **Track drafter.** A device that allows the drafting pencil to rest against the blade of the scale, and be held stationary while the whole track drafter is moved to draw (track) a line. Look at the track on the left side of the drafting table in Figure 1.2.
2. **Adjustable triangle.** A triangle used to draft odd angles such as those found in the pitch (slope) of a roof.
3. **Triangles of various sizes.** Triangles range in size from extremely small ones, used for detailing or lettering, to very large ones, used for dimension lines, perspectives, and so on.
4. **Lettering guide.** A device used for drafting guidelines of varying heights.
5. **Flat scales.** The scales shown in Figure 1.2 are smaller than those shown in Figure 1.1 and are flat. They provide greater ease of handling, but they do not have as many different scales.
6. **Specialty templates.** Specialty templates include furniture, trees, electrical and mechanical equipment, geometric shapes, and standard symbols.

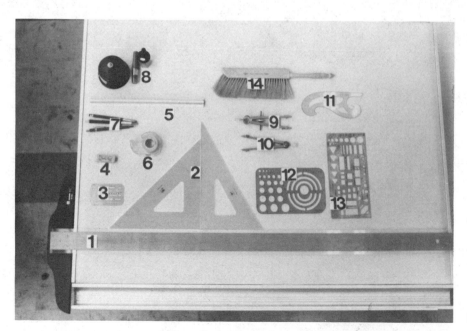

Figure 1.1 Basic drafting equipment.

7. **Proportional dividers.** Dividers used to enlarge or reduce a drawing to any proportion.

8. **Electric eraser.** Particularly useful when you are working with erasable sepias or ink.

9. **Parallel straightedge.** Shown in Figure 1.3, this device is often preferred over a T-square, because it always remains horizontal without the user's constantly checking for alignment. This straightedge runs along cords on both sides, which are mounted on the top or the underside of the drafting board. Parallel straightedges are available in lengths up to 72 inches.

10. **Drafting machine.** Shown in Figure 1.4, this machine uses a pair of scales attached on an arm. These scales move in a parallel fashion so parallel horizontal and vertical lines can be drawn. A protractor mechanism allows the drafter to rapidly move the scales to any desired angle. The drafting machine can be mounted onto a drafting board as shown in the illustration or on a drafting desk.

This list is by no means complete. Your selection of tools will be dictated by office standards and the requirements of particular projects.

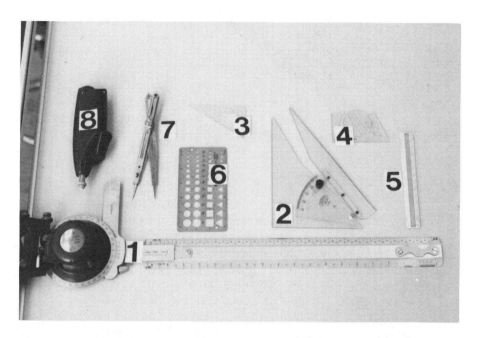

Figure 1.2 Additional drafting equipment.

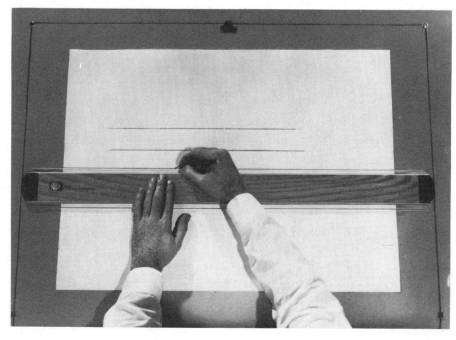

Figure 1.3 Parallel straightedge. (Courtesy of Kratos/Keuffel & Esser.)

Figure 1.4 Drafting machine. (Courtesy of Kratos/Keuffel & Esser.)

Using Drafting Equipment

Using the T-square

To use a T-square properly, you must have a true straight-edge along which to guide the T-square head. As you guide the head against the edge, keep pressure between the edge and the head of the T-square. See Figure 1.5. Notice that the right-handed person keeps pressure against the blade portion while drawing horizontal lines. See Figure 1.6. Never use the T-square on a drafting board in a vertical direction because the board may not be absolutely square or the head of the T-square may not be at a 90° angle with the blade portion; in these instances you will create a line that is not perpendicular with the horizontal line. Even if the T-square is off, say 2 degrees, it will still produce parallel horizontal lines.

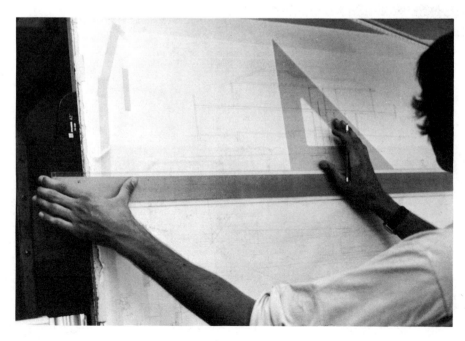

Figure 1.5 T-square and triangle.

Figure 1.6 Drawing with a T-square.

Using the Triangle

The triangle is used in conjunction with the T-square to draft vertical lines and angular lines. See Figures 1.7 and 1.8. In both photographs, note how the draftsperson holds down the T-square firmly with the left palm, and holds the triangles tight against the T-square with the fingers of the left hand, allowing freedom to draw the line with the right hand. You can use the 45° and the 30°/60° triangles in tandem with each other to obtain additional angles as shown in Figures 1.9 and 1.10. Used correctly, triangles enable you to draw lines every 15°. Figure 1.9 shows how a 45° triangle is placed on a 30° triangle to achieve a 75° angle. A 30° triangle can also be placed on a 45° triangle to achieve the same result.

In Figure 1.10, a 45° triangle is used as a base, and correct placement of a 30°/60° triangle gives a 15° angle. To draw these angles in the opposite direction, simply flip both triangles over together.

Drawing Parallel Lines. To draw parallel lines, look at Figure 1.11 and follow these directions:

Figure 1.7 Correct use of a triangle for drawing 90° angles.

Figure 1.8 Using a triangle to draw an angle.

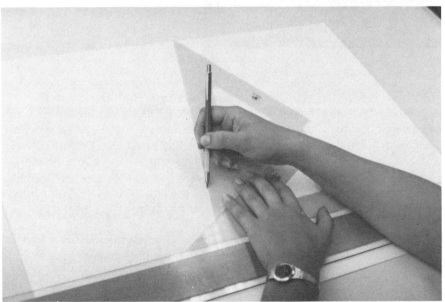

Figure 1.9 Combining triangles to produce a 75° angle.

Figure 1.10 Combining triangles to produce a 15° angle.

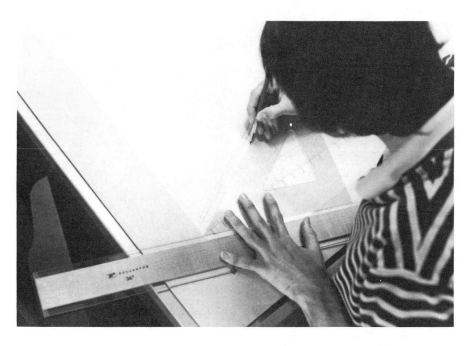

Figure 1.11 Drawing parallel lines on an angle.

1. Place one of the triangles on top of a T-square (30° works well).
2. Move the triangle and the T-square together until they line up with the existing line.
3. Holding the T-square with one hand, slide the triangle away from the existing line.
4. As the triangle is moved, draw the parallel lines.
5. The procedure can also be done with two triangles.

Drawing Perpendicular Lines. The procedure for drawing perpendicular lines is illustrated in Figure 1.12 and is similar to the procedure for drawing parallel lines. However, after the triangle surface is aligned with the line, the triangle must be rotated clockwise, so that the 60° surface is against the T-square.

Using Erasing Shields and Erasers

Drawing Dotted Lines. Dotted lines, which are usually called **hidden lines** in drafting, can be drawn rapidly by using an erasing shield and an eraser. An electric eraser is more effective than a regular eraser.

First draw the lines as if it were a solid line, using the correct pressure to produce the desired darkness. Second, lay the erasing shield over the line so that the row of uniformly drilled holes on the shield aligns with the solid line. Next, erase through the small holes. The results will be a uniform and rapidly produced hidden (dotted) line.

This technique is particularly effective for foundation plans, which use many hidden lines. See Figure 1.13.

Using the Scale

The Triangle Scale. The most convenient scale to purchase is a triangular scale because it gives the greatest variety in one single instrument. There are usually 11 scales on a triangle scale, one of which is an ordinary 12-inch ruler. See Figure 1.14.

Reading the Scale. Since structures cannot be drawn full scale, the 12-inch ruler which is full scale is seldom used. Reading a scale is much the same as reading a regular ruler. Translating a full-size object into a reduced scale—1½ scale for example—is more a matter of your visual attitude than of translating from one scale to another. For example, you can simply imagine a 12-inch ruler reduced to 1½ inches in size and used to measure at this reduced scale. The scale is written on a drawing as 1½" = 1'–0". See Figure 1.15.

On an architectural scale, inches are measured to the left of the zero. Numbers are often printed here to indicate the inches to be measured. Note the 1½ standing by itself on the extreme left. The number explains the scale.

All 3 sides of the triangle scale (except the side with the 12-inch scale) have 2 scales on each usable surface. Each of these 2 scales uses the full length of the instrument, but one is read from left to right and the other from right to left. Typically, a scale is either one half or double the scale it is paired with. For example, if one end is a ¼-inch scale, the opposite end is a ⅛-inch scale; if one end is a ⅜-inch scale, the opposite end is a ¾-inch scale. The opposite end of the 3-inch scale would be the 1½-inch scale.

Figure 1.12 Drawing perpendicular lines.

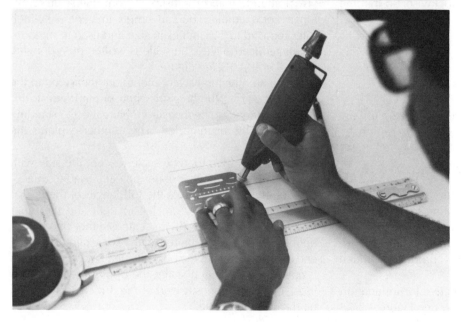

Figure 1.13 Drawing a dotted (hidden) line.

8

Figure 1.14 The triangle scale.

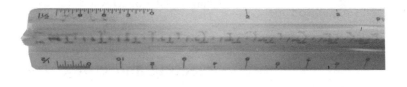

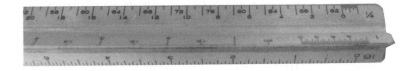

Figure 1.15 Reading the scale.

Confusion is often caused by the numbers between the two scales. Look carefully at these numbers and notice two sets. One set is closer to the groove that runs the length of the scale and the other is closer to the outside edge. The numbers near the edge will be the feet increments for the smaller scale, and the other numbers will be the feet increments for the larger scale. In Figure 1.15A, notice a lower and a higher 2. The upper, right-hand 2 is 2 feet on the 1½-inch scale, and the lower, left-hand 2 is the number of feet from 0 on the opposite side, which is the 3-inch scale and not seen in the photograph. Since the lower 2 falls halfway between the 0 and the upper 2, in this example, it is read as 1 on the 1½-inch scale. Starting from the opposite direction, the upper 2 is read as 1½ feet since it is found halfway between the 1 and 2, of the 3-inch scale.

Figure 1.15B shows a ¼-inch scale. Notice, again, the two sets of numbers. Since the opposite end (not

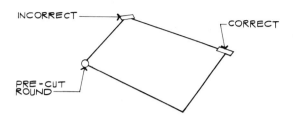

Figure 1.16 Correct placement of drafting tape.

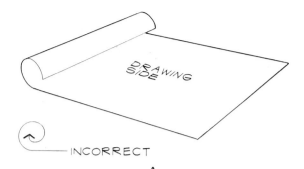

Figure 1.17A Incorrect way to roll a drawing.

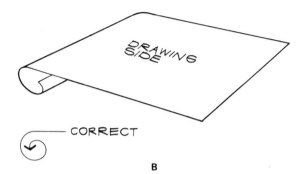

Figure 1.17B Correct way to roll a drawing.

shown) contains the ⅛-inch scale, the lower numbers belong to the ¼-inch side. Notice that they are read 0, 2, 4, 6, 8, etc. In between are numbers that read (from right to left) 92, 88, 84, 80, etc. These numbers belong to the ⅛-inch scale on the opposite side.

An easy error to make is to read the wrong number because the "32" on the ⅛-inch scale is so close to the "32" on the ¼-inch scale. Similar pitfalls occur in other pairs of scales on the triangle scale.

Most engineering scales use the same principles as architectural scales, except that measurements are divided into tenths, twentieths, and so on, rather than halves, quarters, and eighths. The section on metrics explains these metric scales further.

Using Drafting Tape

A simple but effective method of taping original drawings is to keep the edges of the tape parallel with the edges of the vellum (a translucent high quality tracing paper), as shown in Figure 1.16. This prevents the T-square or whatever type of straightedge is used from catching the corner of the tape and rolling it off. Vellum taped at an angle creates unnecessary frustrations for the beginning draftsperson. Drafting supply stores sell tape in a round shape (large dot), which is even better.

Rolling Original Drawings

Most beginners begin rolling drawings in the wrong direction. In their attempt to protect the drawings, they often roll the print or the original so that the printed side is on the *inside*, as shown in Figure 1.17A. However, the correct way is to roll the sheet so that the artwork is on the *outside*, as shown in Figure 1.17B.

When a set of prints is unrolled and read, the drawings should roll toward the table and should not interfere with easy reading by curling up. If originals are rolled correctly, the vellum curls toward the drafting table or blueprint machine, preventing it from being torn when drafting equipment slides across it or when it is being reproduced.

Selecting and Using Drafting Pencils

Types of Leads

Seventeen grades of leads are available, but only a few of these are appropriate for drafting. Harder leads are given an **"H"** designation, while soft leads are given a designation of **"B"**. Between the "H" and "B" range are **"HB"** and **"F"** leads. The softest "B" lead is 6B (number 6) while the hardest "H" head is 9H (number 9). See Figure 1.18.

Selection Factors. Only the central range of leads is used for drafting. 2H, 3H, and 4H are good for light layout, while H is good for a medium weight line. F leads are excellent for dark object lines.

However, many other factors also determine the choice of pencil. Temperature and humidity may dictate that certain leads be used. Manufacturers vary in what they designate as a particular grade. And the natural pressure that the drafter places on the pencil varies from individual to individual. The reproduction method to be used also determines the grade of lead chosen.

For photography, a crisp line is better than a dark one because a dark, broad line may end up as a blur on the negative. Diazo prints (blue or black lines on a white background) need to block out light, and so a dense line is more important.

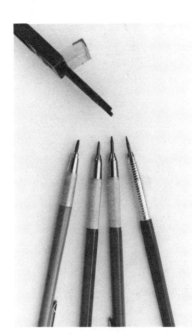

Figure 1.18 Lead hardnesses.

WOOD
PENCILS

MECHANICAL
LEAD HOLDERS

Figure 1.19 Types of lead holders and pencils.

SUPERTHIN
(FINE LINE)
LEAD HOLDERS

Pencils Versus Lead Holders

Wood pencils are fine for the beginner, but serious drafting requires mechanical lead holders. See Figure 1.19. Wood pencils require sharpening of both the wood and the lead, which is time consuming. More important, a lead holder allows you the full use of the lead, whereas a wood pencil cannot.

Lead Pointers

A lead pointer, a tool used to sharpen drafting leads, is a must. Sandpaper can be used for both wood pencils and lead holders, but it is not nearly as convenient, consistent, or rapid as a lead pointer. A good practice after using a lead pointer is as follows: take the sharpened lead and hold the pointer perpendicular to a hard surface such as a triangle; crush the tip of the lead slightly; then hone the tip by drawing a series of circular lines on a piece of scratch paper. You can also use this process with a wood pencil. This stops the lead from breaking on the first stroke. Roll the pencil as you draw to keep a consistent tip on the lead. See Figure 1.20. Draw either clockwise or counterclockwise, depending on whichever produces the best line and is the most comfortable for you. Note the position of the fingers and thumb at the beginning and end of the line.

Superthin Lead Holders

The last type of drafting lead holders, also called fine line lead holders, produces consistent, superthin lines. The diameters of the leads are 0.3 mm, 0.5 mm, 0.7 mm, and 0.9 mm, and the leads come in almost the full

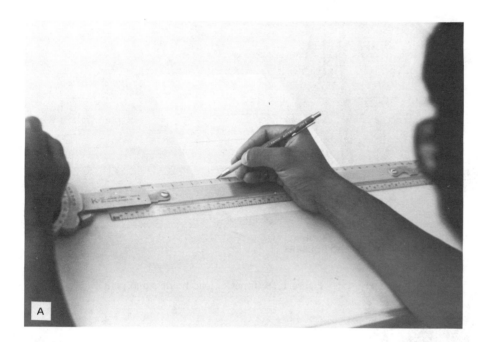

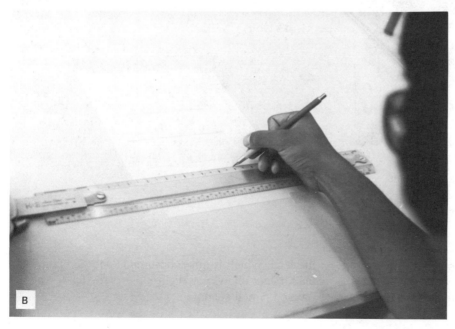

Figure 1.20 Rotating the pencil to keep a rounded point.

range of grades. The most popular of these holders is the 0.5 mm size, because it gives the best thickness of lines. There is no sharpening necessary, so drawing time is maximized. Some drafters still roll this holder as they draw to keep the rounded point, thus avoiding an easily broken chisel point. However, a chisel point is often desirable for lettering. For example, except for the free-hand sketches, all of the lettering in this book is done with a chisel end on a superthin holder.

Lines and Line Quality

Basically, lines can be broken down into three types: light, medium, and dark. Each of these types can be broken down further by variation of pressure and lead.

Light Lines. The lightest lines used are usually the guidelines drawn to help with lettering height. These lines should be only barely visible and should completely disappear when a diazo print is made. Darker than guidelines but still relatively light are the lines used in dimension and extension lines, leaders, and break lines.

Medium Lines. Medium weight lines are used in object and center lines, and in the dashed type of line used for hidden or dotted lines.

Dark lines. The darkest lines are used for border lines and cutting plane lines, major sections, and details. See Figure 1.21.

Choosing Line Quality. Line quality depends on the use of that particular line. An intense line is used to profile and emphasize; an intermediate line is used to show elements such as walls and structural members; and a light line is used for elements such as dimensioning and door swings.

Another way to vary line quality is to increase the width of the line. A thicker line can represent the walls on a floor plan, the outline of a building on a site plan, or the outline of a roof on a roof plan. See Figure 1.21 for line quality examples and uses and Figure 1.22 for an example of the types of lines used to indicate property lines and easements.

Hidden or Dotted Lines. Hidden or dotted lines are used to indicate objects hidden from view. See Figure 1.13. Solid objects covered by earth, such as foundations, can be indicated with hidden lines. This type of line can also depict future structures, items that are not in the contract, public utilities locations, easements, a wheelchair turning radius, or the direction of sliding doors and windows.

A floor plan will often show the roof outline, or a balcony above, or a change in ceiling height with a dotted line. On a site plan, dotted lines indicate the existing grades on the site (see Chapter 6).

Arrowheads. Different types of arrowheads are used in dimensioning. These are shown in Figure 1.23.

Material Designation Lines. Material designation lines are used to indicate the building material used. See Figure 1.24 for a sample of tapered or light-dark lines. (This device saves time; complete lines take longer to draw.) Also note the cross-hatched lines between the parallel lines that represent the wall thickness on Figure 1.25. These diagonal lines represent masonry.

Profiling

Architectural profiling is the process of taking the most important features of a drawing and outlining them. Figure 1.26 shows four applications of this concept.

Example A illustrates the darkening of the lines that represent the walls of a floor plan. The dimension lines or extension lines are drawn as medium weight lines not only to contrast with the walls but to allow the walls of the particular floor plan to stand out. In example B, a footing detail is profiled. Because the concrete work is important here, its outline is drawn darker than any other part of the detail.

Example C shows the top portion (head) of a window. The light lines at the bottom of the detail represent the side of the window. Note how the head section is outlined and the interior parts plus the sides of the walls are drawn lightly.

Example D represents another form of profiling, called "pouche," which enhances the profile technique by using shading. This shading can be done by pencil shading or by lines. Example B also uses this principle: in this instance, the dots and triangles which represent concrete in section are placed along the perimeter (near the profiled line) in greater quantity than toward the center.

In a section drawing, items most often profiled are cut by the cutting plane line. A footing detail, for example, is nothing more than a theoretical knife (a cutting plane) cutting through the wall of the structure. The portion most often cut is the concrete, so it is profiled.

On an elevation, the main outline of the structure should be darkened. See Figure 1.27. This type of profiling is used to simplify the illusion of the elevation to show that the structure is basically an L-shape structure and that one portion does actually project forward.

In the plan view, often the outline of the main structure is heavily outlined (profiled) in order to make the main area stand out more than any other feature of the property. See Figure 1.28 for a finished plan and elevation which have been properly profiled.

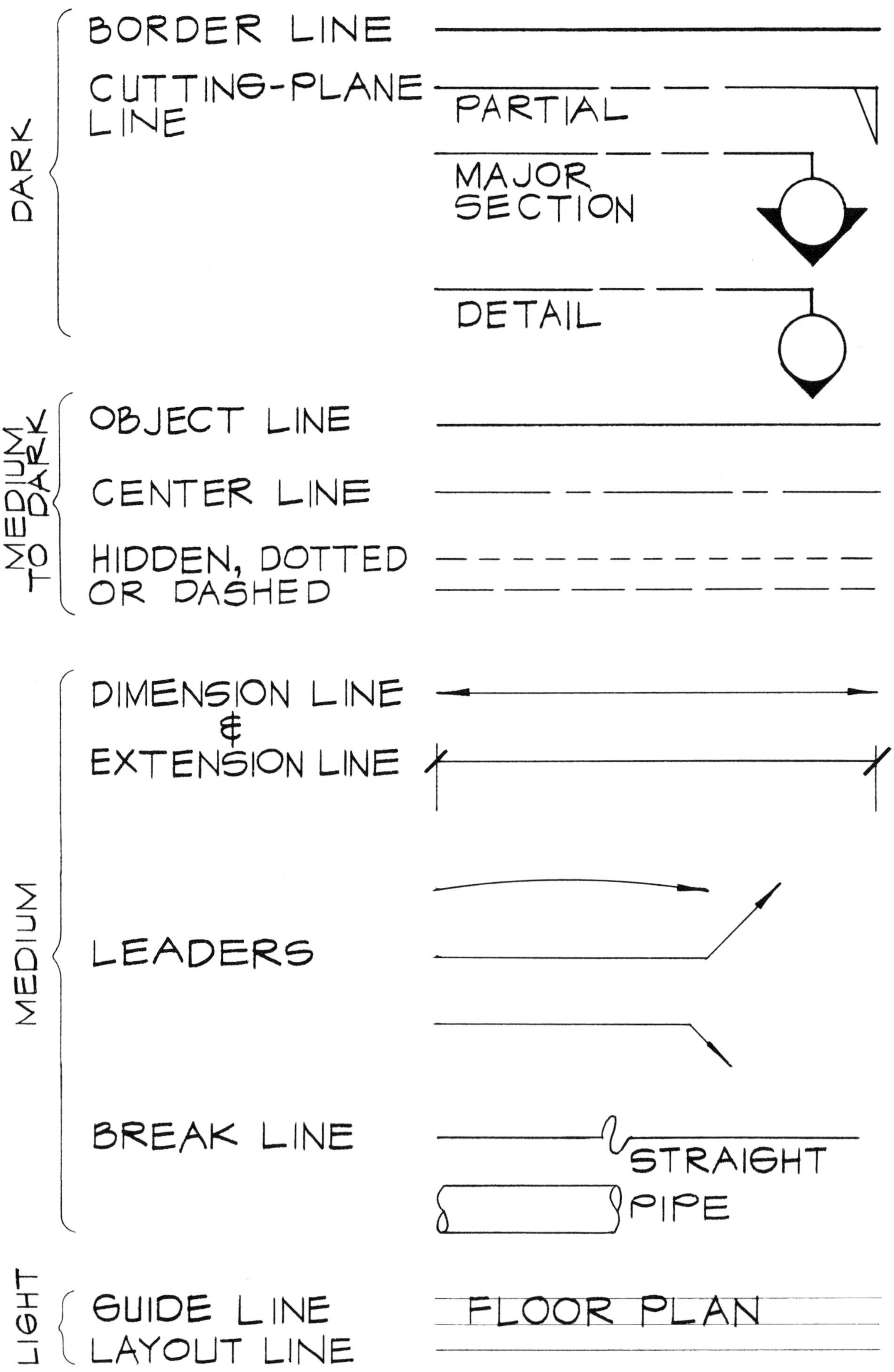

DARK

BORDER LINE

CUTTING-PLANE LINE
- PARTIAL
- MAJOR SECTION
- DETAIL

MEDIUM TO DARK

OBJECT LINE

CENTER LINE

HIDDEN, DOTTED OR DASHED

MEDIUM

DIMENSION LINE & EXTENSION LINE

LEADERS

BREAK LINE
- STRAIGHT
- PIPE

LIGHT

GUIDE LINE
LAYOUT LINE

FLOOR PLAN

Figure 1.21 Vocabulary of architectural lines.

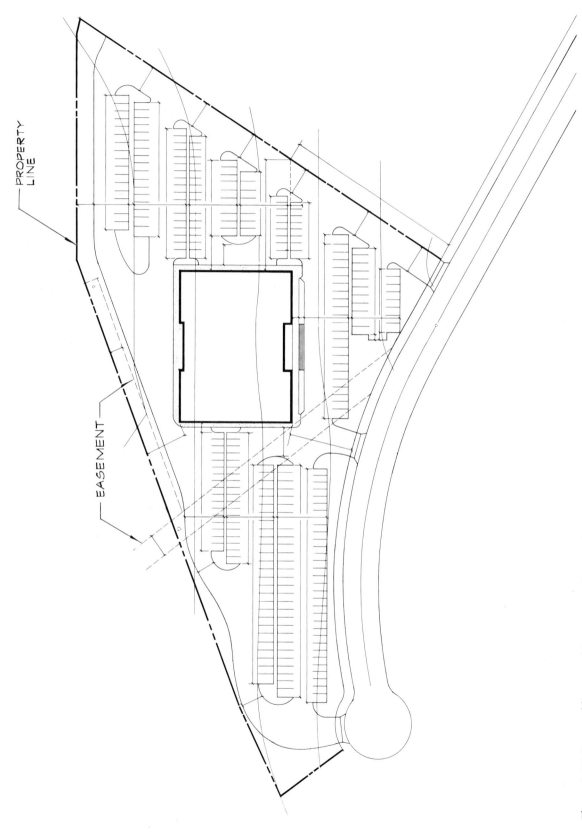

PROPERTY
LINE

EASEMENT

Figure 1.22 Types of lines used for property lines and easements.

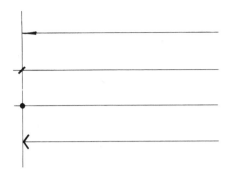

Figure 1.23 Types of arrowheads used in dimensioning.

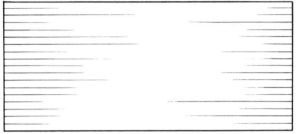

Figure 1.24 Tapered lines.

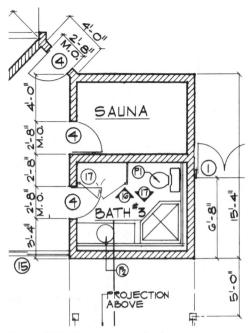

Figure 1.25 Lines representing masonry.

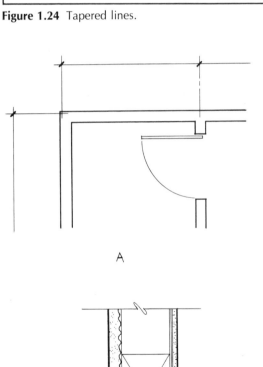

A

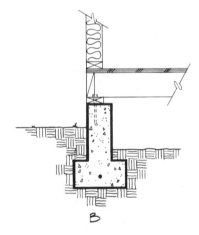

B

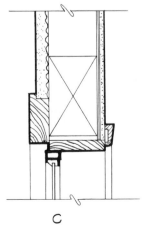

C

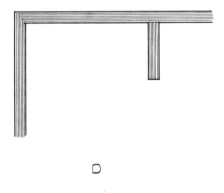

D

Figure 1.26 Profiling.

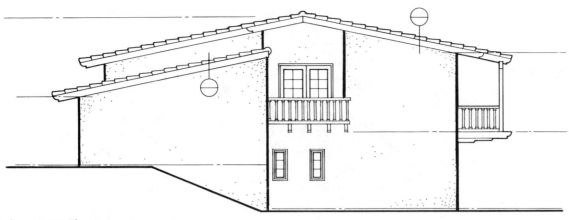

Figure 1.27 Elevation.

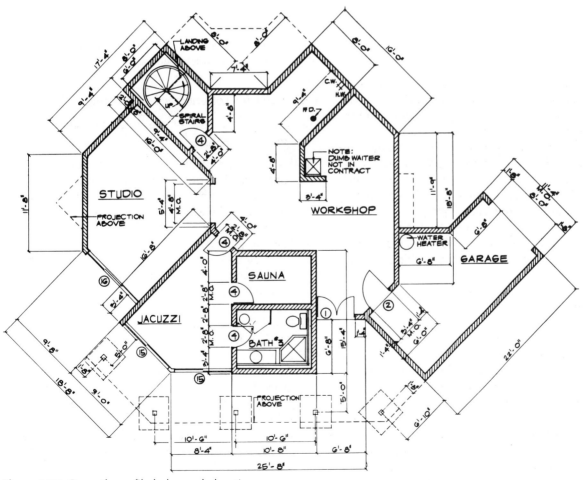

Figure 1.28 Correctly profiled plan and elevation.

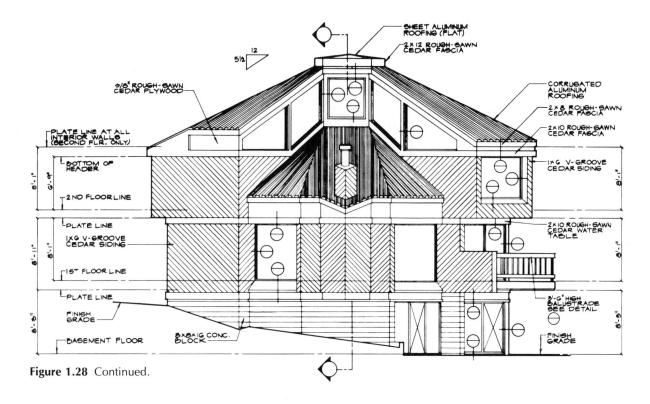

Figure 1.28 Continued.

Lettering

In architectural drafting, as in mechanical drafting, working drawings are not always hand lettered. A variety of different mechanical devices have come on the market in recent years, and large engineering and aircraft firms have been proving their effectiveness.

The architectural industry, however, is and may continue to be a small office industry. A recent survey by the American Institute of Architects (A.I.A.) found that architectural firms usually contain three to six employees and may not use computerized drafting and lettering machines. For this reason, it is important that architecture students become proficient in lettering. In fact, it is good lettering and good line quality that help a student obtain the first job.

Architectural lettering differs somewhat from the Gothic type letters developed by C. W. Reinhardt about fifty years ago and now called "mechanical lettering." Architectural lettering has evolved from a series of influences, including the demand for speed. We must not, however, interpret speed to mean sloppiness.

Another influence on architectural lettering was style. The architecturally drafted plan was in essence an idea or concept on paper, a creative endeavor. So the lines and the lettering took on a characteristic style of their own. In many firms, stylized lettering serves to identify the individual draftsperson. However, most firms attempt to create a uniform style of lettering for their entire staff. Stylizing must not be confused with overdecoration. Let-

tering that looks like a new alphabet should not be justified in the name of stylization.

Basic Rules for Lettering and Numbering

Following are a few simple rules for lettering and numbering:

1. Master mechanical lettering before attempting architectural lettering or any type of stylization. A student who cannot letter well in mechanical drafting has less chance of developing good architectural letters.
2. Learn to letter with vertical strokes first. Sloping letters may be easier to master, but most architectural offices prefer vertical lettering. It is easier to change from vertical to sloping letters than the reverse. See Figure 1.29.
3. Practice words, phrases, and numbers—not just individual letters. Copy a phrase from this book for example.
4. The shape of a letter should not be changed. The proportion of the letter may be slightly altered but one should never destroy the letter's original image. While the "W" in Figure 1.30 is in a style used for speed, it can be misconstrued for an "I" and a "V".
5. Changing the proportions of letters changes their visual effect. See Figure 1.31.
6. Certain strokes can be emphasized so that one letter is not mistaken for another. This also forces the

ANCHOR BOLT   *ANCHOR BOLT*

VERTICAL LETTERS   SLOPING LETTERS

Figure 1.29 Comparison between vertical and sloping lettering.

MECHANICAL   ARCHITECTURAL

　　M W   /Λ \V ΛΛ   ← (Poor)

Figure 1.30 Overworking architectural letters.

MECHANICAL   ARCHITECTURAL

　STUD   STUD   STUD

Figure 1.31 Changing proportions to produce architectural effect.

EXAMPLE:

　　　　　　B L I T R K

Figure 1.32 Emphasis on certain strokes.

EXAMPLE:

　　　　　　B O Q D P

Figure 1.33 Spaces incorrectly left within letters.

EXAMPLE:

　PLYWOOD   PLYWOOD

　　(Poor)   (Good)

Figure 1.34 Producing consistency.

EXAMPLE:

PLYWOOD   P LY WO OD

　(Good)   (Poor)

Figure 1.35 Importance of good spacing.

draftsperson to be more definitive in the formation of individual strokes. The strokes emphasized should be those most important to that letter; for example, a "B" differs from an "R" by the rounded lower right stroke and an "L" from an "I" by the horizontal bottom stroke extending to the right only. The beginning or end of these strokes can be emphasized by bearing down on the pencil to insure a good reprint of that portion. See Figure 1.32.

7. Many draftspersons have picked up the bad habit of mixing upper and lower case letters. This is not good lettering.

8. Some draftspersons also have developed a style of leaving space within the letter that is not there. This too is to be discouraged. See Figure 1.33.

9. Consistency produces good lettering. If vertical lines are used, they must all be parallel. A slight variation produces poor lettering. Even round letters such as "O" have a center through which imaginary vertical strokes will go. See Figure 1.34.

10. Second only to the letter itself is spacing. Good spacing protects good letter formation. Poor spacing destroys even the best lettering. See Figure 1.35.

11. Always use guidelines and use them to the fullest. See Figure 1.36.

Using Guidelines

While a purist might frown on the practice, a guideline or straightedge can be used in lettering to speed up the learning process. Horizontal lines are easier for a beginner than vertical lines and shapes appear better formed when all of the vertical strokes are perfectly perpendicular and parallel to each other. Curved and round strokes are done without the aid of an instrument.

After drawing the guidelines, place a T-square or parallel about 2 or 3 inches below the lines. Locate the triangle to the left of the area to be lettered with the vertical portion of the triangle on the right side. See Figure 1.37. "Eyeball" the spacing of the letters. Position your pencil as if you are ready to make the vertical line without the triangle. Before you make the vertical stroke, slide the triangle over against the pencil and make the stroke. See Figures 1.38 and 1.39. Draw nonvertical lines freehand. See Figure 1.40.

Using a straightedge helps build up skills. Eventually you should discontinue its use as practice improves your lettering skills.

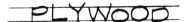

　　　　　POOR   GOOD
　　　　EXAMPLE   EXAMPLE

Figure 1.36 Full use of guidelines.

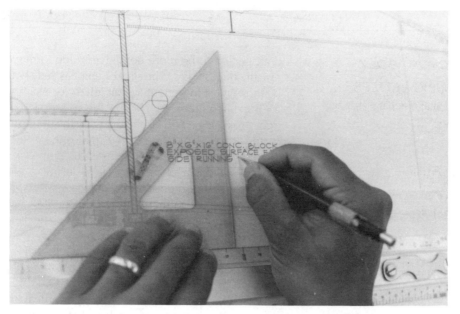

Figure 1.37 Pencil placement for vertical lettering.

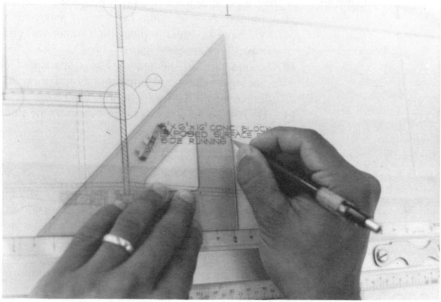

Figure 1.38 Placing the triangle against the pencil.

Figure 1.39 Drawing the vertical stroke.

Figure 1.40 Completing the letter.

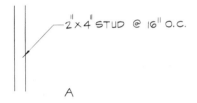

A

B

Figure 1.41 Net and nominal notation.

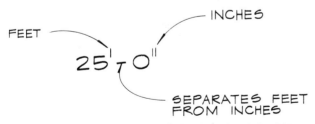

Figure 1.42 Expressing feet and inches.

3⁶   4⁰

Figure 1.43 Dimensions in a restricted area.

Drafting Conventions and Dimensions

Using Net and Nominal Sizing. Many architectural offices have adopted the practice of separating the **net size** and the **nominal size** of lumber in their notations. The nominal size (call out size) is used to describe or order a piece of lumber. The net size is the size of the actual piece of wood drawn and used. For example, the nominal size of a ''two by four'' is 2 × 4 but the net or actual size is 1½″ × 3½″. The distinction between the two sizes is accomplished by the use of inch (″) marks. Figure 1.41A would be very confusing because the nominal size is listed but inch marks are used. Compare this notation with that of Figure 1.41B. The 16″ o.c. (on center) is to be translated as precisely 16 inches while the 2 × 4 is used to indicate nominal size.

Dimensions. Dimensions in feet are normally expressed by a small mark to the upper right of a number (′), and inches by two small marks (″) in the same location. To separate feet from inches, a dash is used. See Figure 1.42. The dash in this type of dimension becomes very important because it avoids dimensions being misread and adds to clarity. If space for dimensions is restricted, an acceptable abbreviated form can be used. This is illustrated in Figure 1.43. The inches are raised and underlined to separate them from the feet notation.

Placement of Dimensions. Dimension lines can be broken to show the numerical value, but it is faster simply to put numerical values above the lines. See Figure 1.44. When dimension lines run vertically, place the numbers above the dimension line as viewed from the right. See Figure 1.45.

ACCEPTABLE

BETTER

Figure 1.44 Placement of dimensions above or between dimension line.

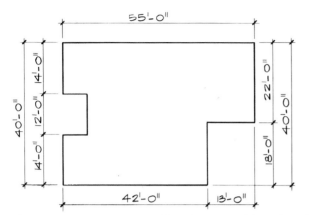

Figure 1.45 Dimensions read from bottom and from the right.

CHANGE DIRECTIONS
HERE

CHANGE DIRECTIONS
HERE

Figure 1.46 Dimension placement.

Not all dimension lines, however, are horizontal or vertical. Often dimension lines are angled, and this can cause problems when you position the numerical value. Figure 1.46 suggests a possible location for such values.

Dividing a Line into Equal Parts. Dividing a line or plane into an equal number of parts has many useful applications. There are two main ways of doing this.

The first way is illustrated in Figure 1.47, Method A.

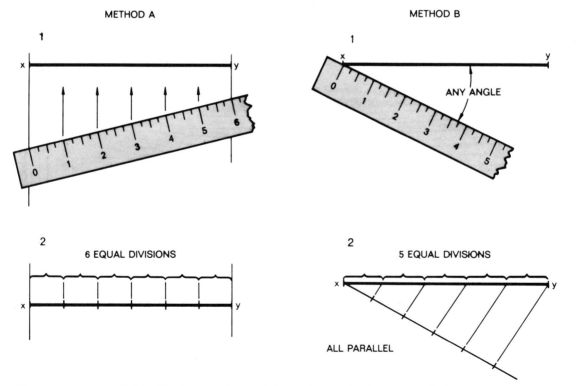

Figure 1.47 How to divide a line into equal parts. (Wakita, *Perspective Drawing: A Student Text/Workbook*, Kendall/Hunt Publishing Co., 1978. Reprinted with permission).

Line XY is to be divided into 6 equal divisions. The initial step is to draw two lines perpendicular to XY, one through point X and one through point Y. Next, lay a scale across these newly drawn parallel lines so that 0 is on one of the lines, and a point divisible by six, such as 6 inches, is on the other line. If the line XY had been 7 inches long, 12 inches could have been used, or 9 inches, or any number larger than 7 inches that is divisible by 6.

A small tick mark is drawn above the desired division and parallel lines drawn until they touch line XY, dividing it into 6 equal divisions. The angle of the scale should not be of any concern.

Method B uses a slightly different approach. See Figure 1.47, Method B. To start with, a line is drawn intersecting line XY at any angle; the new line can be any length. The angle should be larger than 20° to 30°. Next, place a scale on this newly drawn line so that 0 on the scale touches the intersection of line XY and the new line. Find a value divisible by the division desired. For example, if the desired division is 5, find a value on the scale divisible by 5. Draw a line connecting this end point with point Y to form a triangle. Then draw a series of lines parallel to this line toward line XY. See Step 2. These intersections produce the desired division.

Using Terminology: Mechanical Versus Architectural

Mechanical Drafting

While mechanical drafting resembles architectural drafting, the terms used vary greatly. The basis for mechanical drafting is a method of multi-view drawing known as orthographic projection. This method uses a concept in which an object is first housed in a theoretical glass box, as shown in Figure 1.48; second, unfolded as shown in Figure 1.49; and third, viewed in this unfolded form as a flat form. Portions of this six-sided form are given names such as top view, front view, and right side view. The back, left side, and bottom are eliminated, as Figure 1.50 shows.

Architectural Drafting

The architectural version of orthographic projection is shown in Figure 1.51. The top view (as viewed from the helicopter) is now called the **plan,** and the views all the way around from all four sides are referred to as **elevations.** Each of these elevations has a special name and will be discussed in the chapter on exterior elevations (Chapter 11).

In brief, a top view of the total property is called the site or plot plan. A horizontal section (drawn as if the structure were cut horizontally, the top portion removed, and the exposed interior viewed from above) is simply called a plan. There are many types of plans: floor plans, electrical plans (showing electrical features), framing plans (showing how a floor, ceiling, or roof is assembled), and foundation plans, to mention just a few.

A vertical cut through a structure is called a cross-section or a longitudinal section, depending on the direction of the cut. The cross-section is a cut taken through the short end of a structure.

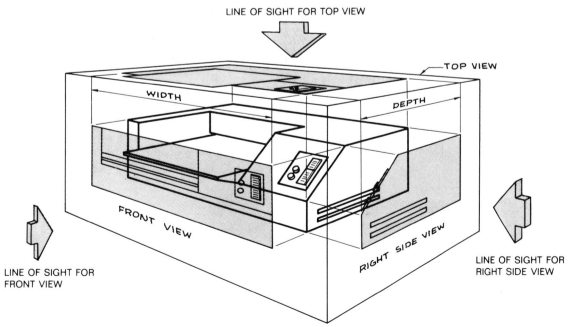

Figure 1.48 The glass box. (Wakita, *Perspective Drawing: A Student Text/Workbook,* Kendall/Hunt Publishing Co., 1978. Reprinted with permission.)

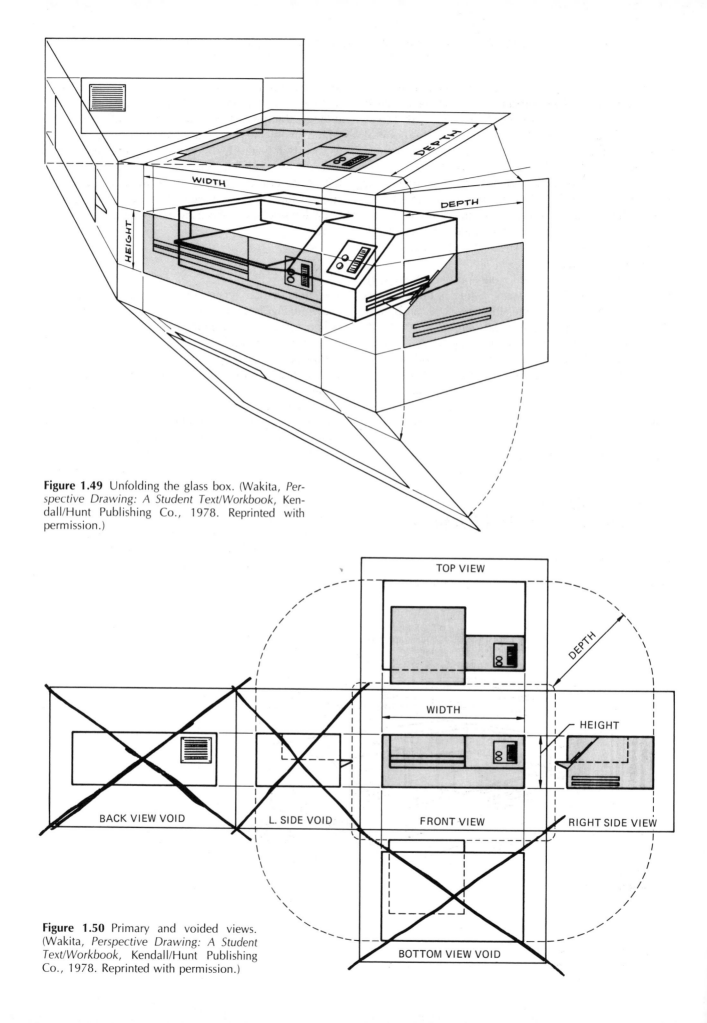

Figure 1.49 Unfolding the glass box. (Wakita, *Perspective Drawing: A Student Text/Workbook*, Kendall/Hunt Publishing Co., 1978. Reprinted with permission.)

Figure 1.50 Primary and voided views. (Wakita, *Perspective Drawing: A Student Text/Workbook*, Kendall/Hunt Publishing Co., 1978. Reprinted with permission.)

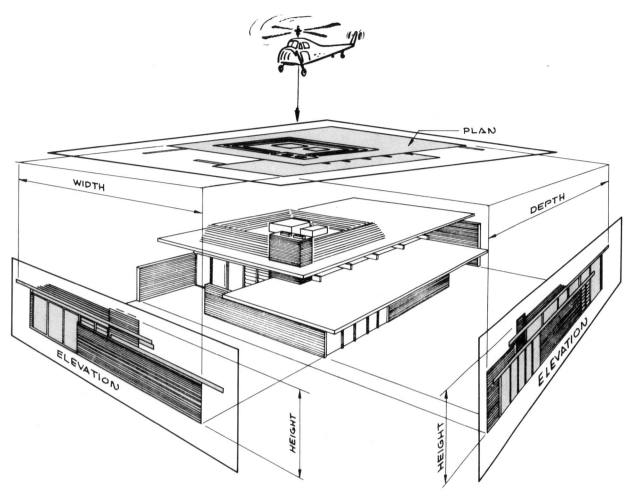

Figure 1.51 Multi-view drawing of a structure. (Wakita, *Perspective Drawing: A Student Text/Workbook*, Kendall/Hunt Publishing Co., 1978. Reprinted with permission.)

REPRODUCTION, STANDARDS, AND DRAWING GUIDELINES

2

Reproduction Methods

The Blueprint Process

Decades ago, the prevalent method of reproduction was the "blueprint." Blueprints have a blue background and white lines. Bond paper was coated with light-sensitive chemicals much like photographic film. The original, drawn on a translucent medium such as vellum, was placed over the paper and exposed to light. The light bleached out the chemicals except where they were screened off by lines. The paper was then dipped in a developing solution which would react to those sections not exposed to the light. The print was then washed and dried. As you can imagine, this process was time consuming.

The Diazo Process

Today, blueprints are seldom used in architecture. The diazo has replaced it and is now used almost exclusively. Much as in the blueprint process, an original translucent medium (usually vellum) is placed over a bond paper which has a coating of light-sensitive chemicals. As the sheets are exposed to the light, the chemicals are bleached out, leaving only those areas that are screened by lines. The print is then exposed to ammonia or another chemical, which develops the unexposed chemicals. The result is a white background and dark lines. Color lines are also available, including brown and green. This diazo process usually only takes from fifteen seconds to one minute.

The Sepia Process

When diazo chemicals are placed onto vellum instead of bond paper, the resulting print is called a sepia print, or simply a sepia. This sepia copy becomes a second master. Sepia displays as reddish-brown lines on a white vellum background. The sepia print can be drawn on or, depending on the type, erased with an electric or chemical eraser called an eradicator. Some sepia papers "ghost" back unwanted lines when the effect of the eradicator wears off.

The advantages of a sepia are twofold: first, as another master; and, second, as a time saving device. As a second master, it is often used to make diazo copies so that normal wear and tear takes place on the sepia rather than on the original. If a structure is being built in a different city from the office, sepia prints can be sent from which necessary sets of diazo prints can be made for permits, bids, and contractors.

Sepias have unlimited use as a time-saving device. For example, a floor is initially drawn; before the drawing becomes too complicated, a number of sepia prints are

made. Sepias are more effective if they are made in reverse so the drafter can draw on the sheet and make corrections without erasing the original print. These sepia copies can be used for electrical plans, structural drawings, and heating and air-conditioning plans. If a consulting engineer provides information, it, too, can be placed on the sepia sheet. Information such as dimensions and equipment locations is thus accurate; the architect and consultant are both using the same original drawings. The structural consultant may even be given a slightly lighter sepia so that the structural work stands out on the sheet when regular diazo copies are made.

Transparent and Translucent Films. Diazo chemicals are also used with transparent or translucent film materials; the result is simply called "film." This transparent or translucent material can also be purchased with an adhesive on one side and is called applique film. After you expose this applique film to the image, you can mount it directly onto a vellum original or sepia. Most types of applique film are erasable.

Plain Paper Copiers

Types and Sizes. A variety of plain paper copiers are now on the open market for sale or lease. Some require special paper; others can copy on almost any paper surface. Some machines can enlarge as well as reduce, but presently only in certain proportions. Some copiers do not copy the original to its exact size; they change the size slightly and often in only one direction. Plain paper copiers usually use the standard paper formats of 8½" × 11" and 8½" × 14". The larger copiers can take copy widths up to 36" and unlimited length since the machine accepts roll stock. But on most copiers the maximum reproducible size is presently about 24"; a 36" master must be reduced to a 24" size for reproduction. A 24" master can be reproduced full size. Paper copiers can reproduce on bond paper, vellum, or acetate. Therefore, a 24" × 36" drawing can be reduced onto vellum and used as a master to produce diazo copies.

Reproducing an acetate is advantageous because prints on acetate can be used with an overhead projector for enlarging sketches or for presentations. Acetate film is also available with an adhesive backing for applique uses.

Appliques. Most adhesive films for plain paper copiers have two sheets: one sheet of adhesive film and a backing sheet or carrier. Since the adhesive film has a sticky substance on one side, the carrier is a non-stick material. This material is either a plastic film or a wax impregnated paper similar to wax paper.

When you use adhesive film on a plain paper copier of the heat developing variety, do not choose a wax carrier type; the heat from the developer portion of the copier melts the wax and jambs the copier.

Standard decals can be made with adhesive film for symbols, title block information, and even construction notes.

Shortcut Procedures

Freehand Drawing. One of the best shortcuts you can learn is drawing freehand. Most of the preliminary design procedures and conceptual design details in this book were done freehand. You still should use a scale to maintain accuracy, and adhere to the drafting vocabulary of lines and techniques. Freehand skill is useful in field situations, for informal office communications, and for communications with contractors, building department officials, and clients. Examples of freehand details can be found in the chapter on architectural details (Chapter 14).

Typewritten notes. Because of the applique film technique and the ease of reproducing spliced drawings, typing is being used more frequently for working drawings. For example, lengthy construction notes may be typed on applique film. However, hand lettering is *still* encouraged at the beginning.

Computer-Aided Drafting. The recent surge of interest in computers has found its way into the architectural office. Both the large and minicomputers (home variety) are now being used to draft. The size and scope of the drafting to be done is only limited by the equipment used.

Experience has shown, however, that the computer drafter must have a minimum of three years and sometimes as many as fifteen years of on-the-board drafting experience to be effective as a computer-aided drafter. This individual must know such things as the symbology used in architecture and the logic of dimensioning, as well as comprehend materials and other aspects of architecture.

The information, approach, and logic are the same for computer drafting as for conventional drafting; only the tools of the drafter change.

Word Processing. The growing popularity of word processing in architectural offices is due mainly to its competitive price and its easy application to architectural uses. Also, the advent of minicomputers has made word processing accessible to even small firms.

The basic equipment used in word processing is as follows:

1. Hardware
   - A monitor (almost any television can be adapted)
   - A minicomputer
   - A disk drive (similar to a record player but smaller in size)
   - A printer (similar to a typewriter without a keyboard)
2. Software
   - A program (contains the instructions that make the processor work)

These instructions are stored on a disk (like a small record) and loaded into the computer memory by way of the disk drive. The desired text is then typed into the computer on the keyboard, which is usually mounted on the computer, and the text is saved (memorized) on the disk. This information can be retrieved at any time and can be changed, corrected, or updated through the program.

The program allows you to change the margin, remove undesirable items, and select the type of printing and medium desired. The medium can be a sheet of typing paper, vellum, or even adhesive film. Specifications can be typed and stored for future use; engineering calculations can be stored; reports, letters—even employee records—can be stored and easily retrieved.

Drafting Appliques and Manufacturers' Literature. Architectural offices often use manufacturers' literature and their details. More recently, offices have been using manufacturers' literature and drawings together with applique film. Erasable applique film is used, and the desired drawing supplied by the manufacturer is first printed by a plain paper copier or with the diazo process; second, changed or corrected to meet specific needs; and last, applied to the original vellum sheet. This saves time and the cost of developing the detail from scratch.

Recognizing the practicality of this method, many manufacturers now provide appliques upon request as part of product promotion.

Screen Drafting. This method adds a screen to the printing of the original drawing. The screen is film made up of microscopic dots which produce a partial light barrier. Screens are available in a variety of percentages: some block 20% of the light, others 80%, and so on. When used with an original drawing, the screen produces a gray copy instead of black.

Diazo (screen) Drafting. For diazo (screen) drafting, a sepia print is made first. The diazo machine is reduced in speed in order to produce a light but readable and reproducible sepia print. This sepia print can now serve as the background for a structural or electrical plan, or a heating and air-conditioning layout, for example. When reprinted on the diazo machine, the reproduction emphasizes the material that has been drafted on and deemphasizes (or "screens") the original drawing, while still showing the relationship between them.

Photography and Drafting. Photography plays a large part in architectural drafting. "Blueprint service" companies have rapidly begun to employ methods of reproduction other than diazo. Many use plain paper copiers and many companies have also added photography. The older photographic method used produced a "photostat." This is rapidly being replaced by the "photo mechanical transfer" (PMT) system. In this process, there is no real negative. Rather, there is an intermediate paper negative that takes about 30 seconds to make; then the image is transferred from this throw-away master to a positive.

Still the best process and the most versatile is regular camera photography. The only limit to the size of print is the equipment itself, and 36" × 42" negatives are now available. Since negatives can be spliced together, the final limit is only restricted by the size of the positive paper available. Uses of photography are described later.

Some stationery suppliers and reproduction centers can take 35 mm slides and produce transparent 8½" × 11" copies by using a 35 mm projector, a plain paper copier, and acetate film.

Reprodrafting

"Reprodrafting" is a term used to describe a number of approaches to improving or revising drafted material in a way that takes advantage of photographic or photocopying processes. These approaches have spawned a number of new terms, including eraser drafting, paste-up drafting, photo drafting, overlay drafting, pen drafting, and scissors drafting. Reprodrafting, then, actually consists of many processes.

Restoration. Restoration refers to the process of taking a photograph of an old original or an old print and, by repairing the negative, producing a new master.

Composite drafting. Composite drafting is the photographic process of making a single drawing from many, or of taking parts of other drawings to make a new drawing. You will often hear the terms "paste-up," "scissors," "eraser," and "photo-drafting" being used in connection with this process.

Paste-up drafting simply refers to the process of pasting pieces onto a single master sheet, and then photographing and reproducing them. The lines on the negative made by edges of the pieces can be eliminated by the photo retoucher.

Scissors drafting takes an existing drawing and eliminates undesirable or corrected portions by cutting them out before the paste-up process. **Erasure drafting** is similar, but the unwanted portions are simply erased. In both cases, the original is never touched. A good copy on good quality paper is produced first. The copy must be printed in a way that allows easy erasure.

Photo-drafting, as the name indicates, uses drafting and photography. It begins with a photograph of any drawing, such as a plan, elevation, or detail. The drawing is printed on a matte-surfaced film and additional information drafted onto it.

Photo-drafting is an ideal method for dealing with historical restoration drawings. The building to be restored is photographed and printed (to scale) on a matte-surfaced film. Required information, such as dimensions, and methods of restoration are added to this photographic reprint.

All of these methods can be intermixed. For example, a floor plan for an apartment can be drawn once, printed onto an applique film, and then cut and joined on the master sheet to produce a composite of the apartment units. A print of this drawing on a new master allows for the addition of notes and dimensions.

Photo-drafting can be used in conjunction with appliques to show surrounding areas, structural location of various parts of a building, and proposed structural additions or relocations. Applique film is either opaque or transparent. Opaque applique is used in a part of scissors drafting and requires photography, while the transparency applique becomes part of the original and can use the diazo process.

Erasable copies of details can be made, updated, and changed to meet the needs of the specific job, and can be applied right onto a portion of an existing drawing. This allows more than one person to work on a given sheet at the same time.

As with diazo drafting, a screen can also be used photographically to produce a gray image for printing on vellum. This allows any added materials to stand out against the gray. This process enables the same master to be reproduced over and over again for the various plans, such as the electrical and framing plans, thus avoiding errors.

Another advantage of photography is the ease with which it allows the scale of a drawing to be changed accurately. If a floor plan drafted at ¼" = 1'–0" scale is to be used for another drawing, such as a roof framing plan at ⅛" or ¹⁄₁₆" scale, it can be reduced photographically, thus saving many hours of work.

One of the best uses for photography is in preparing plans for highly repetitive structures such as apartments, hospitals, schools, and industrial buildings.

Overlay drafting. One of the most significant changes in the production of architectural working drawings is the introduction of overlay drafting or registration drafting. It is a system approach and works mainly for plans. While this is a difficult procedure to learn, with practice and organization, the time savings can be great. Some governmental agencies require this procedure.

The concept of overlay drafting has been used in the printing industry for many years and more recently in

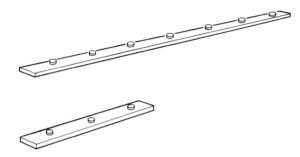

Figure 2.1 Pin registration strips.

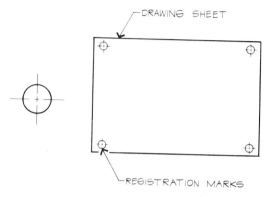

Figure 2.2 Registration marks.

the aircraft industry. Overlay drafting combines a base drawing and a series of overlays, ending up with a single drawing. To keep the base sheet aligned with the overlays, a registration bar with pins is used. For this reason, overlay drafting is often called **pin registration.** See Figure 2.1.

Another way to keep the base sheet aligned with the overlay sheets is to use registration marks similar to those in Figure 2.2. Note the two strips of metal shown in Figure 2.1; one is 26½" long with seven ¼"-round registration buttons, and the other much shorter with three buttons. The longer strip is for drawings and the smaller for photographic negatives. The negatives of all the drawings are made at a reduced scale for storage and cost purposes.

A floor plan can be drawn on a prepunched base sheet. See Figure 2.3 Using a pin registration strip, a second prepunched sheet is layed over the base sheet, and the notes and dimensions are placed on the overlay sheet. A title block and border line can be drawn on the third sheet. If the plan follows a specific module, a grid might be drawn on a fourth sheet.

A reduced negative of each sheet is then made, and the four negatives are exposed onto a single print at the original size. This print is called a **blow back.** The result is a composite of the original floor plan with notes and dimensions, title block, and a grid forming the finished product.

Copies are made of the original floor plan and sent to the consultants. Each of the consultants then overlays the original copy of the floor plan and places particular information on the overlay. Reduced negatives are again made of each of the overlays completed by the consultants. These negatives are combined with the original negative of the original floor plan and grid, and printed on a blow back form.

At this point, a dot screen can be introduced to reduce the darkness of the lines. The screen can be placed so that the floor plan and the grid are gray while the consultant's information is dark, thus providing sharp contrast. See Figure 2.4. This procedure is most effective in preparing plans for a multi-story building where the greater the combination of overlays, the less the drafting, and thus the greater effectiveness of the whole system. See Figures 2.5 and 2.6.

If the overlay system is used in conjunction with another system, the possibilities are endless. For example, in a structure where there is a repetition of a basic plan, the floor plan can be drafted at ¼" scale, photographically reduced in quantity at ⅛" scale, assembled by scissors drafting, and used as a base sheet for subsequent drawings. See Figure 2.7. Applications for site work are shown in Figure 2.8, applications for planning and urban planning in Figure 2.9.

Other Shortcut Methods

Any time you combine lines and words in chart form, you can take a number of approaches. Drawing lines in pencil and then lettering directly on the chart is not always the best approach.

Drawing on the Reverse Side. You can draw lines on the reverse side of the drawing surface and letter on the opposite side. This allows easy correction. You can then erase lettering without disturbing the lines.

Combining Ink and Pencil. You can use ink for the lines and pencil for the lettering. The ink lines can be drawn on either side of the vellum.

Saving the Original Drawing. A sepia print can be made from the original, whether it is in pencil or ink. The lettering is then done on the sepia, saving the original.

Using Standardized Sheets. If an office uses a standardized sheet for all jobs or specializes in a particular building type which calls for the same information each time, a more permanent procedure can be followed. The standardized form can be xeroxed onto vellum or reproduced photographically in one of two ways. First obtain a negative to make a print plate and print the image on vellum. This can usually be done through a blueprint reproduction service that also provides

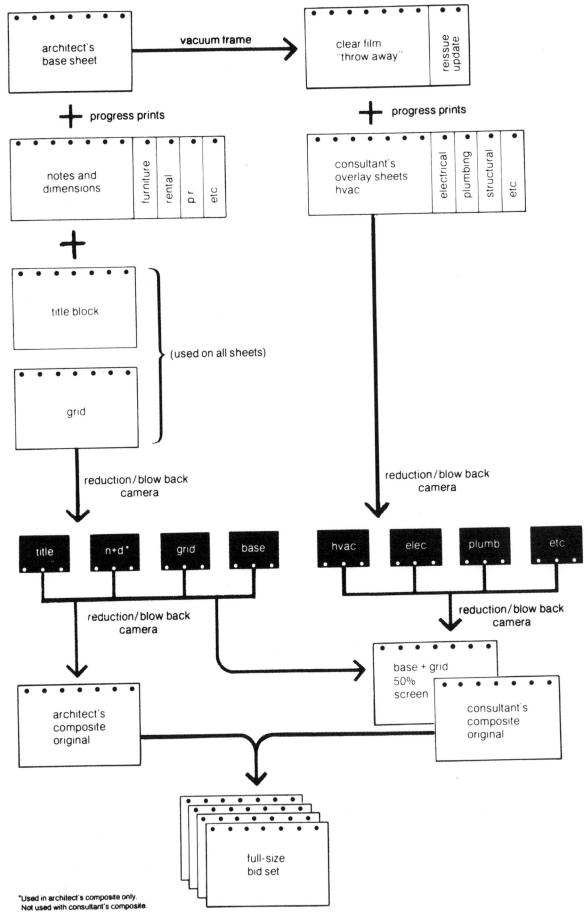

Figure 2.3 Multidwelling residential. (Courtesy of Keuffel & Esser Co., Morristown, N.J.)

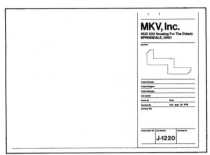

Title Block

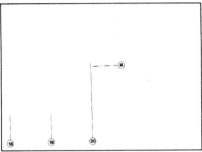

Grid

Base

Title block

The Title Block, which is often one separate sheet, can be printed onto punched mylar for all sheets except the Grid and Architectural Base. This allows each consultant to fill out the specific information as to drawings number, name, etc. more readily. This also applies to the Architectural Notes and Dimension sheets, and reduces cost of printing progress prints. Printed and punched sheets are useful for quickly putting down detail sheets on drafting table's pin bar.

Grid

Grid is best kept as separate sheet since for many plan drawings it is not wanted, for some drawings it is screened, for others it is kept solid.

Composite

Composite sheet can be developed in a number of ways for different purposes. Offset colored prints can be issued as half size as an information set for the bidding contractors. It can be used in-house as check sets for the architect and his consultants for final coordination prior to bidding. Notes and dimensions that interfere from one trade to the next can be blocked out on the negative to allow clearer reading. Such a composite sheet is also a valuable guide for preparation of coordinated ceiling shop drawings.

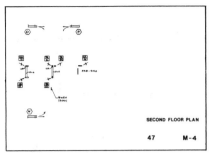

Air Conditioning

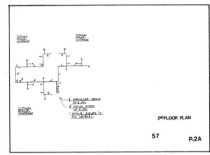

Plumbing

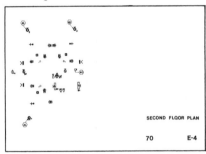

Electrical

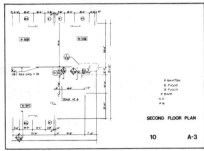

Notes & Dimensions

Courtesy of
**Maple Knoll Village, Inc.
Springdale, Ohio**
Gruzen & Partners, Architects

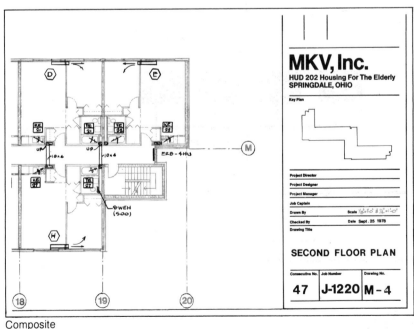

Composite

Figure 2.4 Composite drafting. (Courtesy of Keuffel & Esser Co., Morristown, N.J.)

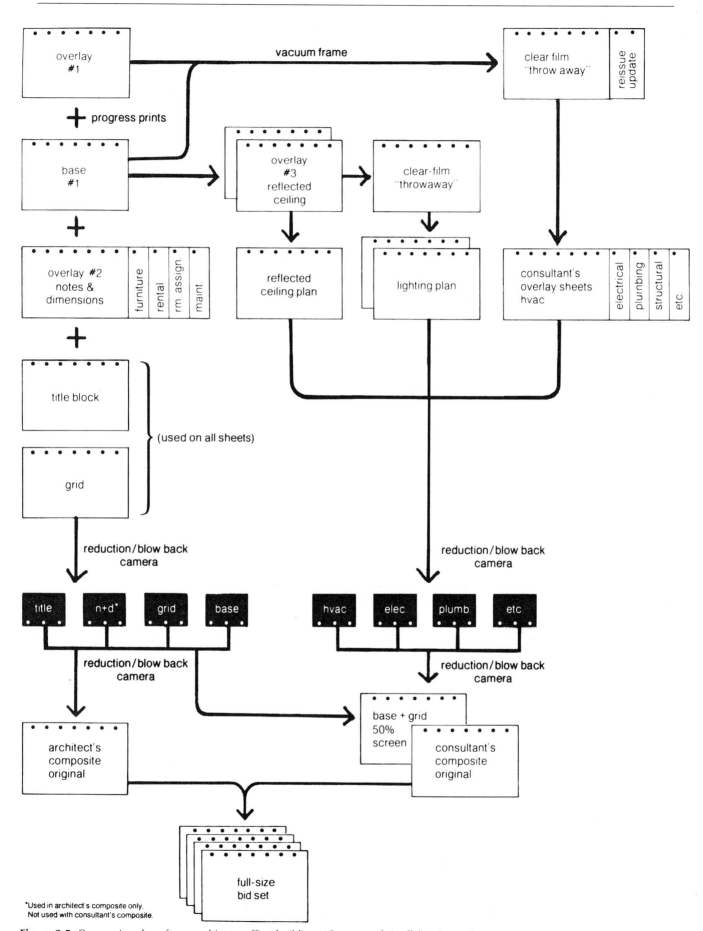

Figure 2.5 Composite plans for a multistory office building. (Courtesy of Keuffel & Esser Co., Morristown, N.J.)

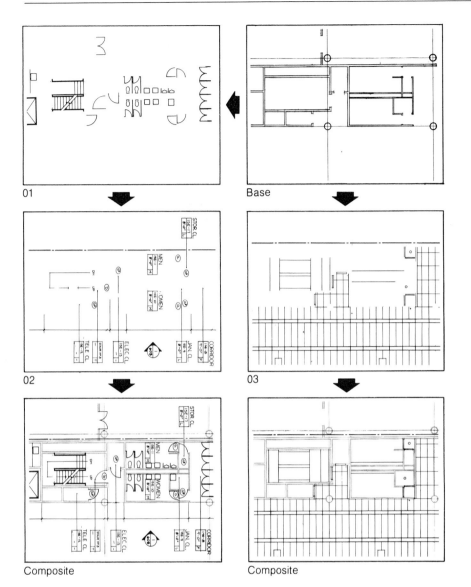

01

Base

02

03

Composite

Composite

Base Sheet: This is the only sheet that is printed with every overlay to produce necessary composites. It contains grid, columns, and structure, interior partitions and exterior walls. Basic information *not applicable* to reflected ceiling plan was included on Overlay 1.

Overlay 1: This sheet includes doors and door swings, stair treads and risers, laboratory benches, toilet partitions, plumbing, drinking fountains, and *most important,* floor edges which are different from ceiling above the respective floor. This is to avoid conflict with the reflected ceiling overlay.

Overlay 2: Contains verbal information such as dimensions, room boxes, wall tags (i.e., construction type designation) door tags, notes, reference symbols for cross sections, plan sections, elevation (floor heights) and exterior elevation symbols.

Overlay 3: The reflected ceiling plan. When sufficiently complete, it is issued to electrical engineer as a clear film throwaway for establishing circuiting overlay. Note that this requires architect to initiate location and dimensioning of lighting layout (a good idea). Reflected ceiling plan is thus the lighting design overlay. Switching plan is the technical overlay completed after the lighting design composite is made.

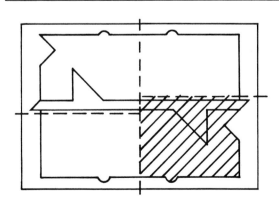

Client's standard sheet size, measuring 34"x22", necessitated laying out the building into four compass quadrants (NW, NE, SE, and SW) to accommodate 1/8" scale drawings. Careful planning and organization was required to keep track of drawings and reproduction orders.

Figure 2.6 Laboratory office building: Architectural drawings, ⅛" scale. (Courtesy of Keuffel & Esser Co., Morristown, N.J.)

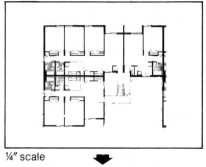

¼" scale

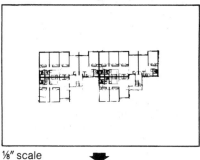

⅛" scale

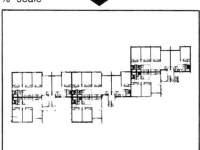

Repetition of Design

Where individual elements of a building require repetitive drafting they can be effectively handled by composite drafting. This is particularly true for many types of housing such as low and high rise housing, hotels, motels, nursing homes, housing for the elderly, criminal justice facilities, and of course, hospitals. Large scale plans of individual units, dwelling units for the elderly in the case history shown here, are prepared at ½" scale. These are then reproduced at ⅛" scale on clear film; left-hand, right-hand, and if necessary in mirror images in the quantity necessary to produce an entire typical floor plan.

Typical Floor Plan

"Created" by taping the clear film dwelling units to a prepunched mylar sheet following blue pencilled guide lines for alignment. Connective lines are carefully drafted and all in-fill such as stairs, elevators, central shafts, special rooms, are completed.

Scales

Final product scale must be anticipated and drafting techniques coordinated. Line weight of ½" or ¼" prototype must be sufficient to take reductions to ⅛" scale and to 1/16" scale for ½ size bidding documents. If 8½" X 11" clear films are wanted for public relation purposes or for printed copies the required reduction must also be taken into account.

Typical Floor Plan in Multi-Story Projects

The single story plan becomes the basis for expanding to additional floors without redrafting. The pin registered plan is reproduced on wash-off film for each floor wanted. This can be done most accurately using a full size negative, although the reduction/blow-back camera process can also be used. Individual floor variations can be incorporated on the wash-off film or the procedure can be often simplified by changing the full size negative working drawing to the simplest or "key" floor plan and then adding variations as required to each wash-off film.

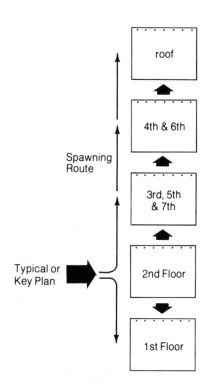

Courtesy of
**Stony Brook Housing
Stony Brook, New York**
Gruzen & Partners, Architects
Preiss/Breismeister, Architects

Furniture, public relations, rental, room assignments, etc.

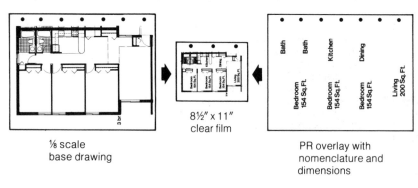

⅛ scale
base drawing

8½" x 11"
clear film

PR overlay with
nomenclature and
dimensions

Figure 2.7 Composite drafting with pin-bar drafting. (Courtesy of Keuffel & Esser Co., Morristown, N.J.)

Site Work

Readily lends itself to the advantages of Pin Registered Drafting since it consists of many different pieces of information on a common base or background. Two backgrounds, contours and/or hard lines are usual. The hard lines or edges consist of major man-made plan elements such as: walks, roadways, terraces and other paved elements; planters, planting beds, seeded areas; walls, sitting benches, retaining walls, pools; and of course building structures.

Site Utilities

All plan aspects of sitework can benefit from pin registration. The surveyor can be supplied with title overlay and punched polyester film to produce survey working drawing base suitable to many uses. Boring information and locations; existing

and new site utilities; chilled water; high temperature hot water; steam; storm and sanitary drainage; electrical, signal, and computer distribution; water and standpipe; gas; materials handling; and others.

Example:

Danish Village is a HUD 202 housing project for the elderly in Michigan designed by Gruzen & Partners. The landscape architects, Gold, Gomberg, Piermont, Ltd. used the man-made hardline drawing as the base, B-8, which combined with 4 overlays produced the following drawings:

Site Grading, SL-1

Site Materials, SL-2

Site Dimension Plan, SL-3

Planting & Pavement Pattern Plan, SL-4

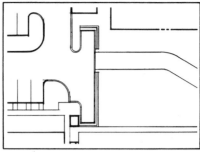

Hard Line Base B-8

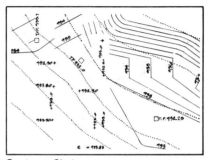

Contours SL-1

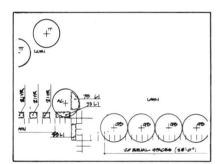

Planting SL-4

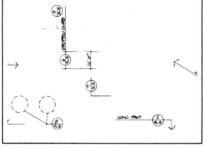

Materials SL-2

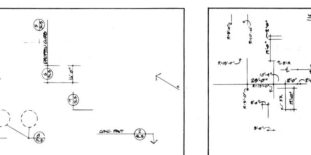

Dimensions SL-3

This project was the landscape architect's first experience with pin registered overlay drafting. Dennis Piermont's records show that drafting plus printing costs equalled budgeted drafting costs without pin registration. Available time was used to advantage on other creative work. Now the system is fully integrated in the firm's operation.

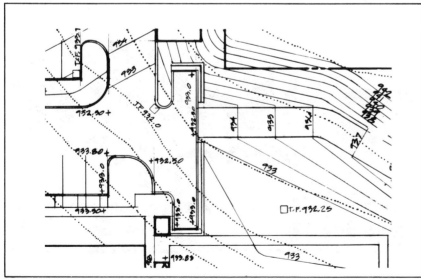

Composite (Hard Line Base B-8 and Contours SL-1)

Figure 2.8 Site work. (Courtesy of Keuffel & Esser Co., Morristown, N.J.)

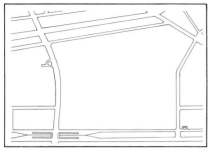
Curbs

Bldgs.

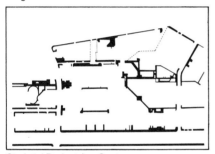
Skeletal Pedestrian System

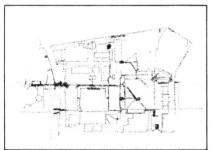
Winter Pedestrian System

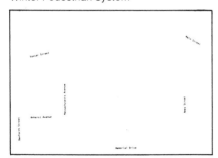
Notes

Living Documents

In general, planning studies become frozen in time in the form of an immutable printed report. Since these documents serve little purpose other than for historical reference, there is a way through the pin register system to make them useful *living documents*. As projects become actual structures or forms, they can be photographically incorporated as background information, with future plans retained as overlays. As new data is collected, it can also be produced in the form of an overlay. Therefore, such information as traffic densities, neighborhood character, urban demolition, environmental influences, etc., can be incorporated with the original report to form a complete and living document.

Planning and Urban Design

Master Planning, Regional Planning, Urban Design, Feasibility Studies and all other planning efforts are made easier and more effective with the use of overlay drafting. The illustration on this page is a good example of a living document. It shows the overlays used in the 1978 planning study of Massachusetts Institute of Technology. The development of this 20 year plan for the Institute's East Campus is the work of Mitchel-Giurgola/Gruzen & Partners.

"As-Builts"

As a result of the pin register system, M.I.T. will easily be able to keep vital data of campus information current and incorporate as-built data at large scale. Through the use of reduction/blow back camera, 1/8" or 1/16" = 1'-0" can be turned into more useful campus plans at smaller engineering scales of 1" = 50', 100', and 200'.

By overlays, information can be stored and updated separately such as: campus steam, chilled water, water supply, standpipe and sprinkler systems, storm and sanitary, natural gas, electric service, lighting, signal, computer cable systems, roads, pedestrian walks, fire fighting access, security, building delivery, landscaping, planting maintenance and watering systems.

Overlays shown are skeletal pedestrian system, winter pedestrian system, and annotations of titles. Large composite drawing illustrates winter pedestrian system.

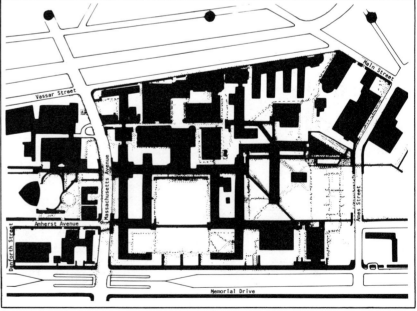
Composite

Figure 2.9 Planning and urban design. (Courtesy of Keuffel & Esser Co., Morristown, N.J.)

photographic services. This negative can then be used to expose a sensitized vellum and make a photographic reproduction on vellum.

Using Standard Titles. Using any number of the procedures previously described, you can produce standard titles such as those found under a drawing or title block, to keep the lettering of titles uniform. Lettering machines which produce letters on a sticky-backed tape are now available with interchangeable type styles and sizes. The final product resembles rub-on letters on adhesive tape.

For example, you can produce the term "floor plan" with rub-on letters or a lettering machine and then reproduce the term in quantity. You can cut out the multiple copies, position them on a sheet, which you can then use as a master to produce appliques with a plain paper copier and adhesive transparent film. In this way, you can cut titles from the adhesive and apply them to the various sheets as needed.

Office Standards

Sheet Size

The drawing sheet size varies from office to office depending on the type of work performed, the method of reproduction used, and the system of drafting used in the office. The most common sheet sizes are 24″ × 36″, 28″ × 42″ and 30″ × 42″.

When sheets are used horizontally, they are usually bound on the left side. Because of this, the border is larger on the left side. A typical border line is ⅜″ to ½″ around three sides and 1″ to 1½″ on the left side.

Title blocks can run the full height of the right side rather than simply filling a square in the bottom right corner, as in mechanical drafting. The long title band contains such information as sheet number, client's name or project title, name of firm, name or title of the drawing, person drafting, scale, date, and revision dates. The title block sheets are usually preprinted or can be applied to sheets in the form of decals or appliques.

This location of the title block allows you to leave a rectangular area for drawing purposes, whereas a title block in the lower right corner produces an L-shaped drawing area. (Even when drawing on a large sheet, take care to draft so that you use the sheet to its fullest.)

Many offices establish a sheet module. Here is an example of this method with a 24″ × 36″ sheet:

Binding side	1½″ border
Other 3 sides	½″ border
Title block	1½″

This leaves a drawing area of 23″ × 32½″. The vertical 23″ distance can be divided into four equal parts, while the horizontal 32½″ can be divided into 8 equal parts. This provides 32 spaces 4¹⁄₁₆″ wide by 5¾″ high. This office procedure may be followed so that each sheet has a consistent appearance. Whether the sheet is full of details or a combination of a plan and details and/or notes, the module gives you parameters within which to work. You should draft from the right side of the sheet so that any blank spaces remaining are toward the inside (on the binding side).

Lettering Height

The height of lettering depends on the type of reproduction used. If you use normal diazo methods, use the following standards as a rule of thumb:

Main titles under drawings	¼″ maximum
Subtitles	³⁄₁₆″
Normal lettering	³⁄₃₂″–⅛″
Sheet number in title block	½″

Increase these sizes when you are reducing drawings. For example, increase normal lettering from ³⁄₃₂″ or ⅛″ or ³⁄₁₆″, depending on the reduction ratio.

Scale of Drawings

The scale selected should be the largest practical scale based on the size of the structure and the drawing space available. Listed below are the most common sizes used by offices, with the most desirable size being underlined where there is a choice.

Site Plan: ⅛″ = 1′–0″ for small sites. Drawings are provided by a civil engineer and scales are expressed in engineering terms such as 1″ = 30′, 1″ = 50′, etc.

Floor Plan: ¼″ = 1′–0″, ⅛″ or ¹⁄₁₆″ = 1′–0″ for larger structures.

Exterior Elevations: Same as the floor plan.

Building Sections: ½″ = 1′–0″ if possible or the same as exterior elevations.

Interior Elevations: ¼″ = 1′–0″, ⅜″ = 1′–0″, ½″ = 1′–0″.

Architectural Details: ½″ = 1′–0″ to 3″ = 1′–0″, depending on the size of the object being drawn or the amount of information that must be shown. Footing detail: ¾″ = 1′–0″ or 1″ = 1′–0″. Eave details: 1½″ = 1′–0″. Wall sections: typically, ¾″ = 1′–0″.

Framing (Roof, Floor, Ceiling): Either the same size as the floor plan, so that it can be superimposed on the floor plan, or smaller.

Materials in Section

Figures 2.10, 2.11, 2.12, and 2.13 show the various methods used throughout the United States to represent different materials in section.

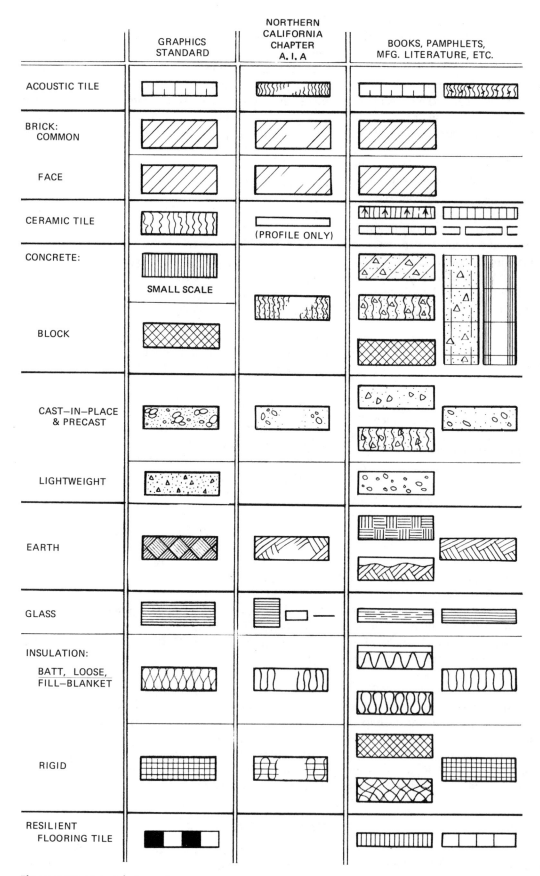

Figure 2.10 Materials in section.

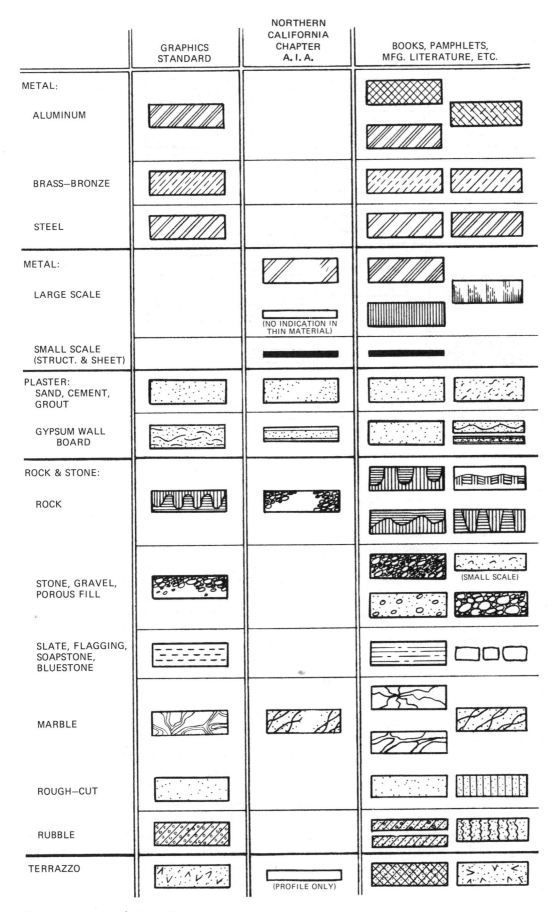

Figure 2.11 Materials in section.

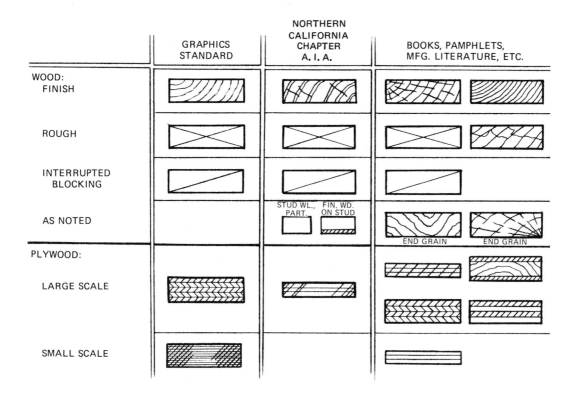

* TO SAVE VALUABLE DRAFTING TIME, THE NORTHERN CALIFORNIA
CHAPTER RECOMMENDS THAT THE TOTAL DETAIL IN SECTION
NOT BE FILLED IN COMPLETELY BUT JUST ENOUGH TO INDICATE
THE MATERIAL IN QUESTION.

Figure 2.12 Materials in section.

In the first column are material designations assembled by the Committee on Office Practice, American Institute of Architects (National) and published in *Architectural Graphic Standards*. The second column designations are prepared by the Task Force on Production Office Procedures of the Northern California Chapter of the American Institute of Architects and published in September 1974. The final column lists items from other sources such as pamphlets, manufacturers' literature, textbooks, governmental agencies, and trade and technical organizations or associations.

Clearly, there is standardization and there are variations. For example, all groups agree on the method of representing brick in section, yet there is a great variation in the way concrete block is represented in section.

The last figure shows specialty items from a variety of sources.

Graphic Symbols

The symbols in Figure 2.14 are the most common and acceptable, to judge by the frequency of use by the architectural offices surveyed. This list can be and should be expanded by each office to include those symbols generally used in its practice and not indicated here.

Again, each professional is urged to accept the task force recommendation by adopting the use of these symbols.

Abbreviations

Suggested abbreviations compiled by Task Force #1, National Committee on Office Practice, American Institute of Architects, and published in the AIA *Journal* in January 1974, can be found in the Appendix at the end of the book.

Dimensioning

Dimensioning is the act of incorporating numerical values into a drawing as a means of sizing various components and also locating parts of a building. This is accomplished on dimension lines, in notes, and by referral to other drawings or details.

Grouping Dimensions. Group dimensions whenever possible to provide continuity. This takes planning. Try running a diazo print of the drawing in question and dimension it on this check print first. This will allow you to identify dimensions and decide how they can be effectively grouped.

ADDITIONAL MATERIALS IN SECTION

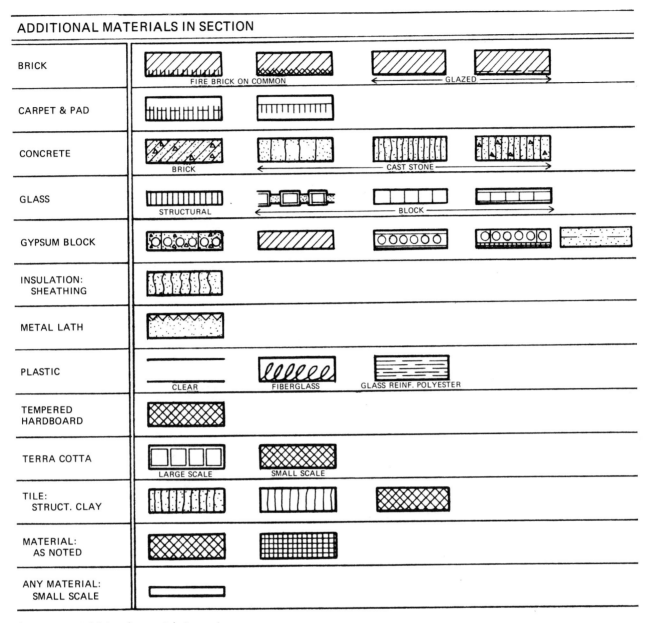

Figure 2.13 Additional materials in section.

Maintaining a Dimension Standard. The most important dimensions dictate subsequent dimensions. For example, if a wall is dimensioned to the center of the wall first, all subsequent dimensions using this wall as a reference point should be dimensioned at its center.

Size Dimensions and Location Dimensions. The two basic kinds of dimensions are size and location. See Figure 2.15. Size dimensions indicate overall size. Location dimensions deal with the actual placement of an object or structure, such as a wall, a window, a concrete patio slab, a barbecue grill, or a planter.

The Dimensional Reference System. The dimensional reference system is based on a three-dimensional axis. See Figure 2.16. Critical planes are located by a series of reference bubbles and used as **planes of reference.** Figure 2.17 shows a box; reference bubbles describe the three planes of height, width, and depth. Now examine this box sliced in two directions as shown in Figures 2.18 and 2.19. The first slice produces a **horizontal control plane** and the second a **vertical control plane.**

The shaded area in Figure 2.20 represents a horizontal plane at a critical point on the structure, such as the floor line. The shaded area on Figure 2.21 represents a vertical plane at a critical point of the structure, such as the location of a series of columns or beams. There is a definite relationship between the vertical control plane

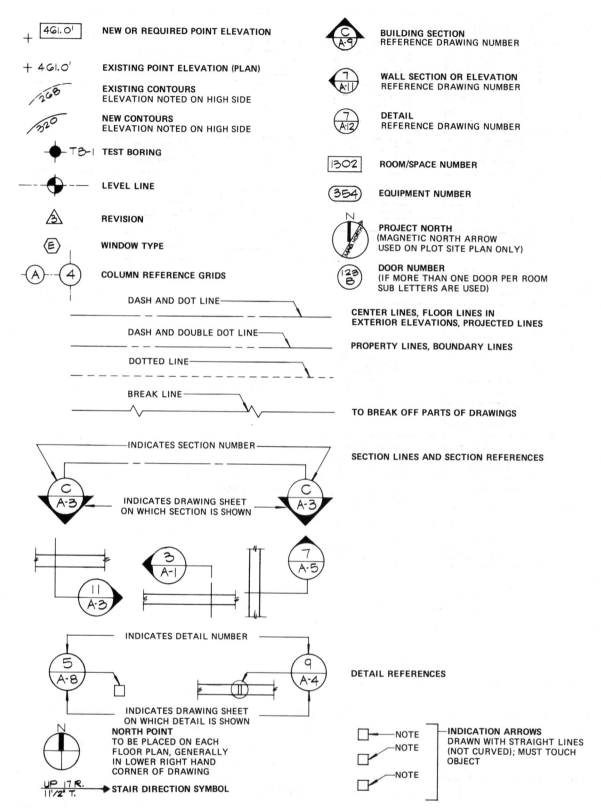

Figure 2.14 Graphic symbols from AIA standards.

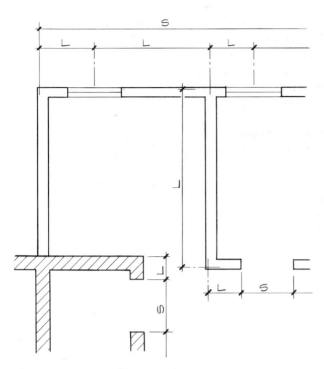

Figure 2.15 Size and location dimensions.

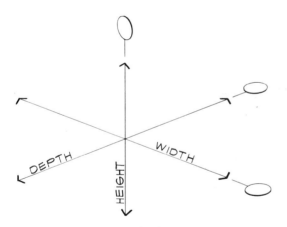

Figure 2.16 Dimensional reference system.

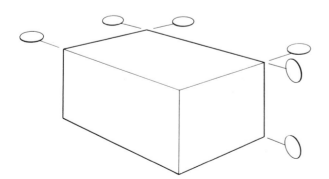

Figure 2.17 Three principle planes using dimensional reference system.

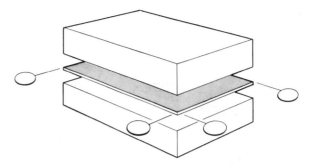

Figure 2.18 Horizontal control plane.

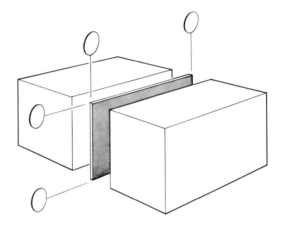

Figure 2.19 Vertical control plane

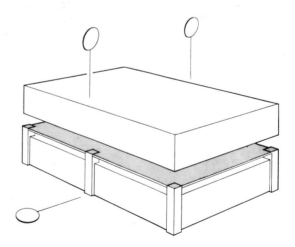

Figure 2.20 Horizontal plane.

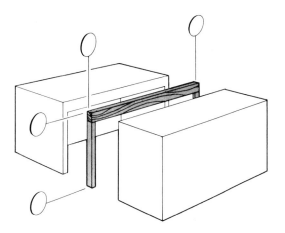

Figure 2.21 Vertical plane.

and the horizontal control plane. Compare the **plan** and the **section** shown in Figure 2.22. The section is a vertical cut as in Figure 2.21 and the plan is a horizontal cut as in Figure 2.20. The two vertical and one horizontal reference bubbles on Figure 2.20 are an attempt to show this relationship

Types of Planes. There are two types of planes. The first is the **axial plane,** which goes through the center of critical structural items as shown in Figure 2.23. Note how the columns are dimensioned to the center. When pilasters (widening of a masonry wall for support) are used, they become a good location for control dimensions, as they support the structural members above.

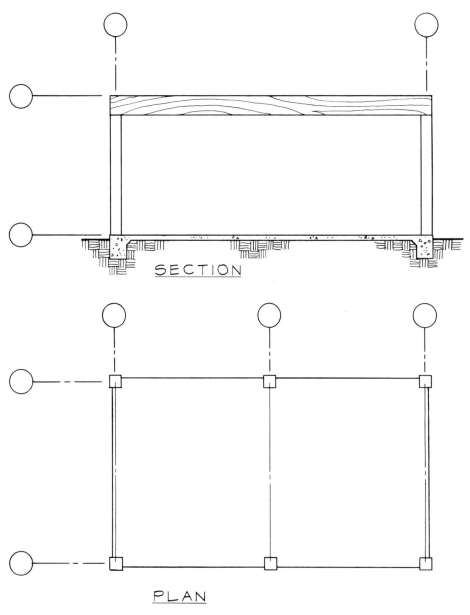

Figure 2.22 Section and plan.

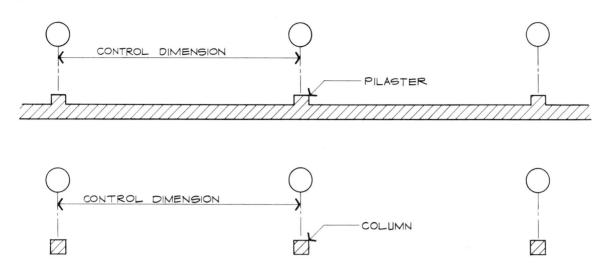

Figure 2.23 Axial control planes.

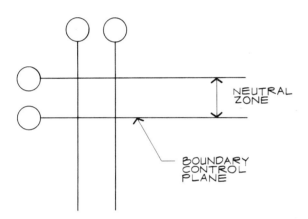

Figure 2.24 Boundary control planes.

The second type of plane is called a **boundary control plane.** See Figure 2.24. In this case, columns and walls are not dimensioned to the center; instead, their boundaries are dimensioned. Figure 2.25 shows examples of columns and walls located in the **neutral zone.** These neutral zones are especially valuable in dealing with the vertical dimensions of a section and with elevations. See Figure 2.26. A neutral zone is established between the ceiling and the floor above. The floor to ceiling heights can be established to allow the structural, mechanical, and electrical consultants to perform their work. Once that dimension is established, the neutral zone and floor-to-floor dimensions follow. See Figure 2.27 for a practical application of the **vertical control dimension** and control zone (another term for netural zone).

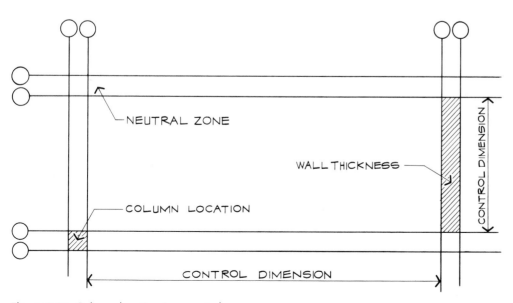

Figure 2.25 Column location in a neutral zone.

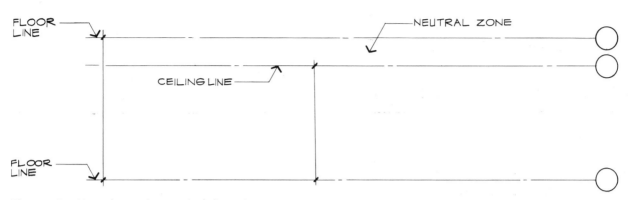

Figure 2.26 Neutral zone in a vertical dimension.

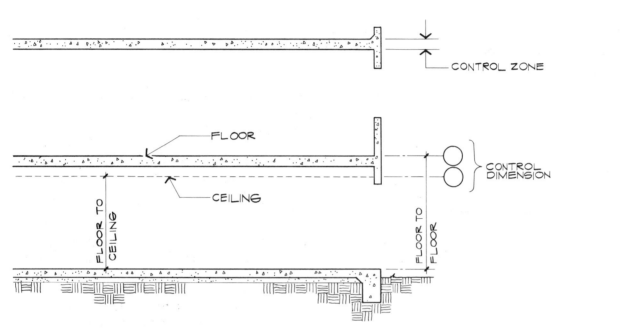

Figure 2.27 Vertical control dimension.

Metrics

Conversion to metric numbers is a change in total concept and attitude that must be incorporated at the basic design stage. Never design in feet and inches and then convert to metric; it creates undesirable metric measurements. Unfortunately, manufacturers of building materials have not been converting consistently to the metric system. Lumber, steel, and masonry units will soon have standards established, but until they are in effect, there is an interim period which involves simple conversion of numbers.

The English system used different basic units. Liquid is measured differently from linear measurements and weight; for example, 4 quarts = 1 gallon, 12 inches = 1 foot, and 16 ounces = 1 pound.

In the metric system, while the names for liquid, weight, and linear measurements are different, their units are based on tenths, which avoids so much memorizing.

Nomenclature. Since the architectural field deals predominantly with linear measurements, this discussion emphasizes the conversion of feet and inches to metric equivalents.

The largest metric unit of measurement for use in the construction industry is the meter. The most recent standard measurement of a meter is the measurement of the swing of a pendulum during a one-second period. This swinging pendulum is made of platinum and is located at 45° latitude in France. Because of the nature of the way the standard meter is measured and the location of this standard, the length of a meter varies slightly throughout the world. It is hoped that attempts at standardization by the International Standards Organization (I.S.O.) will prove successful, because if different lengths are used for the standard meter, building products made in one country might not correspond to the needs of another.

A meter comprises ten decimeters which, in turn, each comprise ten centimeters. The smallest unit of conversion is the millimeter. Ten meters make a decameter; ten times that is a hectometer; and ten times that is a kilometer. Here is a chart showing these values.

kilometer	= 1,000 meters	km
*hectometer	= 100 meters	hm
*decameter	= 10 meters	dam
meter		m
*decimeter	= $\frac{1}{10}$ meter	dm
centimeter	= $\frac{1}{100}$ meter	cm
millimeter	= $\frac{1}{1000}$ meter	mm

*Seldom used in modern drawings.

For architectural drafting, the millimeter and the meter are the most desirable units to use.

Notation Method. Locate the decimal point in the center of the line of numerical value rather than close to the bottom of the line. For example, 304.65 is best written 304·65. However, the original notation is acceptable.

Commas are not used. Rather, spaces are left to denote where commas would have been. For example 10·34674 meters would be written 10·346 74 meters, and 506,473·21 meters would be written as 506 473·21 meters.

Abbreviations of metric units do not have special plural forms. For example, fifty centimeters is written 50 cm, *not* 50 cms. Note, also, the space between the number and the letters. It should read 50, space, centimeters: 50 cm.

Once a standard, such as "all measurements shall be in meters," is established for a set of drawings, it need not be noted on each drawing. A 4 by 8 sheet of plywood should be called out not as 121 9·2 m × 243 8·4 m plywood but rather as 121 9·2 × 243 8 plywood. However, if a size is in a measure other than meters, this should be noted.

English Equivalents. Here is a quick reference chart for converting linear measurements into metrics:

Length:	inches ×	2·54	= centimeters (cm)
	feet ×	0·304 8	= meters (m)
	yards ×	0·914 4	= meters (m)
	miles ×	1·609 34	= kilometers (km)
Mass:	pounds ×	0·453 592	= kilograms (kg)
	ounces ×	28·35	= grams (g)

General Conversion Rules. Using the equivalent values just given, you can convert by multiplication. For example, 16 inches is:

(times)
inches × 2·54 = cm
16 in. × 2·54 = 40·64 cm

To convert 25 feet into metric measurements:

feet × 0·304 8 = m
25 ft. × 0·304 8 = 7·62 m

To convert 75 yards into meters:

yards × 0·914 4 = m
75 yd. × 0·914 4 = 68·58 m

Unit Change. To convert 17 feet 8 inches, follow this procedure:

17 ft. × 0·304 8 = 5·181 6 m
8 in. × 2·54 = 20·32 cm

In this example, conversion of feet results in meters, and conversion of inches results in centimeters. You cannot add these quantities unless you convert them to the same unit of measurement. Do this simply by moving the decimal point. In this example, if meters are desired, simply move the decimal point of the centimeter unit two units to the left: 20·32 cm are equal to .203 2 m. Thus,

$$\begin{array}{rl} 17 \text{ ft.} = & 5·181 \ 6 \text{ m} \\ 8 \text{ in.} = & \underline{·203 \ 2 \text{ m}} \\ & 5·384 \ 8 \text{ m} \end{array}$$

Actual versus Nominal. Presently, lumber uses an odd system of notation. When a piece of lumber is drawn, it is drafted to its actual size (net size). In the notes describing this particular piece of wood, it is called out in its nominal size (call out size). For example, a 2 × 4 piece of wood is drawn at 1½″ × 3½″, but on the note pointing to this piece, it is still called a 2 × 4.

Therefore, when converting to metric, the 1½″ × 3½″ size must be converted and drawn to the actual size. There is no set procedure for the call out. Some drawings convert the 2 × 4 size metrically and note this piece of wood with the 1½″ × 3½″ size converted. A sample note might read as follows:

·0381 × ·0889 (net) STUD

It is hoped that when metric lumber size is established, the net and nominal sizes will be identical.

Using Double Standards. Due to the newness of using metrics in the American architectural profession, we are not yet geared to note things metrically. Lumber, reinforcing, glass, and other materials are still ordered in the English system. Their sizes, weights, and shapes are also still described in the English system.

There are three approaches to this situation. First, we can note only those things we have control over in metrics, such as the size of a room, the width of a footing, and so on, while noting 2 × 4 studs, #4 reinforcing rods, ½″ anchor bolts, and the like, according to the manufacturer until they change to the metric system.

A second method is dual notation. This system requires dimensions, notes, and all call outs to be recorded twice. For example, a 35'–6" dimension has a metric value of 10·820 4 written directly below it. If most workers are operating under the old system, they can ignore the metric value and refer to the English system. If, however, the majority of the workers use the metric figure, you have prepared a value that cannot be measured accurately because the decimal is carried out too far. This problem is dealt with later.

The third and final method is to approach everything metrically. This may not be the best way in an office going through a transition, but it is the best student method because you will eventually be asked to work totally in metrics.

Conversion of Drafting. If we are to convert everything to metrics, there are three procedures to consider. First is that of "holding" certain dimension notes and call outs. If, for example, we are dealing with a #4 rebar (which is a steel reinforcing bar ½" in size) and the manufacturer has not changed to metrics, we must convert the ½" by multiplying ½" × 2·54 and note the rebar as:

> 1·27 cm rebar
> or
> 0·0127 rebar

The second procedure requires "rounding off." See Figure 2.28. In this figure, the scale on the top is an enlarged one that you are accustomed to seeing. The scale directly below is in the same enlarged proportion but in metric units. The numbers in this scale are in centimeters. Notice that 2·54 centimeters equal an inch. Notice also that one centimeter is less than ½ inch. Initially, this is a hard proportion to relate to for anyone making the transition. Also note that half a centimeter (0·5 cm) is smaller than ¼ inch and that one millimeter (one tenth of a centimeter) is less than ¹⁄₁₆ of an inch.

Now compare this knowledge with an actual number. Assume that you wish to dig a trench 12 inches wide for a footing.

> 12 inches = (12 × 2·54) = 30·48 cm

Hence, there are 30 + units less than ½ inch in size that we can measure. The .4 is less than ³⁄₁₆", which is very difficult to measure and impossible to deal with on the job for a worker This is the point when we should begin to round off.

The final number (0·08) is even worse. It amounts to just a little more than ¹⁄₃₂ of an inch—a measurement that a draftsperson would have difficulty even reading on the scale, and that the person digging the trench would have to ignore. The final rounded off value should be 31·0 cm or 0·31. This trench is about ³⁄₁₆ inches

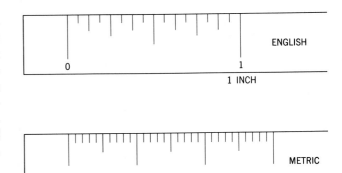

Figure 2.28 Comparison of english and metric scales.

wider than the desired 12 inches but is something the people out in the field can measure with their metric scales.

The third conversion procedure requires judgement about whether to increase or decrease. Certain measurements must be increased in the rounding off process—the trench discussed previously is a good example. If we round this number off to 30·0 cm or 0·30, the measurement is less than 2 inches. If the 12 inch requirement had been imposed by the local code, you would have thus broken the code. Had it been set at 12 inches for structural reasons, the building could be deemed unsafe. Another example is a planned opening for a piece of equipment. To round off to the smaller number might result in the equipment's not fitting.

You must be aware of situations that are dictated by health and safety. The minimum depth of a step might be 10½" or 26·67 cm. If we rounded this off to 26·0 cm, it would not meet the minimum standards for a stair. Another kind of danger lies in *exceeding* a required maximum. For example, the note for an anchor bolt reads:

> ½" × 10"; to anchor bolt embedded 7" into concrete 6'–0" o.c. and 12" from corners.

The spacing of 6'–0" on center is used to maintain a minimum number of anchor bolts per unit of length. If we increase the distance between bolts, we exceed the required spacing, and as stated in the note reduce the number of bolts per unit of length below the minimum required.

The 12-inch measurement has the same effect. The intent is to have an anchor bolt 12 inches or less from each of the corners. We must, therefore, decrease the measurement when we round off after converting to metric, to insure that there is an anchor bolt closer than 12 inches from every corner. The ½" × 10" Φ (Φ is a symbol for round) becomes what is called a "holding" measurement since it comes from the manufacturer that way. The final numerical value that reads "embedded 7 inches into concrete" must be thought out wisely. The bolt must be embedded enough for strength, yet left exposed adequately to penetrate a sill (the first piece of wood to come into contact with concrete) and still leave enough space for a washer and a nut.

The second and third processes are called soft conversion; that is, an English measurement is converted directly into a metric equivalent and then rounded off into a workable metric value. A hard conversion is the name given to changing the total approach. It is not just a numerical conversion but a change of media as well. If bricks are the medium for example, the procedure would be to subscribe to a brick that was sized metrically and dimension accordingly.

Listed below are some of the recommended rounding off sizes:

⅛″	=	3·2 mm	1¾″ =	44·0 mm
¼″	=	6·4 mm	2″ =	50·0 mm
⅜″	=	9·5 mm	2½″ =	63·0 mm
½″	=	12·7 mm	3″ =	75·0 mm
⅝″	=	16·0 mm	4″ =	100·0 mm
¾″	=	19·0 mm	6″ =	150·0 mm
⅞″	=	22·0 mm	8″ =	200·0 mm
1″	=	25·0 mm	10″ =	250·0 mm
1¼″	=	32·0 mm	12″ =	300·0 mm
1½″	=	38·0 mm		

Zero is used to avoid error in metrics. For example, .8 is written 0.8 or 0·8.

When other conversions are needed, round off fractions to the nearest 5 mm, inches to the nearest 25 mm, and feet to the nearest 0·1 meter.

Metric Scale. The metric scale is used in the same way as the architectural scales. It reduces a drawing to a selected proportion. You can purchase scales with the following metric scales.

1:5	1:50
1:10	1:75
1:20	1:100
1:25	1:125
1:33⅓	1:200
1:40	

While these proportions may not mean anything initially, let us take one example and see what it means. The 1:10 scale indicates that we are taking a known measurement (a meter) and making it ten times smaller. See Figure 2.29. In other words, if you visualize a meter (39·37 inches) and squeeze it until it is only one-tenth of its original size, you have a 1:10 ratio scale. Everything you draw is then one-tenth of its original size.

This also applies to any other scale. A 1:50 scale

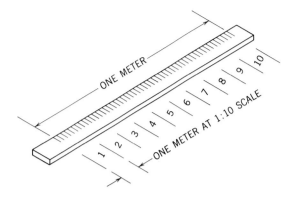

Figure 2.29 Pictorial of reduced metric scale.

means that the original meter has been reduced to one-fiftieth of its original length. Figures 2.30 and 2.31 show the visual appearance of a 1:50, 1:10, 1:20, and 1:100 as they might be seen on an actual scale. Notice how the meter is to be located so you can translate decimeters and centimeters. To measure 12 inches or 30·48 cm (0·3048 m) on a 1:10 scale, see Figure 2.32.

If you find it difficult to transfer a drawing scaled in inches and feet to a metric drawing, the chart below should help.

1:10 is approximately 1″ = 1′–0″ (1:12)
1:20 is approximately ½″ = 1′–0″ (1:24)
1:50 is approximately ¼″ = 1′–0″ (1:48)
1:100 is approximately ⅛″ = 1′–0″ (1:96)

Of the four scales in this chart, the 1:50 and 1:100 come closest to being exact conversions.

The conversion charts for feet to meters, and meters to feet, in Tables 2.1 to 2.5 greatly reduce the need for arithmetic calculations in converting actual dimensions.

Drawing Sheet Size. When the total conversion to metrics takes place, the change will not only affect the drawing but the sheet size of the drawing paper as well. Listed below are some of the typical sizes used internationally. They are expressed in millimeters (mm).

841 × 1189	105 × 148
594 × 841	74 × 105
420 × 594	52 × 74
297 × 420	37 × 52
210 × 297	26 × 37
148 × 210	

A spot check of the various paper companies which sell reproduction paper as well as drawing paper shows that metrically sized paper is already being used for overseas work.

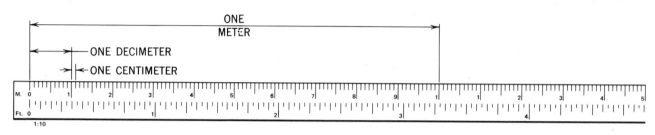

Figure 2.30 How to read an actual scale—1:50 and 1:10.

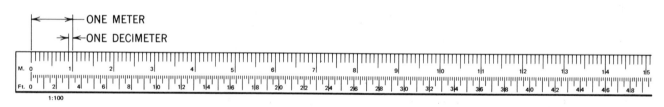

Figure 2.31 How to read an actual scale—1:20 and 1:100.

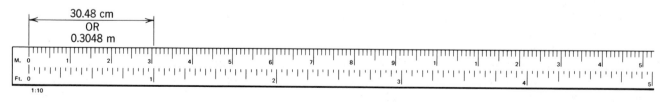

Figure 2.32 One foot equivalent in metric.

Possible Sizes. Because the various manufacturers have not converted to a uniform size, it is difficult to predict the final evolution of the various building materials. Suggested sizes and those used by other countries are listed below.

Wood (in mm)

38 × 75	44 × 75	50 × 75	63 × 150
38 × 100	44 × 100	50 × 100	63 × 175
38 × 150	44 × 150	50 × 125	63 × 200
38 × 175	44 × 175	50 × 150	63 × 225
38 × 200	44 × 200	50 × 175	
38 × 225	44 × 225	50 × 200	75 × 200
		50 × 300	75 × 300

Brick (in mm)

300 × 100 × 100	200 × 100 × 100
200 × 100 × 75	200 × 200 × 100

Gypsum Lath (in mm)

9·5   12·7 or 12·00

Miscellaneous

12 mm diameter for rebar   3 mm for sheet glass
25 mm for sheathing

Modules. As indicated in Figure 2.33, the standard module in metrics is 100 mm. Groups of this standard 100 mm module are called a multi-module. When you select the multi-module, you should consider quantities such as 600 mm, 800 mm, 1200 mm, 1800 mm, and 2400 mm. All of these numbers are divisible in a way that allows you flexibility. For example, the 600 mm multi-module is divisible by 2, 3, 4, and 5. The result of this division gives numbers such as 200, 300, 120, and 150. All of these are numbers for which building materials may be available. This is especially true in masonry units. Most of the sizes listed under "Possible sizes" work into a 600 mm module. See Figure 2.34.

Sweet's Catalog[1]

Sweet's Catalog File is a retrieval system for the most up-to-date product information. It is a set of volumes that helps people in the construction industry obtain literature and information from the thousands of manufacturers of materials. The beginning of each volume has a complete description of its use. The six basic types of *Sweet's Catalog File* are:

A. Products for General Building (green binding)
B. Products for Industrial Construction and Renovation and Renovation Extension

[1]"Sweet's" is a trademark of McGraw-Hill Inc. Sweet's Catalog Files are copyrighted by McGraw-Hill Inc.

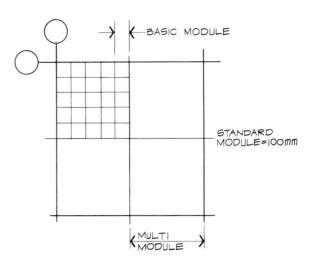

Figure 2.33 Standard module.

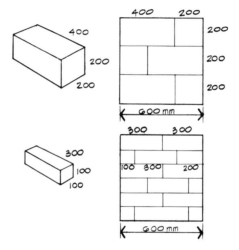

Figure 2.34 Brick and block dimensions.

C. Products for Light Residential Construction (yellow binding)
D. Products for Interiors
E. Products for Engineers
    1. Mechanical and related products
    2. Electrical and related products
    3. Civil and related products
F. Products for Canadian Construction

Sweet's Catalog Files are a distribution system for catalogs of building product manufacturers who pay to insert their literature. Construction professionals are qualified to receive Sweet's Catalog Files acording to the volume and type of projects they carry out.

Architectural offices use mostly the volumes covering "Products for Light Residential Construction" and "Products for General Building."

All sets are based on the "Uniform Construction In-

Table 2.1

Fractions of Inch	64ths of Inch	Decimals	Millimeters	Fractions of Inch	64ths of Inch	Decimals	Millimeters
—	1	.015625	0.397	—	33	.515625	13.097
$\frac{1}{32}$	2	.031250	0.794	$\frac{17}{32}$	34	.531250	13.494
—	3	.046875	1.191	—	35	.546875	13.891
$\frac{1}{16}$	4	.062500	1.588	$\frac{9}{16}$	36	.562500	14.288
—	5	.078125	1.984	—	37	.578125	14.684
$\frac{3}{32}$	6	.093750	2.381	$\frac{19}{32}$	38	.593750	15.081
—	7	.109375	2.778	—	39	.609375	15.478
$\frac{1}{8}$	8	.125000	3.175	$\frac{5}{8}$	40	.625000	15.875
—	9	.140625	3.572	—	41	.640625	16.272
$\frac{5}{32}$	10	.156260	3.969	$\frac{21}{32}$	42	.656250	16.669
—	11	.171875	4.366	—	43	.671875	17.066
$\frac{3}{16}$	12	.187500	4.763	$\frac{11}{16}$	44	.687500	17.463
—	13	.203125	5.159	—	45	.703125	17.859
$\frac{7}{32}$	14	.218750	5.556	$\frac{23}{32}$	46	.718750	18.256
—	15	.234375	5.953	—	47	.734375	18.653
$\frac{1}{4}$	16	.250000	6.350	$\frac{3}{4}$	48	.750000	19.050
—	17	.265625	6.747	—	49	.765625	19.447
$\frac{9}{32}$	18	.281250	7.144	$\frac{25}{32}$	50	.781250	19.844
—	19	.296875	7.541	—	51	.796875	20.241
$\frac{5}{16}$	20	.312500	7.938	$\frac{13}{16}$	52	.812500	20.638
—	21	.328125	8.334	—	53	.828125	21.034
$\frac{11}{32}$	22	.343750	8.731	$\frac{27}{32}$	54	.843750	21.431
—	23	.359375	9.128	—	55	.859375	21.828
$\frac{3}{8}$	24	.375000	9.525	$\frac{7}{8}$	56	.875000	22.225
—	25	.390625	9.922	—	57	.890625	22.622
$\frac{13}{32}$	26	.406250	10.319	$\frac{29}{32}$	58	.906250	23.019
—	27	.421875	10.716	—	59	.921875	23.416
$\frac{7}{16}$	28	.437500	11.113	$\frac{15}{16}$	60	.937500	23.813
—	29	.453125	11.509	—	61	.953125	24.209
$\frac{15}{32}$	30	.468750	11.906	$\frac{31}{32}$	62	.968750	24.606
—	31	.484375	12.303	—	63	.984375	25.003
$\frac{1}{2}$	32	.500000	12.700	1	64	1.000000	25.400

dex,'' one of the three major numbering systems used widely in the construction industry. This particular system uses sixteen major divisions:

1. General data
2. Site work
3. Concrete
4. Masonry
5. Metals
6. Wood and plastics
7. Thermal and moisture protection
8. Doors and windows
9. Finishes
10. Specialties
11. Equipment
12. Furnishings
13. Special construction
14. Conveying systems
15. Mechanical
16. Electrical

Each of these major divisions is subsequently subdi-vided into smaller sections. For example, in Division 8, Doors and Windows, Section 8.1 deals with entrances and storefronts, Section 8.2 with metal doors and frames, and Section 8.32 with exit devices.

An alpha (lower case) numerical system is used when further breakdown is necessary. For example, in Division 11, Equipment, 11.45b deals with incinerators, 11.45c with chutes and collectors. After the number, there is a diagonal slash followed by letters indicating the manufacturer's name. The number 9.13/Du, for example, deals with Division 9, Finishes, and the subsection Wall Coverings; the "Du" stands for DuPont, the manufacturer.

Every volume has the topic and sub-topic listed on the spine, on the cover, and on each division sheet. In addition, the front of each volume contains a classification guide listing all of the volumes and subheadings, and a cross reference to other index systems. There is also an index in the front of each book which lists firm name, product name, and trade name. This system is especially helpful if only the trade name or the manufacturer or a broad general classification is known.

Table 2.2

Feet	Meters	Feet	Meters	Feet	Meters	Feet	Meters	Feet	Meters
0	0.00000	50	15.24003	100	30.48006	150	45.72009	200	60.96012
1	.30480	1	15.54483	1	30.78486	1	46.02489	1	61.26492
2	.60960	2	15.84963	2	31.08966	2	46.32969	2	61.56972
3	.91440	3	16.15443	3	31.39446	3	46.63449	3	61.87452
4	1.21920	4	16.45923	4	31.69926	4	46.93929	4	62.17932
5	1.52400	5	16.76403	5	32.00406	5	47.24409	5	62.48412
6	1.82880	6	17.06883	6	32.30886	6	47.54890	6	62.78893
7	2.13360	7	17.37363	7	32.61367	7	47.85370	7	63.09373
8	2.43840	8	17.67844	8	32.91847	8	48.15850	8	63.39853
9	2.74321	9	17.98324	9	33.22327	9	48.46330	9	63.70333
10	3.04801	60	18.28804	110	33.52807	160	48.76810	210	64.00813
1	3.35281	1	18.59284	1	33.83287	1	49.07290	1	64.31293
2	3.65761	2	18.89764	2	34.13767	2	49.37770	2	64.61773
3	3.96241	3	19.20244	3	34.44247	3	49.68250	3	64.92253
4	4.26721	4	19.50724	4	34.74727	4	49.98730	4	65.22733
5	4.57201	5	19.81204	5	35.05207	5	50.29210	5	65.53213
6	4.87681	6	20.11684	6	35.35687	6	50.59690	6	65.83693
7	5.18161	7	20.42164	7	35.66167	7	50.90170	7	66.14173
8	5.48641	8	20.72644	8	35.96647	8	51.20650	8	66.44653
9	5.79121	9	21.03124	9	36.27127	9	51.51130	9	66.75133
20	6.09601	70	21.33604	120	36.57607	170	51.81610	220	67.05613
1	6.40081	1	21.64084	1	36.88087	1	52.12090	1	67.36093
2	6.70561	2	21.94564	2	37.18567	2	52.42570	2	67.66574
3	7.01041	3	22.25044	3	37.49047	3	52.73051	3	67.97054
4	7.31521	4	22.55525	4	37.79528	4	53.03531	4	68.27534
5	7.62002	5	22.86005	5	38.10008	5	53.34011	5	68.58014
6	7.92482	6	23.16485	6	38.40488	6	53.64491	6	68.88494
7	8.22962	7	23.46965	7	38.70968	7	53.94971	7	69.18974
8	8.53442	8	23.77445	8	39.01448	8	54.25451	8	69.49454
9	8.83922	9	24.07925	9	39.31928	9	54.55931	9	69.79934
30	9.14402	80	24.38405	130	39.62408	180	54.86411	230	70.10414
1	9.44882	1	24.68885	1	39.92888	1	55.16891	1	70.40894
2	9.75362	2	24.99365	2	40.23368	2	55.47371	2	70.71374
3	10.05842	3	25.29845	3	40.53848	3	55.77851	3	71.01854
4	10.36322	4	25.60325	4	40.84328	4	56.08331	4	71.32334
5	10.66802	5	25.90805	5	41.14808	5	56.38811	5	71.62814
6	10.97282	6	26.21285	6	41.45288	6	56.69291	6	71.93294
7	11.27762	7	26.51765	7	41.75768	7	56.99771	7	72.23774
8	11.58242	8	26.82245	8	42.06248	8	57.30251	8	72.54255
9	11.88722	9	27.12725	9	42.36728	9	57.60732	9	72.84735
40	12.19202	90	27.43205	140	42.67209	190	57.91212	240	73.15215
1	12.49682	1	27.73686	1	42.97689	1	58.21692	1	73.45695
2	12.80163	2	28.04166	2	43.28169	2	58.52172	2	73.76175
3	13.10643	3	28.34646	3	43.58649	3	58.82652	3	74.06655
4	13.41123	4	28.65126	4	43.89129	4	59.13132	4	74.37135
5	13.71603	5	28.95606	5	44.19609	5	59.43612	5	74.67615
6	14.02083	6	29.26086	6	44.50089	6	59.74092	6	74.98095
7	14.32563	7	29.56566	7	44.80569	7	60.04572	7	75.28575
8	14.63043	8	29.87046	8	45.11049	8	60.35052	8	75.59055
9	14.93523	9	30.17526	9	45.41529	9	60.65532	9	75.89535

1 inch	= 0.02549 meter	4 inches = 0.10160 meter	7 inches = 0.17780 meter	10 inches = 0.25400 meter
2 inches	= 0.05080 meter	5 inches = 0.12700 meter	8 inches = 0.20320 meter	11 inches = 0.27940 meter
3 inches	= 0.07620 meter	6 inches = 0.15240 meter	9 inches = 0.22860 meter	12 inches = 0.30480 meter

Table 2.3

Feet	Meters	Feet	Meters	Feet	Meters	Feet	Meters	Feet	Meters
250	76.20015	300	91.44018	350	106.68021	400	121.92024	450	137.16027
1	76.50495	1	91.74498	1	106.98501	1	122.22504	1	137.46507
2	76.80975	2	92.04978	2	107.28981	2	122.52985	2	137.76988
3	77.11455	3	92.35458	3	107.59462	3	122.83465	3	138.07468
4	77.41935	4	92.65939	4	107.89942	4	123.13945	4	138.37948
5	77.72416	5	92.96419	5	108.20422	5	123.44425	5	138.68428
6	78.02896	6	93.26899	6	108.50902	6	123.74905	6	138.98908
7	78.33376	7	93.57379	7	108.81382	7	124.05385	7	139.29388
8	78.63856	8	93.87859	8	109.11862	8	124.35865	8	139.59868
9	78.94336	9	94.18339	9	109.42342	9	124.66345	9	139.90348
260	79.24816	310	94.48819	360	109.72822	410	124.96825	460	140.20828
1	79.55296	1	94.79299	1	110.03302	1	125.27305	1	140.51308
2	79.85776	2	95.09779	2	110.33782	2	125.57785	2	140.81788
3	80.16256	3	95.40259	3	110.64262	3	125.88265	3	141.12268
4	80.46736	4	95.70739	4	110.94742	4	126.18745	4	141.42748
5	80.77216	5	96.01219	5	111.25222	5	126.49225	5	141.73228
6	81.07696	6	96.31699	6	111.55702	6	126.79705	6	142.03708
7	81.38176	7	96.62179	7	111.86182	7	127.10185	7	142.34188
8	81.68656	8	96.92659	8	112.16662	8	127.40665	8	142.64669
9	81.99136	9	97.23139	9	112.47142	9	127.71146	9	142.95149
270	82.29616	320	97.53620	370	112.77623	420	128.01626	470	143.25629
1	82.60097	1	97.84100	1	113.08103	1	128.32106	1	143.56109
2	82.90577	2	98.14580	2	113.38583	2	128.62586	2	143.86589
3	83.21057	3	98.45060	3	113.69063	3	128.93066	3	144.17069
4	83.51537	4	98.75540	4	113.99543	4	129.23546	4	144.47549
5	83.82017	5	99.06020	5	114.30023	5	129.54026	5	144.78029
6	84.12497	6	99.36500	6	114.60503	6	129.84506	6	145.08509
7	84.42977	7	99.66980	7	114.90983	7	130.14986	7	145.38989
8	84.73457	8	99.97460	8	115.21463	8	130.45466	8	145.69469
9	85.03937	9	100.27940	9	115.51943	9	130.75946	9	145.99949
280	85.34417	330	100.58420	380	115.82423	430	131.06426	480	146.30429
1	85.64897	1	100.88900	1	116.12903	1	131.36906	1	146.60909
2	85.95377	2	101.19380	2	116.43383	2	131.67386	2	146.91389
3	86.25857	3	101.49860	3	116.73863	3	131.97866	3	147.21869
4	86.56337	4	101.80340	4	117.04343	4	132.28346	4	147.52350
5	86.86817	5	102.10820	5	117.34823	5	132.58827	5	147.82830
6	87.17297	6	102.41300	6	117.65304	6	132.89307	6	148.13310
7	87.47777	7	102.71781	7	117.95784	7	133.19787	7	148.43790
8	87.78258	8	103.02261	8	118.26264	8	133.50267	8	148.74270
9	88.08738	9	103.32741	9	118.56744	9	133.80747	9	149.04750
290	88.39218	340	103.63221	390	118.87224	440	134.11227	490	149.35230
1	88.69698	1	103.93701	1	119.17704	1	134.41707	1	149.65710
2	89.00178	2	104.24181	2	119.48184	2	134.72187	2	149.96190
3	89.30658	3	104.54661	3	119.78664	3	135.02667	3	150.26670
4	89.61138	4	104.85141	4	120.09144	4	135.33147	4	150.57150
5	89.91618	5	105.15621	5	120.39624	5	135.63627	5	150.87630
6	90.22098	6	105.46101	6	120.70104	6	135.94107	6	151.18110
7	90.52578	7	105.76581	7	121.00584	7	136.24587	7	151.48590
8	90.83058	8	106.07061	8	121.31064	8	136.55067	8	151.79070
9	91.13538	9	106.37541	9	121.61544	9	136.85547	9	152.09550
								500	152.40030

1 inch	= 0.02540 meter	4 inches = 0.10160 meter	7 inches = 0.17780 meter	10 inches = 0.25400 meter
2 inches	= 0.05080 meter	5 inches = 0.12700 meter	8 inches = 0.20320 meter	11 inches = 0.27940 meter
3 inches	= 0.07620 meter	6 inches = 0.15240 meter	9 inches = 0.22860 meter	12 inches = 0.30480 meter

Table 2.4

Meters	Feet	Meters	Feet	Meters	Feet	Meters	Feet	Meters	Feet
0	0.00000	50	164.04167	100	328.08333	150	492.12500	200	656.16667
1	3.28083	1	167.32250	1	331.36417	1	495.40583	1	659.44750
2	6.56167	2	170.60333	2	334.64500	2	498.68667	2	662.72833
3	9.84250	3	173.88417	3	337.92583	3	501.96750	3	666.00917
4	13.12333	4	177.16500	4	341.20667	4	505.24833	4	669.29000
5	16.40417	5	180.44583	5	344.48750	5	508.52917	5	672.57083
6	19.68500	6	183.72667	6	347.76833	6	511.81000	6	675.85167
7	22.96583	7	187.00750	7	351.04917	7	515.09083	7	679.13250
8	26.24667	8	190.28833	8	354.33000	8	518.37167	8	682.41333
9	29.52750	9	193.56917	9	357.61083	9	521.65250	9	685.69417
10	32.80833	60	196.85000	110	360.89167	160	524.93333	210	688.97500
1	36.08917	1	200.13083	1	364.17250	1	528.21417	1	692.25583
2	39.37000	2	203.41167	2	367.45333	2	531.49500	2	695.53667
3	42.65083	3	206.69250	3	370.73417	3	534.77583	3	698.81750
4	45.93167	4	209.97333	4	374.01500	4	538.05667	4	702.09833
5	49.21250	5	213.25417	5	377.29583	5	541.33750	5	705.37917
6	52.49333	6	216.53500	6	380.57667	6	544.61833	6	708.66000
7	55.77417	7	219.81583	7	383.85750	7	547.89917	7	711.94083
8	59.05500	8	223.09667	8	387.13833	8	551.18000	8	715.22167
9	62.33583	9	226.37750	9	390.41917	9	554.46083	9	718.50250
20	65.61667	70	229.65833	120	393.70000	170	557.74167	220	721.78333
1	68.89750	1	232.93917	1	396.90083	1	561.02250	1	725.06417
2	72.17833	2	236.22000	2	400.26167	2	564.30333	2	728.34500
3	75.45917	3	239.50083	3	403.54250	3	567.58417	3	731.62583
4	78.74000	4	242.78167	4	406.82333	4	570.86500	4	734.90667
5	82.02083	5	246.06250	5	410.10417	5	574.14583	5	738.18750
6	85.30167	6	249.34333	6	413.38500	6	577.42667	6	741.46833
7	88.58250	7	252.62417	7	416.66583	7	580.70750	7	744.74917
8	91.86333	8	255.90500	8	419.94667	8	583.98833	8	748.03000
9	95.14417	9	259.18583	9	423.22750	9	587.26917	9	751.31083
30	98.42500	80	262.46667	130	426.50833	180	590.55000	230	754.59167
1	101.70583	1	265.74750	1	429.78917	1	593.83083	1	757.87250
2	104.98667	2	269.02833	2	433.07000	2	597.11167	2	761.15333
3	108.26750	3	272.30917	3	436.35083	3	600.39250	3	764.43417
4	111.54833	4	275.59000	4	439.63167	4	603.67333	4	767.71500
5	114.82917	5	278.87083	5	442.91250	5	606.95417	5	770.99583
6	118.11000	6	282.15167	6	446.19333	6	610.23500	6	774.27667
7	121.39083	7	285.43250	7	449.47417	7	613.51583	7	777.55750
8	124.67167	8	288.71333	8	452.75500	8	616.79667	8	780.83833
9	127.95250	9	291.99417	9	456.03583	9	620.07750	9	784.11917
40	131.23333	90	295.27500	140	459.31667	190	623.35833	240	787.40000
1	134.51417	1	298.55583	1	462.59750	1	626.63917	1	790.68083
2	137.79500	2	301.83667	2	465.87833	2	629.92000	2	793.96167
3	141.07583	3	305.11750	3	469.15917	3	633.20083	3	797.24250
4	144.35667	4	308.39833	4	472.44000	4	636.48167	4	800.52333
5	147.63750	5	311.67917	5	475.72083	5	639.76250	5	803.80417
6	150.91833	6	314.96000	6	479.00167	6	643.04333	6	807.08500
7	154.19917	8	318.24083	7	482.28250	7	646.32417	7	810.36583
8	157.48000	8	321.52167	8	485.56333	8	649.60500	8	813.64667
9	160.76083	9	324.80250	9	488.84417	9	652.88583	9	816.92750

Table 2.5

Meters	Feet	Meters	Feet	Meters	Feet	Meters	Feet	Meters	Feet
250	820.20833	300	984.25000	350	1,148.29167	400	1,312.33333	450	1,476.37500
1	823.48917	1	987.53083	1	1,151.57250	1	1,315.61417	1	1,479.65583
2	826.77000	2	990.81167	2	1,154.85333	2	1,318,89500	2	1,482.93667
3	830.05083	3	994.09250	3	1,158.13417	3	1,322.17583	3	1,486.21750
4	833.33167	4	997.37333	4	1,161.41500	4	1,325.45667	4	1,489.49833
5	836.61250	5	1,000.65417	5	1,164.69583	5	1,328.73750	5	1,492.77917
6	839.89333	6	1,003.93500	6	1,167.97667	6	1,332.01833	6	1,496.06000
7	843.17417	7	1,007.21583	7	1,171.25750	7	1,335.29917	7	1,499.34083
8	846.45500	8	1,010.49667	8	1,174.53833	8	1,338.58000	8	1,502.62167
9	849.73583	9	1,013.77750	9	1,177.81917	9	1,341.86083	9	1,505.90250
260	853.01667	310	1,017.05833	360	1,181.10000	410	1,345.14167	460	1,509.18333
1	856.29750	1	1,020.33917	1	1,184.38083	1	1,348.42250	1	1,512.46417
2	859.57833	2	1,023.62000	2	1,187.66167	2	1,351.70333	2	1,515.74500
3	862.85917	3	1,026.90083	3	1,190.94250	3	1,354.98417	3	1,519.02583
4	866.14000	4	1,030.18167	4	1,194.22333	4	1,358.26500	4	1,522.30667
5	869.42083	5	1,033.46250	5	1,197.50417	5	1,361.54583	5	1,525.58750
6	872.70167	6	1,036.74333	6	1,200.78500	6	1,364.82667	6	1,528.86833
7	875.98250	7	1,040.02417	7	1,204.06583	7	1,368.10750	7	1,532.14917
8	879.26333	8	1,043.30500	8	1,207.34667	8	1,371.38833	8	1,535.48000
9	882.54417	9	1,046.58583	9	1,210.62750	9	1,374.66917	9	1,538.71083
270	885.82500	320	1,049.86667	370	1,213.90833	420	1,377.95000	470	1,541.99167
1	889.10583	1	1,053.14750	1	1,217.18917	1	1,381.23083	1	1,545.27250
2	892.38667	2	1,056.42833	2	1,220,47000	2	1,384.51167	2	1,548.55333
3	895.66750	3	1,059.70917	3	1,223.75083	3	1,387.79250	3	1,551.83417
4	898.94833	4	1,062.99000	4	1,227.03167	4	1,391.07333	4	1,555.11500
5	902.22917	5	1,066.27083	5	1,230.31250	5	1,394.35417	5	1,558.39583
6	905,51000	6	1,069.55167	6	1,233.59333	6	1,397.63500	6	1,561.67667
7	908.79083	7	1,072.83250	7	1,236.87417	7	1,400.91583	7	1,564.95750
8	912.07167	8	1,076.11333	8	1,240.15500	8	1,404.19667	8	1,568.23833
9	915,35250	9	1,079.39417	9	1,243.43583	9	1,407.47750	9	1,571.51917
280	918.63333	330	1,082.67500	380	1,246.71667	430	1,410.75833	480	1,574.80000
1	921.91417	1	1,085.95583	1	1,249.99750	1	1,414.03917	1	1,578.08083
2	925.19500	2	1,089.23667	2	1,253.27833	2	1,417.32000	2	1,581.36167
3	928.47583	3	1,092.51750	3	1,256.55917	3	1,420.60083	3	1,584.64250
4	931.75667	4	1,095.79833	4	1,259.84000	4	1,423.88167	4	1,587.92333
5	935.03750	5	1,099.07917	5	1,263.12083	5	1,427.16250	5	1,591.20417
6	938.31833	6	1,102.36000	6	1,266.40167	6	1,430.44333	6	1,594.48500
7	941.59917	7	1,105.64083	7	1,269.68250	7	1,433.72417	7	1,597.76583
8	944.88000	8	1,108.92167	8	1,272.96333	8	1,437.00500	8	1,601.04667
9	948.16083	9	1,112.20250	9	1,276.24417	9	1,440.28583	9	1,604.32750
290	951.44167	340	1,115.48333	390	1,279.52500	440	1,443.56667	490	1,607.60833
1	954.72250	1	1,118.76417	1	1,282.80583	1	1,446.84750	1	1,610.88917
2	958.00333	2	1,122.04500	2	1,286.08667	2	1,450.40927	2	1,614.17000
3	961.28417	3	1,125.32583	3	1,289.36750	3	1,453.12833	3	1,617.45083
4	964.56500	4	1,128.60667	4	1,292.64833	4	1,456.69000	4	1,620.73167
5	967.84583	5	1,131.88750	5	1,295.92917	5	1,459.97083	5	1,624.01250
6	971.12667	6	1,135.16833	6	1,299.21000	6	1,463.25167	6	1,627.29333
7	974.40750	7	1,138.44917	7	1,302.49083	7	1,466.53250	7	1,630.57417
8	977.68833	8	1,141.73000	8	1,305.77167	8	1,469.81333	8	1,633.85500
9	980.96917	9	1,145.01083	9	1,309.05250	9	1,473.09417	9	1,637.13583
								500	1,640.41667

In 1982, the *Sweet's Catalog* set became one volume larger. A new volume called *Selection Data* has now become Volume I. The primary purpose of this volume is to provide generic information that will help drafters, designers, and architects in the design and development of ideas, and aid them in the selection of the proper product for a specific design problem.

Twenty major categories were selected for this volume:

Cement and Concrete	Floors and Roofs
Stone and Masonry	Roofing
Metals	Insulation
Wood and Wood	Sealants and
Products	Waterproofing
Glass and Glazing	Facings
Windows and Skylights	Coatings
Entrances and Doors	Partitions and Doors
Curtain Walls	Flooring
Bearing Walls	Ceilings
Enclosures	Solar Control

Each of the major categories contains six topics:

A. Introduction to the material
B. Evaluation charts
C. Selection checklist
D. Firm and product checklist
E. Information sources
F. Energy notes

This gives the reader the proper information to analyze, compare, and select the proper product and manufacturer for a specific design or structural problem.

"Entrances and Doors," alone, contains almost 50 pages, starting with a basic historical background to door definitions and a description of types. This introduction is followed by a visual description of the various types of shapes. Next comes a checklist to aid in selection. An evaluation chart comparing such items as operation, material selection, hinges, locks, weatherstripping, and so on, also will aid in the proper selection of a door.

Availability, by manufacturer, is the next major topic. This is followed by a list of information sources: industry associations, government agencies dealing with doors, professional institutes and agencies, and various regulatory agencies. This list is similar to the Trade, Technical, and Standard organization list found at the end of the book, but deals solely with doors.

Next is the related literature, standard specifications, and testing methods section. The last section has energy notes on the product.

Each category is treated in the same fashion as described for doors, making Volume I a comprehensive tool for anyone involved in architectural decisions.

As a further service "Sweet's Buyline" provides a toll free telephone number you can call for information on local product distributors or for further manufacturer information.

Manufacturers' Literature

A wealth of product information is available directly from manufacturers in the form of brochures, pamphlets, catalogs, manuals, and even hardbound books. This information may include:

1. Advantages of this product over others
2. Quantitative comparison with others in the trade
3. How the system works or is assembled
4. Necessary engineering
5. Detailed drawings—sometimes on vellum sheets for ease or reproduction
6. Pictorial explanation of the parts and how they are put together.
7. Special design features
8. Colors, textures, and patterns available
9. Safety tests that have been performed
10. Dimensions
11. Variations of the products available
12. Ordering instructions
13. Charts and graphs showing advantages and/or comparisons
14. Guarantees
15. Installation procedures
16. Information particular to this specific product

The material is usually available upon request. Sales representatives may also call to explain the product. These sales representatives can also obtain samples for color, texture, or other finish selection.

Other Reference Sources

Retail Sources. Many major book publishers produce architectural reference books, and most major book stores carry some of them. Many art supply and drafting supply stores also have reference materials.

Public Libraries. Public libraries contain a variety of professional reference materials—books, journals, and magazines. Colleges and universities offering architecture courses also carry architectural resource materials. These fall into one of two categories: broad, general coverage of an area such as architectural drafting, graphics, engineering, or design; or the narrow, specific coverage found in highly technical publications dealing, for example, with acoustics or masonry. An example of a highly technical resource is the A.I.A. *Architectural Graphic Standards,* published by John Wiley & Sons. This book carries the maximum, minimum, and average sizes of a variety of items, and contains such diverse information as the sizes of a baseball diamond or a bowling alley and the various dimensions of most musical instruments, as well as the standard sizes of most major kitchen utensils and appliances.

Guides and Indexes.   Two invaluable general book indexes are the *Subject Guide to Books in Print* and *Books in Print* (author and title volumes). All major bookstores carry these annual reference books. They can also be found in the reference department of many libraries. The *Reader's Guide to Periodical Literature,* which can be found in most libraries, is excellent for locating magazine articles on specific building types, new procedures and methods used in architecture, or specific architects. Four additional sources of architectural information are the *Art Index, Applied Science and Technology, The Humanities Index,* and the *Social Science Index.* These are available in most college and university libraries and in large public libraries.

Trade, Technical, and Standard Organizations

The appendix lists many of the larger organizations that deal with the field of architecture. They represent various associations, societies, and institutes that deal with a building product or industry. Many of these provide a great service to the professional by acting as consulting organizations, and most offer informative literature. For additional information consult the *Encyclopedia of Associations* found in most local libraries.

Working Guidelines for Preparing Construction Documents

In this time of technological advance and specialization, you might easily assume that working guidelines would be precise and mathematically logical. This is not the case. Guidelines are too important to reduce to a series of steps and formulas to memorize. In fact, working guidelines for drafting are actually attitudes and ideals that are fundamental to good communication. It is this ingredient that makes a success or failure out of a basically skilled draftsperson.

You may well think that much of this material is obvious, common knowledge, or common sense. Yet if these guidelines are assumed but *not acted upon,* mass confusion and anguish result! They have been arrived at through research in supervision, communication, human relationships, and field experiences, particularly with prospective employers. This material is, therefore, not original, but its application often is.

The Rules in Summary

1. Plan every step of your drawing.
2. Establish some manner in which you can check your work.
3. Understand the decisions you will be asked to make.
4. Find out the standards under which you will function.
5. Draft from the other person's point-of-view.
6. Cooperate, communicate, and work with others.
7. Find out your primary and secondary responsibilities. Don't assume.
8. Think for yourself.
9. Concentrate on improving one aspect of your skills with each task.

The Rules in Detail

1. *Plan every step of your drawing.*   Do not get a piece of vellum and start immediately on the top left corner. Each drawing has a distinct procedure and an order. Use your mind's eye to completely draw the object first. Picture yourself at the drafting desk. Watch yourself perform the task. Make mental and/or written notes about the sequence and anticipated problems. Every sheet of a set of architectural plans subscribes to a basic system. The system may be based on the materials used, methods of erection, limits of the technology at the present time, or even the limits of the person, to mention just a few. Whatever the control factors, be aware of them, understand them, digest them intellectually, and put them into effect.

2. *Establish some manner in which you can check your work.*   Every office has some method of checking. The method may be a check sheet developed by the principal draftsperson or a person whose primary function is that of checking others. Whatever the system, establish a method to check yourself before you submit a drawing to a senior in the firm. This does two things. First, it builds trust, trust between you and your employer. If your employer thinks that you not only perform the task asked of you but are conscientious enough to double check your work, the rapport built between you and your employer will be enhanced. Second, it builds the employer's confidence that you have done your best to perform your duty.

    This checking method differs with each person and each drawing. However, remember that the checking method is also based on the construction system used. If you understand the system, you will usually discover the method needed to check it.

    Accuracy transcends all systems—accuracy of representation as well as of arithmetic, grammar, and spelling. Nothing causes as many problems in the field as an "L" that looks like an "I," and an "E" that looks like an "F," or arithmetical totals that are not equal to their parts, or dimensions that do not reflect an established module.

3. *Understand the decisions you will be asked to make.* Know your job. Know what decisions you will be allowed to make, and know when to ask a superior.

If, every time you are confronted with a decision, you ask a superior for help, you are taking that person's valuable time and reducing the superior's effectiveness. On the other hand, making decisions that are not part of your job will also create problems. For example, if a production draftsperson (a person drafting working drawings), were to change a design decision, the draftsperson might not be aware of all of the factors that led to that decision and might make the wrong decision. It might seem obvious to the draftsperson that a particular change would produce a better effect, but the original may have been based on a code requirement, a client's request, cost of production, or any one of hundreds of reasons of which the draftsperson may not be aware.

Make sure your duties, responsibilities, and, above all, the decisions you are allowed to make are clearly defined by your superior.

4. *Find out the standards under which you will function.* There are many standards you will encounter. Just as there are office dress and behavior standards, so there are drawing standards.

Each sheet you draw will have a set-up standard. Certain sheet sizes are used by certain offices. Title blocks, border lines, and sheet space allocation are usually set up in advance. Certain drawing conventions are used by each office. Certain symbols and abbreviations are acceptable. In fact, some offices produce what is called a manual of "office standards." The standard may call for something as simple as all vertical lettering, or as professional as a standard based on building erection procedures followed by a particular contractor. Again, whether it be a building code or state regulated requirement, or a personal whim of an employer, you must immediately incorporate this standard into your assignments.

5. *Draft from the other person's point of view.* Your work involves three people: the person in the field, the person who assigns you your duties, and the client. All of these people influence your attitudes. For example, when you draft for the person in the field, your work becomes a medium of communication between the client's needs and the people who execute those needs, but it must also express an understanding of the limits and capabilities of the workers themselves. Prior to drafting, for example, a detail,

plan, or section, you must sufficiently understand the trade involved so that you do not ask a person or machine to perform an unreasonable task.

As for drafting from your employer's point of view, first and foremost understand what your task is. It is better to spend a few minutes with your supervisor at the beginning of a drawing, outlining your duties, and his objectives and needs, than to spend countless hours on a drawing only to find that much of the time you have spent is wasted. We are often so eager to "get on" with a job that we have not spent the proper amount of time understanding what is expected of us. As the ironic saying goes, "There is never enough time to do a job but always enough time to do it over, CORRECTLY."

Finally, look at things from the client's standpoint. The client and the designer have made a number of design and construction decisions. No matter what the reasons are for these decisions, the office and the client have an understanding, which must be respected by you. In other words, you, as a technician, must abide by and subscribe to these decisions and do everything you can to support them. This is not to say you cannot question a decision, but do not make changes without approval. If you know of a better solution or method, verify its appropriateness with a superior before you employ it.

6. *Cooperate, communicate, and work with others.* One of the main criticisms that comes from employers is that employees do not know how to work as members of a team. While education requires you to perform as an individual, each person in an office is a member of a team and has certain responsibilities, duties, and functions on which others rely. There may be many people working on a single project, and you must understand your part and participate with others towards achieving a common goal.

The method of communication is as important as the need for it. Be clear about the way you communicate your ideas. Sketch ideas when possible so others can visualize them. If the office is large, write memos and notes; write formal letters to other companies. Keep in mind that you are a representative of your firm and that proper presentation, grammar, spelling, and punctuation reflect the abilities in the firm.

Communication helps you know what the other people in the firm are doing. The more you understand the overall picture, the more you can participate. Communication also helps you to develop an appreciation of attitudes, goals, and aims of others with whom you will be working. Know what is going on in the office.

7. *Find out your primary and secondary responsibilities.*

Don't assume. Nothing gets an office or an employee in as much trouble as making assumptions. Phrases such as "I thought John was going to do it," or "I didn't think, Kay; I assumed you would do it" not only break down the communication process in an office but can create discord and disturb the office harmony. Many bad feelings emerge and ultimately break down office morale.

Know your responsibilities and how and whom to ask for guidance in case of a change in your responsibilities.

A classic example of this was a large office that had two divisions: an architectural division and a structural engineering division. Each prepared a set of drawings: the architectural drawings and the structural drawings. Each division assumed the other would develop a set of details for the project. Thus on the architectural drawings there were notations that read, "See structural drawings for details." The structural group did the same but made the detail reference to the architectural set. Needless to say, the details were never drawn, and when the total set was assembled and the lack of details discovered, a great delay followed and caused much embarrassment to the firm. The client was obviously unhappy.

The size of the firm is not always to blame. Any time there is more than one person working on a project, you need to understand not only your primary responsibilities, but your not-so-obvious secondary responsibilities as well.

8. *Think for yourself.* There is a natural tendency for a draftsperson to feel that all decisions should be made by a superior. However, your supervisor will tell you that certain decisions have been delegated to you. The process of thinking for yourself also involves fully understanding your primary and secondary responsibilities.

If, each time a problem arises, you ask Bob for help, Bob will not be able to do his job effectively. There is also a cost factor involved. Your immediate supervisor or head-draftsperson is earning two to five times as much as you are because of additional responsibilities. Therefore, each time you ask a question and stop production, the cost is that of your salary plus that of your supervisor.

The solution to this dilemma is a simple one. Research the solution before you approach your seniors, look through reference and manufacturers' literature, construction manuals, *Sweet's Catalog File,* reference books, and so on. Make a list of problems and questions and work around them until your superior is free and available to deal with them. Arrange your time to suit your supervisor's convenience. THINK and be able to propose solutions or suggestions yourself. In this way, you will be prepared to understand the answers you are given, and a potential frustration will have become a learning situation.

Above all, don't stop production and wait around for superiors to be free; don't follow them around. Employers react very negatively to this.

9. *Concentrate on improving one aspect of your skills with each task.* Make a special effort with each new assignment to improve some part of your skills. Constantly improve your lettering, your line quality, your accuracy. As athletes work to perfect some part of their ability, so should you. Work on your weakness first. Because it is your weakness, you may want to shy away from it. For example, if spelling is your problem, carry a dictionary around with you. If sketching is your weakness, practice and use it as a communication method whenever possible. The most valuable athlete is often the most versatile one—the person who can throw and catch and play defense as well as offense. A draftsperson who can draft, sketch, do simple engineering, and do research is a valuable commodity in an office and will always be employed, because an office cannot afford to lose such a versatile person.

An employer wants an employee who is punctual, dependable, and accurate, has a high degree of integrity, and is able to work with a minimum amount of supervision.

We have said many of the principles listed here are obvious. Yet if they are so obvious, why do teachers, employers, and supervisors lament the absence of these principles when desirable employee traits are discussed? To admit to your shortcomings is to confront and deal with them. To ignore them and act as if they don't exist is to run away from them.

PRELIMINARY STEPS IN PREPARING CONSTRUCTION DOCUMENTS

Making the Transition from Preliminary Drawings to Construction Documents

Making the transition from approved preliminary drawings to construction documents is important because it completes the process of making decisions about the physical characteristics of the building. Once this transition is made, the production of construction documents can proceed.

Accomplishing this transition—the design development phase—requires that the following basic requirements be satisfied and thoroughly investigated:

1. Building code and other requirements, such as those set by the zoning department, fire department, health department, planning department, and architectural committees
2. Primary materials analysis
3. Selection of the primary structural system
4. Requirements of consultants, such as mechanical and electrical engineers
5. Regional considerations
6. Energy conservation considerations and requirements
7. Interrelationship of drawings
8. Project programming

Building Code Requirements

Building code requirements are extremely important to research. Figure 3.1, for example, shows a small office building with a code requirement of a minimum dimension between required exit stairs. The correct placement of these stairs is important because the whole structural concept, the office layouts, and many other factors will be affected by their location.

Many people frequently overlook the building code requirements for correct stair dimensions. Often they give a little attention to the width of stairs and landings or to the provisions for the necessary number of risers

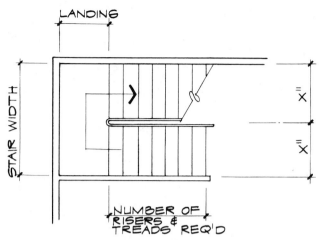

Figure 3.2 Stair dimensions (commercial).

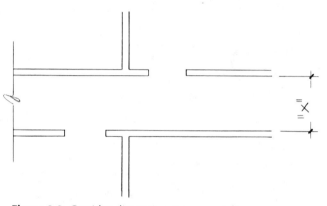

Figure 3.3 Corridor dimension (commercial).

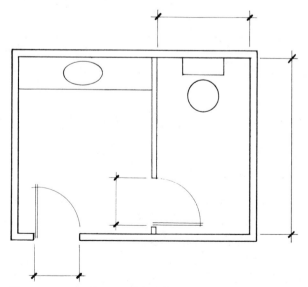

Figure 3.4 Handicap toilet requirements.

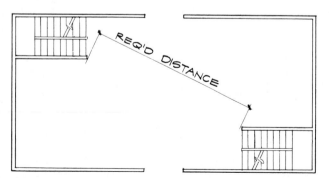

Figure 3.1 Stair separation (commercial).

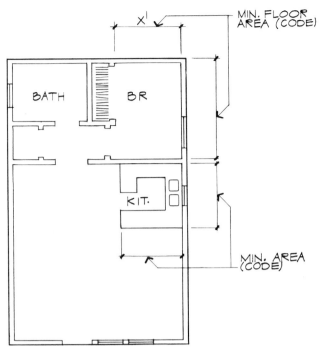

Figure 3.5 Apartment unit.

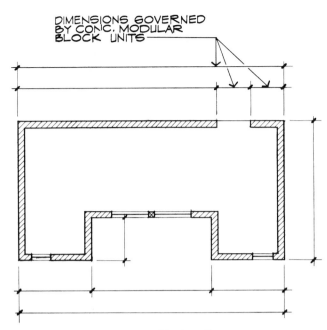

Figure 3.6 Exterior concrete block walls.

(stair height) and treads (step width) to satisfy the vertical dimensions between floors. See Figure 3.2.

Two further examples of satisfying the physical requirements dictated by the code are illustrated in Figure 3.3, which shows corridor dimensions, and Figure 3.4, which shows handicapped toilet access.

In multiple housing projects as well as in residential projects, building codes establish minimum physical requirements for various rooms. Figure 3.5 shows the minimum floor areas and dimensions required for the bedroom and kitchen.

Primary Materials Analysis

The most important building materials to be selected are for foundations and floors, exterior and interior walls, and ceiling and roof structures. There are several factors that influence selection, and many of these require considerable investigation and research:

A. Architectural design
B. Building codes
C. Economics
D. Structural concept
E. Region
F. Ecology
G. Energy conservation

An example of the importance of selection is given in Figure 3.6. Concrete block units have been selected as the material for the exterior walls of a structure. Using this material affects the exterior and interior dimensions because concrete blocks have fixed dimensions. Establishing the exterior and interior dimensions *before* the production of construction documents is most important because other phases, such as the structural engineering, are based on these dimensions.

Modular and Nonmodular Units

The term "module" refers to a predetermined dimension from which structures are designed. "Block module" is usually used in conjunction with masonry units, such as bricks, concrete blocks, or structural clay tiles.

Masonry units can be broadly classified as either modular or nonmodular. The mortar joint between two units is usually either $3/8''$, $7/16''$, or $1/2''$ thick. Modular sizes are designed to ensure that final measurements including mortar joints are in whole numbers. Nonmodular units result in fractional measurements.

As an example, an $8 \times 8 \times 16$ modular concrete block unit measures $7^5/8'' \times 7^5/8'' \times 15^5/8''$, so that a $3/8$ inch mortar joint produces a final $8 \times 8 \times 16$ measurement to work with. There are also half sizes available, so that when the units are stacked on top of each other, lapping each other by one half the length of the block, the end of the structure comes out even. See Figure 3.7.

Certain lengths are commonly available. See Table 3.1, Table A. These measurements follow three rules:

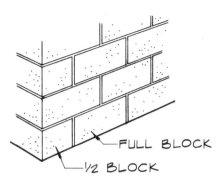

Figure 3.7 Use of half block.

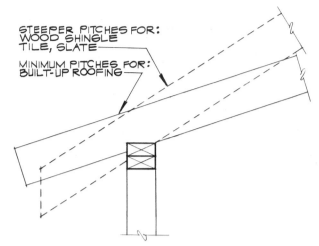

Figure 3.8 Roof material and roof pitches.

first, all even numbers of feet are available (2'–0", 8'–0", 24'–0", etc.); second, all odd numbered feet have four inches added to them (for example, the length closest to 3 feet is 3'–4", the length closest to nine feet is 9'–4", etc.); third, all even numbered feet are also available in 8" increments, such as 4'–8", 8'–8", and 32'–8".

Using the rules above or Table 3.1, Table A, check to see if the following measurements are good for lengths of a concrete block structure using an 8 × 8 × 16 modular construction.

A. 28'–8"
B. 42'–9"
C. 101'–4"
D. 89'–4"
E. 93'–8"

All but B and E are correct. B should be 42'–8" and E should be 93'–4".

In Table A, the height is calculated in the same way and presented in two columns—one for 4"-high blocks and one for 8"-high blocks. The 4"-high blocks do not completely follow the rules mentioned earlier. A careful examination of the chart will reveal a single rule: all modular dimensions will be 4", 8", or 0" (for example, 3'–4", 6'–8", or 10'–0").

Tables B and C are for a nonmodular system. The same size concrete block is used here but with a different mortar joint. Odd fractions begin to appear. Only heights are shown. The mortar joints—both $^7/_{16}$" and $^1/_2$"—affect window and door sizes and heights.

Brick also comes in modular and nonmodular sizes. Examples of sizes for a modular unit are 5$^5/_8$" × 2$^1/_4$" × 7$^5/_8$" for a $^3/_8$" joint and 3$^1/_2$" × 2$^3/_{16}$" × 7$^1/_2$" for a $^1/_2$" joint. 2$^1/_2$" × 3$^7/_8$" × 8$^1/_4$" is a nonmodular size. See Table 3.2 for an interpretation of nonmodular height and length implications.

Here are some of the things you should consider when deciding whether or not to use the block module system:

1. Heights of the structure
2. Ceiling heights
3. Size of foundation if walls are masonry units
4. Size of floor plan if foundation wall is made of masonry units
5. Window and door openings
6. Window and door heights

If you have a choice of modular or nonmodular materials, use modular. The dimensions are easier to figure out, and, as contractors report, the structure is faster, easier, and cheaper to build.

Why then would you choose nonmodular? You may be forced into nonmodular sizes. For example, building function might dictate overall size, as in an assembly plant. The client may require that a building occupy the full width or depth of a piece of property to maximize the site use. An auditorium size is often dictated by seating arrangement or acoustics. A fire department regulation may determine certain size corridors for schools. These are only a few of the reasons for using a nonmodular system. If all these kinds of restraints can be satisfied by using modular units, use modular units.

Because of the state of the technology, the cost of cutting masonry units is rapidly decreasing, thus giving greater selection for almost any size structure. Cutting reduces the visual unity of the building and should be used with discretion.

The importance of selecting primary building materials is further shown in Figure 3.8. The roofing material selected here actually governs the roof pitch. This in turn establishes the physical height of the building and also dictates the size of the supporting members relative to the weight of the finished roof material.

TABLE A (MODULAR) 3/8" HORIZ. AND VERTICAL MORTAR JOINTS					TABLE B (NON-MODULAR) 7/16" HORIZONTAL MORTAR JOINT				TABLE C (NON-MODULAR) 1/2" HORIZONTAL MORTAR JOINT			
LENGTH	NO. 16" LONG BLOCKS	HEIGHT	NO. 4" HIGH BLOCKS	NO. 8" HIGH BLOCKS	HEIGHT	NO. 4" HIGH BLOCKS	HEIGHT	NO. 8" HIGH BLOCKS	HEIGHT	NO. 4" HIGH BLOCKS	HEIGHT	NO. 8" HIGH BLOCKS
0'-8"	1/2	0'-4"	1		0'-4 1/16"	1			0'-4 1/8"	1		
1'-4"	1	0'-8"	2	1	0'-8 1/8"	2	0'-8 1/16"	1	0'-8 1/4"	2	0'-8 1/8"	1
2'-0"	1 1/2	1'-0"	3		1'-0 3/16"	3			1'-0 3/8"	3		
2'-8"	2	1'-4"	4	2	1'-4 1/4"	4	1'-4 1/8"	2	1'-4 1/4"	4	1'-4 1/4"	2
3'-4"	2 1/2	1'-8"	5		1'-8 5/16"	5			1'-8 5/8"	5		
4'-0"	3	2'-0"	6	3	2'-0 3/8"	6	2'-0 3/16"	3	2'-0 3/4"	6	2'-0 3/8"	3
4'-8"	3 1/2	2'-4"	7		2'-4 7/16"	7			2'-4 7/8"	7		
5'-4"	4	2'-8"	8	4	2'-8 1/2"	8	2'-8 1/4"	4	2'-9"	8	2'-8 1/2"	4
6'-0"	4 1/2	3'-0"	9		3'-0 9/16"	9			3'-1 1/8"	9		
6'-8"	5	3'-4"	10	5	3'-4 5/8"	10	3'-4 5/16"	5	3'-5 1/4"	10	3'-4 5/8"	5
7'-4"	5 1/2	3'-8"	11		3'-8 11/16"	11			3'-9 3/8"	11		
8'-0"	6	4'-0"	12	6	4'-0 3/4"	12	4'-0 3/8"	6	4'-1 1/2"	12	4'-0 3/4"	6
8'-8"	6 1/2	4'-4"	13		4'-4 13/16"	13			4'-5 5/8"	13		
9'-4"	7	4'-8"	14	7	4'-8 7/8"	14	4'-8 7/16"	7	4'-9 3/4"	14	4'-8 7/8"	7
10'-0"	7 1/2	5'-0"	15		5'-0 15/16"	15			5'-1 7/8"	15		
10'-8"	8	5'-4"	16	8	5'-5"	16	5'-4 1/2"	8	5'-6"	16	5'-5"	8
11'-4"	8 1/2	5'-8"	17		5'-9 1/16"	17			5'-10 1/8"	17		
12'-0"	9	6'-0"	18	9	6'-1 1/8"	18	6'-0 9/16"	9	6'-2 1/4"	18	6'-1 1/8"	9
12'-8"	9 1/2	6'-4"	19		6'-5 3/16"	19			6'-6 3/8"	19		
13'-4"	10	6'-8"	20	10	6'-9 1/4"	20	6'-8 5/8"	10	6'-10 1/2"	20	6'-9 1/4"	10
14'-0"	10 1/2	7'-0"	21		7'-1 5/16"	21			7'-2 5/8"	21		
14'-8"	11	7'-4"	22	11	7'-5 3/8"	22	7'-4 11/16"	11	7'-6 3/4"	22	7'-5 3/8"	11
15'-4"	11 1/2	7'-8"	23		7'-9 7/16"	23			7'-10 7/8"	23		
16'-0"	12	8'-0"	24	12	8'-1 1/2"	24	8'-0 3/4"	12	8'-3"	24	8'-1 1/2"	12
16'-8"	12 1/2	8'-4"	25		8'-5 9/16"	25			8'-7 1/4"	25		
17'-4"	13	8'-8"	26	13	8'-9 5/8"	26	8'-8 13/16"	13	8'-11 1/4"	26	8'-9 5/8"	13
18'-0"	13 1/2	9'-0"	27		9'-1 11/16"	27			9'-3 3/8"	27		
18'-8"	14	9'-4"	28	14	9'-5 3/4"	28	9'-4 7/8"	14	9'-7 1/2"	28	9'-5 3/4"	14
19'-4"	14 1/2	9'-8"	29		9'-9 13/16"	29			9'-11 5/8"	29		
20'-0"	15	10'-0"	30	15	10'-1 7/8"	30	10'-0 15/16"	15	10'-3 3/4"	30	10'-1 7/8"	15
20'-8"	15 1/2	10'-4"	31		10'-5 15/16"	31			10'-7 7/8"	31		
21'-4"	16	10'-8"	32	16	10'-10"	32	10'-9"	16	11'-0"	32	10'-10"	16
22'-0"	16 1/2	11'-0"	33		11'-2 1/16"	33			11'-4 1/8"	33		
22'-8"	17	11'-4"	34	17	11'-6 1/8"	34	11'-5 1/16"	17	11'-8 1/4"	34	11'-6 1/8"	17
23'-4"	17 1/2	11'-8"	35		11'-10 3/16"	35			12'-0 3/8"	35		
24'-0"	18	12'-0"	36	18	12'-2 1/4"	36	12'-1 1/8"	18	12'-4 1/2"	36	12'-2 1/4"	18
24'-8"	18 1/2	12'-4"	37		12'-6 5/16"	37			12'-8 5/8"	37		
25'-4"	19	12'-8"	38	19	12'-10 3/8"	38	12'-9 3/16"	19	13'-0 3/4"	38	12'-10 3/8"	19
26'-0"	19 1/2	13'-0"	39		13'-2 7/16"	39			13'-4 7/8"	39		
26'-8"	20	13'-4"	40	20	13'-6 1/2"	40	13'-5 1/4"	20	13'-9"	40	13'-6 1/2"	20
27'-4"	20 1/2	13'-8"	41									
28'-0"	21	14'-0"	42	21								
28'-8"	21 1/2	14'-4"	43									
29'-4"	22	14'-8"	44	22								
30'-0"	22 1/2	15'-0"	45									
30'-8"	23	15'-4"	46	23								
31'-4"	23 1/2	15'-8"	47									
32'-0"	24	16'-0"	48	24								
32'-8"	24 1/2	16'-4"	49									
40'-0"	30	16'-8"	50	25								
50'-0"	37 1/2	17'-0"	51									
60'-0"	45	17'-4"	52	26								
70'-0"	52 1/2	17'-8"	53									
80'-0"	60	18'-0"	54	27								
90'-0"	67 1/2	18'-4"	55									
100'-0"	75	18'-8"	56	28								
200'-0"	150	19'-0"	57									
300'-0"	225	19'-4"	58	29								
400'-0"	300	19'-8"	59									
500'-0"	375	20'-0"	60	30								

Notes:

1—For exact wall length or height dimensions subtract thickness of one mortar joint.

2—For exact opening dimensions add thickness of one mortar joint to height and width.

3—For design simplicity and economy of construction plan dimensions should be determined from table A (modular).

4—When using combinations of 8" high and 4" high blocks a detailed wall section should be made to establish height dimensions.

Table 3.1 Concrete Block Dimensional Chart

VERTICAL BRICK COURSES

NUMBER OF BRICKS AND JOINTS	HEIGHT 3/8" JOINTS	HEIGHT 1/2" JOINTS
1 brk. & 1 jt.	2 5/8"	2 3/4"
2 brks. & 2 jts.	5 1/4"	5 1/2"
3 brks. & 3 jts.	7 7/8"	8 1/4"
4 brks. & 4 jts.	10 1/2"	11"
5 brks. & 5 jts.	1'- 1 1/8"	1'- 1 3/4"
6 brks. & 6 jts.	1'- 3 3/4"	1'- 4 1/2"
7 brks. & 7 jts.	1'- 6 3/8"	1'- 7 1/4"
8 brks. & 8 jts.	1'- 9"	1'-10"
9 brks. & 9 jts.	1'-11 5/8"	2'- 0 3/4"
10 brks. & 10 jts.	2'- 2 1/4"	2'- 3 1/2"
11 brks. & 11 jts.	2'- 4 7/8"	2'- 6 1/4"
12 brks. & 12 jts.	2'- 7 1/2"	2'- 9"
13 brks. & 13 jts.	2'-10 1/8"	2'-11 3/4"
14 brks. & 14 jts.	3'- 0 3/4"	3'- 2 1/2"
15 brks. & 15 jts.	3'- 3 3/8"	3'- 5 1/4"
16 brks. & 16 jts.	3'- 6"	3'- 8"
17 brks. & 17 jts.	3'- 8 5/8"	3'-10 3/4"
18 brks. & 18 jts.	3'-11 1/4"	4'- 1 1/2"
19 brks. & 19 jts.	4'- 1 7/8"	4'- 4 1/4"
20 brks. & 20 jts.	4'- 4 1/2"	4'- 7"
21 brks. & 21 jts.	4'- 7 1/8"	4'- 9 3/4"
22 brks. & 22 jts.	4'- 9 3/4"	5'- 0 1/2"
23 brks. & 23 jts.	5'- 0 3/8"	5'- 3 1/4"
24 brks. & 24 jts.	5'- 3"	5'- 6"
25 brks. & 25 jts.	5'- 5 5/8"	5'- 8 3/4"
26 brks. & 26 jts.	5'- 8 1/4"	5'-11 1/2"
27 brks. & 27 jts.	5'-10 7/8"	6'- 2 1/4"
28 brks. & 28 jts.	6'- 1 1/2"	6'- 5"
29 brks. & 29 jts.	6'- 4 1/8"	6'- 7 3/4"
30 brks. & 30 jts.	6'- 6 3/4"	6'-10 1/2"
31 brks. & 31 jts.	6'- 9 3/8"	7'- 1 1/4"
32 brks. & 32 jts.	7'- 0"	7'- 4"
33 brks. & 33 jts.	7'- 2 5/8"	7'- 6 3/4"
34 brks. & 34 jts.	7'- 5 1/4"	7'- 9 1/2"
35 brks. & 35 jts.	7'- 7 7/8"	8'- 0 1/4"
36 brks. & 36 jts.	7'-10 1/2"	8'- 3"
37 brks. & 37 jts.	8'- 1 1/8"	8'- 5 3/4"
38 brks. & 38 jts.	8'- 3 3/4"	8'- 8 1/2"
39 brks. & 39 jts.	8'- 6 3/8"	8'-11 1/4"
40 brks. & 40 jts.	8'- 9"	9'- 2"
41 brks. & 41 jts.	8'-11 5/8"	9'- 4 3/4"
42 brks. & 42 jts.	9'- 2 1/4"	9'- 7 1/2"
43 brks. & 43 jts.	9'- 4 7/8"	9'-10 1/4"
44 brks. & 44 jts.	9'- 7 1/2"	10'- 1"
45 brks. & 45 jts.	9'-10 1/8"	10'- 3 3/4"
46 brks. & 46 jts.	10'- 0 3/4"	10'- 6 1/2"
47 brks. & 47 jts.	10'- 3 3/8"	10'- 9 1/4"
48 brks. & 48 jts.	10'- 6"	11'- 0"
49 brks. & 49 jts.	10'- 8 5/8"	11'- 2 3/4"
50 brks. & 50 jts.	10'-11 1/4"	11'- 5 1/2"
51 brks. & 51 jts.	11'- 1 7/8"	11'- 8 1/4"
52 brks. & 52 jts.	11'- 4 1/2"	11'-11"
53 brks. & 53 jts.	11'- 7 1/8"	12'- 1 3/4"
54 brks. & 54 jts.	11'- 9 3/4"	12'- 4 1/2"
55 brks. & 55 jts.	12'- 0 3/8"	12'- 7 1/4"
56 brks. & 56 jts.	12'- 3"	12'-10"
57 brks. & 57 jts.	12'- 5 5/8"	13'- 0 3/4"
58 brks. & 58 jts.	12'- 8 1/4"	13'- 3 1/2"
59 brks. & 59 jts.	12'-10 7/8"	13'- 6 1/4"
60 brks. & 60 jts.	13'- 1 1/2"	13'- 9"
61 brks. & 61 jts.	13'- 4 1/8"	13'-11 3/4"
62 brks. & 62 jts.	13'- 6 3/4"	14'- 2 1/2"
63 brks. & 63 jts.	13'- 9 3/8"	14'- 5 1/4"
64 brks. & 64 jts.	14'- 0"	14'- 8"
65 brks. & 65 jts.	14'- 2 5/8"	14'-10 3/4"
66 brks. & 66 jts.	14'- 5 1/4"	15'- 1 1/2"
67 brks. & 67 jts.	14'- 7 7/8"	15'- 4 1/4"
68 brks. & 68 jts.	14'-10 1/2"	15'- 7"
69 brks. & 69 jts.	15'- 1 1/8"	15'- 9 3/4"
70 brks. & 70 jts.	15'- 3 3/4"	16'- 0 1/2"
71 brks. & 71 jts.	15'- 6 3/8"	16'- 3 1/4"
72 brks. & 72 jts.	15'- 9"	16'- 6"
73 brks. & 73 jts.	15'-11 5/8"	16'- 8 3/4"
74 brks. & 74 jts.	16'- 2 1/4"	16'-11 1/2"
75 brks. & 75 jts.	16'- 4 7/8"	17'- 2 1/4"
76 brks. & 76 jts.	16'- 7 1/2"	17'- 5"

HORIZONTAL BRICK COURSES

NUMBER OF BRICKS AND JOINTS	LENGTH OF COURSE 3/8" JOINTS	LENGTH OF COURSE 1/2" JOINTS
1 brk. & 0 jt.	0'- 8"	0'- 8"
1 1/2 brks. & 1 jt.	1'- 0 3/8"	1'- 0 1/2"
2 brks. & 1 jt.	1'- 4 3/8"	1'- 4 1/2"
2 1/2 brks. & 2 jts.	1'- 8 3/4"	1'- 9"
3 brks. & 2 jts.	2'- 0 3/4"	2'- 1"
3 1/2 brks. & 2 jts.	2'- 5 1/8"	2'- 5 1/2"
4 brks. & 3 jts.	2'- 9 1/8"	2'- 9 1/2"
4 1/2 brks. & 4 jts.	3'- 1 1/2"	3'- 2"
5 brks. & 4 jts.	3'- 5 1/2"	3'- 6"
5 1/2 brks. & 5 jts.	3'- 9 7/8"	3'-10 1/2"
6 brks. & 5 jts.	4'- 1 7/8"	4'- 2 1/2"
6 1/2 brks. & 6 jts.	4'- 6 1/4"	4'- 7"
7 brks. & 6 jts.	4'-10 1/4"	4'-11"
7 1/2 brks. & 7 jts.	5'- 2 5/8"	5'- 3 1/2"
8 brks. & 7 jts.	5'- 6 5/8"	5'- 7 1/2"
8 1/2 brks. & 8 jts.	5'-11"	6'- 0"
9 brks. & 8 jts.	6'- 3"	6'- 4"
9 1/2 brks. & 9 jts.	6'- 7 3/8"	6'- 8 1/2"
10 brks. & 9 jts.	6'-11 3/8"	7'- 0 1/2"
10 1/2 brks. & 10 jts.	7'- 3 3/4"	7'- 5"
11 brks. & 10 jts.	7'- 7 3/4"	7'- 9"
11 1/2 brks. & 11 jts.	8'- 0 1/8"	8'- 1 1/2"
12 brks. & 11 jts.	8'- 4 1/8"	8'- 5 1/2"
12 1/2 brks. & 12 jts.	8'- 8 1/2"	8'-10"
13 brks. & 12 jts.	9'- 0 1/2"	9'- 2"
13 1/2 brks. & 13 jts.	9'- 4 7/8"	9'- 6 1/2"
14 brks. & 13 jts.	9'- 8 7/8"	9'-10 1/2"
14 1/2 brks. & 14 jts.	10'- 1 1/4"	10'- 3"
15 brks. & 14 jts.	10'- 5 1/4"	10'- 7"
15 1/2 brks. & 15 jts.	10'- 9 5/8"	10'-11 1/2"
16 brks. & 15 jts.	11'- 1 5/8"	11'- 3 1/2"
16 1/2 brks. & 16 jts.	11'- 6"	11'- 8"
17 brks. & 16 jts.	11'-10"	12'- 0"
17 1/2 brks. & 17 jts.	12'- 2 3/8"	12'- 4 1/2"
18 brks. & 17 jts.	12'- 6 3/8"	12'- 8 1/2"
18 1/2 brks. & 18 jts.	12'-10 3/4"	13'- 1"
19 brks. & 18 jts.	13'- 2 3/4"	13'- 5"
19 1/2 brks. & 19 jts.	13'- 7 1/8"	13'- 9 1/2"
20 brks. & 19 jts.	13'-11 1/8"	14'- 1 1/2"
20 1/2 brks. & 20 jts.	14'- 3 1/2"	14'- 6"
21 brks. & 20 jts.	14'- 7 1/2"	14'-10"
21 1/2 brks. & 21 jts.	14'-11 7/8"	15'- 2 1/2"
22 brks. & 21 jts.	15'- 3 7/8"	15'- 6 1/2"
22 1/2 brks. & 22 jts.	15'- 8 1/4"	15'-11"
23 brks. & 22 jts.	16'- 0 1/4"	16'- 3"
23 1/2 brks. & 23 jts.	16'- 4 5/8"	16'- 7 1/2"
24 brks. & 23 jts.	16'- 8 5/8"	16'-11 1/2"
24 1/2 brks. & 24 jts.	17'- 1"	17'- 4"
25 brks. & 24 jts.	17'- 5"	17'- 8"
25 1/2 brks. & 25 jts.	17'- 9 3/8"	18'- 0 1/2"
26 brks. & 25 jts.	18'- 1 3/8"	18'- 4 1/2"
26 1/2 brks. & 26 jts.	18'- 5 3/4"	18'- 9"
27 brks. & 26 jts.	18'- 9 3/4"	19'- 1"
27 1/2 brks. & 27 jts.	19'- 2 1/8"	19'- 5 1/2"
28 brks. & 27 jts.	19'- 6 1/8"	19'- 9 1/2"
28 1/2 brks. & 28 jts.	19'-10 1/2"	20'- 2"
29 brks. & 28 jts.	20'- 2 1/2"	20'- 6"
29 1/2 brks. & 29 jts.	20'- 6 7/8"	20'-10 1/2"
30 brks. & 29 jts.	20'-10 7/8"	21'- 2 1/2"
30 1/2 brks. & 30 jts.	21'- 3 1/4"	21'- 7"
31 brks. & 30 jts.	21'- 7 1/4"	21'-11"
31 1/2 brks. & 31 jts.	21'-11 5/8"	22'- 3 1/2"
32 brks. & 31 jts.	22'- 3 5/8"	22'- 7 1/2"
32 1/2 brks. & 32 jts.	22'- 8"	23'- 0"
33 brks. & 32 jts.	23'- 0"	23'- 4"
33 1/2 brks. & 33 jts.	23'- 4 3/8"	23'- 8 1/2"
34 brks. & 33 jts.	23'- 8 3/8"	24'- 0 1/2"
34 1/2 brks. & 34 jts.	24'- 0 3/4"	24'- 5"
35 brks. & 34 jts.	24'- 4 3/4"	24'- 9"
35 1/2 brks. & 35 jts.	24'- 9 1/8"	25'- 1 1/2"
36 brks. & 35 jts.	25'- 1 1/8"	25'- 5 1/2"
36 1/2 brks. & 36 jts.	25'- 5 1/2"	25'-10"
37 brks. & 36 jts.	25'- 9 1/2"	26'- 2"
37 1/2 brks. & 37 jts.	26'- 1 7/8"	26'- 6 1/2"
38 brks. & 37 jts.	26'- 5 7/8"	26'-10 1/2"
38 1/2 brks. & 38 jts.	26'-10 1/4"	27'- 3"
39 brks. & 38 jts.	27'- 2 1/4"	27'- 7"
39 1/2 brks. & 39 jts.	27'- 6 5/8"	27'-11 1/2"
40 brks. & 39 jts.	27'-10 5/8"	28'- 3 1/2"
40 1/2 brks. & 40 jts.	28'- 3"	28'- 8"
41 brks. & 40 jts.	28'- 7"	29'- 0"
41 1/2 brks. & 41 jts.	28'-11 3/8"	29'- 4 1/2"
42 brks. & 41 jts.	29'- 3 3/8"	29'- 8 1/2"
42 1/2 brks. & 42 jts.	29'- 7 3/4"	30'- 1"
43 brks. & 42 jts.	29'-11 3/4"	30'- 5"
43 1/2 brks. & 43 jts.	30'- 4 1/8"	30'- 9 1/2"
44 brks. & 43 jts.	30'- 8 1/8"	31'- 1 1/2"
44 1/2 brks. & 44 jts.	31'- 0 1/2"	31'- 6"
45 brks. & 44 jts.	31'- 4 1/2"	31'-10"
45 1/2 brks. & 45 jts.	31'- 8 7/8"	32'- 2 1/2"
46 brks. & 45 jts.	32'- 0 7/8"	32'- 6 1/2"
46 1/2 brks. & 46 jts.	32'- 5 1/4"	32'-11"
47 brks. & 46 jts.	32'- 9 1/4"	33'- 3"
47 1/2 brks. & 47 jts.	33'- 1 5/8"	33'- 7 1/2"
48 brks. & 47 jts.	33'- 5 5/8"	33'-11 1/2"
48 1/2 brks. & 48 jts.	33'-10"	34'- 4"
49 brks. & 48 jts.	34'- 2"	34'- 8"
49 1/2 brks. & 49 jts.	34'- 6 3/8"	35'- 0 1/2"
50 brks. & 49 jts.	34'-10 3/8"	35'- 4 1/2"
50 1/2 brks. & 50 jts.	35'- 2 3/4"	35'- 9"
51 brks. & 50 jts.	35'- 6 3/4"	36'- 1"
51 1/2 brks. & 51 jts.	35'-11 1/8"	36'- 5 1/2"
52 brks. & 51 jts.	36'- 3 1/8"	36'- 9 1/2"
52 1/2 brks. & 52 jts.	36'- 7 1/2"	37'- 2"
53 brks. & 52 jts.	36'-11 1/2"	37'- 6"
53 1/2 brks. & 53 jts.	37'- 3 7/8"	37'-10 1/2"
54 brks. & 53 jts.	37'- 7 7/8"	38'- 2 1/2"
54 1/2 brks. & 54 jts.	38'- 0 1/4"	38'- 7"
55 brks. & 54 jts.	38'- 4 1/4"	38'-11"
55 1/2 brks. & 55 jts.	38'- 8 5/8"	39'- 3 1/2"
56 brks. & 55 jts.	39'- 0 5/8"	39'- 7 1/2"
56 1/2 brks. & 56 jts.	39'- 5"	40'- 0"
57 brks. & 56 jts.	39'- 9"	40'- 4"
57 1/2 brks. & 57 jts.	40'- 1 3/8"	40'- 8 1/2"
58 brks. & 57 jts.	40'- 5 3/8"	41'- 0 1/2"
58 1/2 brks. & 58 jts.	40'- 9 3/4"	41'- 5"
59 brks. & 58 jts.	41'- 1 3/4"	41'- 9"
59 1/2 brks. & 59 jts.	41'- 6 1/8"	42'- 1 1/2"
60 brks. & 59 jts.	41'-10 1/8"	42'- 5 1/2"

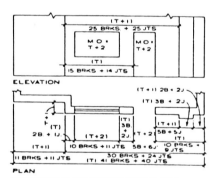

ELEVATION

PLAN

EXAMPLE SHOWING USE OF TABLE

T: Dimensions and number of joints as given in the table, that is, one joint less than the number of bricks.

T + 1: One brick joint added to figure given in the table, that is, the number of bricks is equal to the number of joints.

T + 2: Two brick joints added to figure given in the table, that is, one joint more than the number of bricks.

Table 3.2 Brick Dimensional Chart

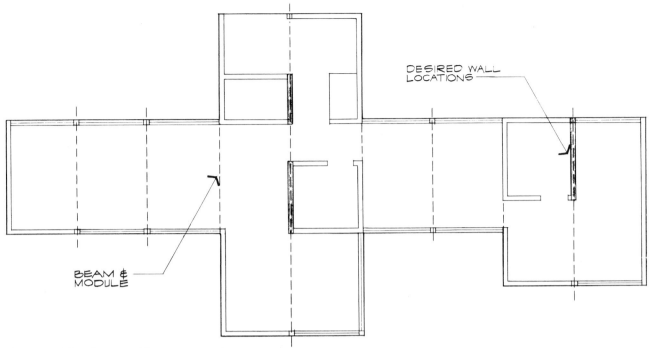

Figure 3.9 Wood post and beam structural system.

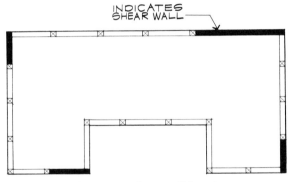

Figure 3.10 Plan view—shear wall locations.

Selecting the Primary Structural System

The selection of a structural system and its members is influenced by the following: meeting building code requirements, satisfying design elements, and using the most logical system based on sound engineering principles, economic considerations, and simplicity.

For most projects, the architect consults with the structural engineer about systems or methods that will meet these various considerations. Figures 3.9 and 3.10 illustrate the importance of establishing a structural concept before producing construction documents. Figure 3.9 shows a residential floor plan in which an exposed wood post and beam structure system has been selected. Here, the walls should fall directly beneath the beam

module. To achieve these desired wall locations and to accommodate the modular structural system, you may need to adjust the floor plan.

Another example of structural factors is the need, at times, for shear (earthquake resistant) walls to resist lateral forces. Figure 3.10 shows a retail store floor plan which has an extensive amount of glass. However, preliminary structural engineering calculations also require the use of shear walls at various locations in order to resist earthquake (seismic) or wind forces. To satisfy these requirements, you would need to make a physical adjustment to the floor plan.

Requirements of Consultants

Early involvement of structural, electrical, mechanical, and civil engineering consultants is highly recommended. Their early involvement generally results in physical adjustments to the finalized preliminary drawings in order to meet their design requirements. For example, the mechanical engineer's design may require a given area on the roof to provide space for various sizes of roof-mounted mechanical equipment. See Figure 3.11.

For projects that require mechanical ducts to be located in floor and ceiling areas, necessary space and clearances for ducts must be provided. Figure 3.12 shows a floor and ceiling section with provisions for mechanical duct space.

The electrical engineer should also be consulted about any physical modifications to the building that may be

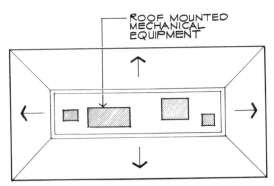

Figure 3.11 Roof plan—mechanical equipment area.

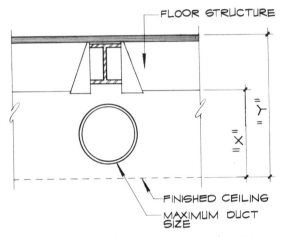

Figure 3.12 Mechanical duct space requirement.

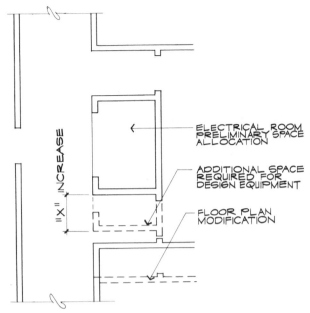

Figure 3.13 Electrical equipment room modification.

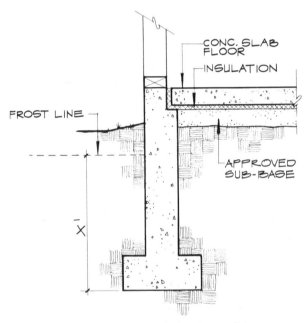

Figure 3.14 Foundation—cold climate conditions.

required to provide space for electrical equipment. In most cases, the architect or project manager provides for an electrical equipment roof or cabinet in the plans. However, with the increasing sophistication and size of equipment, additional space may be required. This increase in the electrical room dimension may require a floor plan adjustment, which can even result in a major or minor plan modification. Figure 3.13 illustrates a floor plan modification to satisfy space requirements for electrical equipment.

Regional Considerations

Regional differences in construction techniques are mainly controlled or influenced by climatic conditions, soil conditions, and natural events such as very high winds and earthquakes. These are considered in greater detail later.

In brief, regional differences influence:

1. Foundation design
2. Exterior wall design
3. Framing system
4. Roof design
5. Structural considerations
6. Insulation

Figure 3.14 illustrates a type of foundation used in regions with cold climatic conditions: an exterior foundation wall and footing with a concrete floor. The depth of the foundation is established from the frost line, and insulation is required under the concrete floor.

Where temperatures are mild and warm, the foundation design and construction techniques are primarily governed by soils investigations and local building codes. Figure 3.15 illustrates an exterior foundation detail where

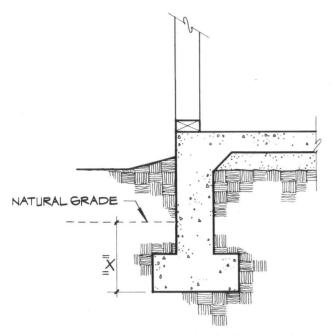

NATURAL GRADE

Figure 3.15 Foundation—recommended depth in warm climate.

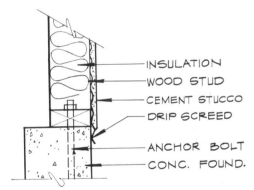

INSULATION
WOOD STUD
CEMENT STUCCO
DRIP SCREED
ANCHOR BOLT
CONC. FOUND.

Figure 3.16 Exterior wall—open frame construction.

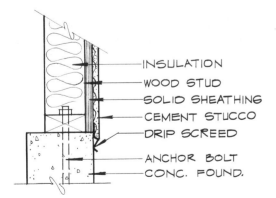

INSULATION
WOOD STUD
SOLID SHEATHING
CEMENT STUCCO
DRIP SCREED
ANCHOR BOLT
CONC. FOUND.

Figure 3.17 Exterior wall—sheathed frame construction.

the depth of the footing is established to a recommended depth below the natural grade.

Another example of regional influence is the change in exterior wall design. Figure 3.16 shows a section of

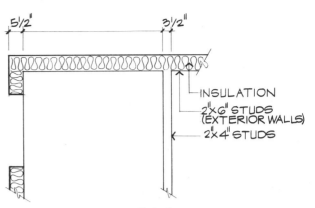

INSULATION
2"x6" STUDS (EXTERIOR WALLS)
2"x4" STUDS

Figure 3.18 Floor plan wall thickness.

an exterior wall with wood frame construction. This open frame construction is suitable for mild climates. A wood frame exterior wall recommended for Eastern regions is shown in Figure 3.17. Here, solid sheathing is used, and this in turn requires the wood studs to be set in from the face of the foundation wall. This one regional difference can affect many procedures and detailing throughout the construction documents such as wall dimensioning, window details, and door details.

Energy Conservation

To determine what you must do to satisfy local and federal energy conservation requirements, you must complete preliminary research. These requirements can affect exterior wall material and thickness, amount and type of glazing, areas of infiltration (leakage of air), amount of artificial lighting to be used, thickness and type of insulation, mechanical engineering design, and so forth. For example, a wood building requires exterior walls to be 2″ × 6″ studs instead of 2″ × 4″ to allow for the thickness of the building insulation. This particular requirement dictates procedures in the construction document process, such as floor plan wall thickness and dimensioning, window and exterior door details, and other related exterior wall details. Figure 3.18 shows a segment of a floor plan and indicates the thickness of walls and the locations of required insulation.

Interrelationship of Drawings

When you develop construction documents, you must have consistent relationships between the drawings for continuity and clarity. These relationships vary in their degree of importance.

For example, the relationship between the foundation plan and the floor plan is most important because continuity of dimensioning and correlation of structural components are both required. See Figure 3.19. The dimensioning of the floor plan and the foundation plan are identical and this provides continuity for dimensional accuracy.

The relationship between drawings for the electrical plan and the mechanical plan is also important. This relationship is critical because the positioning of electrical fixtures must not conflict with the location of mechanical components, such as air supply grilles or fire sprinkler heads.

Cross reference drawings with important relationships such as these and constantly review them throughout the preparation of the construction documents. Only in this way will you avoid conflicts.

This cross-referencing and review is not as critical with drawings that are not so closely related, such as the electrical plan and the civil engineering plans, or the interior elevations and the foundation.

Figure 3.20 indicates which relationships are important or not important and which are merely convenient. The clarity of construction documents depends not only on graphic or drafting skills; it also depends on this consistent relationship between the drawings.

Project Programming

For many construction projects, a construction firm uses a time schedule process to coordinate all trades and services necessary to finish the project on the scheduled completion date. Architects also use a time schedule for programming phases of a project.

The primary phases of a project are preliminary design, client review, preliminary budget, agency review (when required), construction documents, final construction bids, and building department approvals and permits.

A helpful aid for reviewing the scheduling of phases is a bar chart. It is flexible and allows for changes of scheduling for some or all of the phases. Figure 3.21

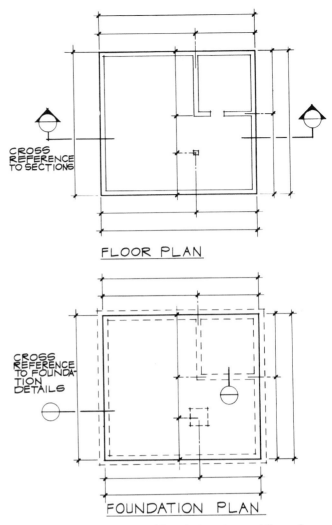

Figure 3.19 Relationship of foundation plan and floor plan.

shows a bar chart used for project programming. Initial communications and programming with consultants such as structural, mechanical, civil, and electrical engineers is most important.

RELATIONSHIP OF CONSTRUCTION DOCUMENT DRAWINGS

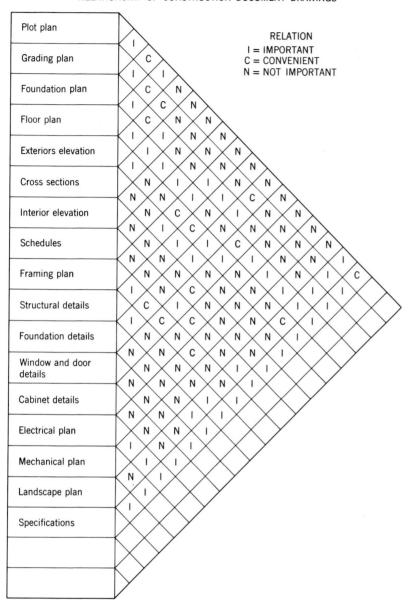

RELATION
I = IMPORTANT
C = CONVENIENT
N = NOT IMPORTANT

Figure 3.20 Matrix chart example.

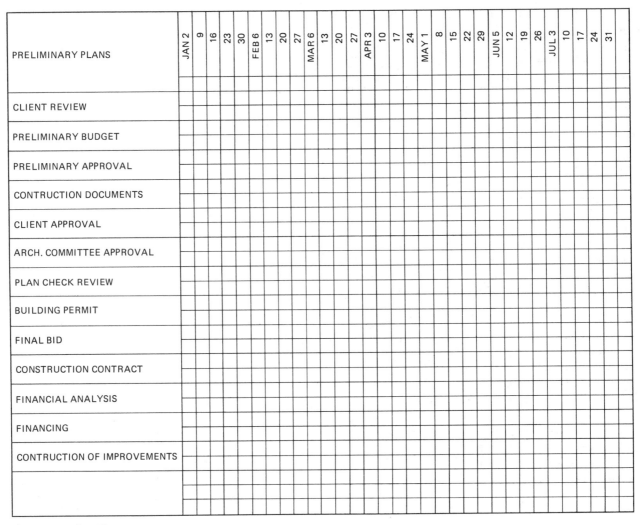

Figure 3.21 Bar Chart

CONCEPTUAL
DESIGN

Basic Influences on the Design Process

Before construction documents can be developed, much time and effort must be devoted to the conceptual design process. This process involves developing preliminary design studies and schematic drawings for site planning, area relationships within the structure, exterior designs and structural concepts, as well as developing solutions for primary user requirements for a specific structure.

In developing conceptual and preliminary designs, the architect—the primary designer—is influenced by many factors. The basic influences on the design process for a specific structure, regardless of the architect's design philosophy are:

1. Site configuration and orientation
2. Topography
3. Geology and soil conditions
4. Environment
5. Region
6. Zoning regulations, codes, etc.
7. Economics
8. Biophysical factors
9. Use and users of the structure

Site Configuration

Site configuration and desired building orientation immediately influence the physical characteristics of a specific structure. The orientation depends on desired exposure to views, sun, and wind. Examples of site configurations and their influences are given in Figures 4.1, 4.2, and 4.3. Note that Figure 4.3 has some existing trees that are to remain. Factors such as these, together with site configuration and building orientation, influence the architect's conceptual design approach.

Topography

The topography of a site—that is, the natural grade condition of the land prior to the development of the construction project—must be considered early in the design stages. The design should involve minimum grading for site development. Figure 4.4 shows how this can be done. The figure shows a cross-section of a building, indicating a change of floor levels compatible with the sloping site, and therefore requiring minimum grading.

Geology and Soils

Sites can have geographical and/or soil condition problems. A portion or portions of a site may have experienced slippage or slide conditions. Unfavorable soil conditions might include uncompacted fill areas or portions with poor soil-bearing capacities. The conceptual design

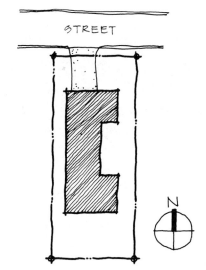

Figure 4.1 Site orientation.

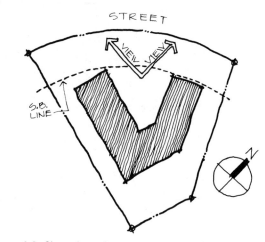

Figure 4.2 Site orientation.

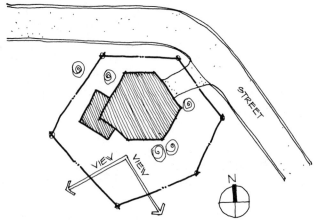

Figure 4.3 Site orientation.

can provide solutions to such problems. An obvious solution is to eliminate any construction in these areas. Figure 4.5 illustrates this.

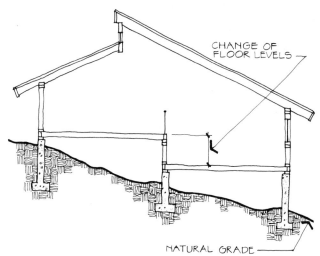

Figure 4.4 Cross section of sloping lot.

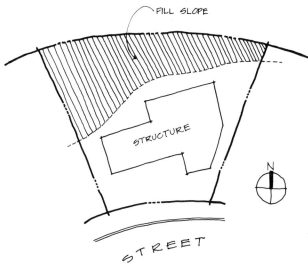

Figure 4.5 An unfavorable soil condition.

Figure 4.6 A snow load design.

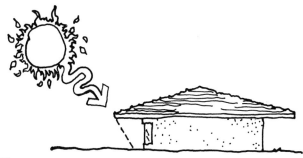

Figure 4.7 An overhang for sun control.

Environment

Environment and region together influence the conceptual design of a structure. Climate influences selection of construction techniques and materials. In regions susceptible to heavy snow loads, for example, steep-pitch roofs are used; in warm regions where sun control is desired, large roof overhangs are used. Figures 4.6 and 4.7 illustrate these contrasting situations.

Zoning Regulations, Codes, and Committees

An architect's designs are regulated and influenced by zoning regulations, codes, and other restrictions established by local, state, and federal laws and agencies.

Before work on a conceptual design is begun, all rel-

evant site restrictions must be discovered. Generally, restrictions apply to the type and use of the building permitted on a specific site, and to building height. In addition, there are usually requirements for front, rear, and sideyard setbacks, and for the amount of landscaping and open space included in the design. Moreover, if a committee has been established to critique the architectural design, it may have placed restrictions on the choice of roof and wall materials as well as on the architectural style.

Figures 4.8 and 4.9 provide examples of these restrictions. Figure 4.8 illustrates building setback requirements established by zoning regulations; Figure 4.9 shows a site design for a commercial building with required areas for parking, open space, and landscaping.

Economics

Economics must also be considered at the conceptual design stage. For example, the size or area of the structure relative to the cost factor, or the site design relative to the existing topography, soils, and geological conditions are all economic considerations. Such forethought in the early design stages has a significant economic impact on the final construction documents.

For example, designing a structure over unfavorable

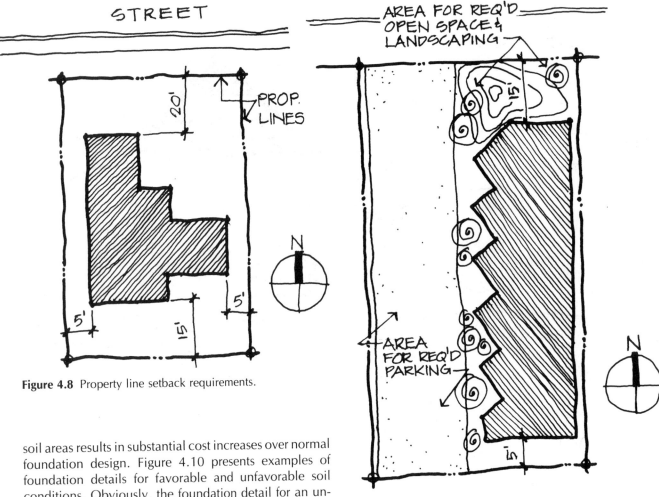

Figure 4.8 Property line setback requirements.

Figure 4.9 Open space requirements.

soil areas results in substantial cost increases over normal foundation design. Figure 4.10 presents examples of foundation details for favorable and unfavorable soil conditions. Obviously, the foundation detail for an unfavorable soils condition involves higher costs for concrete, trenching, forming, and even, possibly, steel reinforcing.

Biophysical Factors

Biophysical factors must be considered. These involve provision of optimum environments for users. Factors include heating, cooling, lighting, water, fuel, and sanitation.

Solar energy, for example, may be used to supply or supplement a desired heating system. Figure 4.11 illustrates a roof and wall orientation best suited to the installation of solar collectors in the Northern Hemisphere (which includes all of North America).

Use and Users

Most influential of all are the use and users. If, for example, the structure is to be a custom residence, the architect's conceptual planning will be influenced by the family's size, living habits, and personal tastes. The client or users of a proposed industrial building inform

the architect of the physical requirements of their manufacturing process, which will influence the architect's conceptual design. From the conceptual design phase on, a constant input of requirements and output of solutions are necessary to satisfy user needs.

Special Client Needs

The architect must maintain constant communication with the client before and during the whole conceptual design process. It is here that primary planning criteria are set: area or room relationships, desired proportions or sizes of required areas, ingress (entrance) and egress (exit) locations, as well as the optimum circulation

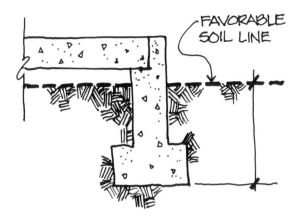

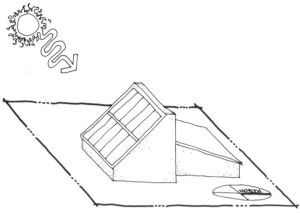

Figure 4.11 Solar orientation.

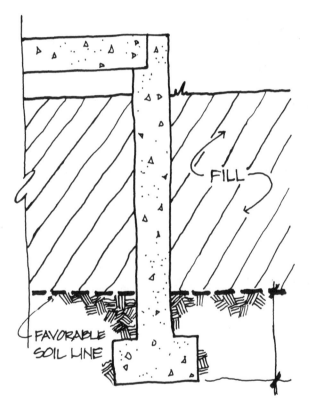

Figure 4.10 Favorable and unfavorable site condition.

throughout the structure. The architect must do considerable research to satisfy and improve upon specific building requirements.

With all the input and communications from the client, as well as the findings from research, the architect then programs the total concept in order to begin schematic drawings.

Schematic Drawings

Evaluating Solutions

Schematic drawings provide the architect with a visual way of evaluating solutions to requirements: now these solutions take shape in area relationships and circulation patterns. Figure 4.12 provides an example of a schematic drawing for a proposed office building. This figure deals only with room relationships and circulation patterns.

Incorporating Predetermined Elements

Schematic drawings are also used for studies incorporating predetermined design elements, as, for example, when the shape of the building must be compatible with a preselected roof design and roof material. The schematic drawing in Figure 4.13 is a visual study that relates building shape to roof design.

Presenting Preliminary Designs

After finishing schematic drawings and design studies, the architect develops these concepts into preliminary design drawings to present to the client. These preliminary drawings generally include the site development, floor plans, exterior elevations, and exterior and interior sketches.

Choosing the Medium

Various media commonly used for presentation of preliminary drawings include ink, felt-tip pens, pencil, and tape. These media, used on reproducible paper, enable

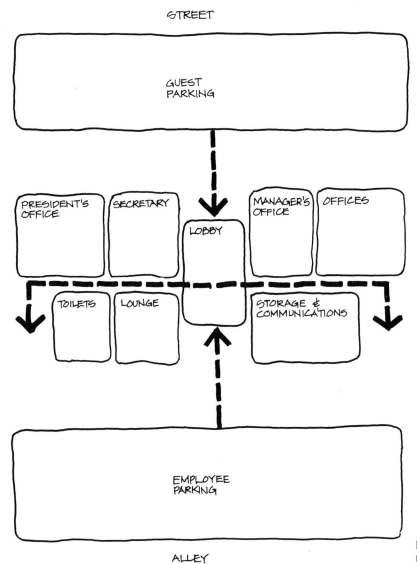

Figure 4.12 Schematic room relationships and desired circulation.

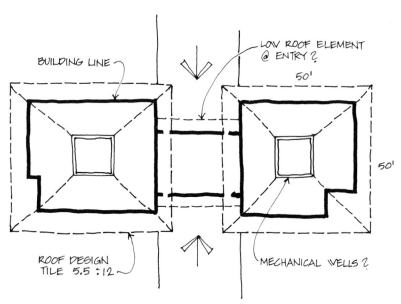

Figure 4.13 Conceptual roof design.

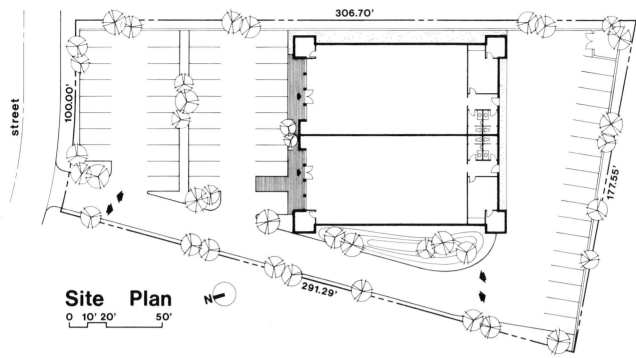

Figure 4.14 Preliminary site development.

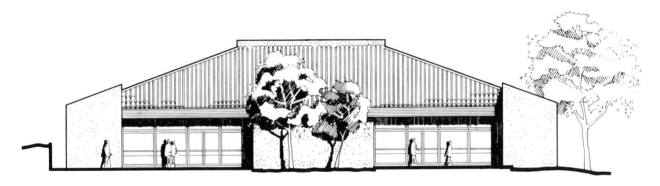

North

Figure 4.15 Preliminary site elevation.

the architect to provide numerous copies of the drawings—a necessity since local agencies and institutions will review them at this preliminary design stage.

Accuracy

While the character and technique of preliminary drawings vary from office to office, the drawings must always be relatively accurate as they largely determine client and agency acceptance as well as the format for the final construction documents.

Combining Drawings

In most cases, the floor plan and site development are delineated on one drawing. This enables the client to see the total design concept—that is, the development of the entire site and its relationships to the planning of the structure. These relationships include vehicular and pedestrian circulation patterns, automotive parking, landscaping, and any other elements necessary to meet specific design requirements.

Figure 4.14 shows a preliminary site development and floor plan presentation for a small office building. Only the main design elements are shown in this drawing. Preliminary exterior elevations should use shades and shadows and also depict the exterior materials to be used, as well as landscaped areas directly related to the structure. Figure 4.15 shows an exterior elevation for a small office building.

Figure 4.16 Exterior perspective.

Figure 4.17 Interior sketches.

Exterior and Interior Sketches

Exterior perspectives (fixed views) and interior three-dimensional sketches are extremely important in preliminary presentations. They help the client and reviewing agencies understand and visualize the architect's concept. The technique and media of these drawings should be compatible with the site plan, floor plan, and exterior elevations.

Three-dimensional sketches often help the architect and project designer to analyze specific design elements. These drawings may never be used for presentation purposes but they do provide visual help for those involved in the design process. Figure 4.16 shows an exterior perspective of a small office. Figure 4.17 shows interior sketches of the same structure.

Using Models

Another way to present preliminary designs is with models. Models constructed for preliminary studies may consist only of the main design elements such as the roof configuration and wall masses. This type of model can be constructed of illustration board, styrofoam, or balsa wood and is usually built in the architect's office. The scale of a model may vary from $\frac{1}{16}''$ to $\frac{1}{4}'' = 1$ foot. See Figures 4.18 A and B.

Figure 4.18A Model for mass study.

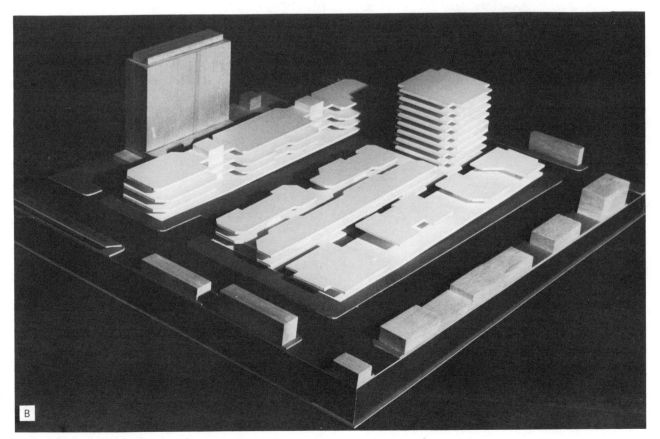

Figure 4.18B Model for mass study.

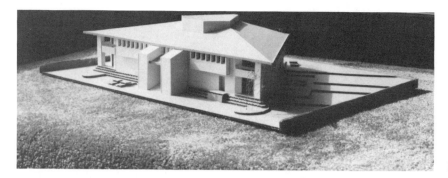

Figure 4.19 Finished model.

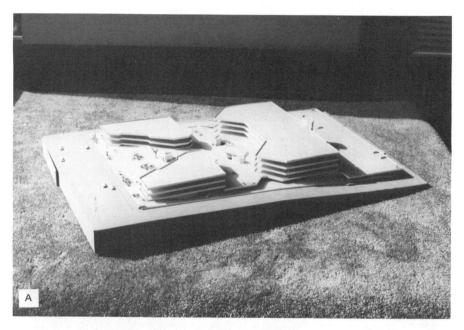

Figure 4.20A Finished model.

Figure 4.20B Model with section removed to show underground parking.

Finished models that include windows, doors, wall materials, and so forth are excellent for preliminary presentation purposes and can be photographed for brochures and other promotional material. The cost of an intricate finished model may be prohibitive for many projects; in most cases, they must be built by a professional model maker. However, models provide the best likeness to the finished structure. As with preliminary presentation drawings, techniques in model building vary. Examples of finished models are shown in Figures 4.19, 4.20A, and 4.20B.

Using Photographs

Photographic enlargements or reductions can also illustrate preliminary designs and can be used in many ways. A model or a structure can be photographed and then reduced to an approximate scale compatible with an aerial photo of the site. The model photograph may then be superimposed onto the site photograph for presentation. This process gives viewers a realistic understanding of the structure and its relationship to the site and the surrounding area. Figure 4.21 illustrates a reduced photograph of a model for a shopping center superimposed onto an aerial photograph of the site.

Another technique is photographing a direct elevation of the site to be developed and the facades of the adjacent buildings. This allows the architect to superimpose a photograph of the facade of the new structure and then photograph it with the adjacent structures.

A series of photographs should be taken when the model is completed, as the model may be damaged or may deteriorate as it is transported to various locations. Photographs of models are excellent for public presentations and for occasions when the model is unavailable or not transportable.

Photographs of architectural **renderings** (finished drawings) are more common than photographs of models, since many exhibits are required for presentation to agencies, architectural committees, and lending institutions. These color or black and white photographs are generally reduced to aid in handling, for submission to publications, or to reduce costs. See Figures 4.22 and 4.23.

Refining Preliminary Designs

After completion and acceptance of preliminary designs by the client and governing agencies, the architect begins to refine the preliminary designs in preparation for construction documents. This phase includes attention to such major factors as economics of the structure, client or user review, and building codes and agencies.

For example, economics can influence the choice of floor plan which must satisfy an economical framing system. In the course of the refinement of preliminary designs, the architect presents any changes or adjustments to the client or users for review. This is essential because the next step after this design phase is the preparation of construction documents and specifications. Obviously, it is vital to have complete approval.

Figure 4.21 Photo of model superimposed on photo of existing area.

Figure 4.22 Reduced architectural rendering.

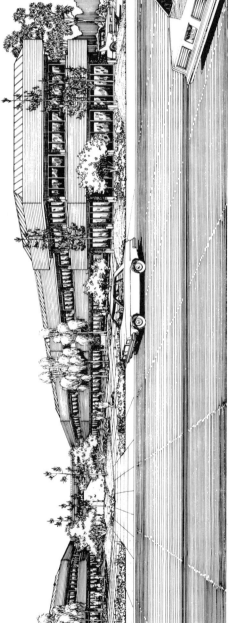

Figure 4.23 Reduced architectural rendering.

Other refinements and adjustments at this stage are made according to governing **building codes** and agencies. A preliminary review by the local building authority, for example, may necessitate refinements such as more exits in the structure, or a fire separation wall. Other agencies, such as the planning department, may introduce refinements in parking arrangements and landscaped areas relative to the side design. These are just a few examples of what can influence the refinement of the preliminary design. In many projects, there may be other related design development criteria, for example, for landscape design, or interior design.

This process of refining drawings continues until all the design factors are integrated through the preparation of construction documents.

CONSTRUCTION
PRINCIPLES
AND METHODS

Today's buildings use various construction principles, methods, and building systems. These principles, methods, and systems are generally selected according to the type and use of the structure, code requirements, logical and simple structural solutions, economic considerations, and satisfactory planning and design elements. So when you are asked to provide solutions for a specific building, you should investigate these various construction principles and methods.

The *primary components* of a structure include *the foundation system, the wall system,* and *the roof system.*

Foundation and Floor Systems

Foundation systems are usually designed to use either wood structural members or a concrete slab as the floor support. When you select a foundation system for a structure, consider the following criteria:

1. Structural considerations
2. Type of structure and its use
3. Desirability of wood or concrete to support the finish floor
4. Finish floor material
5. Topography of the site
6. Soil conditions
7. Client preference

If a foundation for a wood floor has been selected, you should also select a wood floor system.

Wood Floor: Joist System

The most conventional wood floor system uses **floor joists** as structural members and plywood as a subfloor for supporting the finish floor material. Floor joists are generally spaced at 16″ on centers (o/c) and may vary in size from 2″ × 6″ to 2″ × 12″, depending on their spans. These members are supported on the exterior perimeter of the structure by a concrete foundation and, in the interior, by a concrete foundation and/or wood girders and concrete piers.

Advantages. Major advantages of this method of floor construction include (1) being able to produce greater spans length if needed, by using recommended joist sizes and developing a beam in the floor system by nailing or bolting joists together; (2) being able to use fewer internal supporting foundation walls, girders, and piers; and (3) being able to cantilever the floor joists if this is called for by the design. A **cantilever** is a projecting structural member supported at only one end.

Disadvantages. This system should not be selected in regions where buildings are susceptible to termite infestation and/or dry rot; the wood deteriorates and reduces the structural integrity of the wood members. And, in buildings where noise transmission through the floor system needs to be minimized, other floor systems such as concrete are more desirable. Figure 5.1 shows a foundation plan using floor joists, concrete piers, wood girders, and concrete foundation walls. Symbols for construction assemblies are shown for further explanations and reference.

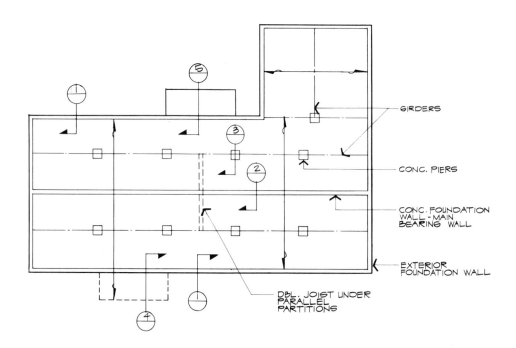

Figure 5.1 Foundation plan— floor joist and pier and girder.

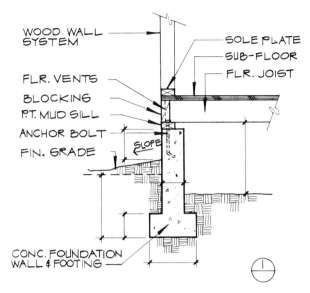

NOTE:
DIMENSIONS AS PER REGIONAL
AND SOILS REQUIREMENTS

A

Figure 5.2A Exterior foundation wall—wood floor joist.

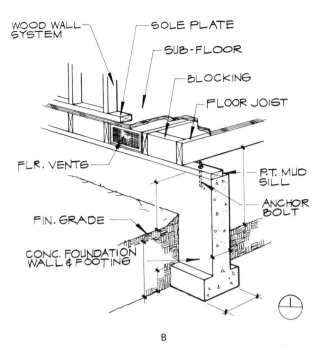

B

Figure 5.2B Isometric of exterior foundation wall with wood floor joist.

Construction Principles. There are some primary construction principles for this system:

1. Ensure floor members are not in direct contact with concrete.
2. Provide recommended underfloor clearance from soil.
3. Provide proper flashing to protect wood from possible moisture problems. (Flashing is a general term for any sheet metal barrier at a joint, etc., to prevent water infiltration.)
4. Provide more than minimum-size joists, blocking and supporting members to avoid deflection or floor movement.
5. Provide adequate ventilation.

Example of Floor Joists. In Figure 5.1 an exterior foundation wall, footing, and floor assembly using wood floor joists is referenced. ⊕ It is illustrated in detail in Figure 5.2A and three dimensionally in Figure 5.2B. The depth of the foundation wall and footing will vary depending on soils and geological conditions, frost line depth, vertical loads acting along the foundation wall, and local code requirements.

Load Bearing Foundations

Supporting Internal Walls. Before you position and dimension internal foundation walls and piers, pay attention to the interior walls. These walls are subjected to heavy loads from the roof, ceiling, and other structures.

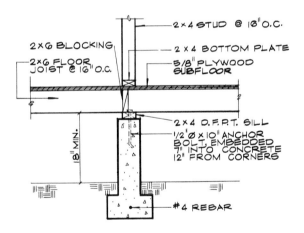

INTERIOR BEARING FOOTING ②
SCALE: 1" = 1'-0"

Figure 5.3 Drafted detail of interior bearing footing with wood floor.

When heavy loads accumulate on a particular wall, position a concrete foundation wall directly below that wall. Figure 5.3 shows a floor and foundation assembly for a load-bearing interior wall. Solid blocking is provided between the floor joists directly beneath the wall for stability.

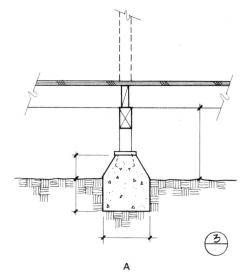

Figure 5.4A Interior pier.

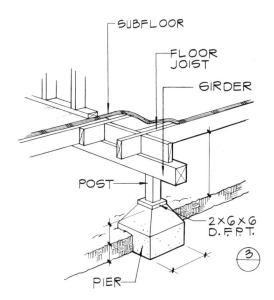

NOTE:
DIMENSIONS AS PER REGIONAL
AND SOILS REQUIREMENTS

Figure 5.4B Isometric of interior pier.

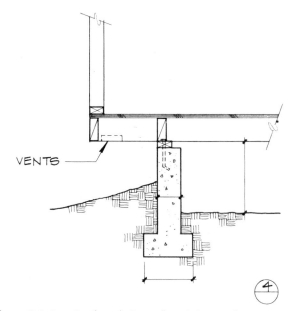

Figure 5.5 Exterior foundation—floor joist cantilever.

Intermediate Supports. For intermediate supports of wood floor joists, use wood **girders** and concrete **piers** (column footings). Positioning of these members depends on the size of the floor joists and their allowable spans. It is good practice to add an additional row of piers and girders where the joists have been extended to their maximum span. This decreases the amount of deflection in the floor system and therefore provides a stiffer floor at minimum construction cost. Whenever possible, locate wood girders directly beneath partition walls. Figure 5.4A shows a pier and girder assembly where solid blocking between the wood joists is pro-

vided directly above the wood girder. Figure 5.4B is an isometric drawing of Figure 5.4A.

Using floor joists in a wood floor system allows the designer to cantilever the floor joists, thereby solving certain design problems. The length of the cantilever depends on the size and spacing of the floor joists as well as on structural loads from above. Figure 5.5 shows a detail of floor joists cantilevered beyond the exterior foundation wall. The underfloor vents may be located underneath the cantilevered joist rather than in the blocking area. Visually, this is a more desirable location than the face of the exterior wall.

Flashing. Moisture in the floor system can cause dry rot and swelling or buckling of wood floor members. Wood floor systems, therefore, always require adequate **flashing** (sheet metal protection of wood) as a deterrent to moisture infiltration. Figure 5.6A shows an exterior foundation wall adjacent to a concrete porch or patio. The metal flashing is positioned to shield against water seepage into the wood floor. Always provide flashing when you are dealing with conditions like these. An isometric view of Figure 5.6A is shown in Figure 5.6B.

Joining Floor Joists. Using wood floor joists allows you to develop floor beams under load-bearing walls and columns. This is a great asset. In many cases, two or three joists may be joined together to form a beam for a structural support. These members may be joined by nails or bolts.

Figure 5.7 shows floor joists joined to develop a beam for the support of a load-bearing wall.

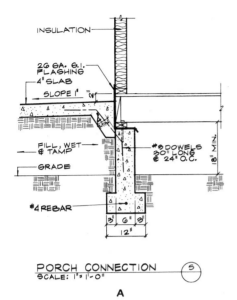

PORCH CONNECTION
SCALE: 1" = 1'-0"

A

Figure 5.6A Porch slab to wood floor system.

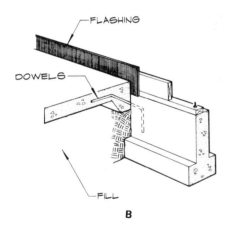

B

Figure 5.6B Isometric of porch slab to wood floor system.

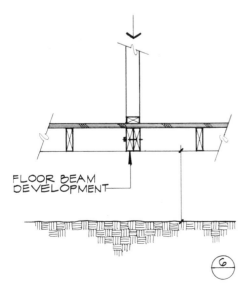

Figure 5.7 Floor beam.

Wood Floor: Tongue-and-Groove System

Frequently, 2-inch thick (2") **tongue-and-groove planking** is used to span over wood girders and concrete foundation walls. Figure 5.8 shows a foundation plan with 2" tongue-and-groove planking for a floor system. Additional rows or piers and girders are necessary because of the short spans. Symbols for details of construction assemblies are shown for reference and further explanation.

Figure 5.9A shows an exterior foundation wall of a wood floor system using 2" tongue-and-groove planking (referenced as ⊖ on Figure 5.8). Here you can immediately see two major differences between this and the floor joist system: first, the height is less from finish grade to the sub-floor; second, a block-out is required in the foundation wall forming (molding) for installing the under-floor vents. As mentioned earlier, the width and depth of the foundation wall and footing depend on numerous factors. Figure 5.9B shows the tongue-and-groove planking in section.

If an interior wall must support a large tributary area of roof and ceiling loads, a concrete foundation wall should be positioned directly beneath the wall, instead of a girder-and-pier support. This is shown in Figure 5.10.

Remember, this floor system needs additional rows of piers and girders because of the span limitations of the 2" tongue-and-groove planking. The pier-and-girder detail resembles the floor joist system, as you can see in Figure 5.11. This system, too, requires metal flashing to protect wood floor members against moisture infiltration, as you can see in detail in Figure 5.12.

Because this floor system, unlike the floor joist system, does not permit floor beams, additional girders must be positioned directly below load-bearing walls. Another method for positioning a beam for the support of a load-bearing wall is to locate the beam at the base of the wall and span between the girders. This is shown in Figure 5.13.

Advantages. There are some major advantages to using this system:

1. Tongue-and-groove provides a stiff floor.
2. The system has a lower noise factor than that of a wood joist floor system.
3. It has a lower exterior height silhouette because the depth of the floor joists has been eliminated.
4. It provides a more rigid subfloor when concrete or a grouted tile floor is to be applied directly above.

Disadvantages. There are also disadvantages in using this system:

1. Some regions are subjected to excessive termite infestation and dry rot.

94

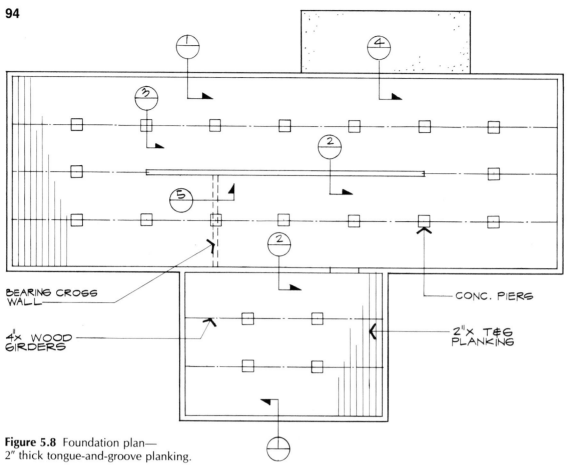

Figure 5.8 Foundation plan—
2″ thick tongue-and-groove planking.

BEARING CROSS WALL

4″× WOOD GIRDERS

CONC. PIERS

2″× T&G PLANKING

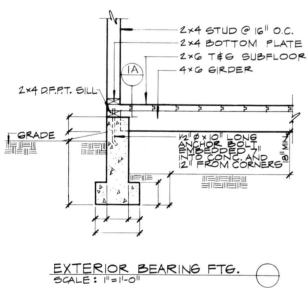

2×4 STUD @ 16″ O.C.
2×4 BOTTOM PLATE
2×6 T&G SUBFLOOR
4×6 GIRDER

2×4 D.F.P.T. SILL

GRADE

½″∅ ×10″ LONG ANCHOR BOLT EMBEDDED INTO CONC. AND 2″ FROM CORNERS

8″ MIN.

EXTERIOR BEARING FTG.
SCALE: 1″=1′-0″

A

Figure 5.9A Exterior foundation wall with 2″ tongue-and-grove planking.

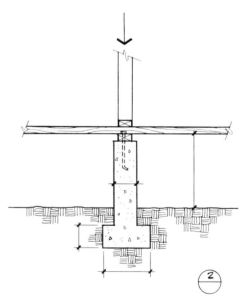

Figure 5.10 Interior bearing concrete foundation—2″ tongue-and-groove planking.

2×6 T&G SUBFLOOR
SCALE: 3″=1′-0″

B

Figure 5.9B Tongue-and-groove subfloor in section.

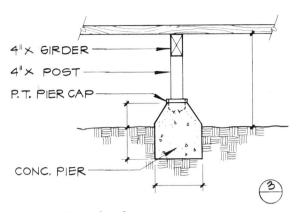

Figure 5.11 Pier and girder.

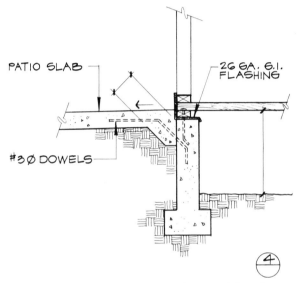

Figure 5.12 Exterior foundation and patio slab—2″ tongue-and-groove floor.

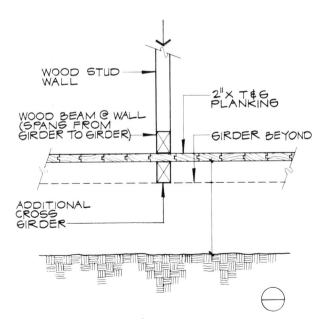

Figure 5.13 Wall support beam.

2. Short spans require additional girders and foundation walls.

3. The system does not allow joining joists together to make beams.

4. The system does not permit floor cantilevers.

This system, too, requires metal flashing to protect wood floor members against moisture infiltration, as you can see in detail in Figure 5.12.

Concrete Floor

When concrete has been selected as the supporting material, the factors influencing the choice of construction methods resemble those influencing wood floor construction: soils and geological conditions, waterproofing and insulation requirements, varying temperature conditions, reinforcing requirements, and finished flooring.

Suppose, for example, that the **soils report** indicates that the proposed site has expansive soil, as shown in Figure 5.14; expansive soil generates upward and downward forces that can fracture or crack concrete members. Given this condition, the following construction methods should be considered:

1. Deeper footings
2. Reinforcing at top and bottom of foundation wall
3. Sand bed at base of footing

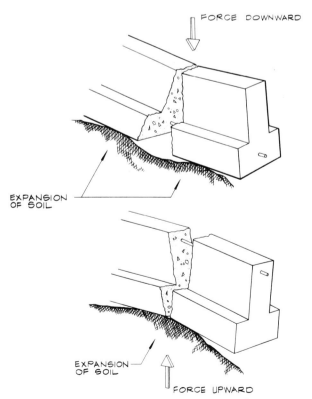

Figure 5.14 Forces on concrete in expansive soil.

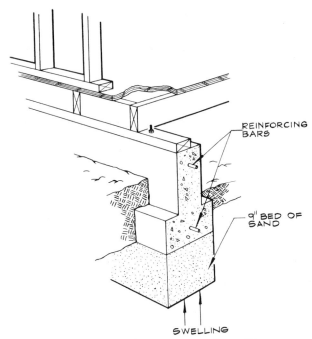

Figure 5.15 Reinforcing for expansive soil conditions.

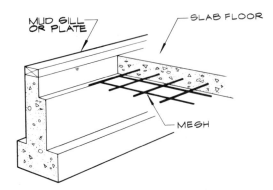

Figure 5.16 Use of mesh in slab.

4. Crushed rock or sand below concrete floor slab
5. Concrete slab reinforcing
6. Water saturation of soil prior to pouring of concrete

Figure 5.15 shows a concrete foundation and floor section on grade, detailed for expansive soil conditions.

Concrete Floor Reinforcing. In much the same way that the foundation needs reinforcing, the concrete floor also needs reinforcing to prevent cracking. Current methods include using either deformed reinforcing bars running in each direction or welded wire mesh.

The welded wire mesh is usually made of number 10 wire spaced 6 inches apart in each direction. The size and spacing of reinforcing bars is based on the soil report recommendations and determined by the engineer. Figure 5.16 shows on-grade concrete floor reinforcing.

Types of Concrete Floor Foundations. There are two main types of concrete floor foundations or footings: the monolithic **one-pour system,** where the concrete floor and foundation are poured in one operation, and the **two-pour system,** where the foundation and concrete floor are poured independently.

These two differ in construction: in the monolithic footing, the trenches themselves become the forms, as shown in Figure 5.17; in the two-pour method, formwork is provided, as shown in Figure 5.18. More concrete is used in the monolithic footing.

One way to hold two different pours of concrete together is to use steel **dowels.** These dowels resemble

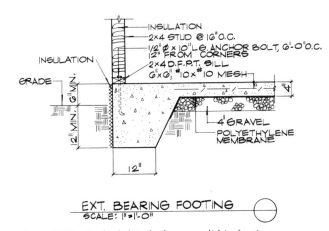

EXT. BEARING FOOTING
SCALE: 1"=1'-0"

Figure 5.17 Drafted detail of a monolithic footing.

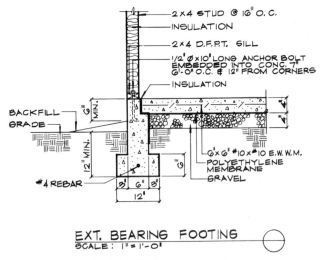

EXT. BEARING FOOTING
SCALE: 1"=1'-0"

Figure 5.18 Drafted detail of a two-pour structure.

reinforcing bars but work differently. An application of steel dowels holding a porch slab to the foundation of a structure is shown in Figure 5.19.

An interior two-pour bearing (supporting) footing resembles the exterior footing and carries the vertical loads

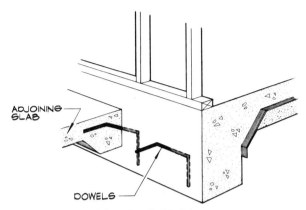

Figure 5.19 Use of dowel to hold slab to structure.

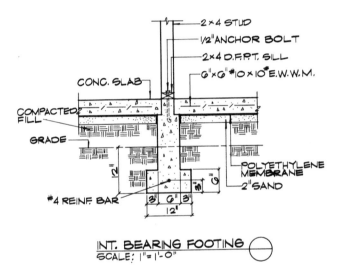

Figure 5.20 Drafted detail of a two-pour interior bearing footing.

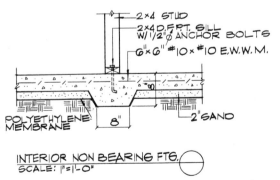

Figure 5.21 Drafted detail of an interior nonbearing footing.

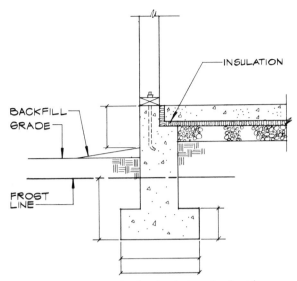

Figure 5.22 Measuring the footing below the frost line.

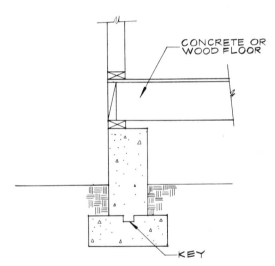

Figure 5.23 Use of a key in a two-pour system.

from the structure above. Figure 5.20 shows a drafted detail for a two-pour bearing footing. Nonbearing footings support the wall weight only. Bearing footings support heavy loads from the roof, ceiling, or floor above.

The purpose of the interior nonbearing footing, how-ever, is to give support for the wall load above and to provide only sufficient thickness to accommodate the anchor bolts that secure the sill, as you can see in Figure 5.21.

Where temperatures are very cold, wider footings are needed to accommodate heavy snow loads, and the footing must be placed far below the frost line. Colder climates also require **insulation** under the concrete floor and around the perimeter of the foundation. Figure 5.22 shows foundation detail and concrete floor detail for colder temperatures.

When the footing is poured separately from the foundation wall, a key should be provided in the footing to give lateral stability. This is shown in Figure 5.23.

You must also be aware of areas that are potentially weak and may produce cracks in the concrete, such as

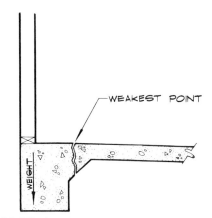

Figure 5.24 Weak points.

the connection between a concrete floor slab and the foundation in a monolithic pour operation. This area must be "beefed up," or strengthened, as you can see in Figure 5.24.

Wall Systems

Two main types of wood wall-framing methods are used in construction: the **balloon frame** and the **Western or** **platform-framing** method. The main differences between these systems lie in the construction methods for the walls and floor assembly.

Balloon Frame

In two-story construction, the balloon frame system uses continuous wall studs from the first floor level up to the roof assembly. The second floor supporting members are then framed to the continuous studs. Stud sizes are 2" × 4" or 2" × 6" at 16" center to center and 2" thick blocking to be fitted to fill all openings in order to provide firestops and prevent drafts from one space to another.

Wood or metal members at a 45° angle, attached securely at the top and bottom of the studs, provide horizontal bracing for walls. Where exterior walls are solid sheathed, additional bracing may not be required. However, this may be determined by the governing building code or structural engineering requirements.

This system has minimum vertical shrinkage or vertical movement and may be used with brick veneer or stucco exteriors. Figure 5.25 gives an isometric (three dimensional) view and shows an exterior wall section. It also shows solid sheathing on the exterior walls. Use of sheathing such as this depends on the region and on the exterior materials selected.

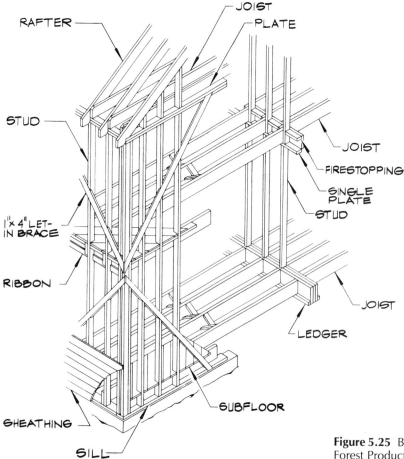

Figure 5.25 Balloon frame construction. (Courtesy of National Forest Products Association.)

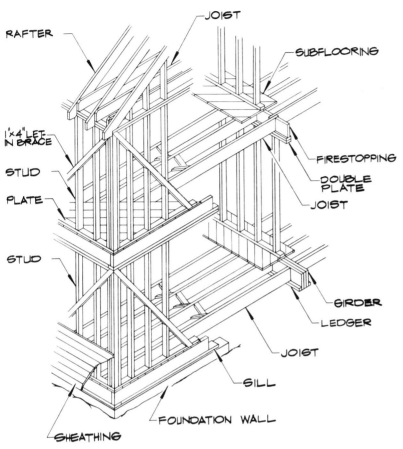

Figure 5.26 Western or platform framing. (Courtesy of National Forest Products Association.)

RAFTER

JOIST

SUBFLOORING

1"x4" LET-IN BRACE

STUD

PLATE

STUD

FIRESTOPPING

DOUBLE PLATE

JOIST

GIRDER

LEDGER

JOIST

SILL

FOUNDATION WALL

SHEATHING

Western or Platform Framing

Western or platform framing uses a different procedure. First, the lower floor walls are assembled. Then the supporting floor members and subfloor for the upper floor are framed. The upper subfloor then provides a platform for assembling the upper floor walls. The walls are framed with 2″ × 4″ or 2″ × 6″ studs at 16″ center to center. Required blocking is 2″ thick and fitted to prevent drafts between spaces.

Solid sheathing or diagonal braces may provide bracing for walls, regional differences determining which is used. Figure 5.26 shows an isometric and wall section using Western framing.

Post and Beam Frame

A third method for framing wood structures is the **post and beam** system. Less common than platform or balloon framing, this method uses a beam-to-post spacing that allows the builder to use 2″ roof or floor planking. Figure 5.27 compares the system with conventional framing. For best use of this system for residential construction, you should provide a specific module of plank-and-beam spacing for planning. Supplementary framing is put on the exterior walls so that exterior and interior finishes can be attached.

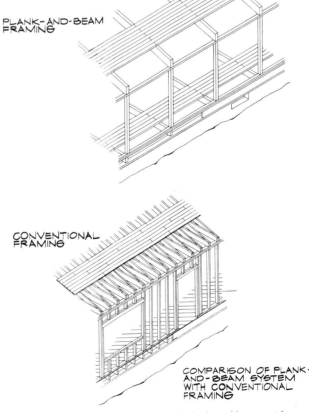

PLANK-AND-BEAM FRAMING

CONVENTIONAL FRAMING

COMPARISON OF PLANK-AND-BEAM SYSTEM WITH CONVENTIONAL FRAMING

Figure 5.27 Pictorial comparison of plank and beam with conventional framing. (Courtesy of National Forest Products Association.)

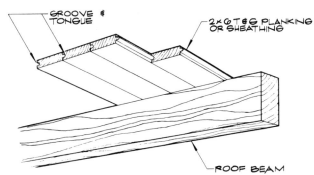

Figure 5.28 Pictorial of roof planking.

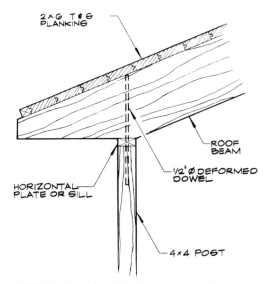

Figure 5.29 Section of post to beam connection.

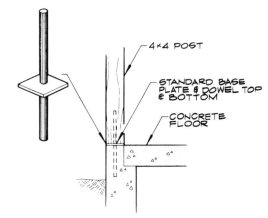

Figure 5.30 Section of post base dowel.

The term **planking** is used to refer to members that have a minimum depth of 2″ and a width from 6″ to 8″. The edges of these members are normally tongue-and-grooved. Using such edges enables a continuous joining of members so that a concentrated load is distributed onto adjacent members. Figure 5.28 illustrates a commonly used planking with tongue-and-grooved edges.

You must provide a positive connection between the post and beam and secure the post to the floor. You can use different types of metal framing connectors. However, if these connectors are visually undesirable, you may use dowels. Examples of doweled post-to-beam and post-to-floor connections are shown in Figures 5.29 and 5.30.

When you are asked to provide architectural details for this framing method, detail members that are properly fastened together. Because fewer pieces are used with this method, pay special attention to connections where beams abut (touch) each other and where beams join posts. When connections are securely fastened together, the building acts as a unit in resisting external forces.

Types of Walls

Masonry.   Masonry for exterior structural walls is widely used in commercial, industrial, and residential construction. The main masonry units used are brick and concrete block. These are available in many sizes, shapes, textures, and colors.

Masonry is fire resistant, providing excellent fire ratings ranging from 2 to 4 hours or more (the time it takes a fire-testing flame temperature to penetrate a specific wall assembly). It also acts as an excellent sound barrier. When solid brick units are used for an exterior structural wall, the primary assembly is determined by geophysical conditions. For example, steel reinforcing bars and solid grout may be needed to resist earthquake forces. Figure 5.31 shows a reinforced grouted brick masonry wall. The size and placement of horizontal and vertical reinforcing steel is determined by local codes and regional requirements.

In regions without high wind conditions or earthquakes, reinforcing steel and grout are not needed. The unreinforced masonry wall or brick cavity wall is excellent for insulating exterior walls. Two 3″ or 4″ walls of brick are separated by a 2″ airspace or cavity. This cavity provides a suitable space for insulating materials and the two masonry walls are bonded together with metal ties set in mortar joints. A wall section illustrating the cavity wall is shown in Figure 5.32.

Concrete block units for structural walls are generally 6″ to 8″ in thickness, depending on the height of the wall. The hollow sections of these units are called **cells.** These vertical cells may be left clear or filled solid with grout and reinforcing steel. This depends on regional and code requirements. In regions where reinforcing steel and solid grout are not required, the open cells may be filled with a suitable insulating material. When you detail concrete block wall, dimension the height of the wall

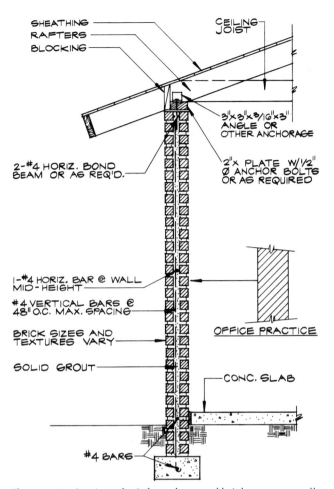

SHEATHING
RAFTERS
BLOCKING
CEILING JOIST

3"x3"x3/16"x3" ANGLE OR OTHER ANCHORAGE

2-#4 HORIZ. BOND BEAM OR AS REQ'D.

2"x PLATE W/1/2" Ø ANCHOR BOLTS OR AS REQUIRED

1-#4 HORIZ. BAR @ WALL MID-HEIGHT

#4 VERTICAL BARS @ 48" O.C. MAX. SPACING

BRICK SIZES AND TEXTURES VARY

OFFICE PRACTICE

SOLID GROUT

CONC. SLAB

#4 BARS

Figure 5.31 Section of reinforced grouted brick masonry wall.

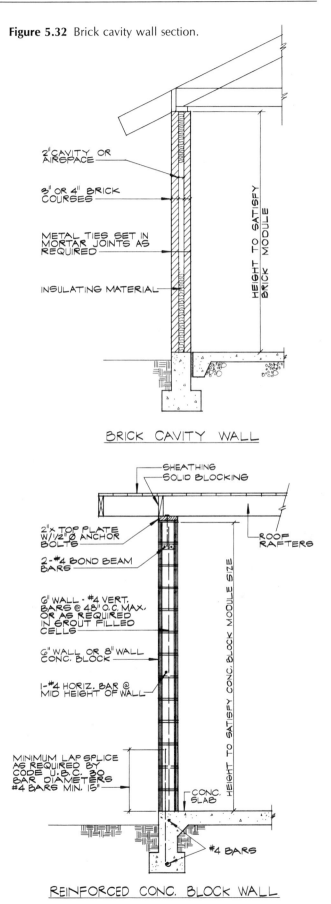

Figure 5.32 Brick cavity wall section.

2" CAVITY OR AIRSPACE

3" OR 4" BRICK COURSES

METAL TIES SET IN MORTAR JOINTS AS REQUIRED

INSULATING MATERIAL

HEIGHT TO SATISFY BRICK MODULE

BRICK CAVITY WALL

SHEATHING
SOLID BLOCKING

2"x TOP PLATE W/1/2" Ø ANCHOR BOLTS

ROOF RAFTERS

2-#4 BOND BEAM BARS

6" WALL - #4 VERT. BARS @ 48" O.C. MAX. OR AS REQUIRED IN GROUT FILLED CELLS

6" WALL OR 8" WALL CONC. BLOCK

1-#4 HORIZ. BAR @ MID HEIGHT OF WALL

MINIMUM LAP SPLICE AS REQUIRED BY CODE U.B.C. 30 BAR DIAMETERS #4 BARS MIN. 15"

CONC. SLAB

HEIGHT TO SATISFY CONC. BLOCK MODULE SIZE

#4 BARS

REINFORCED CONC. BLOCK WALL

to satisfy the modular heights of the masonry units selected. Figure 5.33 shows a reinforced concrete block wall.

Masonry Veneer Wall. Masonry veneer includes the use of brick, concrete block units, or stone. The maximum thickness of masonry veneer is regulated by most building codes and generally recognized as 5". The term ''masonry veneer'' may be defined as a strictly masonry finish that is nonstructural and generally used for appearance.

Code requirements for the attachment of masonry or stone veneer may vary, depending on regional differences. In areas with seismic disturbances, a positive bond between the veneer and a stud wall is needed. A wall section using masonry veneer as an exterior wall finish is illustrated in Figure 5.34.

Figure 5.33 Reinforced concrete block wall section.

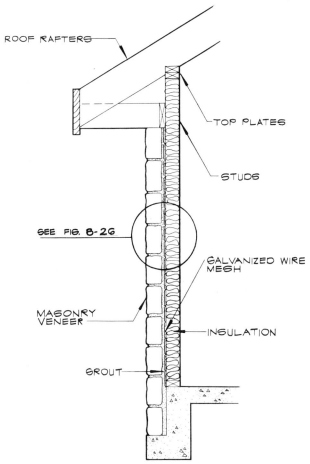

Figure 5.34 Wall section, masonry veneer.

Steel Stud Walls. Using lightweight, cold-formed, steel members provides a solid wall-framing system for load-bearing walls. These walls provide an incombustible support for fire-rated construction and are well suited for pre-assembling. Moreover, shrinkage is of no concern with steel stud walls. The material of the studs varies from 14-gauge to 20-gauge galvanized steel with sizes from 3⅝″ to 10″.

These walls are constructed with a channel track at the bottom and top of the wall with the steel studs attached to the channels. Horizontal bridging is achieved with the use of a steel channel positioned through the stud punch-outs and secured by welding.

An isometric (a type of three-dimensional drawing) of a steel stud wall assembly is shown in Figure 5.35. The attachment of wood sheathing to steel framing members can be achieved with the use of self-tapping screws. A partial section of a steel stud wall using exterior stucco is shown in Figure 5.36.

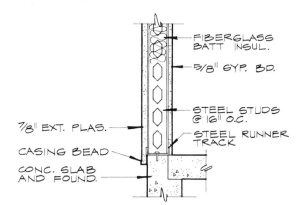

Figure 5.36 Partial steel stud wall section.

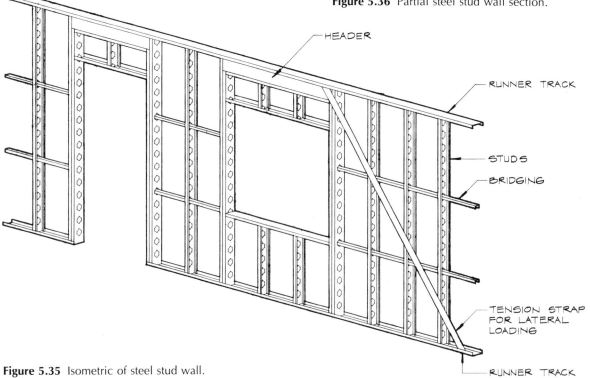

Figure 5.35 Isometric of steel stud wall.

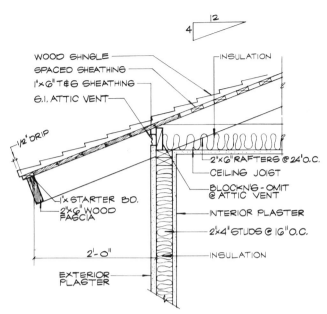

Figure 5.37 Eave detail.

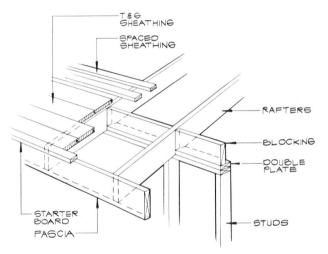

Figure 5.38 Pictorial, eave detail.

Roof Systems

The principles underlying roof systems and the methods of developing these systems depend on the finish roof material. While roofing applications may vary, roofing manfuacturers' literature should be consulted for installation recommendations. The four roofing materials generally used in construction are:

1. Wood shingle and shake
2. Asphaltic composition
3. Clay or concrete tile
4. Aluminum

Wood Shingles and Shakes

Each of these materials has its own set of requirements and construction methods for installation. For example, if you select wood shingles as the roof material, consider the following:

1. 4-in-12 minimum **roof pitch** (degree of inclination)
2. Spaced sheathing or stripping for air space requirements
3. Shingle exposure relative to roof pitch
4. Ventilation
5. Attachment technique
6. Flashing assemblies
7. Weathering qualities
8. Fire resistance
9. Cost

Figure 5.37 shows a drafted eave detail using wood shingles as the roofing material. This detail is shown in pictorial form in Figure 5.38.

If a boxed-in eave is selected for architectural reasons, allow for ventilation. Provide a continuous vent or spaced vents in the soffit (overhead) area. Figure 5.39 shows a drafted detail of this condition. In this case, spaced

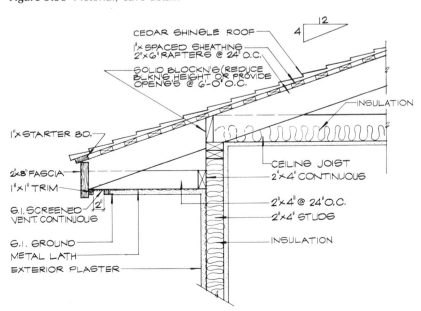

Figure 5.39 Boxed-in eave.

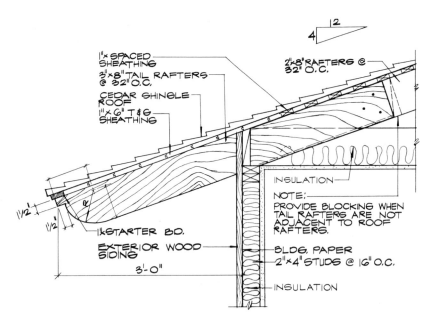

Figure 5.40 Eave detail.

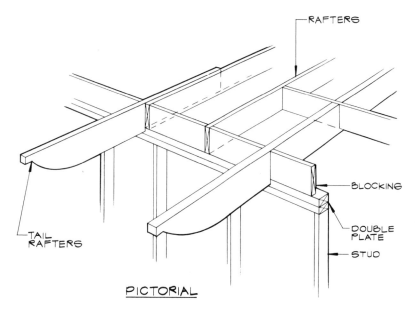

PICTORIAL

Figure 5.41 Pictorial, eave detail.

sheathing is used at the overhang since the plaster soffit becomes the finish of the underside of the eave.

Roof construction methods vary depending on the building's architectural design. If the exterior design calls for exposed tail rafters, this requires a different construction method for the roof system. An example of this is shown in drafted form in Figure 5.40 and in pictorial form in Figure 5.41.

Built-up Asphaltic Composition Roof

Using a built-up asphaltic composition roof requires methods and principles contrary to those of a wood roof.

The recommended pitch for wood shingles is a minimum of 4 in 12, while the recommended maximum pitch for a built-up roof is 3 in 12. Also, using spaced sheathing is unsatisfactory for a built-up roofing system.

The quality of this type of roofing depends on the number and weight of the layers of asphaltic paper and hot tar mopping applications. The roof paper and hot mopping application are the primary deterrents against roof leaks, while the finish material is selected for beauty and architectural style. Two examples of built-up asphaltic composition roofs are shown in Figures 5.42 and 5.43.

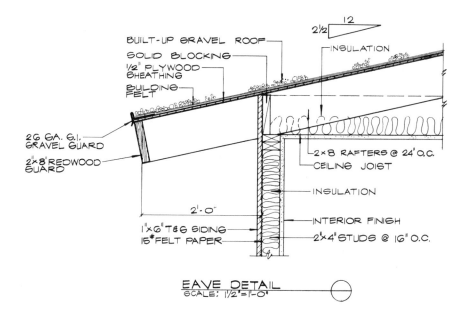

EAVE DETAIL
SCALE: 1/2"=1'-0"

5.42 Eave detail.

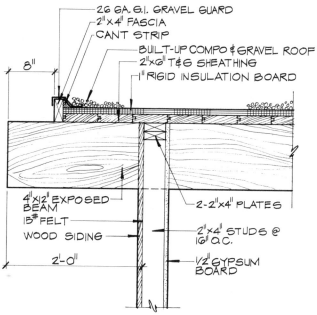

Figure 5.43 Eave detail.

Clay or Concrete Roof Tile

Clay or concrete roof tiles are one of the heaviest finish materials used and require larger framing members such as rafters and supporting beams to carry the additional weight. Figure 5.44 shows a drafted eave detail using mission clay as a finish roof material.

Two acceptable methods for securing the tile to the framing members are, first, using 12-gauge galvanized nails secured to sheathing and, second, using wires spaced along the roof plane with wire ties attached to each individual tile. The wire ties are made from either 12-gauge galvanized wire, 10-gauge copper wire, or .084 diameter stainless steel wire. Figure 5.45 gives a pictorial representation of the use of nails for attaching tiles. Figure 5.46 shows wire ties used in tile attachment. Using wire ties reduces the risk of potential roof leaks because wires are secured only at the ridge and eave.

Aluminum Roofing

Aluminum roofing is available in various shapes, gauges, and colors. Panel thickness may range from 0.032" to 0.040" with baked-on enamel colors. The versatility of the aluminum roof permits application directly to steel girders or purlines (horizontal roof supports), or to plywood or solid sheathing roof decks, with insulation installed directly under the aluminum sheets.

Attachment of the aluminum sheet depends on the structure supporting the finish roofing. Generally, anchor clips or metal fasteners are used for attachment. The configuration of the aluminum varies in design. An example of an aluminum roof is shown in Figure 5.47. The shingle principle of lapping applies also to aluminum roofs. A drafted section for the assembly of an aluminum roof is illustrated in Figure 5.48.

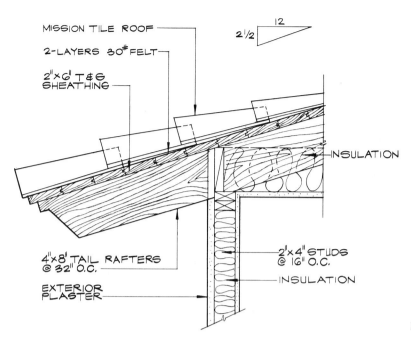

MISSION TILE ROOF

2-LAYERS 30# FELT

2"×6" T&G SHEATHING

INSULATION

4"×8" TAIL RAFTERS @ 32" O.C.

2"×4" STUDS @ 16" O.C.

INSULATION

EXTERIOR PLASTER

2½   12

Figure 5.44 Eave detail—tile roof.

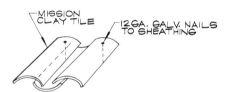

MISSION CLAY TILE

12 GA. GALV. NAILS TO SHEATHING

Figure 5.45 Pictorial, tile roof fastening—nailing.

WIRE TIES @ 10½" O.C. (SPACED ALONG ROOF PLANE)

Figure 5.46 Pictorial, tile roof fastening—wire ties.

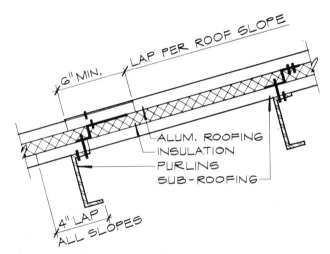

LAP PER ROOF SLOPE

6" MIN.

ALUM. ROOFING
INSULATION
PURLINS
SUB-ROOFING

4" LAP
ALL SLOPES

Figure 5.48 Aluminum roofing section.

Figure 5.47 Aluminum roofing.

6

DEVELOPING
THE SITE PLANS

The Plat Map

The Function of a Plat Map

The site plan is developed through stages, each dealing with new technical information and design solutions. The first step in site plan development is the **plat map**. This map, normally furnished by a civil engineer, is a land plan which delineates the property lines with their bearings, dimensions, streets, and existing easements. The plat map forms the basis of all future information and site development. An example of a plat map is shown in Figure 6.1. The property line bearings are described by degrees, minutes, and seconds; the property line dimensions are noted in feet and decimals.

Even when the architect or designer is only furnished with a written description of the meets and bounds of the plat map, a plat map can still be delineated from this information. Lot lines are laid out by polar **coordinates**; that is, each line is described by its length plus the angle relative to the true North or South. This is accomplished by the use of compass direction, degree, minutes, and seconds. A lot line may read N 6° 49′ 29″ W. The compass is divided into four quadrants. See Figure 6.2.

Drawing a Plat Map

Figure 6.3A shows a plat map with the given **lot lines**, **bearings**, and dimensions. To lay out this map graphically, start at the point labelled **P.O.B. (point of beginning)**. From the P.O.B., you can delineate the lot line in the North-East quadrant with the given dimension. See Figure 6.3B. The next bearing falls in the North-West quadrant, which is illustrated by superimposing a compass at the lot line intersection. See Figure 6.3C. You can delineate the remaining lot lines with their bearings and dimensions in the same way you have delineated the previous lot lines, closing at the P.O.B. See figures 6.3D, 6.3E, and 6.3F. For a site plan layout, accuracy within ½° is acceptable.

The Topography Map

The Function of a Topography Map

For most projects, the architect adjusts the existing contours of the site to satisfy the building construction and site improvement requirements. Because **finish grading**—that is, the adjusting of existing contours—is a stage in the site improvement process, the architect or designer needs a topography map to study the slope conditions which may influence the design process. Usually, a civil

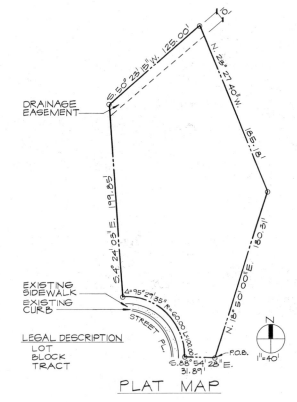

Figure 6.1 Plat map.

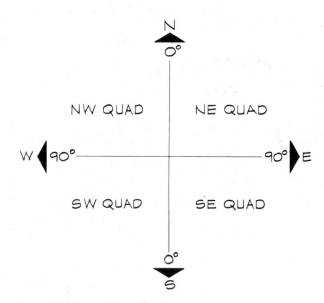

Figure 6.2 Compass quadrants.

engineer prepares this map and shows in drawing form the existing **contour lines** and their accompanying numerical elevations. Commonly, these contour lines are illustrated by a broken line.

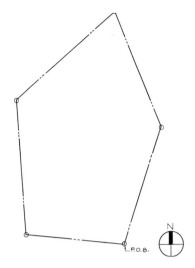

Figure 6.3A Point of beginning.

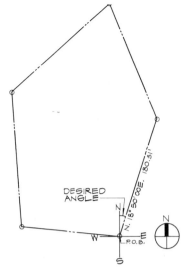

Figure 6.3B Point of beginning and first angle.

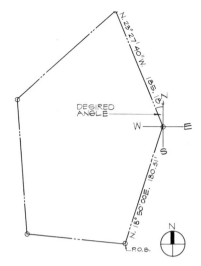

Figure 6.3C P.O.B. and second angle.

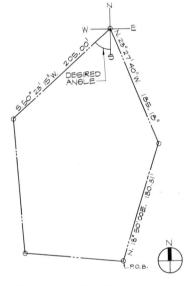

Figure 6.3D P.O.B. and third angle.

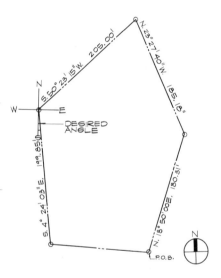

Figure 6.3E P.O.B. and fourth angle.

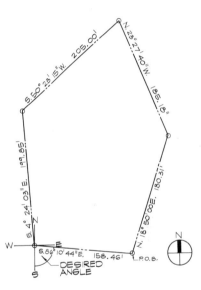

Figure 6.3F P.O.B. and fifth angle.

The topography map is therefore, actually a plat map and its broken lines and numbers indicate the grades, elevations and contours of the site. Figure 6.4 is a topography map showing existing contour lines.

Site Cross Sections

A topography map can appear complex. However, a cross section through any portion of the site can make the site conditions clearer and will also be valuable for the finish grading. Figure 6.5 shows a cross section of a portion of a topography map. The fall of the contours from the front of the site to the rear is almost as high as a two-story building. This site slopes to the North at approximately 1' for every 15'.

To make a cross section, draw a line on the topography map at the desired location. This is called the section line. Next, on tracing paper, draw a series of horizontal lines using the same scale as the topography map and spacing equal to the grade elevation changes on the topography map. Project each point of grade change to the appropriate section line. Now connect the series of grade points to establish an accurate section and profile through that portion of the site.

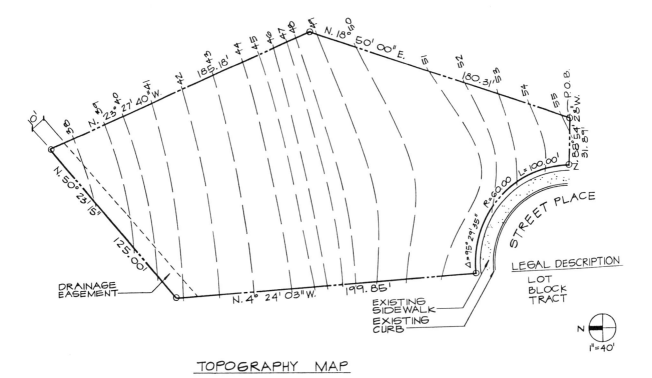

Figure 6.4 Topography map.

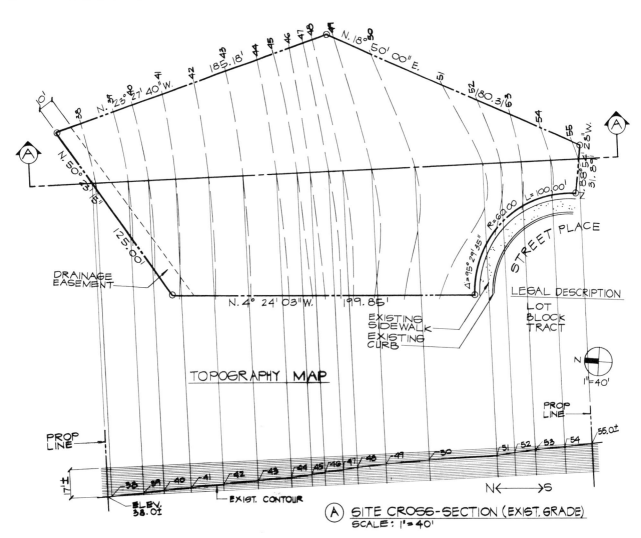

Figure 6.5 Topography map with section lines and cross section.

The Soils and Geology Map

Soils and geology investigations evaluate soil conditions such as type of soil, moisture content, expansion coefficient, and soil bearing pressure. Geological investigations evaluate existing geological conditions as well as potential geological hazards.

Field investigations may include test borings at various locations on the site. These drillings are then plotted on a plat map, with an assigned test boring identification and a written or graphic report. This report provides findings from the laboratory analysis of boring samples under various conditions.

When there are geological concerns and soil instability, the particular problem areas may be plotted on the **soils and geology map** for consideration in the design process. Figure 6.6 shows a plat map with each test boring identified. This map becomes a part of the soils and geological report. Sometimes, the architect or structural engineer requests certain locations for borings according to building location or area of structural concern. Figure 6.7 shows a **boring log** in graphic form. Notice the different types of information presented in the sample boring log. Figure 6.8 shows a geological cross section.

Normally, architectural technicians are not involved

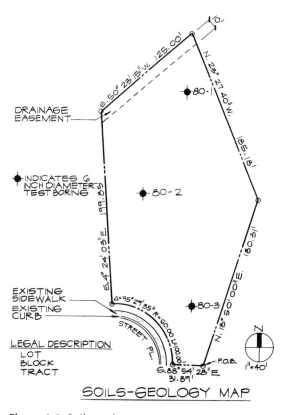

Figure 6.6 Soils-geology map.

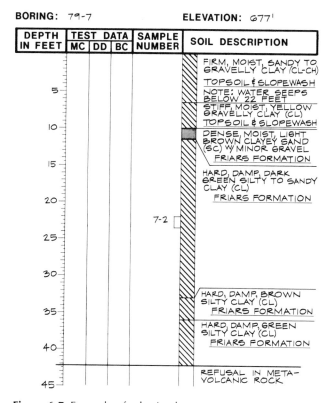

Figure 6.7 Example of a boring log.

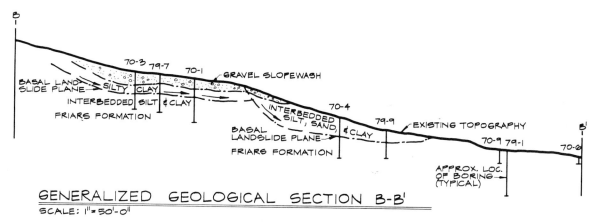

Figure 6.8 Geological cross section.

in **preparing** drawings for geology and soils information; however, it is important to have some understanding of their content and presentation.

The Utility Plan

Plotting existing utilities is necessary to the site improvement process. See Figure 6.9. Such a plan should show the location of all existing utilities, including sewer laterals, water and gas lines, and telephone and electrical services. This drawing then provides a basis for new utility connections. It may also influence the locations of electrical rooms and meter rooms in the structure itself.

The Grading Plan

The **grading plan** shows how the topography of the site will be changed to accommodate the building design. This plan shows the new grades or finished grades. It should also indicate the existing and finished **grade elevations** and the elevations of floors, walks, and walls. Existing grade lines are shown with a broken line and finished grades with a solid line. Finished grading lines show how the site is to be graded.

Floor Elevations

The basis of the finished grades for most projects is the building floor or floor elevations. Floor elevations are determined by the structure's location in relation to the existing grades. In Figure 6.10, the floor elevation on Level-1 is initially established at +44.5 feet. This elevation relates to the existing grade elevation of +44.0, but also requires relocation or reshaping of the contour line to provide for proper drainage. The other existing contours (such as 45, 46 and 47) are reshaped to satisfy this condition.

Cut and Fill Procedures

The contour change just described requires a removal of soil—a **"cut"** into the existing contours. The opposite of this condition, the addition of soil to the site, is called **"fill."** In Figure 6.10 reshaping contours with cut and fill procedures has provided a relatively level area for construction. Depending on the soils condition and soil preparation, the allowable ratio for cut and fill slopes may vary from 2:1 to 3:1. A ratio of 2:1 means that for each foot of change in elevation, there is a minimum of 2' separation on the horizontal. To clarify grading conditions, grading sections should be taken through these areas. See Figure 6.10.

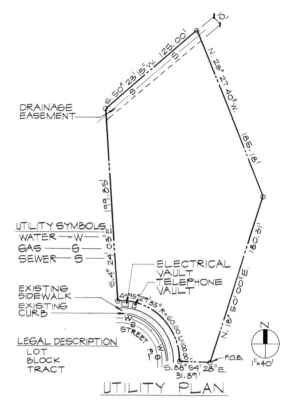

Figure 6.9 Utility plan.

The Landscape Plan and the Irrigation Plan

Landscape Plan and Plant List

The final stage of site development for most projects is landscaping. The landscape drawing shows the location of trees, plants, ground covers, benches, fences, and walks. Accompanying this is a **plant list**, identifying plant species with a symbol or number and indicating the size and number of plants. See Figure 6.11.

Irrigation Plan

An irrigation plan often accompanies the landscape plan. This shows all the water lines, control valves, and types of watering fixtures needed for irrigation.

The Site Improvement Plan: An Overview

The basic requirement for all construction documents is clarity. The site improvement plan is no exception. It can incorporate any or all of the plans just discussed,

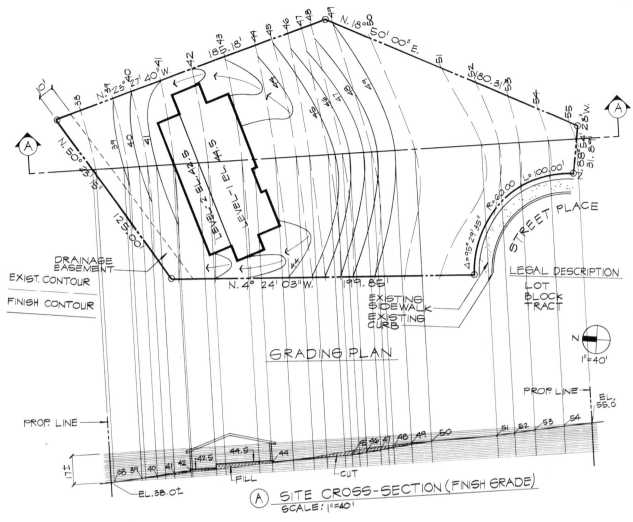

Figure 6.10 Grading plan and site cross section with finish grades.

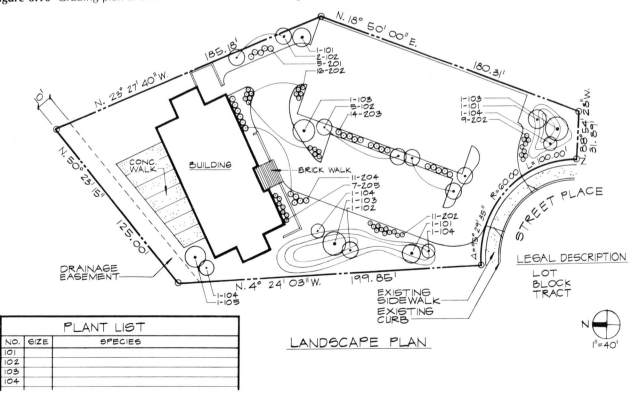

Figure 6.11 Landscape plan and plant list.

113

depending on the complexity of the information and on office practice.

The primary information to be found on the site improvement plan is:

1. Site lot lines with accompanying bearings and dimensions.
2. Scale of the drawing.
3. North arrows.
4. Building location with layout dimensions.
5. Paving, walks, walls with their accompanying material call-outs and layout dimensions.

Figure 6.12 shows the primary information found on a site improvement plan. The building layout dimension

lines at the East and West property lines are parallel to their respective property lines, providing two measuring points at the East and West property lines. This, in turn, provides off-set dimensions to each corner of the building. This is helpful when the property lines do not parallel the building. This method may apply to patios, walks, paving, and walls, also dimensioned on the site improvement plan.

Site plans for large sites such as multiple-housing projects must show primary information such as utility locations, driveway locations, and building locations. See Figure 6.13. Further examples of site development plans appear in later chapters. See Figure 6.14 for a Site Plan Check List.

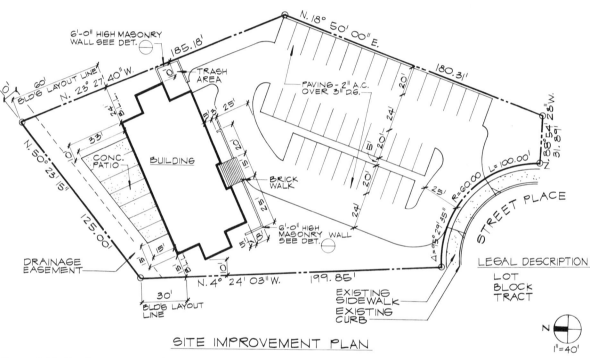

Figure 6.12 Site improvement plan.

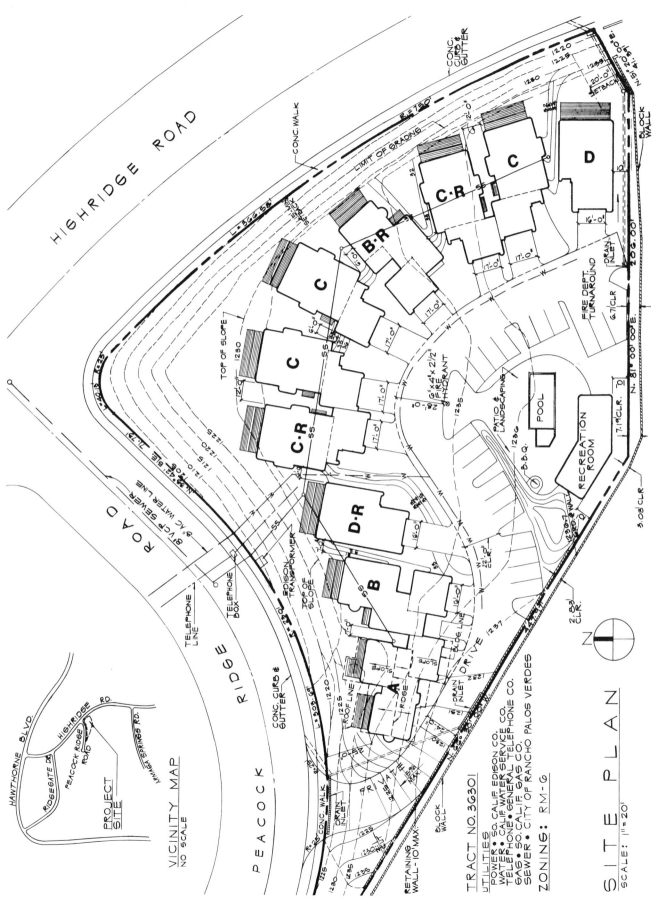

Figure 6.13 Site development plan for multiple housing.

1. Vicinity Map
2. Property lines
   a. lengths - each side
   b. correct angles if not 90°
   c. direction
3. Adjoining streets, sidewalks, parking, curbs, parkways, parking areas, wheel stops, lanes and lighting.
4. Existing structures and buildings and alleys
5. Structures and buildings to be removed
   a. Trees
   b. Old foundations
   c. Walks
   d. Miscellanea
6. Public utilities locations
   a. Storm drain
   b. Sewer lines
   c. Gas lines
   d. Gas meter
   e. Water lines
   f. Water meter
   g. Power line
   h. Power pole
   i. Electric meter
   j. Telephone pole
   k. Lamp post
   l. Fire plugs
7. Public utilities easement if on property
8. Contours of grade
   a. Existing grade—dotted line
   b. Finish cut or fill—solid line
   c. Legend
   d. Slopes to street
9. Grade elevations
   a. Finish slab or finish floor
   b. Corners of building (finish)
   c. Top of all walls
   d. Amount of slope for drainage

10. Roof plan—new building
    a. Building—hidden line
    b. Roof overhang—solid line
    c. Garage
    d. Slopes (arrows)
    e. Projecting canopies
    f. Slabs and porches
    g. Projecting beams
    h. Material for roof
    i. North arrow
    j. Title and scale
    k. Show ridges and valleys
    l. Roof drains and downspouts
    m. Parapets
    n. Roof jacks for T.V., telephone, electric service
    o. Note building outline
    p. Dimension overhangs
    q. Note rain diverters
    r. Sky lights
    s. Roof accessways
    t. Flood lite locations
    u. Service pole for electrical
11. New construction
    a. Retaining walls
    b. Driveways and aprons
    c. Sidewalks
    d. Pool location and size
    e. Splash blocks
    f. Catch basins
    g. Curbs
    h. Patios, walls, expansion joints, dividers etc.
12. North arrow (usually towards top of sheet.)
13. Dimensions
    a. Property lines
    b. Side yards
    c. Rear yards
    d. Front yards

    e. Easements
    f. Street center line
    g. Length of fences and walls
    h. Height of fences and walls
    i. Width of sidewalks, driveways, parking
    j. Utilities
    k. location of existing structures
    l. Note floor elevation
    m. Dimension building to property line
    n. Set backs
14. Notes
    a. Tract no.
    b. Block no.
    c. Lot no.
    d. House no.
    e. Street
    f. City, county, state
    g. Owner's name
    h. Draftsman's name (title block)
    i. Materials for porches, terraces, drives, etc.
    j. Finish grades where necessary
    k. Slope of driveway
    l. Scale (⅛", 1"-30', 1"-20' etc.
15. Landscape lighting, note switching
16. Area drains, drain lines to street
17. Show hose bibs
18. Note drying yard, clothes line equipment.
19. Complete title block
    a. Sheet no.
    b. Scale
    c. Date
    d. Name drawn by
    e. Project address
    f. Approved by
    g. Sheet title
    h. Revision box
    i. Company name and address (school)

Figure 6.14 Site Plan Check List

7

FOUNDATION
PLANS

A foundation plan is a drawing that shows the location of all concrete footings, concrete piers, and structural underpinning members required to support a structure. The main purpose of all the foundation footings is to distribute the weight of the structure over the soil.

Types of Foundations

Two types of floor systems are usually used in foundation plans. These floor systems are constructed of concrete or wood or a combination of both. Each floor system requires foundation footings to support the structure and the floor.

Concrete Slab Floor: Foundation Plans

If you have selected concrete as the floor material for a specific project, first investigate the types of **foundation footing details** required to support the structure before drawing the foundation plan. The **footing design** will be influenced by many factors such as the vertical loads or weight it is to support, regional differences, allowable soil bearing values, established frost line location, and recommendations from a soils and geological report which will determine a minimum footing depth as well as reinforcing requirements. Figure 7.1 illustrates a concrete footing and concrete floor with various factors influencing design.

You may sketch the foundation details in freehand form. Figure 7.2A shows a freehand drawing with an exterior bearing wall footing and concrete slab floor. The sketch then becomes the guide for drawing an exterior bearing footing on the foundation plan. See Figure 7.2B. The broken line represents the footing and foundation wall, located under the concrete slab or grade. This broken line as you will remember, is referred to as a hidden line. The solid line shows the edge of the concrete floor slab as projected above the grade level. Broken lines are mainly used to show footing sizes, configurations, and their locations below grade level or below a concrete floor; solid lines show those above.

The investigation and freehand sketch for a required interior bearing footing might look like Figure 7.3A. If it does, draw the plan view of this detail only with broken lines, because all the configurations are under the concrete slab floor and grade. See Figure 7.3B.

An interior nonbearing footing (a footing that supports a much lighter load than a bearing footing) is drawn in plan view as the section configuration dictates, Figure 7.4A shows a section through a nonbearing footing. Figure 7.4B shows this footing in plan view. Note here that only the width of the footing is shown since the foundation wall and footing are in this case one and the same.

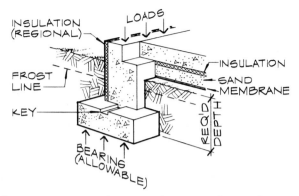

Figure 7.1 Concrete footing and concrete floor with various influencing design factors.

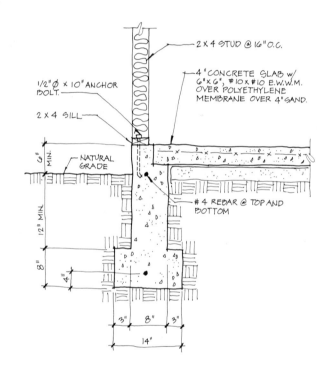

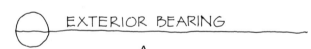

Figure 7.2A Exterior bearing—Beach House

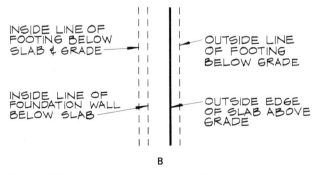

Figure 7.2B Plan view of foundation detail.

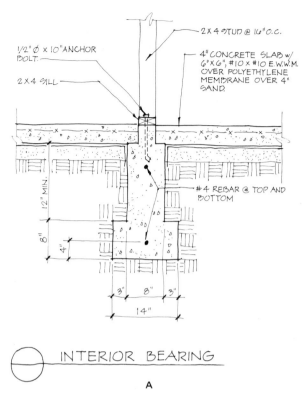

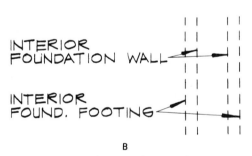

Figure 7.3A Detail of interior bearing footing—Beach House

Figure 7.3B Plan view of interior bearing footing.

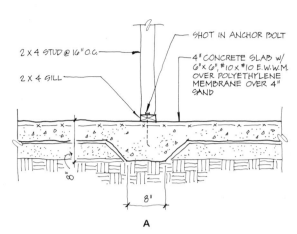

Figure 7.4A Interior nonbearing footing.

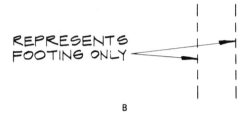

Figure 7.4B Plan view of interior nonbearing footing.

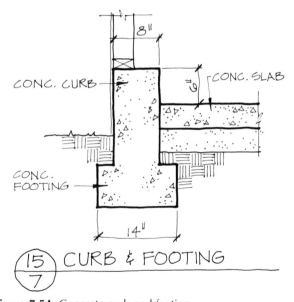

Figure 7.5A Concrete curb and footing.

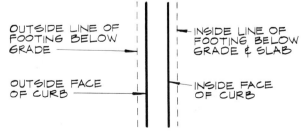

Figure 7.5B Plan view—concrete curb.

Often, concrete curbs above the concrete floor levels are used, as, for example, in garage areas where wood studs need to be free from floor moisture. As with the other foundation conditions, draw a freehand sketch of this detail. See Figure 7.5A for an example. The plan view of this detail is shown in Figure 7.5B, and Figures 7.6A and 7.6B show this photographically.

When you are faced with drawing concrete steps and a change of floor level, a freehand sketch of the section clarifies this condition. See Figure 7.7A. A plan view may then be drawn reflecting this section. See Figure 7.7B.

Figure 7.6A Forms for concrete curb.

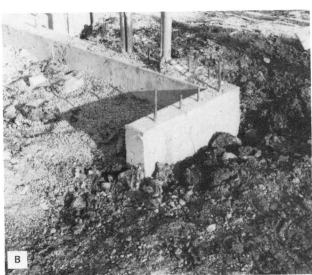

Figure 7.6B Poured concrete curb.

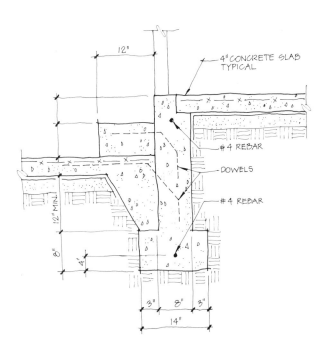

12"

4" CONCRETE SLAB
TYPICAL

#4 REBAR

DOWELS

#4 REBAR

12" MIN.

8"

4"

3"   8"   3"

14"

③
⑦   CHANGE OF LEVEL w/ STEP
      (BEARING FOOTING)

A

Figure 7.7A Change of level with step (bearing footing).

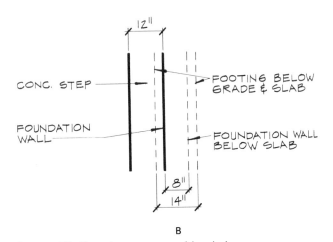

12"

CONC. STEP

FOOTING BELOW
GRADE & SLAB

FOUNDATION
WALL

FOUNDATION WALL
BELOW SLAB

8"

14"

B

Figure 7.7B Plan view—steps and level change.

120

Drawing the Foundation Plan

You are now ready to draw the foundation plan for a concrete slab floor. Lay your tracing over a tracing of the floor plan drawing, then lightly draw the configuration of the floor plan, as well as the internal walls, columns, fireplaces, and so on, that require foundation sections. (Do not trace the foundation plan from a reproduction of the floor plan, because reproductions alter the scale of the original drawing.) After this light tracing, you are ready to finalize the drafting.

The final drafting is a graphic culmination in plan view of all the foundation walls and footings. Start with all the interior bearing and nonbearing foundation conditions. Represent these with a dotted line according to the particular sections in plan view. Figure 7.8 shows an example of a foundation plan for a two-story residence, incorporating the plan views in Figures 7.2B, 7.3B, 7.4B, 7.5B, and 7.7B as previously discussed. Note reference symbols on foundation details and Figure 7.8.

Usually, various notes are required for items to be installed prior to the concrete pouring. An item like a **post holdown**, (a U-shaped steel strap for bolting to a post and embedded in concrete for the use of resisting lateral forces) should be shown on the foundation plan because its installation is important in this particular construction phase. Note the call-out for this item on Figure 7.8. A photograph of this is shown in Figure 7.9.

Drawing Fireplaces. A drawing of a masonry fireplace on the foundation plan should have the supporting walls cross-hatched. (To **crosshatch** is to shade with crossed lines, either diagonal or rectangular.) Show its footing with a broken line. When numerous vertical reinforcing bars are required for the fireplace, show their size and location, because they are embedded in the fireplace

Strengthening Floors. Requirements for strengthening concrete floors with reinforcing vary for specific projects, so it is important to show their size and spacing on the foundation plan. Figure 7.8's foundation plan calls for a 6″ × 6″—#10 × #10 welded wire reinforcing mesh to strengthen the concrete floor. This **call-out** tells us that the mesh is in 6″ × 6″ squares and made of number 10 gauge wire. Figure 7.10 shows how the reinforcing mesh and a plastic membrane are placed before the concrete is poured. Deformed reinforcing bars are also installed to strengthen concrete slab floors. The size and spacing of these bars are determined by factors such as excessive weights expected to be carried by the floor and unfavorable soils conditions.

Sloping Concrete Areas. When concrete areas have to be sloped for drainage, indicate this, too, on the foun-

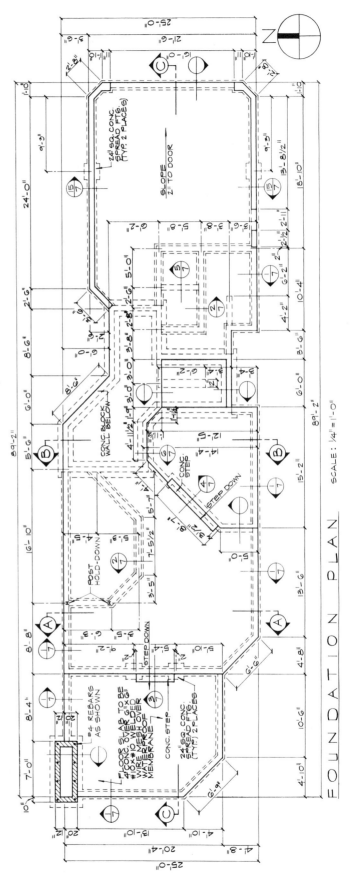

Figure 7.8 Foundation plan—concrete floor. (Residence of Mr. & Mrs. Ted Bear.)

Figure 7.9 Post hold-down.

Figure 7.10 Reinforcing mesh and plastic.

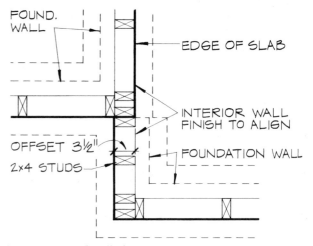

Figure 7.11 Stud wall alignment.

dation plan. You can do this with a directional arrow, noting the number of inches the concrete is to be sloped. See Figure 7.8; here a garage slab is sloped to a door.

Your foundation plan dimensioning should reflect the identical dimension line locations of the floor plan. For example, center line dimensions for walls above should match center line dimensions for foundation walls below. This makes the floor and foundation plans consistent. When you lay out dimension lines, such as perimeter lines, leave space between the exterior wall and first dimension line for foundation section symbols. As Figure 7.8 shows, you must provide dimensions for every foundation condition and configuration. Observe offset dimensioning where angled walls occur. Remember, people in the field do not have the luxury of protractors or other measuring devices and therefore rely on all the dimensions you have provided on the plan.

In some cases, the foundation dimensioning process may require you to make adjustments for stud wall alignments. For example, if studs and interior finish need to be aligned, be sure to dimension for foundation offset correctly to achieve the stud alignment. See Figure 7.11. In this figure, the 3½″ stud, the foundation wall, and footing of the exterior wall are not aligned with the interior foundation wall and footing.

Provide reference symbols for foundation details for all conditions. Provide as many symbols as you need, even if there is some repetition. Remove any guess work

for the people in the field. As Figure 7.8 shows, the arrowheads on these circular reference symbols face the direction in which the detail is drawn and also have enough space within the circle for letters and/or numbers for detail and sheet referencing.

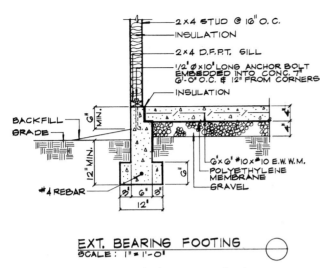

Figure 7.12 Drafted detail of a two-pour footing.

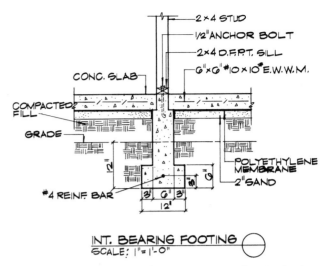

Figure 7.13 Drafted detail of a two-pour interior bearing footing.

Foundation Details for Concrete Slab Floor. You can now draft finished drawings of the foundation details, using freehand sketches as a reference. For most cases, foundation details are drawn using an architectural scale of ½" = 1'–0", ¾" = 1'–0" or 1" = 1'–0". Scale selection may be dictated by office procedure or the complexity of a specific project.

Different geographical regions vary in depth, sizes, and reinforcing requirements for foundation design. Check the requirements for your region.

Foundation details for the residence shown in Figure 7.12 are drawn to incorporate a **two-pour system**; that is, the foundation wall and footing are poured first and the concrete floor later. Figure 7.12 shows the exterior bearing footing drawn in final form. Notice the joint between the foundation wall and concrete floor is filled with insulation.

The interior bearing footing detail should also be drawn to reflect a two-pour system with call-outs for all the components in the assembly. See Figure 7.13. The nonbearing footing is drafted differently from the exterior and interior bearing footings. This detail, Figure 7.14, is shown as one pour, because it is only deep enough to accommodate the **anchor bolt embedment** and can therefore be poured at the same time as the floor slab. The remaining foundation details are drafted using the freehand sketches for reference.

Wood Floor: Foundation Plans

Prepare a foundation plan for a wood floor the same way you do for a concrete floor. Sketch the different footings required to support the structure.

Your first sketch should deal with the exterior bearing footing, incorporating the required footing and wall dimensions and depth below grade. Show earth-to-wood clearances, sizes and treatment of wood members, floor

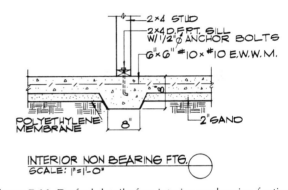

Figure 7.14 Drafted detail of an interior nonbearing footing.

sheathing, and the exterior wall and its assembly of components above the sheathing or sub-floor level. See Figure 7.15A. Figure 7.15B describes the exterior bearing footing in plan view. An investigation of the interior bearing footing requirements can be done with a scaled freehand sketch. See Figure 7.16. In plan view the interior bearing footing looks similar to the exterior bearing footing in Figure 7.16B.

When laying out the foundation plan for a wood floor system, provide intermediate supporting elements located between exterior and interior bearing footings. You can do this with a pier and girder system, which can be spaced well within the allowable spans of the floor joists selected. This layout will be reviewed later in the discussion of the foundation plan. The girder-on-pier detail can be sketched in the same way as the previous details. See Figure 7.17A. Figure 7.17B describes the concrete pier in plan view. The pier spacing depends on the size of floor girder selected. With a 4" × 6" girder, a 5' or 6' spacing is recommended under normal floor loading conditions.

Regional building codes help you to select floor joists and girder sizes relative to allowable spans.

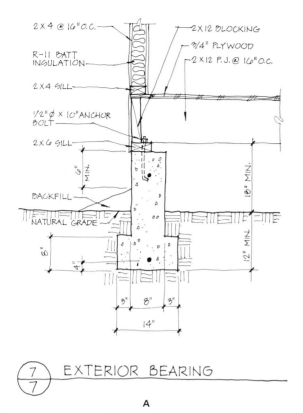

Figure 7.15A Exterior bearing footing detail.

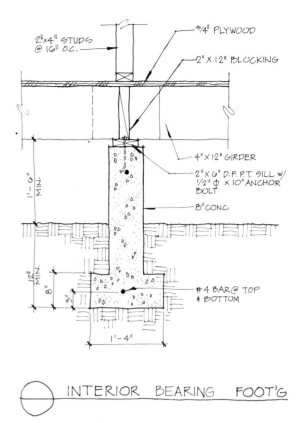

Figure 7.16 Interior bearing footing detail.

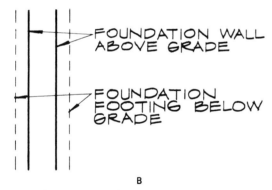

Figure 7.15B Plan view of exterior bearing footing.

Drawing the Foundation Plan

Begin the foundation plan drawing by laying the tracing directly over the floor plan. Lightly trace the outside line of the exterior walls, the center line of the interior load bearing walls (walls supporting ceiling, floor, and roof), and curb and stud edges that define a transition between the wood floor members and the concrete floor. It is not necessary to trace nonbearing wall conditions for wood floors because floor girders can be used to support the weight of the wall.

Refer to your freehand sketches of the foundation details to help finalize the foundation plan. As a review of this procedure, Figure 7.18 shows a foundation plan with wood floor construction, incorporating the plan views

shown in Figures 7.15B and 7.17B. The floor plan is the same one used for the concrete floor foundation plan. The spacing for floor girders and the concrete piers supporting the girders is based on the selected floor joist size and girder sizes. As shown, the floor girders can be drawn with a broken line while the piers, being above grade, can be drawn with a solid line. Dimension the location of all piers and girders. Wherever possible, locate floor girders under walls. Show the direction of the floor joists and their size and spacing directly above the floor girders. The fireplace foundation and reinforcing information can be designated as indicated earlier.

In Figure 7.18 a concrete garage floor is connected to a house floor system with #3 dowels at 24" on center. This call-out should also be designated for other concrete elements such as porches and patios. On this foundation plan, the basement area has supporting walls built of concrete block. The concrete block walls have been cross-hatched on the foundation plan as a reference for the material used and to define the basement area. A sketch of the foundation condition through the basement area is shown in Figure 7.19.

Incorporate dimensioning and foundation detail symbols the same way you did for a concrete foundation. An important note to be located on the foundation plan drawing is the number of foundation vents required, and their sizes, material, and location. This requirement is regulated by governing building codes.

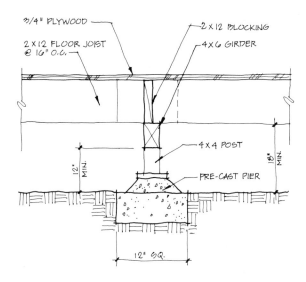

PIER AND GIRDER DETAIL

A

Figure 7.17A Pier and girder detail.

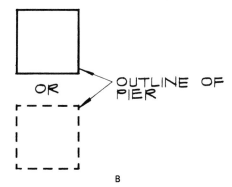

B

Figure 7.17B Plan view of concrete pier.

Foundation Details for a Wood Floor Foundation.

Finished drawings for the foundation details can be drafted with call-outs and dimensions for each specific detail. As with concrete floor foundation sizes, depths and reinforcing requirements vary regionally. Finished details for exterior and interior bearing footings as well as a typical pier and girder are shown in Figures 7.20, 7.21, and 7.22. Figure 7.23 illustrates the use of concrete block for a foundation wall supporting a wood floor. Figure 7.24 combines Figure 7.20 with a porch and stair connected to the exterior foundation detail. Here dowels have been added to tie the concrete porch to the building and metal flashing has been used to protect against dry-rot from water seepage.

A foundation detail through the garage concrete floor and house floor is shown in Figure 7.25. This important detail shows the placement of dowels and provisions for a nailer in which a finished interior material can be secured at the concrete foundation wall. Remaining foundation sections are drafted in the same way using investigative sketches for reference.

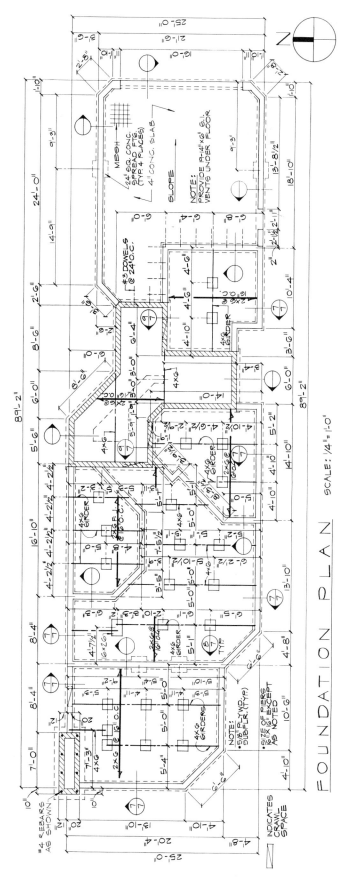

Figure 7.18 Foundation plan—wood floor. (Residence of Mr. & Mrs. Ted Bear.)

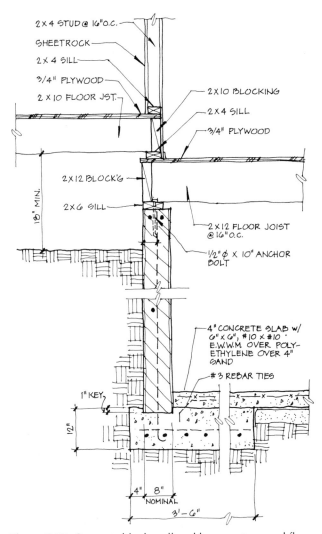

Figure 7.19 Concrete block wall and basement—wood floor.

Labels for Figure 7.19:
- 2 × 4 STUD @ 16" O.C.
- SHEETROCK
- 2 × 4 SILL
- 3/4" PLYWOOD
- 2 × 10 FLOOR JST.
- 2 × 10 BLOCKING
- 2 × 4 SILL
- 3/4" PLYWOOD
- 2 × 12 BLOCK'G
- 2 × 6 SILL
- 2 × 12 FLOOR JOIST @ 16" O.C.
- 1/2" Ø × 10" ANCHOR BOLT
- 18" MIN.
- 4" CONCRETE SLAB w/ 6" × 6", #10 × #10 · E.W.W.M. OVER POLY-ETHYLENE OVER 4" SAND
- #3 REBAR TIES
- 1" KEY
- 12"
- 4" 8" NOMINAL
- 3'-6"

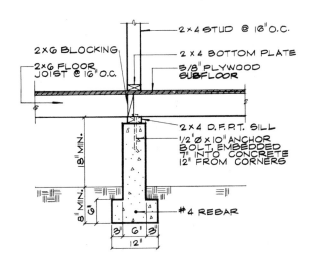

INTERIOR BEARING FOOTING
SCALE: 1" = 1'-0"

Labels for Figure 7.21:
- 2×6 BLOCKING
- 2×6 FLOOR JOIST @ 16" O.C.
- 2×4 STUD @ 16" O.C.
- 2 × 4 BOTTOM PLATE
- 5/8" PLYWOOD SUBFLOOR
- 2×4 D.F.P.T. SILL
- 1/2" Ø × 10" ANCHOR BOLT, EMBEDDED 7" INTO CONCRETE 12" FROM CORNERS
- #4 REBAR
- 18" MIN.
- 8" MIN.
- 6"
- 3" 6" 3"
- 12"

Figure 7.21 Drafted detail of interior bearing footing with wood floor.

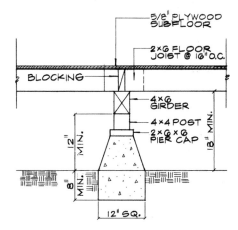

TYPICAL PIER DET.
SCALE: 1" = 1'-0"

Labels for Figure 7.22:
- 5/8" PLYWOOD SUBFLOOR
- 2×6 FLOOR JOIST @ 16" O.C.
- BLOCKING
- 4×6 GIRDER
- 4×4 POST
- 2×6×6 PIER CAP
- 12" MIN.
- 8" MIN.
- 18" MIN.
- 12" SQ.

Figure 7.22 Pier detail perpendicular to girder.

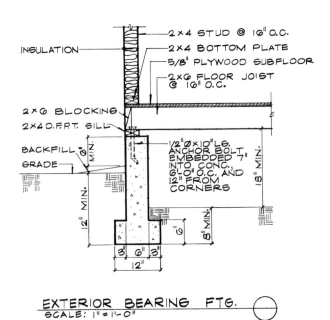

EXTERIOR BEARING FTG.
SCALE: 1" = 1'-0"

Labels for Figure 7.20:
- INSULATION
- 2 × 4 STUD @ 16" O.C.
- 2 × 4 BOTTOM PLATE
- 5/8" PLYWOOD SUBFLOOR
- 2×6 FLOOR JOIST @ 16" O.C.
- 2×6 BLOCKING
- 2×4 D.F.P.T. SILL
- BACKFILL
- GRADE
- 1/2" Ø × 10" LG. ANCHOR BOLT EMBEDDED 7" INTO CONC. 6'-0" O.C. AND 12" FROM CORNERS
- 18" MIN.
- 6" MIN.
- 12" MIN.
- 6"
- 8" MIN.
- 3" 6" 3"
- 12"

Figure 7.20 Drafted detail of typical exterior.

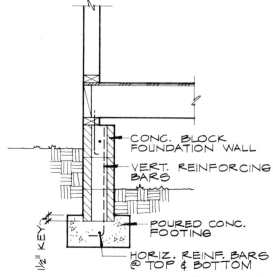

Labels for Figure 7.23:
- CONC. BLOCK FOUNDATION WALL
- VERT. REINFORCING BARS
- POURED CONC. FOOTING
- HORIZ. REINF. BARS @ TOP & BOTTOM
- 1/2" KEY

Figure 7.23 Concrete block foundation wall supporting a wood floor.

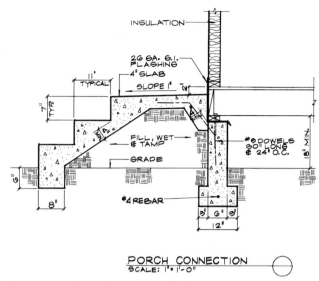

Figure 7.24 Drafted detail of a porch connection.

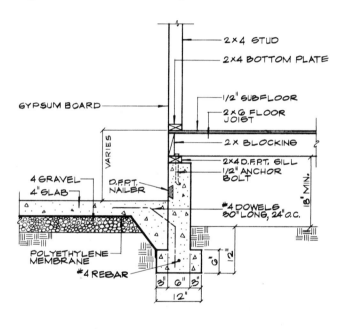

Figure 7.25 Drafted detail of change of level from a wood floor to a concrete slab.

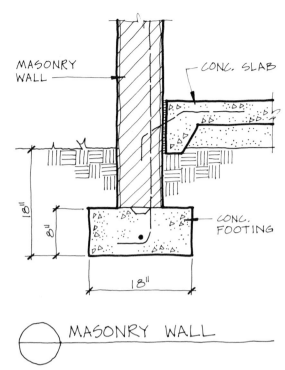

Figure 7.26 Exterior masonry wall and footing.

Examples

Example 1: A Building with Masonry Walls

When projects use concrete or masonry for exterior and interior walls, the walls may continue down the concrete footing. Figure 7.26 shows an exterior masonry wall and concrete footing. If interior walls are constructed of masonry, the foundation section is similar to Figure 7.26. Drawing the foundation plan using masonry as the foundation wall requires delineation of the foundation walls by cross-hatching those areas representing the masonry.

The building in this example is a theatre with exterior and interior masonry walls. Its foundation plan, details, and photographs of the construction of the foundation follow.

The foundation plan, shown in Figure 7.27, defines all the masonry wall locations as per Figures 7.26 and 7.28. The footings are drawn with a broken line. For this project **pilasters** are required to support steel roof beams. A pilaster is a masonry or concrete column designed to support heavy axial and/or horizontal loads. See Figure 7.28. The footing width is not called out but refers to the foundation plan for a specific pilaster footing dimension. Many projects do this because the total loads acting on the pilaster vary.

Steel columns are also required to support heavy axial loads and they, in turn, require a foundation. These foundation members are commonly referred to as concrete piers or **concrete pads**. The size of these pads varies with different loading conditions. Because of the various pad sizes, you may need to use a column pad schedule. This schedule should note the column designation, size, depth, and required steel reinforcing.

An example of a pad schedule is shown in Figure 7.27. Locate the pad schedule directly on the foundation plan sheet for ease of reference. It should show dimensions for all footings, walls, and pad locations with reference symbols clearly defined for specific conditions. Similar notes are provided for items such as ramp and floor slopes, pilaster sizes, and required steel reinforcing.

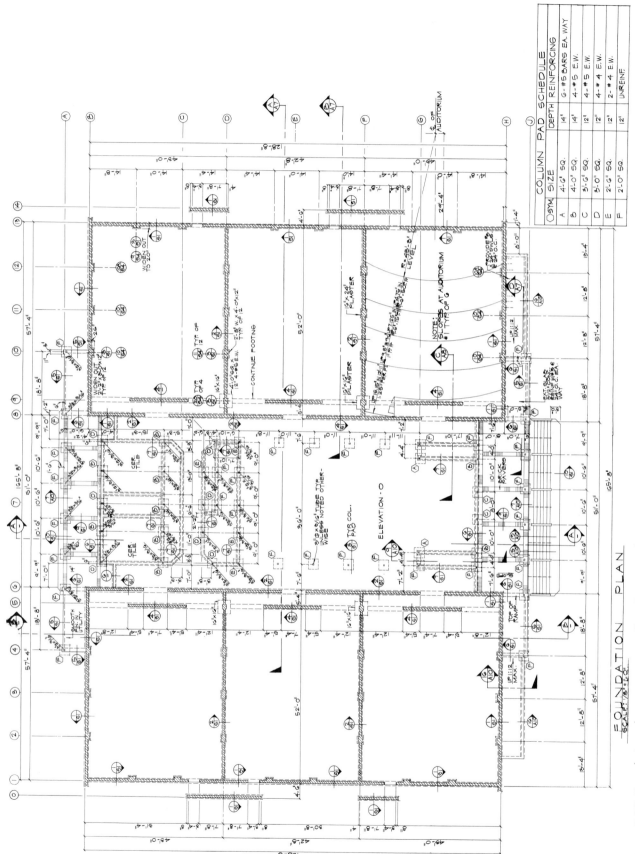

Figure 7.27 Foundation plan—masonry walls. (Courtesy of AVCO Community Developers, Inc. and Mann Theatres Corporation of CA.).

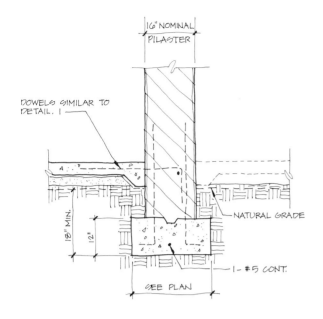

PILASTER FOOTING DETAIL

Figure 7.28 Pilaster footing detail.

From the information on the foundation plan, the various foundation conditions are laid out on the site using chalk lines. In Figure 7.29, the footing for the masonry walls and pilasters is clearly visible on the right side of the structure.

When **chalking** has been completed for the footing locations, trenching for these details is dug and made ready for the pouring of the concrete. Once the reinforcing rods and footings are installed, the masonry work can begin. Figure 7.30 shows masonry work in progress. Note the pilasters and chalking for the various concrete pads.

Example 2: A Foundation Using Concrete Pads and Steel Columns

Drawing foundation plans varies depending on the foundation requirements of the method of construction for a specific structure. The example that follows uses a struc-

Figure 7.29 Chalking for foundation layout. (Courtesy of AVCO Community Developers, Inc. and Mann Theatres Corporation of CA.; William Boggs Aerial Photography. Reprinted with permission.)

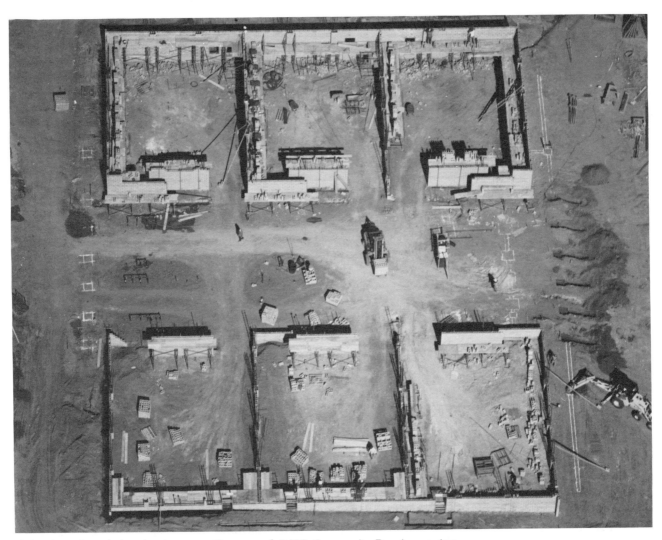

Figure 7.30 Foundation development. (Courtesy of AVCO Community Developers, Inc. and Mann Theatres Corporation of CA.; William Boggs Aerial Photography. Reprinted with permission.)

ture requiring concrete pads to support steel columns with a continuous footing to support masonry walls.

This foundation plan, as Figure 7.31 shows, is handled differently from the foundation plan in Example 1. As you place the tracing paper directly over the floor plan tracing, first establish the column locations as they relate to the **axial reference locations**. Masonry walls are then drawn and delineated. Concrete pads, located under a concrete floor, are represented with a broken line. See Figure 7.31. Figure 7.32 provides a visual example of this column pad footing detail in section. The column pad sizes may vary due to varying loads, and may be sized using a pad schedule or noted directly on the foundation plan. In this case, sizes are noted on the foundation plan. These pads are drawn to scale, relative to their *required* sizes, rather than their actual sizes. Provide, at the bottom of the foundation plan drawing, a **legend** defining the size and shape of the steel column and the base stem that supports it.

Because of all the critical information required in the field, a schedule for column base plates and their required anchorage may be necessary. Put this at the bottom of the plan. Dimensioning this type of foundation depends on the axial reference locations, which are identical to the floor plan referencing. Other foundation conditions are dimensioned from these axial reference lines. See Figure 7.31.

After you complete all the necessary dimensioning, show section reference symbols and notes. Figure 7.31 has a double broken line representing a continuous footing underneath, which connects to all the concrete pads. The main purpose of this footing is to provide continuity for all the components of the foundation.

The concrete pads are the main supports for this structure. Figure 7.33 shows the trenching and some formwork for a concrete pad. Note particularly the placement of the reinforcing steel and the footing, which is used to tie all the pads together. After the concrete is poured

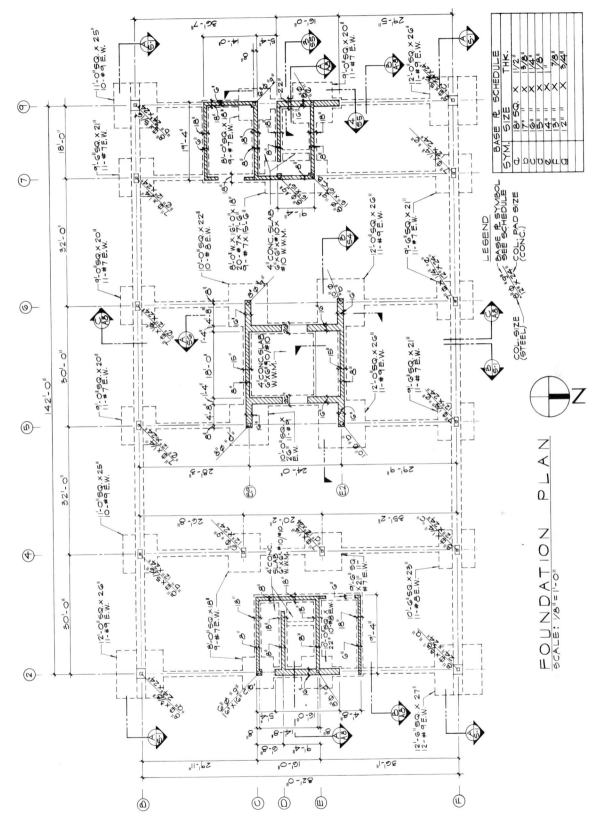

Figure 7.31 Foundation plan—concrete pads. (Courtesy of Westmount, Inc., Real Estate Development, Torrance, CA.)

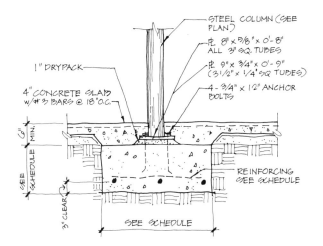

Figure 7.32 Column footing detail.

Figure 7.33 Forming for concrete pad. (William Boggs Aerial Photography. Reprinted with permission.)

Figure 7.34 Steel column on concrete pad.

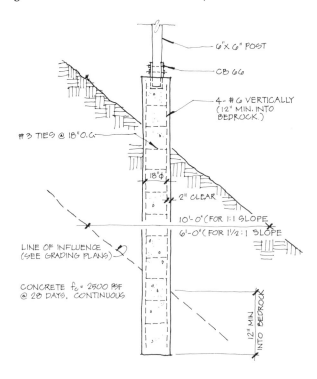

Figure 7.35 Concrete caisson.

and anchor bolts embedded, the steel column with the attached base plate is bolted to the concrete pad. See Figure 7.34.

When columns are used for structural support, **concrete caissons** may be needed in unfavorable soil conditions. A concrete caisson is a reinforced column designed specifically for the loads it will support and is located at a depth that provides good soil bearing. The concrete caisson shown in Figure 7.35 is used on a sloping site to provide firm support for a wood column which in turn is part of the structural support for a building. Figure 7.36 shows a job site drilling rig providing holes for concrete caissons.

Figure 7.36 Drilling holes for concrete caissons. (William Boggs Aerial Photography. Reprinted with permission.)

Example 3: A Concrete Floor at Ground-Floor Level

This foundation plan is for a small two-story residence with a concrete floor at the ground-floor level. See Figure 7.37. The plan view drawing of the foundation sections is similar to those in Figures 7.2B, 7.3B, 7.4B, 7.5B and 7.7B.

Note on the foundation plan everything that is to be installed prior to the pouring of the concrete. If items are located somewhere else in the drawings, the foundation contractor may miss these items, causing problems after the pouring. Specific locations call for anchor bolt placement, steel column embedment, post holdown hardware, and other symbols, all explained in the legend below. Dimensions for the location of all foundation walls and footings are shown with reference symbols for the various footing conditions.

Figure 7.38 demonstrates the importance of noting all the required hardware or concrete accessories on the foundation plan. You can well imagine the problems that would arise if these items were not installed before the concrete was poured! Trenching and formwork for the foundation (see Figure 7.37) is shown photographically in Figure 7.39. The next step in completing the foundation phase of this residence is the pouring of the concrete and finishing of the concrete floor in preparation for the wood framing. See Figure 7.39. Often, a checklist also is furnished that provides specific information required for a project. See Figure 7.40.

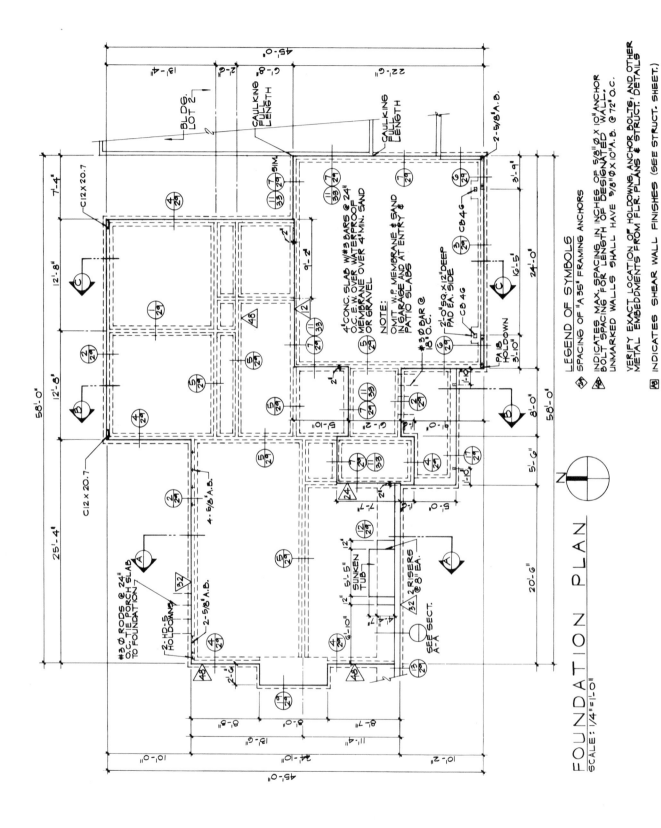

Figure 7.37 Foundation plan with concrete floor. (Courtesy of William F. Smith-Builder.)

Figure 7.38 Embedded hardware (concrete accessories). (Courtesy of William F. Smith-Builder.)

Figure 7.39 Foundation trenching—poured concrete floor and foundation. (Courtesy of William F. Smith—Builder; William Boggs Aerial Photography. Reprinted with permission.)

FOUNDATION PLAN AND DETAIL CHECKLIST

1. North arrow
2. Titles and scale
3. Foundation walls 6″ (solid lines)
   a. Overall dimensions
   b. Offset dimensions (corners)
   c. Interior bearing walls
   d. Special wall thickness
   e. Planter wall thickness
   f. Garage
   g. Retaining wall
4. Footings—12″ (hidden lines)
   a. Width of footing
   b. Stepped footing as per code
   c. Fireplace footing
   d. Belled footing
   e. Grade beams
   f. Planter footing
   g. Garage
   h. Retaining wall
5. Girder (center line)
   a. Size
   b. Direction
   c. Spacing (center to center)
6. Piers
   a. Sizes
   b. Spacing (center to center)
   c. Detail
      (1) 8″ above grade (finish)
      (2) 8″ below grade (natural)
      (3) 2″ × 6″ × 6″ redw'd block secure to pier
      (4) 4″ × 4″ post
      (5) 4″ × 6″ girder
      (6) 2 × ? floor joist (o/c)
      (7) Subfloor 1″ diagonal
         (a) T & G
         (b) Plyscord
      (8) Finished floor (usually in finished schedule)
7. Porches
   a. Indicate 2″ lip on foundation (min.)
   b. Indicate steel reinforcing (⅜″– 24″ o/c)
   c. Under slab note: Fill, puddle, and tamp
   d. Thickness of slab and steps
8. Sub-floor material and size

9. Footing detail references
10. Cross section reference
11. Column footing location and sizes
12. Concrete floors:
    a. Indicate bearing and nonbearing footings
    b. Concrete slab thickness and mesh size
13. Fireplace foundation
14. Patio and terrace location
    a. Materials
    b. See porches
15. Depressed slabs or recessed area for ceramic tile, etc.
16. Double floor joist under parallel partitions
17. Joist—direction and spacing
18. Areaways (18″ × 24″)
19. Columns (center line dimension and size)
20. Reinforcing—location and size
    a. Rods
    b. Wire mesh
    c. Chimney
    d. Slabs
    e. Retaining walls
21. Apron for garage
22. Expansion joints (20′ o/c in driveways)
23. Crawl holes (interior foundation walls)
24. Heat registers in slab
25. Heating ducts
26. Heat plenum if below floor
27. Stairs (basement)
28. Detail references
    a. "Bubbles"
    b. Section direction
29. Trenches
30. Foundation details
    a. Foundation wall thickness (6″ min.)
    b. Footing width and thickness (12″ min.)
    c. Depth below natural grade (12″ min.)

d. 8″ above finish grade (FHA) (6″—UBC)
   e. Redwood sill or as per code (2″ × 6′)
   f. ½″ × 10″ anchor bolts, 6′–0″ o/c, 1′ from corners, imbedded 7″
   g. 18″ min. clearance bottom floor joist to grade
   h. Floor joist size and spacing
   i. Sub-floor (see pier detail)
   j. Bottom plate 2″ × 4″
   k. Studs—size and spacing
   l. Finish floor (finish schedule)
31. All dimensions—coordinate with floor plan dimensions
32. Veneer detail (check as above)
33. Areaway detail (check as above)
34. Garage footing details
35. Planter details
36. House-garage connection detail
37. Special details
38. Retaining walls over 3′–0″ high (special design)
39. Amount of pitch of garage floor (direction)
40. General concrete notes
    a. Water-cement ratio
    b. Steel reinforcing
    c. Special additives
41. Note treated lumber
42. Special materials
    a. Terrazzo
    b. Stone work
    c. Wood edges
43. Elevations of all finish grades
44. Note: solid block all joists at mid-span if span exceeds 8′–0″
45. Specify grade of lumber (construction notes)
46. Poché all details on back of vellum
47. Indicate North arrow near plan
48. Scale used for plan
49. Scale used for details
50. Complete title block
51. Check dimensions with floor plan
52. Border lines heavy and black

Figure 7.40 Foundation plan checklist.

FLOOR PLANS

8

Types of Floor Plans

A floor plan is a drawing viewed from above. It is called a plan, but actually it is a horizontal section taken at approximately eye level. See Figure 8.1.

To better understand this, imagine a knife slicing through a structure and removing the upper half (the half with the roof on a single-story structure). The remaining half is then viewed from the air. This becomes the floor plan. See Figure 8.2.

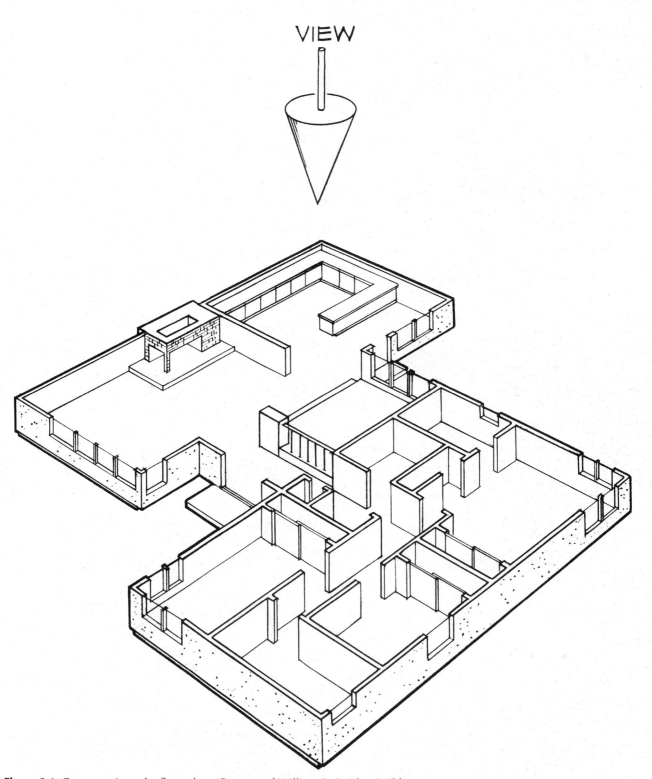

Figure 8.1 Cutaway view of a floor plan. (Courtesy of William F. Smith—Builder.)

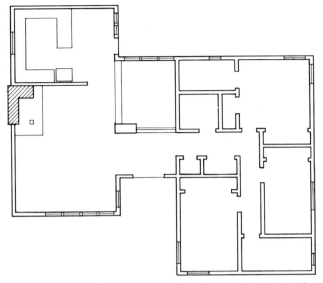

Figure 8.2 Floor plan. (Courtesy of William F. Smith—Builder.)

The floor plan for a split-level residence is more complicated. This plan requires a lower, middle, and upper level. In the example, the entry, powder room, and garage are at the mid-level, which is also the level of the street and sidewalk. Use this level as a point of reference.

The stairs at the rear of the entry lead to the upper and lower level. The lower level contains the master bedroom, master bath, study, bedroom, laundry, and bathroom. See Figure 8.3. The upper level contains the living room with a wet bar, and the dining room, kitchen, breakfast room, and foyer. See Figure 8.4. When these are translated into a floor plan, they appear as in Figures 8.5 and 8.6. The mid-level is duplicated and common to both drawings. Another approach is to use a **break line** (a line with a jog in it to indicate that a portion has been deleted), showing only a part of the garage on one of the plans. Another approach is to use a straight break

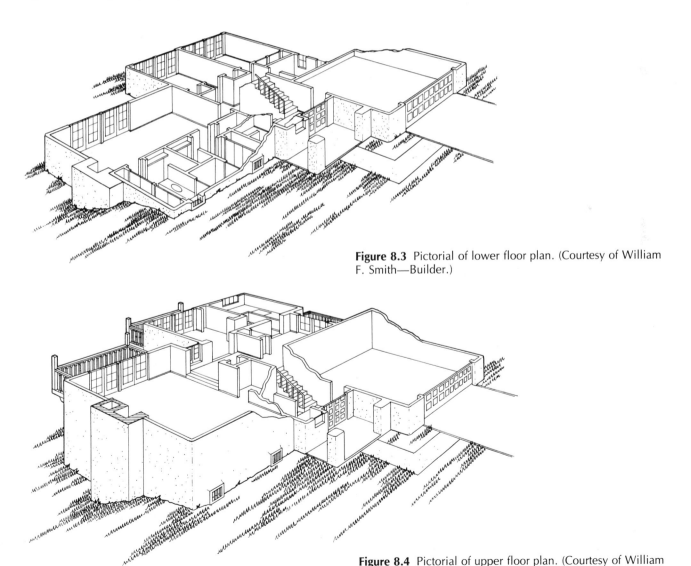

Figure 8.3 Pictorial of lower floor plan. (Courtesy of William F. Smith—Builder.)

Figure 8.4 Pictorial of upper floor plan. (Courtesy of William F. Smith—Builder.)

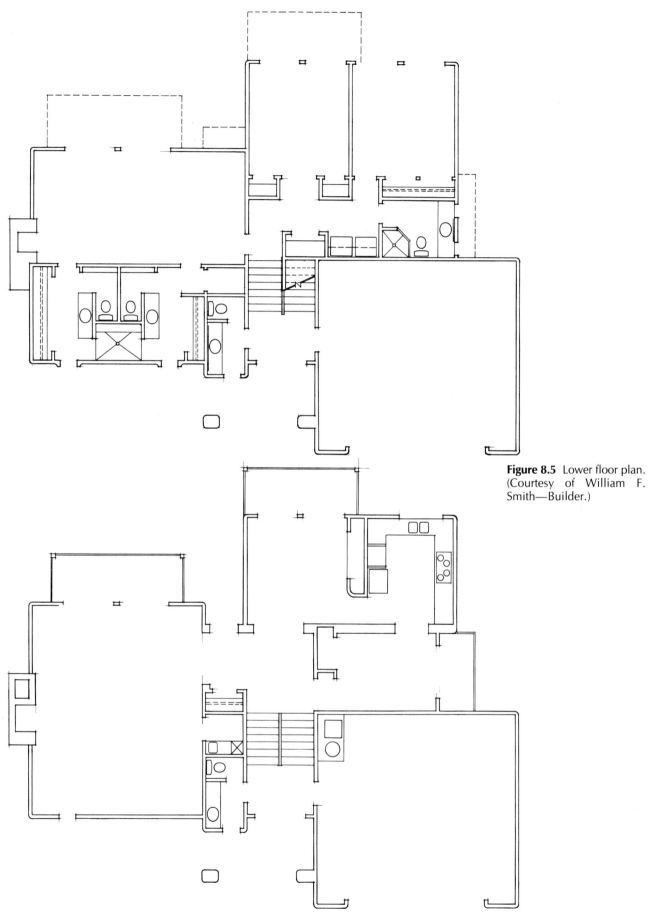

Figure 8.5 Lower floor plan. (Courtesy of William F. Smith—Builder.)

Figure 8.6 Upper floor plan. (Courtesy of William F. Smith—Builder.)

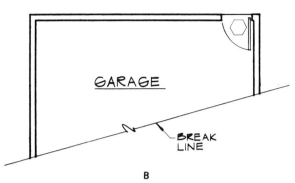

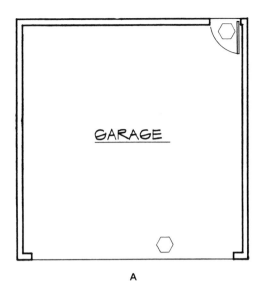

Figure 8.7B Partial garage shown with break lines.

Figure 8.7A Full garage.

line as drafted on Figure 8.7B, showing only part of the garage on one of the plans.

In a two-story building, a single room on the first floor is sometimes actually two stories high. If this room were a living room for example, it would be treated as a normal one-story living room on the first floor plan; however, the area would be repeated on the second floor plan and labeled as upper living room or just labeled "open."

To simplify the image to be drafted, not every structural member is shown. For example, in a wood framed structure, if every vertical piece of wood were shown, the task would be impossible. Simplifying this image of the wood structure is done with two parallel lines. Sometimes the insulation is shown in symbol form and is not shown through the total wall. See Figure 8.8. The same parallel series of lines can also be used to represent a masonry wall by adding a series of diagonal lines. See Figure 8.9. Steel frame can be represented as shown in Figure 8.10.

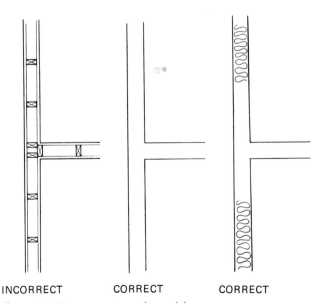

INCORRECT   CORRECT   CORRECT

Figure 8.8 Representation of wood frame.

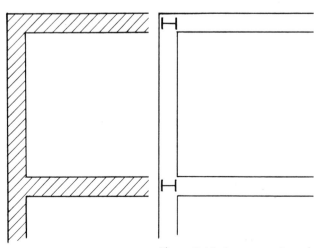

Figure 8.9 Representation of masonry.

Figure 8.10 Representation of steel frame.

Wood Framing

Figures 8.11 and 8.12 show the appearance of a corner of a wood frame structure. Each side of the wall is built separately. An extra stud is usually placed at the end of the wall; it extends to the edge of the building. It therefore acts as a structural support, and gives a greater nailing surface to which wall materials can be anchored. Figure 8.13 shows a plan view of the condition at the corner of the wall.

Figures 8.14 and 8.15 show the intersection of an interior wall and an exterior wall. Figure 8.16 is the plan view of this same intersection.

Walls are not the only important elements in the framing process, of course. You must also consider the locations of doors and windows and the special framing they require. See Figure 8.17.

Various photographic views of intersections are shown in Figures 8.18, 8.19, and 8.20. Figure 8.21 shows how **sills** and **headers** are precut and aligned with the anchor bolts. (A sill is the bottom portion of a door or window. Headers are the structural members above a door or window.)

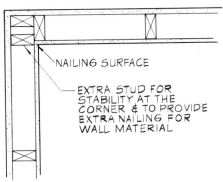

Figure 8.13 Actual appearance of the corner of a wood-framed wall.

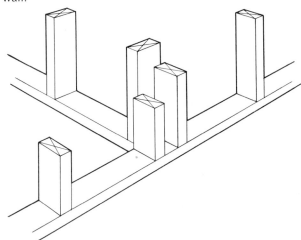

Figure 8.14 Intersection of exterior wall and interior wall.

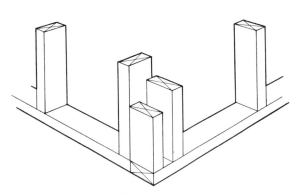

Figure 8.11 Corner at sill.

Figure 8.12 Corner at sill.

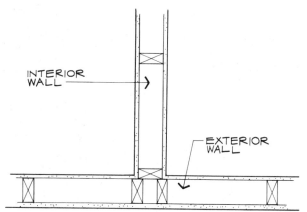

Figure 8.16 Plan view of the intersection of an exterior and interior wall.

Figure 8.15 Intersection of exterior wall and interior wall.

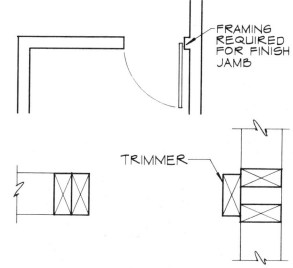

Figure 8.17 Framing for a door.

Figure 8.18 Intersection of interior walls at the sill.

Figure 8.19 Intersection of interior walls at the top plates. (Courtesy of William F. Smith—Builder.)

Figure 8.20 Top plates showing intersections of exterior and interior walls. (Courtesy of William F. Smith—Builder.)

Figure 8.21 Precutting of sills and headers. (Courtesy of William F. Smith—Builder.)

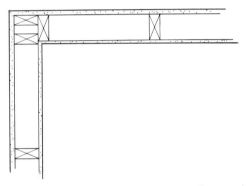

Figure 8.22 Dimensioning a corner of a wood-framed wall.

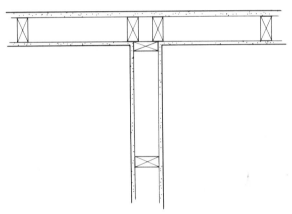

Figure 8.23 Dimensioning an intersection of an interior wall and an exterior wall.

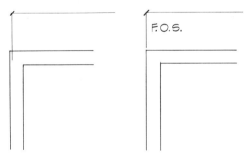

F.O.S.

Figure 8.24 Dimensioning corners.

Interior Dimensioning. Since a wood-framed wall is a built-up system, that is, a wall frame of wood upon which plaster or another wall covering is added, dimension lines must sometimes be drawn to the edge of studs and sometimes to their center.

Figure 8.22 shows how the corner of a wood-framed wall is dimensioned to the stud line. Figure 8.23 shows how an interior wall intersecting an exterior wall is dimensioned. It is dimensioned to the center so that the two studs which the interior wall will join can be located.

The process of drawing each stud in a wall becomes tiresome. So usually two lines drawn 6″ apart (in scale) are used to represent wood. To make sure that the person reading this set of plans does know that the stud is being dimensioned and not the exterior surface, the extension is often brought inside the 6″-wide wall lines. Another way to make this clear is to take extension lines to the outside surface and write **"F.O.S." (face of stud)** adjacent to the extension lines. See Figure 8.24.

Dimensioning interior walls requires a center line or an extension line right into the wall intersection, as shown in Figure 8.25. A center line is more desirable than a solid line.

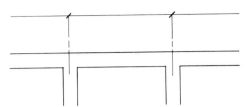

Figure 8.25 Dimensioning interior walls.

Windows and doors are located to the center of the object, as shown in Figure 8.26. When a structural column is next to a window or door, they are dimensioned as in Figure 8.27. The size of a particular window or door can be obtained from a chart called a schedule. This schedule can be found by locating the sheet number on the bottom half of the **reference bubble** adjacent to the window or door. See Figure 8.28. (A reference bubble is a circle with a line drawn through it horizontally.)

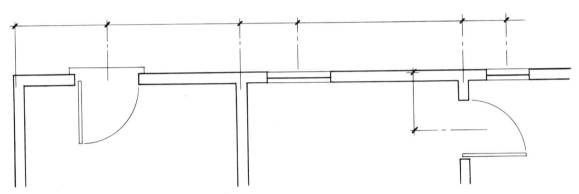

Figure 8.26 Dimensioning doors and windows.

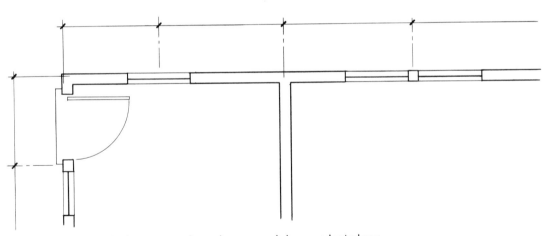

Figure 8.27 Dimensioning structural members around doors and windows.

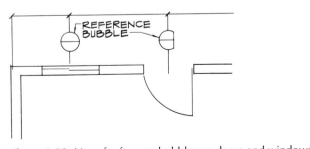

REFERENCE
BUBBLE

Figure 8.28 Use of reference bubbles on doors and windows.

Exterior Dimensioning. There are normally three dimension lines needed on an exterior dimension of a floor plan. The first dimension line away from the object includes the walls, partitions, centers of windows and doors, and so forth. See Figure 8.29. The second dimension line away from the object (floor plan) includes walls and partitions only. See Figure 8.30. If, in establishing the second dimension line, you duplicate a dimension, eliminate the dimension line closest to the object. See Figure 8.31. The third dimension line away from the object is

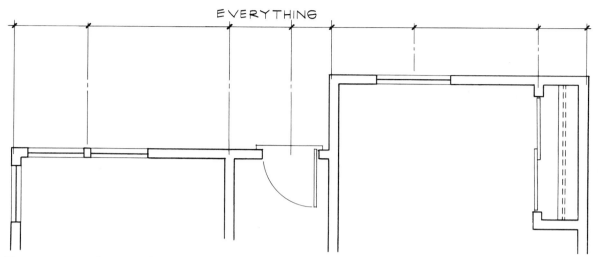

Figure 8.29 First dimension line away from the object.

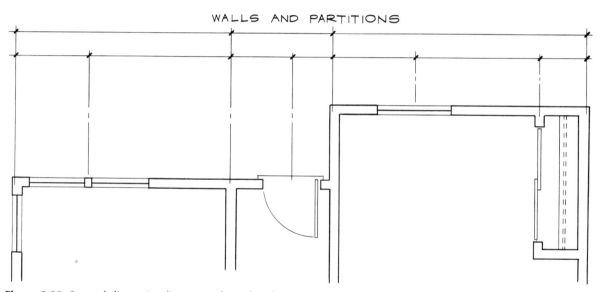

Figure 8.30 Second dimension line away from the object.

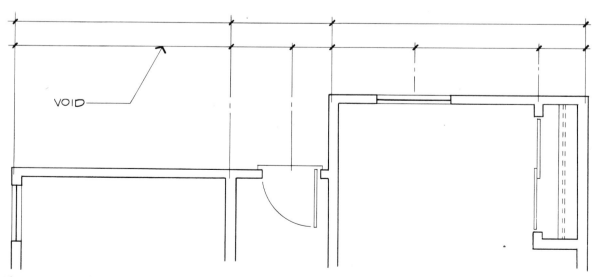

Figure 8.31 Void duplicating dimension lines.

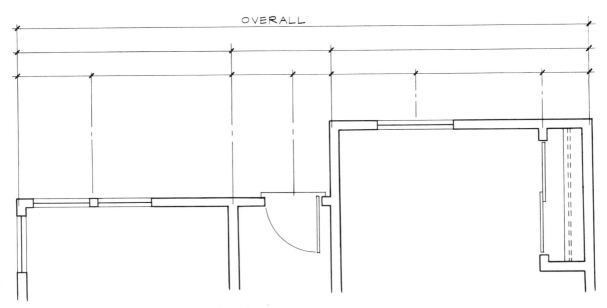

OVERALL

Figure 8.32 Third dimension line away from the object.

for overall dimensions. See Figure 8.32. The first dimension line away from the structure should be measured ¾″ to 1½″ from the outside lines of the plan to allow for notes, window and door reference bubbles, equipment that may be placed adjacent to the structure, and so on. The second dimension line away from the structure should be approximately ⅜″ to ½″ away from the first dimension line. The distance between all subsequent dimension lines should be the same as the distance between the first and second dimension lines.

A large jog in a wall is called an **offset**. Because the jog is removed from the plane that is being dimensioned, you must decide whether to use long extension lines or whether to dimension the offset at the location of the jog. See Figure 8.33.

Objects located independently or outside of the structure, such as posts (columns), are treated differently. First, the order in which the items are to be built must be established. Will the columns be built before or after the adjacent walls? If the walls or the foundation for the walls are to be erected first, then major walls near the columns are identified and the columns are located from them. Never dimension from an inaccessible location! See Figure 8.34.

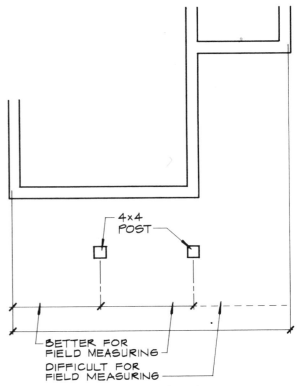

ACCEPTABLE HERE

BETTER HERE

Figure 8.33 Offset dimension locations.

4x4 POST

BETTER FOR FIELD MEASURING

DIFFICULT FOR FIELD MEASURING

Figure 8.34 Locating columns from the structure.

Masonry

When walls are built of bricks or concrete block instead of wood frame, the procedure changes. Everything here is based on the size and proportion of the masonry unit used. Represent masonry as a series of diagonal lines. See Figure 8.35. Show door and window openings the same way you did for wood frame structures. You may represent concrete block in the same way as brick for small scale drawings, but be aware that some offices do use different material designations. See Figure 8.36. (These methods of representing concrete blocks were obtained from various sources, including association literature, A.I.A. standards, and other reference sources.) Extension lines for dimensioning are taken to the edge (end) of the exterior surface in both exterior and interior walls. See Figure 8.37. Pilasters, that is, columns built into the wall by widening the walls, are dimensioned to the center. The size of the pilaster itself can be lettered adjacent to

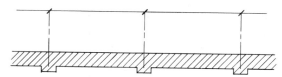

Figure 8.38 Dimensioning pilasters.

one of the pilasters in the drawing. Another method of dealing with the size of these pilasters is to refer the reader of the plan to a detail with a note or reference bubble. See Figure 8.38. All columns consisting of masonry or masonry around steel are also dimensioned to the center.

Windows and Doors. Windows and doors create a unique problem in masonry units. In wood structures, windows and doors are located by dimensioning to the center and allowing the framing carpenter to create the proper opening for the required window or door size. In masonry, the opening is established before the installation of the window or door. This is called the **"rough opening"**; the final opening size is called the **"finished opening."**

The rough opening, which is the one usually dimensioned on the plan, should follow the masonry block module. See Figure 8.39. This block module and the specific type of detail used determine the most economical and practical window and door sizes. See Figure 8.40. Therefore, you should provide dimensions for locating windows, doors, and interior walls or anything of a masonry variety to the rough opening. See Figure 8.41.

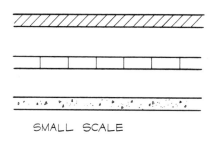

Figure 8.35 Masonry floor plan.

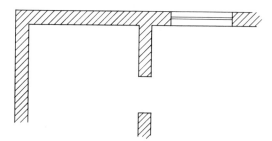

SMALL SCALE

LARGE SCALE

Figure 8.36 Concrete block material designations used on floor plans.

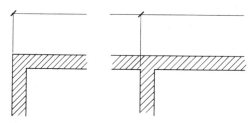

Figure 8.37 Dimensioning masonry walls.

Figure 8.39 Rough opening in masonry wall.

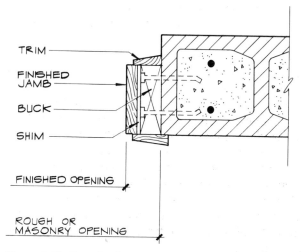

TRIM

FINISHED JAMB

BUCK

SHIM

FINISHED OPENING

ROUGH OR MASONRY OPENING

Figure 8.40 Door jamb at masonry opening.

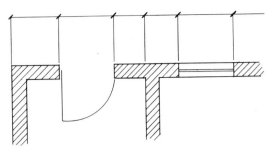

Figure 8.41 Locating doors and windows.

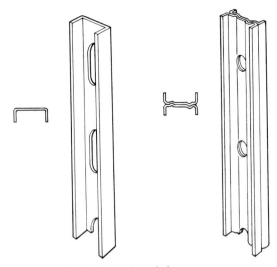

Figure 8.42 Basic steel stud shapes.

Steel

There are two main types of steel systems: **steel stud** and **steel frame**. Steel studs can be treated like wood stud construction. As with wood stud construction, you need to dimension to the stud face rather than to the wall covering (skin).

There are various shapes of steel studs. See Figures 8.42 and 8.43. Drawings A and B in Figure 8.43 show how these shapes appear in plan view. Drawing each steel stud is time consuming and so two parallel lines are drawn to indicate the width of the wall. See drawing C in Figure 8.43. Steel studs can be called out by a note.

If only a portion of a structure is steel stud and the remainder is wood or masonry, you can shade (**pouché**) the area with steel studs or use a steel symbol. See Figure 8.44.

Dimensioning Columns. Steel columns are commonly used to hold up heavy weights. This weight is distributed to the earth by means of a concrete pad. See Figure 8.45. This concrete pad is dimensioned to its center, as Figure 8.46A shows. When you dimension the steel columns, which will show in the floor plan, dimension them to their center. See Figure 8.46B. This relates them to the concrete pads. Dimensioning a series of columns follows the same procedure. See Figure 8.47. The dimensions are taken to the centers of the columns in each direction.

Sometimes, the column must be dimensioned to the face rather than to the center. As Figure 8.47 shows, the extension line is taken to the outside face of the column. Axial reference planes are often used in conjunction with steel columns as shown in Figure 8.48 and the column may be dimensioned to the face. (The dimensional reference system was discussed in Chapter 2.) A sample of a portion of a floor plan dimensioned with and without a series of axial reference planes is shown in Figures 8.49A and 8.49B. Because of the **grid** pattern often formed by the placement of these columns, a center line or a plus (+) type symbol is often used to help the drawing. See Figure 8.50.

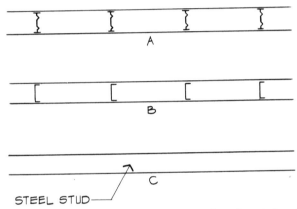

Figure 8.43 Method of representation of steel studs in a floor plan.

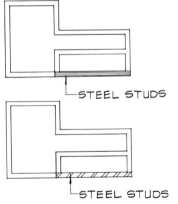

Figure 8.44 Combination of wood and steel.

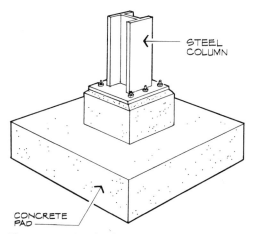

Figure 8.45 Steel column and concrete pad.

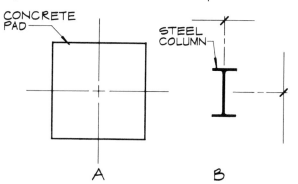

Figure 8.46 Dimensioning concrete pads and steel columns.

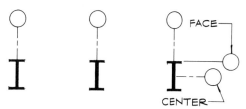

Figure 8.47 Dimensioning a series of columns.

Figure 8.48 Dimensioning a series of columns by way of the axial reference plane.

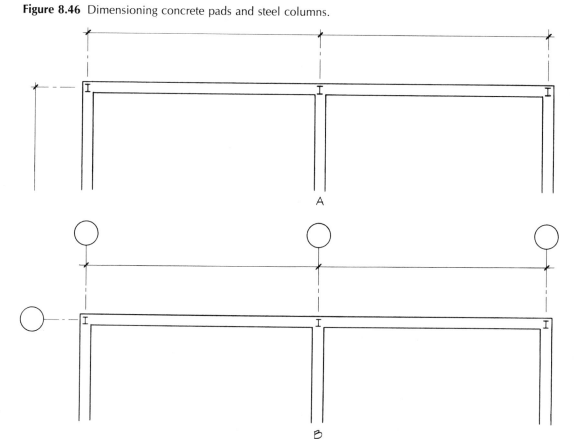

Figure 8.49 Dimensioning a floor plan with steel columns.

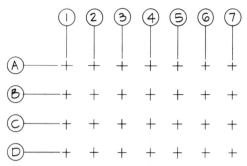

Figure 8.50 Columns forming a grid pattern.

Dimensioning Walls. Walls, especially interior walls that do not fall on the established grid, need to be dimensioned—but only to the nearest dimension grid line. Figure 8.51 is a good example of an interior wall dimensioned to the nearest column falling on a grid.

Combinations of Materials

Due to design or code requirements for fire regulations or structural reasons, materials are often combined: concrete columns with wood walls; steel mainframe with wood walls as secondary members; masonry and wood; steel studs and wood; and steel and masonry, for example. Figure 8.52 shows how using two different systems requires overlapping dimension lines with extension lines. Since dimension lines are more critical than extension lines, extension lines are *always* broken in favor of dimension lines. The wood structure is located to the column on the left side once, then dimensioned independently.

Wood and Masonry. Wood and masonry, as shown in Figure 8.53, are dimensioned as their material dictates: the masonry is dimensioned to the ends of the wall and

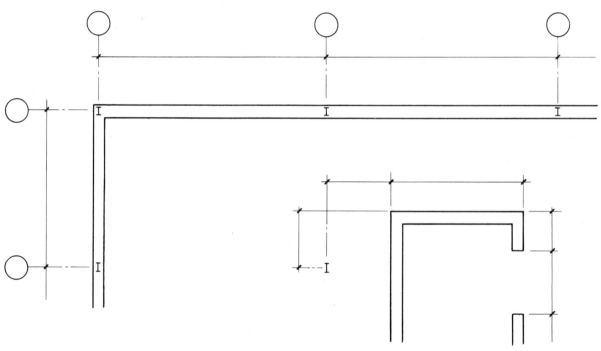

Figure 8.51 Locating interior walls from axial reference bubbles.

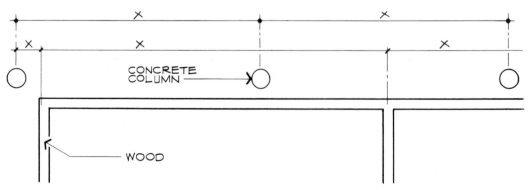

Figure 8.52 Concrete and wood.

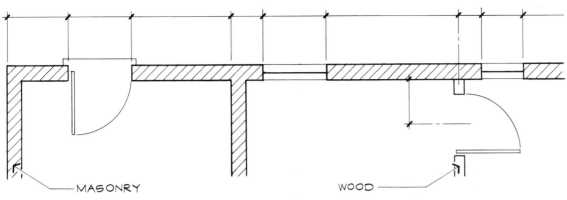

Figure 8.53 Wood and masonry.

the rough opening of windows, while the wood portions are dimensioned to the center of interior walls, center of doors, and so forth. The door in the wood portion is dimensioned to the center of the door and to the inside edge of the masonry wall. This assumes the block wall will be built first.

Masonry and Concrete. Masonry walls and concrete columns, in Figure 8.54, are treated in much the same way as wood and concrete columns. In both instances, the building sequence dictates which one becomes the reference point. See Figure 8.55. Here, steel and masonry are used in combination. Using the dimensional reference system, the steel is installed first. The interior masonry wall is then located from the nearest axial reference plane, and dimensioned according to the block module for that kind of masonry. Additional axial reference plane sub-bubbles are provided. Numbers are in decimals. Since one face of the masonry wall is between 1 and 2, $7/10$ of the distance away from axial reference plane 1, the number 1.7 is used in the sub-bubble. And, since the same wall is also halfway between A and B, A.5 is used as a designation. Another example of the

process is found in Figure 8.56. The fabricators will locate the steel first, then the masonry wall. Dimension "X" relates one system to another.

Doors in Plan View

The general method of dimensioning a window or a door was discussed earlier. Here, we examine a variety of doors and windows and how to draft them. Figure 8.57 shows a sampling of the most typically drafted doors.

Hinged. Doors A and B in Figure 8.57 show the main difference in drafting an **exterior and interior hinged door**. A straight line is used to represent the door and a radial line is used to show the direction of swing. Door "I" shows the same kind of door with its thickness represented by a double line. Doors A, B, and I are used in the floor plans to show flush doors, panel doors, and sculptured doors (decorative and carved).

Flush. Flush doors, as the name indicates, are flush on both sides. They can be solid on the interior (solid slab) or hollow on the inside (hollow core).

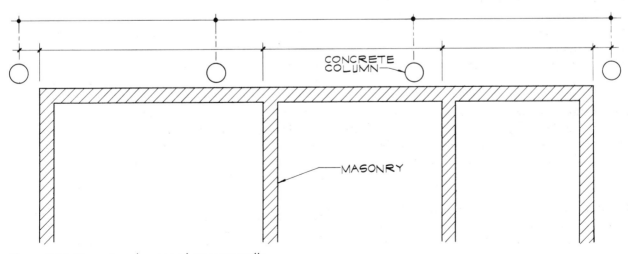

Figure 8.54 Concrete columns and masonry walls.

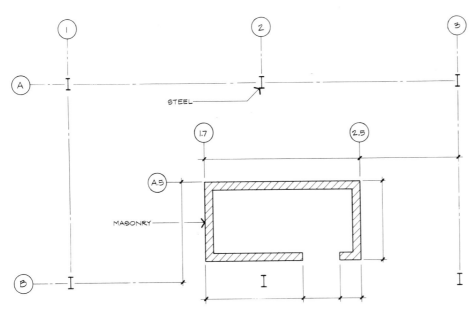

Figure 8.55 Steel and masonry.

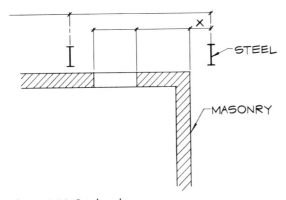

Figure 8.56 Steel and masonry.

Panel. Panel doors have panels set into the frame. These are usually made of thin panels of wood or glass. A variety of patterns are available. See *Sweet's Catalog File* under Doors for pictures of door patterns. Also see the earlier discussion of elevations for a drafted form of these doors.

Sculptured and Decorative. Sculptured and decorative doors can be carved forms put into the doors in the form of a panel door or added onto a flush door in the form of what is called a "planted" door. Different types of trim can also be planted onto a slab door.

Double Action. Door C in Figure 8.57 represents a double action door, a door that swings in both directions. Double action doors can be solid slab, panel, or sculptured.

Sliding. Two types of sliding doors are shown in Figure 8.57. Door D, when used on the exterior, typically is made of glass framed in wood or metal. Pocketed sliding doors are rarely found on the exterior because the pocket is hard to weatherproof, and rain, termites, and wind are hard to keep out of the pocket.

Folding. Doors F and G are good doors for storage areas and wardrobe closets.

Revolving. Where there is a concern about heat loss or heat gain, a revolving door is a good solution. See door H, which shows a cased opening, that is, an opening with trim around the perimeter with no door in it.

Windows in Plan View

Typical ways of showing windows in plan view are shown in Figure 8.58. When a plan is drawn at a small scale, each individual window, of whatever type, may simply be drawn as a fixed window (Window A, Figure 8.58), depending for explanation on a pictorial drawing (as shown in Chapter 9). Ideally, casement, hopper, and awning-type windows should be used only on the second floor or above, for the sake of safety. If they are used on the first or ground floor, they should have planters or reflection pools or something else around them to prevent accidents.

Sizes of Doors and Windows

The best way to find specific sizes of windows and doors (especially sliding glass doors) is to check *Sweet's Cat-*

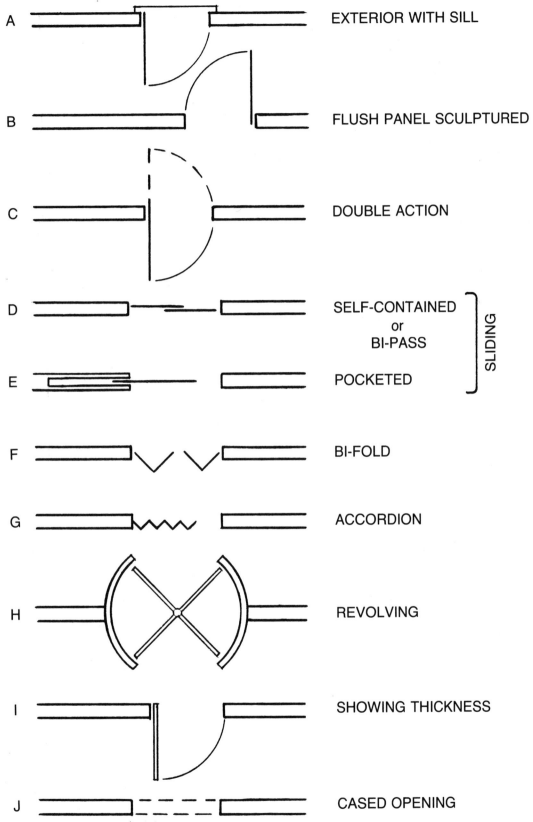

A EXTERIOR WITH SILL

B FLUSH PANEL SCULPTURED

C DOUBLE ACTION

D SELF-CONTAINED
or
BI-PASS

E POCKETED

SLIDING

F BI-FOLD

G ACCORDION

H REVOLVING

I SHOWING THICKNESS

J CASED OPENING

Figure 8.57 Doors in plan view.

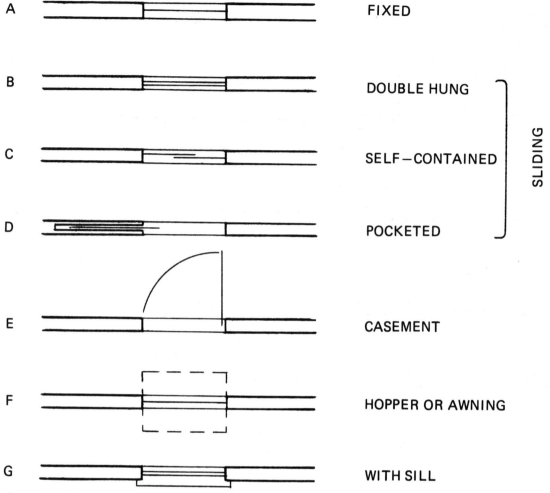

Figure 8.58 Windows in plan view.

alog File. There you will find interior doors ranging from 1'–6" to 3'–0" and exterior doors from 2'–4" to 3'–6". Sizes of doors and windows also depend on local codes. Local codes require a certain percentage of the square footage to be devoted to windows and doors to provide light and ventilation. These percentages often come in the form of minimum and maximum areas as a measure of energy efficient structures. Still another criteria for door size is consideration of wheel chairs and the size required for "barrier free design."

Symbols

Just as chemistry uses symbols to represent elements, architectural floor plans use symbols to represent electrical and plumbing equipment. Figure 8.59 shows the most typical ones used. These are symbols only. They do not represent the shape or size of the actual item. For example, the symbol for a ceiling outlet indicates the *location* of an outlet, not the shape or size of the

fixture. The description of the specific fixture is given in the specifications document.

Electrical Symbols

Some symbols are more generally used than others in the architectural industry. A floor plan, therefore, usually contains a legend or chart of the symbols being used on that particular floor plan.

Number Symbols. Symbols 1, 2, and 3 in Figure 8.59 show different types of switches. Number 2 shows a situation where there might be a number of switches used to turn on a single light fixture or a series of light fixtures. See Figure 8.60. A center-line type line is used to show which switch connects with which outlet. This is simply a way of giving this information to the electrical contractor. (However, Figure 8.60 is not a wiring diagram.) If *one* switch controls one or a series of outlets, it is called a two-way switch. A three-way switch is *two*

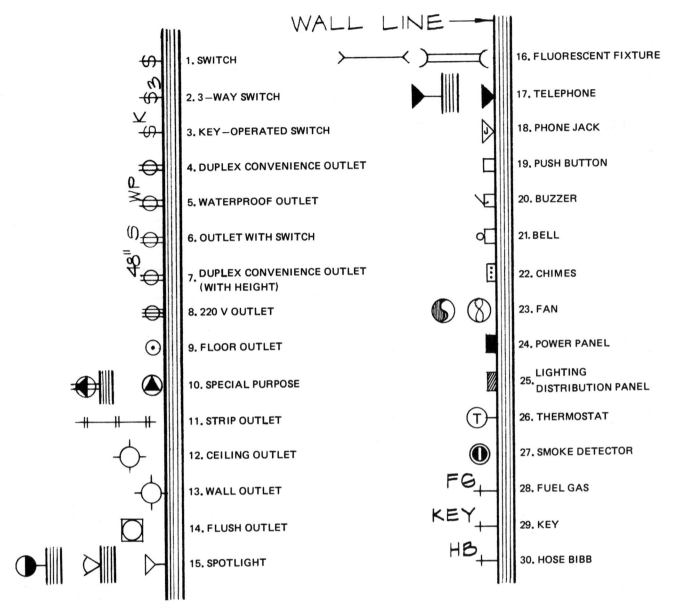

Figure 8.59 Electrical symbols.

1. SWITCH
2. 3—WAY SWITCH
3. KEY—OPERATED SWITCH
4. DUPLEX CONVENIENCE OUTLET
5. WATERPROOF OUTLET
6. OUTLET WITH SWITCH
7. DUPLEX CONVENIENCE OUTLET (WITH HEIGHT)
8. 220 V OUTLET
9. FLOOR OUTLET
10. SPECIAL PURPOSE
11. STRIP OUTLET
12. CEILING OUTLET
13. WALL OUTLET
14. FLUSH OUTLET
15. SPOTLIGHT

WALL LINE

16. FLUORESCENT FIXTURE
17. TELEPHONE
18. PHONE JACK
19. PUSH BUTTON
20. BUZZER
21. BELL
22. CHIMES
23. FAN
24. POWER PANEL
25. LIGHTING DISTRIBUTION PANEL
26. THERMOSTAT
27. SMOKE DETECTOR
28. FUEL GAS
29. KEY
30. HOSE BIBB

switches controlling one outlet or a series of outlets. *Three* switches are called a four-way, and so on. Thus you will always have a number placed next to the switch symbol equal to the number of switches plus one. For example, a number 3 is placed next to the switch when there are two switches, the number 4 for three switches and so on. See Figure 8.60 for examples of switches, outlets, and their numbering system.

Numbers are used to indicate the number of outlets available other than the duplex, the most typical. For example, if a triplex (3) outlet is required, the number 3 is placed beside the outlet symbol. A number in inches, such as 48″, may be used to indicate the height of the outlet from the floor to the center of the outlet. See Figure 8.59, number 7.

Letter Symbols. A letter used instead of a number represents a special type of switch. For example, "K" is used for key-operated, "D" for dimmer, "WP" for weatherproof, and so forth. (A duplex convenience outlet is generally referred to by the public as a wall plug.) As with switches, letter designations are used to describe special duplex convenience outlets: "WP" for waterproof, "S" for outlet and switch, etc. See Figure 8.59, numbers 3, 5, and 6.

Figure 8.60, example E, left half, shows a duplex convenience outlet that is half hot at all times: one outlet is controlled by a switch and the other is a normal outlet. The switch half can be used for a lamp and the normal outlet for an appliance. The symbol "½ SW" identifies this type of outlet.

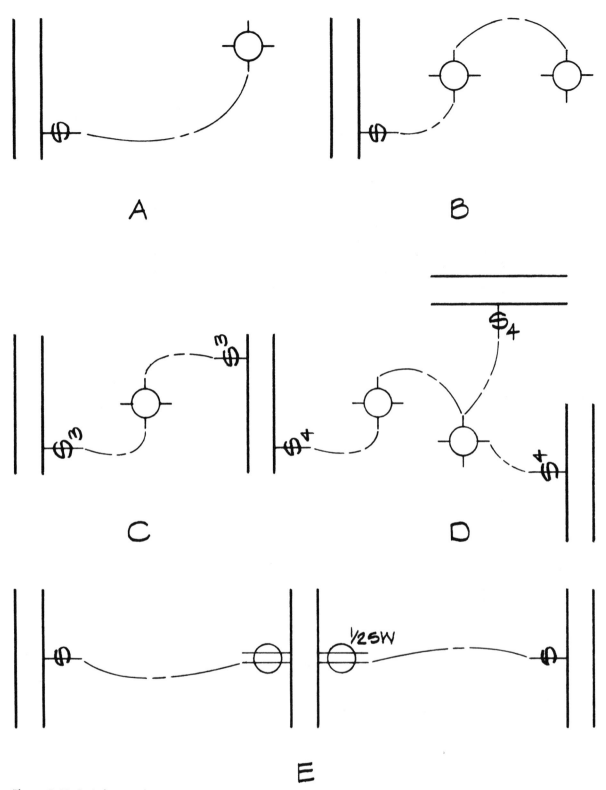

Figure 8.60 Switch to outlet.

Other Symbols. A round circle with a dot in it represents a floor outlet. See number 9, Figure 8.59. A special purpose outlet (number 10 in Figure 8.59) may be needed for a color television set, an ironer, a freezer, a garage door opener, or an electric air conditioner, for example.

Light outlets are shown in numbers 12 through 16, Figure 8.59. A flush outlet is one in which the fixture will be installed flush with the ceiling. The electrician and carpenter must address the problem of framing for the fixture in the members above the ceiling surface.

A selection of miscellaneous equipment is shown in numbers 17 through 27. Number 28 represents a gas outlet while number 29 represents a control for fuel gas. Number 28 would be used to indicate a gas jet in a fireplace. Number 29 would be used to indicate the *control* for the gas, probably somewhere near the fireplace. Number 30 is a hose bibb, a connection for a water hose.

Appliance and Plumbing Fixture Symbols

Many templates are available for drafting plumbing fixtures and kitchen appliances. A good architectural template contains such items as:

Circles	Various kitchen appliances
Door swings	Various plumbing fixtures
Electrical symbols	Typical heights marked along edges

Figure 8.61 shows some of these fixtures and appliances.

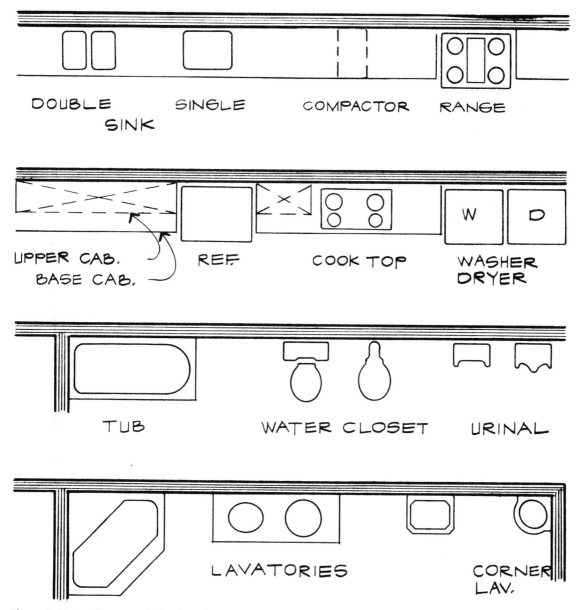

Figure 8.61 Appliance and plumbing fixtures.

Other Floor Plan Considerations

It is often necessary to show more than one or two building materials on a floor plan. Let us take a college music building as an example of a structure that has a multitude of walls of different materials including:

1. Masonry
2. Wood studs
3. Two types of sound proof partitions
4. Low walls
5. Low walls with glass above

We need to establish an acceptable symbol for each material and to produce a legend similar to that in Figure 8.62. A sample of a partial floor plan using some of these materials symbols is shown in Figure 8.63.

Combining Building Materials

Because of ecological requirements (such as insulation); structural reasons; aesthetic concerns; and fire regulations, materials must often be combined. For example, insulation may be adjacent to a masonry wall, a brick veneer may be on a wood stud wall, and steel studs may be next to a concrete block wall. Figure 8.64 shows examples of what some of the walls will look like on the floor plan.

Repetitive Plans and Symmetrical Items

If a plan or portions of a plan are symmetrical, a center line can be used and half of the object dimensioned. If a plan is repetitive—for example, an office building or an apartment or condominium—each unit is given a letter designation (Unit A, Unit B, etc.). These are then referenced to each other and only one is dimensioned.

For example, suppose you were drafting a floor plan for an eight-unit apartment structure; these eight units are to be divided into four one-bedroom units and four two-bedroom units, all using the same basic plans. Your approach could be to draft the overall shape of the structure and then to draft the interior walls only on one typical unit and label it completely. The remaining units (three of each) are referenced to the original unit by a note such as, "See Unit A for dimensions and notes."

This type of plan lends itself well to the use of ad-

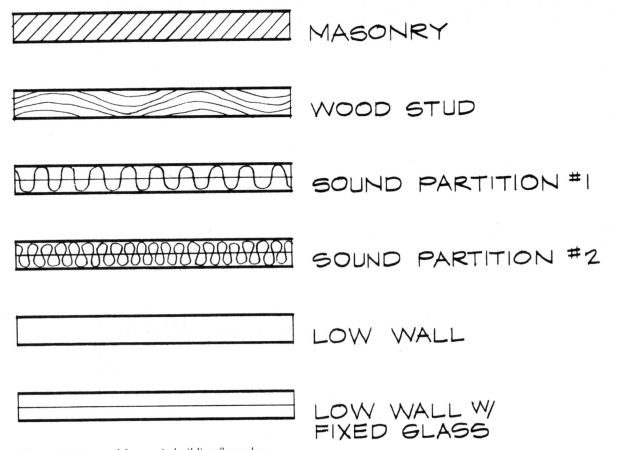

Figure 8.62 Legend for music building floor plan.

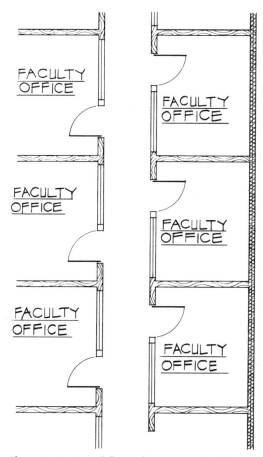

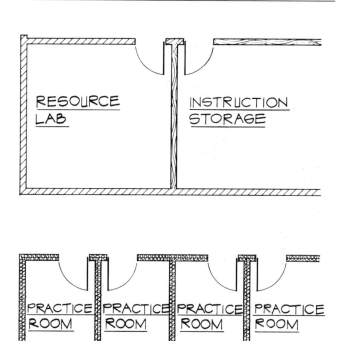

Figure 8.63 Partial floor plan—music building.

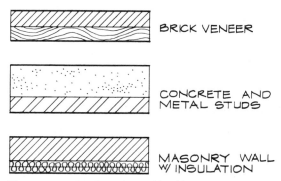

Figure 8.64 Combinations of building materials.

hesives (see Chapter 2). A typical unit is drawn at the proper scale; then a series of adhesives are made of this plan. The whole plan is made by putting the adhesive plans in the proper position to produce the overall shape.

Dimensional Reference Numbers and Letters

The dimensional reference system has already been discussed earlier. Responsibility for placement of the letters

and numbers and often the drafting of the dimensional reference bubbles rests with the structural engineer. Because the structural engineer is responsible for sizing and locating the columns for proper distribution of the building weight, only the structural engineer can make the proper decision. This information can then be taken and put in the reference bubbles on the foundation plan, building section, framing plans, and so forth.

Pouché Walls

The word *pouché* was mentioned earlier. This is the process of darkening the space between the lines which represent wall thickness on a floor plan. Special pouché pencils can be purchased at most drafting supply stores. Graphite pencils, like drafting pencils or colored pencils, can be used to pouché. Do not use red, yellow, or orange; they will block light in the reproduction of the plan and leave the walls black. Do not use wax-based pencils.

Stairs

An arrow is used on the plan of the stair to show the

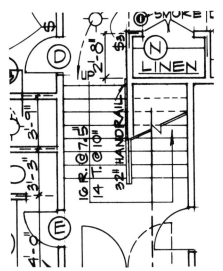

Figure 8.65 Stair direction and number of treads. (Residence of Mr. & Mrs. Ted Bear.)

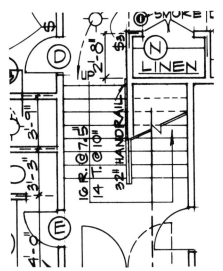 LINEN

direction in which the stair rises. See the partial floor plan, Figure 8.65. Notice how the arrowheads show direction and how the number and size of the treads and risers are indicated.

Noting Logic

The basic approach used here is to show a complete set of working drawings as if a complete set of specifications were included. Specifications are the written documentation of what is drafted; they give information that is not given in the drawings. Brand names, model numbers, installation procedures, and quality of material are just a few of the items discussed in a set of specifications. So the inclusion of the specifications affects the noting of the floor plan.

Because of the precise descriptions contained in the specifications, only general descriptions are necessary on the floor plan. For example, it is sufficient to call out a "cook top" as a generic name and let the specifications take care of the rest of the description. "Tub" and "water closet" are sufficient to describe plumbing fixtures. Further description would only confuse the drawing, and these items should be described in the "specs" (short for specifications).

In other words, specific information should not be duplicated. If it is, changes can present problems. For example, suppose brand "A" is selected for a particular fixture and is called brand "A" on the floor plan rather than by its generic term. Later, it is changed to brand "B." Now both the floor plan and specs need to be changed; if one is missed, confusion results.

Electrical Rating

Many architectural firms that superimpose the electrical plan on top of the floor plan note the **electrical rating** necessary for a particular piece of equipment; for example, range 9KW, oven 5KW, dishwasher 1.5KW, and refrigerator 110V. Electrical ratings can also be included in an electrical appliance schedule if one exists.

Room Sizes

Because sizes of rooms are often found on presentation drawings (scaled drawings), some people think that sizes of rooms (9 × 12, 10 × 14) belong on a floor plan. They do not. These approximate sizes are fine for client consumption but are useless in the construction process.

Providing Satisfactory Dimensions

One of the most common criticisms from the field (workers on the job) is that the floor plans do not contain enough dimensions. Because these people cannot scale the drawings (something we would not want them to do anyway), they are dependent on dimensions, so be sure they are all included. Remember that notes take precedence over the drawing itself. If a member is called 2 × 10 but is drawn as a 2 × 8, the note takes precedence.

Checklist: Checking Your Own Drawing

There are so many minute things to remember in the development of a particular drawing that most offices have worked out some type of checking system. A checklist (or check sheet) is one frequently used device. It lists the most commonly missed items in chart form, making it easy for you to pre-check your work before a checker is asked to review a particular drawing. See Figure 8.66 for a floor plan checklist.

FLOOR PLAN CHECK SHEET

1. Walls
   a. Accuracy of thickness
   b. Correctness of intersections
   c. Accuracy of location
   d. 8-inch wall
   e. Openings
   f. Pony walls designated
   g. Pouché
2. Doors and windows
   a. Correct use
   b. Location
   c. Correct symbol
   d. Schedule reference
   e. Header size
   f. Sills, if any
   g. Show swing
   h. Direction of slide if needed
   i. Door swing
3. Steps
   a. Riser and treads called out
   b. Concrete steps
   c. Wood steps
4. Dimensioning
   a. Position of lines
   b. All items dimensioned
   c. All dimensions shown
   d. All arrowheads shown
   e. Openings
   f. Structural posts
   g. Slabs and steps
   h. Closet depth
   i. Check addition
   j. Odd angles
5. Lettering
   a. Acceptable height and appearance
   b. Acceptable form
   c. Readable
6. Titles, notes, and call-outs
   a. Spelling, phrasing, and abbreviations
   b. Detail references
   c. Specification references
   d. Window and door references
   e. Appliances
   f. Slabs and steps
   g. Pumbing fixtures
   h. Openings
   i. Room titles
   j. Ceiling joist direction
   k. Floor material
   l. Drawing title and scale
   m. Tile work
      (1) Tub
      (2) Shower
      (3) Counter (kitchen and bath)
   n. Attic opening—scuttle

   o. Cabinet
   p. Wardrobe
      (1) Shelves
      (2) Poles
   q. Built-in cabinets, nooks, tables, etc.
7. Symbols
   a. Electrical
   b. Gas
   c. Water
   d. Heating, ventilating, and air conditioning
8. Closets, wardrobes, and cabinets
   a. Correct representation
   b. Doors
   c. Depths, widths, and heights
   d. Medicine cabinets
   e. Detail references
   f. Shelves and poles
   g. Plywood partitions and posts
   h. Overhead cabinets
   i. Broom closets
9. Equipment (appliances)
   a. Washer and dryer
   b. Range
   c. Refrigerator
   d. Freezer
   e. Oven
   f. Garbage disposal
   g. Dishwasher
   h. Water heater
   i. Forced draft vent
10. Equipment (special)
    a. Hi-fi
    b. TV
    c. Sewing machine
    d. Intercom
    e. Game equipment (built-in)
    f. Others
11. Legend
12. Note exposed beams and columns
13. Special walls
    a. Masonry
    b. Veneers
    c. Partial walls, note height
    d. Furred walls for plumbing vents
14. Note sound and thermal insulation in walls
15. Fireplaces
    a. Dimension depth and width of firepit
    b. Fuel gas and key
    c. Dimension hearth width
16. Mail slot
17. Stairways
    a. Number of risers

    b. Indicate direction
    c. Note railing
18. Medicine cabinet, mirrors at bath
19. Attic and underfloor access ways
20. Floor slopes at wet areas
21. Hose bibbs
22. Main water shut-off valve
23. Fuel gas outlets
    a. Furnace
    b. Range
    c. Oven
    d. Dryer
    e. Water heater
    f. Fireplace
24. Water heater: gas fired
    a. 4" vent through roof
    b. 100 sq. in. combustion air vent to closet
25. Furnace location: gas fired
    a. Exhaust vent through roof
    b. Combustion air to closet
    c. Return air vent
26. Electric meter location
27. Floodlights, wall lights, note heights
28. Convenience outlets, note if 220V, note horse power if necessary
29. Note electric power outlets
    a. Range 9 KW
    b. Oven 5 KW
    c. Dishwasher 1.5 KW
    d. Refrigerator 110 V
    e. Washer 2 KW
    f. Dryer 5 KW
30. Clock, chime outlets
31. Doorbell
32. Roof downspouts
33. Fire extinguishers, fire hose cabinets
34. Interior bathroom, toiletroom fans
35. Bathroom heaters
36. Kitchen range hood fan and light
37. Telephone, television outlets
38. Exit signs
39. Bathtub inspection plate
40. Thermostat location
41. Door, window, and finish schedules
42. Line quality
43. Basic design
44. Border line
45. Title block
46. Title
47. Scale

Figure 8.66 Floor plan checklist.

SCHEDULES: DOOR, WINDOW, AND FINISH

The Purpose of Schedules

A schedule is a list or catalog of information that defines the doors, windows, or finishes of a room. The main purpose for incorporating schedules into a set of construction documents is to provide clarity, location, sizes, materials, and information for the designation of doors, windows, roof finishes, and plumbing and electrical fixtures.

Tabulated Schedules: Doors and Windows

Schedules may be presented in **tabulated** or **pictorial** form. While tabulated schedules in architectural offices vary in form and layout from office to office, the same primary information is provided.

Figures 9.1 and 9.2 are examples of tabulated **door and window schedules**. The door schedule provides a space for the symbol, the width and height, and the thickness of the door. It also indicates whether the door is to be solid core (SC) or hollow core (HC). The "type"

column may indicate that the door has raised panels, or that it is a slab door or french door, and so forth.

Information

The material space may indicate what kind of wood is to be used for the door, such as birch or beech. Space for remarks is used to provide information such as the closing device or hardware to be used, or the required fire rated door. In some cases, where there is insufficient space for remarks, an asterisk (*) or symboled number may be placed to the left of the schedule or in the designated box and referenced to the bottom of the schedule with the required information. This information must under no circumstances be crowded or left out. For any type of schedule including lettering, provide sufficient space in each frame so that your lettering is not cramped or unclear.

Symbols

Symbol designations for doors and windows vary in architectural offices and are influenced by each office's

DOOR SCHEDULE

SYM.	WIDTH	HEIGHT	THK.	TYPE	MATERIAL	HC/SC	GLAZ. AREA	REMARKS
1	PR.2'-9"	7'-0"	1 3/4"	SLAB	WOOD	SC		
2	PR.2'-10"	"	"	FRENCH	"	"	11.3 ♯	1/4" TEMP. GL./TINTED GL.
3	PR.3'-1"	"	"	"	"	"	"	" "
4	3'-6"	"	"	"	"	"	13.8 ♯	" "
5	3'-0"	"	"	SLAB	"	"		
6	2'-8"	"	"	"	"	"		
7	2'-8"	"	"	"	"	"		1HOUR SELF-CLOSING
8	2'-6"	"	"	"	"	"		
9	2'-4"	6'-8"	1 3/8"	SLAB	WOOD	HC		
10	2'-0"	"	"	"	"	"		
11	2'-6"	"	"	"	"	"		
12	PR.3'-7"	"	"	BI-FOLD	WOOD	"		
13	PR.3'-8"	"	"	"	"	"		
14	PR.3'-2"	"	"	"	"	"		
15	8'-8"	8'-0"	3"	GARAGE	WOOD	—		2x3 W/1x6 T&G R/S CEDAR
⬡								
⬡								

Figure 9.1 Door schedule.

WINDOW SCHEDULE

SYM.	WIDTH	HEIGHT	TYPE	FRAME	SCR.	GLAZ. AREA	VENT. AREA	REMARKS
A	5'-8"	7'-0"	FIXED/AWNING	WOOD	YES	39.6 #	9.9 #	PR. 1'-9" HIGH AWNING BELOW
B	4'-6"	"	FIXED	"	NO	31.5 #		1/4" TEMP. GLASS
C	5'-6"	"	"	"	"	38.5 #		"
D	4'-0"	3'-0"	AWNING	"	YES	12.0 #	12.0 #	
E	5'-8"	7'-0"	FIXED	"	NO	39.7 #		1/4" TEMP. GLASS
F	4'-0"	3'-6"	GARDEN	WOOD	YES	14.0 #	5.0 #	OPERABLE SIDE VENTS
G	1'-8"	3'-3"	CASEMENT	"	"	5.4 #	5.4 #	
H	PR. 2'-0"	4'-0"	"	"	"	16.0 #	16.0 #	
I	4 @ 1'-4"	5'-8"	FIXED	"	NO	30.2 #		
J	3 @ 1'-8"	4'-0"	FIXED/CASEMENT	WOOD	YES	20.0 #	6.7 #	MIDDLE IS CASEMENT
K	PR. 1'-3"	"	CASEMENT	"	"	10.0 #	10.0 #	
L	5'-6"	7'-0"	FIXED	"	NO	38.5 #		1/4" TEMP. GLASS

NOTES: ALL WINDOWS DOUBLE GLASS-THERMAL EXCEPT WINDOW F
ALL WINDOWS TINTED GLASS, EXCEPT WHERE NOTED BY •

Figure 9.2 Window schedule.

procedures. For example, a circle, hexagon, or square may be used for all or part of the various schedules. Figure 9.3 illustrates symbol shapes and how they may be shown. There are various options, such as using a letter or number or both, and choosing various shapes. Door and window symbol shapes should be different from each other. To clarify reading the floor plan, the letter "D" at the top of the door symbol and the letter "W" at the top of the window symbol are used. The letter "P" is used for plumbing fixtures, "E" for electrical fixtures, and "A" for appliances. Place the letter in the top part of the symbol. Whatever symbol shape you select, be sure to make the symbol large enough to accommodate the lettering that will be inside the symbol.

Whenever possible, the door and window schedules should be on the floor plan sheet. This helps locate the various doors and windows on the floor plan. If you cannot place these schedules on the floor plan sheet, use an adjacent sheet.

Draw the lines for the schedules with ink on the front side of the vellum or with lead on the reverse side of the sheet. In this way, when changes are made in the sched-ule information, you run no risk of erasing the lines. When you provide lines for the anticipated number of symbols to be used, allow extra spaces for door and window types that may be added.

Pictorial Schedules: Doors and Windows

Pictorial Representations

In many cases, tabulated schedules cannot clearly define a specific door or window. In this case, you can add to a schedule a call-out with a pictorial drawing of a door or window adjacent to your schedule, as in Figure 9.4; Door 1 is difficult to explain, so a pictorial representation makes it clearer.

Pictorial Schedules

A pictorial schedule, as distinct from a pictorial repre-

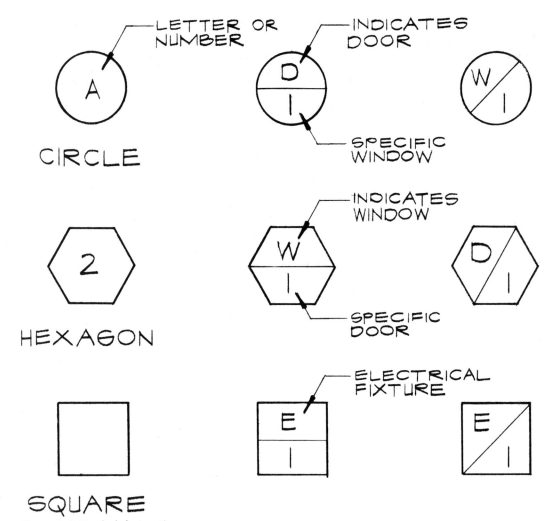

Figure 9.3 Symbol designations.

sentation, is totally pictorial. Each item is dimensioned and provided with data such as material, type, and so forth. Figure 9.5 provides a pictorial schedule of a window. A pictorial schedule provides section references for the head, jamb, and sill sections, so you no longer need to reference the exterior elevations. (The head is the top of a window or door, the jamb refers to the sides of a window or door, and the sill is the bottom of the window or door.)

Choosing a Tabulated or Pictorial Schedule

Tabulated

Your choice of a tabulated schedule may involve the following factors:

1. Specific office procedures.
2. Standardization or simplicity of doors and windows selected.
3. Large number of items with different dimensions.
4. Ease of changing sizes.

Pictorial

Choice of a pictorial schedule may involve the following factors:

1. Specific office procedures.
2. Unusual and intricate door or window design requirements.
3. Very few doors and windows in the project or very few types used.
4. Desired clarity for window section referencing.

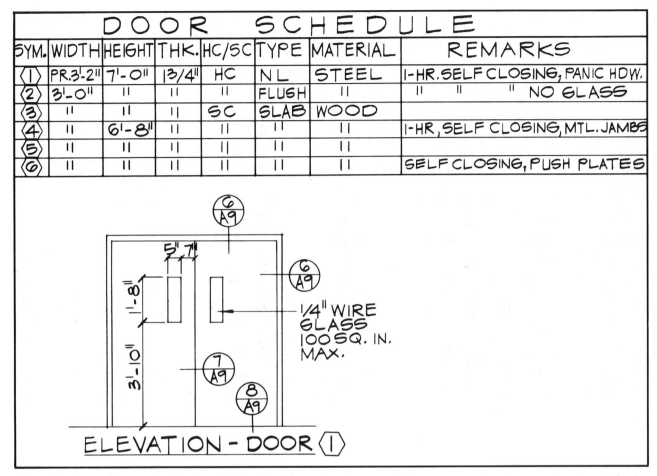

Figure 9.4 Pictorial representation on a tabular schedule.

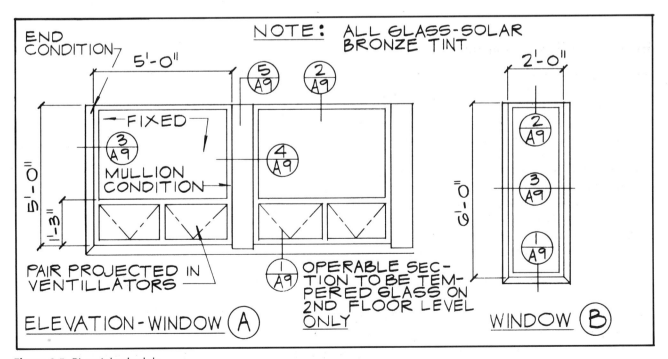

Figure 9.5 Pictorial schedule.

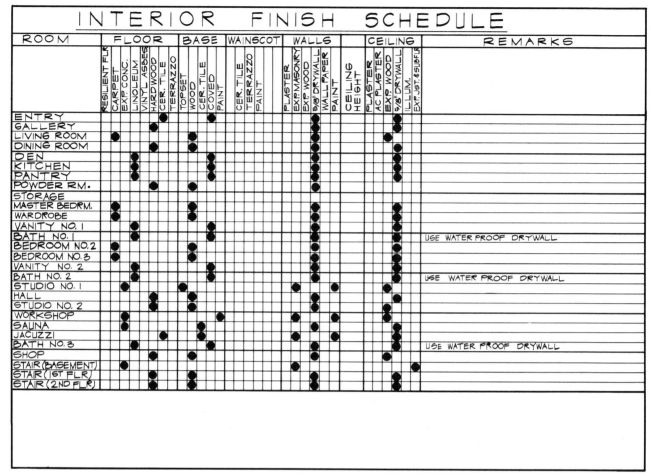

Figure 9.6A Interior finish schedule.

A

Interior Finish Schedules

Interior finish schedules provide information such as floor and wall material, trim material, and ceiling finish. Architectural offices vary in their layout of an interior finish schedule because of their office philosophy and specific information they receive for various types of projects.

Figure 9.6A shows an interior finish schedule. The column allocated for room designation may show the room name or an assigned space number or both. This selection may be dictated by the project itself. See Figure 9.6B. Another method of defining finishes combines the room finish schedule with a room finish key, which uses numbers and letters to indicate the various materials to be used for floors, walls, and so forth. An example of this type of schedule is shown in Figure 9.6C. Using space numbers is more logical for a large office building, for example, than for a very small residence. Once again, when extensive information is required in the remarks section of the schedule, use an asterisk (*) or footnote number for reference at the bottom of the schedule.

Figure 9.6B Interior finish schedule. (opposite, top)

Figure 9.6C Roof finish schedule—key type. (opposite, bottom)

INTERIOR FINISH SCHEDULE

	ROOM	FLOOR			BASE			WALLS	CEILING		AREA	REMARKS
		CARPET	LINOLEUM	TILE	WOOD	VINYL TOPSET	COVED	5/8" SHEETROCK	CEILING HEIGHT	5/8" SHEETROCK	SQUARE FEET	
101	ENTRY			●	●			●	17'-6"	●	73	
102	KITCHEN		●			●		●	8'-0"	●	184	
103	LIVING	●			●			●	9'-3"	●	270	CEILING SLOPES
104	DINING	●			●			●	8'-6"	●	284	
105	FAMILY	●			●			●	7'-9"	●	167	
106	BAR		●			●		●	8'-0"	●	26	
107	LAUNDRY		●			●		●	"	●	39	
108	MUD ROOM		●			●		●	"	●	28	
201	MASTER BATH		●			●		●	7'-6"	●	77	
202	DRESSING	●			●			●	"	●	60	
203	MAST. BEDROOM	●			●			●	8'-0"	●	380	
204	BATH		●			●		●	7'-6"	●	55	
205	BEDROOM	●			●			●	8'-0"	●	146	
206	STAIRS	●			●			●	—	●	54	

ROOM FINISH SCHEDULE

NO.	ROOM	FINISHES				CEIL. HGT.	ROOM AREA	REMARKS
		FLOOR	BASE	WALLS	CEILING			
101	RECEPTION	B	1	A	2	9'-0"	110☐'	
102	OFFICE	A		B	2	8'-0"	170☐'	
103	OFFICE	A		B	2	"	180☐'	
104	OFFICE	A		B	2	"	185☐'	
105	WOMENS TOIL.	C	1	A	1	7'-6"	30☐'	
106	MENS TOILET	C	1	A	1	7'-6"	25☐'	

ROOM FINISH KEY

FLOORS		BASES		WALLS		CEILINGS	
A	CARPET	1	WOOD	A	5/8" SHEETROCK	1	5/8" SHEETROCK
B	OAK PARQUET			B	1x6 T&G CEDAR	2	SUSP. AC. TILE
C	CERAMIC TILE						

PLUMBING FIXTURE SCHEDULE

SYM.	ITEM	MANUFACTURER	CATALOG NO.	REMARKS
1	WHIRLPOOL BATH	FIXTURES INC.	2640.061	FITTING 1108.019
2	LAVATORY	''	0470.039	FAUCET 2248.565
3	BIDET	''	5005.013	FITTING 1852.012
4	TOILET	''	2109.395	

Figure 9.7 Plumbing fixture schedule.

APPLIANCE SCHEDULE

SYM.	ITEM	MANUFACTURER	CATALOG NO.	REMARKS
1	COOKTOP	APPLIANCES INC.	RU38V	WHITE
2	MICROWAVE	''	JKP65G	
3	DISHWASHER	''	GSD2500	WHITE
4	DISPOSER	''	GFC510	

Figure 9.8 Appliance fixture schedule.

Additional Schedules

Other types of schedules used depend on office procedure and the type of project. For example, if a project has many types of plumbing and appliance fixtures in various areas, provide additional schedules to clarify and to locate items with their designated symbols.

Figures 9.7 and 9.8 show a **plumbing fixture schedule** and an **appliance schedule**. If these types of schedules are not used in a project, the fixture types, manufacturers, catalog numbers, and other information needed must be included in the project specifications.

For most projects, the specifications will augment information found in the schedules. Examples of information usually found in the specifications include the window manufacturer, the type and manufacturer of the door hardware, and the type and manufacturer of paint for the trim.

BUILDING SECTIONS

10

Building Sections

A building section cuts a vertical slice through a structure or a part of a structure. Figure 10.1 shows a vertical slice cut through a wood-framed, two-story residence. To further examine the various roof, floor, and wall conditions found at that particular slice location, we can separate the two elements as viewed in Figure 10.2.

Drawing a Building Section

Drawing a building section is done by making a cross section giving relevant architectural and structural information. When given the task of drawing a building section, you first need to gather basic information including:

1. Type of foundation
2. Floor system
3. Exterior and interior wall construction
4. Beam and column sizes and their material
5. Plate and/or wall heights
6. Floor elevations
7. Floor members (size and spacing)
8. Floor sheathing, material and size
9. Ceiling members (size and spacing)
10. Roof pitch
11. Roof sheathing, material and size
12. Insulation requirements
13. Finished roof material

When you have gathered this information, select a suitable architectural scale. Usually, the scale ranges

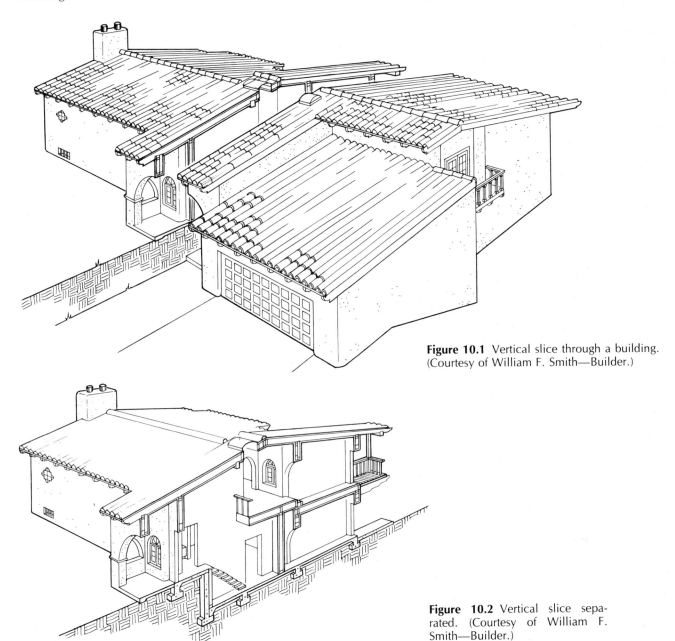

Figure 10.1 Vertical slice through a building. (Courtesy of William F. Smith—Builder.)

Figure 10.2 Vertical slice separated. (Courtesy of William F. Smith—Builder.)

from $\frac{1}{8}$" = 1'–0" to $\frac{3}{4}$" = 1'–0". The scale depends on the size and complexity of a project and should also be chosen for clarity.

As you draw the building section, visualize the erection sequence for the structure and the construction techniques of the material being used. Figure 10.3 shows a building section derived from Figures 10.1 and 10.2.

The first step is to show the concrete floor and foundation members at that particular location. While foundation details should be drawn accurately, they do not need to be dimensioned or elaborated upon; all the necessary information will be called out in the larger scale drawings of the individual foundation details.

Next, establish a **plate height**. (A plate is a horizontal timber that joins the tops of studs.) Here the plate height is 8'–0", measuring from the top of the concrete floor to the top of the two plates (2—2" × 4" continuous) of the wood stud wall. This height also establishes the height to the bottom of the floor joist for the second floor level. Once the floor joists are drawn in at the proper scale, repeat the same procedure to establish the wall height that will support the ceiling and roof framing members.

As indicated, the roof pitch for this particular project is a ratio of 3 in 12; for each foot of horizontal measurement, the roof rises 3 inches (for every 12 feet, the roof rises 3 feet). You can draw this slope or angle with an architectural scale or you can convert the ratio to an angle degree and draw it with a protractor or adjustable triangle. Draw the roof at the other side of the building in the same way, with the intersection of the two roof planes establishing the ridge location. Mission clay tile was chosen for the finished roof member for this project and is drawn as shown.

When you have drawn in all the remaining components, such as stairs and floor framing elevation changes, note all the members, roof pitch, material information, and dimensions.

Figure 10.3 shows various reference symbols. These symbols refer to an enlarged drawing of those particular assemblies. To demonstrate the importance of providing enlarged details, Figure 10.4 shows a building section of a wood-framed structure with critical bolted connections. A reference symbol (the number 1 over the number 8, in a reference bubble) is located at the roof framing and wall connection. This connection is made clear with an enlarged detail showing the exact location and size of bolts needed to satisfy the engineering requirements for that assembly. See Figure 10.5.

Number and Place of Sections

Draw as many building sections as you need to convey the greatest amount of information and clarity for those building the structure.

Usually, building sections are used to investigate various conditions that prevail in a structure. These sections can point out flaws in the building's structural integrity, and this information can lead to modifications in the initial design.

The number of building sections required varies ac-

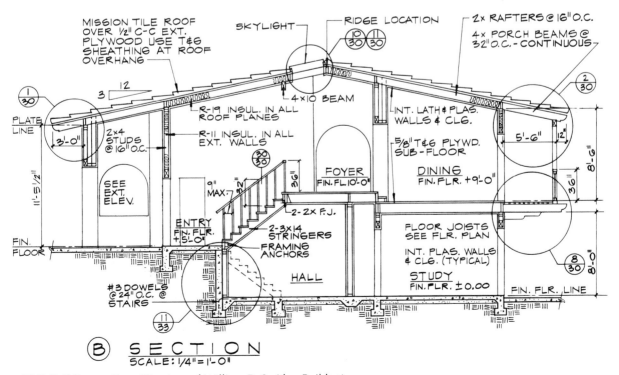

Figure 10.3 Building section. (Courtesy of William F. Smith—Builder.)

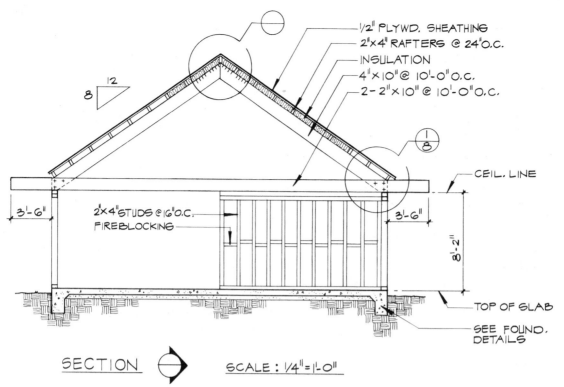

Figure 10.4 Structural section.

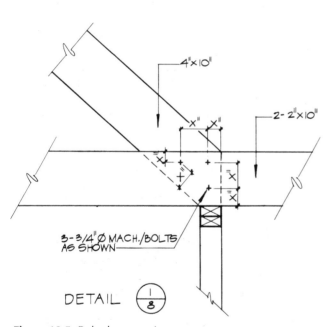

Figure 10.5 Bolted connection.

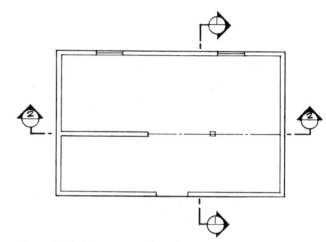

Figure 10.6 Two structural sections.

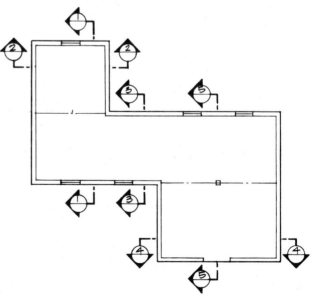

Figure 10.7 Five structural sections.

cording to the structural complexity of the particular building. Figures 10.6 and 10.7 illustrate two buildings varying in complexity. Figure 10.6 shows a rectangular building, which probably needs only two building sections to clearly provide all the information required. However, the building in Figure 10.7 requires at least five sections to provide all the structural information.

allow you to clearly elaborate building connections and call-outs without having to draw separate enlarged details.

Figures 10.8, 10.9, 10.10 and 10.11 show an industrial building and also show how wall sections are incorporated into a set of construction documents. Figure 10.8 shows the floor plan with two main exterior and one interior bearing wall conditions. These wall con-

Types of Sections

Because the design and complexity of buildings vary, types of sections also vary.

Wall Sections

Simple structural conditions may only require wall sections to convey the necessary building information. Structural sections for a small industrial building, for example, might use wall sections.

In most cases, wall sections can be drawn at larger scales such as ½" = 1'–0". These larger scale drawings

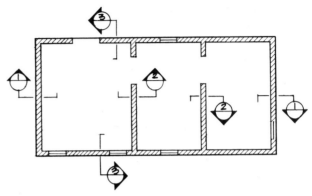

Figure 10.8 Floor plan—industrial building.

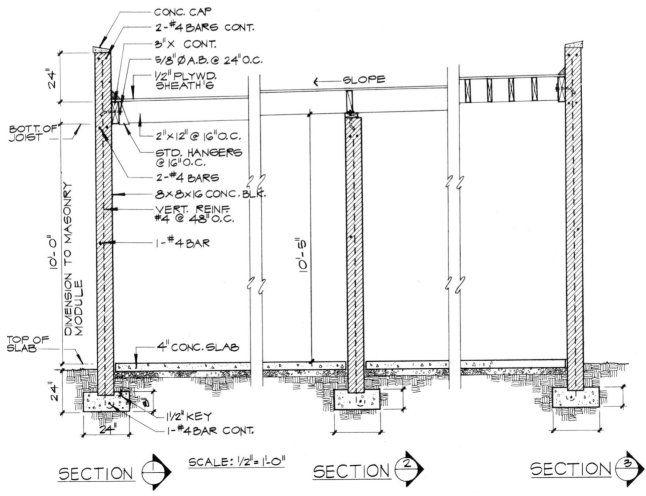

Figure 10.9 Exterior wall section. **Figure 10.10** Interior wall section. **Figure 10.11** Exterior wall section.

ditions are referenced to wall sections and are shown in Figures 10.9, 10.10, and 10.11.

To draw a wall section, first select a scale that clearly shows the wall and foundation assembly details as well as the adjacent structural members and components. Then, using wall section 1, Figure 10.9, as an example, draw and dimension the footing for the masonry wall. Because you are drawing at a large scale, you can note all the footing information directly on the wall section, thereby making separate foundation details unnecessary. Next draw the masonry wall using 8 × 8 × 16 concrete block as the wall material. Because a modular unit is being used for the wall construction, a wall height is established that satisfies the 8″ concrete block increments. Draw the roof-to-wall assembly at the desired height above the concrete floor, with the various framing connections and members needed to satisfy the structural requirements. After you finish the drawing, add notes for all members, steel reinforcing, bolts, and so forth. Other wall sections, as shown in Figure 10.10 and 10.11, are drawn and noted similarly. Note that while Figure 10.11 is similar to Figure 10.9, different roof framing conditions exist.

In short, large-scale wall sections allow the structural components and call-outs to be clearly drawn and usually make larger-scale details such as framing connections and foundation details unnecessary.

Full Sections

For projects with complex structural conditions you should draw an entire section. This gives a better idea of the structural conditions in that portion of the building, which can then be analyzed, engineered, and clearly detailed.

Figure 10.12 shows a building section through a residence that has many framing complexities. Here you can clearly understand the need for a full section to see the existing conditions. To show the full section, you should draw this type of section in a smaller architectural scale, ¼″ = 1′–0″. Again, when you use a smaller scale for drawing sections, you must provide enlarged details of all relevant connections. The circled and referenced conditions in Figure 10.12, for example, will be detailed at a larger scale.

Partial Sections

Many projects have only isolated areas of structural complexities. These areas are drawn in the same way as a cross section but they stop when the area of concern has been clearly drawn. This results in a partial section of a structural portion.

Figure 10.13 shows a partial section that illustrates the structural complexities existing in that portion. Additional detailing is required to make other assemblies clear.

One of these assemblies, for example, may require a

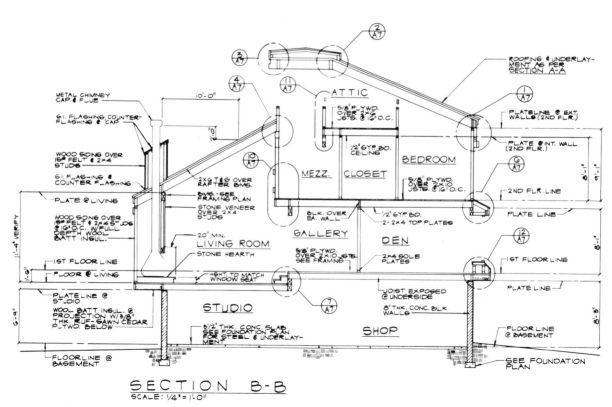

Figure 10.12 Full section. (Courtesy of Steve L. Martin.)

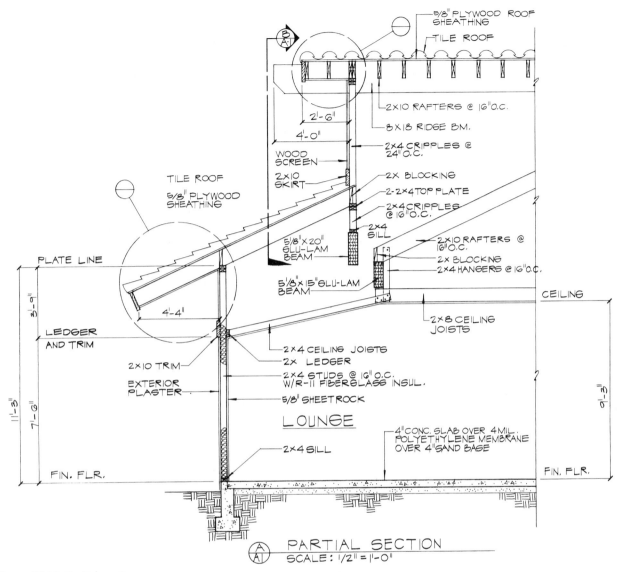

Figure 10.13 Partial section.

partial framing elevation to show a specific roof framing condition. This condition may be referenced by the use of two circles—each with directional arrows, reference letters, and numbers—attached to a broken line. Figure 10.14 shows this partial framing elevation as referenced on Figure 10.13.

Steel Sections

For buildings built mainly with steel members, use elevations to establish column and beam heights. This approach coincides with the procedures and methods for the shop drawings provided by the steel fabricator.

Figure 10.15 shows a structural section through a steel-frame building. In contrast to sections for wood-frame buildings, where vertical dimensions are used to establish plate heights, this type of section may establish column and beam heights using the top of the concrete slab

as a beginning point. Each steel column in this section has an assigned number because the columns are identified by the use of an axial reference matrix on the framing plan, shown in Figure 10.16.

Examples

These two examples of buildings show how their unique structural systems dictate different ways of showing a building section.

Example 1: A Theatre

The first building, constructed of masonry and steel, has a mainly symmetrical floor plan. Therefore, the structural design is similar for both sides, if not identical. As Figure 10.17 shows, the symmetry of this theatre may mean

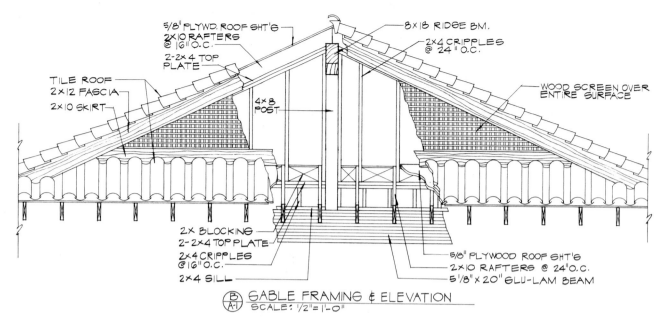

Figure 10.14 Framing elevation.

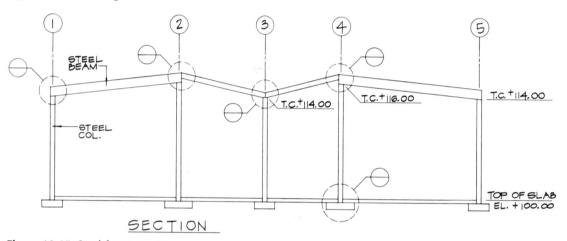

Figure 10.15 Steel frame section.

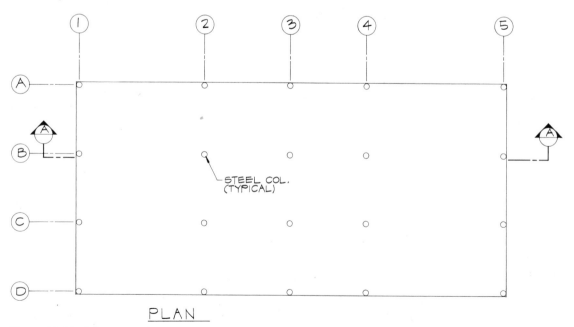

Figure 10.16 Column matrix.

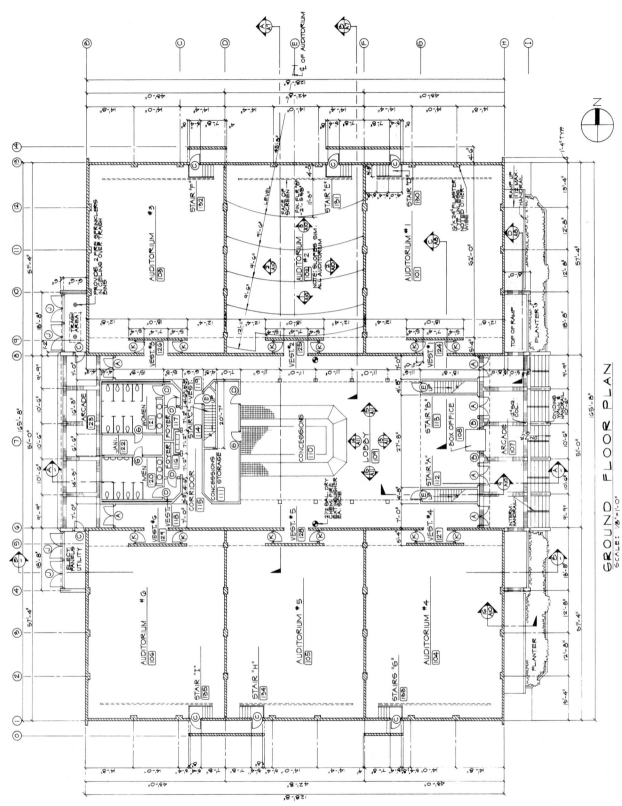

Figure 10.17 Theatre floor plan. (Courtesy of Westmount, Inc., Real Estate Development, Torrance, CA.)

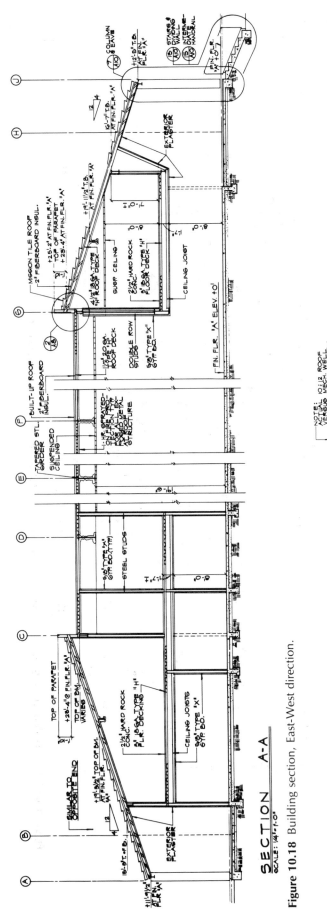

Figure 10.18 Building section, East-West direction.

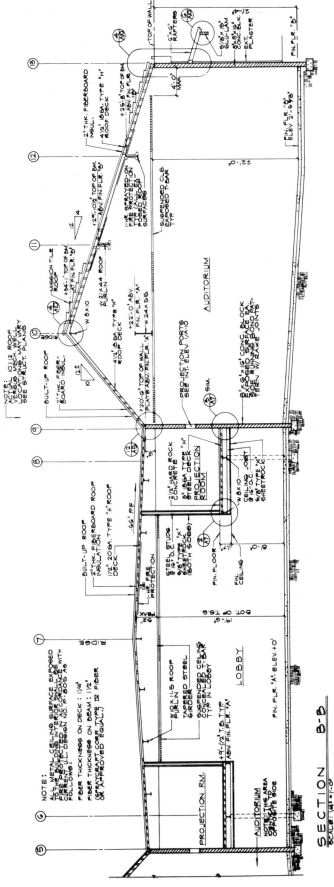

Figure 10.19 Building section, North-South direction.

that only two major building sections are required. The first section has been taken through the lobby in the East-West direction. The other has been taken through one side of the lobby in the North-South direction.

Draw the first building section, Figure 10.18 shows, by first lightly laying out the dimensional reference planes to accurately locate beams, columns, and walls relative to those shown on the floor plan in the East-West direction.

For this type of structure and its overall dimensions, a scale of ¼" = 1'–0" gives enough clarity for the members and required assemblies. Because the overall dimensions of the building are large and the area through the lobby is mainly open space, you may simply provide break lines between supporting members, as indicated between dimensional reference planes Ⓓ and Ⓔ, Ⓔ and Ⓕ, Ⓕ and Ⓖ. This helps when the size of the vellum is restricted.

When you have drawn the foundation members and concrete floor, then draft wall locations and their respective heights in place. In this way, the second floor members are shown in their respective locations. The finished ceiling is attached directly to the bottom of the steel joist. Steel decking with a 2½"-thick concrete topping is drawn in as shown. From the second floor level, plate heights are set and then minimum roof pitches are drawn, establishing the roof height at reference planes Ⓓ and Ⓖ. You can now draw all the remaining structural members, at their respective location and heights.

Because the North and South auditoriums are identical in size and structural design, you may simply provide a section through one auditorium and the lobby. See Figure 10.19. This partial building section is delineated in the same way as Figure 10.18; first, the reference planes are laid out, and then the foundation sections and the concrete floor are drawn relative to the foundation plan. The concrete floor slopes in the auditorium area. This slope ratio is determined by recommended seating and viewing standards for cinema theatres. Next, draw in the various walls and their heights.

The exterior masonry wall height at reference ⑬, established by the recommended interior ceiling height of 22'–0", satisfies the required height for the viewing screen. From the top of this wall, you can draw in the steel decking and roof assembly at a roof pitch of 4 in 12. The ridge location is established by the reference number ⑩. From this point, a roof pitch of 10 in 12 is drawn to where it intersects the lobby roof along the dimensional reference line ⑨. All the structural members for the roof and walls within the lobby area are now drawn in and noted.

For reference, show a portion of the opposite identical side for this type of partial section. In Figure 10.19 this is indicated at reference line ⑤, the back wall of the opposite auditorium. Use the correct material designation for the wall, floor, and roof materials.

Example 2: A Three-Story Office Building

This three-story office building has structural steel beams and columns as the main supporting members. Spanning the steel beams, open web **trusses** are used for the floor joists. Plywood and lightweight concrete are installed directly above the joists. Supporting members, at the ground floor level, are composed of steel columns encased in concrete, and masonry walls located at the lobby and stairway areas.

Figure 10.20 shows the ground floor plan for this structure and the dimensional axial reference planes for column and wall locations. Building section cuts have been referenced in the North-South and East-West directions. The floor plan for the second and third levels, which are similar, is provided so that the building sections can be drawn. See Figure 10.21.

The first section to draw is Section Ⓐ. This is taken between reference planes Ⓓ and Ⓔ in the East-West direction. Begin the drawing by lightly laying out the reference planes and incorporating section break lines between the reference planes as indicated between beam lines ④ and ⑤ as well as between ⑥ and ⑦. See Figure 10.22A, building section Ⓐ.

Starting from the lobby's finished floor elevation of 100.0, we establish a clearance height of approximately 8'–0" in the parking area, in which the **soffit** (finished underside of spanning members) framing elevation is designated at 108.00. Now, consult with the structural and mechanical engineers about what space is required for structural members and plumbing lines. In this case, a height of 4'–10" satisfies their requirements, thus establishing a second floor elevation of 112.8. From the second to the third floor level, a height of 14'–0" is required to satisfy the space requirements for structural and mechanical members, as well as for the desired suspended ceiling height. The space required for mechanical and electrical components is called the **plenum area**. An example of this is shown on Figure 10.22B.

A top plate height of 12'–0" or an elevation of 139.33 establishes the exterior wall height, from which point the roof pitch will be drawn. Roof rafters are drawn in with a roof pitch of 4 in 12, extending 2 feet beyond the exterior walls to provide support for the soffit framing. The steel roof beams at the various reference numbers are drawn in at various elevations to provide adequate roof drainage for the various drains located in the roof well area.

These elevations are shown at the various beam locations. From these locations, wood members are framed between the main steel beams which provide the required roof pitches. When all the required members have been drafted in, the various notes and dimensions can be lettered accordingly. When you provide notes, organize lettering as shown on reference lines ⑤, ⑦, and ⑩ in Figure 10.22A.

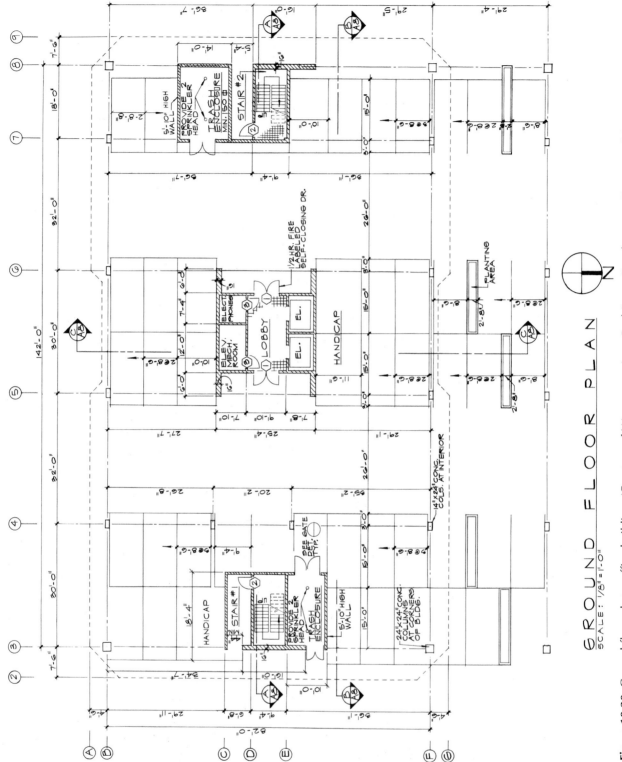

G R O U N D   F L O O R   P L A N
SCALE: 1/8" = 1'-0"

Figure 10.20 Ground floor plan—office building. (Courtesy of Westmount, Inc., Real Estate Development, Torrance, CA.)

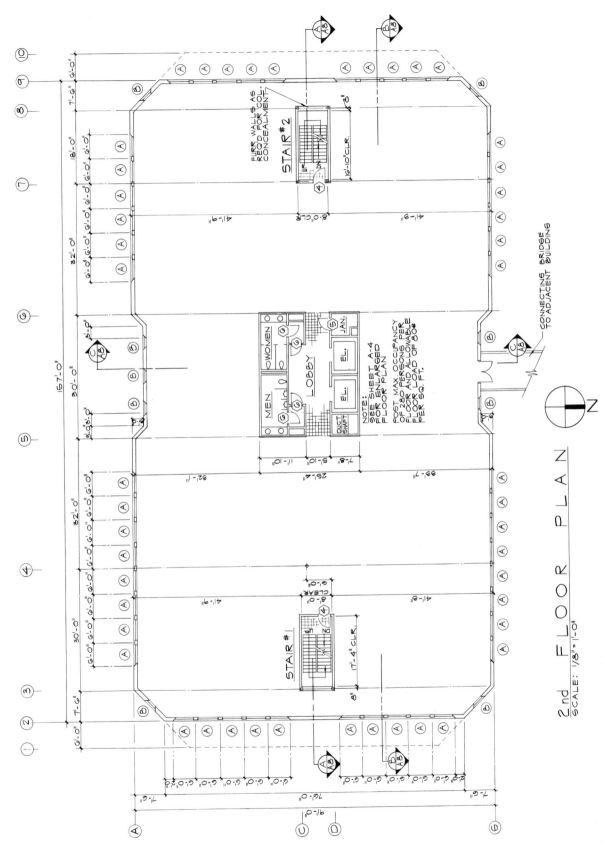

Figure 10.21 Floor plan—2nd level of office building. (Courtesy of Westmount, Inc., Real Estate Development, Torrance, CA.)

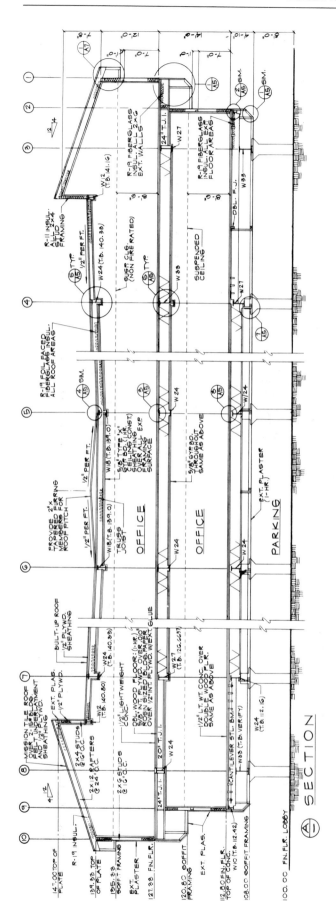

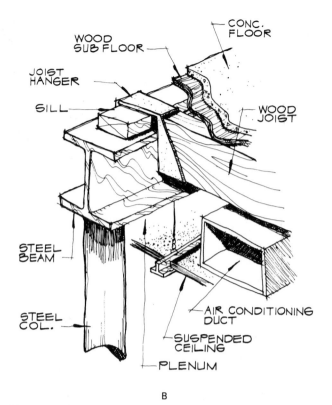

Figure 10.22B Plenum area.

Figure 10.22A Office building section—East-West direction. (Courtesy of Westmount, Inc., Real Estate Development, Torrance, CA.)

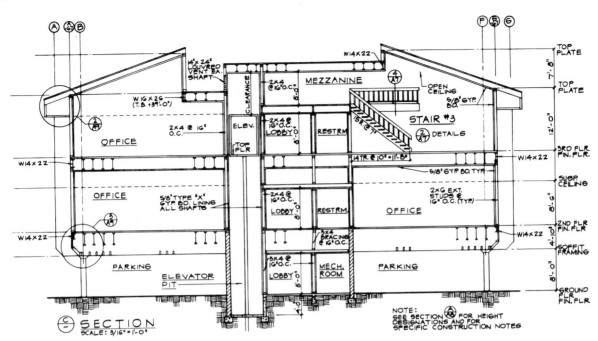

Figure 10.23 Office building section—North-South direction. (Courtesy of Westmount, Inc., Real Estate Development, Torrance, CA.)

Building section ©, cut in the North-South direction, is shown in Figure 10.23. This section is drawn in the same way as building section Ⓐ. However, many of the notes have not been shown because they are identical to those noted in section Ⓐ. This is acceptable practice as long as you make clear they are identical, as is done in this case at the bottom of reference Ⓕ. In this way, changes can be made on one drawing and also corrected elsewhere. The section shown in Figure 10.23 was taken through an area with many elements relevant to the construction process.

Checklist for Building Sections

This checklist covers the basic information that should be found on building sections as well as characteristics of a well-thought-out set of sections.

1. Sections that clearly depict the structural conditions existing in the building.
2. Sections referenced on plans and elevations.
3. Dimensioning for the following (where applicable):
   a. Floor to top plate
   b. Floor to floor
   c. Floor to ceiling
   d. Floor to top of wall
   e. Floor to top of column or beam
   f. Cantilevers, overhangs, offsets, etc.
   g. Foundation details
4. Elevations for top of floor, top of columns and beams.
5. Call-out information for all members, such as:
   a. Size, material, and shape of member
   b. Spacing of members
6. Call-out information for all assemblies if enlarged details are not provided.
7. Column and beam matrix identification if incorporated in the structural plan.
8. Call out for sub-floor and sheathing assembly.
9. Roof pitches and indication of all slopes.
10. Reference symbols for all details and assemblies that are enlarged for clarity.
11. Designation of material for protection of finish for roof, ceiling, wall, and structural members.
12. Structural notes applicable to each particular section, such as:
    a. Nailing schedules
    b. Splice dimensions
13. Structural sections corresponding accurately to foundation, floor, and framing plans.
14. Scale of drawing provided.

EXTERIOR
ELEVATIONS

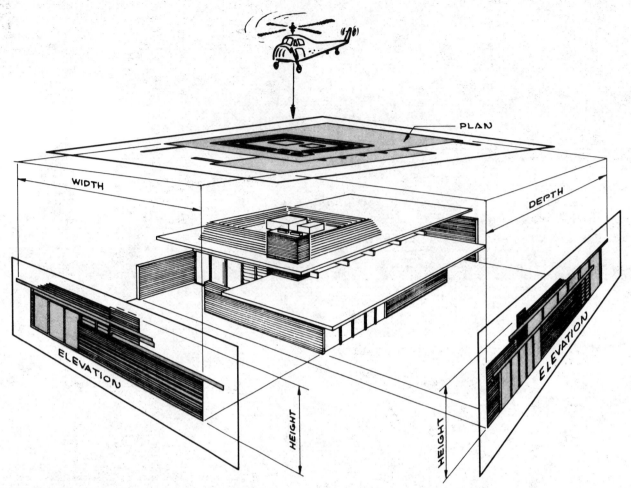

Figure 11.1 Multi-view drawing of a structure (Wakita, *Perspective Drawing: A Student Text/Workbook,* Kendall/Hunt Publishing Co., 1978. Reprinted with permission).

Exterior Elevations

Purpose

Exterior elevations are an important part of a set of construction documents because they can show information not found anywhere else in the set.

The exterior elevations will:

1. Describe exterior materials found on the structure.
2. Provide a location for horizontal and vertical dimensions not found elsewhere.
3. Show, by using hidden lines, structural members that are found inside the walls. (Diagonal bracing is a good example of such hidden members.)
4. Show the relationship of two elements such as the height of the chimney in relationship to the roof of the structure.
5. Incorporate reference bubbles for building, window, and door sections.
6. Show any exterior design elements that cannot be shown elsewhere.

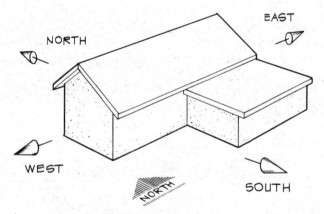

Figure 11.2 Names of elevations.

Basic Approach

In mechanical or engineering drafting, the elevations are described as the front, side, and rear. In architecture, exterior elevations are called North, South, East, and West. See Figure 11.1. Figure 11.2 shows how we arrive at the names for exterior elevations.

Orientation

The North, South, East, and West elevations may not be true North or true East. They might have been taken from an "orientation North," which may not be parallel to true North. For example, if a structure's boundaries are not parallel with true North, an orientation North is established, and used from then on to describe the various elevations. See Figure 11.3.

These terms, then, refer to the direction the structure is facing. In other words, if an elevation is drawn of the face of a structure that is facing south, the elevation is called the South elevation; the face of the structure that is facing west is called the West elevation, and so on. Remember, the title refers to the direction the structure is facing, *not* to the direction in which you are looking at it.

Finally, because of the size of the exterior elevations, they are rarely drawn next to the plan view as in mechanical drafting. See Figure 11.4.

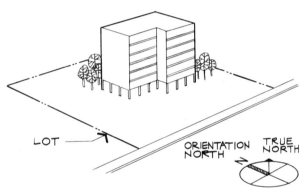

Figure 11.3 Use of orientation North.

Method 1: Direct Projection

Exterior elevations can be drafted by directly projecting sizes from the plan views or sections. Figure 11.5 shows how elevations can be directly projected from a plan view (a roof plan in this case). Figure 11.6 shows how the heights are obtained. Locations of doors, windows, and other details are taken from the floor plan. Figure 11.7 shows a slightly more complex roof being used to form the roof shape on an elevation.

Method 2: Dimensional Layout

Exterior elevations can also be drafted by taking the dimensions from the plans and sections and drafting the elevation from scratch. First, lightly lay out the critical vertical measurements. In the example shown in Figure 11.8, these measurements are the sub-floor line and the plate line, (top of the two top plates above the studs). See Figure 11.9A. This measurement is taken directly from the building section.

The second step establishes the location of the walls and offsets in the structure from the floor plan. Draw these lines lightly because changes in line length may be required later. See Figure 11.9B.

Third, establish the grade line (earth) in relationship to the floor line. See Figure 11.9C. This dimension is from the building sections or footing sections.

Next, as Figure 11.9D shows, the roof configuration is added. To better understand the relationship between the roof and structure, draw the **eave** in a simple form as shown in Figure 11.9E. These dimensions are found on the building section. The finished roof shape depends on the roof framing plan or the roof plan for dimensions. See Figure 11.9F.

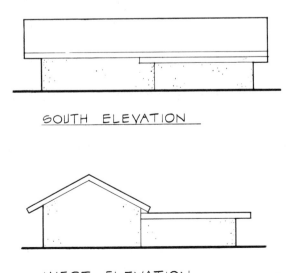

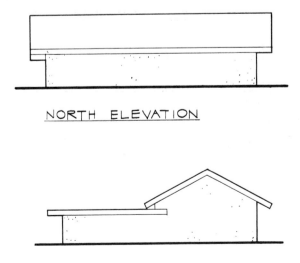

Figure 11.4 Elevation arrangement.

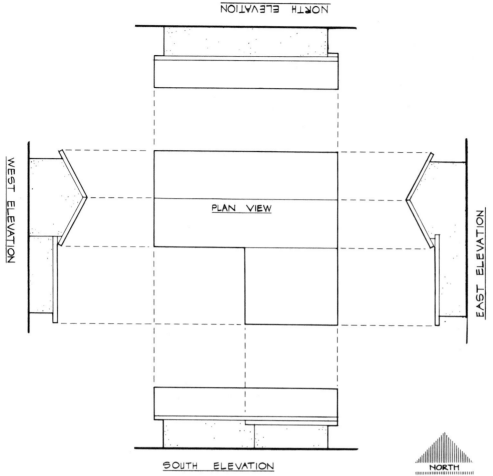

Figure 11.5 Obtaining width and depth dimensions.

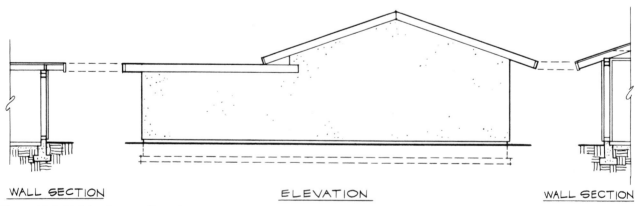

Figure 11.6 Heights from wall sections.

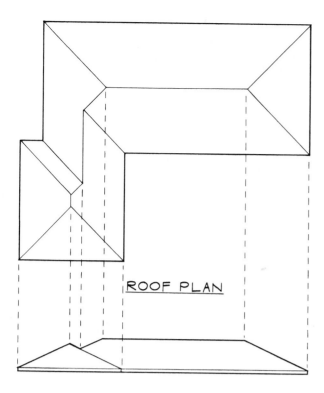

ROOF PLAN

ELEVATION OF ROOF

Figure 11.7 Roof elevation from roof plan.

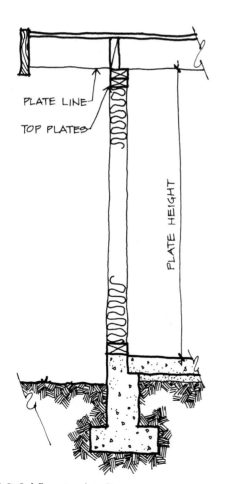

PLATE LINE

TOP PLATES

PLATE HEIGHT

Figure 11.8 Subfloor to plate line.

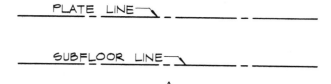

PLATE LINE

SUBFLOOR LINE

A

Figure 11.9A Establishing floor and plate lines.

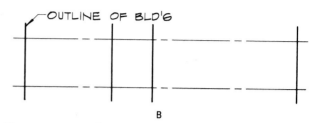

OUTLINE OF BLD'G

B

Figure 11.9B Drafting exterior outline.

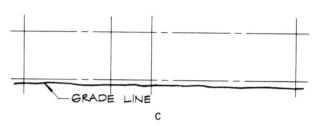

GRADE LINE

C

Figure 11.9C Establishing the grade line.

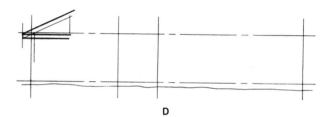

D

Figure 11.9D Incorporating the roof structure into the exterior elevation.

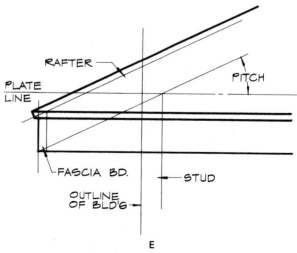

RAFTER

PITCH

PLATE LINE

FASCIA BD.

STUD

OUTLINE OF BLD'G

E

Figure 11.9E Rough eave detail.

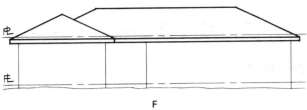

Figure 11.9F Finishing the roof shape.

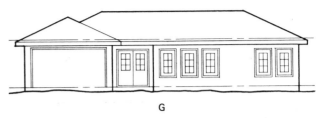

Figure 11.9G Locating doors and windows.

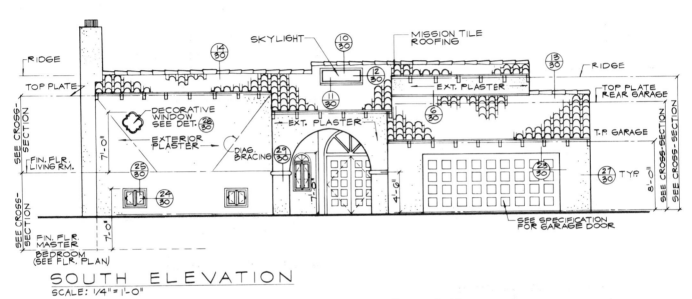

Figure 11.10 Drafted South elevation of a condominium (Courtesy of William F. Smith—Builder).

Figure 11.11 Pictorial view of South elevation of a condominium (Courtesy of William F. Smith—Builder, Aerial Photography by William Boggs. Reprinted with permission).

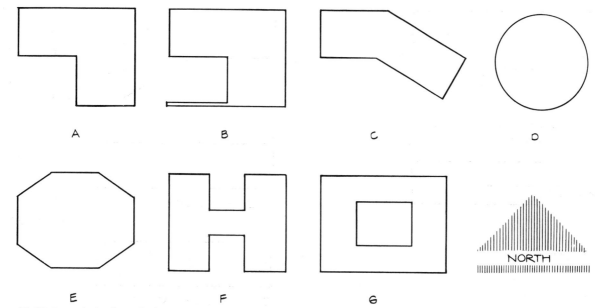

A   B   C   D

E   F   G

Figure 11.12 Irregularly shaped plans.

Finally, windows and doors are located. Sizes are found on the window and door schedule and locations on the floor plan. Material designations, dimensions, notes, and structural descriptions complete the elevation. See Figure 11.9G.

To help you visualize the transition from a drafted elevation to the actual building, see Figures 11.10 and 11.11. Compare the drafted elevation with the photograph.

Choice of Scale

Selection of the scale for elevations is based on the size and complexity of the project and the available drawing space. For small structures, $1/4'' = 1'-0''$ is a common scale. The exterior elevation is usually drawn at the same scale as the floor plan. For medium and large elevations, you may have to decrease the scale in relationship to the floor plans.

Because we are dealing with small structures, two to four stories in height, we are using the largest scale allowed by the available drawing space not exceeding $1/4'' = 1'-0''$.

Odd-Shaped Plans

Not all plans are rectangular; some have irregular shapes and angles. Figure 11.12 shows several building shapes and the North designation.

Shape A. Figure 11.13 shows the exterior elevations for a relatively simple L-shaped building and how these elevations were obtained using the projection method.

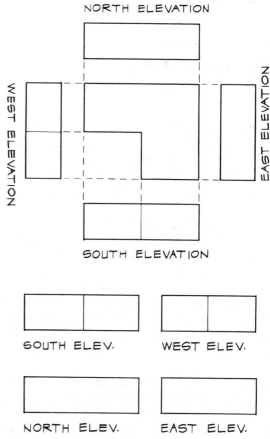

Figure 11.13 Elevations for Shape A.

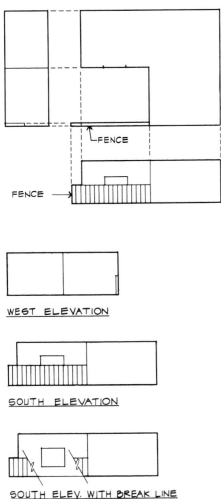

WEST ELEVATION

SOUTH ELEVATION

SOUTH ELEV. WITH BREAK LINE

Figure 11.14 Elevations for Shape B.

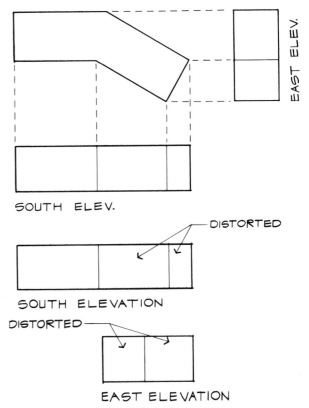

SOUTH ELEV.

SOUTH ELEVATION

EAST ELEVATION

Figure 11.15 Elevations for Shape C.

Shape B. The elevations for Shape B on Figure 11.14 present a unique problem on the East and particularly the South elevation. Because the fence is in the same plane as the south side of the structure, include it in the South elevation. Had the fence been in front of the structure, you could either delete it or include it in order to show its relationship to the structure itself.

The inclusion of the fence may pose additional problems such as preventing a view of portions of the structure behind. You can overcome this difficulty in one of two ways: either eliminate the fence altogether (not show it) or use a break line, as shown in Figure 11.14. This allows any item behind it, such as the window, to be exposed, referenced, and dimensioned. Break lines still allow dimensioning and descriptions of the fence.

Shape C. The two portions on the right of the South elevation and all of the East elevation are *not* true shapes and sizes because they are drawn as direct 90° projections from the *left* portion of the plan view. This is sometimes a problem. See Figure 11.15. The West and North elevations will also have distortions. See Figure 11.12.

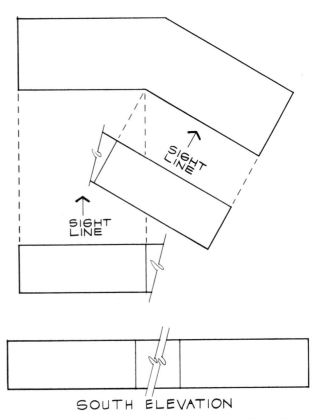

SOUTH ELEVATION

Figure 11.16 Elevations with new sight line. (William Boggs Aerial Photography, Printed with permission).

To solve this problem, we use an auxiliary view: a view that is 90° to the line of sight. The elevations are projected 90° to the sight lines and a break line is used to stop that portion which is not true. Notice on Figure 11.16 how the break line splits the South elevation into two parts. Each part is projected independently of the other, and its continuation, which is not a true shape, is voided.

The South elevation in Figure 11.15 appears to have three parts rather than two, as in Figure 11.16. In the latter case, the third part will be left to the East elevation. With a more complex shape, a break line beyond the true surface being projected can be confusing. See Figure 11.17. To avoid confusion, introduce a pivot point (P.P.) and show it as a dotted (hidden) line or a center-line type line (dots and dashes). See Figure 11.18. Use a **pivot point**. (A pivot point is the point at which the end of one elevation becomes the beginning of another elevation.)

Pivot points can cause a problem in selecting a title for a particular elevation. To avoid confusion, introduce a **key plan**. The key plan is usually drawn on the bottom right corner of the drawing sheet. See Figure 11.19. Draw and label a reference bubble for every necessary elevation. These reference bubbles will become the title for the elevation. If the surface contains important information about the structure or surface materials, it deserves a reference bubble. Figure 11.20 shows how these elevations are represented with titles and pivot point notations.

Shape D. With Shape D, in Figure 11.12, nothing is true shape and size, regardless of the direction of the elevation. See Figure 11.21. Figure 11.22 shows a pivot point together with a fold-out (called a "development drawing" in mechanical drawing).

Shape E. Shape E in Figure 11.12 can be drawn in one of three ways: first, drawing it as a direct projection so that one of the three exposed faces will be in true shape

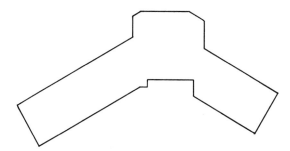

Figure 11.17 Complicated shape.

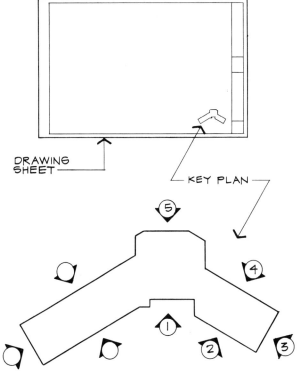

Figure 11.19 Using a key plan.

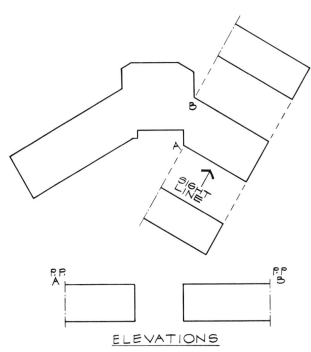

Figure 11.18 Use of pivot point in exterior elevations.

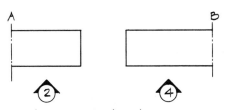

Figure 11.20 Elevations using key plan.

and size; second, using a key plan and drawing each surface individually; and third drawing it as a fold out similar to Figure 11.22. Choose the method that will explain the elevations best. For example, if all other sides are the same, the direct projection method may be the best. If every wall surface is different, then the key plan or fold-out method is best.

Shape F. Surfaces that will be hidden in a direct projection, such as some of the surfaces of Shape F in Figure

11.12, can effectively be dealt with in one of two ways. The first uses a key plan and the second uses a combination of an elevation and a section. Both methods are shown in Figure 11.23. The combination of the section and the elevation shows the structure and its relationship to the elevation more clearly.

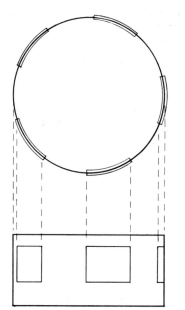

Figure 11.21 Elevations of a cylinder.

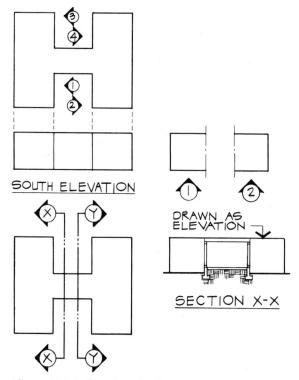

Figure 11.23 Elevations for Shape F.

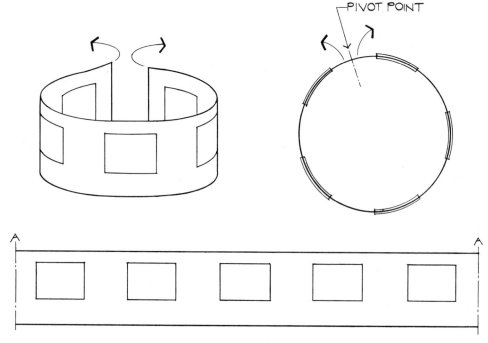

Figure 11.22 Elevation of cylinder using pivot point.

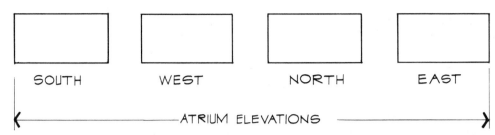

Figure 11.24 Simplified elevation titles.

Shape G. Shape G in Figure 11.12 can be drawn simply as the South elevation, North elevation, East elevation, and West elevation using a direct projection method. The interior space (atrium) can also be drawn as a direct projection with titles "Atrium North Elevation," "Atrium South Elevation," "Atrium East Elevation," and "Atrium West Elevation." A way to simplify this is shown in Figure 11.24.

Drawing Doors and Windows

Draw doors and windows on elevations as closely as possible to the actual configuration. Horizontal location dimensions need not be included because they are on the floor plan; and door and window sizes are contained in the door and window schedule. However, vertical location dimensions are shown with indications of how the doors and windows open.

Doors

Doors and their surface materials can be delineated in various ways. Illustrations A and B in Figure 11.25 show the basic appearance of a door with and without surface materials—wood grain in this instance. Illustration C shows the final configuration of a dimensioned door. Note that the 6'–8" dimension is measured from the floor line to the top of the door. The other line around the door represents the trim. For precise dimensions for the trim, consult the door details. Illustrations D and E of Figure 11.25 show how a door opens or slides. Panel doors are shown in Illustration F, while plant-on doors (doors with decorative pieces attached) are shown in Illustration G.

Windows

Windows are drafted much like doors. Their shape, their operation, and the direction in which they open is rep-

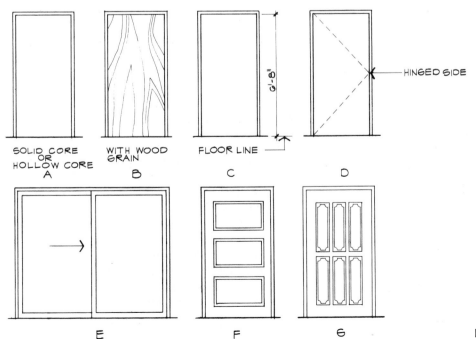

Figure 11.25 Doors in elevation.

resented. Double-hung windows and louver windows are obvious exceptions because of their operation. See Figure 11.26.

On the double-hung and the sliding windows, one portion of the window is shown in its entirety while the moving section shows only three sides of the window. Using the sliding window as an example, the right side of the window shows all four sides because it is on the outside. The left section shows only three sides because the fourth is behind the right section.

Fixed Windows.   If the window is fixed (non-opening), as shown in Figure 11.27, you must know if the window

is to be shop made (manufactured ahead of time) or constructed on the job. If the frame can be ordered—in aluminum for example—treat it like other manufactured windows and include it in the window schedule. If the window is to be job made (made on the site), provide all the necessary information about the window on the window schedule or exterior elevations as shown in Figure 11.28. However, keep all this information in one place for consistency and uniformity.

Referencing Doors and Windows

Reference doors and windows with bubbles. Bubbles can refer to details or to a schedule for size. See Figure 11.28. If, for some reason, there are no schedules or details for a set of drawings, all information pertaining to the windows or doors will be on the exterior elevations near or on the windows and doors. See Figure 11.27.

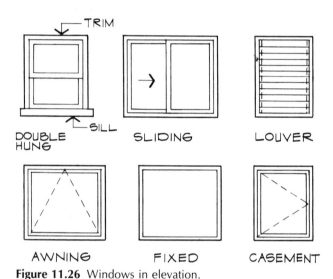

Figure 11.26 Windows in elevation.

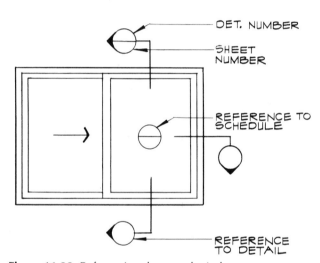

Figure 11.28 Referencing doors and windows.

Material Designations

Describing the Materials

The exterior elevations also describe the exterior wall surface material. For a wood structure, describe both the surface covering and any backing material. **Wood siding**, for example, is described with the backing behind it. See Figure 11.29.

In some cases, one word, such as "stucco," describes the surface adequately unless a special pattern is to be applied. Here, the draftsperson assumes that the contractor understands that the word "stucco" implies building felt, (black waterproof paper) mesh, (hexagonal woven wire) and three coats of exterior plaster. Often a more detailed description of the material is found in the specifications.

Figure 11.27 A fixed window.

Even if the complete wall is made up of one material such as concrete block (as opposed to a built-up system as in wood construction) describe the surface. See Figure 11.30.

Drawing the Materials

In both Figures 11.29 and 11.30 a facsimile of the material is shown. The material represented does not fill the complete area but is shown in detail around the perimeter only, which saves production time. Figure 11.31 shows more of the area covered with the surface material but in a slightly more abstract manner. Another method is to draft the surface accurately and erase areas for notes.

Figure 11.32 shows other materials as they might appear in an exterior elevation. These are only suggestions. Scale and office practice dictate the final technique. See Figure 11.33.

Eliminating Unnecessary Information

Because exterior elevations are vital in the construction document process, unnecessary information should be eliminated. Shades and shadows, cars, bushes and trees, people and flowers add to the looks of the drawings *but* serve no purpose here.

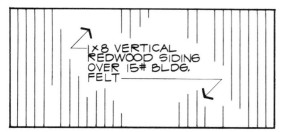

Figure 11.29 Wood siding in elevation.

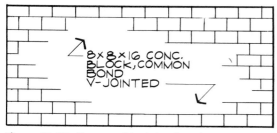

Figure 11.30 Concrete block in elevation.

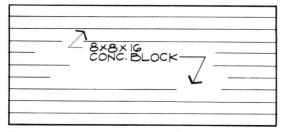

Figure 11.31 Abbreviated concrete block pattern.

Notes

Order of Notes

Notes on elevations follow the same rules as notes on other drawings. The size of the object is first, then the name of the material, and then any additional information about spacing, quantity, or methods of installation. For example,

1″ × 8″ redwood siding over 15# (15 lb) building felt

OR

Cement plaster over concrete block

OR

Built-up Composition Gravel Roof

OR

1″ × 6″ let-in bracing

In the second example, there are no specific sizes needed, so the generic name comes first in the note.

Noting Practices

Noting practices vary from job to job. A set of written specifications is often provided with the construction documents. Wall material on a set of elevations may be described in broad, generic terms such as "concrete block" when the specific size, finish, stacking procedure, and type of joint is covered in the specifications.

If there are differences between the construction documents and the specifications, the specifications have priority. In the construction documents, often the same material note can be found more than once. If an error is made or a change is desired, many notes must be revised. In the specifications, where it is mentioned once, only a single change has to be made.

There are exceptions. When there are complicated changes and variations of material and patterns on an elevation, it is difficult to describe them in the specifications. In this case, the information should be located on the exterior elevations. See Figure 11.33.

Dotted Lines

Doors and Windows

Dotted lines are used on doors and windows to show how they operate. See Illustration D of Figure 11.25 and the awning and casement windows in Figure 11.26. These dotted lines show which part of the door or window is hinged. See Figure 11.34. Not all offices like to show this on an elevation. One reason is that the direction the door swings is shown on the floor plan and therefore does not need to be indicated on the elevations.

the elevations in order to explain the foundation better. Dotted lines are used in various ways relating to the foundation. Dotted lines (center-line type lines are also

Foundations

At times you may have to delineate the foundation on

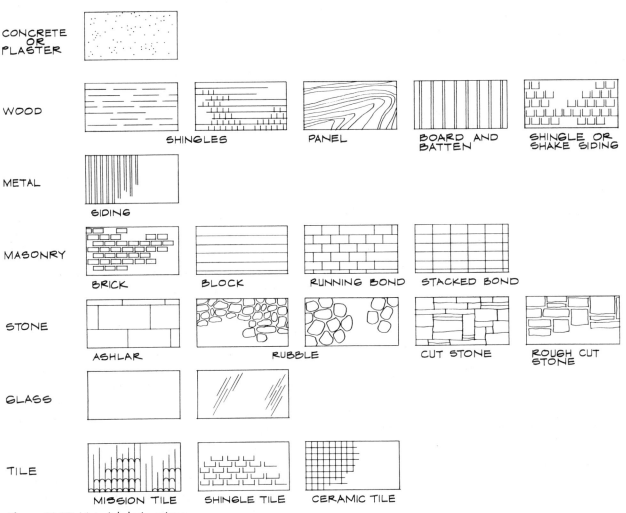

Figure 11.32 Material designations.

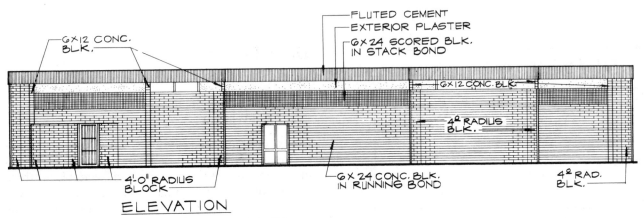

Figure 11.33 Masonry structure with variations in building patterns.

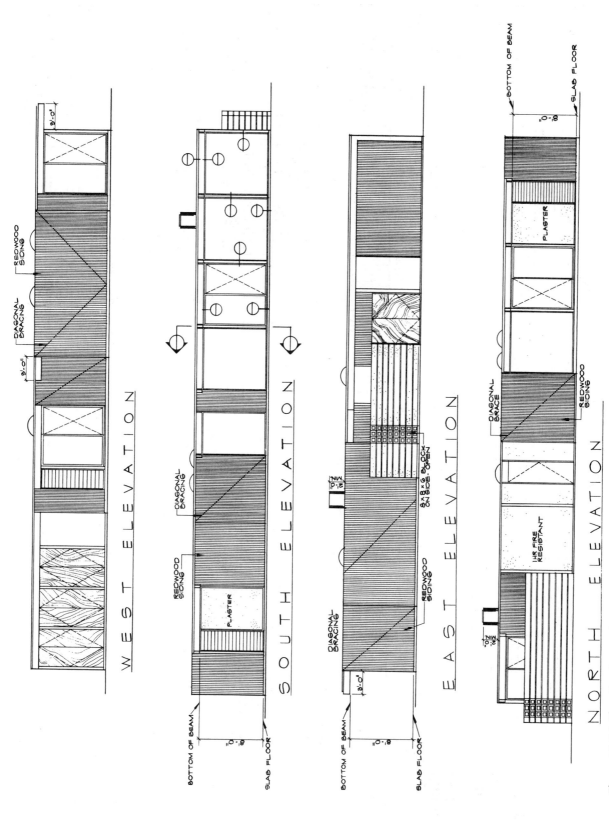

Figure 11.34 Elevation in wood.

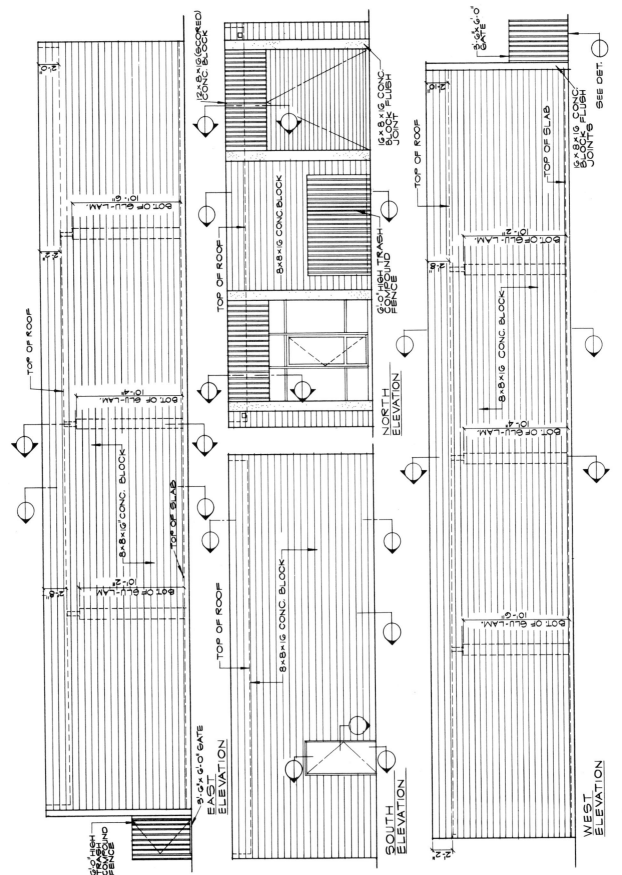

Figure 11.35 Elevation in masonry.

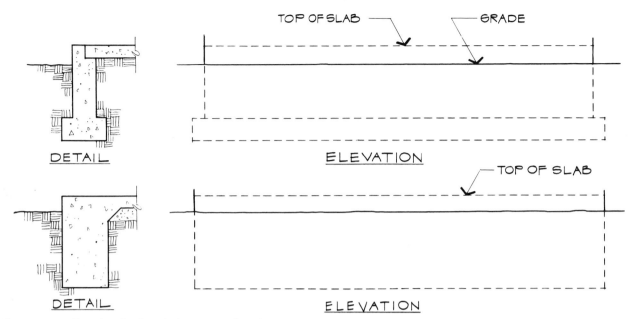

Figure 11.36 Showing the foundation on an elevation.

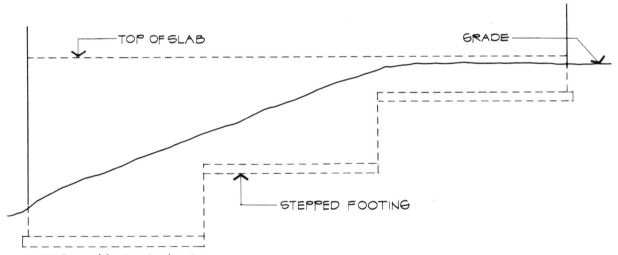

Figure 11.37 Stepped footings in elevation.

used) show the top of a slab as in Figure 11.35. They are used to show the elevation of the footings. See Figure 11.36 for elevations of a two-pour footing and a one-pour footing.

Dotted lines are also used to describe a **stepped footing**. When the property slopes, the minimum depth of the footing can be maintained by stepping the footing down the slope. See Figure 11.37.

Structural Features

Structural features below the grade can be shown by dotted lines if this helps to explain the structure. See Figure 11.38. Dotted lines can also be used to help show

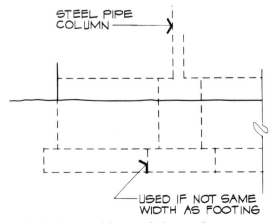

Figure 11.38 Structural features below grade.

structural elements of the building. In Figure 11.10, center-line type lines (which can also be used) show **let-in braces** (structural angular braces in a wall). (The plate line is the top of the two horizontal members at the top of the wall, called **top plates**.) In Figure 11.35, dotted lines show the top of the roof, which slopes for drainage, and a pilaster (a widening of the wall for a beam) and beam (here, a laminated beam called a Glu-lam).

As with doors and windows, the footing on an elevation can be referenced to the foundation plan, details, and cross sections. The system is the same. Reference bubbles are used. See Figure 11.39.

Whatever the feature, the dotted line is used for clarity and communication. How can you keep the message clear for construction purposes? How can you communicate this best on the drawings?

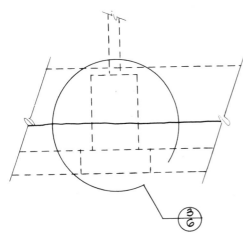

Figure 11.39 Referencing hidden lines.

Controlling Factors

Each type of construction has unique restrictive features that you need to know about to effectively interpret the transition from design elevations to production of exterior elevations in the construction documents.

Wood Frame Structures

With wood frame structures, elevations are usually dictated by plate line heights. The **plate height** is measured from the floor to the top of the two top plates. See Figure 11.8. Efficient use of material is dictated by this dimension because studs are available in certain lengths and sheathing usually comes in 4' × 8' sheets.

Floor, Plate, and Grade Lines. When the floor elevations and plate heights are established, the first thing to

draw is the floor line and its relationship to the grade. Next, draw the plate line. If the structure is of post and beam construction, measure from the floor line to the bottom of the beam. Some offices prefer these dimensions on the building sections.

Find the distance between the floor line and the grade line from the grading plan, foundation plan, footing details, and building sections. If the lot is relatively flat, just draw a grade line with the floor line measured above it and the plate line height above the floor as a start. If the site is not flat, carefully plot the grade line from the grading plan, foundation plan, and details or the site plan.

Some site plans, grading plans, and foundation plans indicate the grade height, marked F.G. (finished grade), in relation to the structure at various points around the structure. In Figure 11.40, the grade line is figured by making a grid where the horizontal lines show grade heights and vertical lines are projected down from the structure. Once this grade line is established, the top of the slab—that is, the floor line—is drawn. The plate line is then measured from the floor line. There is no need to measure the distance between the grade and the floor line. See Figure 11.41.

Masonry Structures

Masonry structures such as brick or concrete block must be approached differently. The deciding factor here is the size of the concrete block or brick, the pattern, the thickness of the joint, and the placement of the first row in relationship to the floor. Unlike wood, which can be cut in varying heights, masonry units are difficult to cut, so cutting is minimized. As Figure 11.33 shows, dimensions of the masonry areas are kept to a minimum. Refer to the discussion of noting, earlier in this chapter, for suggested practices and sample illustrations.

Steel Structures

Structures where the main members are steel and the secondary members are, for example, wood, are treated differently from wood structures or masonry. The configuration is arrived at in the same way and representation of material is the same, but dimensioning is completely different.

In a wood frame structure, the lumber can be cut to size on the job. In masonry, the size of the masonry units often dictates such things as the location of windows and doors, the modular height, and so on. Some of the controlling factors in steel construction are: the size of the structural members; the required ceiling heights; and the **plenum** area (the space necessary to accommodate the mechanical equipment and duct work). See Figure 11.42.

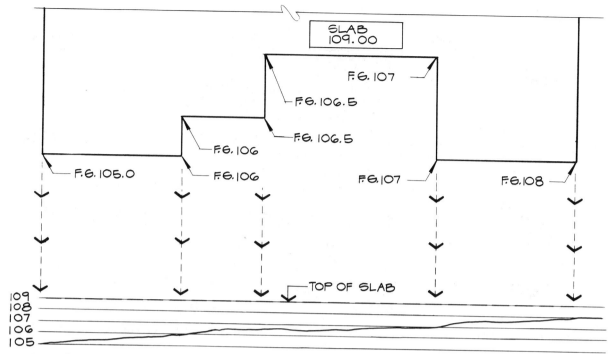

Figure 11.40 Plotting grade lines for an elevation.

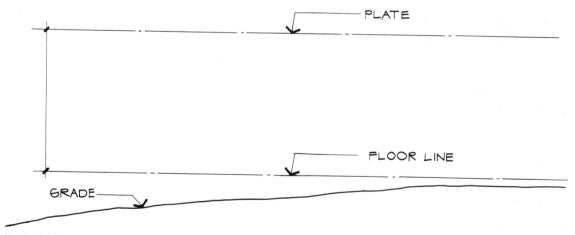

Figure 11.41 Preliminary steps for drafting an elevation with grade variation.

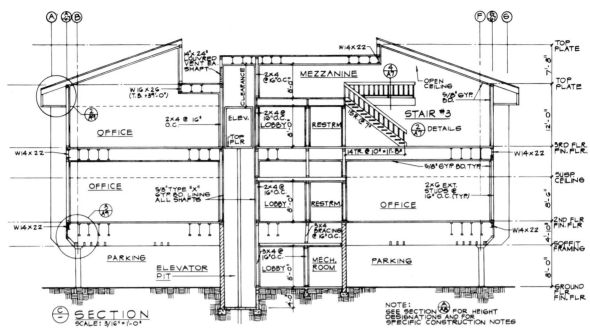

Figure 11.42 Section of a steel and wood structure (Courtesy of Westmount, Inc., Real Estate Development, Torrance, CA.).

Drawing an exterior elevation for a steel structure is a relatively simple task. Usually, the floor elevations on a multi-story structure of steel are established by the designer. The building section usually provides the necessary height requirements. See Figure 11.42. Figure 11.43 is a check list for exterior elevations.

EXTERIOR ELEVATIONS

1. Natural grade
2. Finish grade
3. Floor elevations
4. Foundation (hidden lines)
   a. Bottom of footing
   b. Top of foundation (stepped footing)
   c. Detail reference
5. Walls
   a. Material
      (1) Wood
      (2) Stucco
      (3) Aluminum
      (4) Other
   b. Solid sheathing
      (1) Plywood
      (2) 1 × 6 diagonal
      (3) Other
   c. Diagonal bracing (hidden lines)
      (1) Cut-in
      (2) Let-in
6. Openings
   a. Heights
      (1) Door and window min. 6' -8"
      (2) Post and beam special
   b. Doors
      (1) Type
      (2) Material
      (3) Glass
      (4) Detail reference
      (5) Key to schedule
   c. Windows
      (1) Type

      (2) Material
      (3) Glass - obscure for baths
      (4) Detail reference
      (5) Key to schedule
   d. Moulding, casing and sill
   e. Flashing (gauge used)
7. Roof
   a. Materials
      (1) Built-up composition, gravel
      (2) Asphalt shingles
      (3) Wood shingles or shake
      (4) Metal-terne-aluminum
      (5) Clay and ceramic tile
      (6) Concrete
   b. Other
8. Ground slopage
9. Attic and sub floor vents
10. Vertical dimensions from floor to plate
11. Window, door fascia, etc. detail references
12. Roof slope ratio
13. Railings, note height
14. Stairs
15. Note all wall materials
16. Types of fixed glass and thicknesses
17. Window and door swing indications
18. Window and door heights from floor
19. Gutters and downspouts
20. Overflow scuppers at parapets
21. Mail slot
22. Stepped foundation footings - if occur
23. Dimension chimney above roof

Figure 11.43 Exterior Elevations Checklist

ROOF AND
CEILING FRAMING

12

Methods of Representation

There are two main ways to represent floor, ceiling, and roof framing members as part of construction documents: drawing framing members on the floor plan and drawing them separately.

Drawing Framing Members on the Floor Plan

This first method illustrates and notes ceiling and/or floor framing members directly onto the finished floor plan. It is a good method to use when the framing conditions are simple and do not require many notes and reference symbols that might be confused with the other finished floor plan information.

Figure 12.1 shows the lower floor plan of a two-story residence. This plan contains all the information and symbols needed; no separate drawing of the ceiling framing members is required. Note how the ceiling joist size, spacing, and direction are illustrated in bedroom #1 and the study. Note also the use of broken lines to represent exposed ceiling beams in the master bedroom. As you can see, if a great deal more framing information were required, the drawing would lose its clarity.

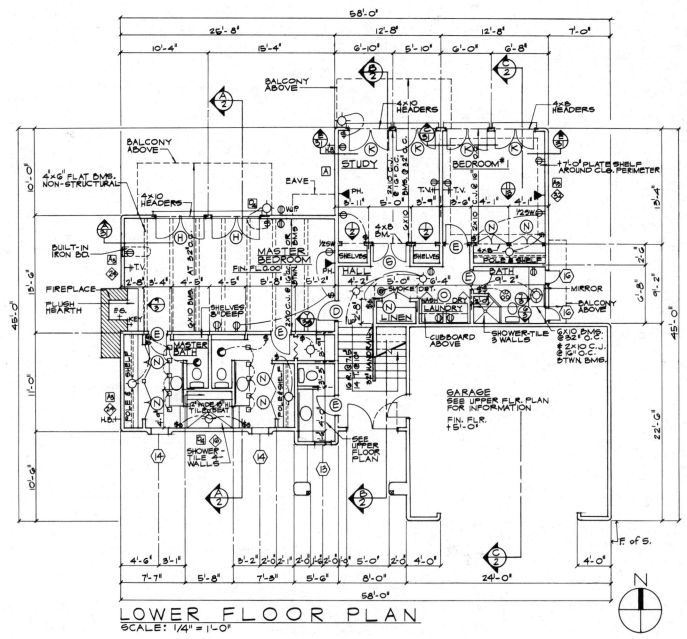

Figure 12.1 Ceiling framing on finished floor plan. (Courtesy of William F. Smith—Builder.)

The upper floor plan of this residence designates ceiling joist sizes, spacing, and direction, as well as roof framing information such as rafter sizes, spacing, and direction; ridge beam size; and the size and spacing of exposed rafter beams in the living room. See Figure 12.2A. **Headers** and beams for framing support over openings are also shown in this figure. If you are using this method to show framing members, you can delineate beams with two broken lines at the approximate scale of the beam or with a heavy broken line.

The structural design of beams and footings is calculated by finding the total loads that are distributed to any specific member. This total load is found by computing the tributary area effecting that member. Figure 12.2B illustrates a cross section showing the various tributary areas which accumulate loads to the ridgebeam, floor beam, and foundation pier.

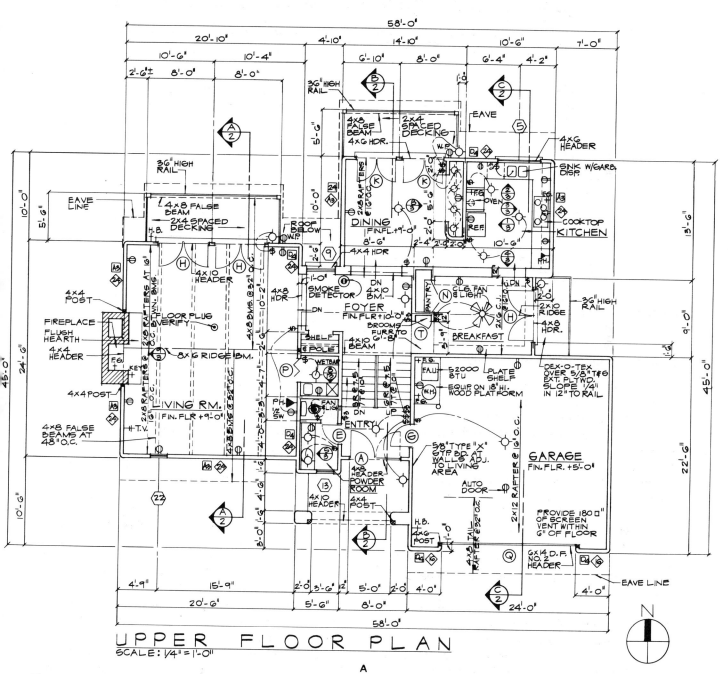

Figure 12.2A Ceiling and roof framing on finished floor plan. (Courtesy of William F. Smith—Builder.)

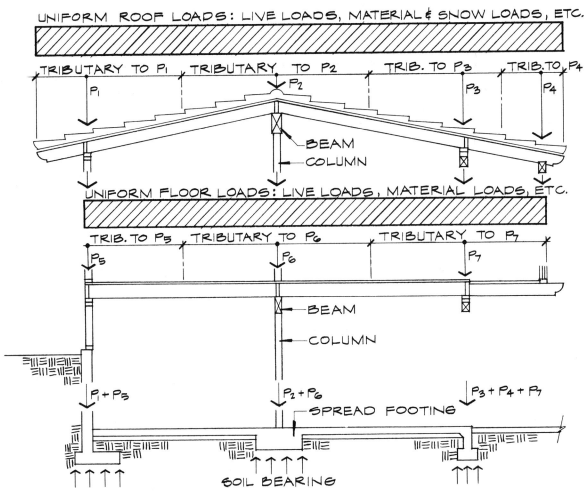

Figure 12.2B Tributary loading section.

Drawing Framing Members Separately

The second way to show ceiling, floor, and roof framing members is to provide a separate drawing that may be titled "ceiling framing," "floor framing," or "roof framing." You might choose this method because the framing is complex or because construction document procedures require it.

The first step is the same as that of the foundation plan's. Lay a piece of tracing paper directly over the floor plan tracing. Trace all the walls, windows, and door openings. The line quality of your tracing should be only dark enough to make these lines distinguishable after you have reproduced the tracing. In this way, the final drawing, showing all the framing members, can be drawn with darker lines like a finished drawing. This provides the viewer with clear framing members, while the walls are just lightly drawn for reference.

Another way to provide a basis for a framing plan is to reproduce the floor plan from the initial line drawing with a mylar or sepia print. By doing this, you can print the floor plan drawing when only the walls and openings

have been established. Later, when you are prepared for framing plans, you can go back to these prints and incorporate all the required information to complete the framing plan.

Figure 12.3 shows the floor plan of the first floor of a two-story, wood framed residence with all the framing members required to support the second floor and ceiling directly above this level. Because the second floor framing and ceiling for the first floor are the same, this drawing is titled "Upper Floor Framing Plan."

First draft in all the floor beams, columns, and headers for all the various openings. Then incorporate the location and span direction of all the floor joists into the drawing. In Figure 12.3, the floor joist locations and span directions are shown with a single line and arrowhead at each end of the line. This is one way to designate these members. Another method is shown later when the roof framing plan is discussed.

Dimensioning for framing plans mainly applies to beam and column locations. Provide dimensioning for all floor beams and columns located directly under load-bearing

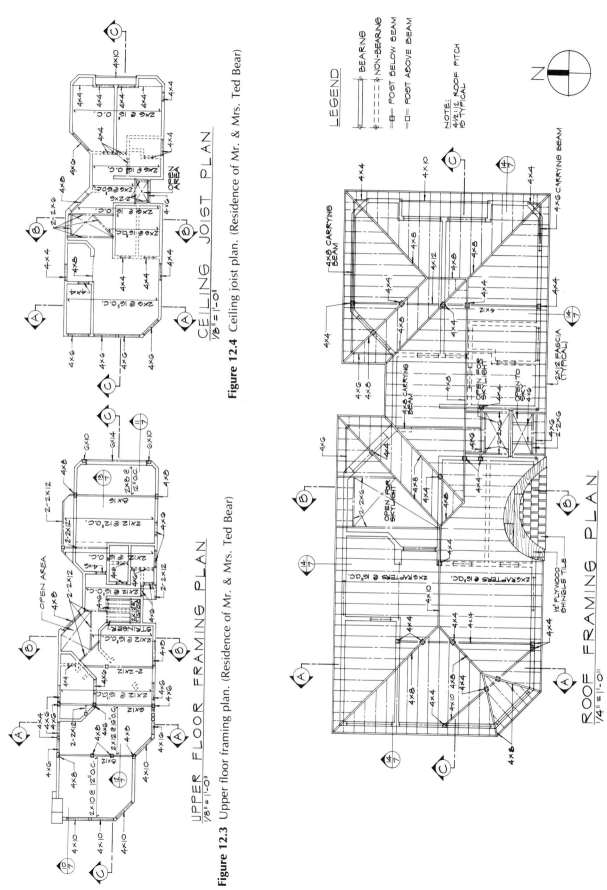

Figure 12.3 Upper floor framing plan. (Residence of Mr. & Mrs. Ted Bear)

Figure 12.4 Ceiling joist plan. (Residence of Mr. & Mrs. Ted Bear)

Figure 12.5 Roof framing plan. (Residence of Mr. & Mrs. Ted Bear)

members. These members, such as walls and columns, are located on the second floor. Dimensioning for these members is similar to that on a floor plan. When you have finished the drawing, provide the required notes for all the members included in the drawing.

Drawing the ceiling plan for the second floor level involves only the immediate ceiling framing members. See Figure 12.4. This drawing deals only with headers over openings and with ceiling joist location, span, direction, size, and spacing for a specific ceiling area. Where applicable, notes and dimensioning are shown as in Figure 12.3.

The final framing plan for this project is the roof framing plan. See Figure 12.5. As mentioned previously, another way to show framing members is to draw in all the members that apply to that particular drawing. This obviously takes more time to draw but is clearer for the viewer.

Framing with Different Materials

Framing Plan: Wood Members

When wood structures have members spaced anywhere from 16" to 48" on centers, show them with a single line broken at intervals. Figure 12.5 shows the roof framing plan for this residence incorporating all the individual rafters, ridges, **hip rafters** (the members that bisect the angle of two intersecting walls), and supporting columns and beams under the rafters. Show the rafters, which are closely spaced, with a single line. Lightly draft the walls so that the members directly above are clear. Provide dimensioning for members with critical locations as well as call-outs for the sizes, lumber grade, and spacing of all members.

Framing Plan: Steel Members

When you are using steel members to support ceilings, floors, and roof, show all the members on the framing plans. The method of drawing the framing plan is similar to the method for drawing wood framing plans.

After you have selected a method, show steel members with a heavy single line. See Figure 12.6, which is a roof framing plan for a theatre using various size steel members and steel decking. The interior walls have been drawn with a broken line, which distinguishes the heavy solid beam line and the walls below. As you can see, all the various beam sizes are noted directly on the steel members. Some members have an abbreviated "DO" as their call-out; this tells the viewer that this member is identical to the one noted in the same framing bay.

In some cases, a beam may also be given a roof beam

number, noted as "RB–1", "RB–2", etc. The structural engineer uses this beam reference in the engineering calculations. It can also be incorporated into a roof beam schedule, if one is needed. Any elements that require openings through a roof or floor should be drawn directly on the plan. On Figure 12.6, an open area for skylights and a roof access hatch are shown with a heavy solid line.

A framing plan can also be useful to show detail reference symbols for **connections** of various members that cannot otherwise be shown on the building sections. Figure 12.6 shows several detail symbols for various connecting conditions. Show building section reference symbols at their specific locations.

Axial reference lines form the basis for dimensioning steel framing members. These lines provide a reference point for all other dimensioning. In Figure 12.6, axial reference symbols are shown on all the major beam and wall lines. From these, subsequent dimension lines to other members are provided. These same reference lines are used on the foundation plan.

Beam and column elevation heights are often shown on the framing plan. See the axial reference point H–10 in Figure 12.6. The diagonal line pointing to this particular beam has an elevation height of 31'–7½" noted on the top of the diagonal line. This indicates that this is the height to the top of the beam. If the height at the bottom of that beam were required, you would note it underneath the diagonal line. Columns usually only require the elevations to the top of the column.

An aerial photograph showing a stage of the roof framing is shown in Figure 12.7. You can clearly see the main supporting steel members, as per axial reference lines ②, ③, ④, ⑩, ⑪, and ⑫, and some placement of the steel decking on top of these members.

Framing Plan: Wood and Steel Members

Framing plans using wood and steel members to support ceilings, floors, and roof are drawn in a similar fashion to framing plans using steel alone. Steel members are drawn with a heavy solid line and the wood members with a lighter line broken at intervals. You can also show wood members with a solid line and directional arrow.

Figure 12.8 shows a floor framing plan using steel and wood members to support the floor. This particular building is supported mainly on round steel columns, with the wall only being used to enclose a lobby and stairwells. For clarity, draw these columns in solid, and be careful to align them with each other. After you have laid out the required columns and walls below, draw in the main steel members with a solid heavy line. The designation of floor trusses spaced at 24" on centers is shown between these steel members.

Because these members are closely spaced, a solid

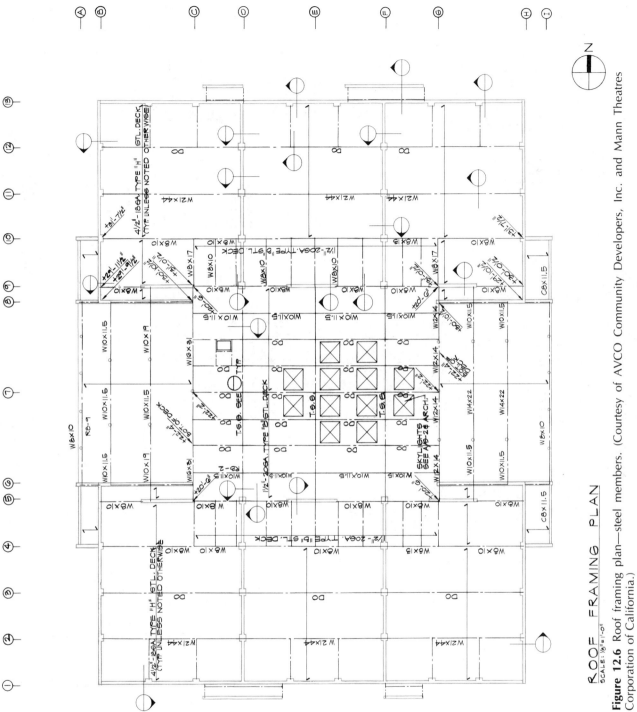

ROOF FRAMING PLAN
SCALE: 1/8"=1'-0"

Figure 12.6 Roof framing plan—steel members. (Courtesy of AVCO Community Developers, Inc. and Mann Theatres Corporation of California.)

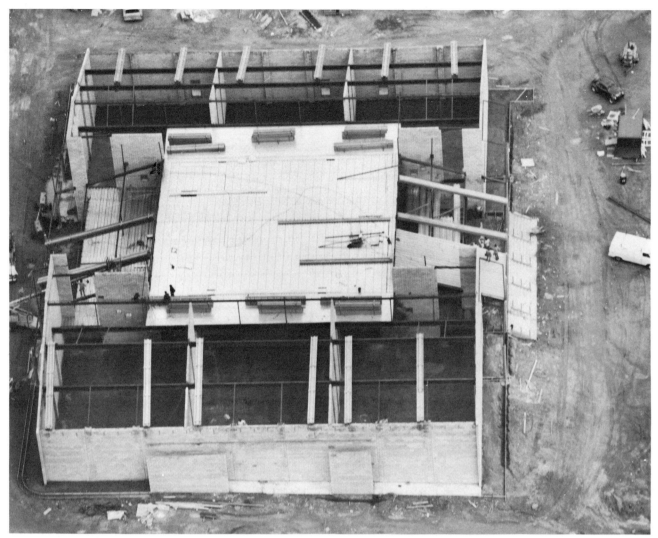

Figure 12.7 Roof framing. (Courtesy of AVCO Community Developers, Inc. and Mann Theatres Corporation of California; William Boggs Aerial Photography. Reprinted with permission.)

line is used with directional arrows at the end and the size and spacing of trusses noted directly above the solid line. The bottom of the line shows a notation, "FJ–3." This is the abbreviation for floor joist number 3, which is referenced in the structural engineer's calculations and may be used in a floor joist schedule. When you are asked to draw a similar framing plan, be sure to show the joist for all bay conditions. As we saw earlier, "DO" is shown between axial reference lines ⑦ and ⑧. When you use this abbreviation, be sure it is clear. Detail reference symbols are shown for the connections of various members. Sizes and shapes for all the steel columns have been designated as well as the elevation height to the top of each column. Building section reference symbols and locations are shown. Whenever possible, take these sections directly through an axial reference plan.

Dimensioning for this type of project relies totally on axial reference planes as they relate to the column locations. Usually, you should locate notes satisfying various requirements on this same drawing. For example,

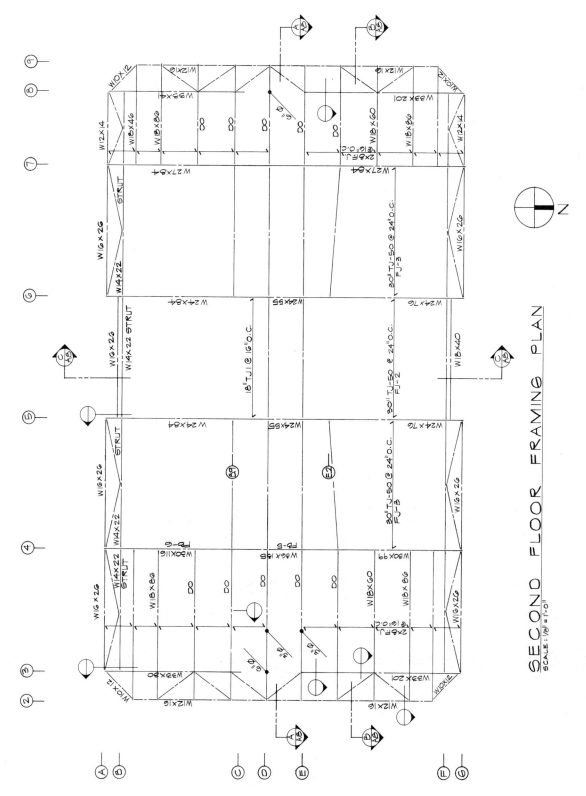

Figure 12.8 Framing plan—second floor. (Courtesy of Westmount, Inc., Real Estate Development, Torrance, CA.)

Figure 12.9 Steel beams for floor framing. (opposite, top) (Courtesy of Westmount, Inc., Real Estate Development, Torrance, CA; William Boggs Aerial Photography. Reprinted with permission.)

Figure 12.10 Main steel floor beam and column with joist hangers. (opposite, bottom) (Courtesy of Westmount, Inc., Real Estate Development, Torrance, CA; William Boggs Aerial Photography. Reprinted with permission.)

these notes might designate the thickness, type, and nailing schedule for the plywood subfloor or the location of the fire draft stops within the floor framing.

To understand this structure better, look at the series of framing photographs. Figure 12.9 gives a general view of the overall steel and wood skeleton used in the erection of this building. The floor joist truss member seen in the foreground will eventually be attached between the main steel beams. Figure 12.10 is a close-up view of a main steel floor beam and column with joists hangers located at the top of the beam in preparation for the attachment of the floor truss members.

In Figure 12.11, floor joist trusses have now been attached to the hangers and nailed in place. Reference symbols for connection details should be located throughout the framing plan drawing. Figures 12.12 and 12.13 give examples of what these details may look like in their construction phase.

Figure 12.11 Floor joist trusses attached to hangers and nailed in place. (Courtesy of Westmount, Inc., Real Estate Development, Torrance, CA; William Boggs Aerial Photography. Reprinted with permission.)

Figure 12.12 Beam and column connection. (Courtesy of Westmount, Inc., Real Estate Development, Torrance, CA.)

Figure 12.13 Floor beam to main beam assembly. (Courtesy of Westmount, Inc., Real Estate Development, Torrance, CA.)

FRAMING PLAN CHECK LIST

1. Titles and scales.
2. Indicate bearing and non-bearing walls.
   a. Coordinate with foundation plan.
   b. Show all openings in walls.
3. Show all beams, headers, girders, purlins, etc.
   a. Note sizes.
4. Show all columns, note sizes and materials.
5. Note accessway to attic - if occurs.
6. Note ceiling joist sizes, direction, spacing.
7. Draw all rafters, note sizes and spacing.
8. Draw overhands.
   a. Indicate framing for holding overhangs up.
   b. Dimension width.
9. Note shear walls.
10. Note roof sheathing type and thickness.
11. Indicate all ridges, valley. Note sizes.
12. Note all differences in roof levels.

INTERIOR
ELEVATIONS

13

Purpose and Content of Interior Elevations

The drawing process for interior elevations resembles the drafting procedure for exterior elevations. You should be familiar with the chapter on exterior elevations before proceeding with this chapter.

Sources of Measurements

Use the floor plan and building sections for accurate measurements of the width and height of an interior elevation wall. When you use these plans, remember that these dimensions are usually to the stud line or center line of the wall. Interior elevations are drafted to the plaster line.

Interior elevations may not always be drafted at the same scale as the floor plans or sections. Since this requires a scale transition, use caution to avoid errors. In this chapter, if the same scale is used and the drawings are directly projected from the plan and section, it is done only to show the theory of where to obtain shapes and configurations.

Information Shown on Interior Elevations

Some architectural offices draft interior elevations for every wall of every room. While this can guard against errors, many wall surfaces are so simple that they do not need a formal drafted interior elevation. These simple walls depend primarily on the interior finish schedule for their proper description.

Use interior elevations when you need to convey an idea, dimension, construction method, or unique feature that you can better describe by drafting than by a written description in the specification. For example, in a residence, the kitchen, bathrooms, special closets, and wet bars have walls that are usually drafted. On a commercial structure, you might select typical office units showing bookcases, cabinets, display cases, and so on. In an industrial structure you might draw the locations of equipment, conveyor belts, and special heights for bulletin boards or tool racks.

In other words, interior elevations are the means of controlling the interior walls of a structure in terms of construction, surface finishes, and the providing of information to subcontractors.

Naming Interior Elevations

In exterior elevations, the titles assigned—North, South, East, and West—are based on the direction the structure faces. In interior elevations this is reversed: the title is based on the direction in which the viewer is looking. For example, if you are standing in a theatre lobby facing north, the interior wall you are looking at has the title "North Lobby Elevation." See Figure 13.1. To avoid confusion when you are naming an interior elevation, you should use reference bubbles like those in Figure 13.2.

The reference symbol shown on the left is the same as the one used in the foundation plans and framing plans when you need to refer to details. Remember that the reference bubble is a circle with a darkened point on one side which points to the elevation being viewed and drawn.

The reference symbol shown on the right in Figure 13.2 shows a circle with a triangle inside it. The point of the triangle tells the viewer which elevation is being viewed, and the placement of the triangle automatically divides the circle in half. The top half contains a letter or number which becomes the name of that interior elevation. The lower half contains the sheet number on which the interior elevation can be found.

Figure 13.3 shows a floor plan and a symbol used to show multiple elevations. Letter "A" is for the North elevation, "C" is for the South elevation, "B" for the West elevation, and "D" for the East elevation. Figure 13.4 shows two types of **title references.**

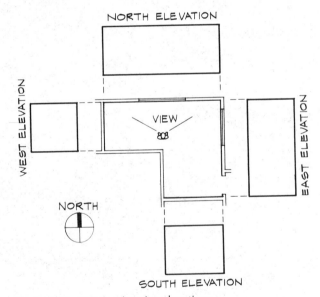

Figure 13.1 Naming interior elevations.

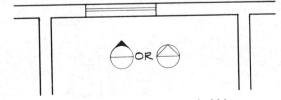

Figure 13.2 Interior elevation reference bubbles.

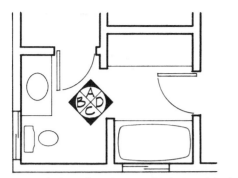

Figure 13.3 Symbol used to show multiple interior elevations.

Figure 13.4 Interior elevation titles.

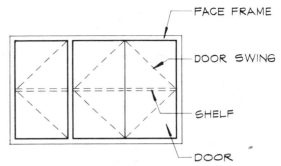

Figure 13.5 Typical elevation of cabinet.

Choosing a Scale

The most desirable scale to use on an interior elevation is ½″ = 1′–0″. Most floor plans are drafted at ¼″ = 1′–0″, so using this scale makes the translation from floor plan to interior elevation easy because you only need to use a pair of dividers and double every measurement. Interior elevations are seldom drawn larger than this.

If the drawing space does not permit you to use a ½″ = 1′–0″ scale, or if the scale of the drawing calls for a smaller interior elevation, you may use a ⅜″ = 1′–0″ or ¼″ = 1′–0″ scale. The scale could also depend on the complexity of the wall to be shown.

Using Dotted Lines

Dotted lines are used extensively on interior elevations. As in the drafting of exterior elevations, the dotted line is used to show door-swing direction—for example, for cabinets or for bi-fold doors on a wardrobe closet. See Figure 13.5. Dotted lines are also used to represent items hidden from view, for example, the outline of a kitchen sink, shelves in a cabinet, or the vent above a hood vent, range, or cook top.

Dotted lines are also used to show the outline of objects to be added later or those **not in the contract** (designated as **"N.I.C."**). For example, the outline of a washer and dryer or refrigerator is shown. Even though the appliances themselves are not in the contract, space must be allowed for them. The wall behind the appliance is shown, including duplex convenience outlets, and moulding or trim at the base of the wall.

Other Drafting Considerations

To draft interior elevations of cabinets, you must know the type, counter top material, heights, general design, and number of cabinet doors.

Types of Cabinet Doors. There are three main types of cabinet doors: **flush, flush overlay,** and **lip.** As Figure 13.6 shows, flush overlay doors cover the total face of the cabinet. The front surface, called the **face frame** of the cabinet, does not show. The flush door is shown in Figure 13.7 and the lip door in Figure 13.8. Because the face frame of the cabinet shows in both the lip and flush

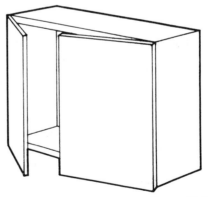

Figure 13.6 Flush overlay doors.

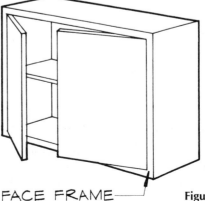

FACE FRAME

Figure 13.7 Flush doors.

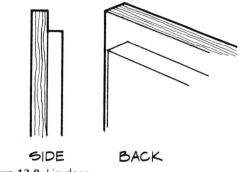

SIDE   BACK

Figure 13.8 Lip door.

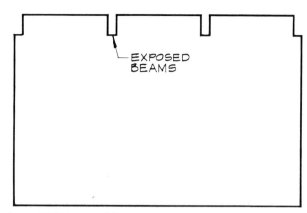

Figure 13.9 Exposed beams.

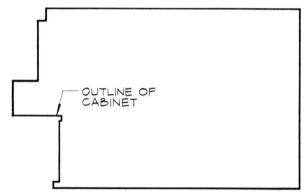

Figure 13.10 Outline of cabinet.

cabinet doors, they appear the same in the interior elevation.

Material Designation and Noting

Materials for interior elevations are represented like the materials for exterior elevations. Refer to Chapter 11, on exterior elevations, for samples.

Noting is kept simple and generic terms are often used. Specific information, brand names, workmanship notes, procedures, applications and finishes are placed in the specifications. Later in this chapter, you will see examples of generic noting for such items as ceramic tile counter tops, an exhaust hood (with a note to "See specs."), and metal partitions.

Outline of Interior Elevations

The outline of an interior elevation represents the outermost measurement of a room. Objects that project toward the viewer, such as cabinets, beams, or air-conditioning ducts, are drawn. Some architectural offices deal with these as if they were in section but most prefer to treat them as shown in Figures 13.9 and 13.10. Note in Figure 13.10 that the tops of the cabinets have been eliminated in drafting the outline of the cabinet.

Using Templates

A useful tool for drafting interior elevations is a plumbing fixture template. Some templates contain side and front views of bath tubs, water closets, urinals, lavatories (washbasin) and sinks, and they come in a range of scales.

Planning for the Handicapped and Children

Always have information available on standards affecting facilities that should be usable by the handicapped and children. Here are some of the standards established by several states for the handicapped:

1. Door opening: minimum size 2'–8"
2. Restroom grab bars: 2'–9" above the floor
3. Towel bars: 3'–4" maximum above floor
4. Top of lavatory: 2'–5½" maximum above floor
5. Drinking fountains: 2'–6" minimum, 3'–0" maximum, 2'–10" optimum above the floor.

Many standards can be obtained by writing to the proper authority, such as the State Architect's office. Most standards are presented in the form of a drawing; see Figure 13.11 for an example.

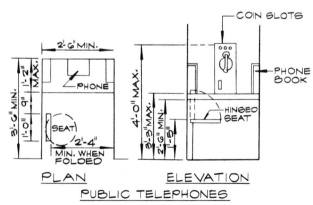

Figure 13.11 Public telephone for the handicapped. (Courtesy of AVCO Community Developers, Inc. and Mann Corporation of California.)

Dimensions and Intersections

Dimensions

When you draft a set of interior elevations, do not repeat dimensions that appear elsewhere. For example, you do not need to indicate the width of rooms on the interior elevation. In fact, avoid repeating dimensions at all costs. In this way, if you need to make changes on one plan—such as the floor plan—you do not risk forgetting to change the interior elevations.

In a similar way, you do not need to dimension the interior elevation of the counter of Figure 13.12, because it will occupy the total width of the room. The boundaries, which are the walls, are already dimensioned on the floor plan.

The interior elevations for Figure 13.12 will show a counter, walls, a window, and an opening. The portion of the counter that returns toward the opening should be dimensioned either on the floor plan or on the interior elevations, but not on both. See Figure 13.13.

Notice how the base cabinet is dimensioned; in fact,

the space between the door and the cabinet could have been dimensioned instead. Deciding whether to dimension the space or the cabinet is based on which is more important. If the space is left for an appliance or some other piece of equipment, then the space should be dimensioned.

The interior elevation is also the place to provide such information as the location of medicine cabinets, the heights of built-in drawers, the locations of mirrors, the required clearance for a hood above a range, and the heights of partitions.

Intersection of Wall and Floor

Interior elevations can also show, in a simple way, the wall and floor intersection. This can be achieved by applying a topset, coving the floor, or using a base or a base and a shoe. This creates a transition between the floor and wall planes. **Topset** is made of flexible material such as rubber and placed on the wall where it touches the floor. **Coving** is a method whereby the floor material is curved upward against the wall. A **base** is used to cover or as a guide to control the thickness of the plaster on the wall, while the **shoe** covers the intersection between the wall and floor. See Figure 13.14.

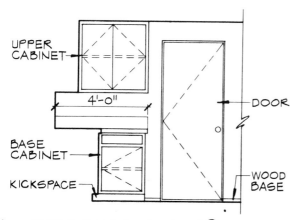

Figure 13.12 Partial plan of food preparation area.

Figure 13.13 Partial interior elevation of ⊕

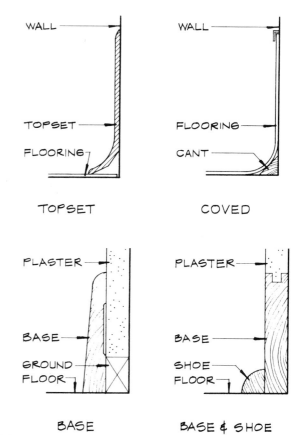

Figure 13.14 Intersection of wall and floor.

Drafting an Interior Elevation: Examples

A Kitchen

Figure 13.15 shows a perspective view of a kitchen. The main portion has lip doors on the cabinets, and the extreme left side (not shown in the perspective) has flush overlay doors. Different types of cabinet doors are not usually mixed on a single project; here the intention is simply to show the different methods used to represent them on an interior elevation. Figure 13.16 shows a floor plan of the perspective drawing in Figure 13.15. Note the flush overlay cabinet on the left and the lip or flush cabinets on the right. The upper and base cabinets, slightly left of center, project forward.

Figure 13.17 shows the drafted interior elevation of one side of floor plan of the kitchen. You should take careful note of these points:

1. The difference in the method of representing a flush overlay and a lip door on the cabinets.
2. The outlining of the cabinet on the extreme right side of the drawing.
3. The use of dotted lines to show door swing, shelves, and the outline of the sink.
4. The handling of the forward projection of the upper and base cabinet slightly to the left of center.
5. Dimensions and eventually the location of notes.

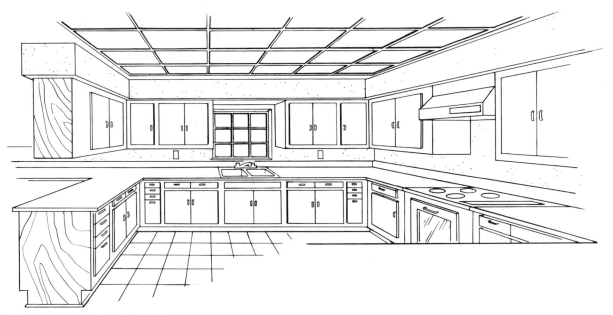

Figure 13.15 Perspective of a kitchen.

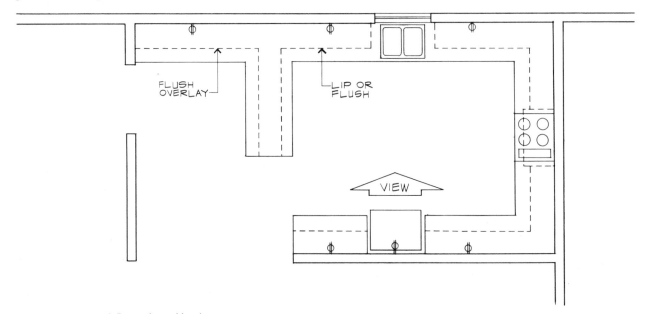

Figure 13.16 Partial floor plan of kitchen.

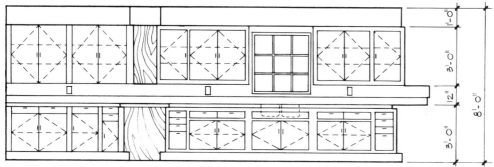

Figure 13.17 Interior elevation of Figure 13.16.

A Condominium

Figures 13.18, 13.19, and 13.20 are partial floor plans of a two-story condominium project. The corresponding interior elevations can be found in Figures 13.21 through 13.28. Different ways of showing door openings, cabinets, appliances, partial walls, open shelves, and other features are given. Notice the dimensioning procedure and the noting method used.

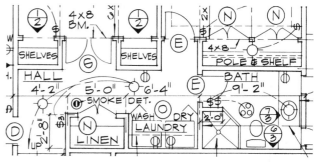

Figure 13.20 Partial lower floor plan. (Courtesy of William F. Smith—Builder.)

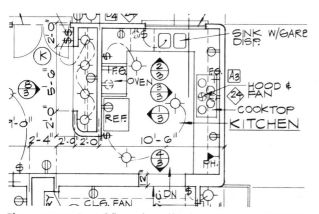

Figure 13.18 Partial floor plan of kitchen. (Courtesy of William F. Smith—Builder.)

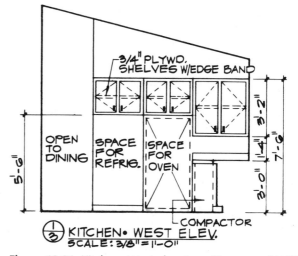

Figure 13.21 Kitchen: West elevation. (Courtesy of William F. Smith—Builder.)

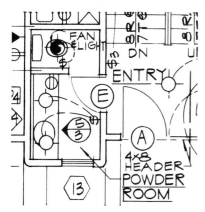

Figure 13.19 Partial floor plan of powder room. (Courtesy of William F. Smith—Builder.)

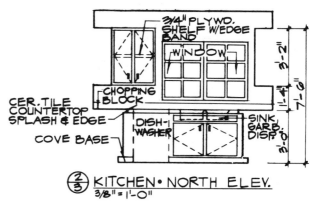

Figure 13.22 Kitchen: North elevation. (Courtesy of William F. Smith—Builder.)

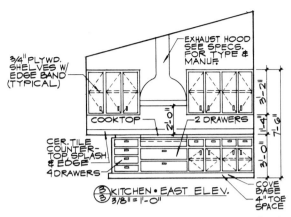

Figure 13.23 Kitchen: East elevation. (Courtesy of William F. Smith—Builder.)

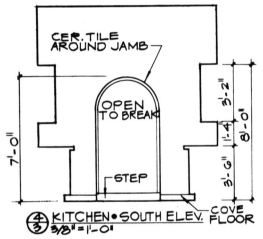

Figure 13.24 Kitchen: South elevation. (Courtesy of William F. Smith—Builder.)

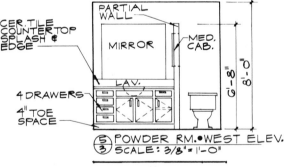

Figure 13.25 Powder room: West elevation. (Courtesy of William F. Smith—Builder.)

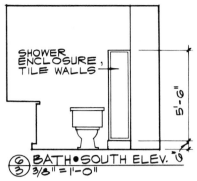

Figure 13.26 Bath: South elevation. (Courtesy of William F. Smith—Builder.)

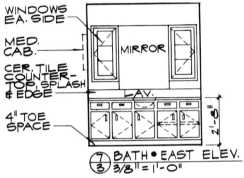

Figure 13.27 Bath: East elevation. (Courtesy of William F. Smith—Builder.)

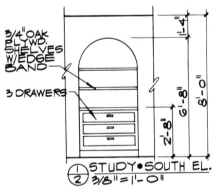

Figure 13.28 Study elevation. (Courtesy of William F. Smith—Builder.)

A Lobby and Restroom

Figure 13.29 shows a partial floor plan for the lobby and restroom area of an office building. Figure 13.20 shows the North elevation of the men's toilet. Because this is a public facility, handicapped access is shown on both the partial floor plan and the interior elevation.

Additional interior elevations for a beach house and for a theatre are found in later chapters.

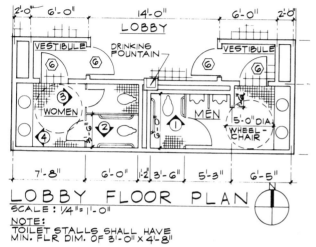

Figure 13.29 Partial floor plan of lobby and restroom. (Courtesy of Westmount, Inc., Real Estate Development, Torrance, CA.)

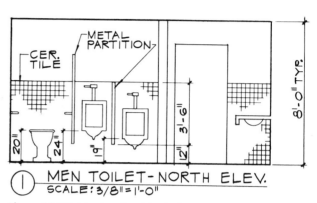

Figure 13.30 Men's toilet: North elevation. (Courtesy of Westmount, Inc., Real Estate Development, Torrance, CA.)

ARCHITECTURAL DETAILS

14

The Purpose of Architectural Details

Architectural details are enlarged drawings of specific architectural assemblies. These details are usually provided by the architect, and structural details are furnished by the structural engineer.

Architectural details are done for many different construction assemblies, including door and window details, fireplace details, stair details, and wall and roof assemblies. The number and kind of details needed for a given project depends entirely on the architect's or designer's estimate of what is needed to clarify the construction process. The contractor may request additional architectural details in the construction stage.

Architectural details often start with **freehand sketches** and an architectural scale in order to solve different construction assemblies in a structure. Once the details have been formulated in a scaled freehand sketch, they are then ready to be drafted in final form. Many details, such as standard foundation and wall assemblies, are relatively straightforward and do not require freehand sketches. The following sections provide examples of sketches and final forms of details for different residences to give you an understanding of what is required.

Using Details in Construction Documents

Freehand Detail Sketches: Mountain Residence

Architectural details encompass many construction assemblies, such as this mountain residence with its unique foundation details. This residence is treated in full in Chapter 16. Figure 14.1 shows a freehand sketch detail of an exterior bearing footing for this residence. There are some nonstandard conditions in this detail such as steel anchor clips for the connection of the floor joists to the mudsill (for lateral support), steel reinforcing placement in the wall for earth retention, and location of (and installation requirements for) a footing drain. Figures 14.2 and 14.3 show two other exterior footing conditions: Figure 14.2 shows a concrete floor condition below grade, and Figure 14.3 shows the wood deck connection to the exterior footing.

An interior foundation and masonry wall is also sketched in detail, showing steel reinforcing placement and floor joist assembly in Figure 14.4. Figures 14.5 and 14.6 show other interior footing conditions: Figure 14.5 shows a bearing footing with a concrete floor; Figure 14.6 shows a square concrete pier and reinforcing bars required to support a heavy concentrated load distributed by a 6″ × 6″ post. Study each of these carefully before proceeding further.

If you are asked to detail a wood beam and masonry wall connection, with the required assembly informa-

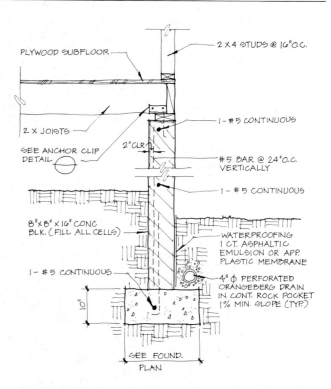

Figure 14.1 Detail of exterior bearing footing.

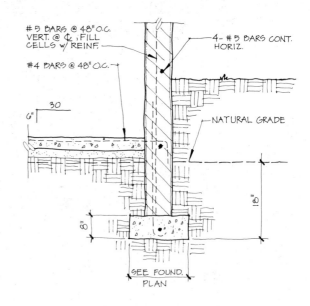

Figure 14.2 Detail of exterior footing.

tion, first draw a freehand sketch including the necessary information. Figure 14.7 shows such a sketch. The size of the steel plate dictates the masonry wall offset and the embedment of the anchor bolts is 10″.

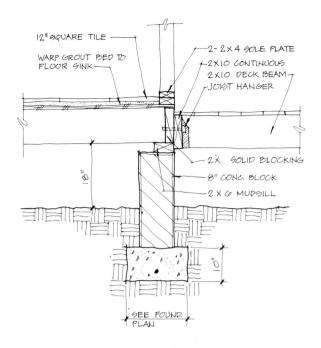

12" SQUARE TILE

WARP GROUT BED TO FLOOR SINK

2- 2×4 SOLE PLATE

2×10 CONTINUOUS

2×10 DECK BEAM

JOIST HANGER

2× SOLID BLOCKING

8" CONC. BLOCK

2×6 MUDSILL

18"

10"

SEE FOUND. PLAN

DECK @ EXTERIOR FOOTING

Figure 14.3 Detail of deck at exterior footing.

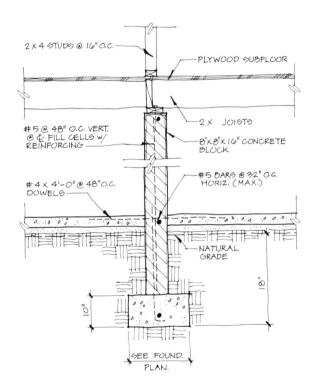

2×4 STUDS @ 16" O.C.

PLYWOOD SUBFLOOR

#5 @ 48" O.C. VERT. @ ℄ FILL CELLS W/ REINFORCING

2× JOISTS

8"×8"×16" CONCRETE BLOCK

#4 × 4'-0" @ 48"O.C. DOWELS

#5 BARS @ 32" O.C. HORIZ. (MAX.)

NATURAL GRADE

18"

10"

SEE FOUND. PLAN.

INTERIOR CONC. BLOCK WALL

Figure 14.4 Detail of interior concrete block wall.

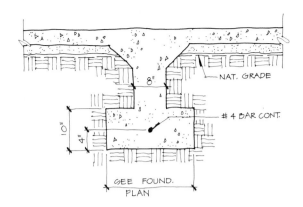

NAT. GRADE

8"

#4 BAR CONT.

10"

4"

SEE FOUND. PLAN

INTERIOR BEARING FOOTING

Figure 14.5 Detail of interior bearing footing.

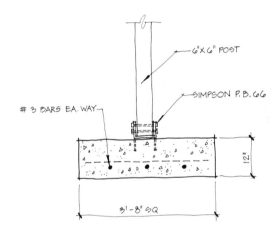

6"×6" POST

SIMPSON P.B. 66

#3 BARS EA. WAY

12"

3'-8" SQ

FOOTING @ WOOD POST

Figure 14.6 Detail of footing at wood post.

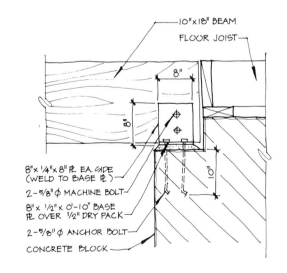

10"×18" BEAM

FLOOR JOIST

8"

8"

10"

8"×1/4"×8" PL. EA. SIDE (WELD TO BASE PL.)

2-5/8" φ MACHINE BOLT

8"×1/2"×0'-10" BASE PL. OVER 1/2" DRY PACK

2-5/8" φ ANCHOR BOLT

CONCRETE BLOCK

WOOD BEAM CONNECTION

Figure 14.7 Detail of wood beam connection.

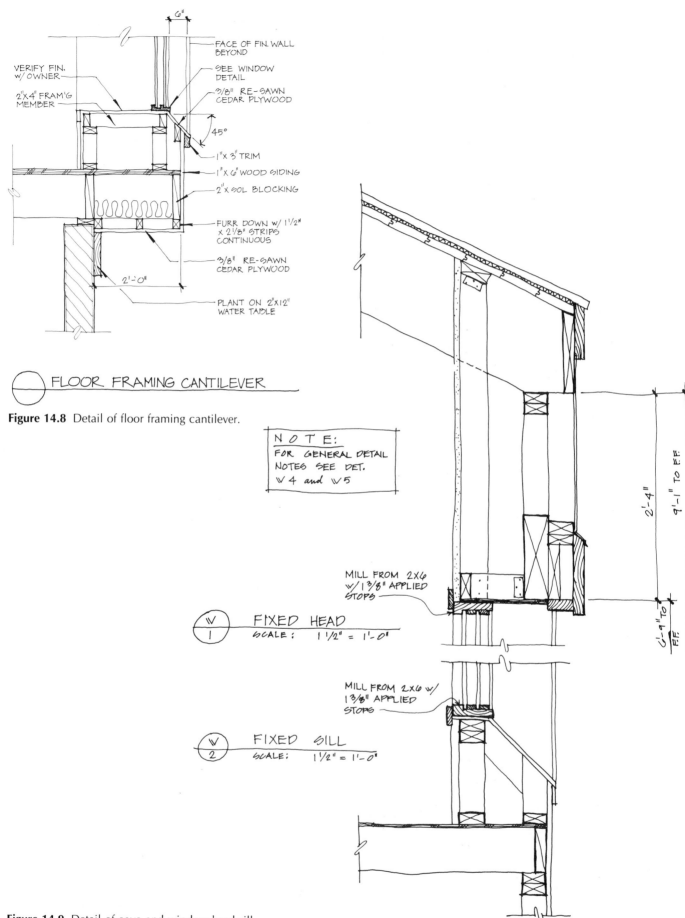

Figure 14.8 Detail of floor framing cantilever.

FLOOR FRAMING CANTILEVER

FACE OF FIN. WALL BEYOND

SEE WINDOW DETAIL

3/8" RE-SAWN CEDAR PLYWOOD

45°

1"X 3" TRIM

1"X 6" WOOD SIDING

2"X SOL BLOCKING

FURR DOWN W/ 1 1/2" X 2 1/8" STRIPS CONTINUOUS

3/8" RE-SAWN CEDAR PLYWOOD

PLANT ON 2"X12" WATER TABLE

VERIFY FIN. W/ OWNER

2"X4" FRAM'G MEMBER

2'-0"

6"

NOTE:
FOR GENERAL DETAIL NOTES SEE DET. W 4 and W 5

MILL FROM 2X6 W/ 1 3/8" APPLIED STOPS

W/1 FIXED HEAD   SCALE: 1 1/2" = 1'-0"

MILL FROM 2X6 W/ 1 3/8" APPLIED STOPS

W/2 FIXED SILL   SCALE: 1 1/2" = 1'-0"

2'-4"

9'-1" TO F.F.

6'-9" TO F.F.

Figure 14.9 Detail of eave and window head sill.

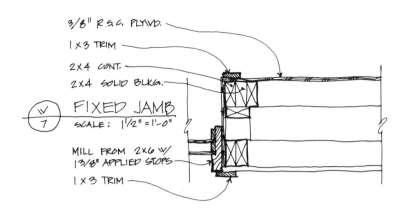

3/8" R.S.C. PLYWD.

1 x 3 TRIM

2x4 CONT.

2x4 SOLID BLKG.

FIXED JAMB

SCALE: 1 1/2" = 1'-0"

MILL FROM 2x6 W/
1 3/8" APPLIED STOPS

1 x 3 TRIM

Figure 14.10 Detail of window jamb.

An important factor in architectural detailing is providing details that are an integral part of the architectural design of the building. For example, if floor cantilevers and wood soffits are an integral part of the design, first design and solve these assemblies in sketch form, as shown in Figure 14.8, before completing the final detail. As this figure shows, creativity and craftsmanship in architectural detailing are as important as any other factors in designing a structure.

In this particular residence, we thought that the top of the head section of the windows and doors should have a direct relationship with the eave assembly. So we detailed the eave assembly with the various wood members forming a wood soffit directly above the head section of the window. See Figure 14.9. We sketched in detail the window sill and exterior wall assembly projecting down from the head section. From both these figures, 14.8 and 14.9, it was possible to design and detail the **jamb** section for this particular opening, using the established head and sill section as a guide for the detailed assembly. Figure 14.10 shows a freehand sketch of the jamb details. We used two wood stud walls at the window area to provide a deep architectural relief at the openings. See Figure 14.9.

Details: Beach Residence

(For additional details, see chapter 7.)

Foundation Details. The architectural details for this project were fairly conventional but were still worth investigating with freehand drawings. For example, we detailed the foundation details for this two-story residence to satisfy the sandy soil requirements. Figure 14.11 shows a detail for the exterior bearing wall. Because this soil did not provide good bearing qualities, we used horizontal reinforcing rods at the top and bottom of the foundation wall. Nonbearing walls still required a minimal footing to support the weight of the wall and a depth

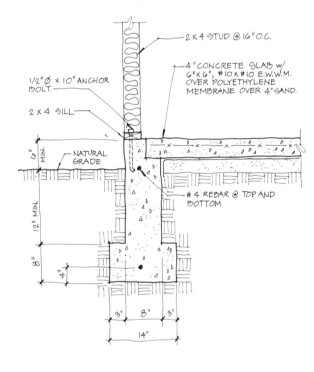

2 X 4 STUD @ 16" O.C.

4" CONCRETE SLAB W/
6" X 6", #10 x #10 E.W.W.M.
OVER POLYETHYLENE
MEMBRANE OVER 4" SAND.

1/2" Ø x 10" ANCHOR BOLT.

2 X 4 SILL

NATURAL GRADE

6" MIN.

12" MIN.

8"

4"

#4 REBAR @ TOP AND BOTTOM

3" 8" 3"

14"

EXTERIOR BEARING

Figure 14.11 Detail of exterior bearing footing.

of concrete to receive the anchor bolts. See Figure 14.12. Because this residence has a change of floor levels, we provided a detail through the floor transitions. Figure 14.13 shows a detail at a location that has incorporated the **risers** and **tread.** (A riser is the vertical dimension of a stair step and the tread is the horizontal dimension.) The risers and tread are dimensioned, as are rebar ties for the connection of the upper concrete floor. (Rebar ties act as dowels to join two concrete elements.)

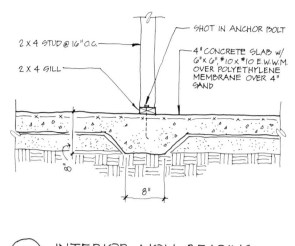

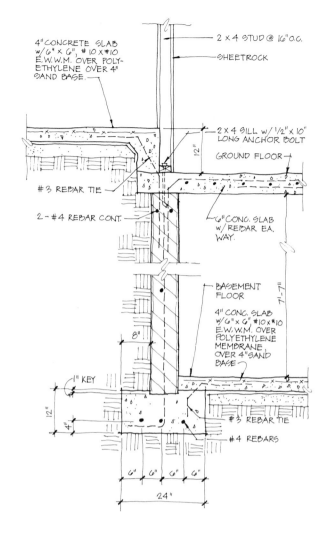

INTERIOR NON-BEARING

Figure 14.12 Detail of interior nonbearing footing.

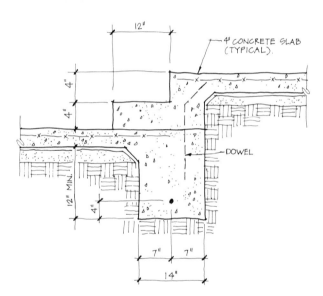

CHANGE OF LEVEL w/STEP

Figure 14.13 Detail of change of level with step.

CONC. BLOCK WALL @ BASEMENT

Figure 14.14 Detail of concrete block wall at basement—slab floor.

A large storage area and a mechanical room were located in the basement. A detail was needed to show the assembly for the basement and floor level changes. See Figure 14.14. The wood stud wall has been offset in front of the upper level concrete floor to provide a nailing surface for the wall finishes at both levels.

Details for Framing Assemblies. Architectural details for framing assemblies were also provided in these construction documents. One example is the eave detail.

First, the project designer did a freehand drawing. Then this freehand drawing was given to a draftsperson for final drawing. Figure 14.15 shows the freehand sketch.

Figure 14.16 shows a study of a deck and handrail detail located directly above a recessed garage door. The deck assembly at the building wall is also detailed, because proper flashing and drainage are needed to prevent water leaks. Figures 14.17 and 14.18 resemble each other but show different floor framing conditions. Other deck and handrail conditions are also detailed. Figure 14.19 shows the flashing and handrail assemblies and a continuous wood soffit to be used at the wall cantilever.

Details: Theatre

In some projects, structural complexities may dictate various construction assemblies. For example, a ma-

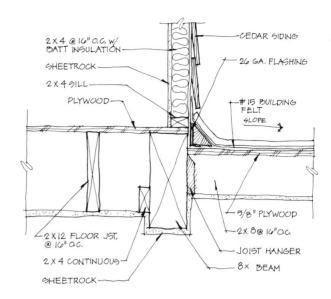

13/7 BEAM AND DECK @ GARAGE

Figure 14.17 Detail of beam and deck at garage.

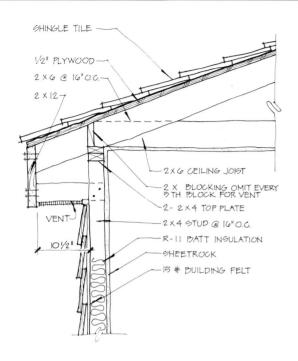

14/7 EAVE DETAIL

Figure 14.15 Eave detail.

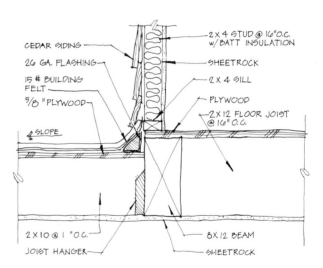

12/7 BEAM & DECK @ LIVING ROOM

Figure 14.18 Detail of beam and deck at living room.

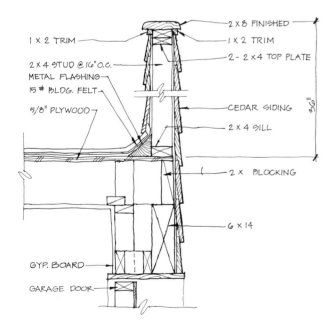

11/7 DECK RAILING & HDR. @ GARAGE

Figure 14.16 Detail of deck railing and header at garage.

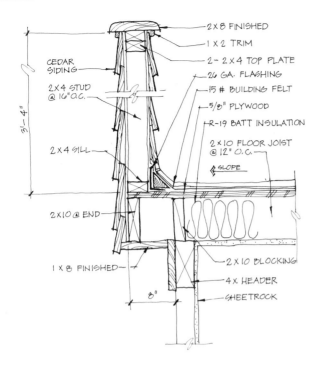

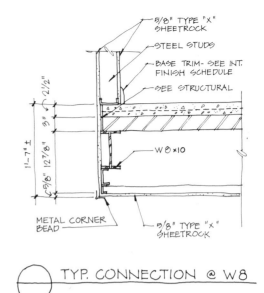

TYP. CONNECTION @ W8

Figure 14.20 Detail of typical connection at a steel beam.

DECK RAILING ABOVE LIVING RM.

Figure 14.19 Detail of deck railing above living room.

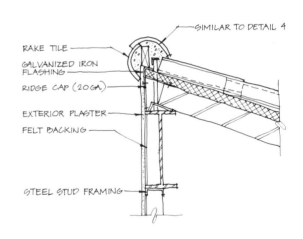

RIDGE @ MECHANICAL WELL

Figure 14.21 Detail of ridge at mechanical well.

sonry and steel structure has many architectural details that are governed by structural engineering requirements. The detailer must coordinate these details with the structural engineer. Figure 14.20 shows a detail for a steel beam connection where the beam, steel decking, and concrete floor thickness have been designed by the structural engineer. From these required members, the architectural detail is developed showing wall materials, ceiling attachment, and underfloor space for mechanical and electrical runs. Figure 14.20 has a note to "SEE STRUCTURAL." This refers the reader to the structural engineer's drawings, which provide such information as type and length of welds for steel connections, and size and weight of steel members. Note the call-out on the steel beam of "W 8 × 10." The "W" refers to the shape of the beam (here a wide **flange**), the "8" refers to the depth of the beam (here 8 inches), and the "10" refers to the weight of the beam per lineal foot (here 10 lb per linear foot).

A second example is shown in Figure 14.21. The steel stud framing is terminated at the bottom of the steel beam and extensive galvanized iron flashing has been used to cover and protect the intersection of the various members at the ridge.

Some architectural details become complex and require much study before the finished detail is drafted. See Figure 14.22. This eave and column detail is intricate and shows the entire column assembly from the foun-

dation to the roof, including the eave detail. Notes refer the viewer to other details for more information. Usually, it is unnecessary and unadvisable to repeat all the information from one detail to another; changes made on one detail must be made on any other affected.

Many projects require a specific architectural detail to show conditions that will satisfy a governing building code requirement. Figure 14.23, for example, shows exactly where a fire protection coating is required under a steel roof decking that covers the structural steel angle on a masonry wall. This information is combined with a roof parapet detail. Figure 14.24 shows another detail for areas requiring fire protection.

Figure 14.25 shows a third example of this kind of detail. This detail of a handicapped ramp shows the required number of handrails, the height of the handrails

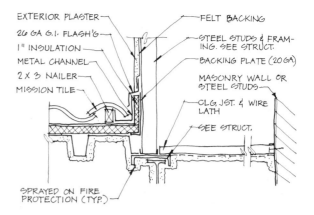

BASE FLASHING DETAIL

EXTERIOR PLASTER
26 GA. G.I. FLASH'G
1" INSULATION
METAL CHANNEL
2 X 3 NAILER
MISSION TILE

FELT BACKING
STEEL STUDS & FRAM-ING. SEE STRUCT.
BACKING PLATE (20 GA)
MASONRY WALL OR STEEL STUDS
CLG. JST. & WIRE LATH
SEE STRUCT.

SPRAYED ON FIRE PROTECTION (TYP.)

BASE FLASHING DETAIL

Figure 14.24 Base flashing detail.

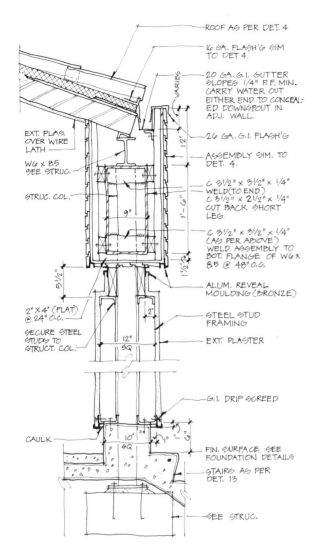

ROOF AS PER DET. 4
16 GA. FLASH'G SIM TO DET. 4.
20 GA. G.I. GUTTER SLOPES 1/4" P.F. MIN. CARRY WATER OUT EITHER END TO CONCEALED DOWNSPOUT IN ADJ. WALL.
VARIES
12"
26 GA. G.I. FLASH'G
ASSEMBLY SIM. TO DET. 4.
C 3 1/2" X 3 1/2" X 1/4" WELD (TO END)
C 3 1/2" X 2 1/2" X 1/4" CUT BACK SHORT LEG.
C 3 1/2" X 3 1/2" X 1/4" (AS PER ABOVE) WELD ASSEMBLY TO BOT. FLANGE OF W6 X 85 @ 48" O.C.
1'-6"
1 1/2"
ALUM. REVEAL MOULDING (BRONZE)
STEEL STUD FRAMING
EXT. PLASTER
G.I. DRIP SCREED
FIN. SURFACE SEE FOUNDATION DETAILS
STAIRS AS PER DET. 13
SEE STRUC.

EXT. PLAS. OVER WIRE LATH
W6 X 85 SEE STRUC.
STRUC. COL.
9"
5 1/2"
2" X 4" (FLAT) @ 24" O.C.
SECURE STEEL STUDS TO STRUCT. COL.
2"
12" SQ
CAULK
10" SQ
1"
6"
2"

EAVE AND COLUMN DETAIL

Figure 14.22 Eave and column detail.

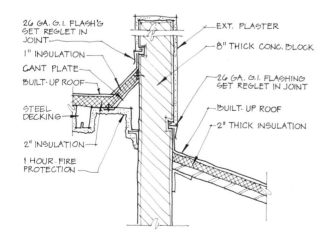

26 GA. G.I. FLASH'G SET REGLET IN JOINT
1" INSULATION
CANT PLATE
BUILT-UP ROOF
STEEL DECKING
2" INSULATION
1 HOUR FIRE PROTECTION

EXT. PLASTER
8" THICK CONC. BLOCK
26 GA. G.I. FLASHING SET REGLET IN JOINT
BUILT-UP ROOF
2" THICK INSULATION

PARAPET DETAIL

Figure 14.23 Parapet detail.

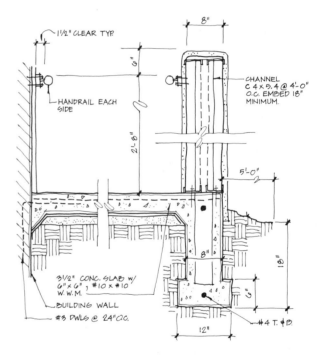

1 1/2" CLEAR TYP.
8"
6"
HANDRAIL EACH SIDE
2'-8"
CHANNEL C 4 X 5.4 @ 4'-0" O.C. EMBED 18" MINIMUM.
5'-0"
8"
18"
6"
3 1/2" CONC. SLAB W/ 6" X 6", #10 X #10 W.W.M.
BUILDING WALL
#3 DWLS @ 24" O.C.
12"
#4 T. & B.

RAMP DETAIL

Figure 14.25 Ramp detail.

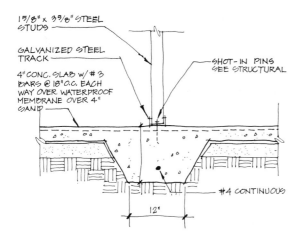

Figure 14.26 Steel stud footing detail.

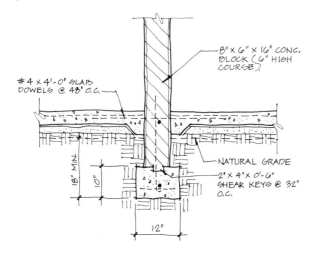

Figure 14.27 Block wall footing detail.

above the ramp, and the clear space required between the handrail and the wall. This information has also been combined with the structural requirements for the support of a low wall on the outside of the ramp.

Footing details may also be sketched for various conditions as an aid to the finished drawings. Figure 14.26 shows a footing detail supporting a steel stud wall and Figure 14.27 a footing detail supporting the masonry wall that separates the auditoriums.

Details: Office Building with Steel Members and Wood

Many commerical projects use a combination of structural steel and wood members. When detailing such

assemblies, coordinate the architectural details with the structural members. For example, Figure 14.28 shows a **furred ceiling** detail (a furred ceiling is a finished surface which provides air space within the inner structure). This detail emphasizes the importance of first locating the required structural members so that the supporting members for the ceiling below can be detailed.

In many cases, a material selection will influence the assembly of structural members. As Figure 14.29 shows, lightweight concrete over a plywood sub-floor has been

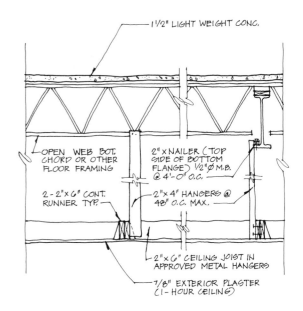

Figure 14.28 Furred ceiling detail.

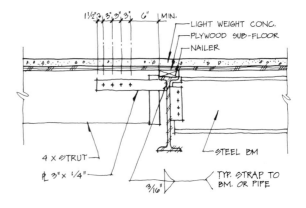

Figure 14.29 Steel beam connection detail.

selected as the main floor for an office building. To accommodate the nailing of the plywood, a wood member, called a **nailer,** will be bolted to the top flange (projecting edge) of the steel beam. This then establishes the top of beam elevation.

Figure 14.30 shows a steel **pipe column** and **tube brace** to be located within a wall. From these requirements, you can provide a detail of a wall accommodating these structural members. Communication with the structural engineer is necessary in order to evaluate such structural conditions and their effects on the details.

Figures 14.31 and 14.32 show structural details that

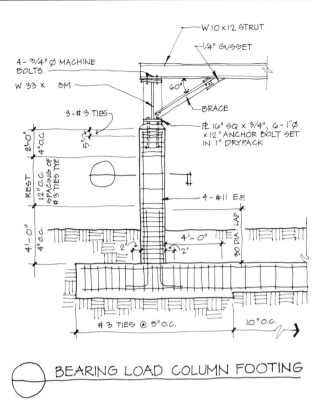

Figure 14.32 Detail of load-bearing column and footing.

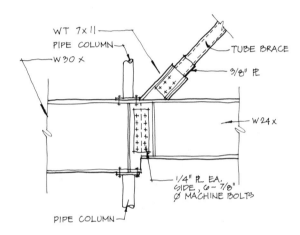

Figure 14.30 Brace connection detail.

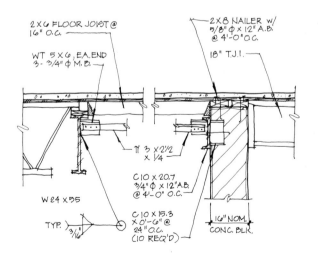

Figure 14.31 Second level framing detail.

may influence the detailing. Figure 14.31 shows the various members for wall and floor assemblies, which may, in turn, dictate a ceiling or wall connection.

In Figure 14.32, the engineer has designed a brace from one steel beam to another. This brace may influence the required height clearance where the brace occurs and beam height adjustments may be necessary.

Once the structural requirements for an assembly have been reviewed, you can then proceed to develop the architectural detail. Figure 14.33 shows cantilevered floor joists trusses, where a detail is required to illustrate the soffit and exterior wall configuration as well as the wall relationship to the sill of the window. This detail shows clearly the advisability of first providing a sketch of how this detail may appear. A note at the top of the 2″ × 6″ stud wall reads "SEE WINDOW DETAIL," referring to the window sill detail that gives an overall view of the wall and window sill assembly. See Figure 14.34. The corresponding head detail for the window assembly is shown in Figure 14.35.

The eave detail for an office building is shown in Figure 14.36. This detail is developed using all wood members to support the roof overhang and wood soffit. It also shows two building code requirements: the **fire-blocking** located at the bottom of the wood soffit and the **waterproofing** (½″ waterproof gypsum board backing for the exterior siding).

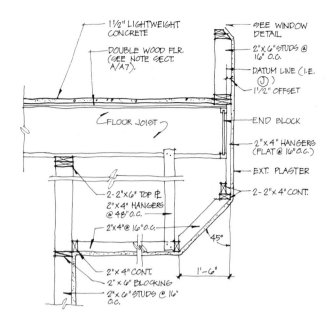

SOFFIT DETAIL

Figure 14.33 Soffit detail.

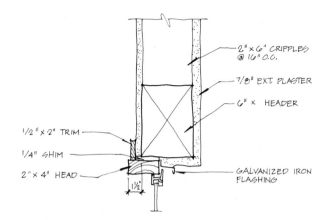

HEAD DETAIL

Figure 14.35 Head detail.

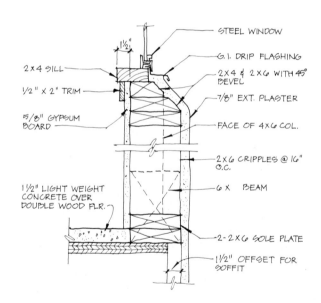

SILL DETAIL

Figure 14.34 Sill detail.

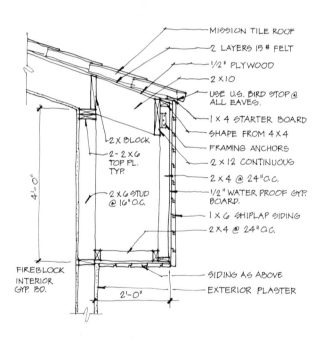

EAVE DETAIL

Figure 14.36 Eave detail.

Architectural details may also be required to satisfy a manufacturer's equipment installation requirements. See Figure 14.37, which details an elevator pit meeting dimensional requirements set by the elevator manufacturer. As well as meeting the manufacturers' dimensional requirements, this detail gives the location of waterproofing and a drain, and the size and location of the reinforcing steel to be used.

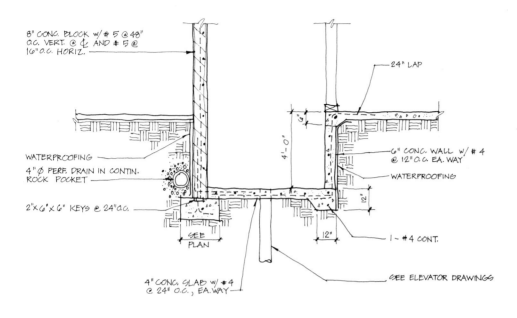

ELEVATOR PIT DETAIL

Figure 14.37 Elevator pit detail.

CONCEPTUAL DESIGN AND CONSTRUCTION DOCUMENTS FOR A WOOD BUILDING— BEACH HOUSE

15

SKYLIGHT

LOCATION OF SOLAR PANELS

SOUTH ELEVATION

Residence of Mr. and Mrs. Ted Bear

Conceptual Design

The site for this project was a small beach lot fronting the ocean in a southern California community. The site dimensions are 35 feet in width and 110 feet in depth, with the 35-foot dimension adjacent to a private road. The site ownership also included an additional 35 feet on the opposite side of the private road easement. Figure 15.1 graphically illustrates the site plan, showing its relationship to the ocean, access road, and compass direction.

Site Development Regulations

Site development regulations, enforced by the community's planning commission, covered building setback requirements, building height limit, parking requirements, and the allowable building coverage of the site. These are considered together with the site and floor plan development.

Other regulatory agencies included a design review board and a State coastal commission. The design review board primarily dealt with the architectural design of the building and the landscaping plan. The coastal commission is concerned with the protection of historical landmarks, access to the public beach, and energy conservation through, for example, the use of solar collectors to augment domestic water heating.

After researching all the site development regulations and gathering the design data for our clients' needs, we started the conceptual design process.

Client's Requirements

The clients, a middle-aged husband and wife whose children no longer live at home, wanted to develop the site to its maximum potential. The site allowed a two-story residence with a maximum floor area of 2,900 square feet measured from the inside wall dimensions. Given these two factors, they wanted the following rooms: living room, dining room, kitchen, study or family room, guest bath, mud room and laundry, and three bedrooms with two full bathrooms. They also wanted a two-car garage and shop area. Because this was a beach site, they also wanted to have sun decks wherever possible, as well as a sheltered outdoor area for winter.

Initial Schematic Studies

Our initial schematic studies worked around relationships among the rooms as well as room orientation on the site. Room orientation required that we locate the major rooms, such as the living room, dining room, and master bedroom, so that they would face the ocean and capture a coastline view. The garage and entry court needed to be adjacent to the private road for accessibility.

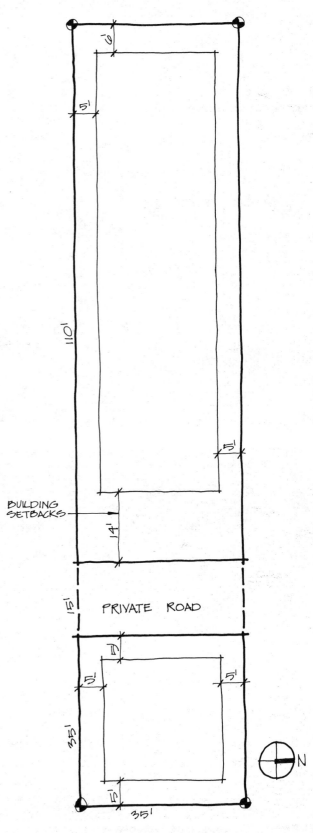

Figure 15.1 Conceptual design—site plan.

Because the site is small and because the setback regulations further reduced the buildable area, we obviously needed to design a two-story building to meet the clients' requested number of rooms.

First Floor. Figure 15.2 shows a schematic study of the first floor level. This figure also illustrates some early decisions we made: locating the entry court on the leeward side of the building; providing a view and access to the beach from the living, dining, and family rooms; locating the mud room and laundry in an area that would afford accessibility from the outside and to the beach; and providing a basement area for the mechanical system for space heating as well as a boiler for the solar collectors.

Second Floor. We developed a schematic study for the second floor level to show the desired location and relationships among the rooms as well as possible sun deck locations. We wanted all bedrooms to have direct access to a sun deck. See Figure 15.3.

Preliminary Floor Plans

Using the schematic studies as a basis for the various room locations, we developed scaled preliminary floor plan drawings.

First Floor. The first floor level, as Figure 15.4 shows, was planned to follow the site contour, which sloped to the beach. So we included floor transitions from the living room, dining room, and family room levels. Our choice of forty-five degree angles on the exterior window wall areas was influenced by a coastline view in the Southwest direction. As you can see, these angles in turn influenced other areas of the floor plan. At this stage, the scaled plan adhered to all the setback requirements and was within the allowable floor area established by the design review board.

Second Floor. The second floor preliminary plan, as Figure 15.5 shows, was basically an extension of the first floor level. It provided a master bedroom with an ocean view and had sun decks adjacent to the bedroom areas. A portion of the hall, which provided the circulation to the various rooms, was opened to the entry below. This gave the entry a high ceiling and allowed both areas to have natural light from a skylight.

Roof and Exterior Elevation Studies

From these preliminary floor plans, we developed roof and exterior elevation studies to investigate any design problems that might require some minor floor plan adjustments. We made these adjustments as we drew the floor plans for the construction documents.

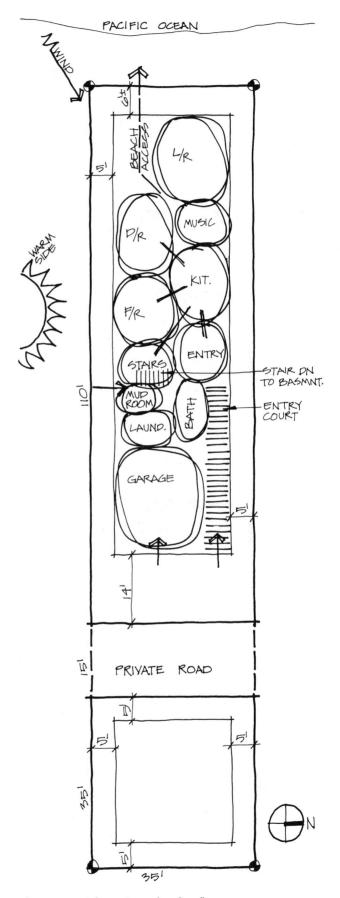

Figure 15.2 Schematic study—first floor.

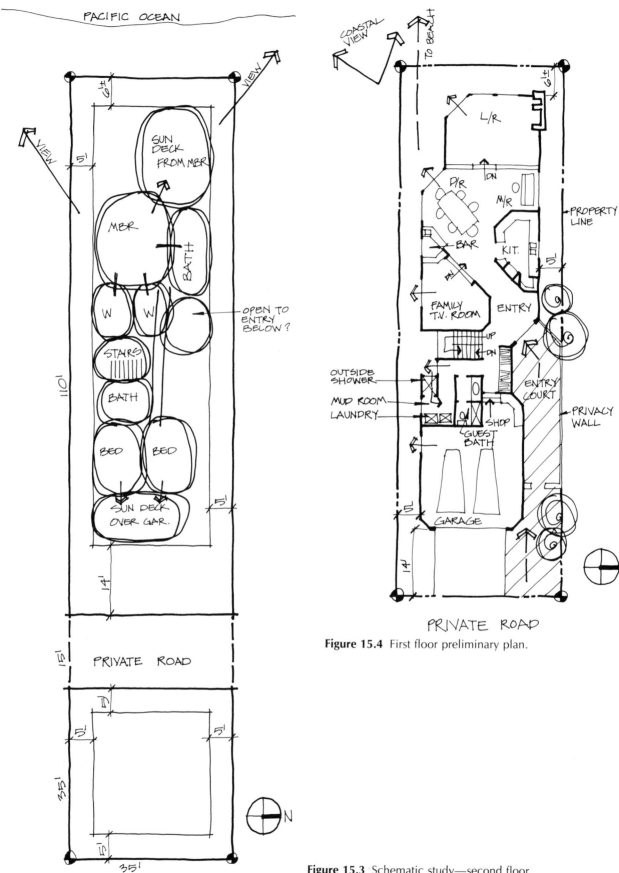

Figure 15.4 First floor preliminary plan.

Figure 15.3 Schematic study—second floor.

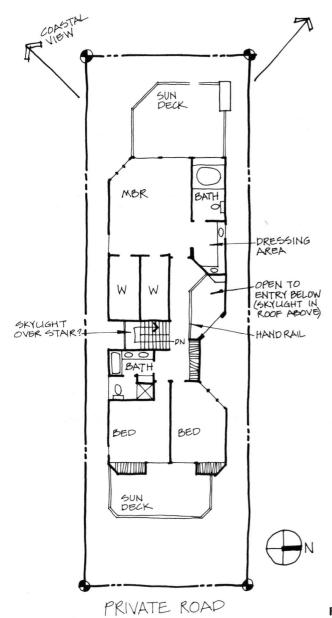

SKYLIGHT OVER STAIR?

PRIVATE ROAD

Figure 15.5 Second floor preliminary plan.

Roof Design. The development of the exterior elevations started with the roof design. We decided to use a roof pitch of 4½ in 12 to achieve an angle conducive to using solar collectors. We planned to locate these collectors on the recommended South side of the plane of the roof. This roof pitch provided the maximum height allowed by the design review board; it also determined the roof material. We selected shingle tile for the roof and cedar shingles for the exterior walls. Because salt air causes metal corrosion, we used wood windows and doors with a creosote stain finish. The glass was double glazing throughout to provide greater insulation during both the winter and summer months.

Exterior Elevations. The window designs combined fixed glass and operable sections as well as separate operable sections. Using the previously mentioned design criteria, we developed sketches of the exterior elevations. Figure 15.6 shows the four sides of this residence using these exterior materials and window elements. Because the material on the exterior was wood, we also exposed the wood lintel over the windows and doors.

After we completed these studies, we submitted them to the clients and to the various regulatory agencies. We incorporated their adjustments and refinements into the final drawing of the construction documents.

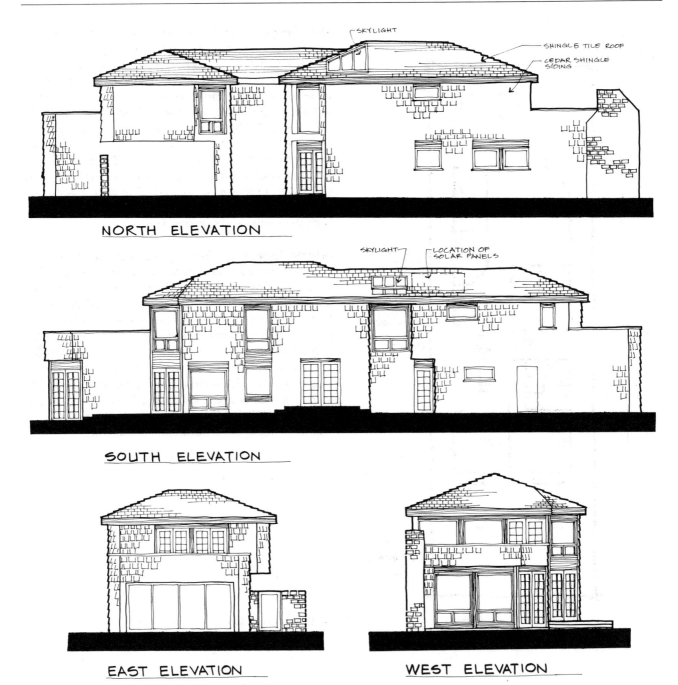

Figure 15.6 Conceptual design—exterior elevations.

Site Plan

Stage I

The first stage of the site plan (see Figure 15.7) eventually results in a combination site plan and roof plan. After planning the sheet layout, we traced the site layout from the civil engineer's drawing. We established the perimeter of the structure from both the ground floor and upper floor plan. We also did a light layout of the vicinity map

at this stage. The set of double lines at each end of the structure are second floor decks. Note the entry patio on one of the sides.

The roof is what is called a hip roof. The horizontal and perpendicular lines represent the top or peak of the roof (called the ridge), while the angular lines (always drawn at 45° to maintain a constant slope of the roof) represent what are called the hip and the valley. The hip and the valley mark the transition from one plane to another. See Figure 15.8.

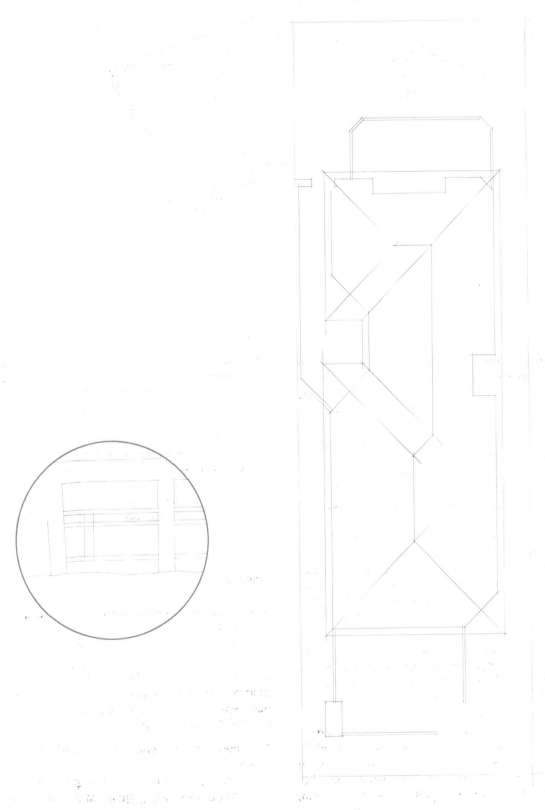

Figure 15.7 Site plan—Stage I.

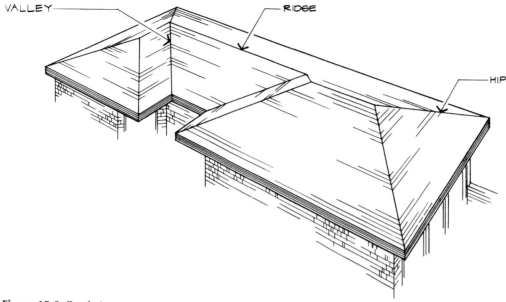

Figure 15.8 Roof view.

Stage II

After confirming the correct setbacks and the size of the structure in relationship to the site, we began the line darkening process. See Figure 15.9. On the vicinity map, we cut the plastic lid from a coffee can as a template for darkening the outline of the beach at the left. This is good practice for irregular lines for a beginner. An experienced drafter performs this freehand.

All lines on the site plan were darkened. Notice the change in the roof outline at the rear of the structure. Figure 15.10 shows the geometry to perform this cutting of the roof.

The outline of the structure was changed to a hidden line. Had the roof plan been separate from the site plan, the building would have been solid and the roof outline would have been dotted. The lines representing the shape of the roof would also have been eliminated. Skylights were put in two locations, at the entry and on the opposite side of the roof.

The round shapes found around the perimeter are planters. We next included the material designation for brick pavers as well as the wood benches at the back of the lot. We also made a correction in the size of the fireplace at this stage.

The series of close parallel lines at the front and the rear of the building indicated the guardrail around the deck created by a smaller second floor. The very small rectangular pieces attached to these parallel guardrail lines represent scuppers. Scuppers are used for draining

water that accumulates on the deck and are usually made of sheet metal. In this case, they project through an opening in the guardrail and allow the water to drip to the ground. They protrude beyond the surface of the guardrail to stop water from flowing onto the surface of the guardrail.

There are various levels on the ground surface. A look at the final stage of the building section (Figure 15.34) shows the different heights. The area adjacent to the family room is the highest; the property slopes downward to the rear and to the front from here. The lot slopes up again on the other side of the private road.

Stage III

Relocating the Vicinity Map. A check at this point showed that the vicinity map was in an inconvenient location. (See Figure 15.7). The general notes and sheet index still had to be located on this sheet. It was better to have the index on the right hand side opposite the binding edge where it is more accessible. So the vicinity map was moved, but not redrawn. (See Figure 15.11). We did this as follows:

1. A new sheet of vellum was placed over the original sheet.
2. Using a mat knife and a straight edge, both sheets were cut in half lengthwise at the same time.

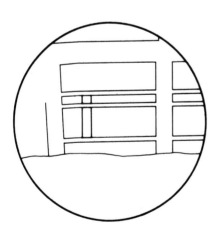

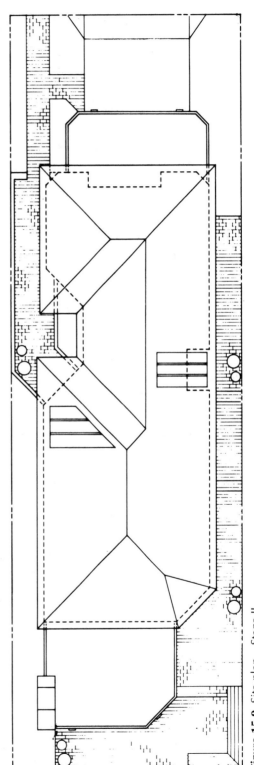

Figure 15.9 Site plan—Stage II.

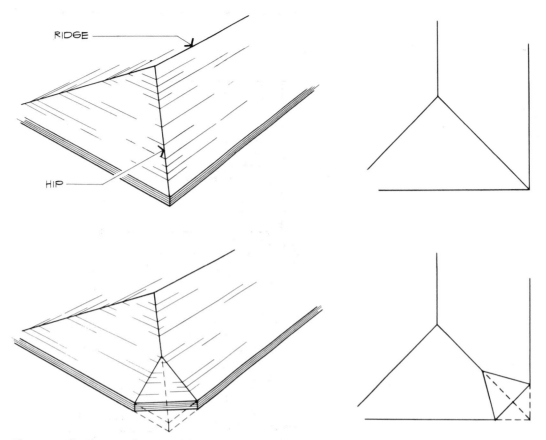

Figure 15.10 Change of a normal hip roof.

3. The upper half of the original sheet was replaced with the newly cut vellum and taped on the reverse side using transparent tape.
4. The original ½ sheet containing the vicinity map was placed over this newly assembled drawing in the now desired position.
5. Another cut around the vicinity map and through the 2 sheets of vellum was then made.
6. The cut out of the vicinity map was then taped in the new location with transparent tape on the reverse side.

The vicinity map was then finished by shading the subject property and identifying adjoining streets and the Pacific Ocean.

Setbacks, Improvements, and Notes. The setbacks—that is, the dimensions needed to locate the structure—were then added to the site plan. All improvements were dimensioned next. These improvements were located from the property line or the building itself. The direction of the slope of the roof, the decks, and even such areas as the driveway we indicated by arrows and/or notes.

Notes were next to be added and we used broad general terms. Utility lines were shown. Notice the abbreviation ''P.O.C.'' (point-of-connection) to the various utility lines. The sewer line is marked with an ''S'', the

gas line with a ''G'', and the water main with a ''W''. We showed hose bibb locations (garden hose connections) as well as the various steps around the lot.

Reference bubbles for the skylight areas were drawn to refer to a specific detail. Finally, we added the legal description at the extreme right.

Stage IV

The final stage for the site plan sheet is shown in Figure 15.12. In the previous stage we nearly finished the site and roof plan. All that remained was to add roof texture, which we did to show a variety of techniques. Some architectural offices prefer not to invest a drafter's time in this type of activity and leave the roof as it was in previous stage.

We made a correction to one of the skylights because we found that the exterior wall below forced a separation. Finally, we added the title, North arrow, construction notes, and sheet index. As you can see, the construction notes are not hand lettered, but they could have been. In this case, the notes were typed onto a piece of vellum cut from the larger sheet, then spliced back in when the typing was completed. Other methods already discussed in earlier chapters could have been used to apply the notes to the larger vellum.

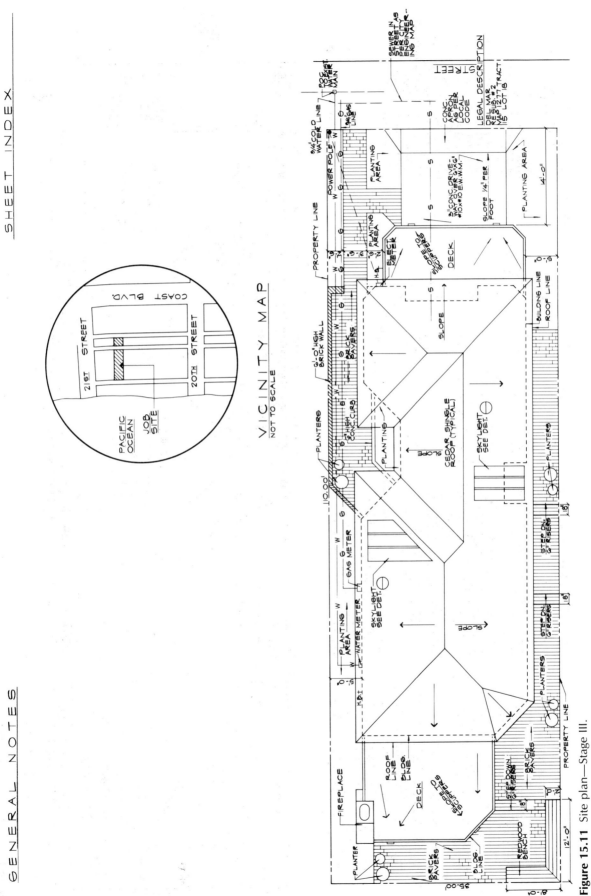

Figure 15.11 Site plan—Stage III.

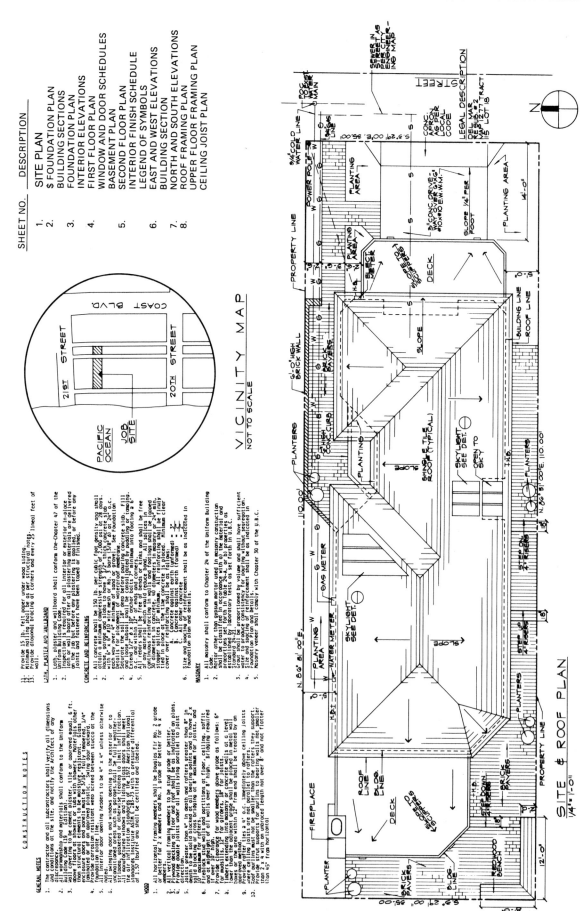

Figure 15.12 Site plan—Stage IV.

Foundation Plan: Slab

There are two foundation plans shown here, concrete slab and wood floor. These are shown to illustrate their differences and how they are drafted.

Stage I

Figure 15.13 shows the layout stage for both the foundation plan and two building sections. The basement retaining wall footing size has been dictated by the fact that the top of the retaining wall is restrained by the concrete floor slab.

The dotted and solid lines of the foundation plan show the shape of the footing and foundation walls. The double solid line around the perimeter of the garage represents a 6" curb that extends above the grade far enough to keep the sill away from termites.

All walls are bearing walls except the two in the laundry room, represented by a pair of dotted lines. The rectangle between the family room and the dining room, drawn with a solid line, represents a step down.

The foundation plan and details are used to figure the shape of the building sections. The horizontal lines between floors in the sections represent the thickness of the slab floor. The three horizontal lines between the lower floor and the upper floor are the header (support beam at openings) line for windows and doors, the plate line, and the floor line.

The two lines between the upper floor and the roof are the header line and the plate line. The angular lines represent the rafters. The building section on the left was taken through the dining room and between the kitchen and living room. The other building section was taken through the family room and entry to show the basement and how the entry extends through both floors (this will become visible in the next stages of the drawing).

Stage II

Figure 15.14 shows the beginning of the dimensioning stage for the foundation and the refinement stage for the building sections. These cross sections could appear on the same sheet as the longitudinal section in order to group similar drawings. However, for learning purposes, the building sections are shown here with the foundation plan.

The sizes for the various members in the building section were obtained from the structural engineer's framing plan. However, with this type of structure, this framing plan could have been done "in house."

Freehand sketches of details help greatly at this stage. See the illustrations in Chapter 14 for architectural details.

The dimensions at the corners of the structure for the angles are not really necessary but they are included to help the contractor. The rectangle at the left top corner is the foundation for the fireplace. Local codes should be checked for fireplace requirements. The dots represent the vertical steel included in earthquake areas. Check the sheets to make sure that every exterior and interior wall (and the foundation under them) can be located from either side. Check for size and location.

Stage III

Building Sections. At this stage the building sections are being refined. See Figure 15.15. The quality of lines is improved, and the material designations for such items as concrete, masonry, and insulation is the delineation of the structural components such as joists, studs, beams, and rafters. Here we tried to show what the roof would look like based on the precise location of the cutting plane. Rather than seeing the ridge at the top of the building section, the cutting plane exposes this end view of the rafters. We could have taken, instead, an offset section by moving the cutting plane running through the building to expose the most comprehensible structure. If we had done this, we would have exposed the ridge at the top rather than the rafters.

Notice the location of the beam on the left building section and the furred (lowered) ceiling. On the right building section, notice too how the stud goes from almost the ground level to the roof, two stories tall. These are 2 × 6 studs rather than the normal 2 × 4 studs because of the increased vertical span. The eaves (intersection of the roof and wall) are closed off by a horizontal member.

Structurally, the building section shows the retaining wall in the basement. Because the slab is pinned (attached) to the outer walls, it stops the walls of the basement from caving inward.

Foundation Plan. This is the stage during which the numerical values are added. The dimensions must coincide with the floor plan. Both *must* be to the stud line. The edge of the concrete foundation wall is also the stud line. Detail reference bubbles are located and the material designation for the masonry in the fireplace is drafted. See Figure 15.15.

Stage IV

This is the noting stage—the final stage for both the building sections and the foundation plan. See Figure 15.16.

Sections. We first established vertical distances which were taken from floor line to plate line. Each room that the building sections cut through is labeled to make its cutting location clear. We next labeled parts of the building: floor, ceilings, and roof coverings, plus special beams, and so forth. Detail reference bubbles, scale, and titles completed this portion of the sheet.

Foundation Plan. After double checking the dimensions, we put in the building section reference bubbles and their symbols. Notes were added next. These notes take the form of descriptions of the slab, sizes of spread footings, or notes describing the drafter lined, as in the case of the steps. Omission of the waterproof (W.P.) membrane in the garage area was also noted, as was the slope of the slab. The title, scale, and North arrow finished this sheet.

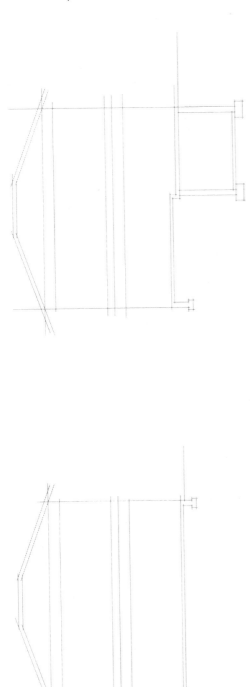

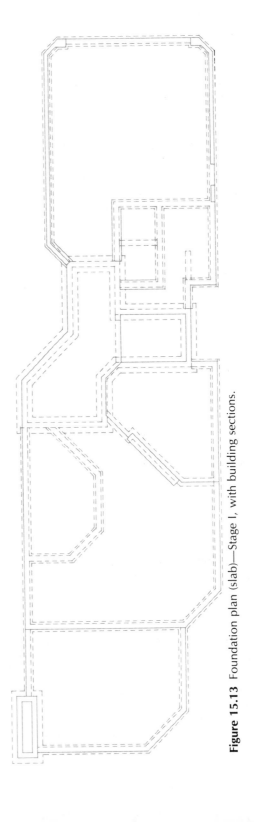

Figure 15.13 Foundation plan (slab)—Stage I, with building sections.

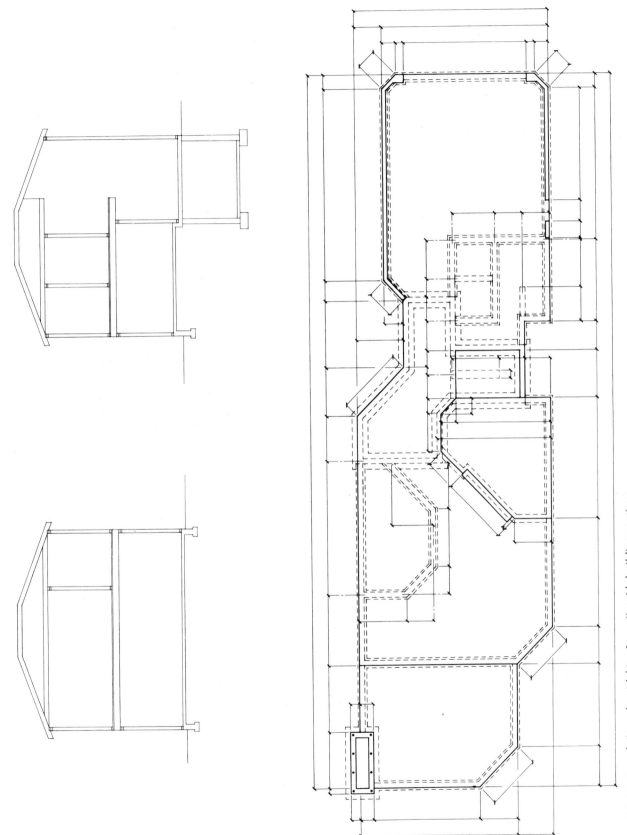

Figure 15.14 Foundation plan (slab)—Stage II, with building sections.

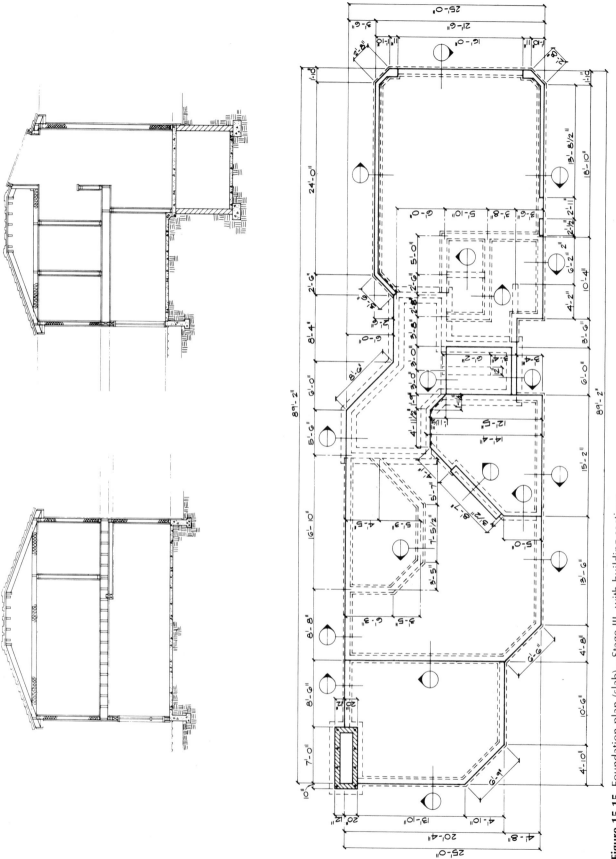

Figure 15.15 Foundation plan (slab)—Stage III, with building sections.

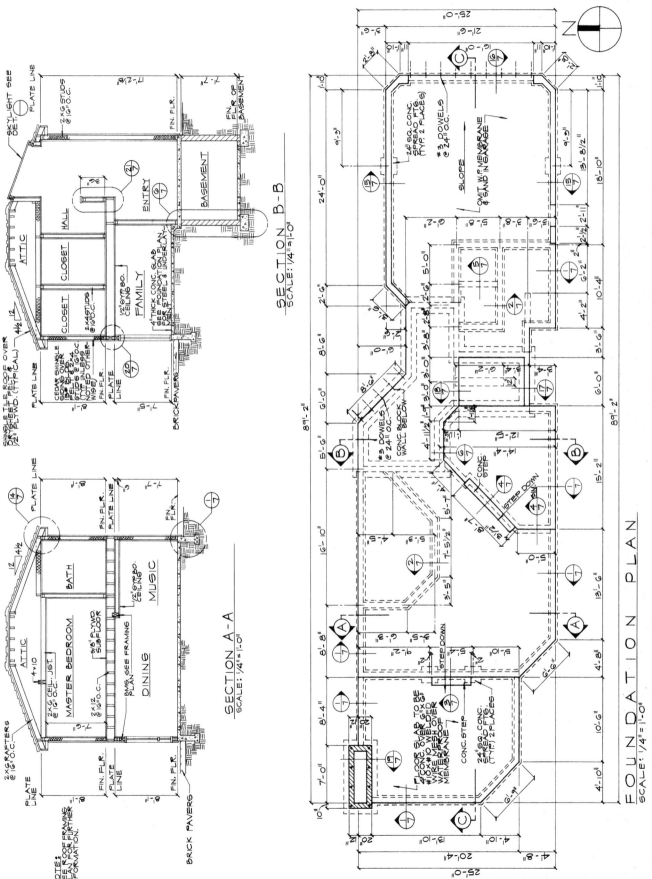

Figure 15.16 Foundation plan (slab)—Stage IV, with building sections.

Foundation Plan: Wood

Both a wood floor and concrete slab floor system were developed for this beach house. While preparing two foundation plans for a single project is not customary, it was done here for comparison so that the reader can see the difference of appearance between a wood and concrete floor. The slab foundation will be used throughout the remainder of this set of drawings.

Stage I

The layout of the foundation plan (Figure 15.17) was done after the floor plan had been finalized to the point where all exterior and interior walls were established.

The structural considerations should always be analyzed so that the design of the foundation can take those considerations into account. Basically, there were three levels in this structure. On the first floor the rooms are on one level with the exception of the living room near the fireplace and the triangular family room. However, the foundation plan shows four levels: the three mentioned above plus the basement located directly below the entry.

The footing for the basement retaining wall is large because it is not restrained at the top and acts as a full cantilever. The dotted lines in the basement area represent footing shape. The dotted lines do not extend into the area below the hall between the garage and entry; because the leg of the footing is so large that the garage and entry overlap each other, they are treated as a solid mass. The garage is the only area that is a slab on the ground. The double lines around the edge represent the width of the 6″ wall. This extends above the ground to keep the wood sill away from the ground level, protecting it from termites.

The square forms represent the piers. One form, adjacent to the kitchen, is not square but rectangular. Because of the design of this structure, two girders were going to land on this pier, so the pier size was increased.

The rectangular shape at the corner of the living room represents the fireplace and the dots represent the reinforcing bars to be placed vertically. The series of center lines between the laundry room and the garage represents dowels that hold the slab of the garage to the foundation wall of the house.

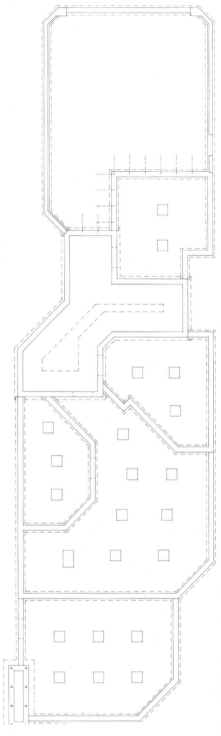

Figure 15.17 Foundation plan (wood)—Stage I.

Note the solid and dotted lines around the perimeter of the foundation walls. The solid line, like the one in the garage, represents a break in the portion that extends above the slab level and is for a door. The dotted lines represent an opening for access from one underfloor area to another. From the basement there is access to any of three underfloor areas. There is also access to the area below the kitchen from the area below the dining room. This access is located where there is no supporting wall or partition. There is also underfloor access near the fireplace.

The basement wall is concrete block and does not follow the block module. We decided to forego the block module measurement because it was costly and unnecessary for this small a use.

Stage II

We made a check print on which freehand dimension lines, actual dimensions, notes, and missing items like girders and so on were drawn. See Figure 15.18. This information was then transferred onto the final drawing. The following stages illustrate the placement of the information from the check print.

The space above the foundation plan on this sheet was allocated to the interior elevations. Stage II of the foundation plan also became Stage I of the interior elevations. The elevation on the top left is the downstair bathroom; the one directly to the right is the bathroom on the upper floor; the last two on the right of the top row are the master bath. The three directly below are interior elevations of the kitchen.

The outline of the foundation plan was now confirmed and checked for size. Dimension lines were introduced. Because of the various angles throughout the structure, dimension lines were often crossed by extension lines and other dimension lines. The extension lines on the bottom left corner were broken for the dimension lines. We did this because dimension lines take precedence over extension lines.

Girders were overlooked and were added at a later stage. A final correction that might be made later using this stage for comparison is a wall that separates the two sets of stairs. The dotted lines representing the end of the retaining wall disappear because the space between the dotted lines is filled with a footing for the new wall. A look at the building sections explains this better.

Stage III

Compare Stage II and III drawings (Figures 15.18 and 15.19) at the stair and notice the change in the pattern of the hidden lines. Because the walls of the basement and the fireplace were masonry units, the material designation for masonry (diagonal lines) was drafted.

We next added the numbers for the dimensions. See Figure 15.19. These dimensions must always coincide with the floor plan's. We also included reference bubbles for details at this stage. We drew vertical dimension lines on the interior elevations, cleaned up all lines, and drafted additional details such as door swing designations, shelves, and handles on doors and drawers.

Stage IV

Interior Elevations. Here we added material designations such as ceramic tile on interior elevation #1 and kick space material. See Figure 15.20. We deleted the solid line for the refrigerator by using the erasing shield method. The numerical values for the vertical dimension lines were next to be included. We eliminated small corrections such as the lines above and below the oven. Finally, we put the notes in. Remember that a set of written specifications is included as part of these construction documents. Our notes, therefore, were general in nature, and descriptive but not specific. Reference bubble numbers and titles completed this step.

Foundation Plan. The main difference between this stage and the previous stage was the inclusion of girders (floor beams to support floor joists). They are shown by a very dark center line. Joists are shown by a dark line and arrows (half arrowheads); these show the size, spacing, and direction of the floor joists. See Figure 15.20.

The floor joists were running parallel to the garage door in the area of the bathroom, stairs, and entry. The rest of the house—family room, dining room, kitchen, music room, and living room—had floor joists running perpendicular to the garage door.

A rectangle with a single diagonal line indicates the break in the foundation wall between one area and the next. A note on the bottom left explains the drafting system being used. Additional notes about venting were added in the garage area. This would show up in drafted form on the exterior elevation if an exterior elevation of a wood floor system were drafted. Reference bubble numbers, title, scale, and North arrow complete this drawing.

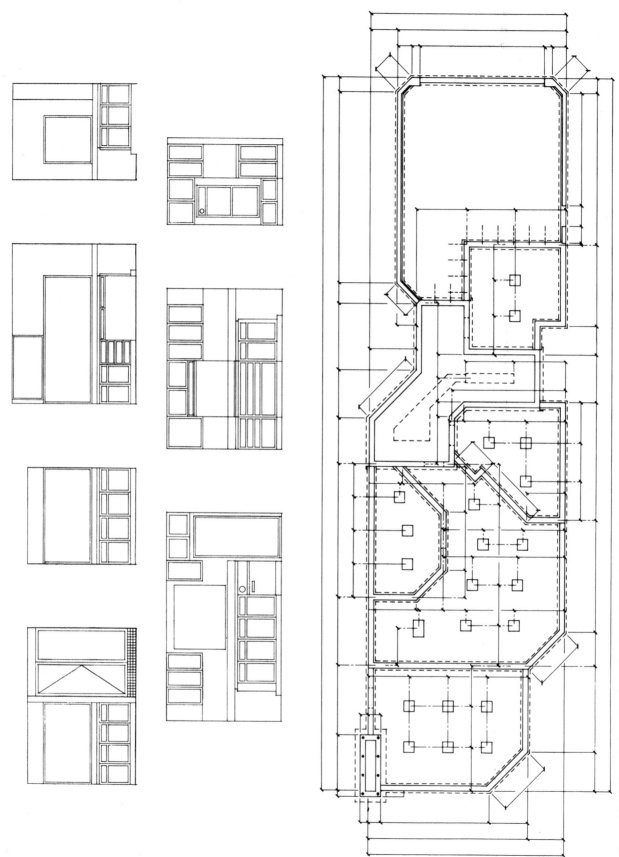

Figure 15.18 Foundation plan (wood)—Stage II, with interior elevations.

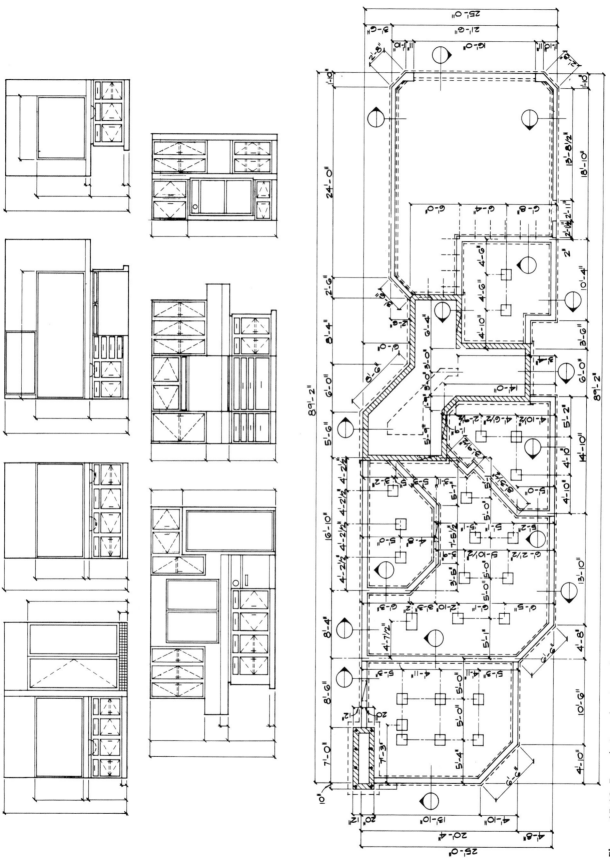

Figure 15.19 Foundation plan (wood)—Stage III, with interior elevations.

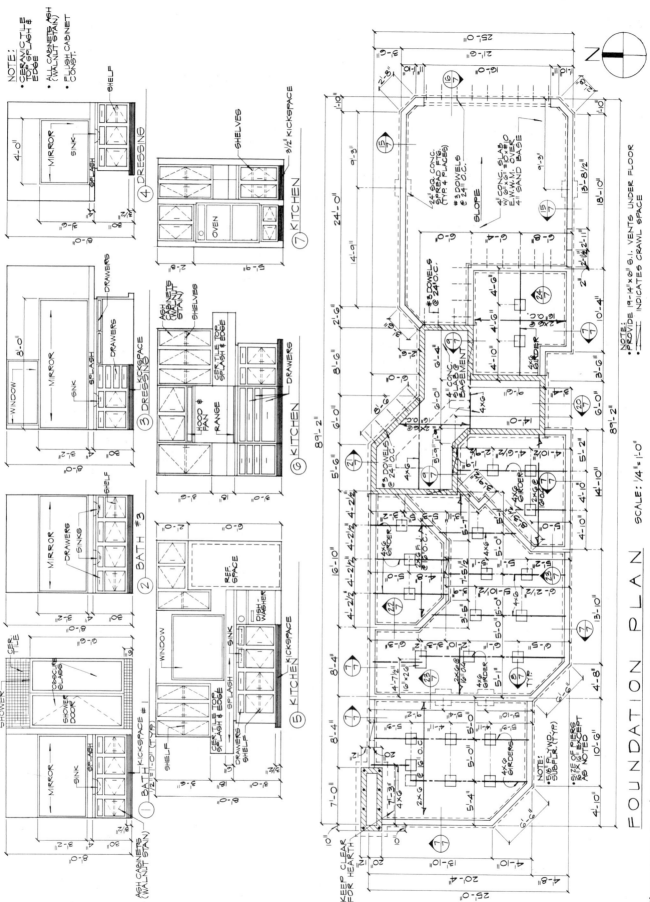

Figure 15.20 Foundation plan (wood)—Stage IV, with interior elevations.

First Floor Plan

Stage I

While the lines in Figure 15.21 appear dark because of the photographic method used in textbook reproduction, this is actually the light block-out stage. Measurements are carefully taken from the preliminary floor plan, verified, and checked against the site plan.

The door jambs of the garage and entry are enlarged to give the illusion of a thicker wall construction. The "U" shaped area in the kitchen was designed to eventually house a built-in oven. The area with the shower adjacent to the laundry room functions as the mud room. Here those coming in from the beach can wash off sand and change out of bathing suits before entering the main portion of the house.

Stage II

At this stage, all equipment was placed in the kitchen and the bathrooms. See Figure 15.22. Note the wet bar between the dining room and the family room. The stairs to the basement and to the upper level are shown. Most important are the level changes that are beginning to show between the living room and dining room and the dining room and family room, and the slight change between the garage and the house. Windows and doors around the perimeter were also located. The wall lines were darkened. Sepia copies were made for the structural, mechanical, and electrical consultants.

Stage III

Figure 15.23 shows the preliminary layout stage for the window and door schedules. The format is normally established by office standards. This format follows the A.I.A. standard with allowances for specific structures. This information usually comes from the designer and/ or architect.

This is also the preliminary stage for the basement plan. The basement is made of concrete block but is so small it will not follow the block module. Had the area been larger, a standard block module would have been used. The basement area was designed to house the boiler for the solar collectors and the mechanical equipment for space heating.

This is a critical step in the plan because it is the dimension line stage. This step also includes variations of line quality because while the dimension lines must be precise, they must not take away from the main body of the drawing. Every wall and partition must be located and every door and window must be sized. See Chapter 8, on floor plans, for a method for wood structures.

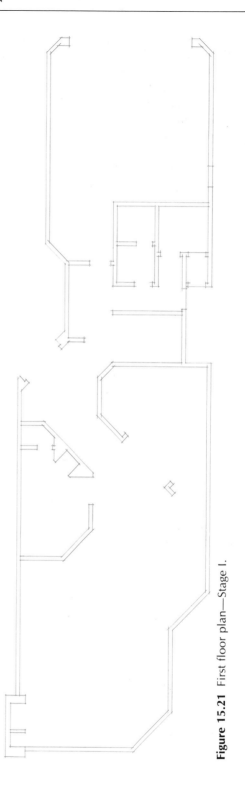

Figure 15.21 First floor plan—Stage I.

The measurements on the angular walls were included to help the contractor check accuracy. These dimensions must not only be graphically correct but trigonometrically correct as well. Because of the many angles, many dimension lines may cross each other. This crossing should be kept to a minimum.

Electrical fixtures are also shown. This floor plan eventually incorporated a complete electrical plan. Larger buildings, however, often have a separate electrical plan.

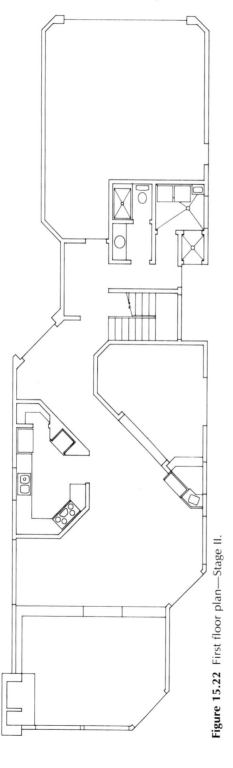

Figure 15.22 First floor plan—Stage II.

At this stage, dimensioning could be established by indicating the dimensions directly on a check print of the floor plan. Door and window designations were also added at this stage.

Stage IV

The window and door schedules were now due to be finished. See Figure 15.24. Remember that each door and window described is different. The schedules do not list every single door and window, just each different *type* of door or window. For example, the #2 window is used frequently in the plan, but is only listed once in the schedule.

Fixed windows are also listed here because they are manufactured and brought to the job. If fixed windows are built on the job site, the size is dimensioned on the exterior elevation and not listed on the schedule. The identification numbers for windows and doors found in the "SYM" (symbol) column of the schedule were put into reference bubbles on the plan. Since both the plan and the schedules were on the same sheet, the reference bubbles did not need to be divided into halves to show the sheet number.

Manufacturers' numbers and brand names are not on this sheet. These will be included on the specifications. However, switches to electrical outlet lines were included at this stage.

On the door schedule, the abbreviation "S.C." is for solid core, "H.C." for hollow core, and "P.P.T." for polished plate tempered. Some schedules also use numbers for doors and letters for windows.

Stage V

Corrections were made on the schedules after checking with the senior drafter. Room titles were now included on the floor plan. See Figure 15.25. Various pieces of equipment such as the range, oven, and sink were described, as were other parts of the structure such as closets, garage doors, lift counter for the bar, and so on. The titles are general and do not include the construction method, finish, or function. Naturally, the dimensions were checked again and corrections made where necessary. Titles, scale, and North arrow completed this sheet.

Second Floor Plan

Stage I

The upper floor plan has many walls that align themselves with the walls below on the ground floor. Therefore, the light blockout of the upper floor plan (Figure 15.26) was done by first overlaying the vellum on top of the ground floor plan and using the information from the preliminary floor plan.

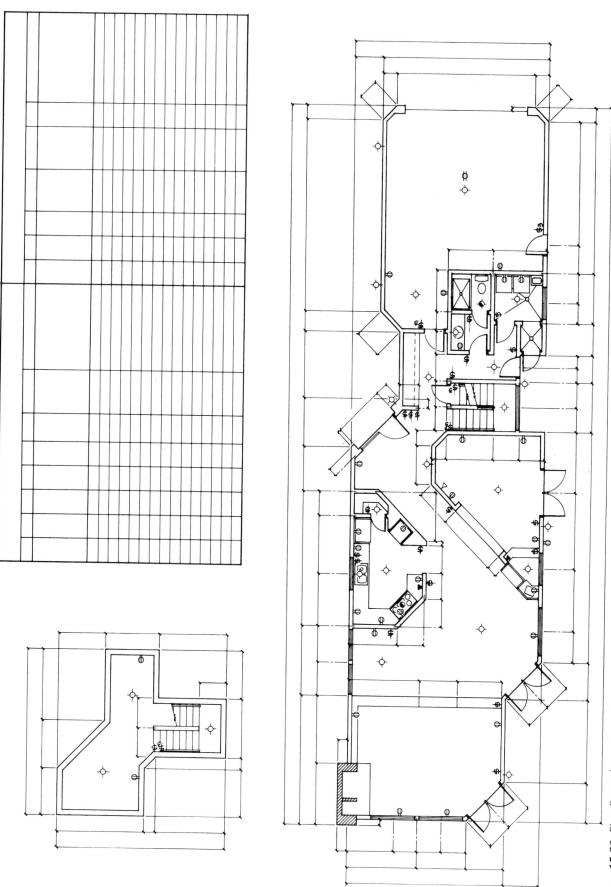

Figure 15.23 First floor plan—Stage III.

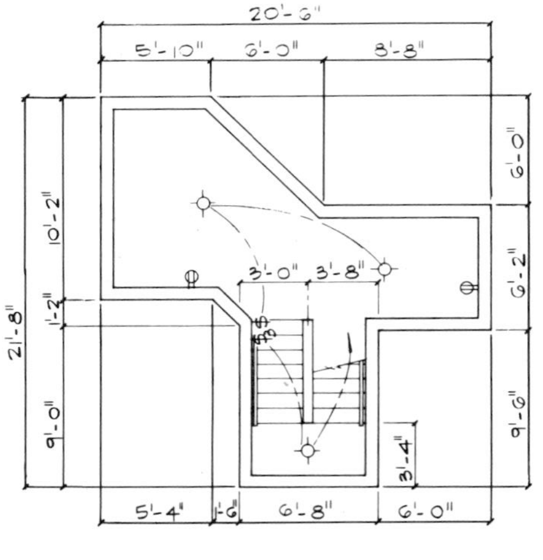

DOOR SCHEDULE

SYM.	WIDTH	HEIGHT	THK	HC/SC	TYPE	MATERIAL	REMARKS
1	PR.3'-0"	6'-8"	1 3/4"	S.C.	GLASS PANEL	WD./GLS.	USE 1/4" GLS. P.P.T.
2	2'-8"	6'-8"	1 3/4"	—	FRENCH DOOR	WOOD	
3	2'-4"	6'-8"	1 3/4"	S.C.	SLAB	WOOD	ASH
4	2'-8"	6'-8"	1 3/4"	S.C.	SLAB	WOOD	ASH
5	2'-6"	6'-8"	1 3/8"	H.C.	SLAB	WOOD	
6	2'-4"	6'-8"	1 3/8"	H.C.	SLAB	WOOD	
7	2'-8"	6'-8"	1 3/8"	H.C.	SLAB	WOOD	
8	2'-0"	6'-8"	1 3/8"	H.C.	SLAB	WOOD	
9	PR.2'-4"	6'-8"	1 3/4"	S.C.	GLASS PANEL	WD./GLS.	USE 1/4" GLS. P.P.T.
10	PR.3'-2"	6'-8"	1 3/8"	H.C.	BI-FOLD	WD. (ASH)	
11	PR.2'-0"	6'-8"	1 3/8"	H.C.	SLAB	WD. (ASH)	
12	9'-0"	6'-8"	1 3/8"	H.C.	BI-FOLD	WD. (ASH)	
13	PR.3'-0"	7'-8"	1 3/4"	—	FRENCH DOOR	WOOD	
14	5'-8"	6'-8"	1 3/8"	H.C.	BI-FOLD	WD. (ASH)	
15	6'-6"	6'-8"	1 3/8"	H.C.	BI-FOLD	WD. (ASH)	

WINDOW SCHEDULE

SYM.	WIDTH	HEIGHT	TYPE	FRAME	SCR	REMARKS
1	3'-6"	4'-0"	FIXED	WOOD		1/4" TEMP. CASEMENT BELOW
2	4'-0"	2'-0"	CASEMENT	WOOD		1/4" TEMP.
3	6'-0"	7'-0"	FIXED	WOOD		1/4" TEMP. CASEMENT BELOW
4	4'-0"	4'-0"	FIXED	WOOD		1/4" TEMP.
5	2'-0"	4'-0"	CASEMENT	WOOD		1/4" TEMP.
6	4'-0"	6'-0"	FIXED	WOOD		1/4" TEMP. CASEMENT BELOW
7	6'-0"	6'-0"	FIXED	WOOD		1/4" TEMP.
8	6'-0"	6'-0"	FIXED	WOOD		1/4" TEMP. CASEMENT BELOW
9						

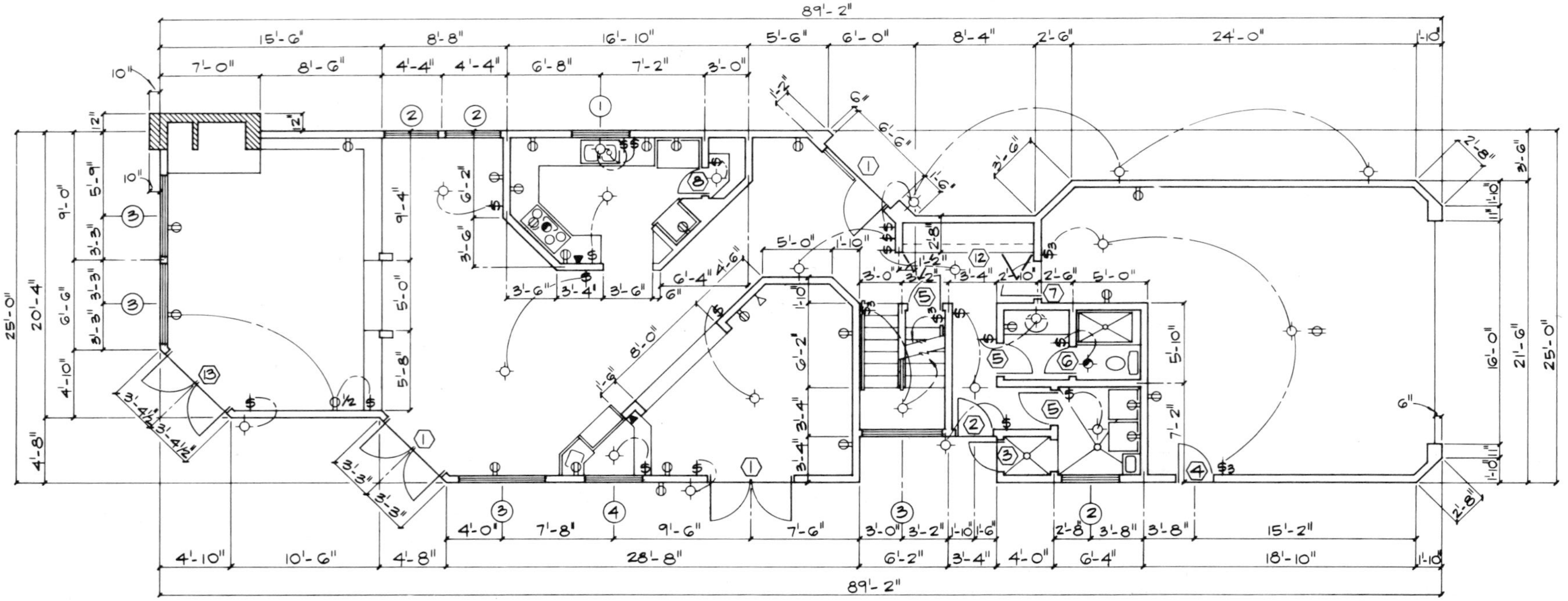

Figure 15.24 First floor plan—Stage IV.

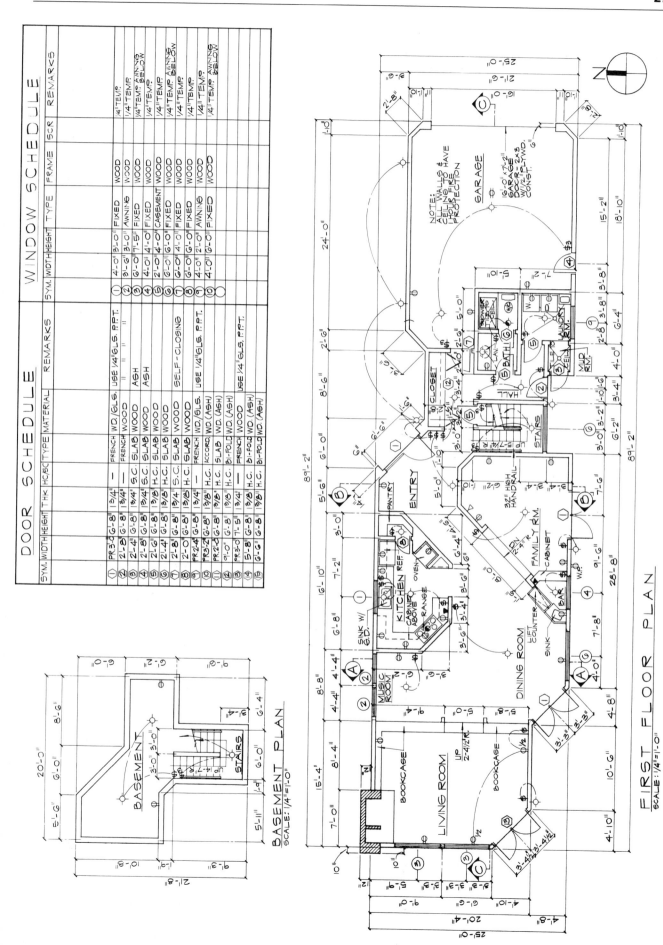

Figure 15.25 First floor plan—Stage V.

The exterior walls, stairs, entry, and fireplace were good locations to register one drawing with another. Check the preliminary upper floor plan (Figure 15.5) for various room names. Note the deck areas, the upper entry area (the entry is two stories high), the cantilever (overhang without support) of one of the bedrooms near the entry, and the two walk-in wardrobe closets in the master bedroom.

Stage II

Figure 15.27 shows the stage at which bathroom equipment, closet poles, stairs, and several windows were located and the handrail around the opening at the upper entry was drawn. Hard lines were drawn for the walls and the intersecting corners were cleaned up with an eraser. The rectangle adjacent to the sunken tub is a planter. A planter over the entry would be added later.

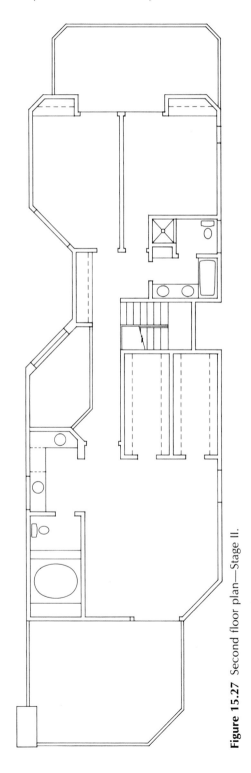

Figure 15.26 Second floor plan—Stage I.

Figure 15.27 Second floor plan—Stage II.

Stage III

A chart, called the finish schedule, for the description of the finish on the various wall and floor surfaces was begun in the top left corner. To the right of the finish schedule is the legend for the various symbols used, such as electrical outlets, switches, and telephone jacks. See Figure 15.28.

We added dimension lines to the floor plan. As with the foundation plan, the dimension lines were not done initially on this plan but rather were done freehand on a check print, checked for accuracy, and transferred to this sheet.

We decided to incorporate the electrical plan into the floor plan. So we included switches, outlets, duplex convenience outlets, and so on here. Doors and windows were also completed. Compare this drawing with the final stage (Figure 15.30) and determine whether any dimensions were changed or corrected.

Stage IV

The symbol legend, showing various symbols used on the floor plan, was now finished. See Figure 15.29. The interior finish schedule was partly finished. Window and door numbers were included on the floor plan. We also placed two smoke detectors in the hall.

After discussion with the clients, we decided to use bi-fold doors rather than sliding doors into the master bath. We changed the wall that separates the stairs. This change then affected the foundation plan. See Stage II of the foundation plan, Figure 15.4. The electrical switch to outlet lines were also included at this stage.

Finally, we added dimensions. These dimensions had to be checked against those on the lower floor plan. It is always important to check walls that line up under one another.

Stage V

We then filled in the interior finish schedule on a check print based on consultation with the clients. The information was then transferred to this sheet. See Figure 15.30.

We added notes at this stage which included titles and necessary area descriptions. As with the ground floor plan, the notes are general in nature and do not describe construction methods, workmanship, or installation requirements that are described in the specifications. Addition of the main title completed this sheet.

Building Section/Elevations

Because of the available space, the longitudinal section and two of the narrow elevations were combined. Many of the lines drawn on the first stages should be lightly identified in pencil and later erased.

Stage I

Elevations. At this preliminary stage (Figure 15.31), floor lines, header lines, plate lines, and ridge lines were lightly blocked out. All of these measurements were taken from the sections.

Building Section. This drawing coordinates the foundation plan, basement plan, first floor plan, second floor plan, and roof plan with preliminary details or structural decisions already made. The stairs were drawn in first, since their horizontal and vertical dimensions are critical.

Stage II

Building Section. Compare the stair footing area in Figure 15.32 with the foundation plan (slab) in Figure 15.16. A basement wall between the stairs was now included. All interior and exterior walls were also outlined using Western frame construction, and the location of walls and guardrails was taken from the floor plan.

The upper floor level was definitely established as were the various horizontal members. Specific sizes of these members were obtained from the structural engineer, architect, or another supervisor. All of the lines were cleaned up and darkened.

Elevations. The previous stage had established all of the horizontal lines. This stage now produced all the vertical and angular roof lines. The vertical lines were obtained from the floor plans. The elevation on the left side now begins to show a cantilever. The elevation on the right begins to show the exterior form of the fireplace. Both elevations also begin to show the outline of the balcony and the roof forms.

A drawing of a roof can be constructed from scratch, like a building section, or the shape can be obtained from the building section itself. Still another way is to orthographically project it from the roof plan, if such a drawing is available. Note that all of the horizontal lines that were drafted in the first stage do not appear here. They are there, but drafted so lightly that the reproduction process did not print them.

Stage III

Building Section. All of the individual members were drafted in at this stage. Of particular interest is the top of the roof. See Figure 15.33. Examine the second floor plan (Figure 15.30) or the roof framing plan (Figure 15.40). These show where this actual section slice was taken.

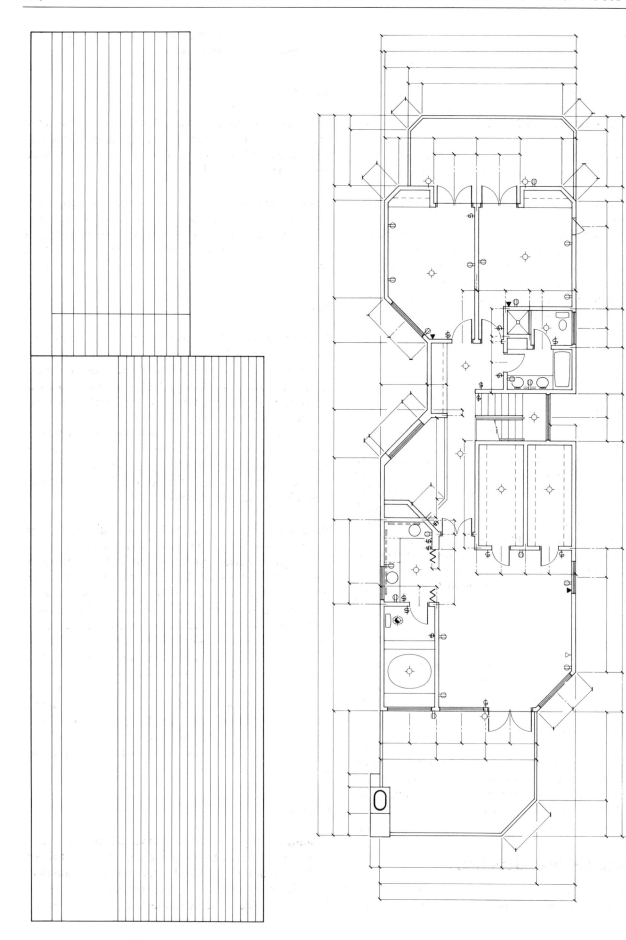

Figure 15.28 Second floor plan—Stage III.

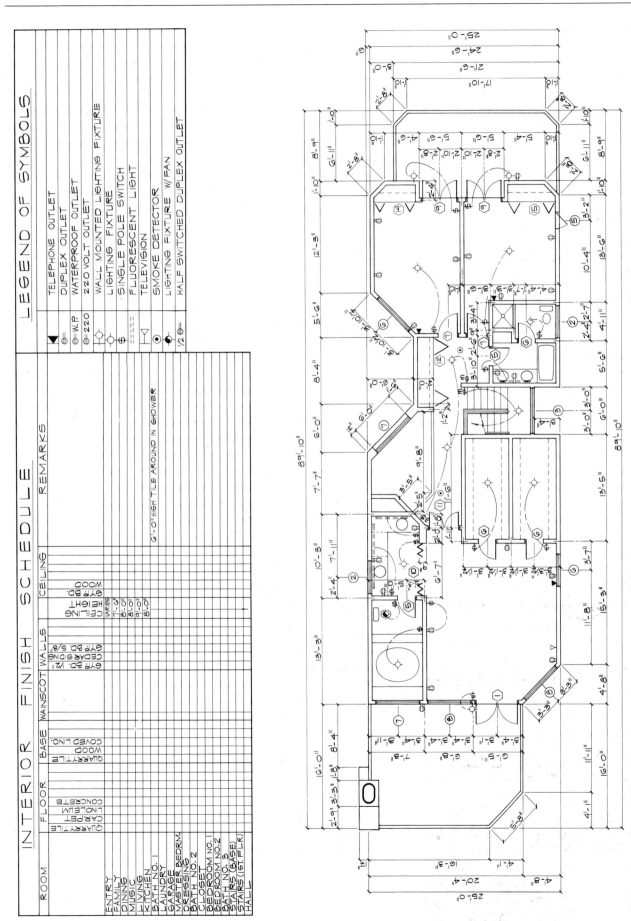

Figure 15.29 Second floor plan—Stage IV.

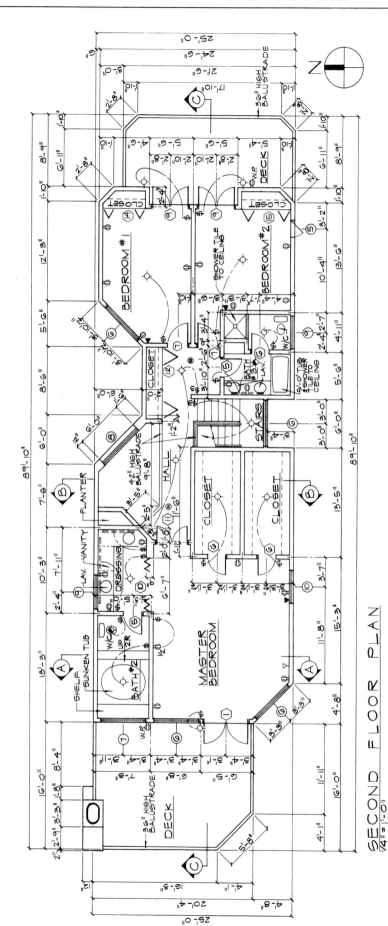

Figure 15.30 Second floor plan—Stage V.

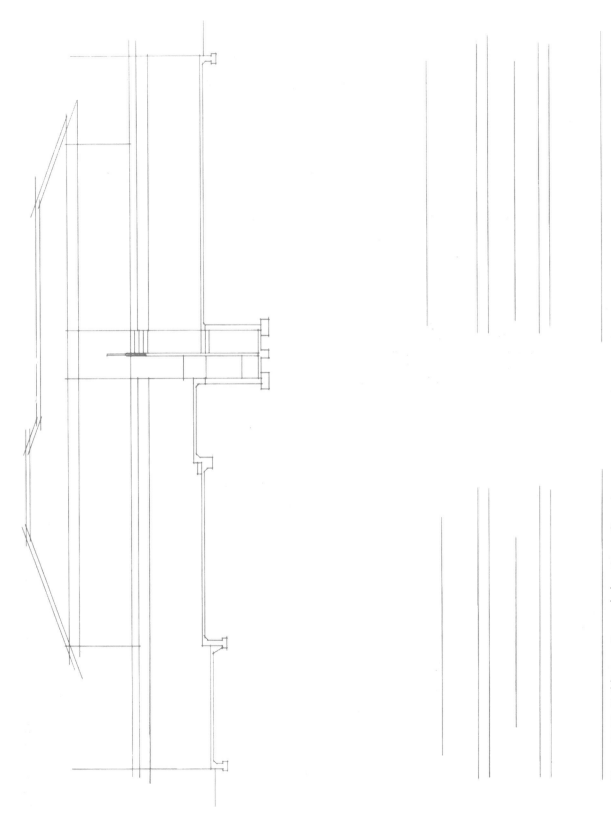

Figure 15.31 Building section and elevations—Stage I.

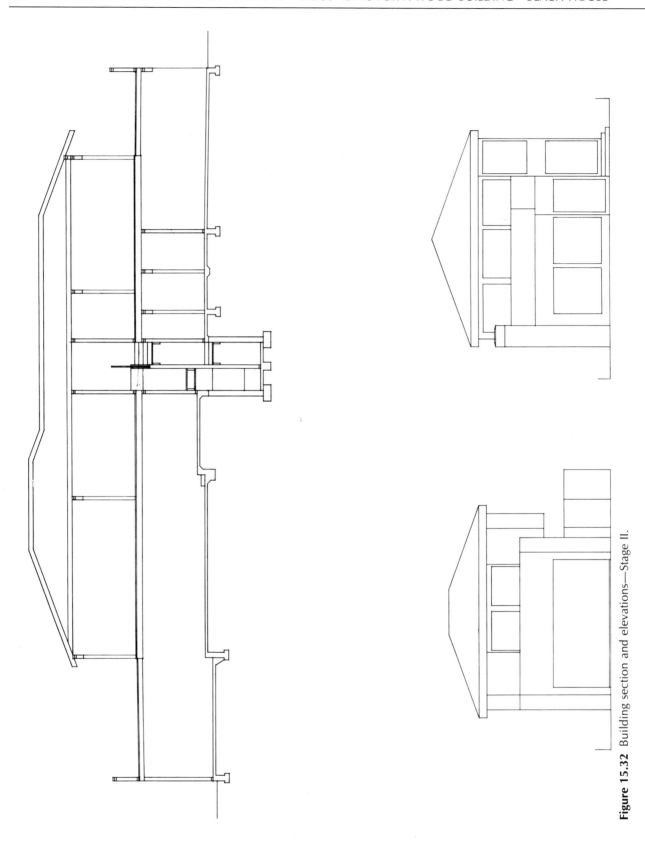

Figure 15.32 Building section and elevations—Stage II.

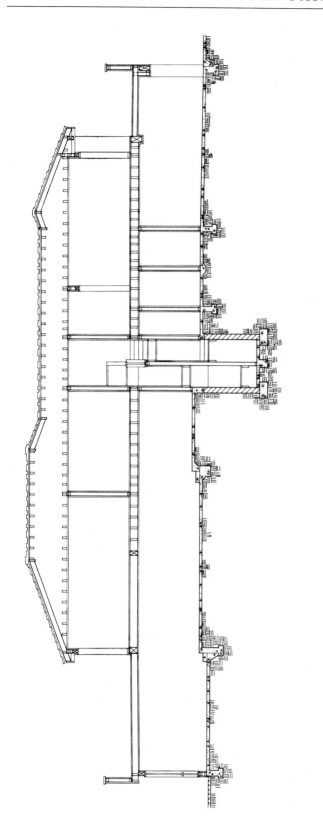

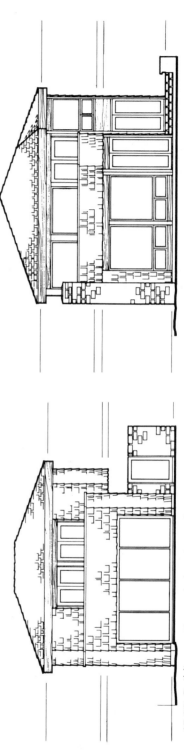

Figure 15.33 Building section and elevations—Stage III.

The ridge, especially at the left, is missed by the slice and therefore shows the rafters coming forward. An offset section would pick up the ridge but we decided to show a straight slice. Not shown is the ridge behind sloping up and back away. You should refer to the details relevant to this structure that are found in Chapter 14. These details, such as footing details, guardrails, and eave details, help explain, in an enlarged form, some of the critical areas in the structure.

Material designations—earth, concrete block, concrete, and shingle tile—were added at this stage.

Elevations.   Material designations for the roof, the surface of the wall, and the masonry units were drafted. The total surface material is *not* shown. There is, however, enough shown to identify the material and to help the profiling, which was also completed at this stage. Windows and door shapes were confirmed from the manufacturer's literature and drawn accurately.

Stage IV

This was the final stage for both the building section and the exterior elevations.

Exterior Elevations.   Vertical dimensions were referred to the building section for the sake of clarity and to avoid duplication. See Figure 15.34. The hidden lines designating the swing of doors and windows were drafted, together with the divisions (called lights) in the french doors. Various notes were placed on the elevations to identify such items as the fascia, shingles, gate, and garage door.

Building Section.   Vertical heights were established based on the type of framing chosen and the head clearance required by local code. We obtained basic framing member sizes and noted them from the structural engineering drawings. You should look at this drawing (Section C-C in Figure 15.34) together with the foundation plan and roof framing plan. Together, they answer many questions. Detail references, room titles, drawing title, and scale finished this drawing.

Exterior Elevations

Stage I

Before starting the exterior elevations, you should always carefully study two drawings: the floor plans and building sections. The floor plans give the width and length of the structure. In this case, the upper floor is not the same size as the lower floor. The building section establishes all the heights.

In Figure 15.35, the heights were laid out lightly first and then identified lightly in pencil. The elevations to be drawn here were the North and South elevations. Looking at the upper (North) elevation, the first two lines at the bottom of the layout are floor lines. The next two lines above these are the header lines (tops of windows). And above these, two lines run the full width of the sheet. The lower is the plate line and the upper is the floor line for the second floor. The next short line is the top of the guardrail on the balcony.

The next two long lines above the guardrail line are the header line and plate line, respectively. Finally, the two top lines are the ridge of the roof. These should usually be lightly drawn in.

The lower (South) elevation resembles the upper, but the lines are reversed (left becomes right and right becomes left) because the elevation being drafted is a view in the opposite direction. Another difference is the variation in the floor lines and header lines for the first floor in the South elevation.

Stage II

Study Figure 15.36. This is the stage that gave the exterior elevation shape. The floor plan was used to locate exterior wall lines and windows, and the roof plan was used to help define the outline of the roof.

Stage III

At this stage, shown in Figure 15.37, lines were polished. Notice the extremely dark line at the bottom of the exterior elevations and the dark lines around the perimeter of the structure as well as those defining the changes of plane. Texture was added to the roof as well as to the walls. We did not waste time covering the entire surface of the wall or roof with the texture; we only did the perimeter to help the profile lines. The wall material shown is cedar shingles and the roof material, tile shingles. Wood graining of the exposed lintel was used above the doors and windows.

Stage IV

Vertical dimensions in Figure 15.38 refer to the building sections. A special note is also included to direct the reader to the building sections for dimensions. All callouts are generic in nature and depend on the specifications for specific material, quality, size, and workmanship. Roof material and wall surface material are called out with such identifying notes as "chimney," "wall," and "fixed glass." Finally, the title and scale were drawn. Note location for future solar panels.

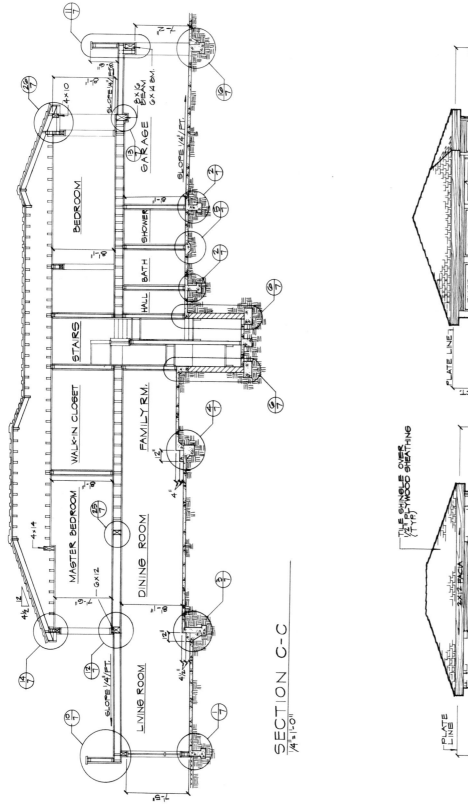

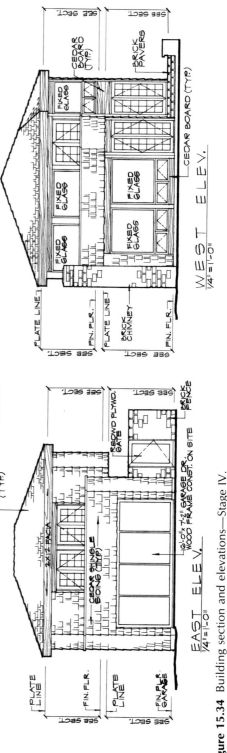

Figure 15.34 Building section and elevations—Stage IV.

Figure 15.35 Exterior elevations—Stage I.

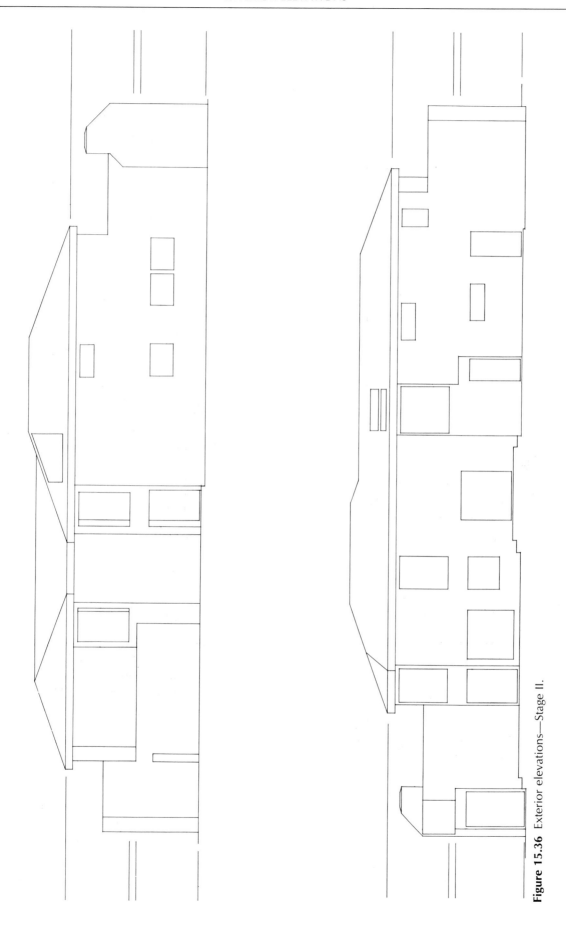

Figure 15.36 Exterior elevations—Stage II.

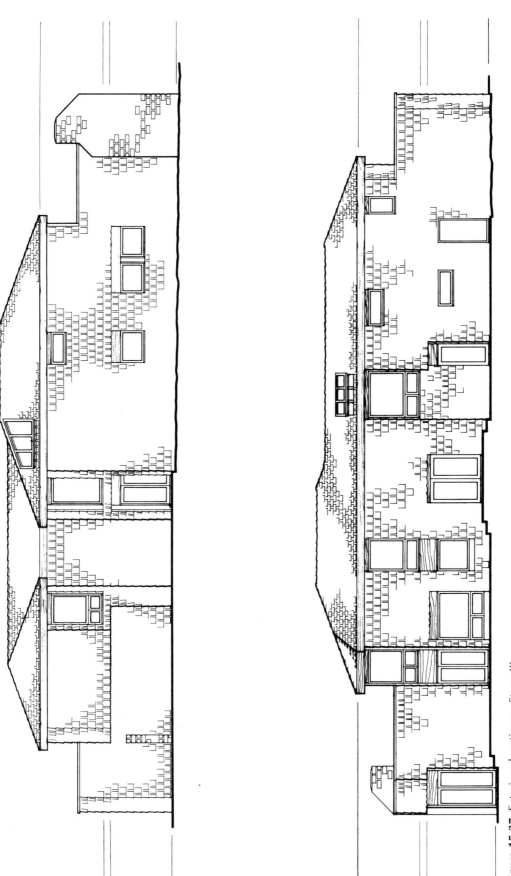

Figure 15.37 Exterior elevations—Stage III.

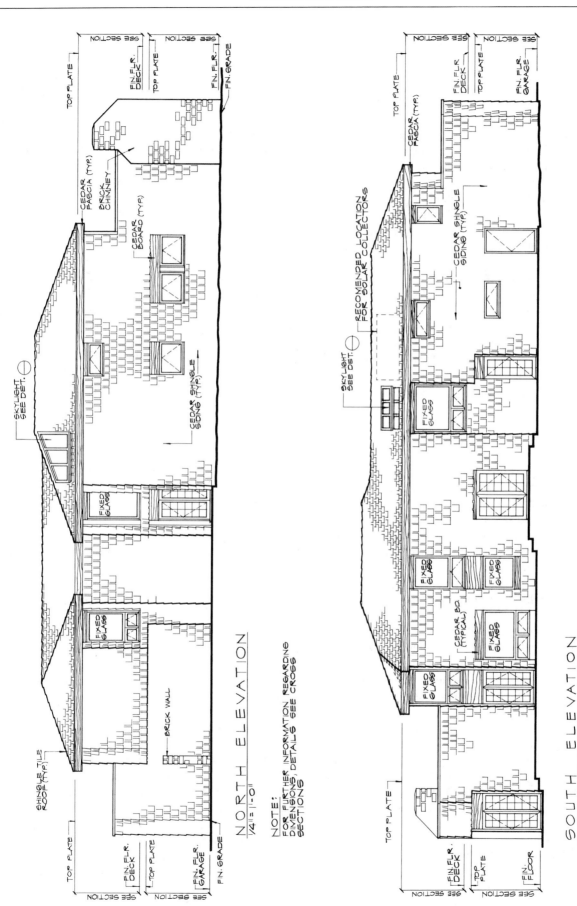

Figure 15.38 Exterior elevations—Stage IV.

Framing Plan

Stage I

Prior to drafting a framing plan we needed to make a number of decisions. These included approach, size, and method. First, we need to decide on our approach— that is, whether to use directional arrowheads or actually draft each framing member. Both approaches are shown in Figure 15.39. Scale (size) was the second major decision. Available sheet size and clarity were the deciding factors here. Third, we had to decide on method. We needed to draft a framing plan over a sepia copy of the specific plan involved.

First Floor and Second Floor Plans. There are three plans here. The top left is the first floor plan showing the floor framing for the second floor. The drawing adjacent to it is a floor plan for the second floor which indicates the ceiling joists for the second floor. The largest of the three plans shows the second floor plan with the roof framing plan.

In our office, the two smaller plans could have been drafted from scratch or the specific floor plan involved could have been reduced photographically or by a plain paper copier onto vellum.

On the small framing plans, we decided to demonstrate the abbreviated method of showing the members, that is, drafting of all beams and headers but not all joists. The floor and ceiling joists are shown by a dimension-type line using a ½ arrowhead on each end. Beams are drafted showing the actual thickness of the members while headers are shown over windows and doors as a center-line type line.

Second Floor with Roof Framing Plan. On the roof framing plan, headers are shown as center lines, beams are drafted to actual size, and the ridge, hip rafters, and valley members are drafted showing their full size. A hip rafter rests on the corner of the structure and is held in place by the forces from the rafters coming against it from either side. Rafters themselves are drafted with a center-line type line.

All exterior walls and interior bearing walls are drafted solid (i.e., using solid lines). All nonbearing walls are drafted using dotted lines.

Three things make this roof unique. First, the framing around the skylights. The skylight above the entry area (see the floor plan for roof description) is a single opening while the one over the stair area is two skylights. The framing around the skylights is not too unlike the opening for a roof access or an opening for an interior chimney.

Most corners of structures have 90° corners. One conventional framing for such a corner is to bisect the 90° corner with a hip rafter. A good example of such framing can be found at the corner where the master bathroom tub is found.

A variation can be found on the opposite corner where the wall angles at 45°. Here, we actually have two corners with a hip rafter near the ridge. This hip rafter joins other members, which in turn bisect the 45° corners. This creates a weak spot in the roof. To strengthen it, 4 × 4 posts are added to the wall and a beam is installed parallel to the 45° wall. Two additional 4 × 4 posts are placed on top of this beam to support the members that bisect the 45° bend in the wall.

If you look carefully, you can tell when a beam sits on a post or a post on a beam. If the beam sits on a post, you will see the two parallel lines that simulate the beam drafted over the post. If the post sits on top of the beam, the lines of the beam stop short of the post.

The use of a roof with a normal 90° angle over walls at 45° angles is also unique. This condition called for cantilevered beams that protrude from the wall parallel to the roof to form a 90° intersection which supports the roof. These beams enter deeply into the wall of the structure. This construction was used in a number of places, as you can see on the framing plan for the roof.

Stage II

To better understand the three drawings in Figure 15.40, look at the final stage of the building section and elevations shown in Figure 15.34. The top left drawing, the second floor framing plan, uses half-arrows to indicate the direction of the various members. A close look at this drawing shows many interesting features. The deck on the left side has 2 × 10 members while the area adjacent has 2 × 12 members. The two-inch difference allows for the difference between the floors of the deck and the inside of the house. The direction of the floor joists changes from one area to another and their spacing also changes. Open areas are crossed out ("X") as in the entry area. Headers (beams over windows and doors) are also noted throughout the drawing as are certain beams to hold up posts which in turn will hold up the roof. Extremely large sizes were selected for the framing plan because the structure is in an earthquake area, and the roof material is heavy.

Above the garage, the members were again placed perpendicular to the floor joists under the floor of the house. Two things result from this change of direction. First, the floor of the deck can be sloped away from the house for water drainage. Second, the reduced size of the floor joists allows for a larger beam over the garage door without sacrificing head clearance.

The ceiling in the garage is therefore *not* flush as in the living room at the rear. The long building section (Figure 15.34) shows this clearly. The change of spacing of the floor joists above the garage was produced by the

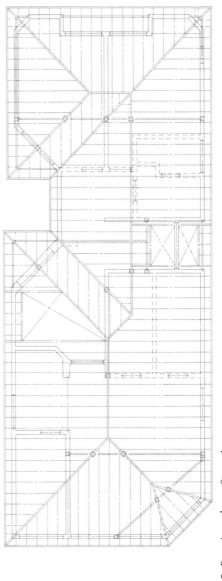

Figure 15.39 Framing plan—Stage I.

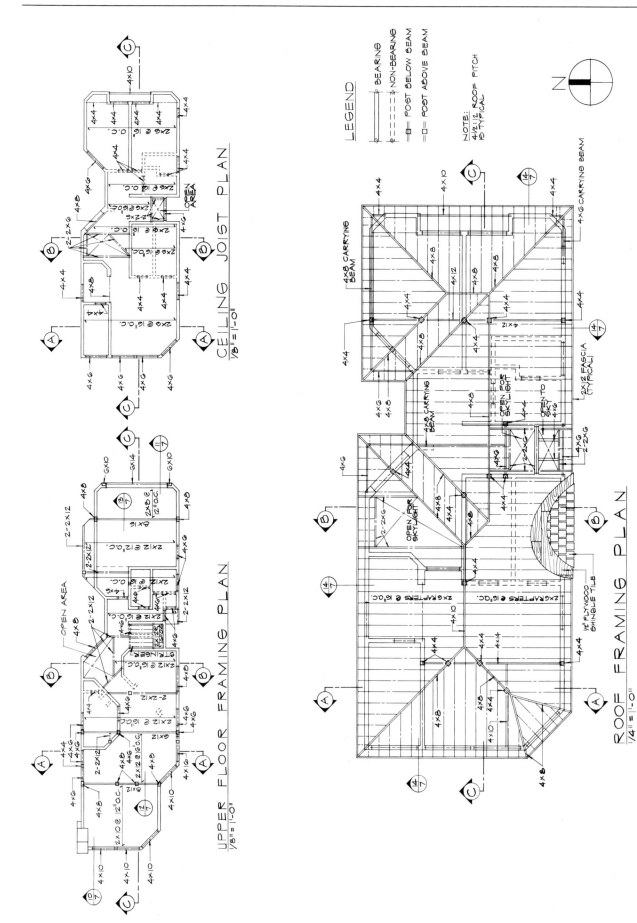

Figure 15.40 Framing plan—Stage II.

distance the joist had to travel: 2 × 12 at 12″ o.c. (on centers) to start and eventually 16″ o.c. A hidden line between these shows where the change of spacing took place.

The posts (square forms) drawn throughout must be looked for very carefully. Some are under the floor plan while others are above and often located inside walls of the second floor. Compare the floor plans here with the roof framing plan and you will find many post locations.

We also used the same method the structural engineer used in the roof framing plan to show the location of these posts. If the post is drawn solid with no lines interrupting the perimeter of the post, the post is above. If the lines of the joist or beam are drawn through it, the post is below. See the legend on Figure 15.40. All sizes and locations were obtained from the structural engineer.

The floor joists of the second floor become the ceiling joists of the lower floor. The ceiling joist plan of the upper floor is shown on the top right. We chose to show all of the headers for the second floor on this drawing rather than on the roof framing plan. Of special interest is the framing around openings like the skylights.

On the roof framing plan, the dotted walls are non-bearing and the solid wall lines are load bearing walls. An explanation is given on the legend on the far right.

The framing of the Northwest corner (top left corner of the roof framing plan) is the most typical framing for a hip roof with no special beams needed to carry the weight of the roof. However, such is not the case with the other corners. A careful look at the various corners reveals how the structural engineer designed the beams and posts to carry the weight of this unique roof.

The rafters are all 2 × 6 @ 16″ o.c. Title, scale, and North orientation completed this drawing.

CONCEPTUAL DESIGN AND CONSTRUCTION DOCUMENTS FOR A WOOD BUILDING— MOUNTAIN CABIN

16

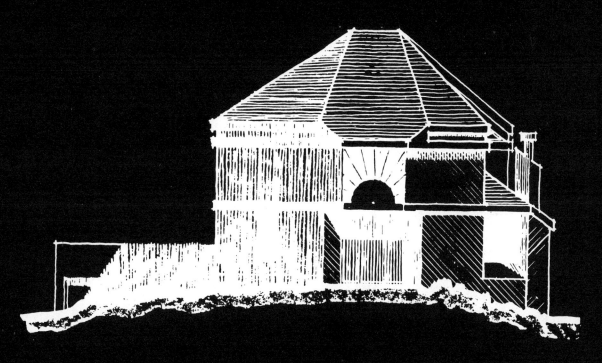

Courtesy of Steve L. Martin

Conceptual Design

Site Requirements

The design purpose for this project was to provide a three-bedroom residence for a young family. The site is located in a mountainous area of Northern California noted for skiing. The area receives as much as 144 inches of snow during the winter. The site is on a cul-de-sac and is irregular in shape with an approximate area of 7,200 square feet. This site has many pine trees, two of which are over 150 feet tall. The clients wished to preserve as many as possible. The topography of the site slopes from North to South with a cross fall of 10 feet.

Clients' Requirements

As well as wanting three bedrooms, the clients requested a formal dining room, kitchen, den, living room, powder room, and two bathrooms. The man, whose hobby is cabinet making, wanted a shop area, and the woman, whose profession is photography, requested a studio.

Both were preferably to be located in the garage or basement area. A single car garage would be adequate for the clients' needs.

Initial Schematic Studies

The conceptual approach was to place the main entrance at the high side of the site, so that the low side of the site would accommodate a basement and garage area. This approach would use the topography to its best advantage. The initial plan was also influenced by the two giant pine trees located on the upper slope.

Near the main entrance, a gallery provided circulation for the living room, dining room, powder room, and kitchen. A circular staircase provided access to the basement and upper floor. Because of the topography, we decided to lower the living room floor, which in turn gave it a higher ceiling.

Schematic drawings—loose freehand sketches—provided us with a visual tool for defining areas and their interrelationships. Figure 16.1 shows the schematic study for the first level. Similar schematic studies defined the upper and basement floor areas.

Figure 16.1 Schematic Studies.

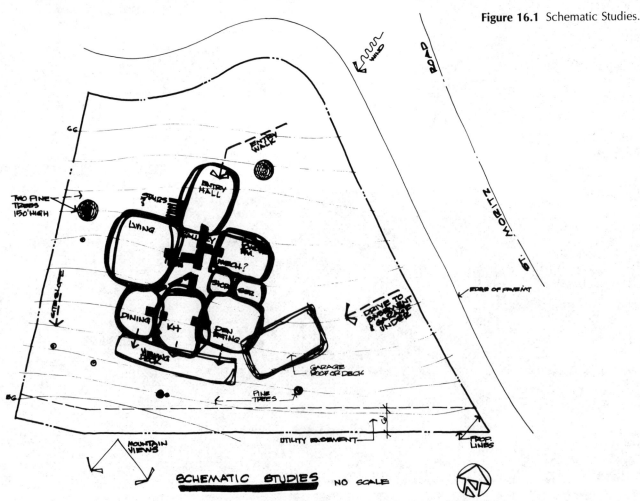

Scaled freehand floor plans that evolved from these schematic studies established the basic format for the finished drawings. Figures 16.2, 16.3, and 16.4 show these preliminary floor plans.

Roof and Exterior Elevation Sketches

As the first and second floor plans were refined, the initial concept and solutions for the roof plan evolved. The geometry of the plan and the need for steep roof pitches became an important design concern. Figure 16.5 shows a freehand sketch of the initial roof plan.

After we completed the floor and roof plan studies, we developed the exterior elevations. We drew scaled freehand elevations incorporating suggested exterior materials and architectural details. With the clients' approval, these drawings became our basic design for the finalized exterior elevations. Figures 16.6 and 16.7 show drawings of the initial exterior conceptual designs.

In addition to these initial conceptual designs, further studies including framing and construction methods and architectural details were analyzed in preparation for the final construction documents.

Figure 16.2 Preliminary—first floor plan.

Figure 16.3 Preliminary—second floor plan.

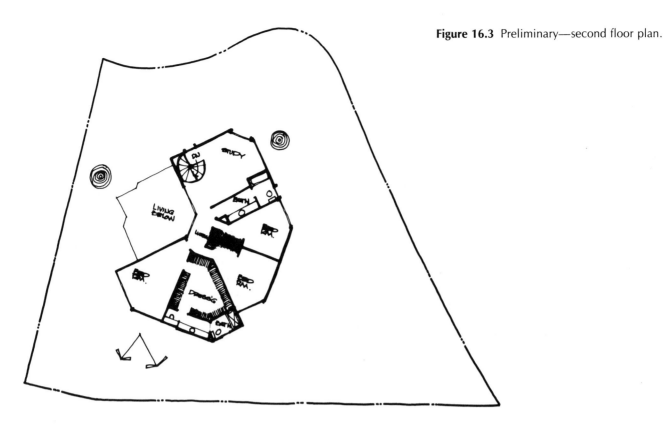

PRELIMINARY - 2ND FLOOR PLAN
1/8"=1'-0"

Figure 16.4 Preliminary—basement floor plan.

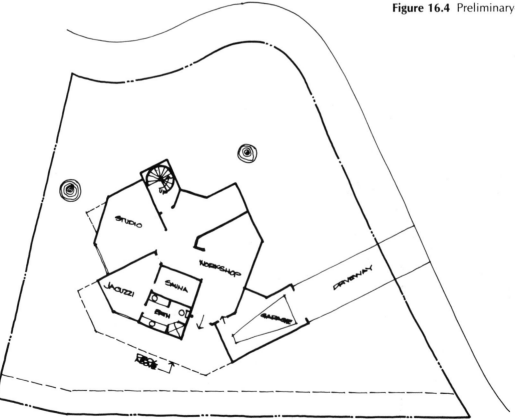

PRELIMINARY - BASEMENT FLOOR PLAN
1/8"=1'-0"

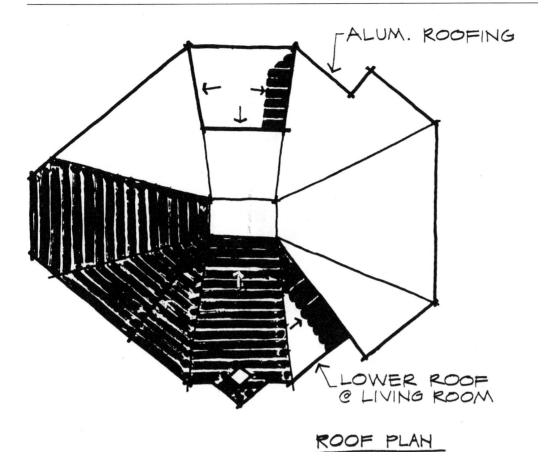

ALUM. ROOFING

LOWER ROOF
@ LIVING ROOM

ROOF PLAN

Figure 16.5 Roof plan—conceptual design.

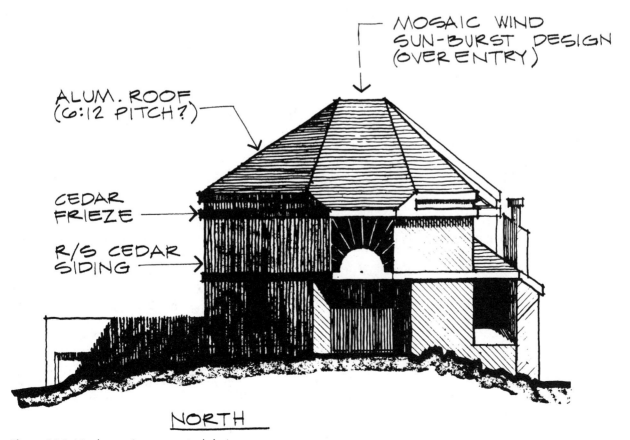

MOSAIC WIND
SUN-BURST DESIGN
(OVER ENTRY)

ALUM. ROOF
(6:12 PITCH?)

CEDAR
FRIEZE

R/S CEDAR
SIDING

NORTH

Figure 16.6 North exterior conceptual design.

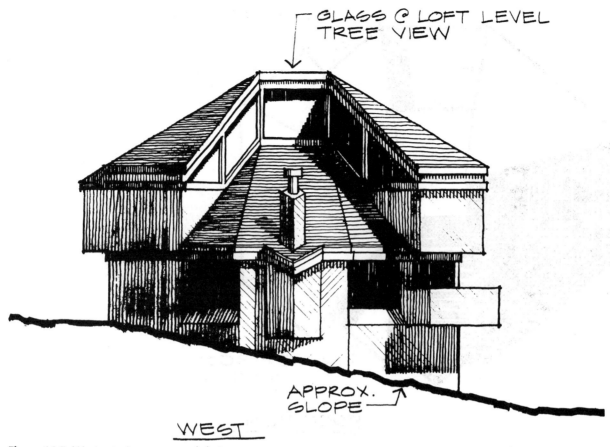

Figure 16.7 West exterior conceptual design.

Site Plan

Stage I

Before beginning to draw the site plan, you must obtain an accurate plat map and/or topography map and description of the site. Usually this information is provided by a civil engineer. See Chapter 6, on site plans.

We first lightly drew the property lines or "perimeter lines" of the site. See Figure 16.8. Next the existing contours were drawn to show the present condition of the site. (Finished contour lines are added at a later stage.)

Any streets, curbs, parkways, and so on are added at this stage. Trees on the site that are to remain are shown as small circles, but new landscaping is not shown. The dotted lines toward the bottom of the page indicate sewer lines.

Stage II

The location of the structure on the site is critical. Many factors govern the placement on the site, including ori-

entation to the sun, prevailing winds, code requirements, setbacks, and easements.

The solid lines on the site plan indicate the outline of the structure, and the dotted lines indicate the walls below. See Figure 16.9. The roof plan was drawn at the top right corner so that the draftsperson could locate and dimension the structure to a solid line. The complex shape of the roof made the accurate drafting of the roof plan difficult.

Stage III

At this stage, the immediately visible items around the perimeter of the structure were added. This included drives, a patio slab on the left side, and the deck and steps at the top. See Figure 16.10. The rectangular object at the right represents a slab for a gas tank to be added later and the small square at the top left represents the water meter. The deck and the trees were textured as was the roof plan. Note how the center portion of the roof was left without texture. This untextured portion represents flat metal as opposed to the corrugated metal used on the rest. We also darkened many of the major lines at this point.

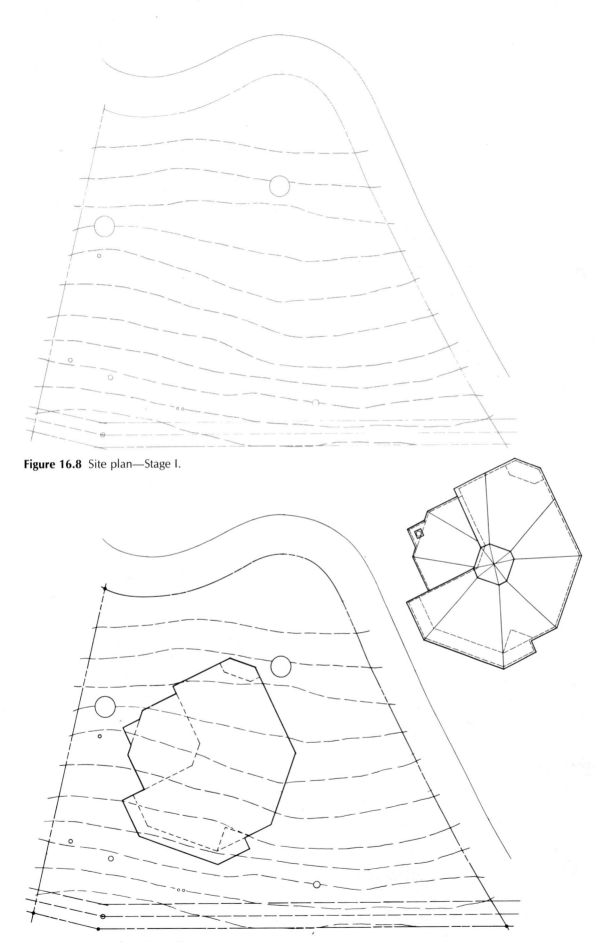

Figure 16.8 Site plan—Stage I.

Figure 16.9 Site plan—Stage II.

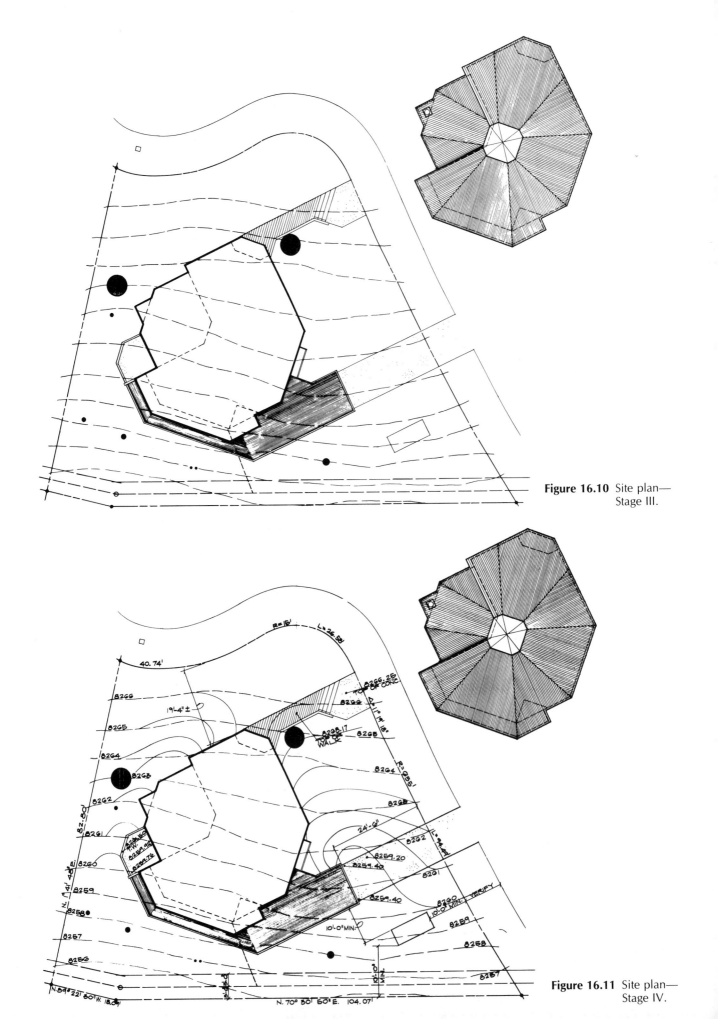

Figure 16.10 Site plan—Stage III.

Figure 16.11 Site plan—Stage IV.

Stage IV

Next we drew the new contour of the ground. Because we drew the original contour using a standard dotted line, we drew the new contour with solid lines. Compare Figure 16.11 with Figure 16.10. Some existing contour lines blend into a new solid line; this shows that part of the earth remained as it was originally and portions of it changed. (The 8265 contour line at the top left corner of the site on Figure 16.11 is a good example of this combination.) Numerical elevation values were then added to each contour line, each number representing a change of one foot. We next added dimensions for the location of the structure on the lot.

Examine how the top of the concrete walk and the driveway height in relationship to the finished grade

(contour) are shown. The top of the wood walk adjacent to the concrete is designated first, followed by the concrete elevation at the patio. ("T.W." means top of wall.) This designation accomplishes two things: it shows the elevation (height), and it insures good water drainage.

The directions and lengths (including radius in the case of an arc) of the lines describing the exterior perimeter of the lot were added next.

Stage V

The final stage involved the noting. See Figure 16.12. The notes described material such as roofing, driveway surface, and porch, and utilities such as water and sewer were called out along with the easement (a right-of-way).

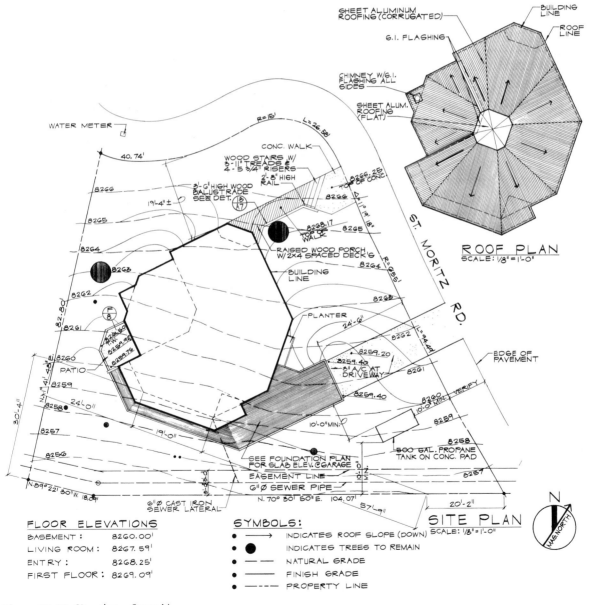

Figure 16.12 Site plan—Stage V.

We also noted special equipment or special construction procedures such as the propane tank on the site plan and the flashing on the roof plan.

We called out the building line and roof lines to avoid any confusion of lines. We designated the slope of the roof by arrows to indicate the direction of water flow.

We labeled the final elevations of the various rooms in chart form, below the site plan itself. These elevations should always correspond with the foundation plan. We also prepared a chart of the various symbols used, to avoid confusion or misinterpretation.

Finally, we added the title, scale, and North orientation symbol. The orientation arrow is carried on every plan, including the floor plans and foundation plans.

Foundation Plan

Stage I

The basic shape of the foundation plan is based on the floor plan and the location of the loads the foundation must carry and distribute to the ground. Here, the floor plan of the basement was traced. See Figure 16.13.

The walls in the foundation plan were drawn with solid lines because the walls are concrete block and act as part of the footing, going above the grade. The spread footings were drawn with hidden lines because they are below the grade.

Normally, sizes of the footings are obtained from structural engineering drawings or from a preliminary detail sketched by the architect. Some walls take heavier loads than others, so the width of the footing varies throughout structures. If structural engineering drawings are not available at this stage, the structural engineer is asked specific questions. A floor plan, a preliminary foundation plan, and rough elevations and sections are also sent to the structural engineer who determines the loads and the necessary sizes of the footings to support the walls. For a simple structure, loads and footing sizes can be determined in the office and a structural engineer need not be consulted.

Figure 16.13 Foundation plan—Stage I.

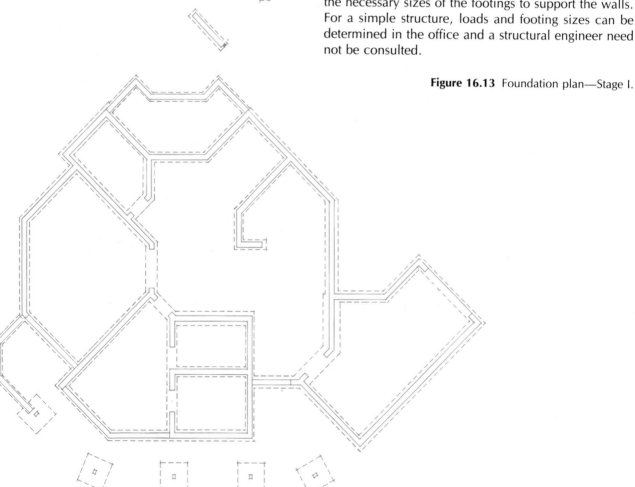

This particular project required a structural engineer because of its location and unique shape. Heavy snow loads were computed for the structure, and what appear on the plan to be excessive sizes of members are actually necessitated by earthquake precautions and snow loads.

The five column pads at the bottom of the structure, as the dotted lines indicate, were realigned in subsequent drawings because these changes took place after additional computations were made.

During the evolution of a set of drawings, there are constant changes. As each drawing progresses, additional information and understanding of the structure produces change.

Stage II

Outlining the decks was the next step, together with the addition of the structural members at the top of the plan. See Figure 16.14. The edge of the patio slab at the bottom was then added, and the structural members for the wood deck were drawn at the top of the plan.

Dimension lines were added next—at the *end* of walls and wall openings because of the use of concrete block modular units. Normally, exterior dimension lines are put in first, followed by interior dimension lines. In this example, the first dimension line is spaced away from the objects ½″, and each subsequent dimension line is spaced ½″ away from the preceding one.

Figure 16.14 Foundation plan—Stage II.

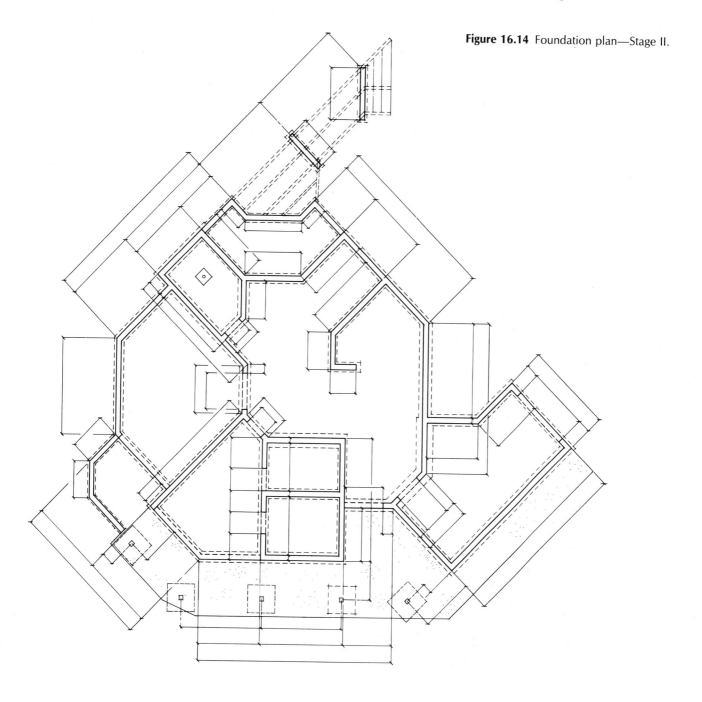

If a dimension line crosses an extension line, the extension line is broken; if a dimension line crosses another dimension line, decide which of the two is the major or more critical and break the other; if a dimension line crosses an object line, allow clarity to dictate which is to be broken.

Stippling (dots) helped to define the concrete patio area. The pad for the column on the right was repositioned at this time, as was the second from the left. Compare its position now with its position in the previous stage, shown in Figure 16.13. We made this change after the structural engineer finished the structural drawings.

Stage III

At the stage shown in Figure 16.15, the dimensioning was added. If you want to know the number of blocks in a given wall in Figure 16.15, divide that dimension by 16" or 1.3', which is the size of the block and mortar.

Masonry opening (M.O.) sizes were carefully selected in conjunction with the door sizes and jamb details. There are basically two ways to dimension widths of footings. One is on the foundation plan as indicated on Figure 16.15; the other is by dimensioning the footing on the foundation detail. One reason for dimensioning on the foundation plan is that footings vary in widths.

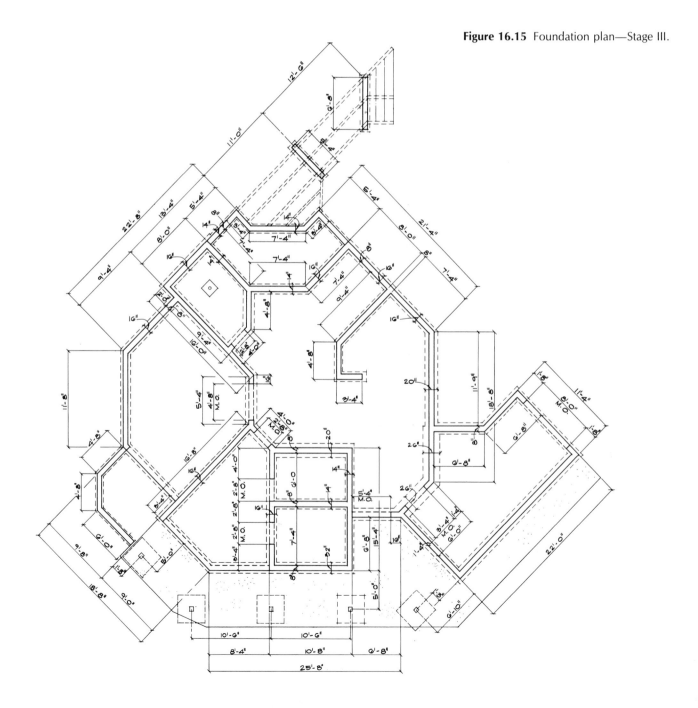

Figure 16.15 Foundation plan—Stage III.

As you look closely at these various dimensions, you will notice that the dimension lines occasionally cross. An example of this is found toward the lower center of the plan. A 5'–4" M.O. horizontal dimension crosses a 15'–4" vertical dimension. Had the 5'–4" dimension been raised higher, the crossing dimension could have been avoided. Proximity was the determining factor here.

The column locations at the bottom have two 10'–6" dimensions. The dimension line to the right of the 10'–6" dimension and above the 6'–8" dimension is missing. We did this to help the contractor locate the columns from the most accessible point.

At this stage of a project, you should make a diazo copy before you put any dimensions on the sheet. All dimensions should be put on the proof copy, checked, then lettered on the original drawing.

Stage IV

Based on decisions made in conference with the head draftsperson or job captain, detail reference bubbles and cross section indications were now included. See Figure 16.16. The bubbles with the large triangles are for the

Figure 16.16 Foundation plan—Stage IV.

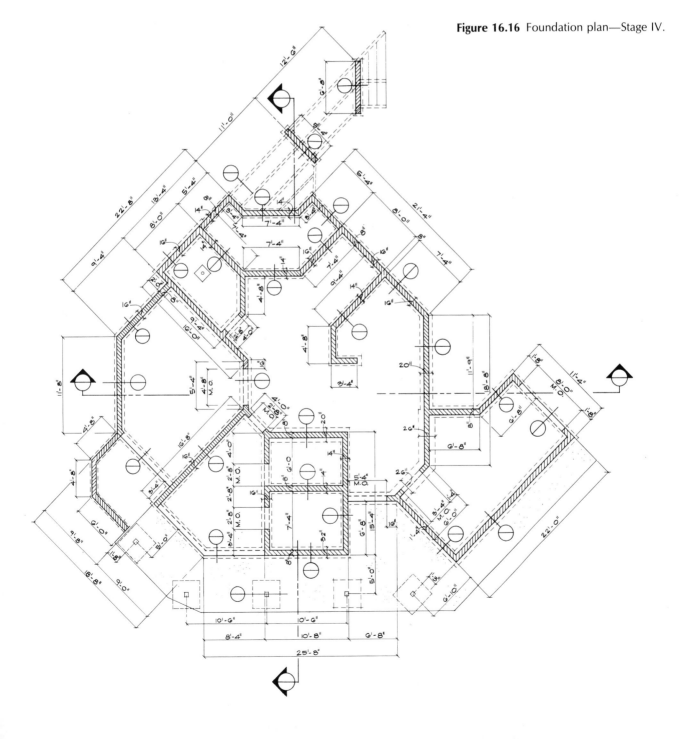

cross section and the others are for the details. The small point on the detail bubbles indicates viewing direction. Detailing should almost always put the inside of the structure on the right and outside on the left.

Stage V

Figure 16.17 shows the final step in the evolution of the foundation plan. Our task here was mainly to note and reference. We added a simplified point to the detail reference bubble. We also included a note in the garage to indicate the elevation of the finish floor (FF) and made a reference notation for the slab at the left. Finally, we added the title, scale, and North orientation.

Figure 16.17 Foundation plan—Stage V.

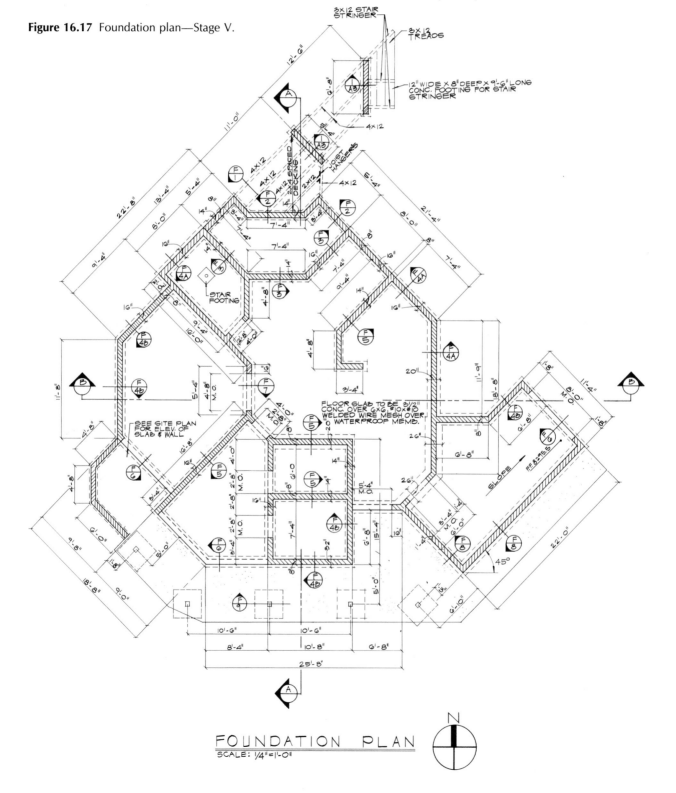

FOUNDATION PLAN
SCALE: 1/4"=1'-0"

Basement Floor Plan

Stage I

There are three levels in this structure. We started with the lowest floor, that is, the basement. See Figure 16.18. This was called the basement rather than the first floor because the entry is on the floor above. To do a preliminary layout of this level, we took measurements from the preliminary floor plan. The walls of the basement are made of concrete block so it was important to check and stay with the multiples of this block module size. (Block module dimensions must also be checked against the foundation plan and all subsequent floors above it.) Note the appearance of the concrete block units in Figure 16.19.

At this stage, the layout was done lightly so that it did not matter if lines overlapped. (Use a 2H lead or harder.) Door swings and windows would be added in Stage II. Portions of the first floor were cantilevered beyond the edges of the basement floor plan and were shown with dotted lines.

The five columns shown at the bottom near the dotted lines support the beam for the floor above. At this stage these supports were tentative and awaited confirmation by the structural engineer, who could increase the size or number of the columns or change their position.

You should always check the preliminary section before drawing this sheet as it gives important information such as critical connections, concrete block size, and possible guidance as to the position of the walls in relation to the first floor walls. In this case, the walls were located at 45° and the columns at 45° and 22½°.

Stage II

Wall locations were checked, verified, and relocated where necessary at this stage. See Figure 16.20. The walls were then darkened and items such as stairs, bathroom fixtures, and a dumbwaiter (the square with an ''X'' inside, near the top right) were included. The round circle at the right is a water heater.

If interior elevations have been sketched, you should view these before locating equipment or fixtures.

Stage III

The first change that was made in Stage III came from the structural and foundation plans and is shown in Figure 16.21. The extreme right column was lined up with the wall to the right (garage wall), and the column second from the left was lined up with the others in the center.

All the door swings and windows were now drafted in. We noticed a conflict of the door swings at the bathrooms. Correction could have been done at a later stage but we chose to do it here.

Figure 16.18 Basement floor plan—Stage I.

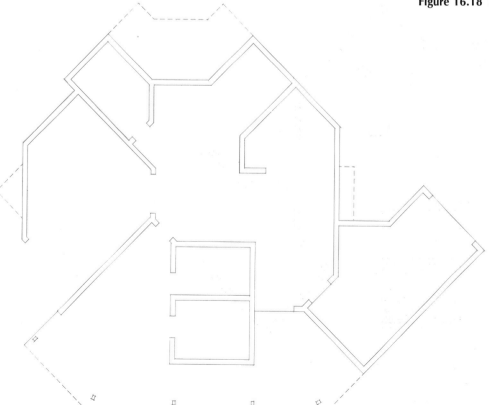

Figure 16.19 Basement wall.

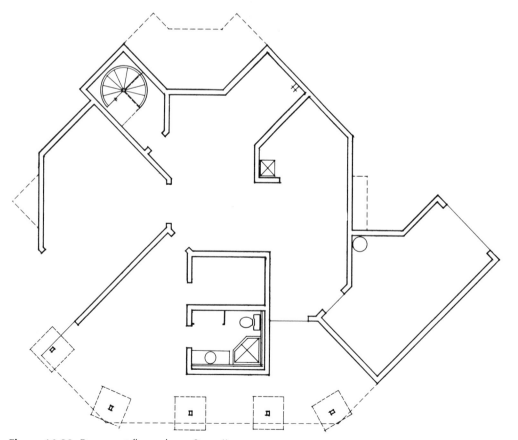

Figure 16.20 Basement floor plan—Stage II.

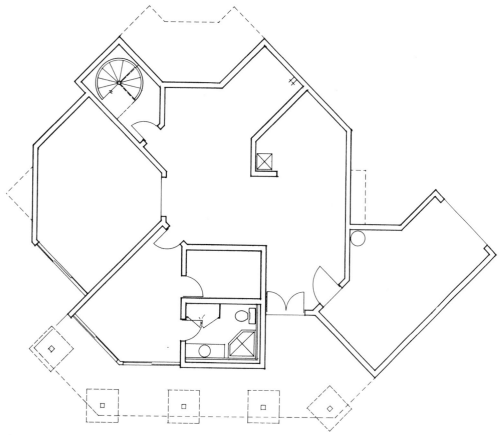

Figure 16.21 Basement floor plan—Stage III.

Stage IV

Hidden lines at the top of the floor plan shown in Figure 16.22 and those extending beyond the rear of the garage indicate the floor above. These dotted lines were dimensioned from known locations such as existing columns and existing parts of the building. We did this because the relationship of one dotted line to the other (columns) could be seen best on this plan. Notice that this decision would mean that the deck did not need to be dimensioned on the first-floor plan.

The extension lines for the columns use center-line type lines as they were dimensioned to the center. Extension lines for all others are solid.

As you study this stage, check the cross section to see the relationship of the columns to the main body of the structure. Remember that the walls are masonry.

Because of the very nature of the unusual shape of the building and the presence of both dimension and extension lines, the extension and dimension lines were broken often.

Again, because the structure is masonry at this level, the dimensions are to the edges of the wall and the interior walls are treated differently from wood stud interior walls, which are dimensioned to the center. Openings, too, are dimensioned to the width of the opening.

Stage V

At this point you can make a check print so that you can put the numerical values on it, check the dimensions against the block module size, and check the overall dimensions against the sum of the individual parts. See Figure 16.23.

In this case, as the dimensions were placed on the original drawing, openings could be called out. Masonry extensions are often labeled "F.O.M.", meaning face of masonry. Each dimension should be and was checked against the foundation plan.

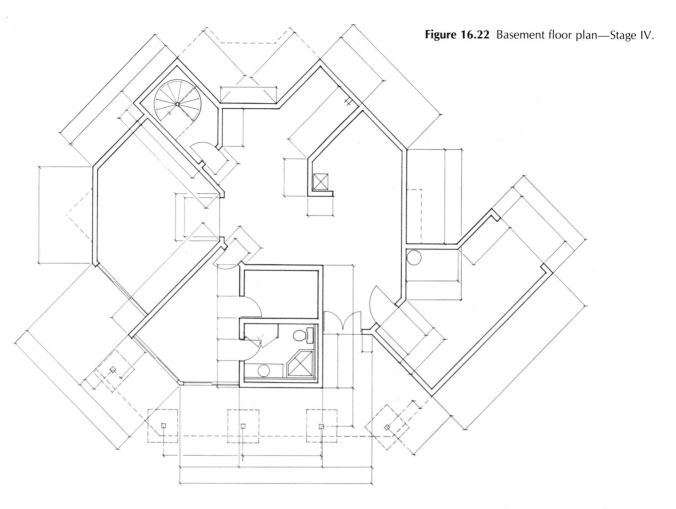

Figure 16.22 Basement floor plan—Stage IV.

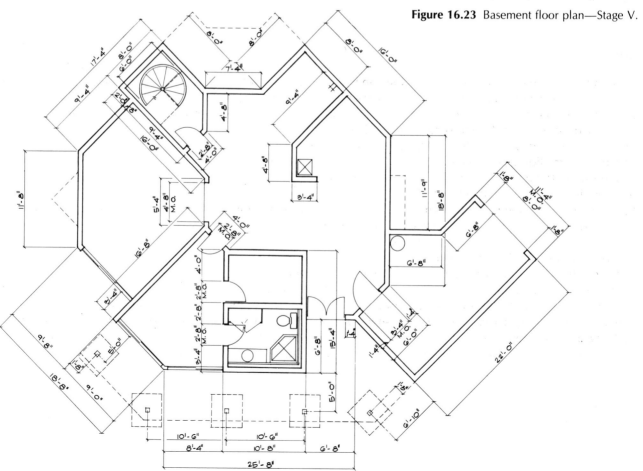

Figure 16.23 Basement floor plan—Stage V.

Stage VI

As the dimensions were located the material designations for the walls were included. These are the diagonal lines between the wall lines and represent concrete block. See Figure 16.24. Some architectural offices do not like this block designation because it is the same as brick's. There are actually at least five different ways of representing concrete block, ranging from drawings of the actual block to a crisscross pattern. We used a series of diagonal lines to represent the masonry walls because of the scale.

We left the material designations step until after the dimensions were located, in case we needed to change anything. We then added room titles and some noting and placed the door and window bubbles.

We also included here a cold water line (CW), a hot water line (HW), and a floor drain (FD) in the room adjacent to the workshop. This area was to be the photographic darkroom, added later and not shown here.

Many of the areas projecting beyond the outer limits of the basement floor above are shown dotted. Many of them are labeled. This helped others to orientate themselves and to visualize the structure. We also included the title and scale.

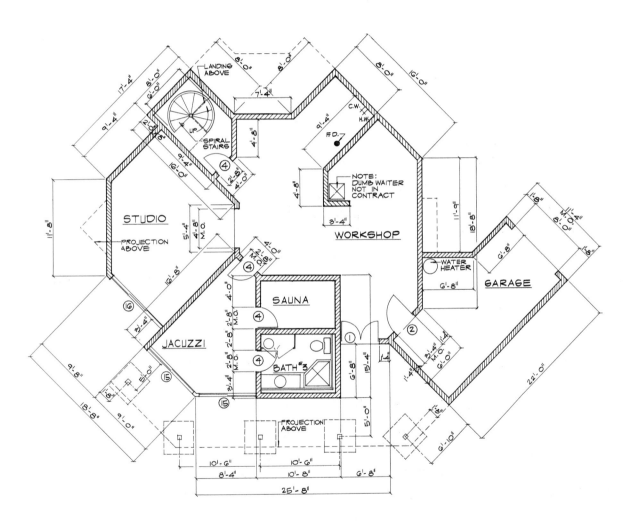

Figure 16.24 Basement floor plan—Stage VI.

Stage VII

During a discussion between the drafter and a senior person, it was decided that the dotted lines which represent the five concrete pads should be eliminated from the plan shown in Figure 16.25. They appear on the foundation plan and would be duplicated here. Also, since the pads are below grade, it would be incorrect to show them on the basement floor plan.

The building section lines were now included, as were the interior elevation reference symbols (see Bath #3 for circles with arrows on them) and the reference bubbles for the plumbing fixtures that refer to the plumbing fixture schedule. Finally, the title and North orientation were located.

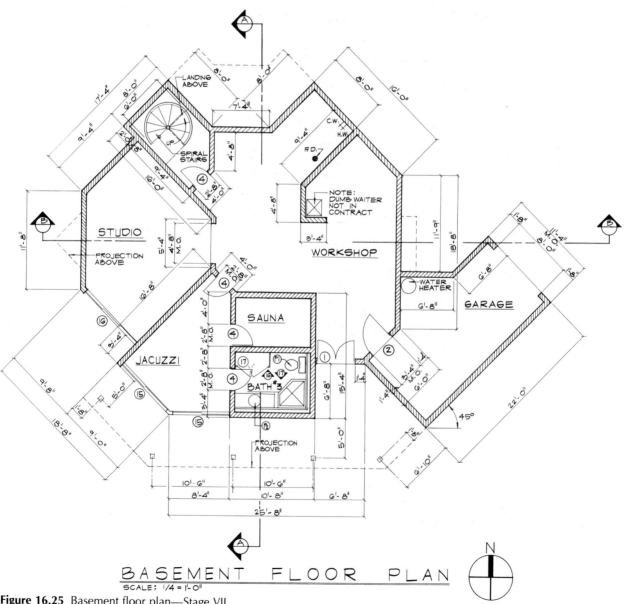

Figure 16.25 Basement floor plan—Stage VII.

First Floor Plan

Stage I

We lightly blocked out all the exterior and interior walls. The first floor plan differs from the basement floor plan in that it overlaps the basement floor plan. Look at the preliminary floor plans in Figure 16.26 and compare them with Figures 16.27 and 16.28. Figure 16.27 looks into the kitchen. The dining room is to the extreme right. Look carefully at the extreme right center of the photograph and see the pass-through between the dining room and the kitchen. Figure 16.28 is a view of the den. The drop in floor level marks the beginning of the sunken living room.

The first task was to identify the walls that line up with the basement walls and block those out. Because of the severe angles involved, many of the intersections of the walls were widened to maintain a rectangular shape. There are two levels with two steps between them; the lower portion at the left is the living room.

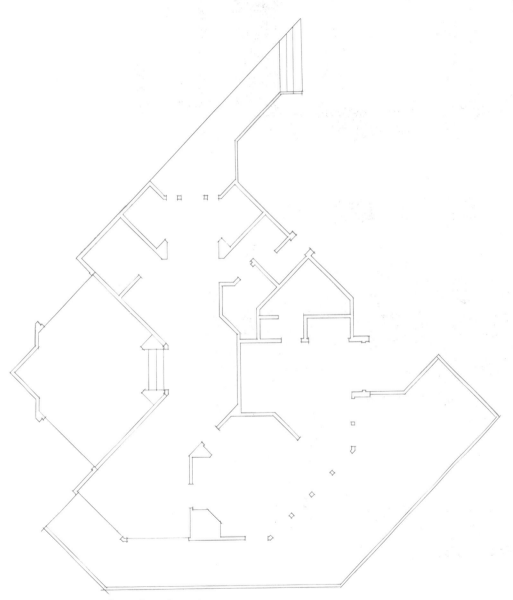

Figure 16.26 First floor plan—Stage I.

Figure 16.27 View looking into the kitchen.

Figure 16.28 View looking toward the den.

Stage II

To differentiate between the deck and the interior, we added wood texture to the deck area. See Figure 16.29. The fireplace is prefabricated, with masonry around the front face. The stairs and all equipment are now drawn. See Figure 16.30. Special hose bibs are shown for the washer and refrigerator. There are built-in seats and window seats in the living room.

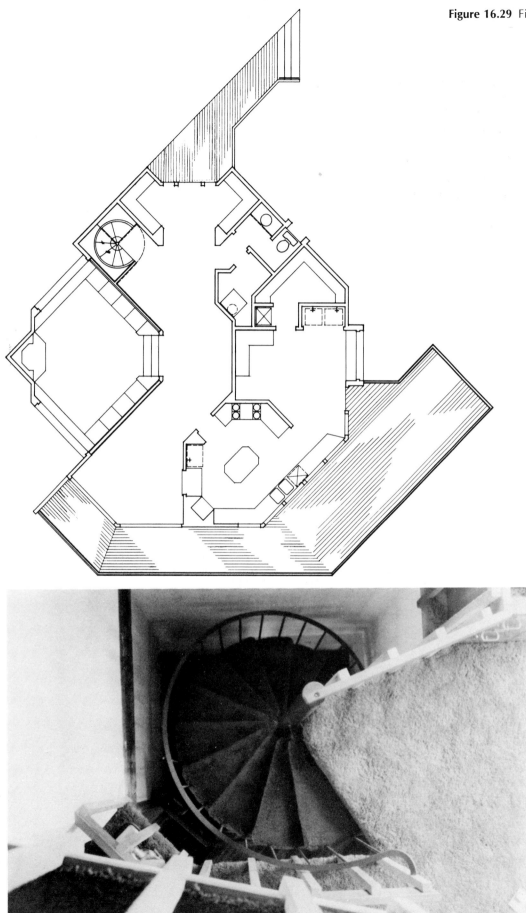

Figure 16.29 First floor plan—Stage II.

Figure 16.30 Top view of spiral staircase.

Stage III

Doors and their swing direction were now added. This includes the bi-fold door in front of the washer/dryer unit at the right of the drawing. See Figure 16.31. Windows were also added. The door at the right leading out to the deck is slightly lost in the lines that represent the deck material. This could change when the reference bubble is added. The designation for the wood texture could have been added after the doors were drawn.

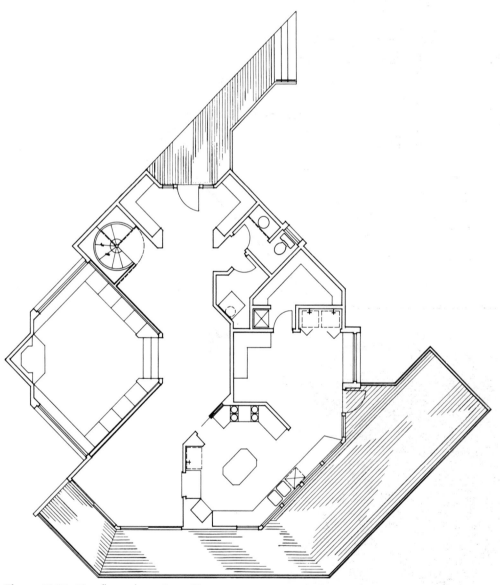

Figure 16.31 First floor plan—Stage III.

Stage IV

It was now time for the dimensioning. You should review the chapter on floor plans (Chapter 8) before reading further. An aid at this stage is to make a print and free-hand draw all dimensions on it before proceeding on the original vellum sheet.

Because of the many angles on the floor plan, many dimension lines and extension lines will probably cross. To maximize clarity and avoid confusion, we drew extension lines to two locations: the edge of the stud (noted at a later stage) and the center of a wall. The centers have a center line, while the outside stud line extension lines have solid medium-weight lines. See Figure 16.32.

We checked all walls that lined up with the basement wall (concrete block) for concrete block modules. In some instances, we located the windows by locating the columns in between; others that were close (within 6" of an adjacent wall) we located by the window detail. The window behind the water closet in the bathroom was located but the size was not dimensioned. The window schedule would determine the size.

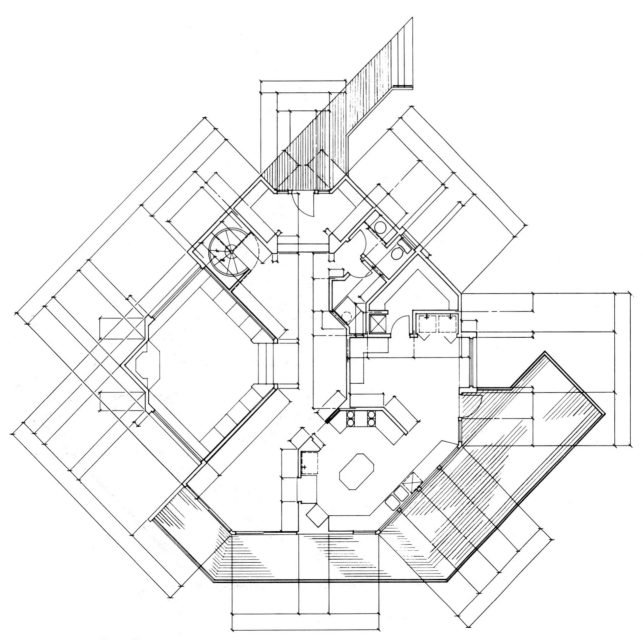

Figure 16.32 First floor plan—Stage IV.

Stage V

To understand the floor plan dimensions compare Figure 16.33 with the plan for the floor below. In both the basement and the foundation plans, sizes are dictated by the concrete block module. Many of the walls here line up with the walls below. Study the garage dimensions, the location of the columns, and the location and size of the stairs. By overlaying the original drawing of this plan on the basement plan, we could check for wall alignment.

Once again, a print was made of the sheet and the numerical values were placed and checked before they were added to the original. We again made certain the overall dimensions totaled the sum of their parts and corresponded with the block modules.

The deck at the bottom, adjacent to the kitchen, was not dimensioned here. The basement floor plan had already dictated its size and shape. While it could have been dimensioned here, it would have been a duplication.

If any dimension is critical, the term "hold" can be placed after it. This was not the case here. Plus and minus ($\pm$) notations, indicating minimum and maximum dimensions, could also be shown at this stage, if required.

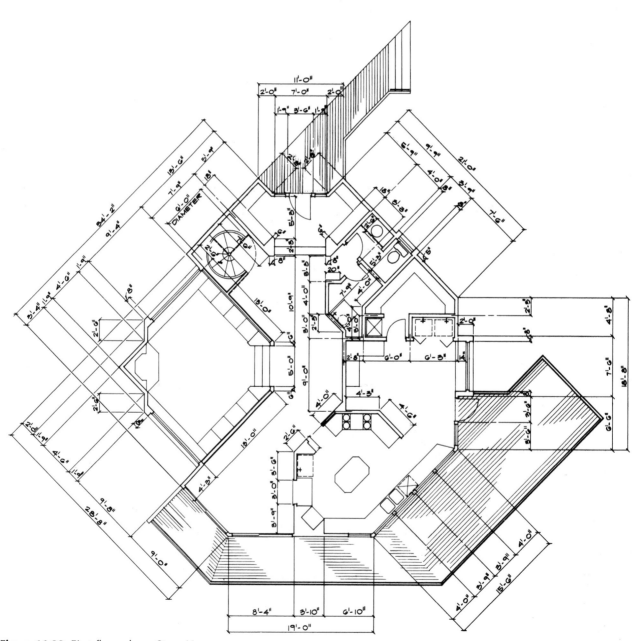

Figure 16.33 First floor plan—Stage V.

Stage VI

The cross-section reference symbol was now included, as well as the reference bubbles for the windows and doors and much of the noting. See Figure 16.34. Many of the items noted are not typical items: window seats, balustrades, and the end of the built-up roofing on the deck, for example. The call-out for the dryer vent on the right side was not spelled correctly and was corrected in the next stage.

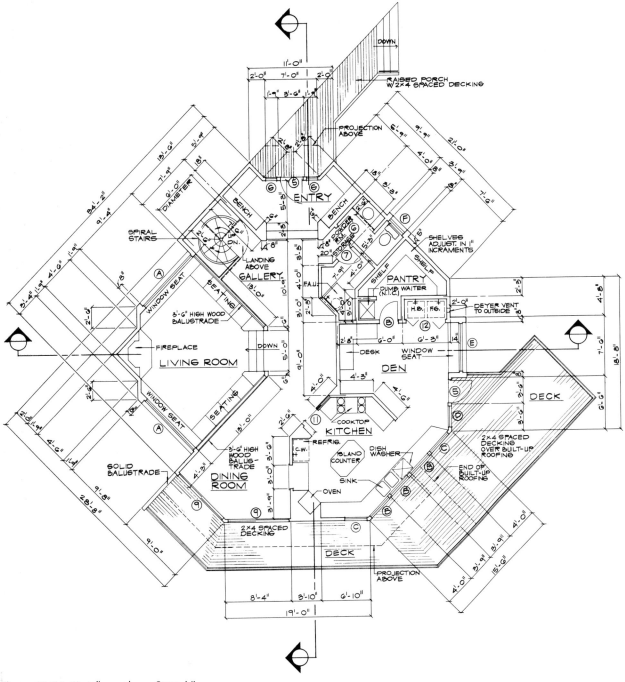

Figure 16.34 First floor plan—Stage VI.

Stage VII

Figure 16.35 shows the final step in the evolution of the first floor plan. Spelling and numerical values are usually checked at this stage by use of a check print. The bulk of the interior elevation reference symbols are in the kitchen; these are circles with arrows on them similar to the cross-section reference symbol. The appliance and plumbing fixtures have a circle and leader pointing to them. These refer to the appliance schedule and plumbing fixture schedule. See Figure 16.70. Finally, the title, scale, and North orientation were added.

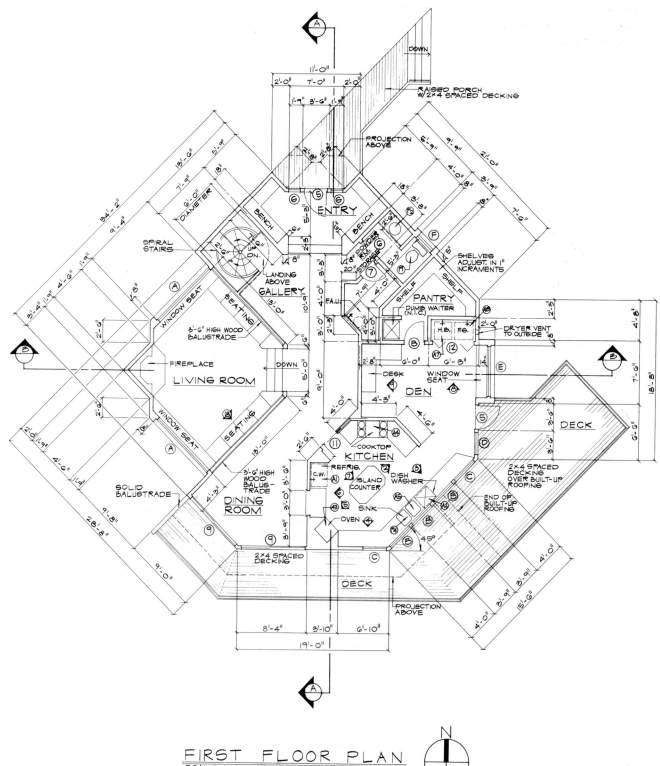

Figure 16.35 First floor plan—Stage VII.

Second Floor Plan

Stage I

The first step for the second floor plan, shown in Figure 16.36, was to identify the walls that lined up with the floor below because these dimensions were set. Any change would affect not only the first floor plan but the basement floor plan and foundation plan as well. Figure 16.37 shows the relationship between the various floors. Figure 16.38 shows the cantilever of the second floor over the first floor and the basement below. The opening

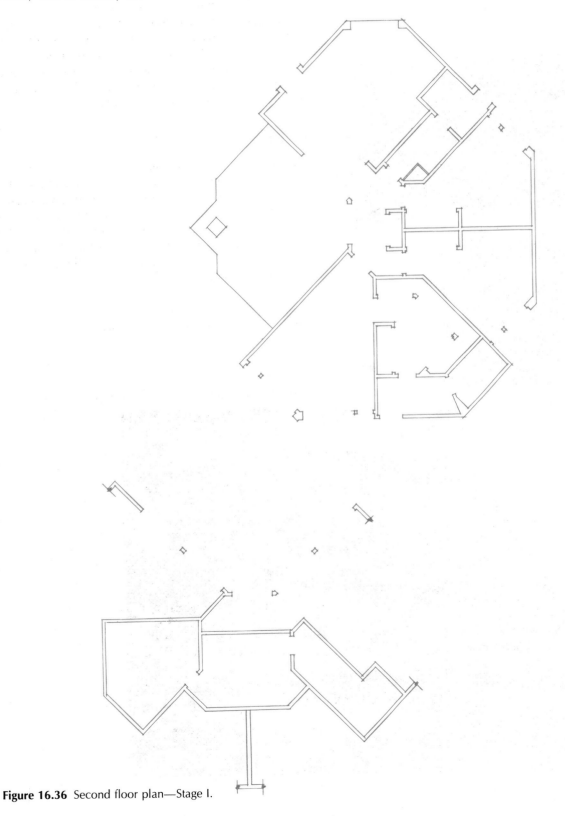

Figure 16.36 Second floor plan—Stage I.

is actually the garage door space, and this is helpful in orienting the photo to the drawing. Because a heavy timber floor was used, it did not matter that the other walls did not line up.

The single line area to the left on Figure 16.36 represents the living room, which can be seen from the hall in the center of the second floor plan.

The attic plans at the bottom of the sheet were turned to fit in this drawing area. Normally, they would have been drawn as if they could be placed on top of the second-floor plan. In this example, the T-shaped wall of the attic plan lines up with the large T-shaped wall on the right side of the second-floor plan.

Stage II

As on the previous floor plans, the next step was to add items such as stairs, bathroom fixtures, and clothes poles in the wardrobes. See Figure 16.39. The rectangular area with an "X" in it toward the center of the plan represents the disappearing stair to the attic. The dotted lines to the right of the disappearing stair represent the attic balcony. These two features will help you orient the attic to the second-floor plan.

Figure 16.37 Relationship of the various floors.

Figure 16.38 Cantilever of second floor over first floor.

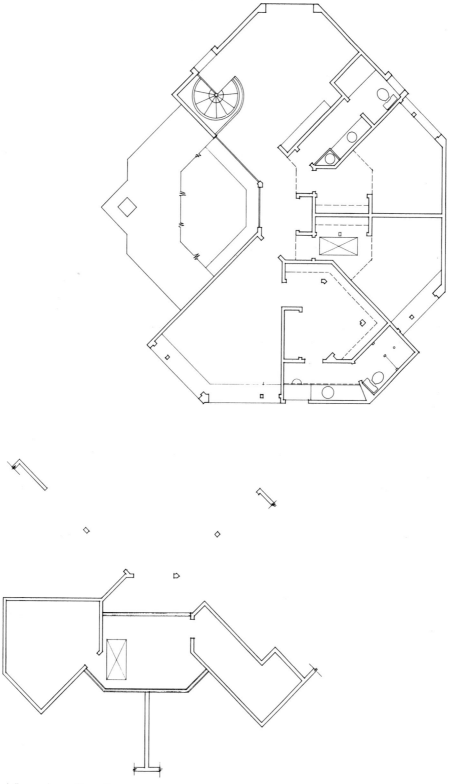

Figure 16.39 Second floor plan—Stage II.

The living room area was dealt with in an unusual way. We used a partial break to expose the interior of the living room. The extreme left area is still the roof of the living room. The line between the edge of the hall and the break line represents the edge of the second floor. The decision to extend the floor beyond the guardrail in the hall was based on aesthetic reasons as well as safety. Look at the section (Figure 16.63) for a better visual picture of this area.

A double line was used around the spiral stair to indicate the handrail. The single line area indicates the place where people actually descend the stair.

Stage III

In Stage II, the disappearing stair was shown as a solid line. Stage III changed this to a hidden line because this section is above eye level. See Figure 16.40. We changed this line simply with an erasing shield and eraser.

Doors, direction of swing, and windows were then added, including bi-fold doors on the wardrobe closets. The chimney flue was added and the windows on the attic plan, located at the bottom. Refer to the sections to understand the relationship between these windows and the second-floor plan. These were the windows that extended above the second floor.

Stage IV

At the dimensioning stage, shown in Figure 16.41, all exterior and interior walls were located. Once again, all walls lining up on the two floors had to have the same dimensions (in this case, concrete block dimensions) if they lined up with the basement.

The windows were then dimensioned. If the windows were within 6″ of an adjacent wall, the jamb detail located the window. The same was true with doors. The attic plan was not dimensioned. We wanted the second-floor plan to dictate the size and shape of the attic, because the walls of the second floor and the attic were aligned.

To understand the vertical relationship of the floors, imagine the disappearing stair to the attic; there are handrails on both sides of the hall. As you stand in front of the shorter of the two handrails, you can look down into the hall below as well as through a high window to the exterior. This gives this area a special open quality.

Stage V

Compare this stage, shown in Figure 16.42, with the previous stage, shown in Figure 16.41. The attic floor plan has a new location at the bottom of the drawing. At first we thought the two plans would not fit on the same sheet unless we isolated the attic plan. Now, having drawn the attic plan, we found that the plan would fit into the upper plan. The drawing was so simple that we just drafted it again. If this had been a complex drawing needing hours to draft over, we could have moved it by splicing the vellum into place with tape or by the photographic method. Review this method if you have forgotten it (see Chapter 2).

The numerical values of the various dimensions were then added.

Stage VI

This was the final step. See Figure 16.43. Reference bubbles were located for the interior elevations. This symbol is a circle with an arrow similar to the one used as a cross-section reference with a number in it. Note Number 14 and Number 15 at the bottom of the floor plan.

Plumbing fixtures were also called out by a circle with a leader pointing to the specific plumbing fixture. The numbers such as P-1, P-2, and P-3 refer to the plumbing fixture schedule. See Figure 16.70.

Door and window reference bubbles were located. Then we added section lines. Examine sections A-A and B-B carefully. Finally, we added the various notes and the main title, scale, and North orientation.

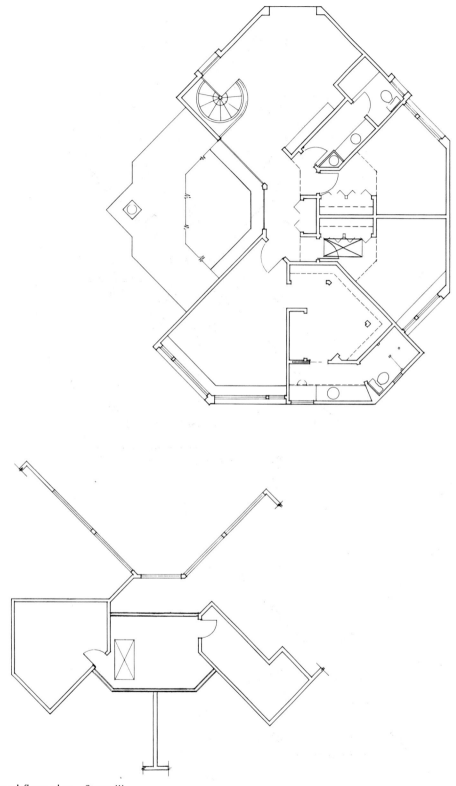

Figure 16.40 Second floor plan—Stage III.

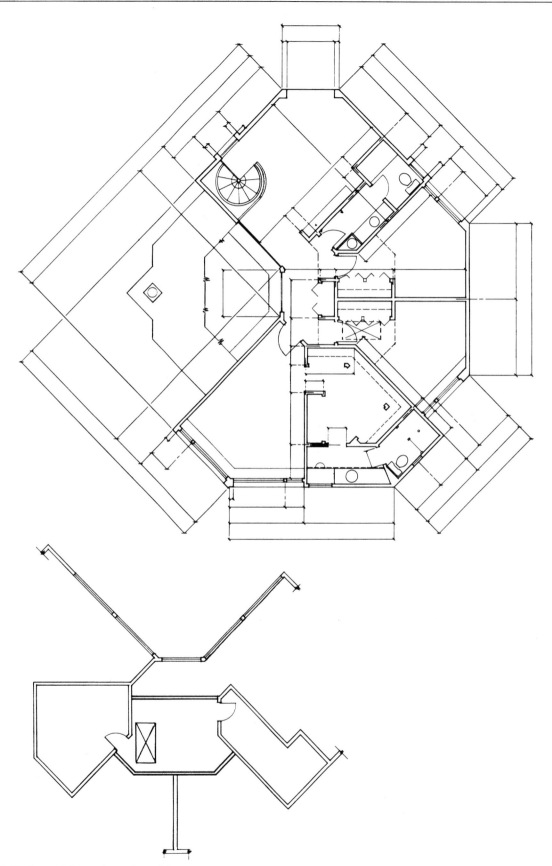

Figure 16.41 Second floor plan—Stage IV.

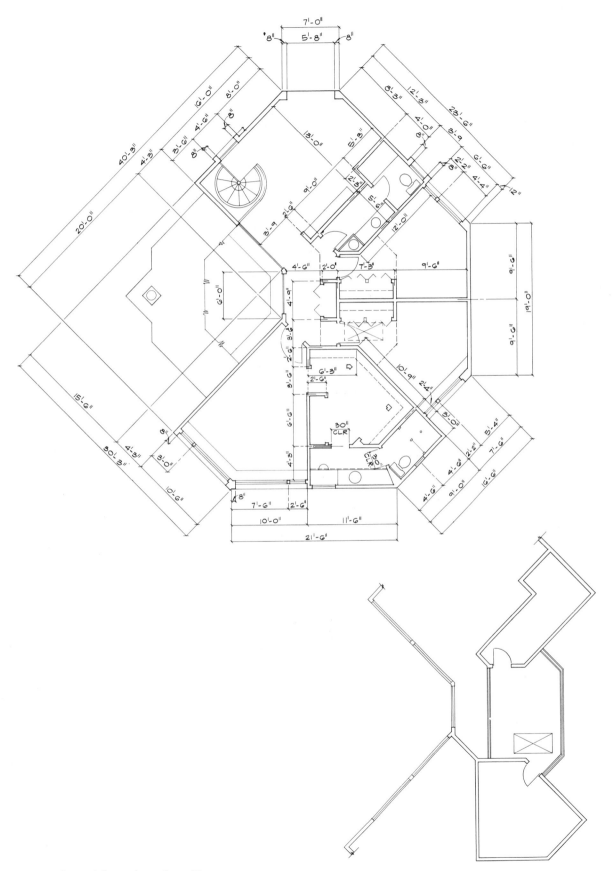

Figure 16.42 Second floor plan—Stage V.

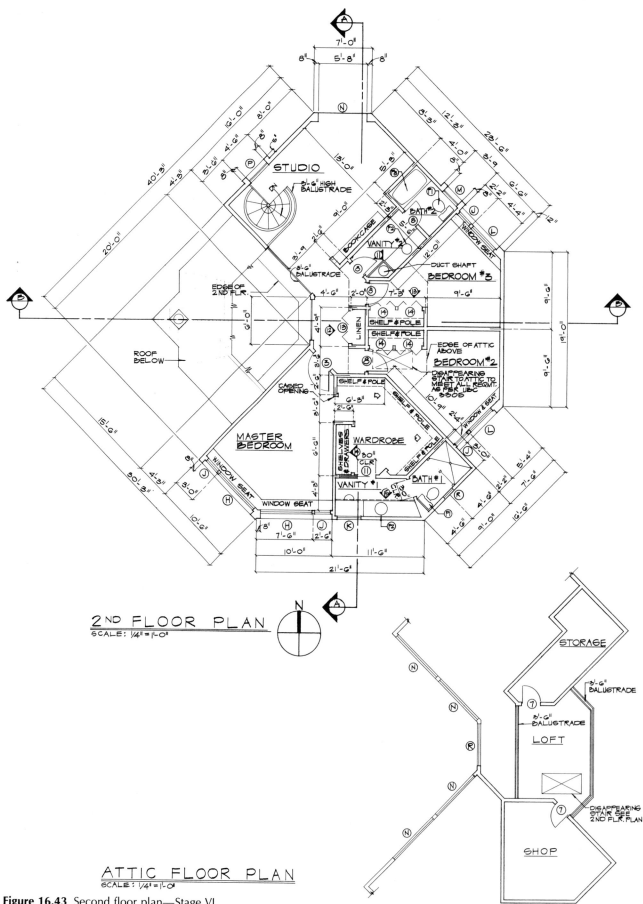

2ND FLOOR PLAN
SCALE: 1/4"=1'-0"

ATTIC FLOOR PLAN
SCALE: 1/4"=1'-0"

Figure 16.43 Second floor plan—Stage VI.

Elevations

Stage I

The elevations are among the last drawings to be done because they depend on the sections and floor plans. See Figures 16.44 and 16.45.

From the cross section we obtained the plate lines and the floor lines. As with the cross section, we put some of the heights on the right side and others, such as the living room, on the left. We checked the bottom floor line with both the cross sections and verified it with the site plan. Most of the finished grade levels were arrived at during this procedure.

Plate lines had to be constantly checked because this structure does not have the customary eight-foot plate heights throughout the building. The plate line in this instance varies from 8'–2" to 9'–2" in height.

The light vertical lines on this drawing are taken from the exterior wall of the floor plans.

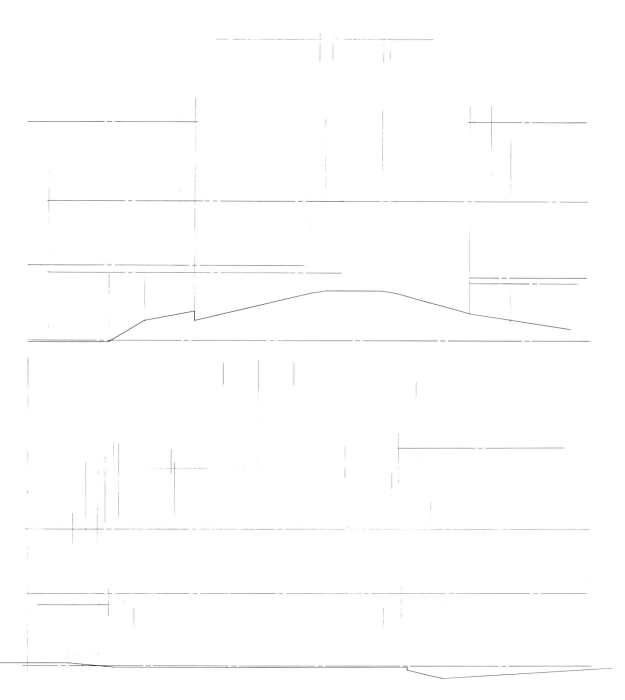

Figure 16.44 North and South elevations—Stage I.

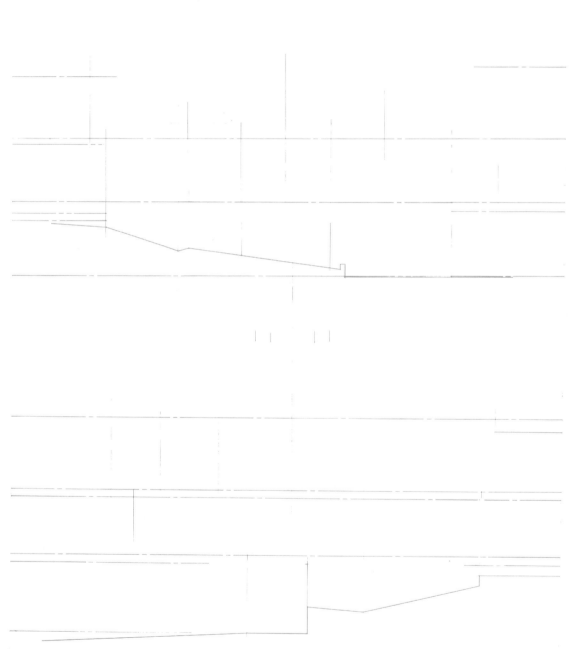

Figure 16.45 East and West elevations—Stage I.

Stage II

Our next step was to determine the basic outline and shape of the building. We checked preliminary elevations with the cross section and any available detail sketches, such as eave and balcony details. We could not draw the elevations until these detail decisions were made. It is not uncommon to draw the structural members lightly to produce accurate elevations.

From the roof plan we developed the roof configuration as shown in Figures 16.46 and 16.47. Direct projection is the desired method for drawing this complicated roof in elevation form.

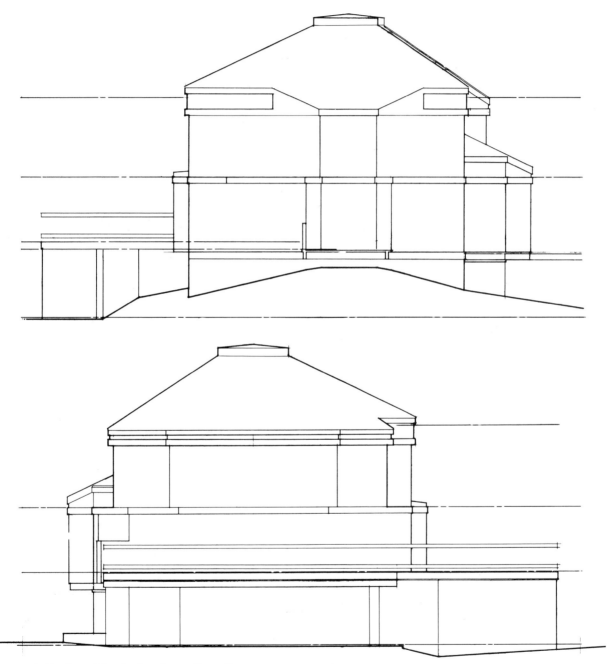

Figure 16.46 North and South elevations—Stage II.

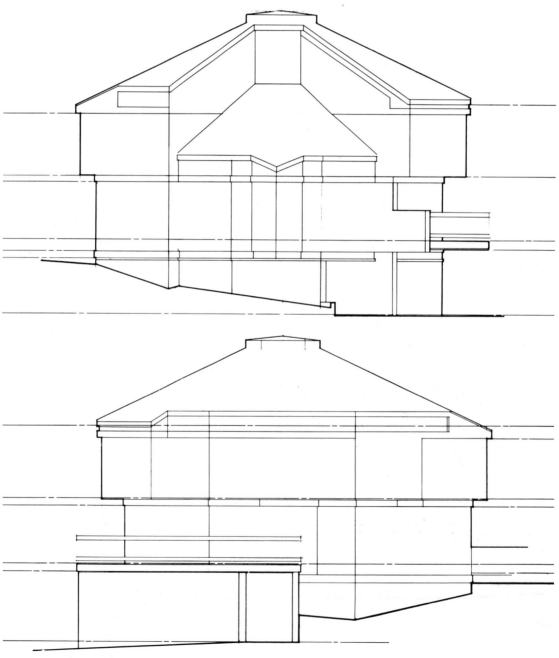

Figure 16.47 East and West elevations—Stage II.

Stage III

All of the doors and windows were now located on the elevation. See Figures 16.48 and 16.49. Many of the windows and doors appear out of scale because the elevations are drawn as direct orthographic projections from the floor plan and because the plan has unusual angles. We also indicated the swing of the doors with a dotted line. The ''X'' in some of the sliding doors indicates that the door can be opened. An arrowhead would also indicate the direction in which the door opens.

The surface (face of the wall) of the structure and the surface of the roof were given a texture, and proper symbols for the various material indications were given to ensure correct selection. The roof was to be made of corrugated sheet aluminum over rigid insulation.

Guardrails and vertical rails around the balcony were also included, as Figures 16.50 and 16.51 show. We also finished the chimney. The client requested a stained glass window above the front door, which we included at this stage.

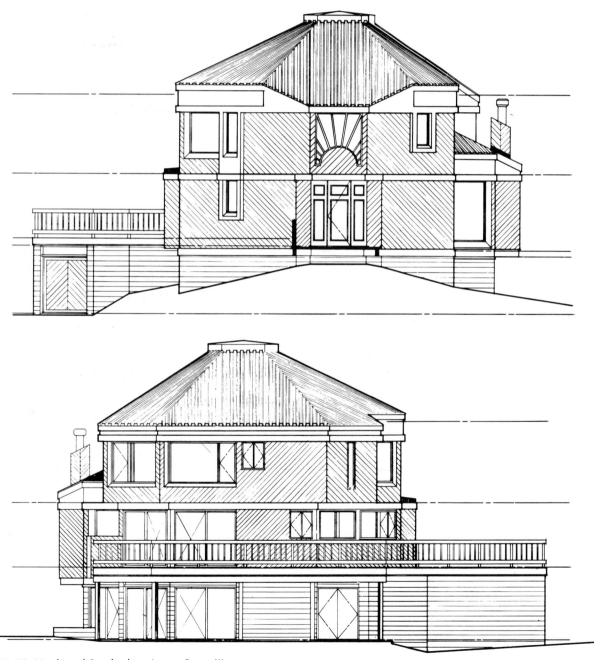

Figure 16.48 North and South elevations—Stage III.

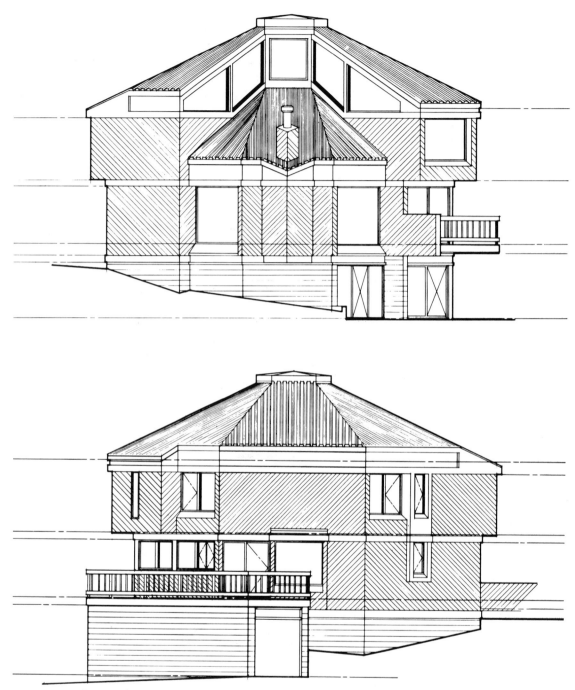

Figure 16.49 East and West elevations—Stage III.

Figure 16.50 Guardrail.

Figure 16.51 Guardrail over garage.

Stage IV

All of the elevations received dimensions at this stage. See Figures 16.52 and 16.53. Because all the vertical heights were based on the sections, the dimensions on the sections had to be verified before we placed them on the elevations. Because of the height variations, many of the floor lines and plate lines were further described by extensive notes. See an example at the top left of the top elevation: "Typical Plate Line, at exterior walls (2nd Floor Only)."

The lowered living room resulted in many different dimensions from one side of the elevation to the other. Because the plate line and floor line notations were placed on the left side of the top elevation (North elevation), the leader then crossed the dimension line. This was later changed in Figure 16.57.

Keep abbreviations to a minimum. When using them,

follow a list that is widely subscribed to, like the list of the American Institute of Architects. For example, one abbreviation used here was "R.S.C.", rough sawn cedar. (See Figure 16.54 for a photograph of this exterior finish.)

After we made a diazo copy of Stage III, we saw that the material texture was drawn too lightly, so we redrew much of the material designation in Stage IV.

The next detail to be drawn was now chosen (see Figure 16.55). Often, the details are already sketched at this stage. Sometimes even the finish details are already drafted, because the elevations are often the last drawing to be prepared. The detail shown in Figure 16.55 is the window on the right side of the North elevation. Since the sketch was taken below the window to expose additional portions of the structure, the reference bubble line had to extend far below the window to simulate this detail section.

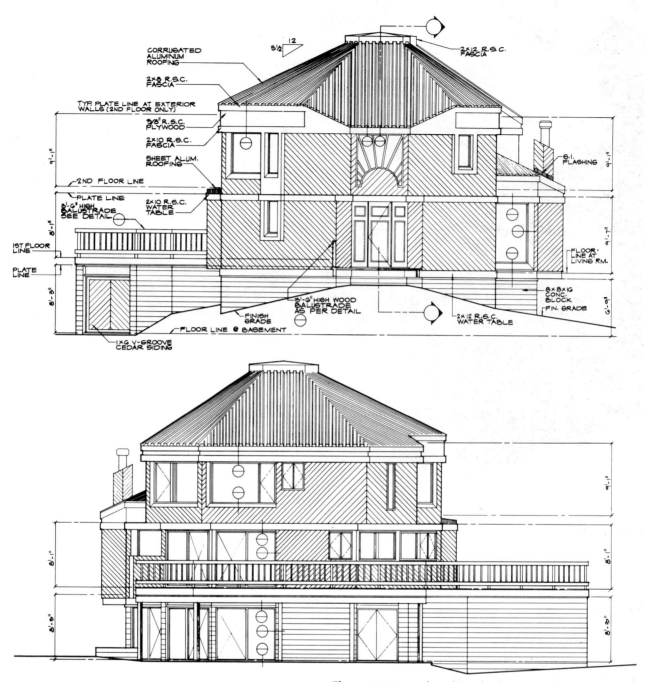

Figure 16.52 North and South elevations—Stage IV.

At this point, the direction the structure faced was noted and titles were given. Figure 16.56 shows a Northwest view of the structure. This drawing helps viewers understand the complicated geometry of the building and reasons for the unusual shape, such as tree location. West and East elevation titles were located.

Material descriptions are not always repeated on all elevations. Here, a note was simply added on the bottom left corner of the East elevation to direct attention to another source for missing information. This note could have been added to the South elevation as well.

Stage V

Since the East and West elevations were now basically finished, we moved on to the North and South elevations. See Figure 16.57. We took three significant steps here. First, we corrected the dimensioning on the North elevation. Because the dimension lines crossed the leaders of some of the notes on the left side, we relocated

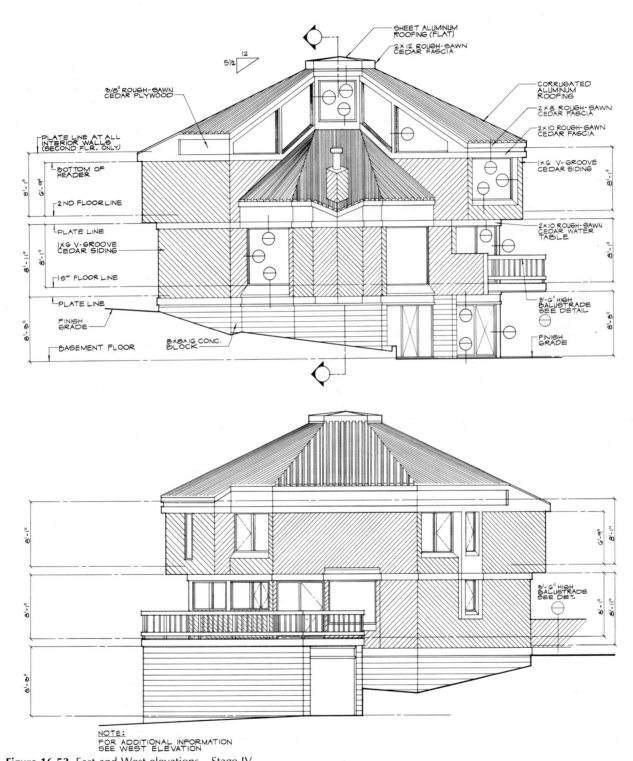

Figure 16.53 East and West elevations—Stage IV.

the notes and dimensions to improve the drawing.

Second, we included a key plan (as described in Chapter 11) at the bottom of the sheet. We then decided that because the structure was such an unusual shape, we should include both titles and numbers on the elevations.

Finally, we placed titles in the proper location for all the elevations, and put the numbers from the key plan in circles after each title. See Figure 16.58.

Figure 16.54 Rough sawn cedar exterior.

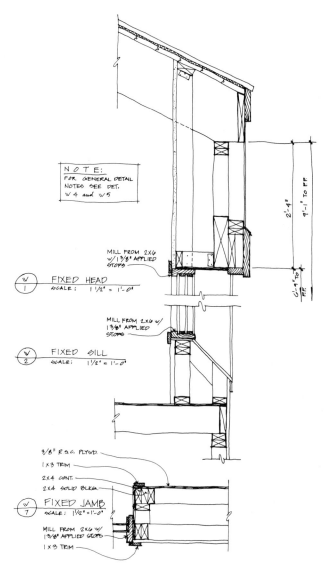

NOTE:
FOR GENERAL DETAIL
NOTES SEE DET.
W 4 and W 5

MILL FROM 2X6
W/ 1 3/8" APPLIED
STOPS

W 1 FIXED HEAD
SCALE: 1 1/2" = 1'-0"

MILL FROM 2X6 W/
1 3/8" APPLIED
STOPS

W 2 FIXED SILL
SCALE: 1 1/2" = 1'-0"

3/8" R.S.C. PLYWD.
1 X 3 TRIM
2X4 CONT.
2X4 SOLID BLKG.

W 7 FIXED JAMB
SCALE: 1 1/2" = 1'-0"

MILL FROM 2X6 W/
1 3/8" APPLIED STOPS
1 X 3 TRIM

2'-4"
9'-1" TO F.F.
0'-4" TO F.F.

Figure 16.55 Eave and window section on the right side of the North elevation—detail.

Figure 16.56 Northwest view of structure.

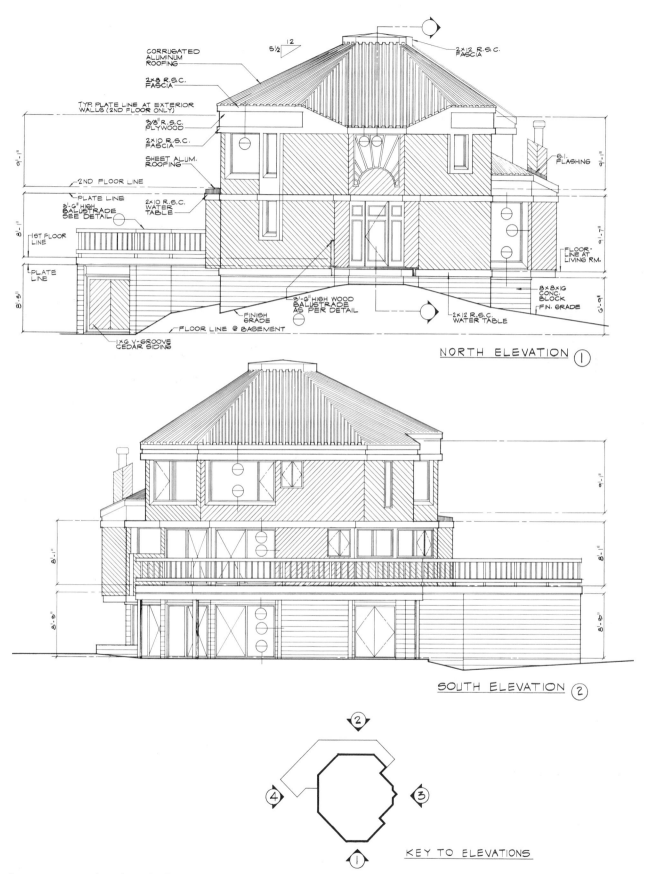

CORRUGATED
ALUMINUM
ROOFING

2×8 R.S.C.
FASCIA

TYP. PLATE LINE AT EXTERIOR
WALLS (2ND FLOOR ONLY)

3/8" R.S.C.
PLYWOOD

2×10 R.S.C.
FASCIA

SHEET ALUM.
ROOFING

2ND FLOOR LINE

PLATE LINE

3'-6" HIGH
BALUSTRADE
SEE DETAIL

2×10 R.S.C.
WATER
TABLE

1ST FLOOR
LINE

PLATE
LINE

FINISH
GRADE

FLOOR LINE @ BASEMENT

1×6 V-GROOVE
CEDAR SIDING

3'-6" HIGH WOOD
BALUSTRADE
AS PER DETAIL

5½ / 12

2×12 R.S.C.
FASCIA

G.I.
FLASHING

FLOOR-
LINE AT
LIVING RM.

8×8×16
CONC.
BLOCK

FIN. GRADE

2×12 R.S.C.
WATER TABLE

NORTH ELEVATION ①

SOUTH ELEVATION ②

KEY TO ELEVATIONS

Figure 16.57 North and South elevations—Stage V.

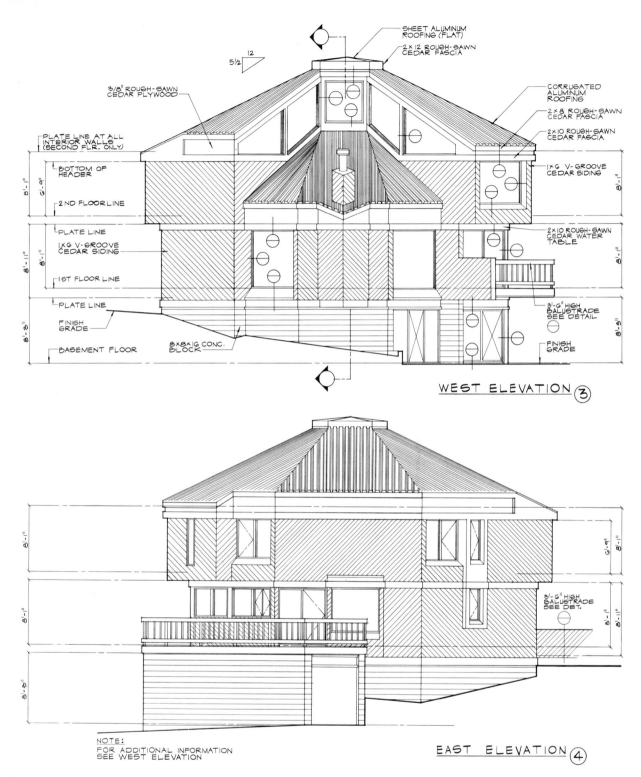

SHEET ALUMINUM ROOFING (FLAT)

2 x 12 ROUGH-SAWN CEDAR FASCIA

3/8" ROUGH-SAWN CEDAR PLYWOOD

CORRUGATED ALUMINUM ROOFING

2 x 8 ROUGH-SAWN CEDAR FASCIA

2 x 10 ROUGH-SAWN CEDAR FASCIA

1 x 6 V-GROOVE CEDAR SIDING

PLATE LINE AT ALL INTERIOR WALLS (SECOND FLR. ONLY)

BOTTOM OF HEADER

2 ND FLOOR LINE

PLATE LINE

1 x 6 V-GROOVE CEDAR SIDING

1 ST FLOOR LINE

2 x 10 ROUGH-SAWN CEDAR WATER TABLE

PLATE LINE

FINISH GRADE

3'-6" HIGH BALUSTRADE SEE DETAIL

BASEMENT FLOOR

8 x 8 x 16 CONC. BLOCK

FINISH GRADE

WEST ELEVATION ③

3'-6" HIGH BALUSTRADE SEE DET.

NOTE:
FOR ADDITIONAL INFORMATION SEE WEST ELEVATION

EAST ELEVATION ④

Figure 16.58 East and West elevations—Stage V.

Building Sections

Stage I

Cross sections should be among the first drawings attempted. If a preliminary section was not drawn, it should be drawn at this stage.

Based on the contour of the property, the roof slope decisions were made with regard to ceiling heights at each level. These heights, translated into precise floor and plate heights, were the first to be drawn.

There were two sections to be drafted. See Figure 16.59. The section at the bottom of the page would have a change of level at the living room, so we decided to put the regular plate lines and floor lines on the right and the living room floor and plate lines on the left. We again checked the basement floor line against the site plan.

Figure 16.59 Building sections—Stage I.

The light vertical lines represent the width of the structure taken from the floor plans.

Most offices construct quick sketches of various details before and during the development of the section drawings. Even pictorial sketches are developed to clarify the architect's intentions and avoid problems.

Stage II

Based on the quick sketches and detail sketches, interior and exterior walls were located from the various plans and thickness was added to the members. See Figure 16.60. The intersection of the various horizontal and vertical planes took much thought, because the aesthetic ideas and structural assembly concepts were largely explained through this drawing.

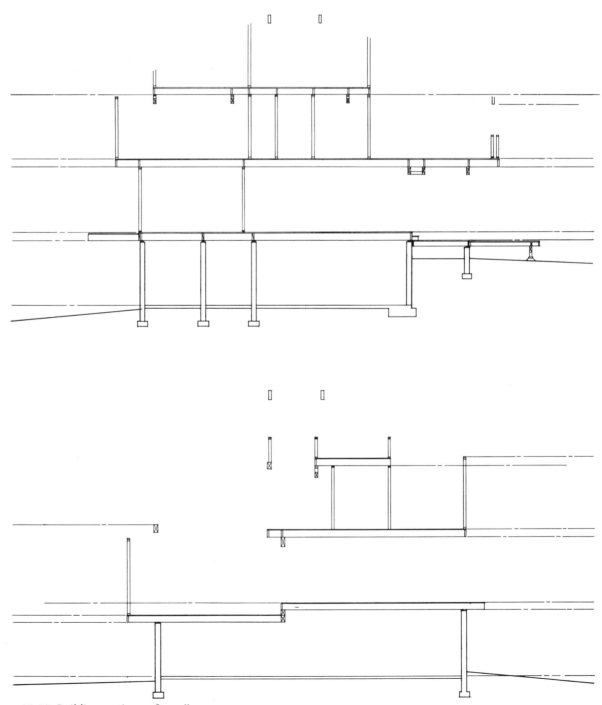

Figure 16.60 Building sections—Stage II.

Stage III

After studying the various detail sketches and framing plans from the structural engineer, we could now accurately draft the roof, ceilings, and floors. See Figure 16.61. We also added special features such as lowered ceilings, steps for the lowered living room, and the prefabricated fireplace. We obtained sizes for items like the prefabricated fireplace from the manufacturer's literature.

The proper material symbols for the materials could now be included, along with symbols for masonry, soil, and insulation. Because of the size of this reproduction, we eliminated items like the gravel or sand under the slab and the plastic membrane. If the scale had been larger than $\frac{1}{8}'' = 1'-0''$, we could have included these.

Now we could lightly lay out the exterior elevations.

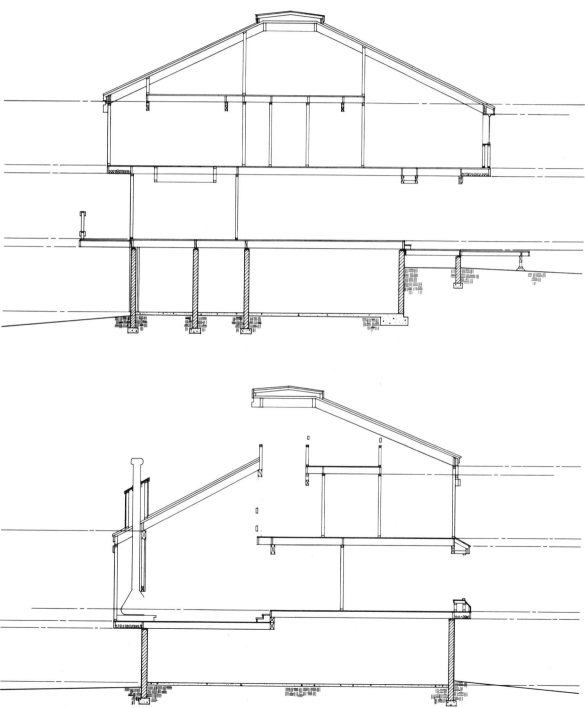

Figure 16.61 Building sections—Stage III.

Stage IV

All items requiring a call-out were next to be added— all the materials and sizes of members and all of the floor and plate lines, including their dimensions. See Figure 16.62. This is such a complicated building, structurally, that our dimensions included unusual dimen- sions like locations of tops of beams, plate lines for interior walls, and even bottoms of headers. We also added the height of the chimney in relation to the roof. Notice the location of the notes and the attempt of the drafter to align the notes so as to produce a margin.

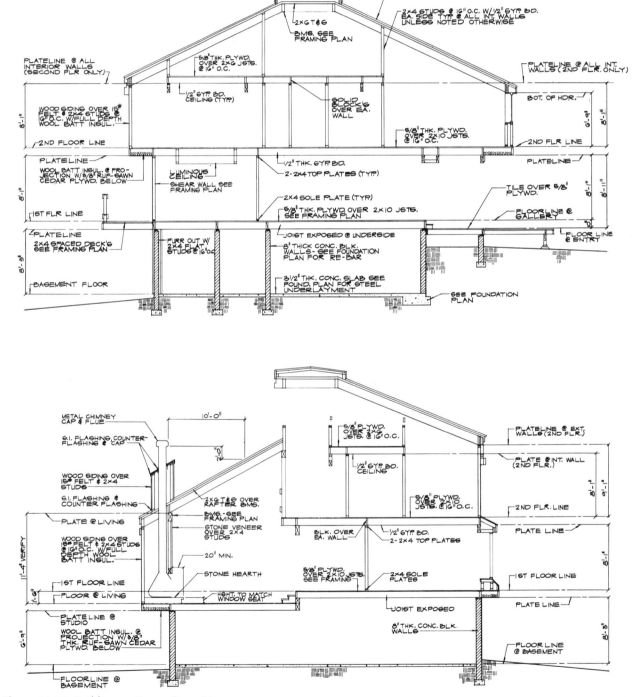

Figure 16.62 Building sections—Stage IV.

Stage V

All of the areas requiring a detail for clarification were now referenced. While we had already drawn most of the details freehand, and had solved many of the problems at the design stage, the need for additional details became apparent as the drawing of the formal architectural section was done. See Figure 16.63. Note how all of the detailed areas are circled and referenced.

Missing notes such as the 3½" concrete slab on Section B-B were now added, as well as room titles, main sheet title, and scale.

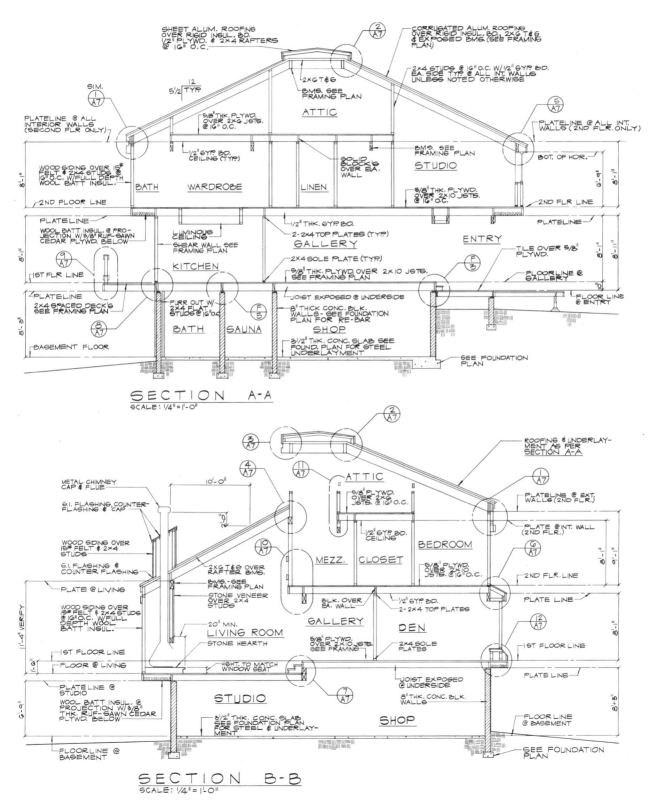

Figure 16.63 Building sections—Stage V.

First Floor Framing Plan

There were various ways the drawing shown in Figure 16.64 could have been done. The easiest was to have a structural engineer (or engineer) compute and draft the plan. The second was to ask the structural engineer to indicate the engineered beams freehand. This information could then be transcribed into drafted form.

To transcribe this information into a finished drafted form, a floor plan is drawn or traced onto a new vellum, and the engineering information is added. Or a reproducible can be made of the floor plan at an early stage and the engineering materials then added. Reproducibles can be made either photographically (the method used in Figure 16.64) or by a diazo process. The sepia process is a common diazo method of obtaining a reproducible.

In anticipation of using the photographic method, we made an early-stage copy of the original floor plan. We placed a piece of vellum over this copy and drafted the structural engineer's drawings. We then sent the two drawings to a blueprint service and combined them photographically. For simplicity, we deleted many connection notes and detail reference bubbles. See Figures 16.65 and 16.66. Figure 16.65 shows the staggered blocking, the joist hangers, and the built-up beam. Figure 16.66 shows clearly on the left the transition and method of construction between wood, steel, and concrete masonry units.

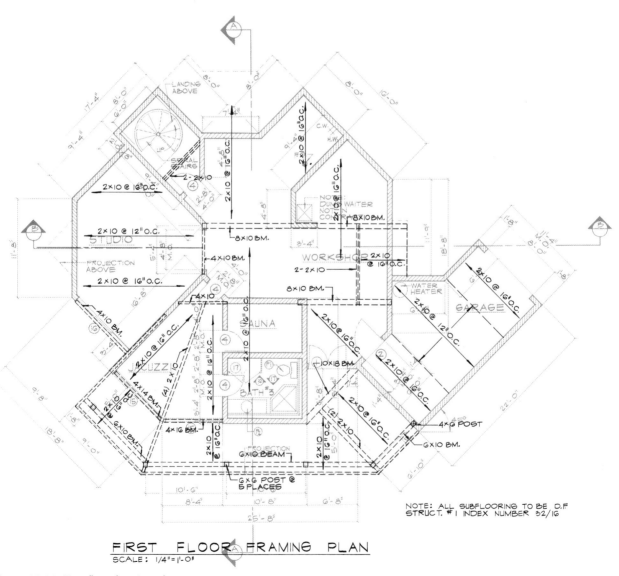

FIRST FLOOR FRAMING PLAN
SCALE: 1/4"=1'-0"

Figure 16.64 First floor framing plan.

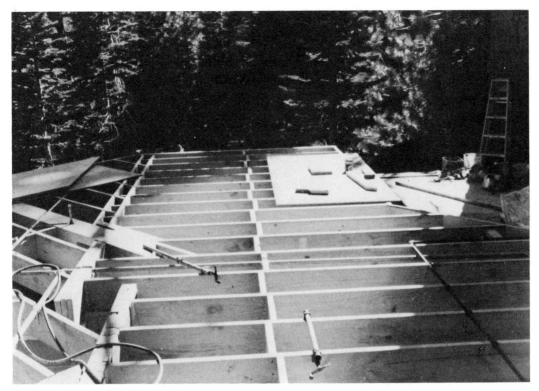

Figure 16.65 First floor framing.

Figure 16.66 Transition between masonry, steel, and wood.

Second-Floor Framing Plan

Like the drawing for the first floor framing plan, the drawing shown in Figure 16.67 applies the principles of composite drafting discussed in Chapter 2. The main members, as usual, were drawn in first—the 10 × 10 beams and the 8¾" × 9¾" glue laminated beams. The smaller beams and headers were drawn next. "HDR DOWN" indicates a header below the level represented. The single dimension-type lines with arrows at each end represent repeated members such as 2 × 10 @ 16" o.c. The single lines represent plywood on the walls chosen to resist seismic or wind problems. Even the nailing is specific (8d or 16d). Placing a vellum over a copy of an early-stage drawing of the second floor plan and carefully aligning the sheets, the structural engineer made a drawing similar to Figure 16.64. A drawing such as this can be roughly done on a print of the floor plan and then transferred to the vellum sheet.

Because this building is constructed of heavy timber, the main members were drawn first: the 10 × 10 beams

and 2 × 10 members were indicated by arrows because of spacing and quantity.

Look at the floor above and see what wall loads are placed on the framing members. Note again that because the structure must withstand heavy snow loads, the framing members are larger than normal. (Figure 16.68.)

Also note the glue laminated beam on the right of the framing plan. Glue laminated beams are many layers of wood glued together for strength. Plywood nailed on the wall below the second floor framing is shown by a single solid line, or by dotted lines (indicating a beam) with a solid line between. This plywood helps offset wind and seismic problems.

Roof and Attic Floor Framing Plans

Figure 16.68 used the same procedure as Figure 16.64, the first floor framing plan, and Figure 16.67, the second floor framing plan. Two interesting features of this plan are the dotted line indicating the roof line (perimeter of the roof) and the note sizing those beams now labeled.

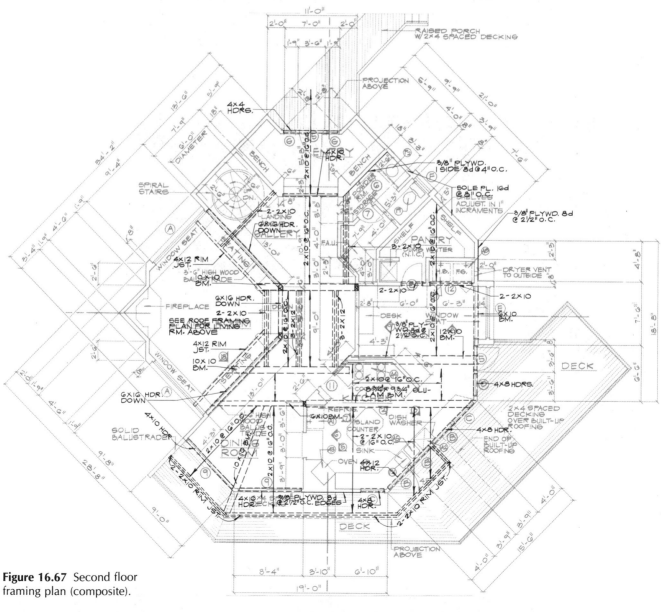

Figure 16.67 Second floor framing plan (composite).

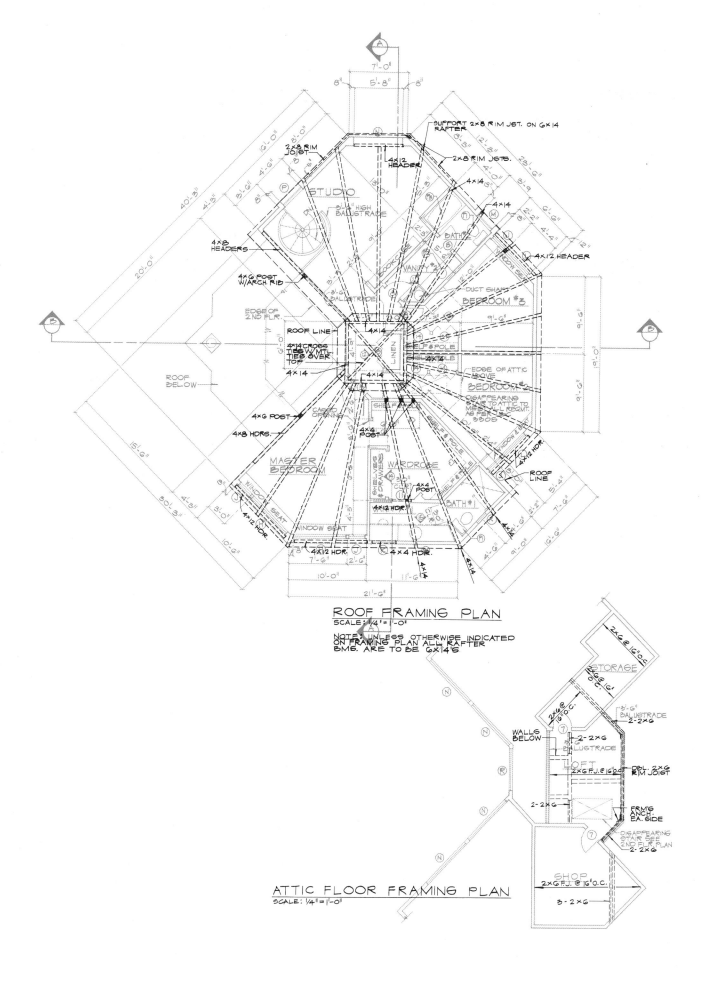

Figure 16.68 Roof framing plan and attic floor framing plan.

Schedules

Five schedules were to be included in this particular set of construction documents: the door, window, finish, plumbing fixture, and appliance schedules.

Stage I

A preliminary form shown in Figure 16.69, was made to ensure that all schedules would fit on one sheet and that the space distribution would be sufficient to contain the required information. Using the scheduling procedure described in Chapter 9, the vellum was inked.

Many finish schedules use angular lines at the top for material descriptions. The form used here has all lines perpendicular for easy reading.

The first stage included gathering the necessary information from the client and then from manufacturers' literature and putting it in order on a preliminary form.

Stage II

Figure 16.70 shows the schedule with information filled in. Because of the complexity of this project, the written specifications would be comprehensive. As a result, we only gave general descriptions for such items as "Wood."

On the window schedule below the remarks area in Figure 16.70 there is a reference to double-pane insulated glass. This was used to protect against the cold climate conditions and to prevent heat loss. Head, jamb, and sill spaces were left for future details.

When items were repeated, as on the door schedule under "Slab," and "Wood," either a line or a line with an arrowhead was drawn to show repetition.

Because the space we had allocated for the interior finish schedule was limited, we deleted various columns. This gave us space for another finish material. We needed space for a "wainscot" column, leaving two spaces for additional wainscot information. One space under the letter "W" was deleted, which allowed for other notations.

The slot titled "ceiling height" on the interior finish schedule, could be left blank or noted as "varies" with an arrow below indicating the lack of a standard height. Check the final drawing on the cross section and note the great variation in ceiling heights.

The schedules were not completed sufficiently to give a clear idea of the choices and their functions.

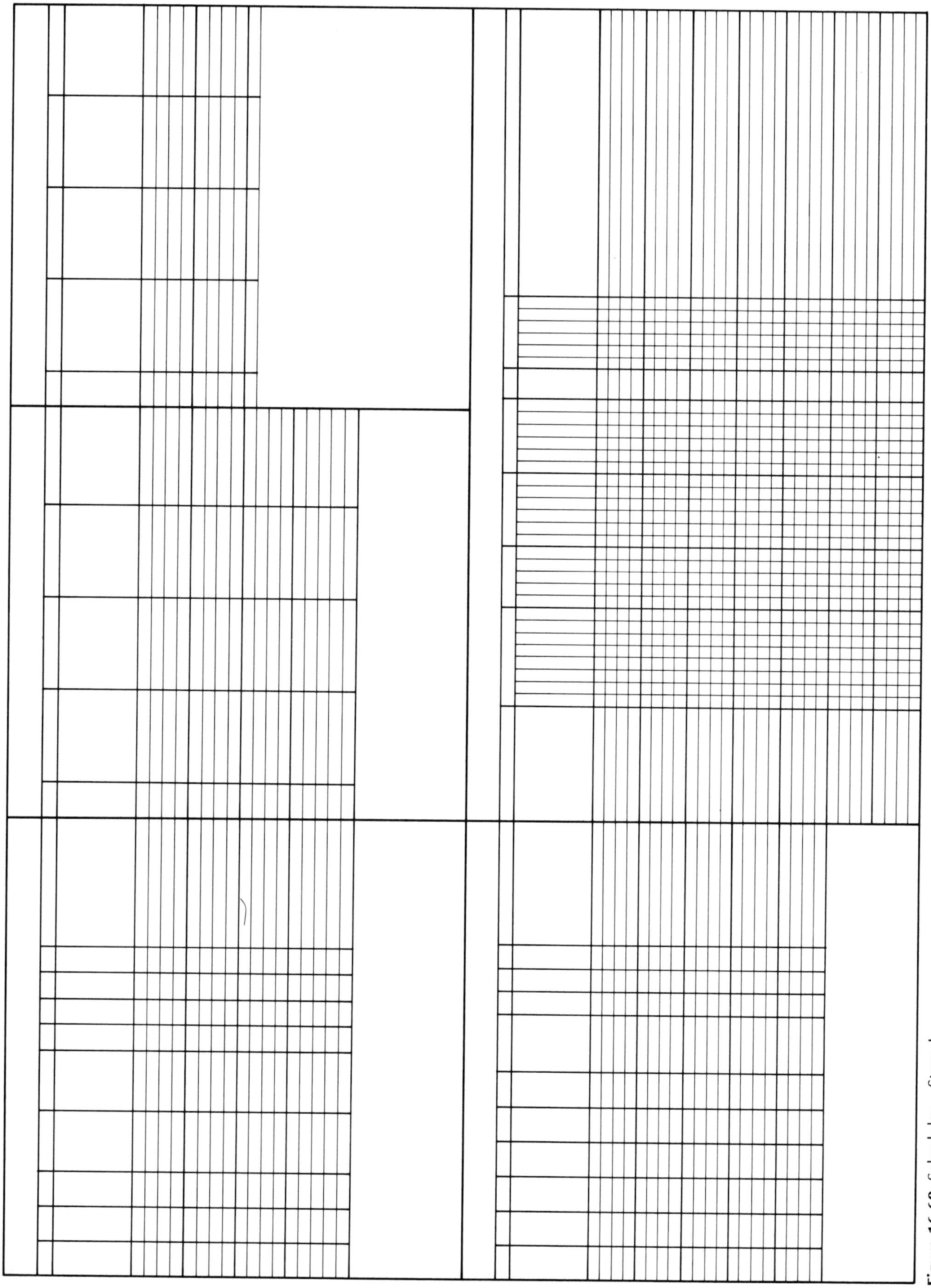

Figure 16.69 Schedules—Stage I.

WINDOW SCHEDULE

SYM.	WIDTH	HGT.	TYPE	FRAME MATERIAL	SCR.	HEAD	JAMB	SILL	REMARKS
A	8'-0"	7'-0"	FIXED	WOOD					
B	8'-0"	4'-0"	FIXED	WOOD					
C	8'-0"	4'-0"	CSMT.	WOOD					
D	8'-0"	7'-0"	FIXED	WOOD					
E	6'-0"	7'-0"	FIXED	WOOD					
F	2'-6"	6'-0"	CSMT.	WOOD					
G	1'-6"	1'-6"	FIXED	WOOD					
H	6'-0"	5'-0"	FIXED	WOOD					
I	2'-0"	5'-0"	CSMT.	WOOD					
K	8'-0"	3'-6"	CSMT.	WOOD					
L	3'-0"	5'-0"	CSMT.	WOOD					
M	2'-6"	5'-0"	CSMT.	WOOD					
N	VERIFY GLASS SIZES W/FRAME OPENING								
O		4'-0"	CSMT.	WOOD					
P	6'-0"	5'-0"	FIXED	WOOD					

NOTE: ALL GLAZING TO BE DOUBLE-PANE INSULATED GLASS UNLESS NOTED OTHERWISE

APPLIANCE SCHEDULE

SYM.	ITEM	MANUFACTURER	CATALOG NO.	REMARKS
1	REFRIGERATOR	SEARS	W46H6406GN	TAWNY GOLD
2	DISHWASHER	KITCHEN AID	KDC-17	HARVEST GOLD
3	DBL OVEN	GENERAL ELECT.	JK25 & PT	GOLD
4	COOKTOP	THERMADOR	TMH45	GOLDEN TONE
5	GARB. DISPOSAL	IN-SINK-ERATOR	77	STAINLESS
6	RANGE HOOD	TRADEWIDE	MASTERPIECE	FAN VC 500
7	WASHER	MAYTAG	A606	HARVEST GOLD
8	DRYER	MAYTAG	D606	HARVEST GOLD
9	FOOD WARMER	CORY	FW 324	GOLD
10	WATER HEATER			
11	FORCED AIR UNIT			
12	SAUNA HEATER			
13	JACUZZI	RIVEARA	7x7 GIBRALTER	WHITE W/BLUE

PLUMBING FIXTURE SCHEDULE

SYM.	ITEM	MANUFACTURER	CATALOG NO.	REMARKS
P1	WATER CLOSET	AMERICAN STD.	CADET	WHITE
P2	LAVATORY	AMERICAN STD.	OVALYN	WHITE
P3	TUB	AMERICAN STD.	BILDOR	WHITE
P4	KITCHEN SINK	COMMERCIAL	790-4 (42 x 21)	HARVEST-GOLD

DOOR SCHEDULE

SYM.	WIDTH	HGT.	THK.	HC/SC	TYPE	MATERIAL	HEAD	JAMB	SILL	REMARKS
1	FR 2'-6"	6'-8"	1-3/4"	S.C.	SLAB	WOOD				DOUBLE HINGED
2	3'-4"	6'-8"	1-3/8"	H.C.						
3	2'-8"	6'-8"	1-3/8"	H.C.						
4	2'-8"	6'-8"	1-3/8"	H.C.						
5	2'-0"	8'-0"	1-3/4"	S.C.						
6	2'-4"	6'-8"	1-3/8"	H.C.						
7	2'-6"	6'-8"	1-3/8"	H.C.	SLAB	WOOD (ASH)				
8	8'-0"	7'-0"	1/4"PT	—	5L&L	ALUM.				
9	2'-0"	6'-8"	1-3/8"	H.C.	POCKET	WOOD (ASH)				
10	2'-8"	6'-8"	1-3/8"	H.C.	BI-FOLD	(ASH)				
11	2'-6"	6'-8"	1-3/8"	H.C.	BI-FOLD	WOOD (ASH)				
12	8'-0"	7'-0"	1/4"PT		5L&L	ALUM.				8 x 12 LOUV. TOP & BOT.
13	3'-0"	6'-8"	1-3/8"		5L&L	ALUM.				
14	FR 2'-6"	6'-8"	1-3/8"	H.C.	SLAB	WOOD				

INTERIOR FINISH SCHEDULE

ROOM	FLOOR	BASE	WAINSCOT	WALLS	CEILING	REMARKS
ENTRY						
GALLERY						
LIVING ROOM						
DINING ROOM						
DEN						
KITCHEN						
PANTRY						
POWDER RM.						
STORAGE						
MASTER BEDRM.						
WARDROBE						
VANITY NO. 1						
BATH NO. 1						USE WATER PROOF DRYWALL
BEDROOM NO. 2						
BEDROOM NO. 3						
VANITY NO. 2						
BATH NO. 2						USE WATER PROOF DRYWALL
STUDIO NO. 1						
HALL						
STUDIO NO. 2						
WORKSHOP						
SAUNA						
JACUZZI						
BATH NO. 3						USE WATER PROOF DRYWALL
SHOP						
STAIR (BASEMENT)						
STAIR (1ST FLR)						
STAIR (2ND FLR)						

Figure 16.70 Schedules—Stage II.

Basement, First Floor, and Second Floor Electrical Plans

Like the framing plans, the electrical plans (Figures 16.71, 16.72, and 16.73) were drawn on separate sheets placed over the drawings of the respective floor plans. The electrical plans and the floor plans were later combined photographically.

As Figure 16.72 shows, these are not exclusively elec-

trical plans. There are items such as "FG" (fuel gas), "HB" (hose bibb), "CW" (cold water) located along with the electrical items. A notation at the top left indicates additional switching on other floors, 220 volt outlets, "WP" (waterproof) outlets, dimmer switches, and references to outlet location information the owner would supply.

Figure 16.73 shows a fire warning system. Many municipalities now require smoke alarms or smoke detectors.

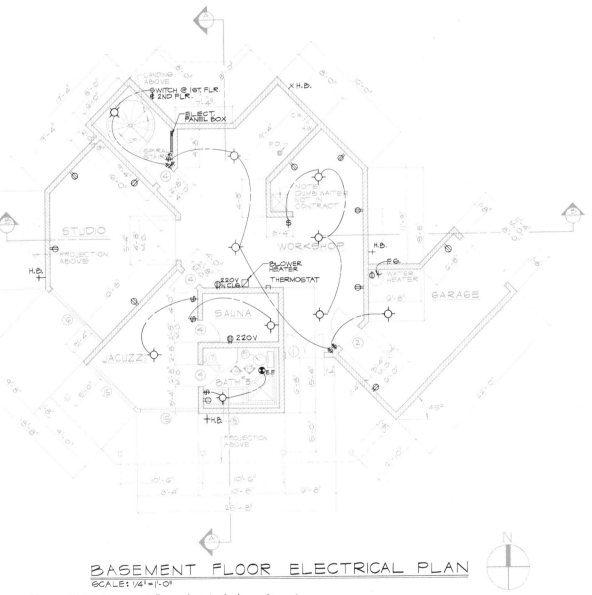

BASEMENT FLOOR ELECTRICAL PLAN
SCALE: 1/4" = 1'-0"

Figure 16.71 Basement floor electrical plan—Stage I.

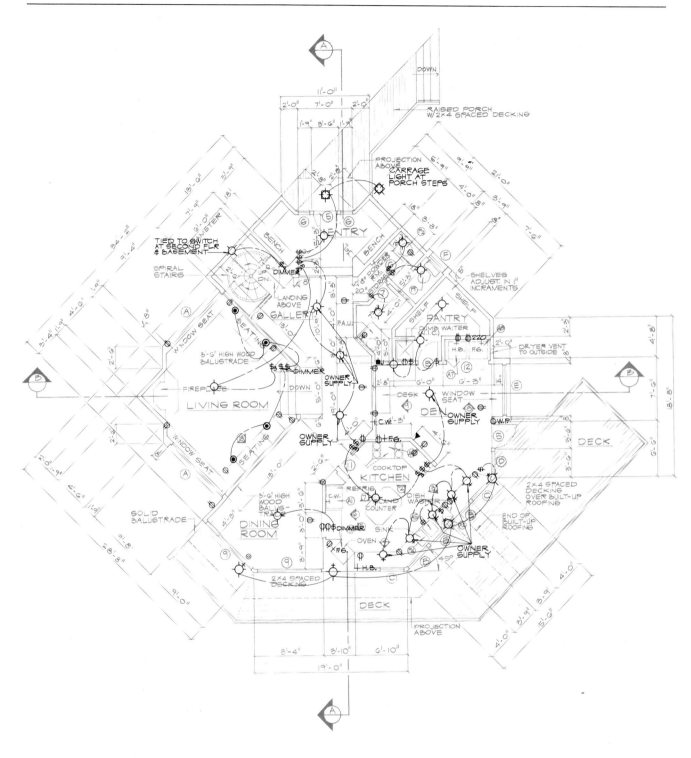

FIRST FLOOR ELECTRICAL PLAN
SCALE: 1/4" = 1'-0"

Figure 16.72 First floor electrical plan—Stage I.

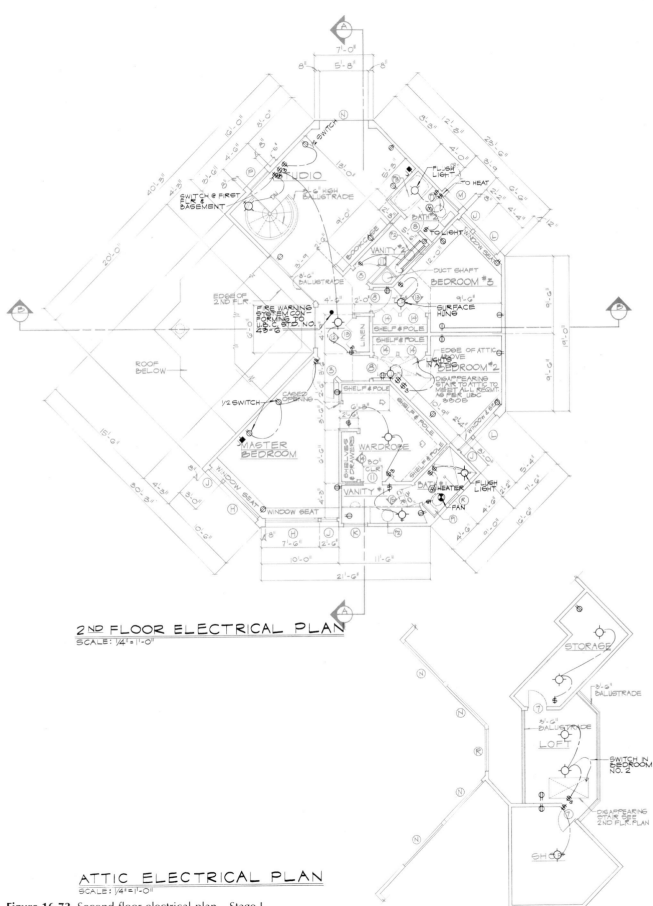

2ND FLOOR ELECTRICAL PLAN
SCALE: 1/4"=1'-0"

ATTIC ELECTRICAL PLAN
SCALE: 1/4"=1'-0"

Figure 16.73 Second floor electrical plan—Stage I.

CONCEPTUAL DESIGN AND CONSTRUCTION DOCUMENTS FOR A STEEL AND MASONRY BUILDING—THEATRE

17

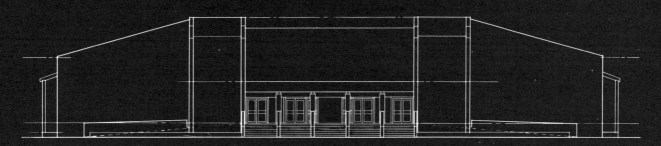

Courtesy of Avco Community Developers, Inc.
and Mann Theatres of California

Conceptual Design

Site and Client Requirements

The client required a theatre building with six separate auditoriums of 200 seats each. The sloping site of approximately three acres also had stringent architectural restrictions.

The proposed structure, with six auditoriums, office, restrooms, storage and food areas, required approximately 26,000 square feet of area. The seating area dictated the required on-site parking of 400 automobiles.

To satisfy fire requirements, the primary building materials selected were structural steel and concrete block. The concrete block also would provide an excellent sound barrier between the auditoriums and the lobby.

The initial concept provided for three auditoriums on each side of a central service core. This core would contain the lobby, toilet facilities, food bar, and storage areas. The core would provide controlled circulation and access to the auditoriums, facilities, and required fire exits. Efficient arrangements for the 200 seats and fire code requirements governed the auditorium dimensions.

The wall dimension also had to be compatible with the concrete block module. The upper floor level would contain the projection rooms, manager's office, employee toilet, and additional storage rooms. Stair location for this upper area was also governed by fire department and building code design criteria.

Initial Schematic Studies

After programming the basic physical requirements for this proposed project, we began schematic site development.

Stage I

The irregularly-shaped site had a West to East cross fall averaging 22 feet from the lowest to the highest grade. See Figure 17.1. Complicating the site further was a 25-foot-wide utility easement located near the center of the site. We could not build any of the structure in this easement.

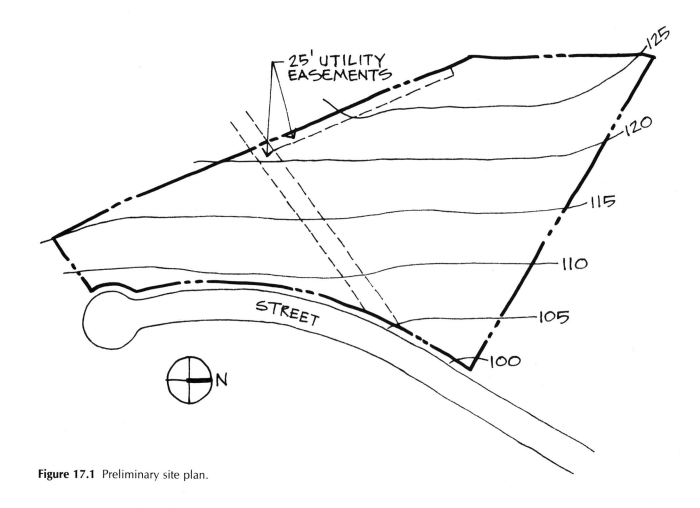

Figure 17.1 Preliminary site plan.

Stage II

In the intial schematic site study, shown in Figure 17.2, the structure is located north of the utility easement on the upper portion of the site. We thought this location would provide the most suitable parking layout for access to the theatre as well as a higher floor elevation for site drainage. The site entrance for automobiles is from the East property line only.

Stage III

After the schematic site development was completed, we designed the scaled preliminary first floor plan (Figure 17.3) and preliminary parking layouts. Client requirements determined the first level floor plan. Parking layouts and automobile circulation were designed to be compatible with the natural topography of the site; we paralleled the parking stalls and driveways with the existing grades. We also terraced the parking levels. This reduced the amount of rough and finish grading to be done. Stairs, as well as ramps for the handicapped, were provided at the front of the theatre.

Stage IV

From the scaled preliminary first floor plan, we made overlay studies of the second floor. Correct projector port locations for each auditorium, and required exit locations, determined the second floor design. Other spaces and their locations were more flexible. See Figure 17.4.

Stage V

Buildings in the area where this theatre is located are subject to the jurisdiction of an architectural review committee, with written criteria being given for exterior appearances and materials. One of these restrictions stated that the roof must be of mission tile with a minimum pitch of 4 in 12. Another requirement was that all roof-mounted mechanical equipment must be shielded from view. By providing the required sloping roof planes over the auditoriums and the rear and front lobby access, we created a well that would screen the roof mounted heating and ventilating equipment.

For aesthetic reasons, we decided to soften the facade of the building by breaking up the long exterior blank walls at the rear of the auditoriums. We added a heavy timber arbor to provide shadows on the blank walls. See Figure 17.5A. The arbor stain and general design were chosen to be compatible with mission tile. To provide an acceptable finish, we covered the concrete block with a plaster finish. To enhance the exterior and further define the design elements, as well as to fulfill building department requirements, we added concrete columns in the colonnade. Instead of using three-dimensional drawings for presentation, a conceptual model was constructed defining the general massing of the building as well as major architectural features. This model is shown in Figure 17.5B.

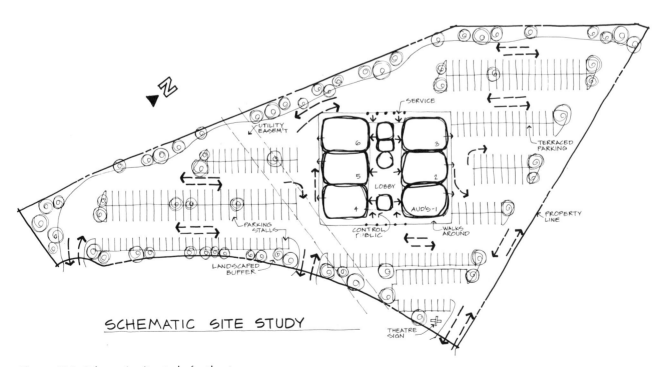

SCHEMATIC SITE STUDY

Figure 17.2 Schematic site study for theatre.

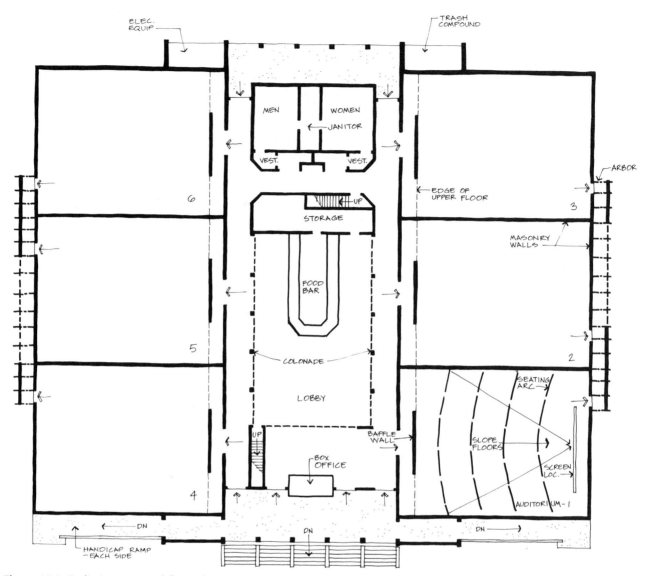

Figure 17.3 Preliminary ground floor plan.

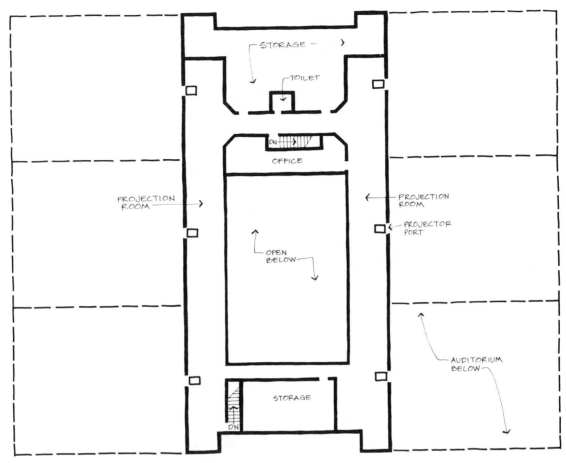

Figure 17.4 Preliminary upper floor plan.

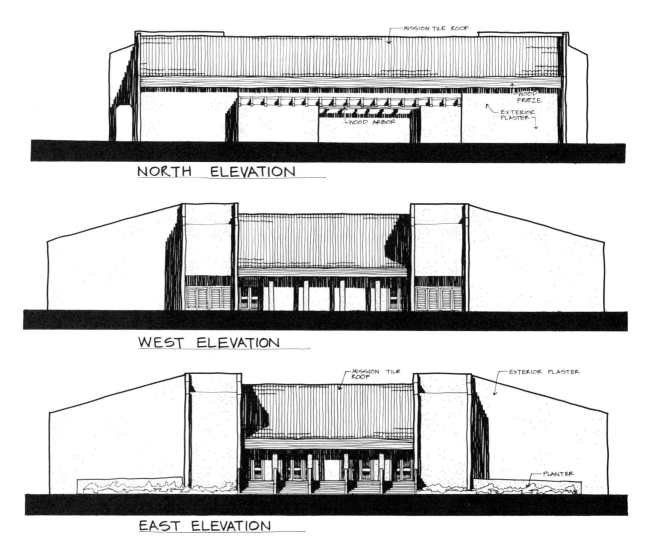

NORTH ELEVATION

WEST ELEVATION

EAST ELEVATION

Figure 17.5A Preliminary exterior elevations.

A

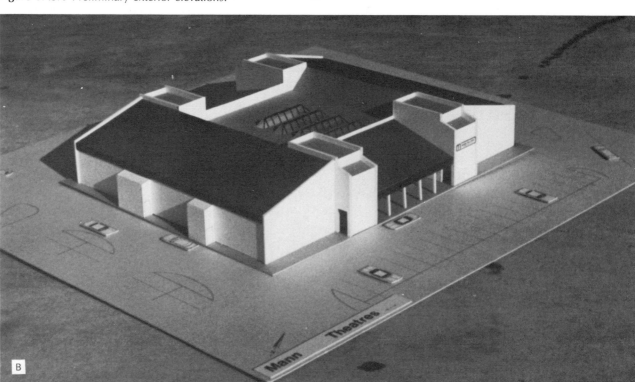

Figure 17.5B Conceptual model.

Site Plan

The primary purpose of the site plan was to locate the structure on the lot and indicate the proposed parking plan. Depending on its complexity, site plan may or may not be combined with the grading plan. For this project, the grading plan, the site plan, and the paving plan were done separately. Figure 17.6 is an aerial photo of the completed project.

Stage I

Our first step was to describe with lines the perimeter of the lot. See Figure 17.7. A formal description of the site is obtained from the client or civil engineer. The civil engineering survey shows and locates easements (right-of-access). In this case, the easement was a sewer easement, shown by dotted lines through the center and at the top of the lot.

The property contour is shown with a center-line type line to contrast it with the dotted lines of the easement. Property contours are shown with dotted lines or central-line type lines.

The center line of the road is shown here as a solid line, as are the road itself and the sidewalk. The circle at the left indicates a cul-de-sac (the end of the road with an area for turning around).

Stage II

Our main task at this stage was to locate the structure. See Figure 17.8. Location must always be done very carefully, using the preliminary site plan and the civil engineer's site plan. In this case, the easement through the center of the lot was a key factor in locating the structure.

Figure 17.6 Aerial photo of finished site. (William Boggs Aerial Photography. Reprinted with permission.)

Figure 17.7 Site plan—Stage I.

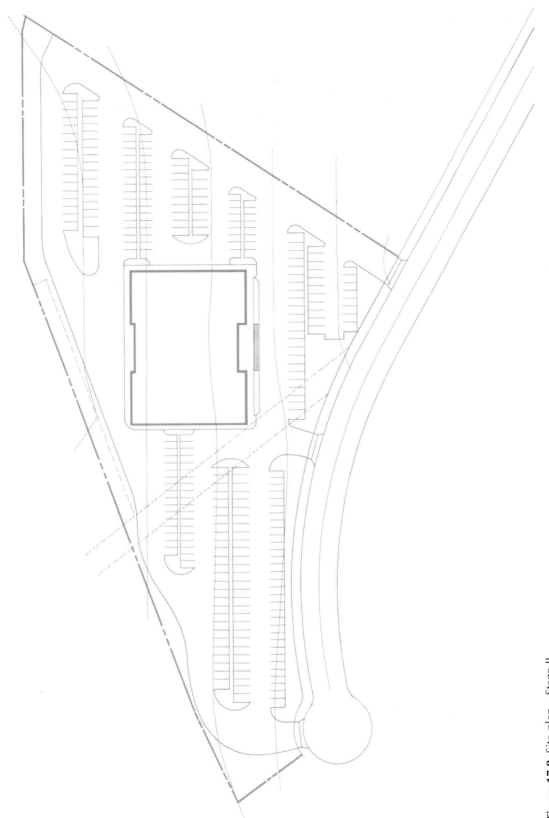

Figure 17.8 Site plan—Stage II.

The 400 parking stalls were next located. We needed to take into account such regulations as:

1. Turning radius of a standard car
2. Parking stall requirements
3. Permissible ratio of compact stalls to regular stalls
4. Aisles required between rows of parking
5. Dedicated green space requirement, if any
6. Ratio of parking spaces for the handicapped; their required distance to the point of entry, etc.

At this stage, also, the property line was darkened.

Stage III

Look carefully around the perimeter of the structure in Figure 17.9 and notice the dimension lines locating the building from the property lines.

Stage IV

Here, we added the property lines with their North orientations and respective lengths. See Figure 17.10. The dimensions that located this structure were added next.

Parking stalls and islands were dimensioned and located next. Notice again that the parking layout follows the contour lines. Streets were labeled, and the drawing titled. The scale and North arrow were added.

The shape of the site was complicated and we had many parking stalls to show, so we drew a separate partial grading plan. Figure 17.11A shows the overall site with a shaded area that is enlarged in Figure 17.11B. The letters "T.C." means "top of curb." The number on the top indicates the height (elevation) to the top, while the bottom number indicates the elevation to the bottom of the curb. These numbers are expressed in decimals; a difference of 0.5 is equal to 6 inches. By following the numbers around the curb, the direction of water flow can be determined. A 1% and 2% slope is also shown periodically.

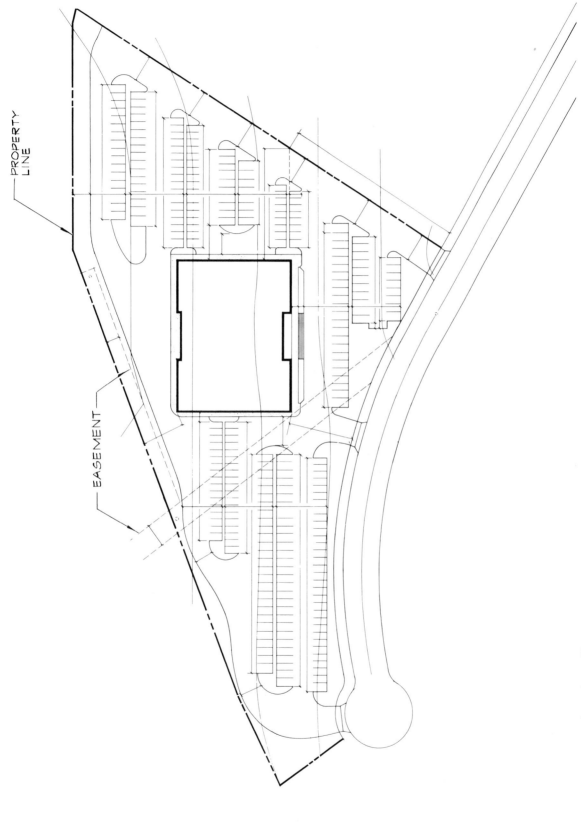

Figure 17.9 Site plan—Stage III.

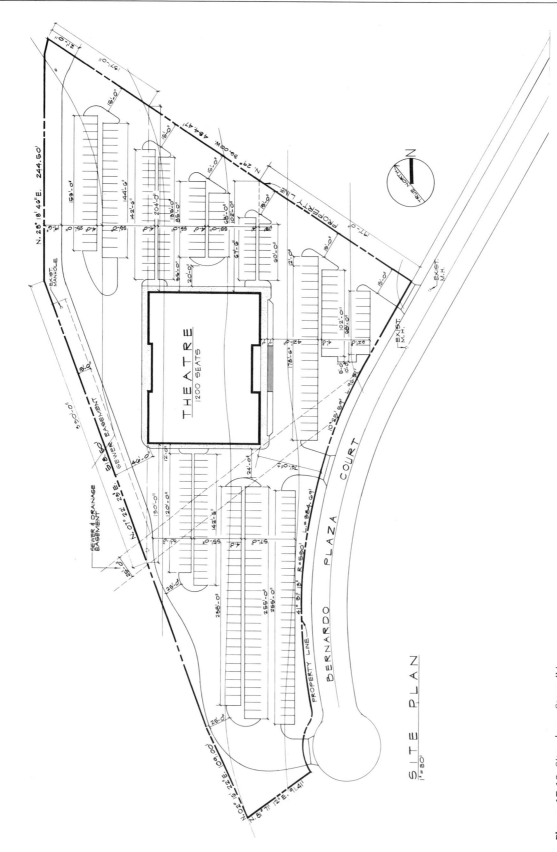

Figure 17.10 Site plan—Stage IV.

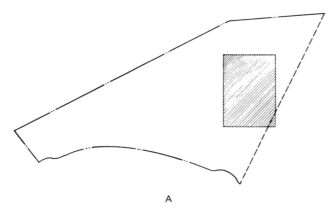

A

Figure 17.11A Portion of grading plan to be enlarged.

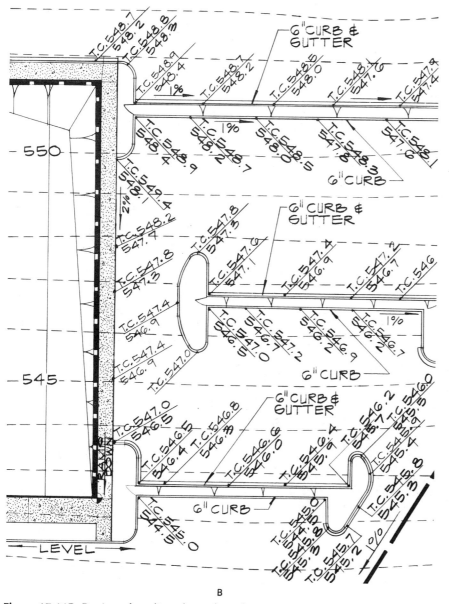

B

Figure 17.11B Portion of grading plan enlarged.

Foundation Plan

Stage I

The foundation plan was traced directly from the floor plan. See Figure 17.26. Sizes and location had to conform to the concrete block module.

To better understand the evolution of this plan, see Figures 17.12 and 17.13. Both the aerial photograph and the ground level view show how the property is graded. Stakes were used to guide the large earth-moving equipment, as you can see in Figure 17.14. Figures 17.15 and 17.16 show the chalk lines indicating the position of the wall columns, and Figure 17.17 shows trenched footings. A back hoe (trenching machine) was then used to dig the required trenches.

Pilasters (periodic widenings of a wall) act as columns to support members above. On interior walls, pilasters are seen from either room, while exterior pilasters can be seen only from the inside, so that the face of the exterior wall can remain flat. Pilaster sizes are obtained from the structural drawing; a few typical sizes are used. If you start a foundation drawing before you have these required sizes, you can still trace the walls and indicate the tentative location of the columns and pilasters with light cross lines to show the center.

Figure 17.18 shows the first stage in the preparation of the foundation plan. In this drawing, lines are dotted lines, but often, at this initial stage, the outline is drawn with light solid lines.

Four lines are needed to represent the walls of concrete block and the footing below the grade. At some locations, where the footing is continuous but the wall is

Figure 17.12 Graded site without structure. (William Boggs Aerial Photography. Reprinted with permission.)

Figure 17.13 Grading the property.

Figure 17.14 Stakes placed by surveyor.

Figure 17.15 Chalk lines for foundation.

Figure 17.16 Chalked lines ready for trenching. (William Boggs Aerial Photography. Reprinted with permission.)

not, there are only two lines. The squares drawn with dotted lines represent concrete pads for steel pipe columns.

The exit doors at the rear of each auditorium are interesting features of this project. Each exit was designed to be sheltered by a wall with a trellis above.

The rectangular areas adjacent to the easterly side are ramps for the handicapped. (Every feature of this theatre had to accommodate the handicapped. These features include restroom facilities, widths of openings and halls, and ramps for wheelchairs.)

The columns toward the center of the structure would hold up the upper floor. Figure 17.19 shows these columns and also the forms placed for the entry stairs adjacent to the ramps for the handicapped. The columns were carefully aligned with the upper floor walls and first floor walls.

Figure 17.17 Trenched footings.

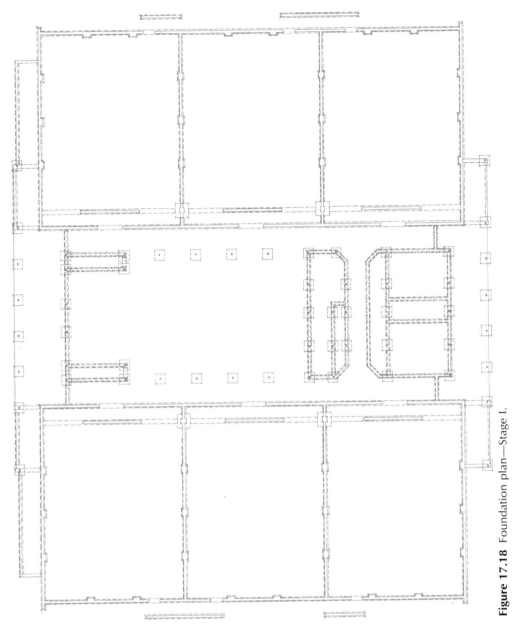

Figure 17.18 Foundation plan—Stage I.

Figure 17.19 Columns to support upper floor and forms for the stairs adjacent to the handicap ramps.

Stage II

The inclusion of the stairs in Figure 17.20 clearly identifies the entry to the theatre. The two lines extending from each column with several perpendicular lines in them represent brick pavers (patterned brick on ground level).

The arc lines within one of the auditoriums represent the subtle changes of levels. This was done only once because the floors in all six auditoriums are the same.

All exterior and interior dimension lines were added next, taking care to ensure a proper block module.

The reference bubbles on the outside of the overall dimension lines are called, collectively, a matrix of the dimensional reference plane. This matrix is used to locate columns, walls, and structural members above (not seen in this drawing).

Stage III

Major section lines were added at this stage, as were detail reference bubbles. See Figure 17.21. Some of the section symbols break the overall dimension lines. This is not desirable but we had to do it because of space limitations.

At the top right auditorium (looking at the building from the side where the entry is) notice two reference bubbles piggy-backed. This indicates that two details of these columns are available elsewhere, one architectural and the other a structural detail. The section bubbles with a flag-like symbol on the opposite side indicate wall sections.

In the lobby, next to the columns, are hexagonal symbols. These are concrete pad symbols and will have numbers or letters in them corresponding with the chart introduced at the bottom right. Each concrete pad for the various columns varied enough to necessitate a chart rather than individual dimensions.

We finally added the material designation for the walls, (the hatching lines within the wall lines).

Stage IV

Noting, referencing, and actual numerical values of dimensions were now added. See Figure 17.22. Noting included describing the floor material, such as the ceramic tile in the restrooms and brick pavers at the front of the theatre. We indicated slopes on the ramps for the handicapped. We noted special widening instructions

along the perimeter of the foundation wall as well as sizing of pilasters. At the center of the structure around the concession stand, a note reads "3" ⌀ × ³⁄₁₆'" tube typ. unless noted otherwise." Many of the columns at the rear of the concession stand and around the restroom area have a diagonal line indicating a different size.

Numerical values were placed, each being checked to ensure that the overall dimensions fell within the block module. Some of the values are missing near the schedule at the bottom. These dimensions are picked up later.

All of the detail and section reference bubbles were noted and the axial reference planes (the numbers across the top and the letters along the right side) were finished.

Stage V

The dimensions overlooked in the previous stage were picked up here. See Figure 17.23. A set of dimensions describes the slope of the floor in the auditorium nearest the column pad schedule.

The hexagon-shaped symbols next to the column pads were now sized, using the column pad schedule. Size, depth, and reinforcing are now indicated. If this structure had had only a few pads, we would have dimensioned them at their location.

The center of the arc that established the slope of the auditoriums was located on the outside of the building. Notice the broken 29'–4" dimension line on Figure 17.23. Since the arcs were symmetrical, we used a center-line type line to designate the middle of the auditorium. From this point we placed a series of numbers on a dimension line with arrowheads on it. Each arrowhead points to a specific arc and each arc was dimensioned with a note indicating two measurements. The first gives the distance traveled versus the change in the height; the second gives a ratio. For example, the first note closest to the center of the building reads, "up 16.15" in 12'–11" and 1.25" per ft," meaning the vertical distance traveled. "In 12'–11" means the horizontal distance the 16.15" vertical distance is measured in. In other words, for every horizontal foot traveled, there is 1.25" vertical distance achieved. This ratio is based on the seating arrangement, viewing requirements, and the most comfortable walking slope for the audience.

Since all the auditoriums were to be the same, only one dimension was necessary, with a note to that effect placed in the center. Section references were labeled and the main sheet title and scale were added. This was the final stage.

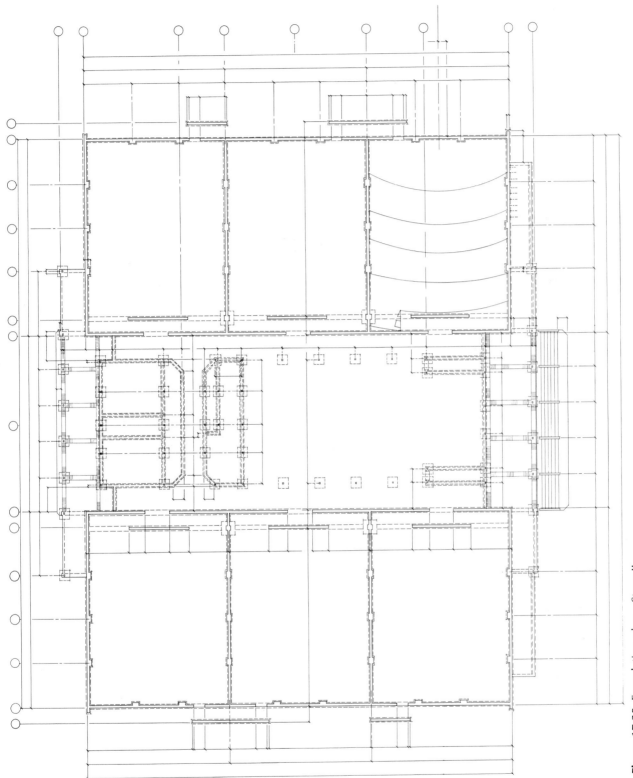

Figure 17.20 Foundation plan—Stage II.

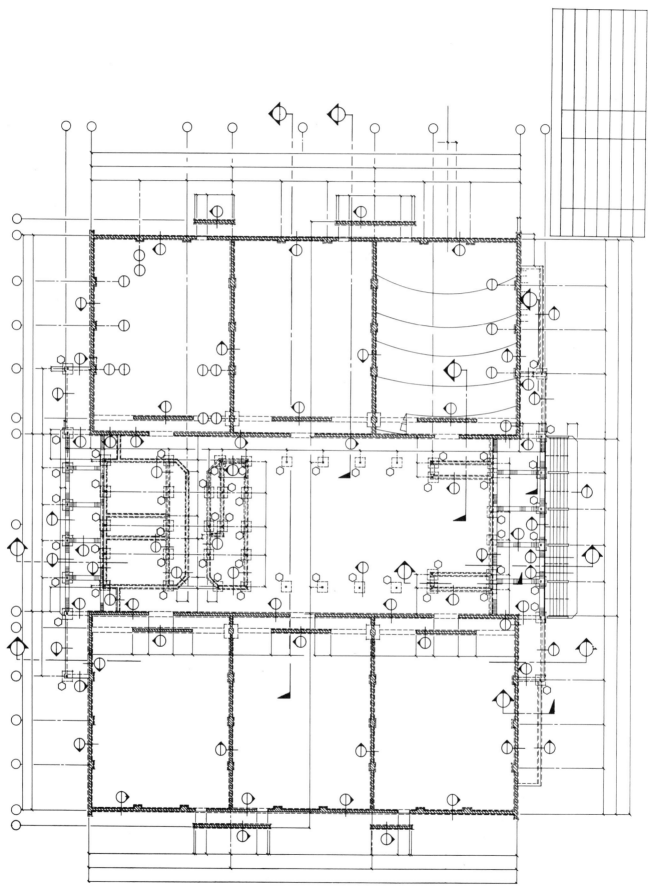

Figure 17.21 Foundation plan—Stage III.

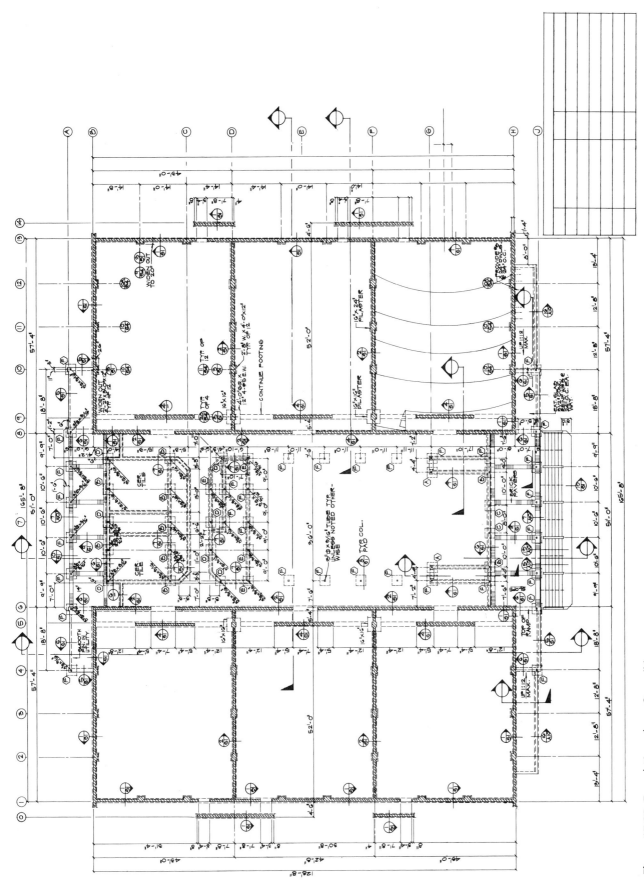

Figure 17.22 Foundation plan—Stage IV.

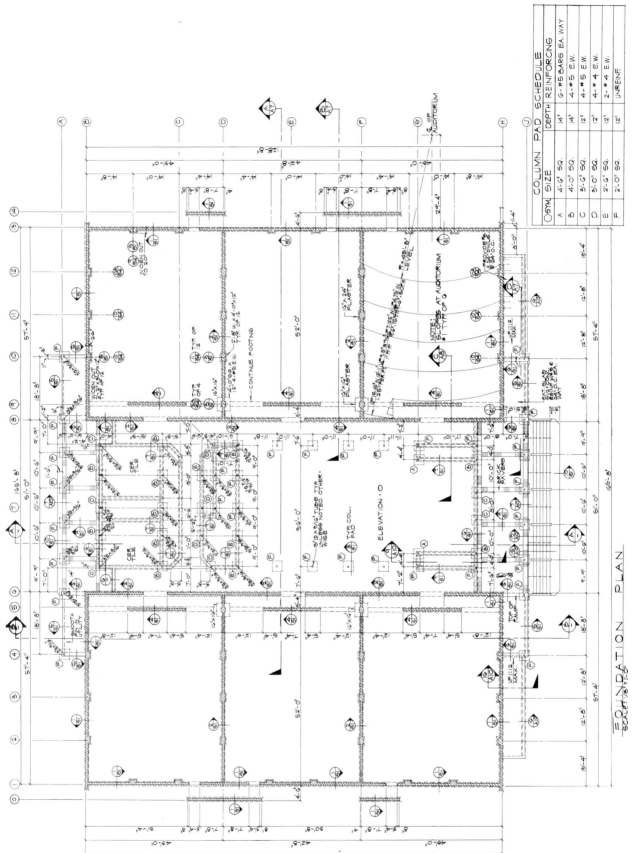

Figure 17.23 Foundation plan—Stage V.

Ground Floor Plan

Stage I

The floor plan is taken from the preliminary floor plan. Because this was the first drawing to be laid out, we had to take care to conform to the block module.

Clients may supply prototype plans based on their experience in a particular business. This particular client had determined that this would be a six-theatre structure with 200 seats in each theatre. Seating, the level for each row of seats, and fire restrictions were all design factors affecting the structure. We researched all of these factors prior to drawing the preliminary floor plan.

Compare the aerial photograph, Figure 17.24, with Figure 17.25 to see what was actually being constructed. Figures 17.24 and 17.25 show the construction sequence in relationship to the floor plan found on Figure 17.26.

In Figure 17.26, the columns toward the center of the theatre support the upper floor. (The upper floor accommodates the projectors and allows projectionists to move from one projector to another.) Near the rear of the building are the restrooms and snack bar storage. The two partial rectangles near the front of the theatre are stairwells.

Stage II

At the bottom of the left and right side of the plan, we added a planter and a ramp for handicapped people. See Figure 17.27. Stairs were added throughout the plan, and we added a set of dotted lines in each auditorium to represent the motion picture screens. The size of the screen was determined by the seating capacity and client needs. Dividing walls were drawn within the stairs at the front. Notice at the front and rear of the building the brick pavers as described in the foundation plan. These pavers were drawn with textured concrete within them.

At the center of the structure is the concession stand. The textured area represents a tile floor and the blank space, the counter. We added toilet partitions and lavatories to the restrooms, leaving larger stalls for handicapped people. Toilets can be added here or later.

At the center of each restroom entry, the small area for telephones also accommodates handicapped people. The small circles with a darkened cross indicate fire extinguishers. We added fire sprinkler symbols in the trash area in the rear of the building. Line quality becomes important here to differentiate between walls, floor patterns, and fixtures.

Stage III

Interior and exterior dimension lines were now added. See Figure 17.28. These dimensions *must* always be double checked with the foundation plan to insure proper alignment of the walls with the foundation. As the floor plan was dimensioned first, the concrete block module was followed.

The axial reference plane bubbles across the top and to the right correspond with walls, columns, and any structural members above, and form the reference plane matrix. We also indicated door swings.

Stage IV

All of the reference bubbles were now located. See Figure 17.29. Full architectural section references, wall sections, door reference bubbles, and interior elevation reference symbols were included. Each room would later receive a number as well as a title, so we drew in underlines for the names and rectangular boxes for the numbers.

At the entry, we drew plants in the planters to clearly differentiate the planter areas from the ramps. The planters and plants were later included in the elevation (Figure 17.49) for clarity and consistency.

The material designation for the walls, indicated by hatching lines in the wall lines, was drafted next.

Stage V

Numerical values for the dimension lines were now included. See Figure 17.30. Each dimension had to be checked with the foundation plan. Accuracy at this stage is critical. Compare the radial dimension line added in Auditorium #2 with Auditorium #1 on the foundation plan (Figure 17.23).

We noted typical items such as pilaster sizes and the location of the screens, and unique items such as the location of fire extinguishers. Area titles and room titles were the next items to be noted.

We labeled the reference plane bubbles next. The stair notations refer to the finish schedule in the same way that the door letters refer to the door schedule. Finally, the drawing title, scale, and North arrow were added.

Figure 17.24 Aerial view of completed walls. (William Boggs Aerial Photography. Reprinted with permission.)

Figure 17.25 View of entry, lobby, and back of theatres.

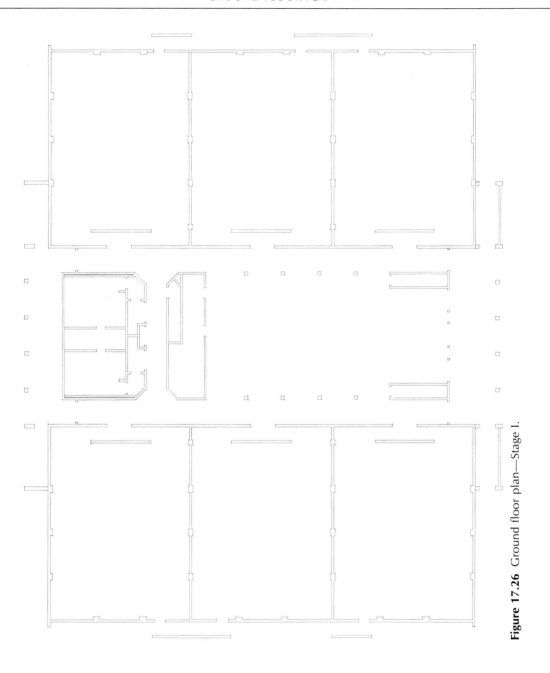

Figure 17.26 Ground floor plan—Stage I.

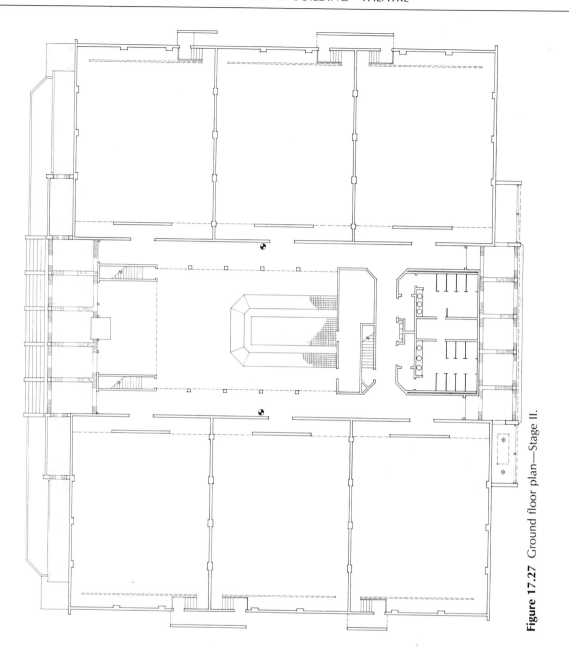

Figure 17.27 Ground floor plan—Stage II.

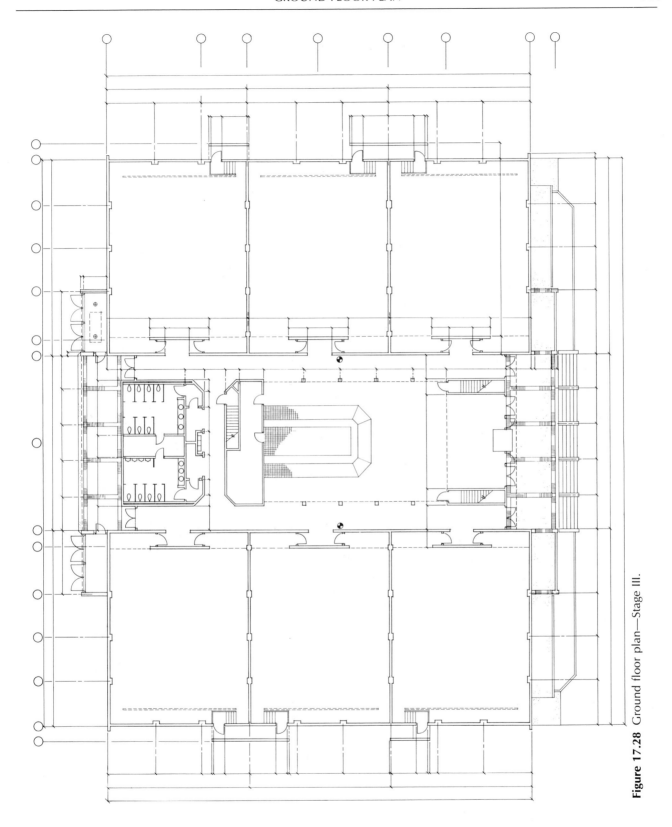

Figure 17.28 Ground floor plan—Stage III.

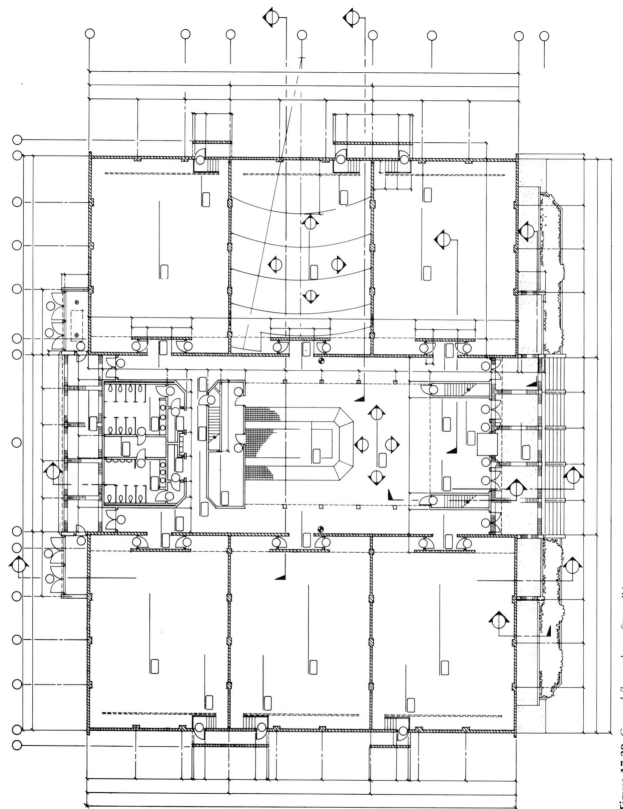

Figure 17.29 Ground floor plan—Stage IV.

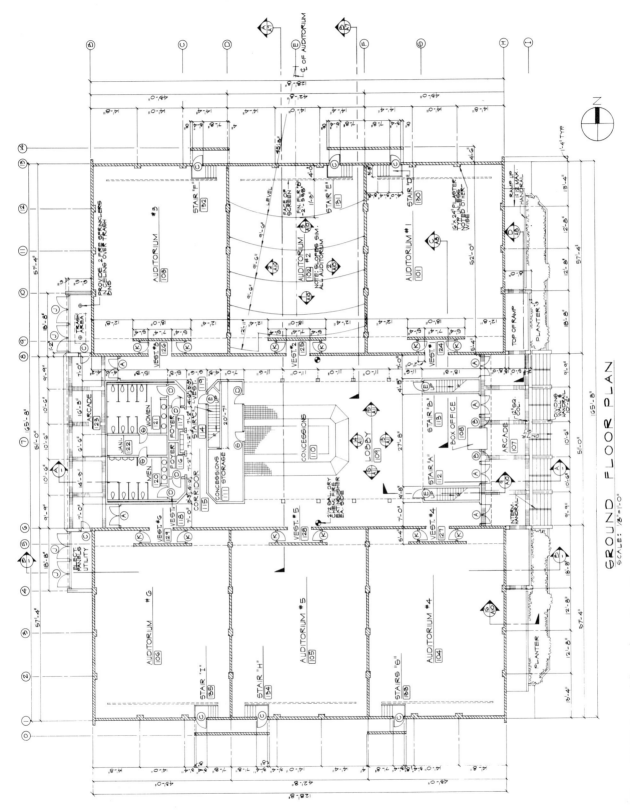

Figure 17.30 Ground floor plan—Stage V.

Upper Floor Plan

Stage I

We included the six auditoriums in the upper floor plan (see Figure 17.31) because the upper portions of the auditoriums were adjacent to the upper floor. The center of the structure is the lobby, which extends to the roof.

We located the projection windows according to their required angle. Figure 17.32 shows the interior of the structure. Note the projection windows and the connectors below to attach the upper floor. We took care to align the walls of the upper floor with the walls below.

Another view of this relationship is seen in the structural sections (for instance, in Section B-B in Figure 17.53).

Stage II

This stage (Figure 17.33) shows the stairs, restroom facilities, two fire extinguishers (one circle on each side) and, most important, the projectors and the space they occupy. A rectangle with a line through it next to a circle was the symbol we selected to represent the projectors.

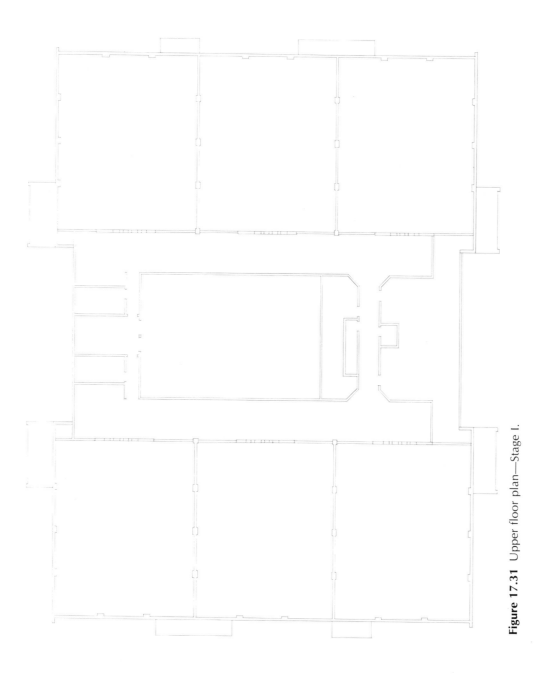

Figure 17.31 Upper floor plan—Stage I.

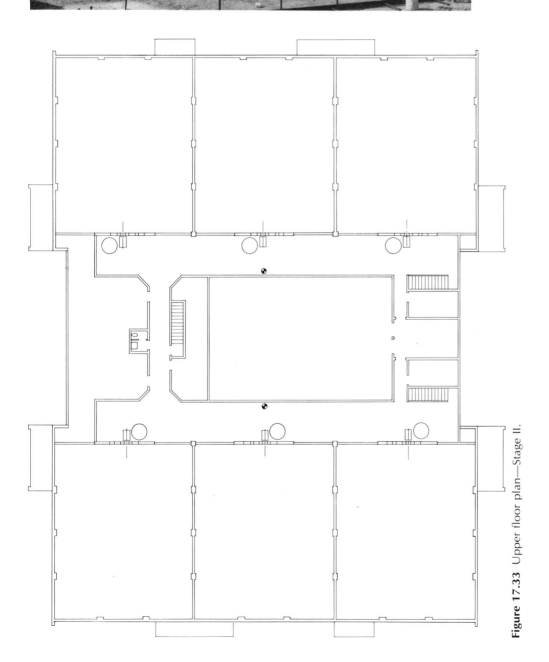

Figure 17.32 View looking toward Lobby.

Figure 17.33 Upper floor plan—Stage II.

Stage III

The upper floor plan affects only the central part of the building, but the dimensions shown on it relate to the overall structure. So our first step was to add the necessary dimension line. See Figure 17.34.

The foundation plan and the first floor plan were consulted to maintain consistency in dimensioning. This correspondence would be checked again when numerical values were added to the drawing. Finally, we drafted the material designation for the concrete block and located the door symbols.

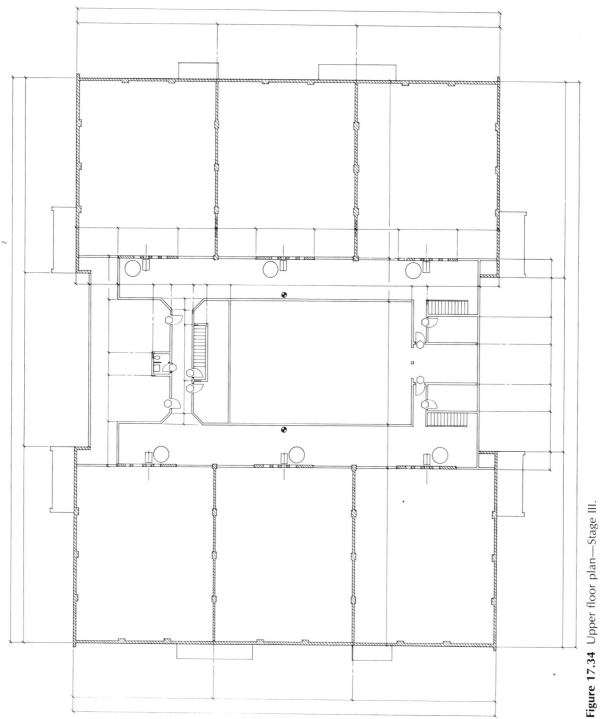

Figure 17.34 Upper floor plan—Stage III.

Stage IV

The main difference between this stage and the last is the addition of most of the dimension numbers. See Figure 17.35. The dimensions had to be checked against the floor plan of the floor below, and both had to be checked to ensure correct concrete block module dimensions.

Stage V

In this final stage, Figure 17.36, interior elevation reference bubbles were added, together with all necessary lettering. Some dimensions that were missing in Figure 17.35 now appear.

Doors and windows were checked with the schedule and filled in. Stair A and Stair B do not indicate the size

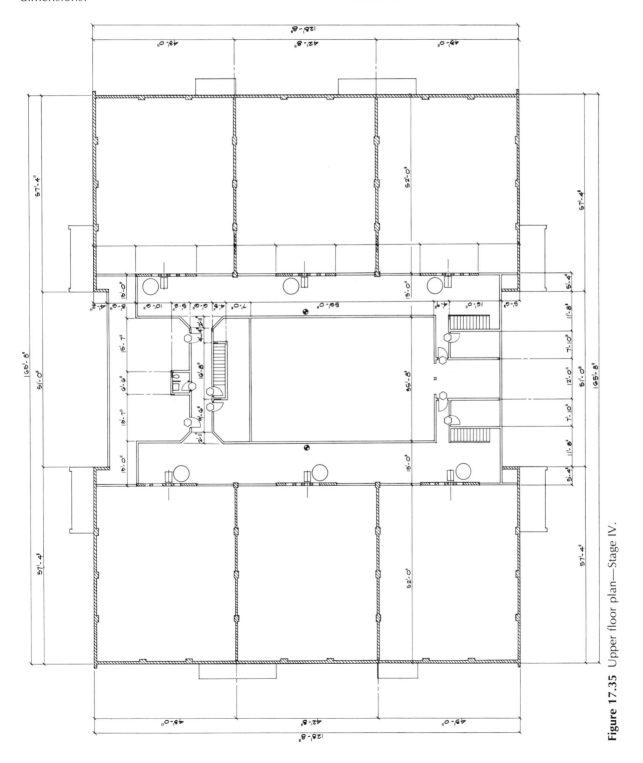

Figure 17.35 Upper floor plan—Stage IV.

or number of treads and risers. Details or sections provide their size, shape, and proportion. Look at the first floor plan (Figure 17.30) at the stair area and note the cutting plane line for a detail section.

The rooms in Figure 17.36 are numbered with three digits beginning with a "2", for the floor reference. The auditoriums were previously numbered on the first floor plan; the upper floor plan shows the upper portion of the auditoriums (without room numbers).

The central portion of the plan is open to the area below as indicated. Using this scale, it was difficult to show the small toilet at the rear. Therefore, we made an enlarged floor plan and elevation of Room 208 on the partial floor plan and the interior elevation sheet.

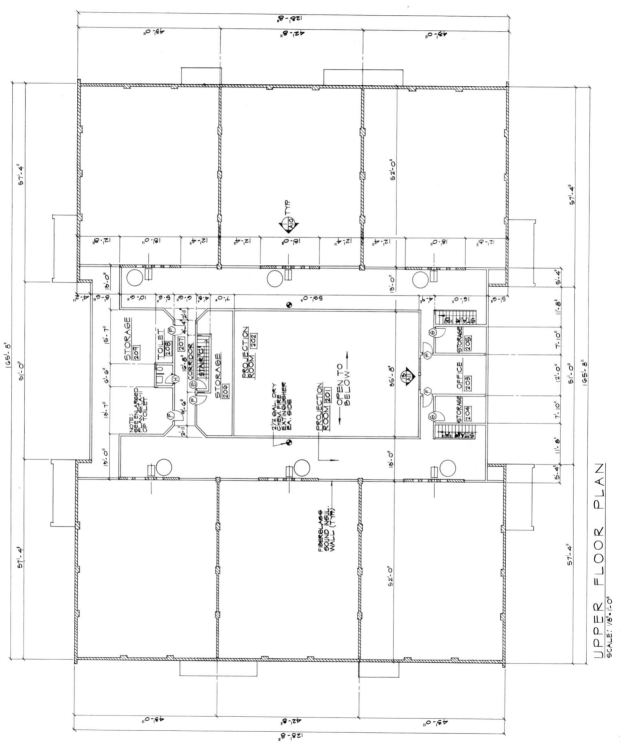

UPPER FLOOR PLAN
SCALE: 1/8" = 1'-0"

Figure 17.36 Upper floor plan—Stage V.

Partial Floor Plan and Interior Elevations

Stage I

The partial floor plan shown in Figure 17.37 was drawn at a larger scale than the other plans. It includes the concession areas and restrooms. Only a few interior elevations are drafted here.

Here, the partial floor plan is drawn twice the size of the first floor plan. We took the measurements from the first floor plan. At this scale, we could also show the double wall for the plumbing. (See the wall with toilets.)

The four rectangles at the bottom of the drawing represent columns. Two more columns appear to be located next to the walls but are actually inside the walls. They were included for visual continuity and have no structural implications.

The left half of the drawing was blocked out to receive the interior elevations, with one exception: the floor plan of the toilet on the upper floor level located slightly left of center on the drawing. The rectangle to the right of the upper floor toilet would become the interior elevation for that toilet, while the long rectangle at the bottom would become the interior elevation of the entry to the restrooms and telephone area.

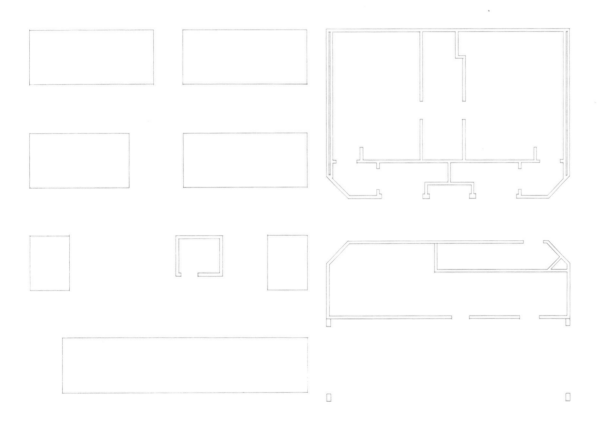

Figure 17.37 Partial floor plan and interior elevations—Stage I.

Stage II

The partial floor plan now shows the plumbing fixtures and the floor material in the restrooms. See Figure 17.38. The rectangles at the center near the entry to the restrooms are drinking fountains. Across the hall are the stairs to the upper level.

The wall material was now added to the interior elevations. Various fixtures such as urinals, paper towel dispensers, grab bars for the handicapped, and drinking fountains were also added.

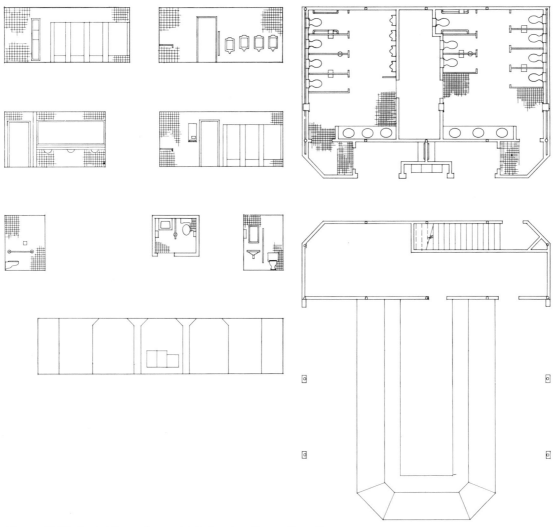

Figure 17.38 Partial floor plan and interior elevations—Stage II.

Stage III

All of the necessary dimension lines not included on the ground floor plan were not located on this sheet (see Figure 17.39), as well as some of the critical dimensions on the interior elevations. Door swings were shown by dotted lines. We added the designation of floor material in the concession area.

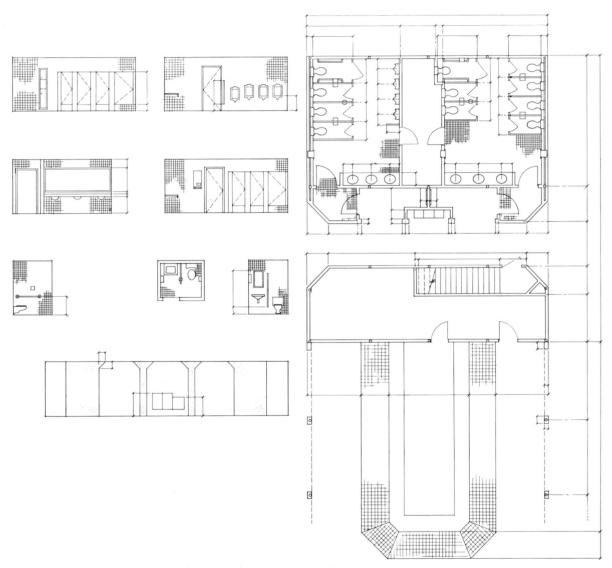

Figure 17.39 Partial floor plan and interior elevations—Stage III.

Stage IV

We established the numerical values for the dimensions shown in Figure 17.40 by checking the upper floor plan, foundation plan, and first floor plan. The dimension to the right side of the concession counter ends in a series of dots, indicating that the structure continues; break lines were not used.

The reference bubbles with arrows on them refer to the interior elevations. Only a few typical examples are shown here; in reality, there should be an interior elevation for every symbol shown.

Among the interior elevations, there is a plan and interior elevation for the upper floor toilet. This is unusual but the available paper space determined place-

ment. Pay attention to the structural columns and the double stud wall behind the water closet designed for the plumbing.

Next, dimensions of the heights of the interior elevations were added. Various typical items such as mirrors were located and given sizes. Handicap requirements were again checked and items such as grab bars were properly located.

Material indications for walls and floors were called out. This was done broadly (generically) because the written specifications would be used for a more definitive explanation. Last, additional notes, main titles, and scale were added.

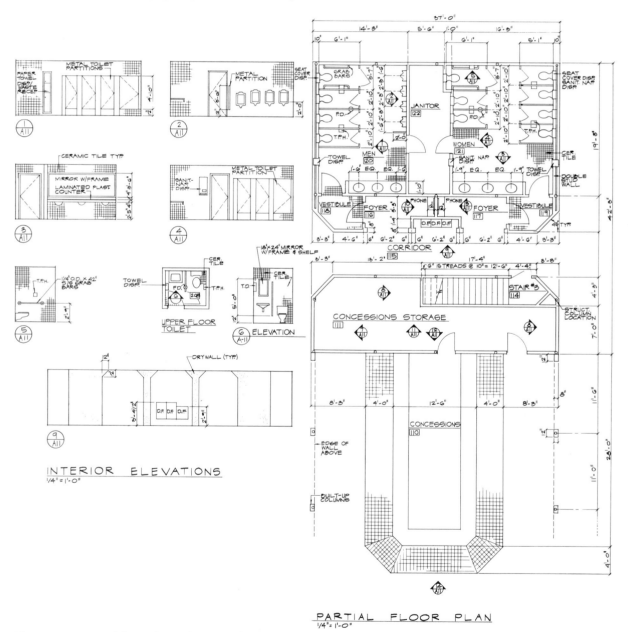

Figure 17.40 Partial floor plan and interior elevations—Stage IV.

Exterior Elevations

Elevations are developed from scratch, and are not traced from any other drawings unless extremely accurate preliminary drawings have been prepared. In most sets of drawings, the elevations are among the last to be completed because they are dependent on the floor plan, sections, roof plan, and so on. To better see how exterior elevations evolve, read the chapter on cross sections first (Ch. 10). Figures 17.41 and 17.42 show how the exterior of the project actually appears as the construction proceeds, and Figures 17.43 and 17.44 show front and rear views of the construction when completed.

Figure 17.41 Front of theatre. (William Boggs Aerial Photography. Reprinted with permission.)

Figure 17.42 Front of theatre showing ramp for the handicapped. (William Boggs Aerial Photography. Reprinted with permission.)

Figure 17.43 Front view of finished structure. (Photography: Kent Oppenheimer.)

Figure 17.44 Rear view of finished structure.

Stage I

We decided to draft only three exterior elevations rather than the normal four because the structure is symmetrical and the North and South elevations are similar. The horizontal lines in Figure 17.45 represent several items; the two floor levels, the top of the parapet, the tops of the beams, and the top of the beam at the canopy over the door. (The sloped, dotted line on the bottom elevation is the angle of the ramp for the handicapped.)

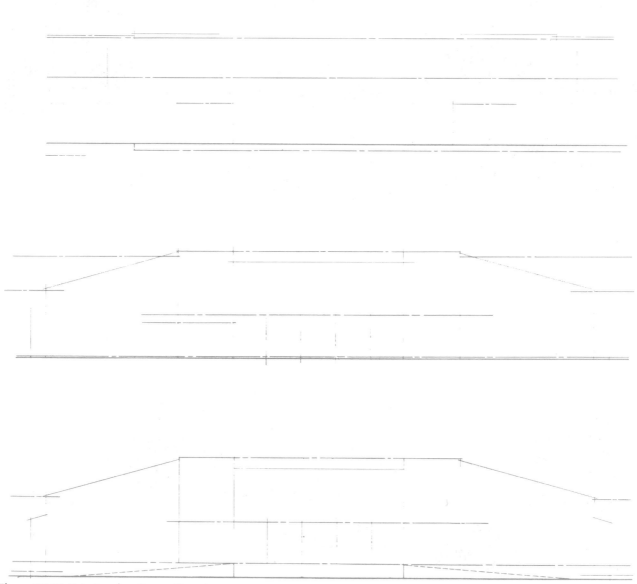

Figure 17.45 Exterior elevations—Stage I.

Stage II

The small, light vertical lines shown in Figure 17.46 locate the various beams and columns. These locations were taken from the reference bubbles on the floor plan. The complete structure would later be referenced by the column locations.

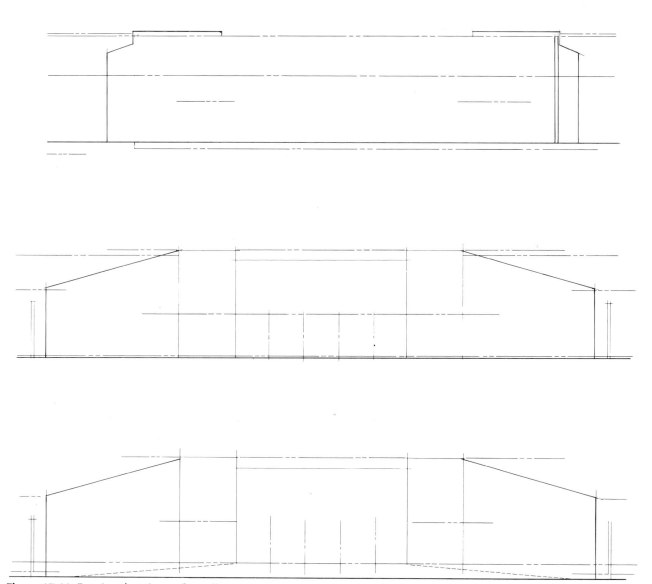

Figure 17.46 Exterior elevations—Stage II.

Stage III

Where Stage II indicated the vertical heights, Stage III established the outline of the building itself. See Figure 17.47. Column locations, wall thicknesses, independent walls at the exit were all established at this point. These measurements were obtained from the various plans, such as the floor plan, foundation plan, and the architectural sections. Each of these drawings used a dimensional system. This was helpful in the development of this structure because it gave specific points of reference. Heights, width, and depth of the structure were all referenced to this system.

For orientation purposes, the top elevation is the North elevation; the center is the West elevation; and the bottom is the East elevation and entry to the theatre. The two rectangular shapes toward the center of the North elevation represent the walls protecting the patrons at the exit.

The top center line on the West elevation is a point of reference. It is the top of the parapet wall extending above the roof plan. The series of vertical lines toward the center represent columns and the two horizontal lines above the columns represent the fascia.

The ramp on either side of the entry is indicated with dotted lines. See the East elevation, Figure 17.47. At the center are columns with handrails drawn in front of them. Stairs would be added later.

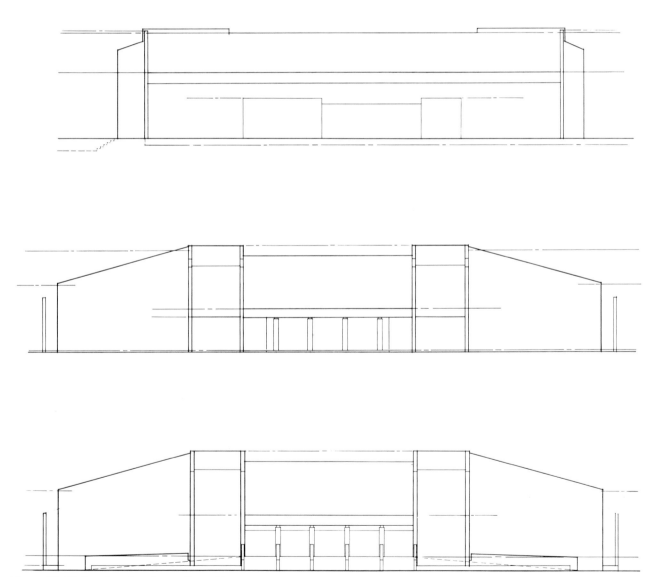

Figure 17.47 Exterior elevations—Stage III.

Stage IV

Now that we had a basic configuration we could describe some of the smaller shapes. See Figure 17.48. We added the arbor, or shaded walk, to the North elevation. Refer back to Figure 17.46. The line above the wood arbor is the wood frieze (band of wood). The opening is located at the left.

To the West elevation, we added rear doors, the doors for the storage area, and the arbor at each end. We positioned step and doors on the East elevation.

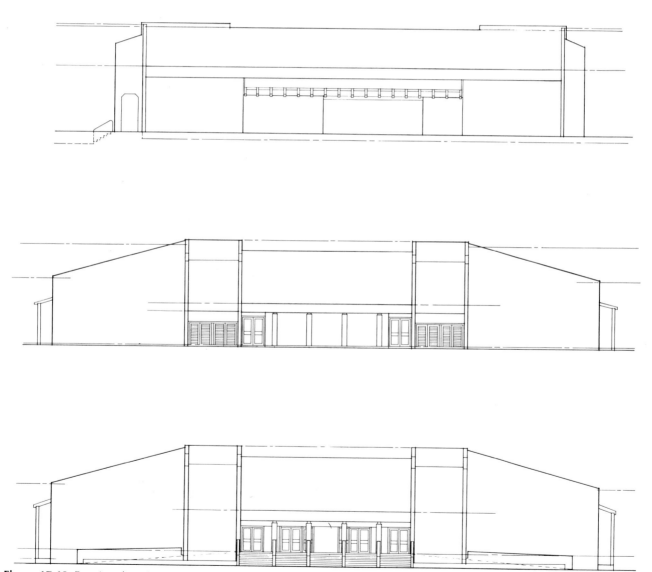

Figure 17.48 Exterior elevations—Stage IV.

Stage V

This was the final stage and included a multitude of items. See Figure 17.49.

Texture. Roof material was designated. We also stippled the cement plaster that was to cover the concrete masonry units. We added plants in the planter on the East elevation to be consistent with the plants we showed on the floor plan.

Dimensions. Dimensions of the two floor levels were added. Some dimensions were referenced to the building sections (Figure 17.53) for clarity.

Notes. The surface material was called out. We also added title and scale.

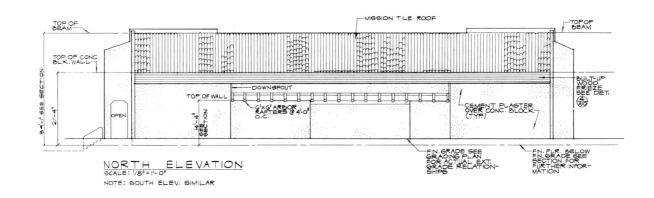

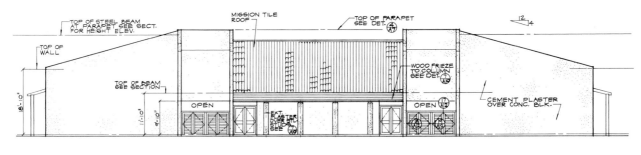

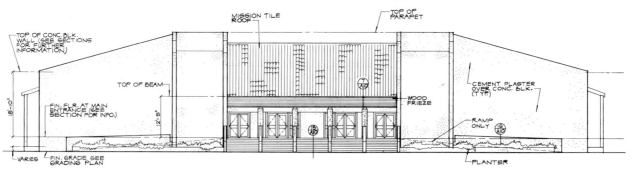

Figure 17.49 Exterior elevations—Stage V.

Building Sections

Stage I

The drawings developed in Figures 17.50 through 17.53 are architectural building sections, not structural sections. This sheet is a classic example of how the available drawing area and number of sections to be drawn dictate the approach.

For example, the top section in Figure 17.50 has six break lines representing the removal of three areas. At this point, we could have changed scales or kept the same scale while eliminating the least important or the most redundant area. (We use the term redundant to mean an area that remains the same for long lengths.) We could either have two areas broken out and lose one major steel girder (see Figure 17.53) or have three areas broken out and save the girder. Because the location of the beams showed so much about heights and the structural assembly method, we decided to have three areas broken away and save the beam.

Another approach we could have taken would have been to use match lines and then slice the structure into two pieces, aligning one above the other. Because of the size of the structure, this would have left a lot of unused space on one side of the sheet and would have required our adding another sheet for the other section. This additional sheet would also have had extra space on it.

We approached the lower section by using a break line and eliminating a large portion of the theatre. The structure is symmetrical and the auditorium to the right would have been duplicated on the left. There would be no break in the center portion of the theatre (the lobby) or the auditorium on the right.

First, we located all of the steel beams as well as their corresponding foundation below. Using the framing and foundation plans together with structural details helped greatly in developing this drawing.

Since the floor of the auditorium sloped, we used two floor levels to describe the structure: Level "A" and Level "B." Level "A" is the top of the auditorium slope and "B" the bottom.

The vertical lines above some of the beams in Figure 17.50 would have reference bubbles added to them in the next stage, so they could be keyed to other drawings.

Stage II

We added reference bubbles for the beams at this stage (Figure 17.51), but only above continuous beams, so some beams on the upper section and many on the lower sections have no reference bubbles.

We also studied available details at this time. When details are not available, freehand details should be sketched to solve many of the intersections of wall and floors or roofs. Based on this information, we drafted the interior walls and upper floor.

Stage III

As drawings become more complicated, the floor plan should always be reviewed to clarify the various parts of the section.

The sections now began to show the wall material designations, the soil under the foundation, the corrugated steel decking at the upper floor level, and the mission tile roof. See Figure 17.52. The steel decking under the mission tile is in side view in the lower section, so the corrugation does not show. The view of the floor decking in the upper section is an end view and shows the corrugation.

The suspended ceiling at various locations was now indicated. Because of the intended use of the structure and the materials chosen, we used many fireproofing techniques. For example, many of the steel beams have a freehand line drawn around them. These represent a sprayed-on fire protection material. A specific description of this spray material would be included later in the specifications.

Stage IV

At this stage, we completed the noting and dimensioning. See Figure 17.53.

Dimensioning. First we had to keep the dimensions consistent with the other drawings. Each letter of the matrix and each number had to align with the proper column, beam, or footing pad. After checking, they were vertically located. The term "T.B." means "top of beam." These beams were dimensioned by notation and were measured from one of the two floor levels. The abbreviation "T.S.G." means tapered steel girder.

Dimension lines were now added to the floors and ceilings, and the top of walls. Because the space between the upper floor and the ceiling below it had been determined by detail, it too was included.

Reference. We drew many reference bubbles showing locations of details or special wall sections. These were carefully selected.

Noting. Most of the noting explained a material or a method of erection or the dimensions themselves. The section titles, scales, and room names were added. There is also a special note about fire protection below the title "Section A-A."

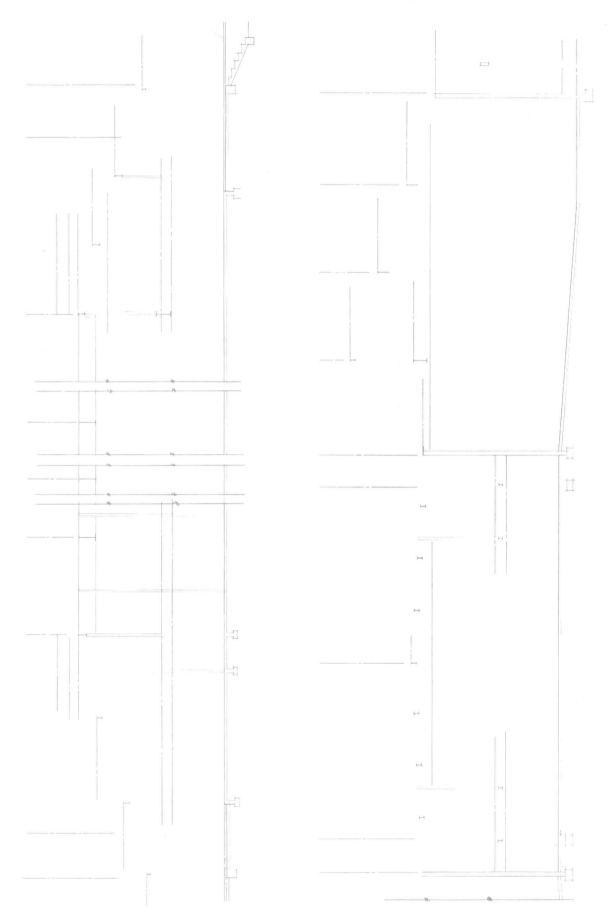

Figure 17.50 Building sections—Stage I.

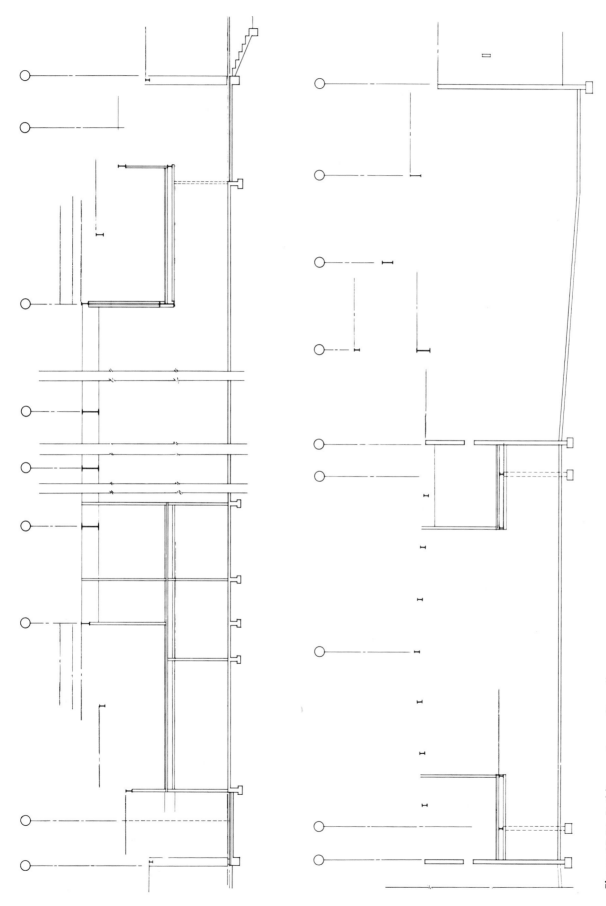

Figure 17.51 Building sections—Stage II.

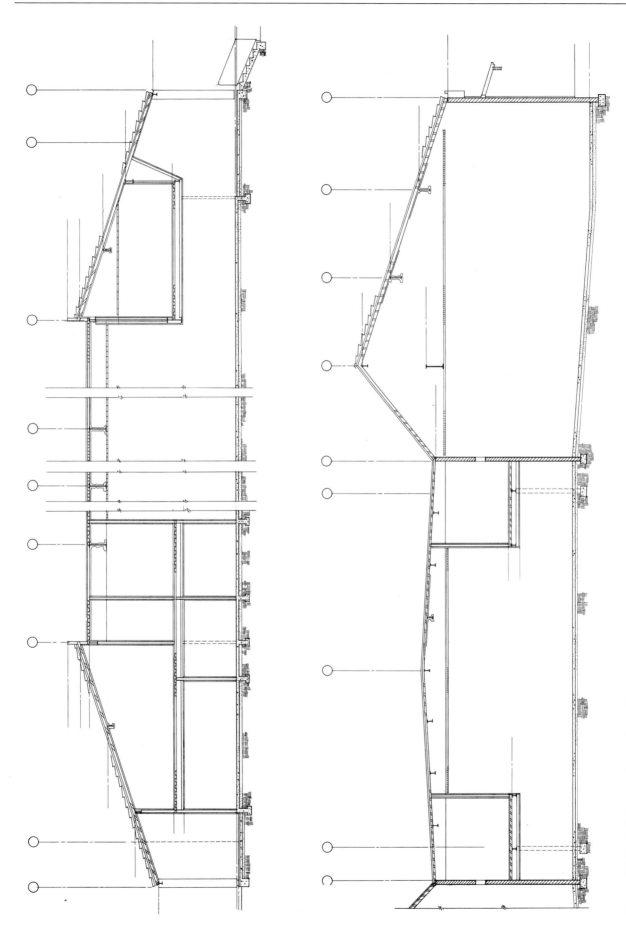

Figure 17.52 Building sections—Stage III.

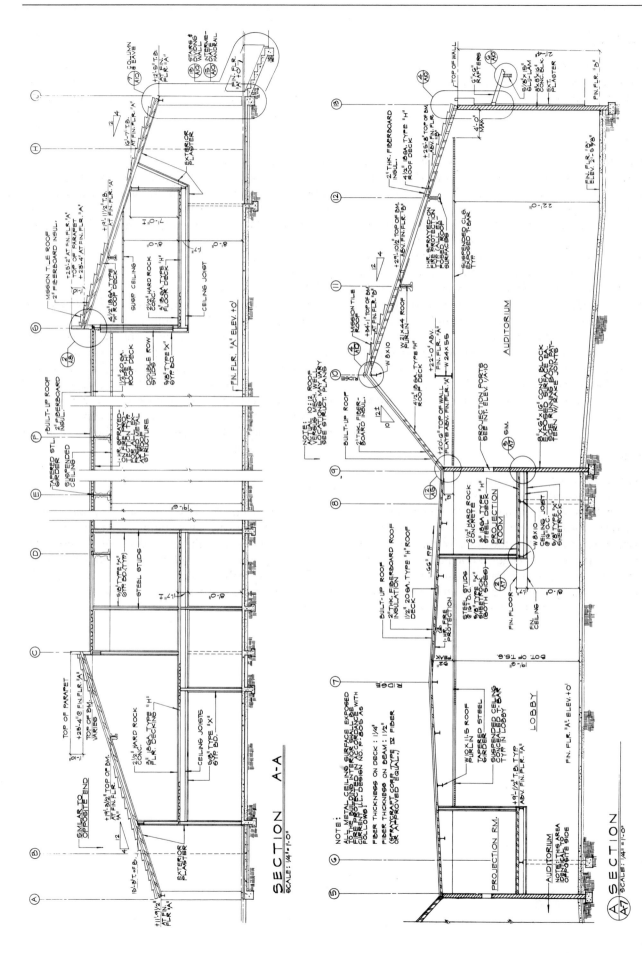

Figure 17.53 Building sections—Stage IV.

Roof Plan

Review the first floor plan, the upper floor plan, the sections, and the preliminary elevations before starting to study this roof plan.

Stage I

First we traced the roof plan from the first floor plan. See Figure 17.54. The dotted lines located the major interior walls. Note that the design called for the exterior walls to extend above and beyond the tops of the roof.

The five major divisions of the roof are, the top, bottom, left, right, and center. The top, bottom, left, and right portions all slope away from the structure. The center portion slopes in two directions with a ridge at the center. Because the four major portions around the center rose higher than the center, roof drains were required. See Figure 17.55. These drains and the surrounding areas will be mentioned later.

The exterior walls on Figure 17.54 were drawn slightly wider than the interior walls because they represented exterior plaster over concrete block. Note the configuration of the arbor over the exterior exits from each auditorium.

Stage II

To better understand this roof, as shown in Figure 17.56, look at the sketch of its central portion in Figure 17.55. The line at the very center is the ridge. This ridge produces a gable type roof at the central portions. The surrounding portions are higher and so the slope of this gable roof needs to be drained at its edges. Roof drains, commonly called scuppers, were added at strategic points.

As you can see by comparing the sketch with the plan, portions of the low point of the gable roof remained flat to accept air-conditioning equipment. Other portions sloped down from the vertical plane like a shed roof. Sheet metal saddles, called crickets, were positioned to control the flow of water on the roof and to direct it toward the roof drains. The small circles near the roof drains represent the overflow drains provided in case the regular scuppers clog.

On two sides of the structure, we added reference bubbles to correspond with those on the plans and sections. Skylights (still visible in Figure 17.61) were not shown because they were deleted earlier at the request of the client.

Stage III

At this stage, the reference bubbles were numbered and lettered. See Figure 17.57. Numerical values for all the dimension lines were added next. The slope of the roofs were designated by arrows. Arrows at the edges of the roof show the slope of the gutters toward the downspout.

All dimensions were verified with the building section in this chapter, and the engineering drawings were checked for correct column and beam locations. Finally, detail reference bubbles were drawn. The details were selected at an earlier stage.

Stage IV

The final roof construction, described by the plan in Figure 17.58, actually differs from the drawing in Figure 17.57. This happens quite often as better solutions, the pressure of economic considerations, or construction restrictions change the final plans. Figure 17.59, the aerial photograph of the finished structure, shows how we departed from the original design.

Figure 17.54 Roof plan—Stage I.

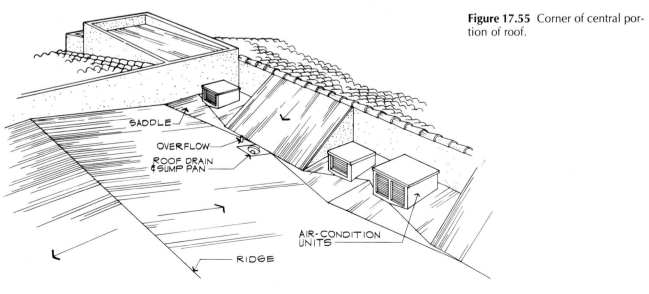

Figure 17.55 Corner of central portion of roof.

SADDLE

OVERFLOW

ROOF DRAIN
& SUMP PAN

AIR-CONDITION
UNITS

RIDGE

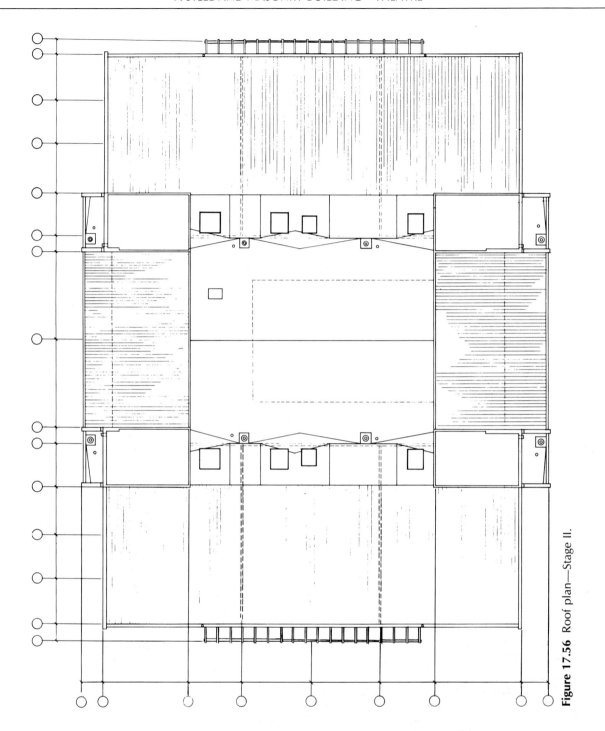

Figure 17.56 Roof plan—Stage II.

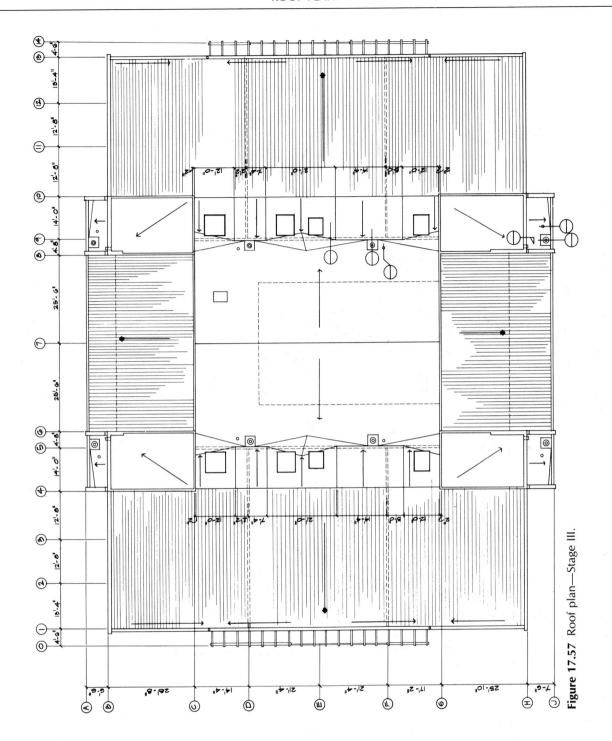

Figure 17.57 Roof plan—Stage III.

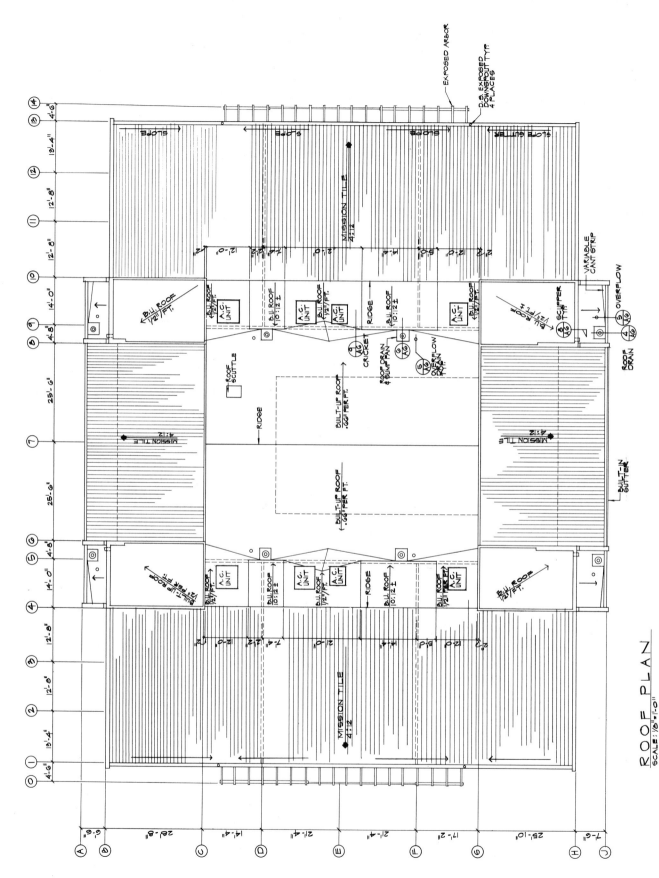

ROOF PLAN
SCALE: 1/8"=1'-0"

Figure 17.58 Roof plan—Stage IV.

Figure 17.59 Aerial photo of finished roof. (William Boggs Aerial Photography. Reprinted with permission.)

All descriptive notes were included at this stage. In many of the notes, measurements, pitches, and ratios are indicated. Detail numbers, titles, and scale were the final items added. At each step, the water drainage system and the location of potential leakage areas were considered.

Roof Framing Plan

For a description of the parts of the roof framing plan, refer to the roof and ceiling framing chapter (Ch. 12). Here, we will describe the approach and method used to obtain the necessary information for this plan, and how the plan was drafted.

Stage I

First, a reproducible and a diazo print were made of the floor plan at an early stage without dimensions or notes. See Figure 17.60. The diazo print was then sent to the structural engineer for structural information (column and beam locations, etc.).

Stage II

The engineer returned the diazo print with his sketches, and the refined sketches were then drafted onto the reproducible. See Figure 17.61. Notice the skylights and recall that they were deleted at a later stage, at the client's request.

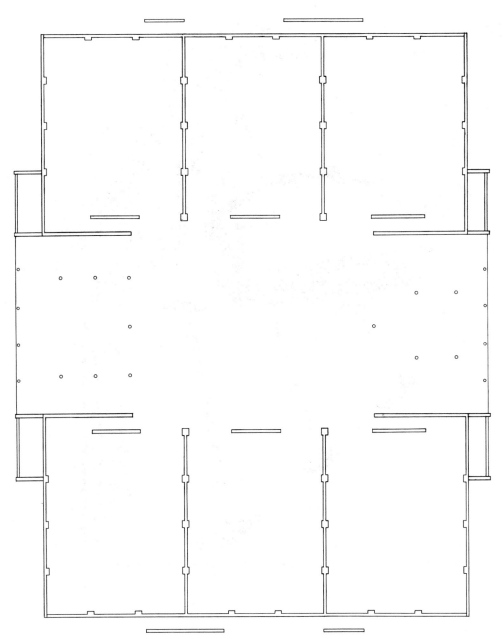

Figure 17.60 Roof framing plan—Stage I.

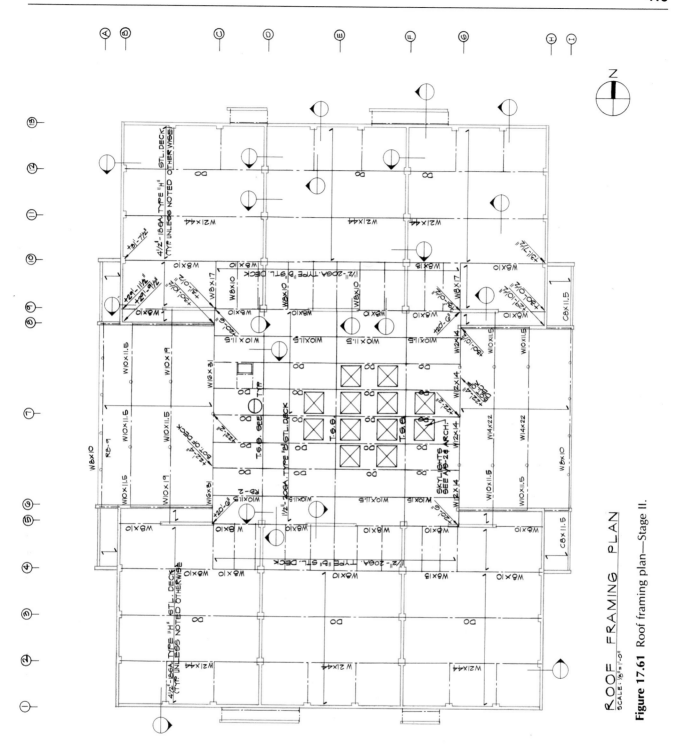

ROOF FRAMING PLAN
SCALE: 1/8"=1'-0"

Figure 17.61 Roof framing plan—Stage II.

CONCEPTUAL DESIGN AND CONSTRUCTION DOCUMENTS FOR AN OFFICE PARK

18

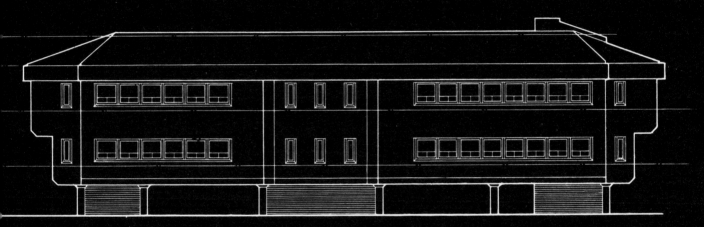

All figures courtesy of Westmount, Inc., Real Estate Development, Torrance, CA.

Conceptual Design

Client's Requirements

The client asked us to design a structure for general office use. From this initial request we developed a concept of an office park: several buildings under individual ownership with all the owners sharing maintenance of common areas for parking and landscaping.

Site Requirements

The gross area of the site is 4.76 acres, with a 607-foot frontage on a secondary highway. The site is broken by areas given over to oil lease rights. This reduced the usable area to approximately 3.25 acres.

A sloping bank influenced automotive access. It began at the Northwest corner at a height of 22 feet above the street and diminished to a grade level with the street in approximately 500 feet.

We located two concrete driveways for auto access at the Southern portion of the site. From these points, we established automobile circulation, a parking layout, and a parking structure. The oil lease easements determined the location of the parking facilities. Figure 18.1 shows the site and the easements.

Initial Schematic Studies

The remaining portions of the site were planned for parking facilities, landscaping, and the buildings themselves. Figure 18.2A shows the preliminary parking study with traffic flow considerations. After the parking plan was refined, the building locations and their configurations were designed together with the parking plan and the required building separations. Also at this stage, the possibility of a future parking structure, located at the southerly portion of the site, was analyzed. The proposed building and parking structure locations are shown in preliminary form in Figure 18.2B.

Once the building locations were established, the building configurations and related design elements such as lobby, stairs, and columns were planned. These elements are shown in Figure 18.3.

Roof and Exterior Elevation Studies

Even before our preliminary studies of the exterior elevations, we decided to use mission clay tile for most of the roof material and to use cement plaster for the exterior walls.

We developed the geometry of the roof plan using hip sections at the building corners. See Figure 18.4. These corners would be reflected in the angled corners of the

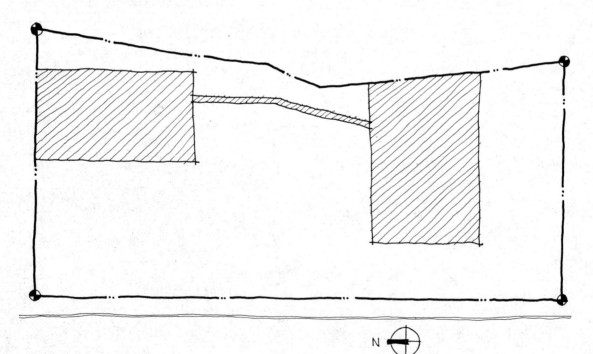

N

Figure 18.1 Site and easements.

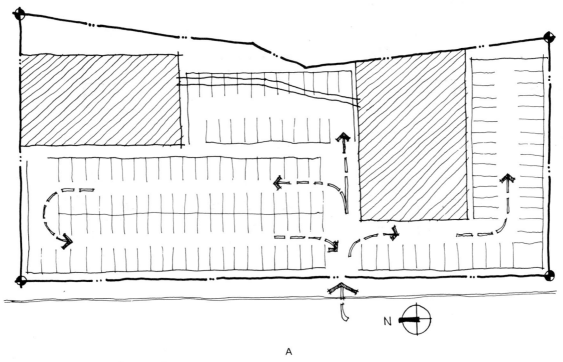

A

Figure 18.2A Preliminary parking study.

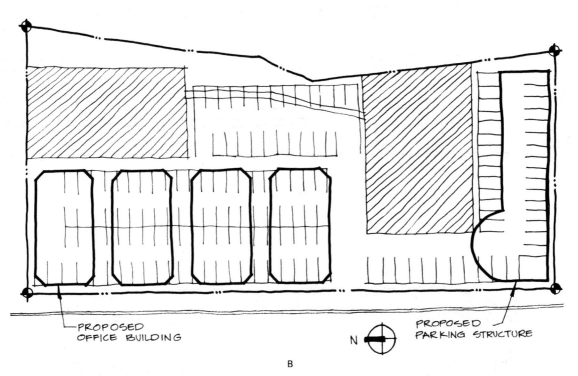

PROPOSED
OFFICE BUILDING

N

PROPOSED
PARKING STRUCTURE

B

Figure 18.2B Preliminary study of building locations.

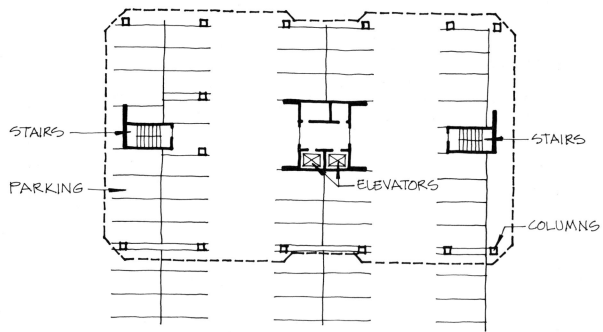

Figure 18.3 Building configuration.

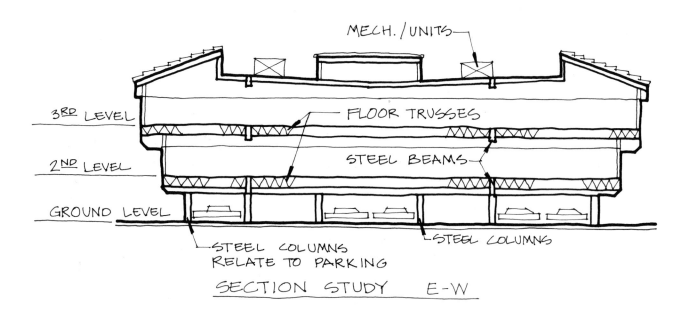

SECTION STUDY E-W

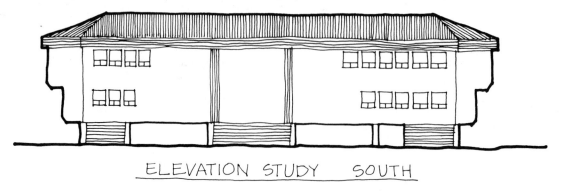

ELEVATION STUDY SOUTH

Figure 18.4 Exterior and sectional studies.

floor plan. The intersection of the hip members determined the height of the roof. Beyond this height, we created a roof well to provide an area for the mechanical equipment, an elevator penthouse, and an enclosure for the stairwell to the roof. These elements would be screened from view by the height of the tile roof area.

To conserve energy, we incorporated into our plans 6-inch stud framing for the exterior walls; these studs would provide greater depth for insulation than the more common 4-inch studs. The thick cement plaster walls allowed us to sculpt and recess the window design. We used both fixed and operable window sections. The operable sections would provide natural ventilation during mild climate conditions, thus cutting energy costs.

Figure 18.4 shows initial conceptual studies of the exterior South elevation and an East-West section. We also constructed a model to study the general massing of the building. See Figure 18.5. After we refined many of the design decisions, we started the final drawings.

Figure 18.5 Scale model of office building.

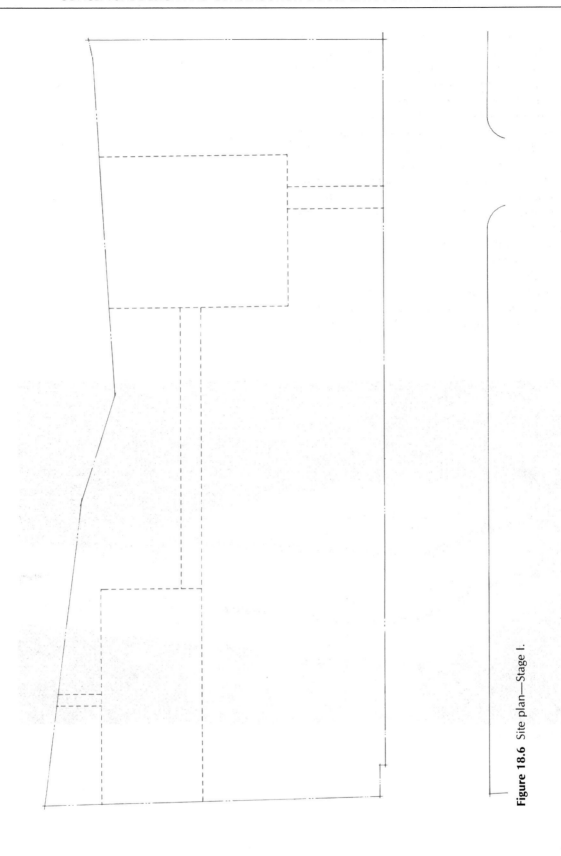

Figure 18.6 Site plan—Stage I.

Site Plan

Stage I

We gathered all of the information available, including easements, boundary descriptions, and the location of the proposed structures. The civil engineer's drawing was the source for this information.

In the first-stage drawing shown in Figure 18.6 the boundaries of the property were laid out and all of the oil easements were located, including the roads that connected them. The adjacent street was located.

The largest space available (left over after excluding the easements and roads) is the area designated for the location of the four structures. The other two available spaces were to be used for a parking area and a future parking structure. Of the four structures whose designs were to be submitted to the Department of Building and Safety, only one was to be built initially.

Figures 18.7 and 18.8 show the property in its original state and after some grading. Figure 18.9 is an aerial photograph of the site, showing the beginning of construction.

Figure 18.7 Undeveloped site.

Figure 18.8 Site with some grading.

Figure 18.9 Overall site. (William Boggs Aerial Photography. Reprinted with permission.)

Stage II

We located the four main structures on the site. See Figure 18.10. Since they were all the same, we drew a typical unit on a separate piece of paper, positioned it under the site plan, and traced it four times. The column locations on the plan are discussed in the next stage.

Stage III

We located all the parking stalls, and regional requirements for compact parking and parking reserved for the handicapped were checked again. The blank areas in Figure 18.11 (identified with dotted lines) are the oil easements. The blank area at the center rear of the lot would be developed later as additional parking. The parking lot at the extreme right would later become a parking stucture shown in the next stage. The "L" shapes outlined with solid lines in each structure are the stairwells. The H-shaped forms in the center of each structure are the restrooms, storage areas, and elevators.

Stage IV

The final stage of the site plan, shown in Figure 18.12, includes all dimensions needed to locate the structure and driveways, size the easements, and dimension the property boundaries. We also added notes describing the various components and indicating the future buildings and parking areas.

We indicated the direction of the flow of vehicular traffic. Because of the many changes in the angle of the property lines and because of the dimensions needed to locate the easements, we used arrows at the ends of the property lines.

Vicinity map, street names, title, and North arrow were the final items added. We could have titled this drawing "Site Plan," but used "Ground Level Plan" because we showed parking stalls on the ground level as well as a partial description of the ground floor of the structures.

We knew that the ground floor plan would also show these parking stalls, but showing all the structures at one time at this stage allowed the viewers to understand the total vehicular traffic flow on the site.

Stage V

Compare Figure 18.12 with Figure 18.13. There are many subtle changes. These changes resulted from our submitting the plans to the Building Department for a plan check and from Fire Department regulations and code interpretations. The Fire Department regulations affected ground level parking, which in turn affected the stair egress (exit).

A trash enclosure and the change in the stairs are also shown here. These would affect the parking configuration around the buildings. Most of the changes are noted by a delta (Δ) symbol, keyed to a written explanation at

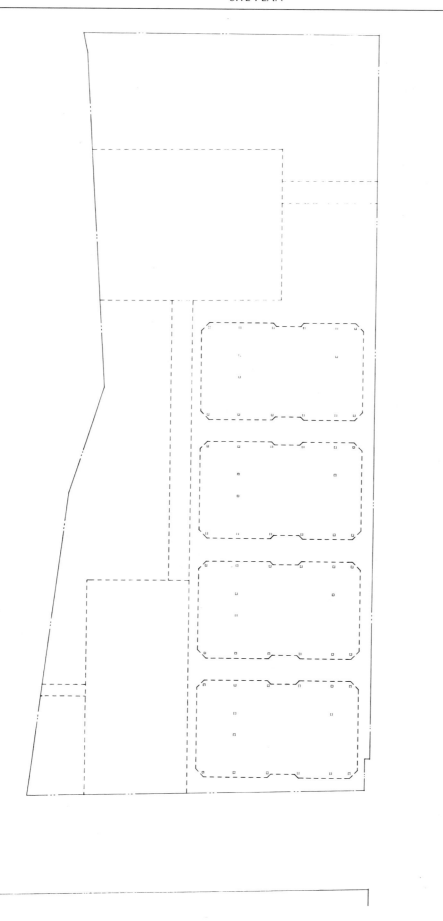

Figure 18.10 Site plan—Stage II.

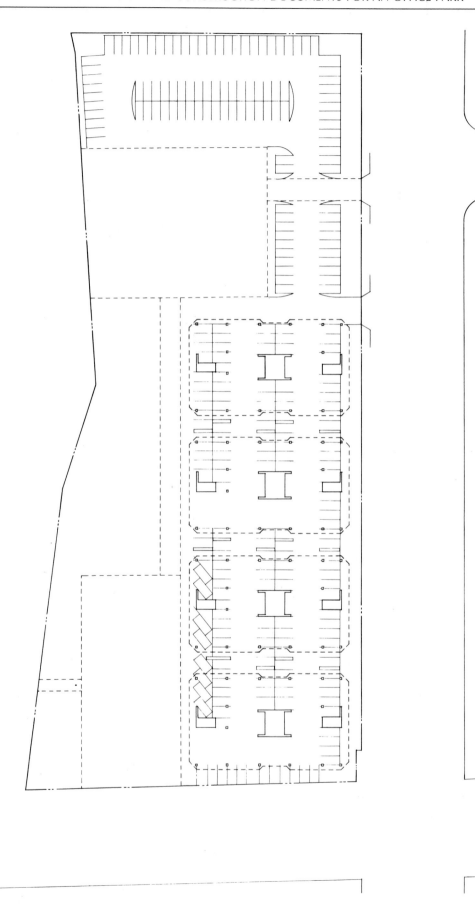

Figure 18.11 Site plan—Stage III.

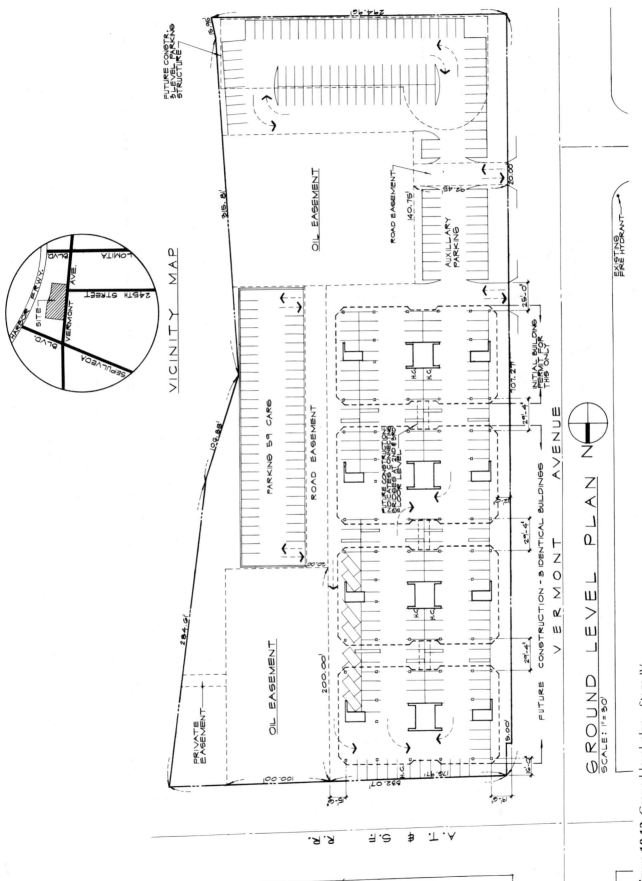

Figure 18.12 Ground level plan—Stage IV.

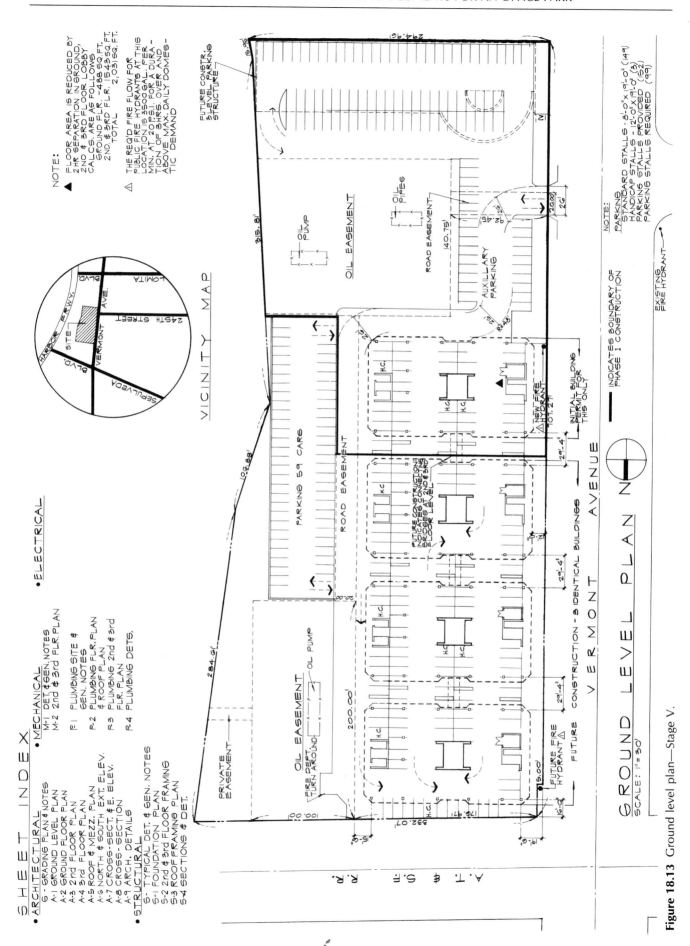

Figure 18.13 Ground level plan—Stage V.

the top of this sheet near the vicinity map. This symbol is usually reserved for revisions and changes.

The parking areas, especially those on the South side, and the turning radius were redefined to allow a fire truck to enter and leave. Notice the hammerhead shaped turnaround on the North side of the site for the fire truck. We also eliminated one of the driveways. Oil pump locations were added.

Finally, standard and handicapped parking stall sizes were defined and a sheet index was added. Because the electrical drawings were still in progress, we left a space for future use.

Foundation Plan

Stage I

The foundation plan shown in Figure 18.14 is unusual because we can see on it an approximation of the basic shape and configuration of the upper levels of the buildings. At this stage, the structural engineer had established the size of the various concrete pads and pipe columns and provided us with engineering details. These important pieces of information would be translated into a drawing in the next stage.

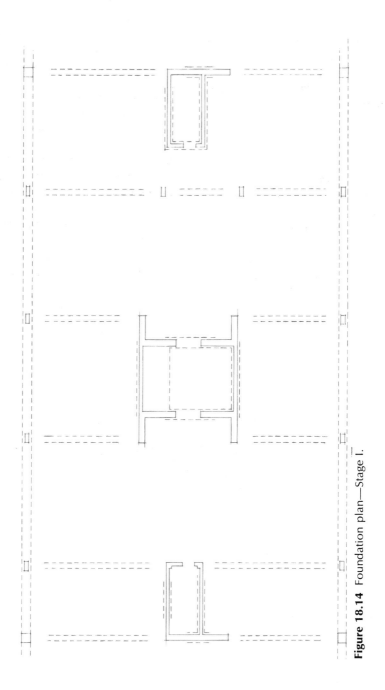

Figure 18.14 Foundation plan—Stage I.

Stage II

As you compare the beginning stages of the ground level plan and the ground floor plan, you will probably be confused because of differences at the stair area. See Figure 18.15. When the complete set of drawings was submitted for Building Department plan check, changes were made. One of these was the addition of a trash area and the requirement for those using the stairs to exit to the outside of the building instead of under the building. We considered the area below the structure as a continuation of the parking area, but the Building Department interpreted it as the ground level parking garage and so made the stair egress requirement.

All other plans and elevations show this change at the last stage. We sent the foundation plan back to the structural engineer because the change was, in effect, a new item requiring structural revisions.

We next drew columns (circles) and their respective support pads (squares). We obtained their sizes and shapes from the structural engineer.

Stage III

Dimension lines were the first addition to the drawing at this stage. We used the reference plane system. See Figure 18.16. All subsequent dimensions were referenced to this basic set on the top and to the left. In the lobby area (central portion of the plan), where the walls do not align with the existing reference bubbles, we added new bubbles. We showed partial and full section designations, but only the full sections are included in the set of drawings in this chapter.

Stage IV

Dimensions were added for the concrete block foundation walls. We also dimensioned the width of all footings. A single detail is used for all of the foundation walls and footings. This detail *does not* have dimensions for the foundation wall or footing, just a note saying "See plan." In this way, a single typical detail took care of every condition and the foundation plan accounted for the variation. At this stage, the material designation for the concrete block walls and variations in dimensions in the footing and width of the walls were added. See Figure 18.17. Also, the section reference notations were filled in in the section designation symbols.

Stage V

At this stage we added all remaining numerical values and filled in the reference bubbles. See Figure 18.18. Of interest is the method of naming locations on the matrix in the dimensional reference system. The reference B.9, for example, indicates there is a column at an intermediate distance between B and C of the axial reference plane. B.9 is approximately $9/10$ of the distance between B and C. If there were another column that was $8/10$ of the way between B and C, it would be designated B.8.

Around the perimeter of the structure are a series of squares drawn with dotted lines. These represent concrete pads that distribute the weight bearing down on the columns. A special type of noting is used here. The leader pointing to the hidden line indicates the size and thickness of the concrete pad and reinforcing. For example, 9'–0" sq. × 20", 11–#7 EW, means the concrete pad is 9' square and 20" thick and that there are 11 Number 7 ($7/8$") reinforcing bars running each way.

At the center of these hidden lines is another rectangle with a smaller rectangle inside, representing a steel column. The leader pointing to this area explains these. For example, 7" ⏀ × $1/4$" "e", 12" × 24", means that the column is a 7"-square column, $1/4$" thick (wall thickness), mounted onto an "e" base plate. This "e" base plate size can be found on the base plate schedule below. Here, "e" is equal to a 14"-square by 1"-thick plate. This plate rests on another concrete pad often called a pedestal, 12" by 24".

Contained within the masonry walls are some steel columns, with concrete pads that are also noted using the schedule. Next to the schedule is a legend explaining the noting method. The title and North arrow finished this sheet.

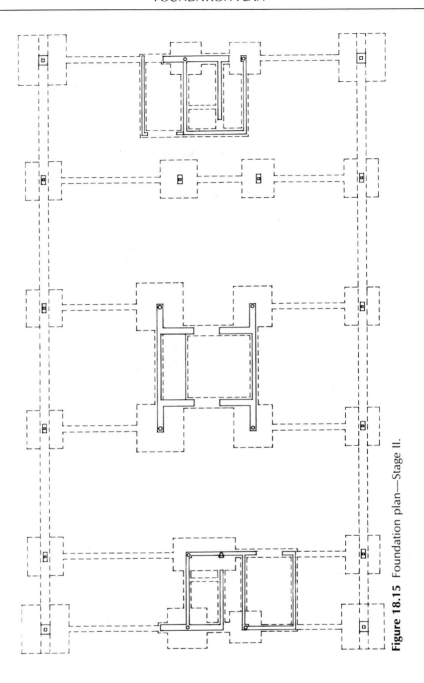

Figure 18.15 Foundation plan—Stage II.

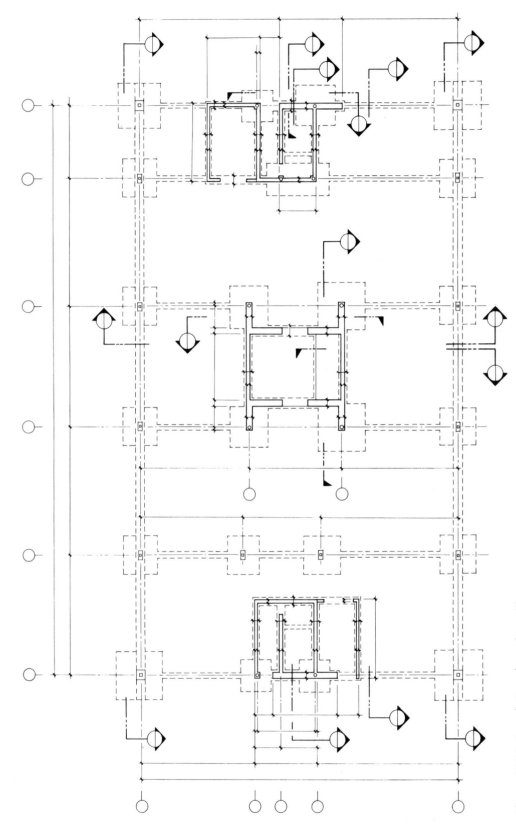

Figure 18.16 Foundation plan—Stage III.

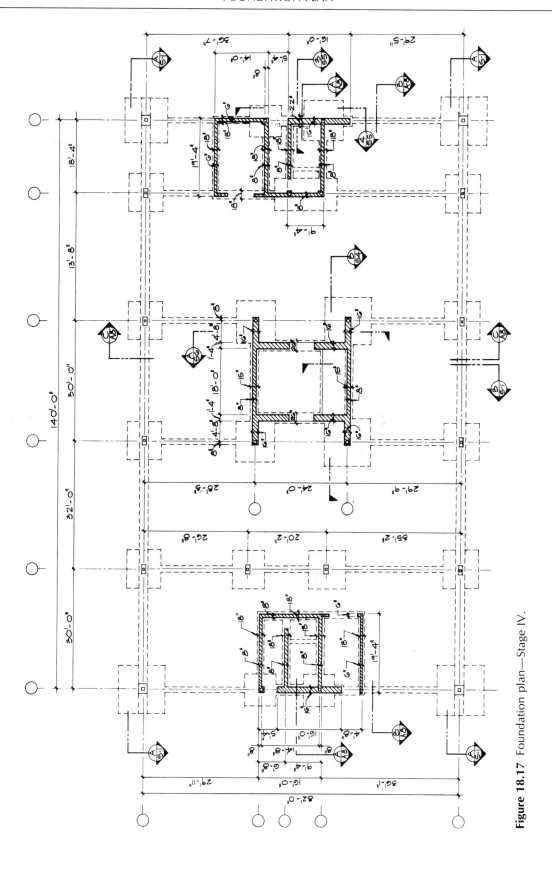

Figure 18.17 Foundation plan—Stage IV.

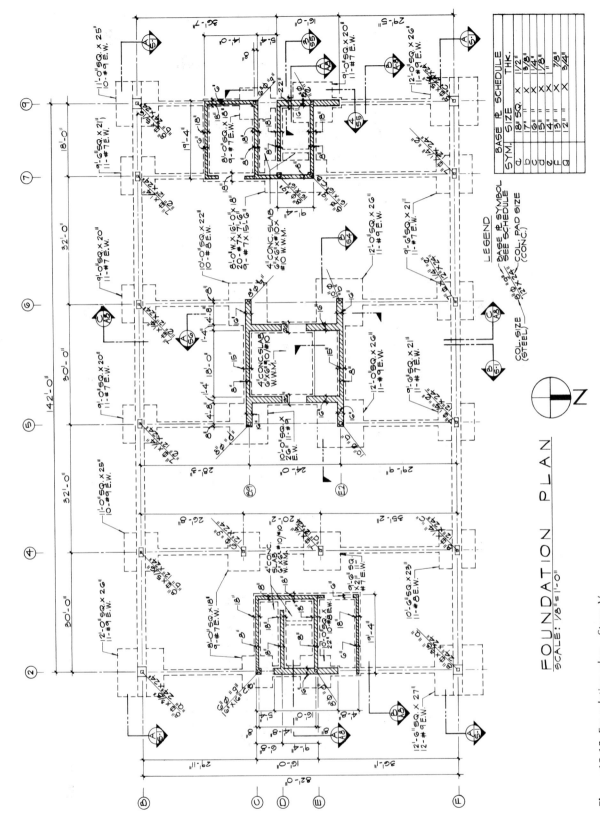

Figure 18.18 Foundation plan—Stage V.

Ground Floor Plan

Stage I

In this light layout stage, shown in Figure 18.19, dimensions of the locations were obtained from the preliminary ground floor plan and any subsequent drawings available, such as structural drawings that precisely located columns, overhangs of floors above, and stair locations.

This whole level is a parking area, and each stall will be layed out on the next step. The rooms in the center of the structure are the elevators, while those on each end of the structure are the stairs. The small rectangular objects around the perimeter near the dotted lines are structural columns. The dotted lines indicate the perimeter of the structure itself.

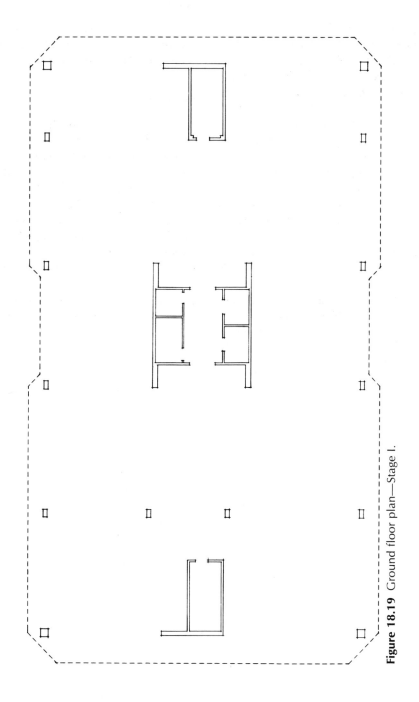

Figure 18.19 Ground floor plan—Stage I.

Stage II

We added the elevators after checking their size. See Figure 18.20. Then we added stairs, showing the risers and treads. Parking stalls were next. We confirmed the parking requirements for the handicapped and the allowed ratio of compact to standard size stalls.

The long rectangles beyond the perimeter of the structure are planter strips and the small rectangles beyond the planter strips are the columns of the next structure. (Remember that the plan includes four structures.)

Stage III

In the dimensioning stage, shown in Figure 18.21, our first step was to dimension the four large columns at each corner, because all other dimensions were to be located from these reference points. We located these four columns on the dimension line farthest away from the structure. The dotted lines representing the perimeter of the floor above were located to these columns.

We then located the other columns and the parts of the structure housing the elevators in the middle and stairs at each end. Notice how the walls around the elevators were extended to align with the columns on the exterior of the structure. All columns were located to their centers using center lines that extended out to dimension lines.

Sizes and locations of parking stalls were next: we used a special method here. The odd-sized parking stalls were all dimensioned. However, the typical ones were dimensioned only once per area; an arrowhead indicated their repetition. This simplified the dimensioning and the appearance of the plan. The final dimension lines were for the planter strips and the parking stalls between structures.

Stage IV

Coordinating this drawing with the structural engineer's drawing, the foundation plan, and the section, we added the axial reference plane bubbles across the top and the left side of the drawing. See Figure 18.22. We also included numerical values. Where dimension lines crossed each other, convenience of location of the dimension lines to the object established precedence or priority. All necessary labeling and door and window symbols were added.

Stage V

This final stage (Figure 18.23) added cross section indications, notations in reference plane bubbles, title, scale, and North orientation.

Stage VI

Review Stage V of the site plan before reading further, and recall that the discussion of Stage II of the Foundation Plan mentioned that the Building Department required a change in the way the stairs exited from the building, as well as the addition of trash enclosures. These changes are shown at this stage. See Figure 18.24. All parking on the West side of the structure was consequently changed to 90° rather than diagonal parking. A special note was added (the fire rating on the lobby door) and two parking stalls for the use of the handicapped were labeled.

We also changed the numbers on the reference plane bubbles because we found an error there. Finally, we placed page numbers in the section indications.

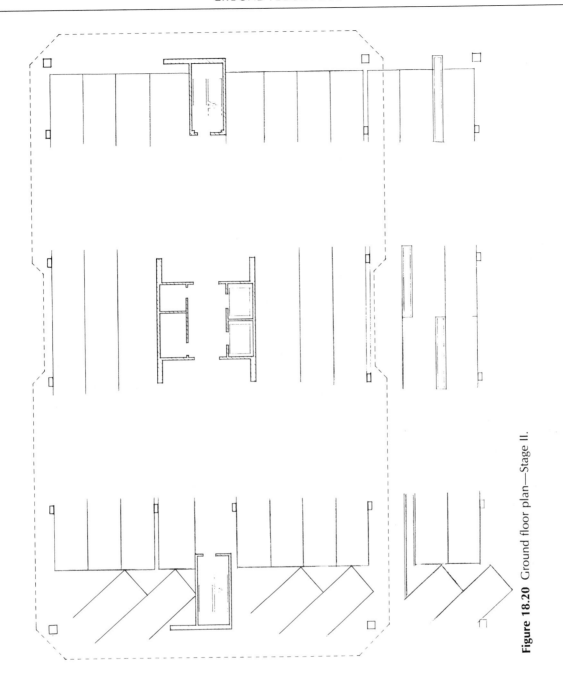

Figure 18.20 Ground floor plan—Stage II.

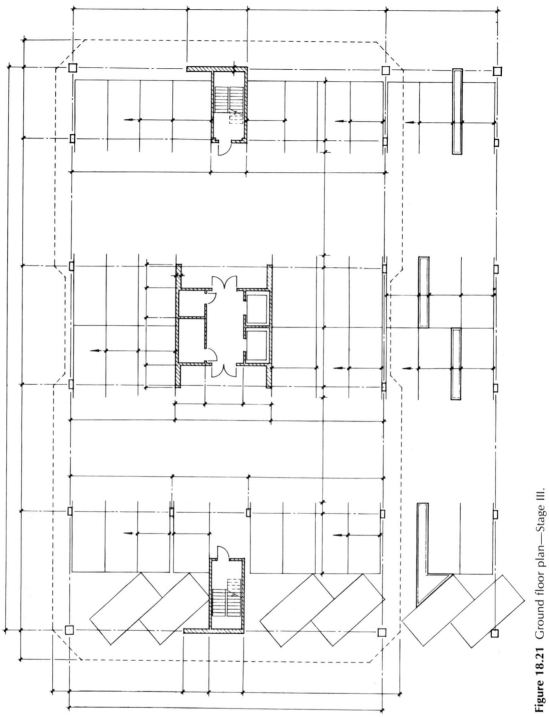

Figure 18.21 Ground floor plan—Stage III.

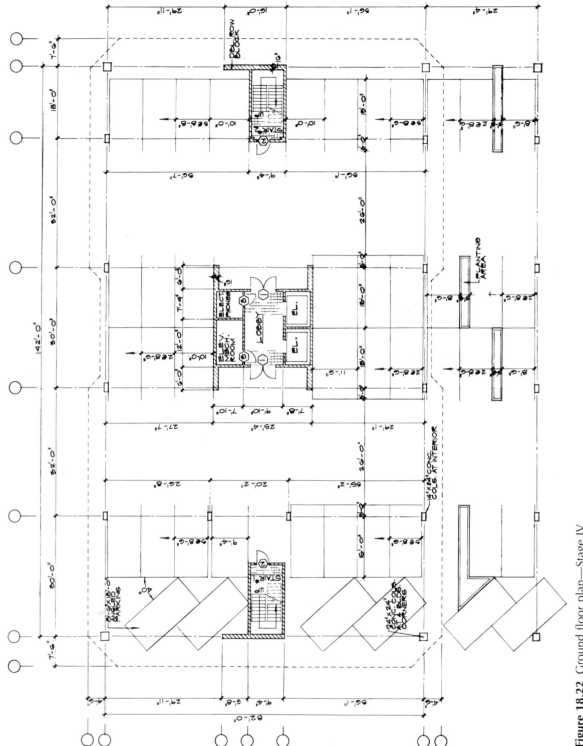

Figure 18.22 Ground floor plan—Stage IV.

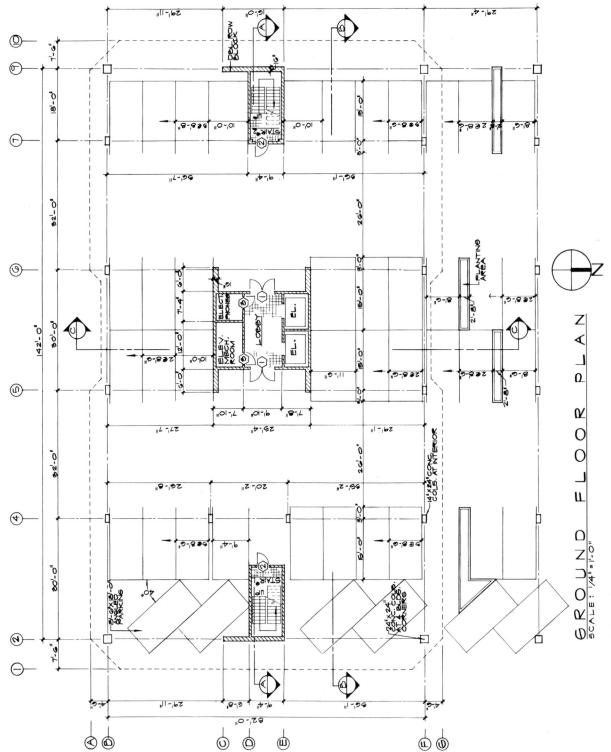

Figure 18.23 Ground floor plan—Stage V.

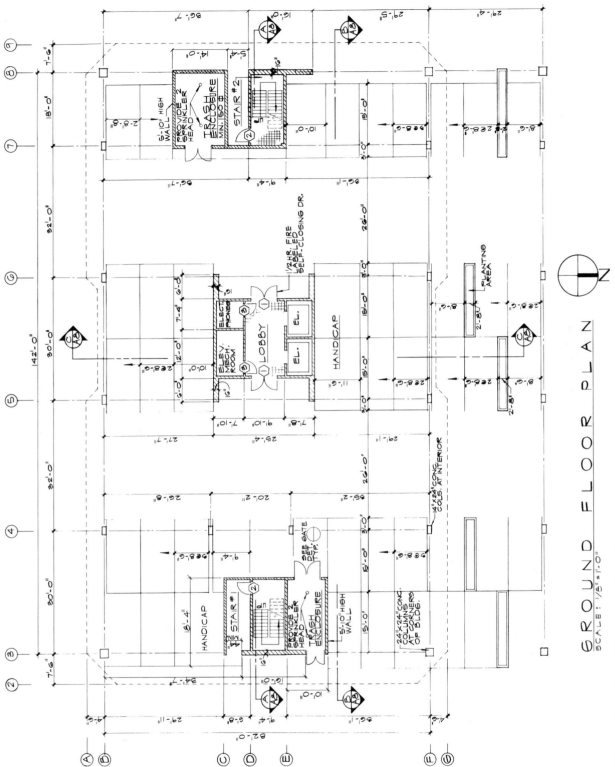

Figure 18.24 Ground floor plan—Stage VI.

Second Floor Plan

Stage I

This light layout stage (Figure 18.25) required checking the preliminary drawings for information that would help in drafting the plan. We also checked the ground floor plan for the location of the elevator and stair wells. To save effort and time, we placed the drawing over the ground floor plan sheet for location.

All walls and windows were then shown. The dotted lines at each end of the structure are the outline of the floor above. We traced the elevator and stairs from the floor below. Plumbing fixtures were included next, using templates provided by the manufacturer.

Stage II

The outside walls were most important in this dimensioning stage, shown in Figure 18.26, because they are located to the significant columns below the ground floor plan. We also located the axial reference plane bubbles. See how these bubbles line up with columns, walls, and so on.

We dimensioned the interior walls next, being careful to align these with the walls below. Door swings were also included. Dimension lines were not complete at this stage because of possible changes in the structure required by additional engineering that was being done simultaneously.

Stage III

The dimensioning is still not complete in Figure 18.27. However, we located window and door symbols at this stage, and included floor texture in the stair and elevator areas. After checking alignment with the ground floor plan, we added the dimensions, filled door bubbles (the door schedule is shown in Figure 18.71) and did some minimal noting.

Stage IV

This stage shown in Figure 18.28, included the remaining lettering for titles and notes. We decided to include a partial, enlarged floor plan of the lobby and the nearby note. Also note the special furring (building up) comment near Stair #2. We checked and indicated reference plane numbers and letters.

Stage V

At first, all four structures were conceived as individual buildings, but after much discussion with the owners and building officials, we decided to join the buildings with bridges. This accomplished many things: for example, if a large tenant wished to occupy two or more buildings, those would be physically tied together and everyone, including handicapped people in wheelchairs, could go from one structure to another without constantly having to go down in the elevator; furthermore, if the structure were treated as one rather than four buildings, additional subdivision maps did not have to be filed. In short, the project was less expensive with the bridges, and expense became the deciding factor. The bridge was therefore included here, as was an additional note about occupancy, required by the building department. See Figure 18.29.

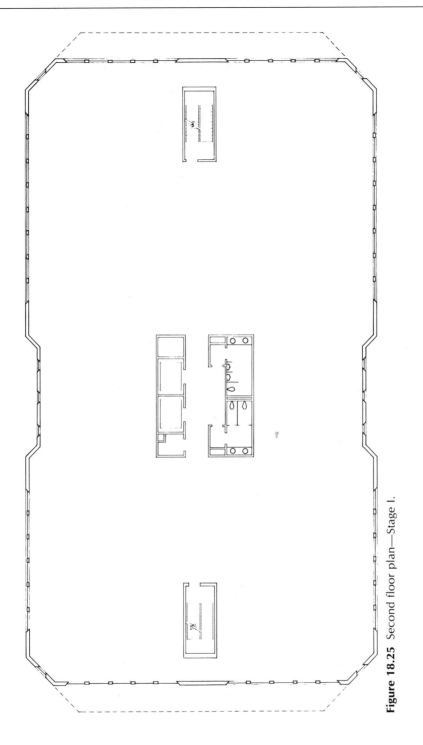

Figure 18.25 Second floor plan—Stage I.

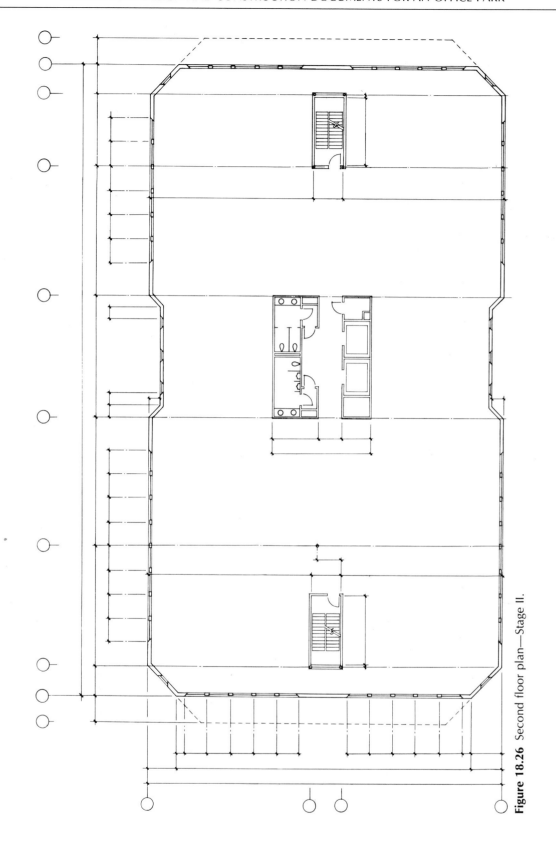

Figure 18.26 Second floor plan—Stage II.

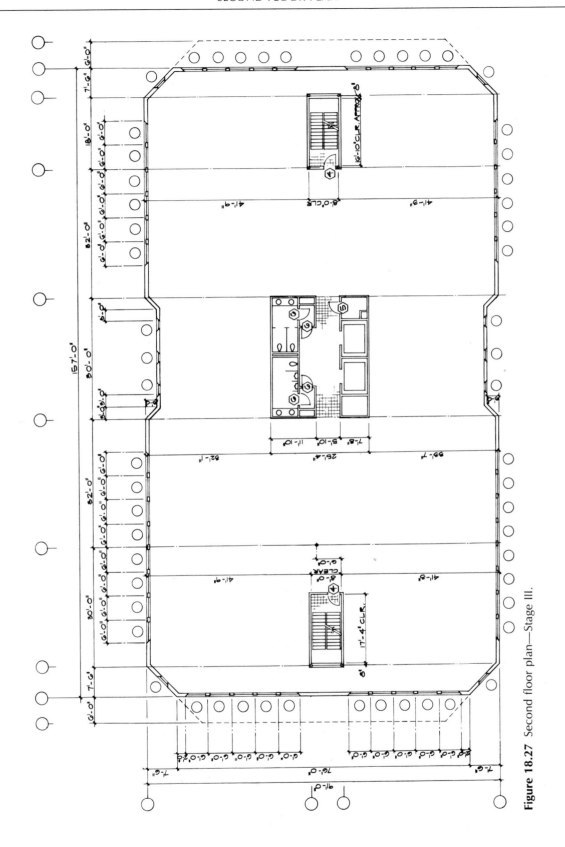

Figure 18.27 Second floor plan—Stage III.

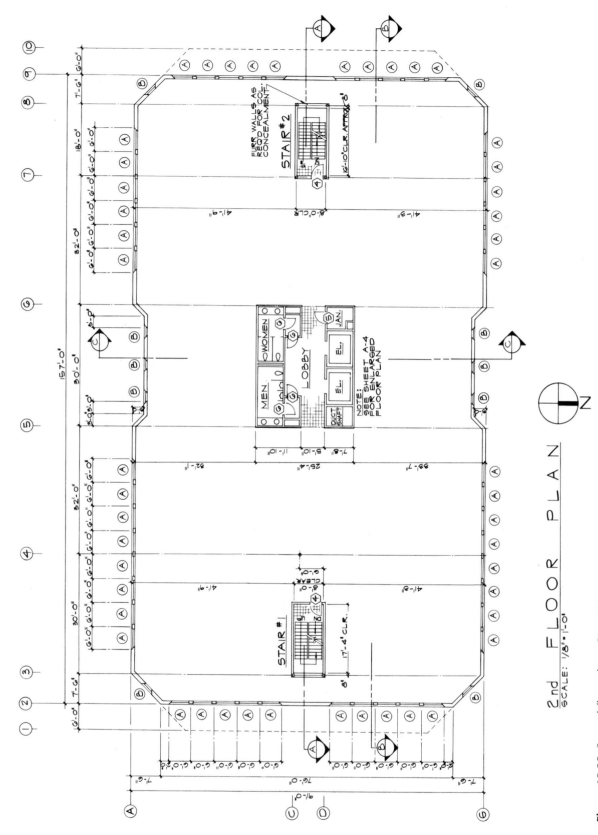

Figure 18.28 Second floor plan—Stage IV.

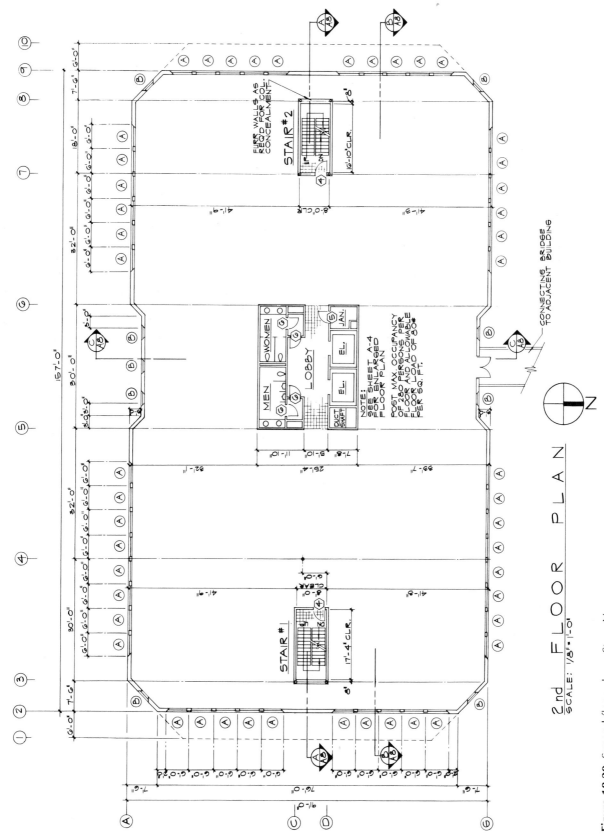

Figure 18.29 Second floor plan—Stage V.

Third Floor Plan

Stage I

As with the first stage of the second floor plan, this was the light layout stage. See Figure 18.30. Refer back to Stage I of the second floor plan. Note the dotted lines on each end, representing the third floor overhang.

As with previous floor plan stages, the third floor plan could be traced off the second floor plan sheet, taking the change in size into account. This would help align the elevator shaft and stairs.

We added the stairs, elevator, plumbing fixtures in the restrooms, and dotted lines adjacent to the restrooms to represent the stairs to the mezzanine and the location of some critical columns.

Stage II

Our first step at this stage (see Figure 18.31) was to check all of the previous floor plans for the location of the dimensional reference bubbles. Each of the important elements in the structure, such as columns, windows, and stairs were located from these reference bubbles. The rest of the dimensions would be placed after verifying them with the structural engineer's drawings.

Stage III

The floor material designations both in the stair area and between the elevator and restrooms were added now. See Figure 18.32. Window and door reference symbols were also put in. We added numerical values for the dimension lines and constantly checked the second floor plan and the sections to verify the information.

Stage IV

Cutting planes for the sections were now drafted. See Figure 18.33. We checked the reference bubbles against the previous floor plan and added them. Wrong numbers would be changed in the next stage.

Notes, room names, title, and North arrow were added next. Most notes were given in general terms, for example, "Typ. fire protection at exposed col." Specific material descriptions and so on were to be described in the specifications (specs.). Window reference bubbles were designated with the proper letter taken from the window schedule, which is shown in Figure 18.71.

Stage V

There was little change in the plan at this stage except for the inclusion of the bridge between the structures. See Figure 18.34. We changed dimensional reference bubble 9 (compare Figure 18.29) and added page numbers for the sections.

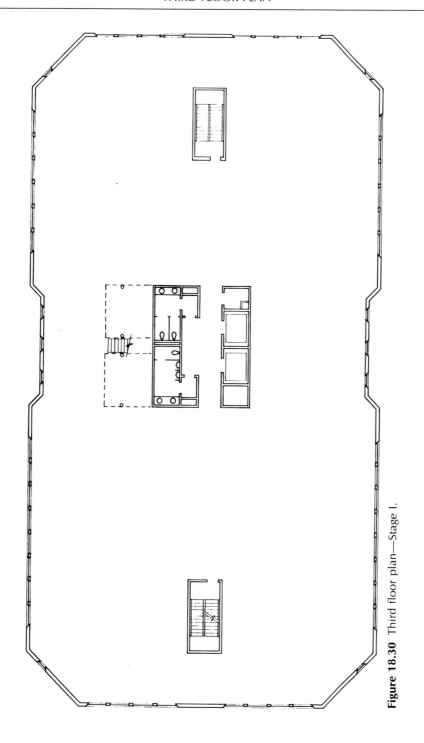

Figure 18.30 Third floor plan—Stage I.

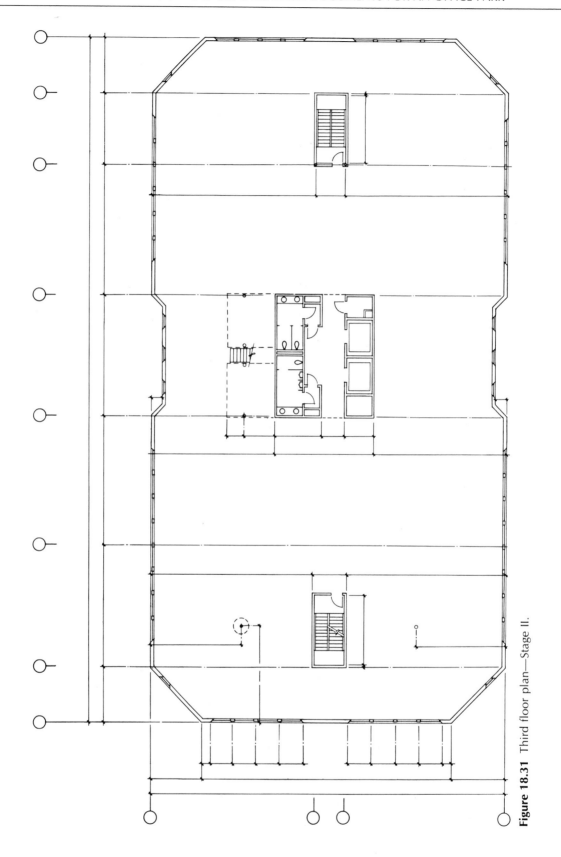

Figure 18.31 Third floor plan—Stage II.

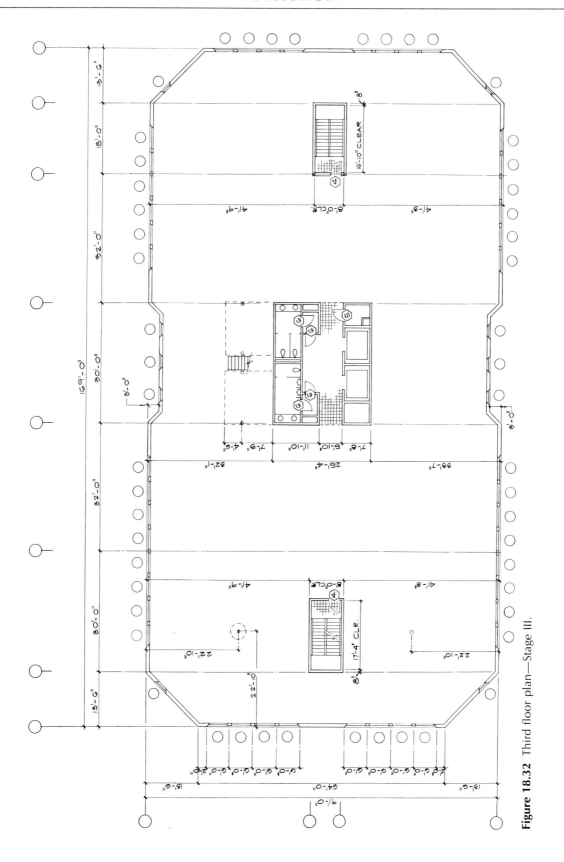

Figure 18.32 Third floor plan—Stage III.

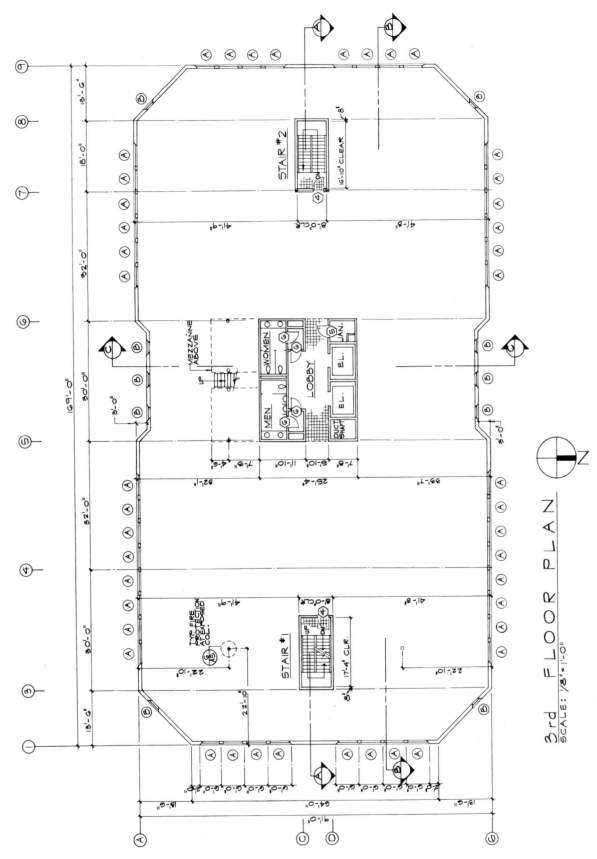

Figure 18.33 Third floor plan—Stage IV.

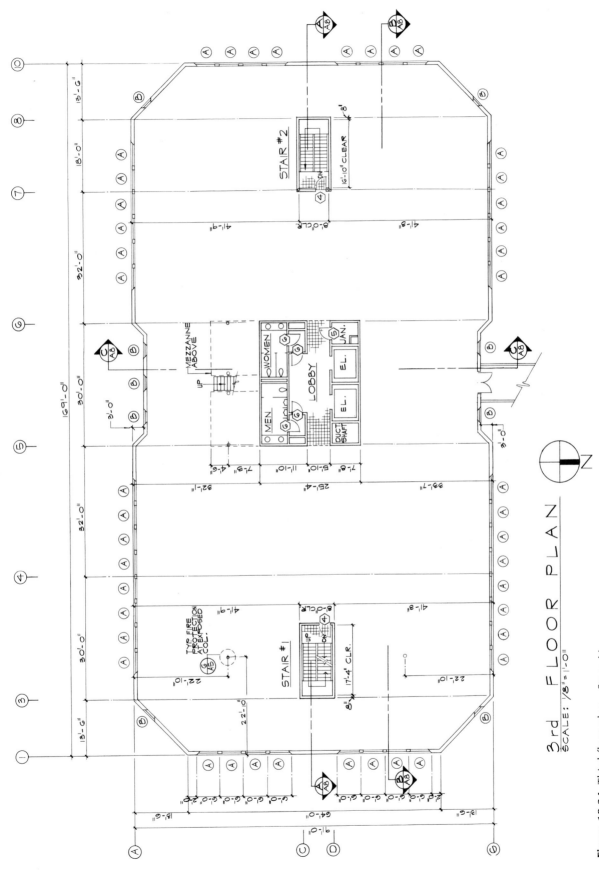

Figure 18.34 Third floor plan—Stage V.

Elevations

Stage I

To save space, we decided to use only three elevations and three sections. The East and West elevations were almost the same, so we did not use the West elevation. The West elevation is found in the next step, section/elevation.

To understand the horizontal lines in Figure 18.35, review the discussion of building sections in Chapter 10. This stage established the shape of the elevation and other information needed to complete the drawing. The position of the horizontal lines could also be obtained from the description of the Stage I building section.

Figures 18.36, 18.37, 18.38, and 18.39 are photographs of the building during and at the completion of construction; they show important features of the elevation.

Stage II

We obtained column locations for the lowest level from the foundation plan, structural details, and floor plan. The dark vertical lines in Figure 18.40 (four in the center and two near the left and right) represent the change in the plane. A quick look at the floor plans and at Figures 18.38 and 18.39 helps clarify the shape of the structure.

The soffit framing at the left and right edges of the elevation drawing would be obtained from the section drawings and from various details that were sketched.

The angular forms at the uppermost portion of the elevation are the stairwell accesses to the roof.

Stage III

At this stage, shown in Figure 18.41, we first added the windows. Those at the extreme ends of the structure were not drawn to true shape and size because the face on which these windows were located slanted away from the viewer.

Next, we added the concrete block material designation and profiled the elevation. We left the central portion of the North (top) elevation blank. This area is the bridge between structures (see the site plan, Figure 18.13) a portion of it would be seen in section and its shape was not yet resolved.

Stage IV

At the stage shown in Figure 18.42 we added material designations for the roof and walls in the form of lines and dots (stipple). All of the material descriptions are general because precise descriptions would be given in the specifications. "Frieze" refers to the decorative band around the structure that is like a fascia. We also added the bridges on the North elevation and the windows and doors around the bridges. A note on the North elevation reads "For further information see Cross Sections." All vertical dimensions were put on the cross sections.

Figure 18.35 Exterior elevation—Stage I.

Figure 18.36 Framing.

Figure 18.37 Surfacing exterior elevation. (William Boggs Aerial Photography. Reprinted with permission.)

Figure 18.38 Elevation.

Figure 18.39 Finished exterior elevation.

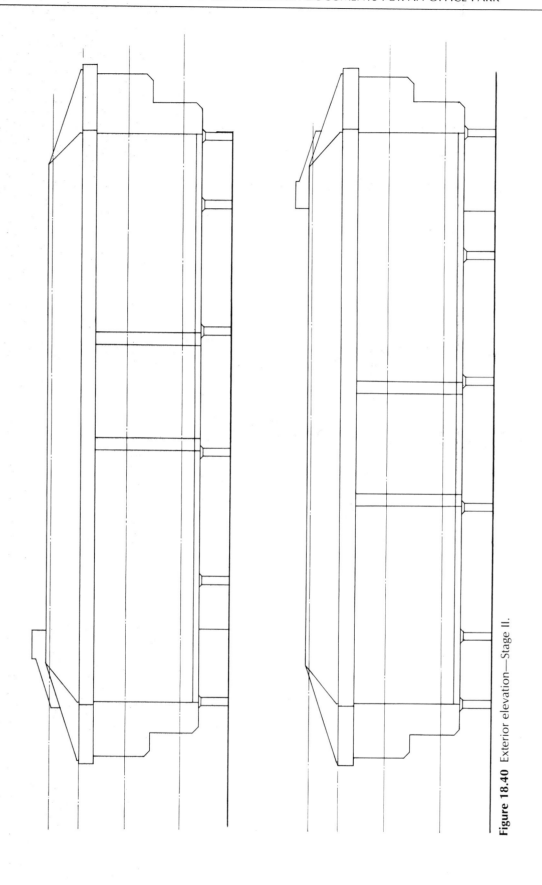

Figure 18.40 Exterior elevation—Stage II.

Figure 18.41 Exterior elevation—Stage III.

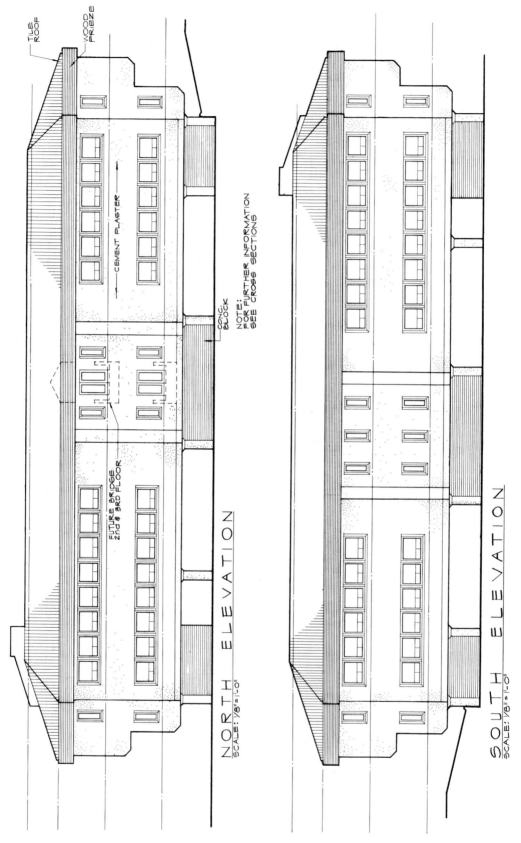

Figure 18.42 Exterior elevation—Stage IV.

Section/Elevations

Stages I and II

The various stages for this series of drawings resemble the other building section stages and the North and South elevation stages. Unique to this section and elevation, however, were the mezzanine and the elevator, and the profile view of the bridge between the buildings. See Figures 18.43 and 18.44.

Study Figure 18.45 for another view of the framing used at the various floors. Note that the photograph does not show all the beams shown in the section in Figure 18.44.

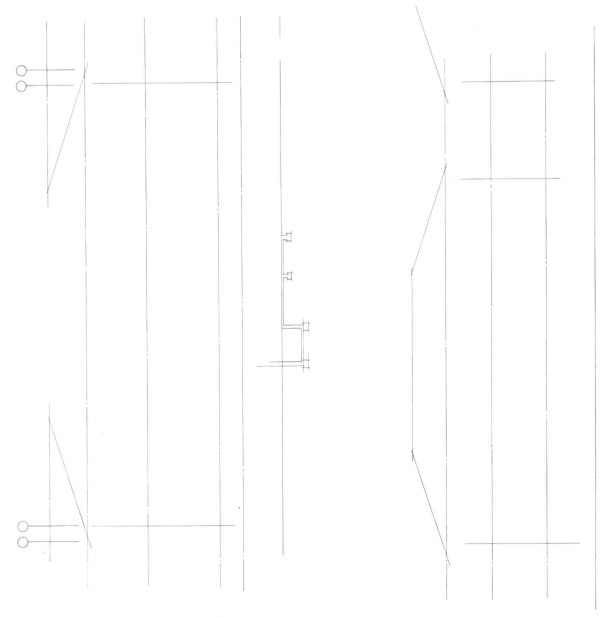

Figure 18.43 Section/elevation—Stage I.

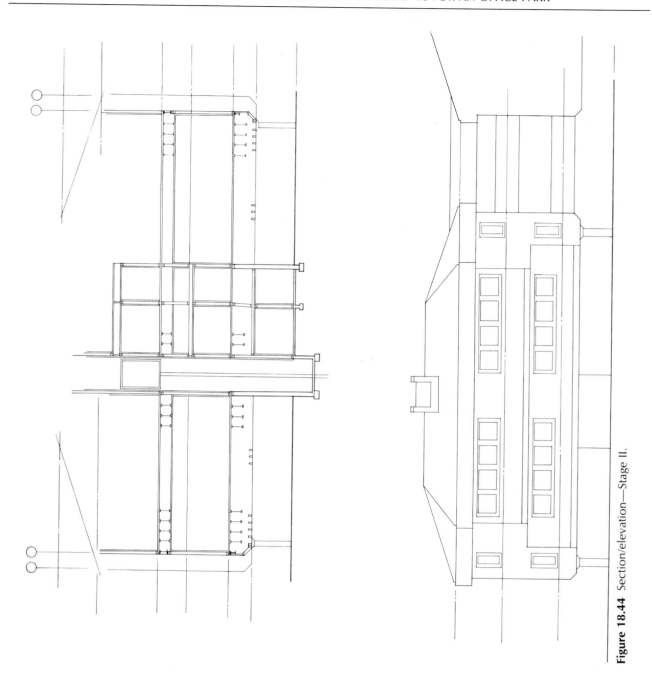

Figure 18.44 Section/elevation—Stage II.

Figure 18.45 Second and third floor framing. (William Boggs Aerial Photography. Reprinted with permission.)

Stage III

Now began the addition to this sheet of the partial floor plan of the lobby area and interior elevations. See Figure 18.46. Additional interior elevations would eventually develop as the building became occupied.

The roof and mezzanine area was now complete on the building section. See Figure 18.47 for a view of the mezzanine framing. The structural engineer provided the sizes of the roof framing members on the roof framing plan.

The dotted horizontal lines represent the level to which the eventual suspended ceiling would be lowered. The guardrail around the mezzanine was next to be drafted, together with the stairs and handrail. Finally, we drafted the material designations for concrete block and earth.

On the elevation below, we represented the windows according to manufacturer's literature. We profiled the whole elevation to emphasize the different planes, added the guardrail on the bridge, and drafted the material designation for concrete block in elevation.

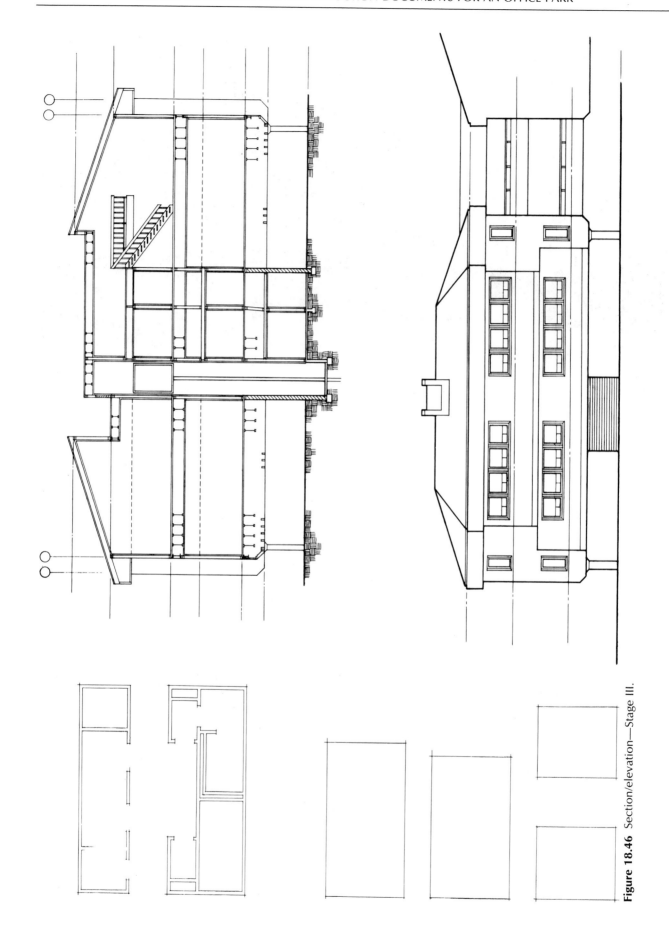

Figure 18.46 Section/elevation—Stage III.

Figure 18.47 View of mezzanine framing.

Stage IV

We next drafted the plumbing fixtures, including grab bars for the handicapped and the drinking fountain (facing the elevator, and located at the wall dividing the restrooms). See Figure 18.48. After the plumbing, we drafted the door swings and dimension lines. The circular dotted lines in both restrooms represent the minimum clearance required for a wheelchair to turn around. The interior elevations below are the restrooms in the partial plan. We made no changes on the building section or exterior elevation at this stage.

Stage V

The ground floor plan and second floor plan show the North arrow pointing downward. We did this so the dimensional reference bubbles would not interfere with the planting area on the ground floor. The lobby plan here has the North arrow pointing toward the top of the sheet. We could have shown dimensional reference bubbles here to clarify location but felt this wasn't necessary. We added numerical values for the dimension lines, as well as all the noting and floor material texture. See Figure 18.49.

The interior elevation references were located on the floor plan. They correspond to the interior elevations below. The interior elevations received notes, dimensions, and titles.

We showed the surface material texture on the East elevation. Each texture helps the profiling process; for example, the stippling (dots) in this drawing are most often placed near an elevation outline.

The building section contains information on building materials. The building section contains vertical dimensions and uses axial reference plane bubbles. Plane "A" aligns with the outside extreme points of the structure while "B" represents the location of the column. A.67 represents the outside wall through which the section is taken.

Various members were noted next, including the top of the beams in the office area, written W 16 × 26 (T.B. + 39'–0"). Finally, we added detail reference bubbles, room names, title, and scale.

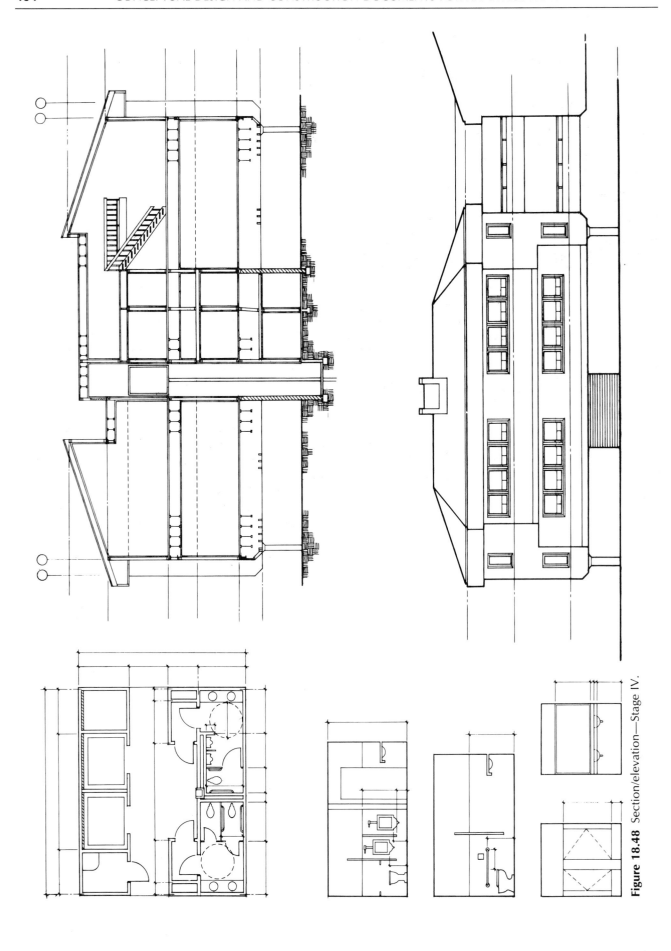

Figure 18.48 Section/elevation—Stage IV.

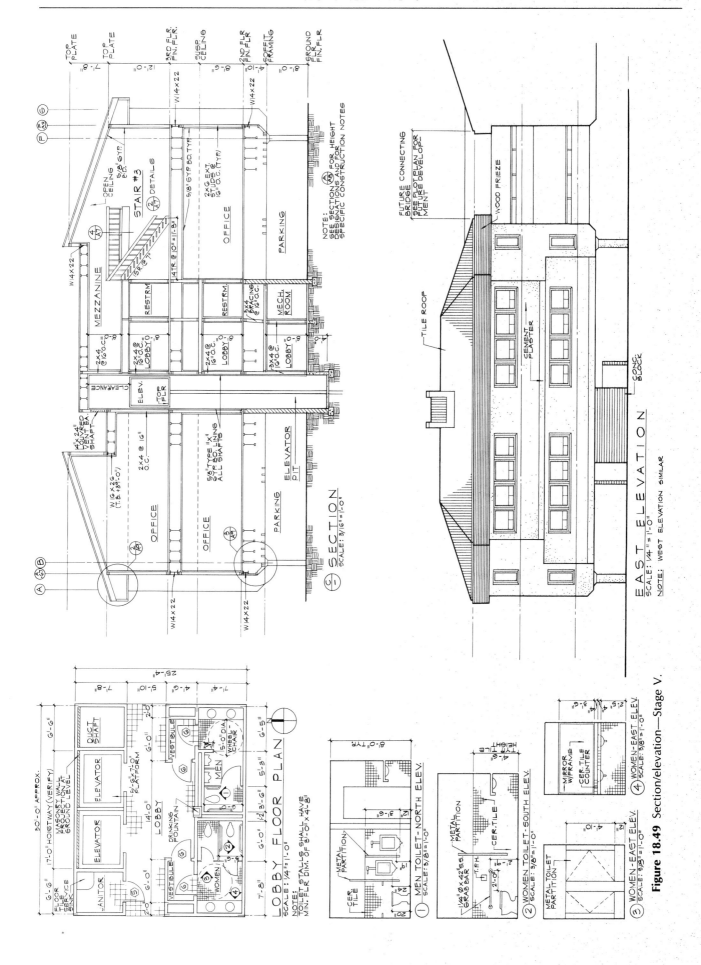

Figure 18.49 Section/elevation—Stage V.

Building Sections

Stage I

The two building sections shown in their first stage in Figure 18.50 were one of the most difficult drawings to perform. Figures 18.51 through 18.63 show photographs of stages of construction at critical locations. Figure 18.51, for example, shows a steel column supporting the second floor beams. The column is encased in a wood form and concrete is poured around the column. Figure 18.52 shows an overall view of the installation of these steel beams. Figure 18.53 shows an aerial view of the process. Between these steel beams would be normal floor joists plus trusses. See Figures 18.54, 18.55, 18.56, 18.57 and 18.58. Figure 18.59 shows the installation of the main members in the structure. Note the assembly numbers on the members in the foreground. Figure 18.60 shows an overall view of the framing for the second and third floor plus the framing around the perimeter of the second floor. Figures 18.61, 18.62, and 18.63 shows various conditions seen from the third floor.

In locating the main steel members, we needed information from the fabricators about the tolerances of these members. We also checked the structural engineer's drawings to locate and size the footings and their respective columns above.

The vertical lines in Figure 18.50 are the axial reference planes. Each of these lines was taken at a specific location to position the main steel members. Each of the horizontal lines represents a location of a specific event. Starting at the top and working downward, they are:

1. The topmost plates
2. The top plate at the exterior walls
3. The soffit level (at the underside of the eave)
4. The floor level on the top floor
5. The underside of the floor
6. The ceiling level
7. The soffit framing at the exterior eave area (close to the previous line)
8. Finished floor of the next level down
9. The soffit framing
10. Finished lobby floor level

Note the concrete block walls and their respective footings on the lower drawing.

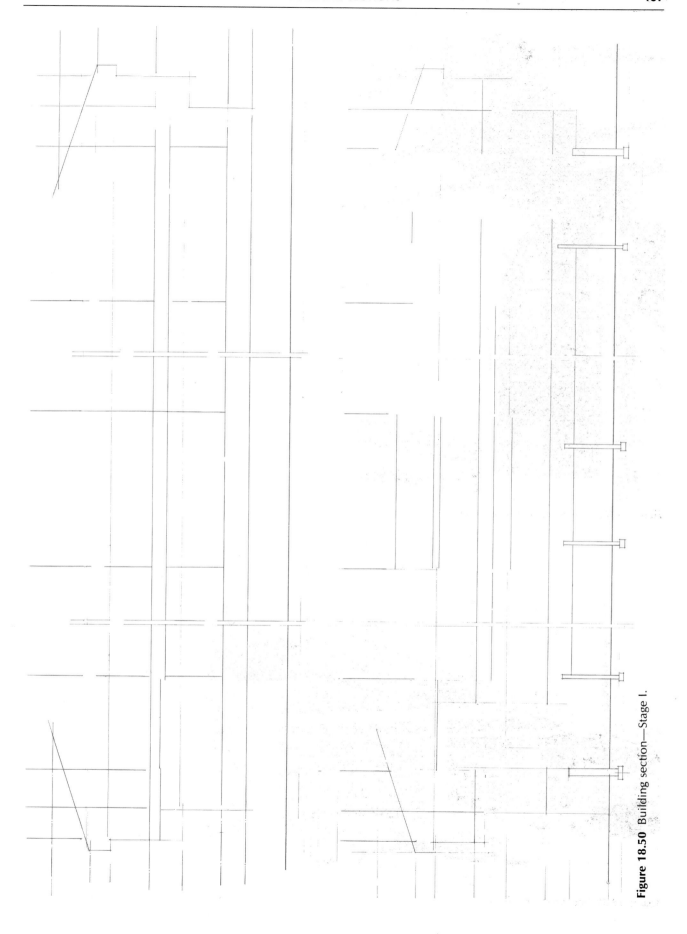

Figure 18.50 Building section—Stage I.

Figure 18.51 Steel column to steel beams.

Figure 18.52 Second floor framing.

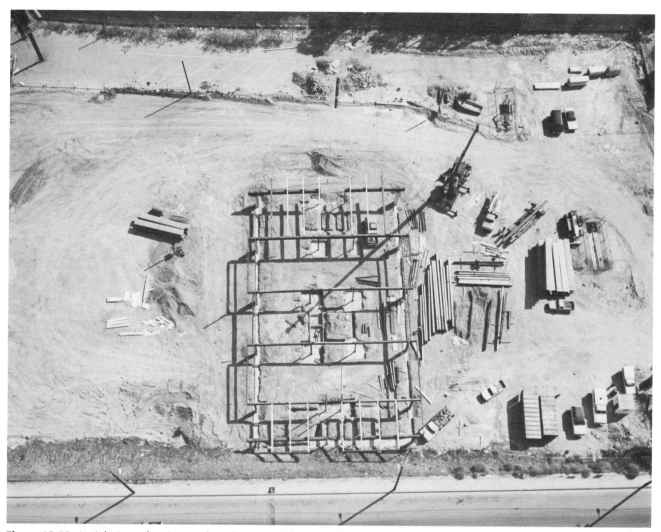

Figure 18.53 Aerial view of main members for second floor. (William Boggs Aerial Photography. Reprinted with permission.)

Figure 18.54 Truss.

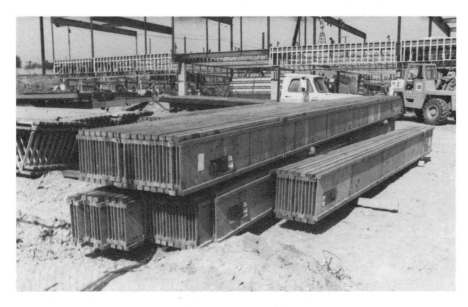

Figure 18.55 Wood trusses.

Figure 18.56 Installation of trusses. (William Boggs Aerial Photography. Reprinted with permission.)

Figure 18.57 Second floor beams with joists and trusses. (William Boggs Aerial Photography. Reprinted with permission.)

Figure 18.58 Truss installation at second floor. (William Boggs Aerial Photography. Reprinted with permission.)

Figure 18.59 Installation of main members. (William Boggs Aerial Photography. Reprinted with permission.)

Figure 18.60 Overall view of second floor and third floor framing. (William Boggs Aerial Photography. Reprinted with permission.)

Figure 18.61 Framing around stairs.

Figure 18.62 Intersection of roof members.

Stage II

Now the outline of the structure began to emerge more clearly. See Figure 18.64. On the upper section, we drew columns. We obtained sizes and shapes from the structural drawings and details and the axial reference bubbles from structural drawings (which were verified on the various plans). We then located the steel beams to coincide with the axial reference bubbles.

We located the soffit around the perimeter, the furred ceiling, and the stair landing from one preliminary freehand detail. The space between the steel beams would house the joists in a web-like form shown in Figure 18.54 that would carry the floor load and transfer this weight to the steel beams. Notice also the lowered (furred) ceiling in some parts of the structure.

Stage III

We had started to show the "pitch (angle)" of the roof on the previous stage, so the roof configuration was the next item to be completed. See Figure 18.65.

Additional steel beams were included near the roof. Steps were added and a diagonal line drawn to represent the block wall. We used dotted lines to represent the eventual location of the ceiling. The space between the ceiling and the underside of the floor above would be the space used for the heating and air conditioning ducts, and electrical lines.

Material designation for soil (earth) was the next thing to be drawn. Finally, after consulting the joist to steel beam detail, we drew the steel joists. These joists are perpendicular to the steel beams and are most easily identified by a series of "W" shapes (webb-members) in their description. On one side of the steel beams there are steel joists, while on the other side, a series of horizontal lines represent wood joists.

Figure 18.63 Framing at roof.

Stage IV

This was one of the critical stages because almost all vertical dimension information would be taken from the drawings on this sheet. All vertical dimensions were drawn at this stage, as well as stair dimensions and ceiling heights. See Figure 18.66.

We next included detail reference bubbles.

Stage V

All vertical dimensions were now added. See Figure 18.67. These had to be constantly verified with the steel fabricator's drawings (shop drawings) and details, and with the structural engineer's details.

On the left side of the top section, all of the horizontal lines are described and dimensioned in reference to the elevation of the finished floor of the lobby. This base level was assigned an elevation of "O" on this drawing and everything else was dimensioned to it. At the next stage, all these dimensions would be changed after realistic and specific vertical dimensions were established—based on a decimal system starting with 100.00. We included the original dimensions to show drawing and design dimensions later changed by the fabricators.

Very detailed stair dimensions were added next; this was one of the few times horizontal dimensions were used. Finally, detail reference bubbles were assigned detail numbers. The bottom half of these detail bubbles has an "A" designation, which indicates that these would be architectural details.

Stage VI

The jump from Stage V to Stage VI looks big, but in fact only the lettering of titles and notes was added. See

Figure 18.68. There are three types of notes. First, there are those that identify the major parts of the structure, such as "2 × 4 c.j. [ceiling joist] @ 16" o.c.," and "Built-up roof over ½" ext. grade plywood." Second, there are those that label space, such as "Lobby," "Parking," and "Duct space." Finally, there are those that describe a procedure: "Keep framing flush with beams," or "Furr out framing as necessary for column concealment."

The materials are selected and used for aesthetic reasons *but*—and just as important—they are also selected to fulfill code requirements such as fire regulations, insulation value for energy laws, and safety and handicapped requirements.

Good practice here is to take a drawing of a stage similar to Stage V, make a print, and begin to label in felt tip pen. Have someone check and correct your drawing before proceeding.

Notice how the horizontal lines at the left are changed from feet and inches to decimal equivalents starting at 100.00 at the floor. This helped the contractor in the erection process as these numbers corresponded with the fabricator's and structural engineer's drawings, done after this drawing was finished. The original feet-and-inch values were used to communicate to the consultants (such as the structural engineer) the desirable height for the structure.

There are many notes unique to the architectural profession used here. "T.B." means "Top of beam" and is used often with the height above the finished floor level. "R" as in "R-19" is the resistive value designation for heat loss and heat gain in a particular material. "T.J.I." is a designation given to a wood truss joist. "W" is a designation given to a particular steel beam shape, and the number next to it is the size.

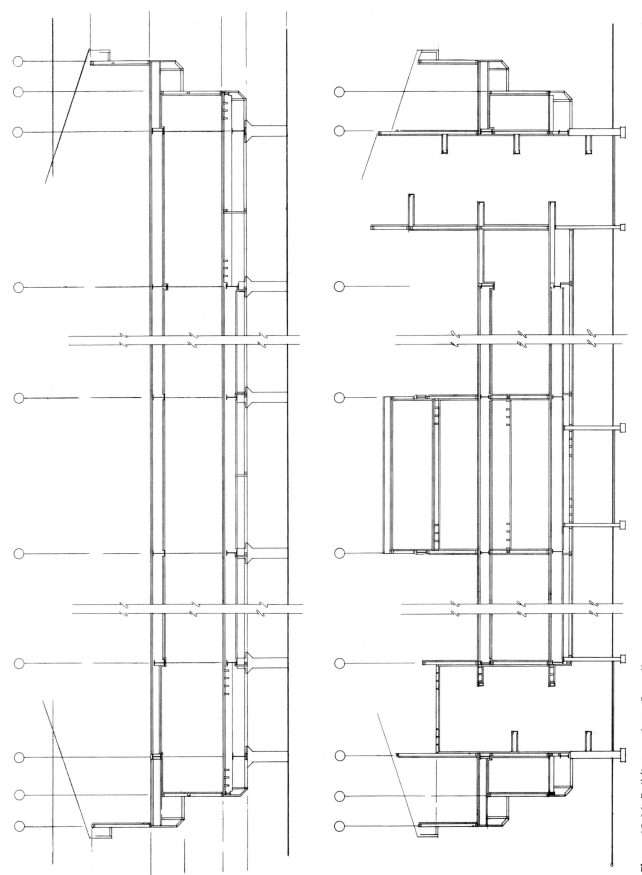

Figure 18.64 Building section—Stage II.

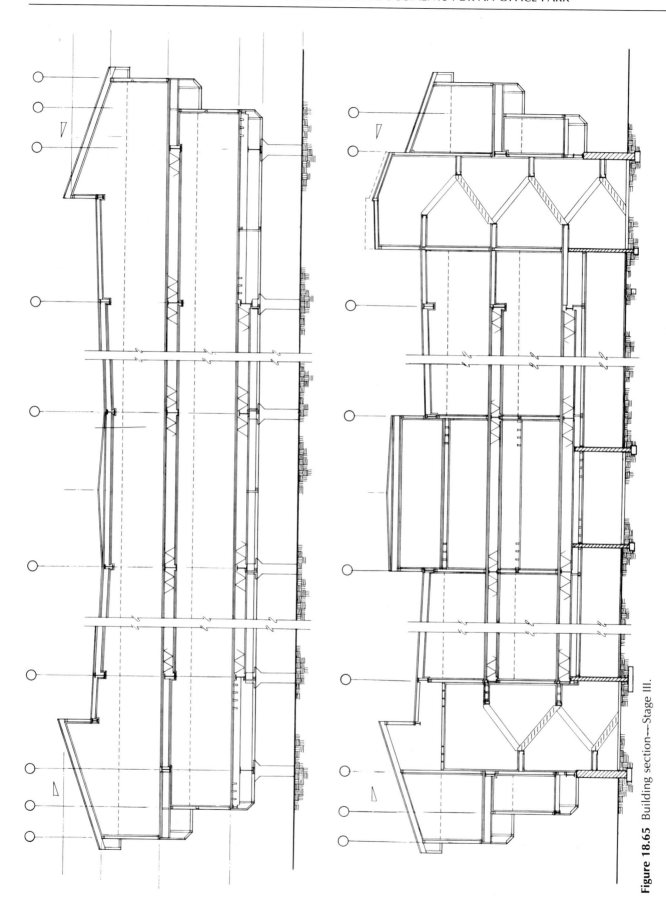

Figure 18.65 Building section—Stage III.

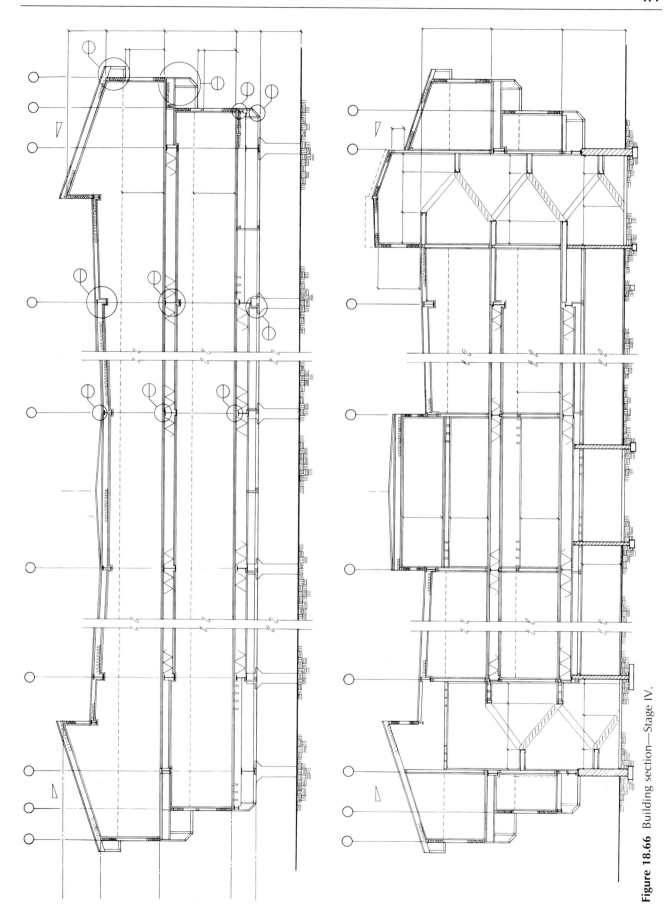

Figure 18.66 Building section—Stage IV.

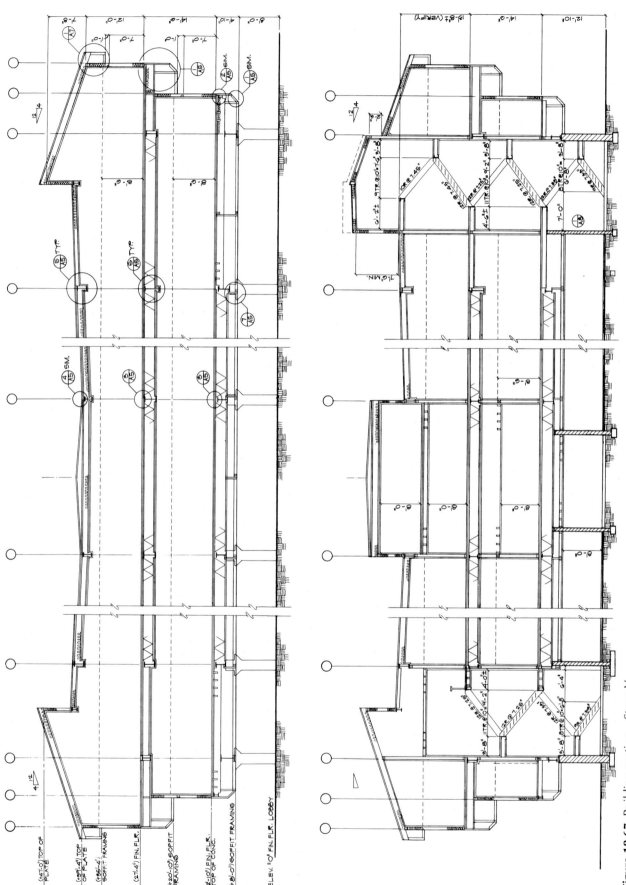

Figure 18.67 Building section—Stage V.

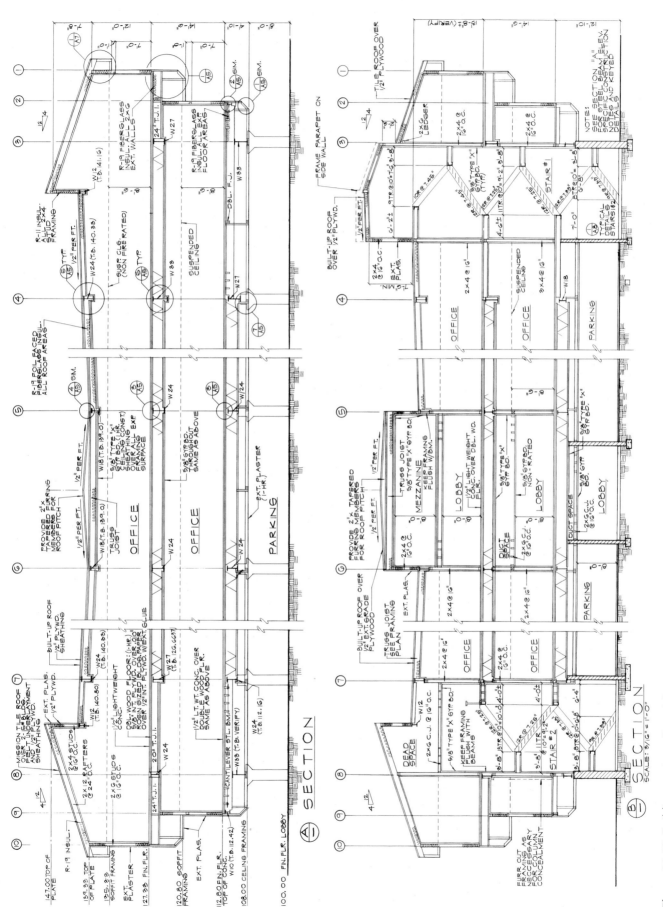

Figure 18.68 Building section—Stage VI.

Roof Plan

Stage I

This plan departs from the normal roof plan; rather than just a view from the top, a portion of the roof has been removed to expose the mezzanine. See Figure 18.69. A break line toward the center of the roof exposes the mezzanine. Review Section B, as well as the third floor plan to clarify this area. The mezzanine area and the stairs leading to it are outlined here. The dimensions for the mezzanine were included because there was no other place to put them, short of drafting a separate mezzanine plan.

The small circles with circles within them represent roof drains. The triangular shapes beside them represent small roof forms called saddles or crickets that help the water drain toward the roof drain. The dotted line around the perimeter is the building line.

Detail bubbles were included to refer to drafted details explaining the construction at that location. Finally, note how the roof of the stairwell is removed to show how the stair ends and how to get to the roof by this stair system.

Stage II

We are really seeing three things in Figure 18.70: the third floor; the stair leading to the mezzanine and the mezzanine itself; and last, the roof. The roof texture for the mission tile roof is stopped at the break line.

Axial reference bubbles, titles, and North arrow completed this portion of the plan.

Door, window, and interior finish schedules were planned and drafted on the reverse side of the sheet.

Stage III

Stage III was the final stage for this sheet. Since the roof and mezzanine plan was finished in the previous stage, we concentrated here on the completion of the door, window, and interior finish schedules. See Figure 18.71.

As well as the normal grid chart schedule, this sheet includes pictorial schedules. Pictorial schedules are often incorporated in schedules that are difficult to describe by a chart. For example, the fixed window with the pair of projecting windows below it is easier to understand when you see a picture of it than when you read a written description of it. Notice the reference below the window schedule to the solar-bronze tinted glass to be used in all the windows.

Compare these schedules with those for the beach house in Chapter 16 and the mountain residence in Chapter 17. Notice the difference in complexity.

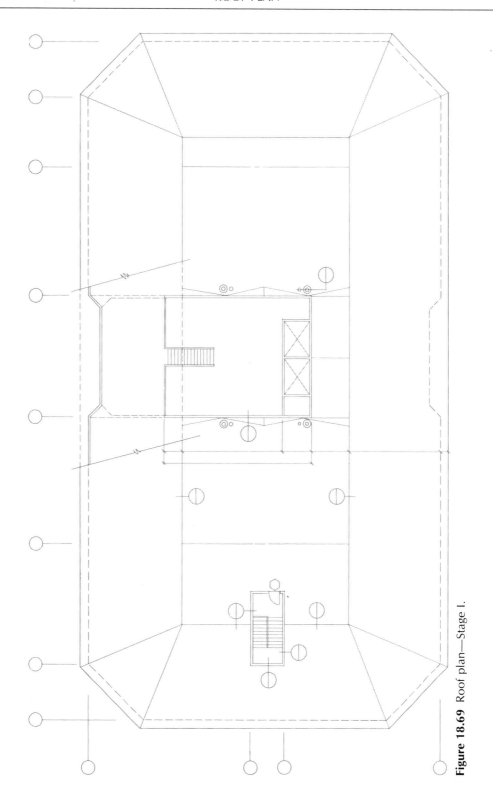

Figure 18.69 Roof plan—Stage I.

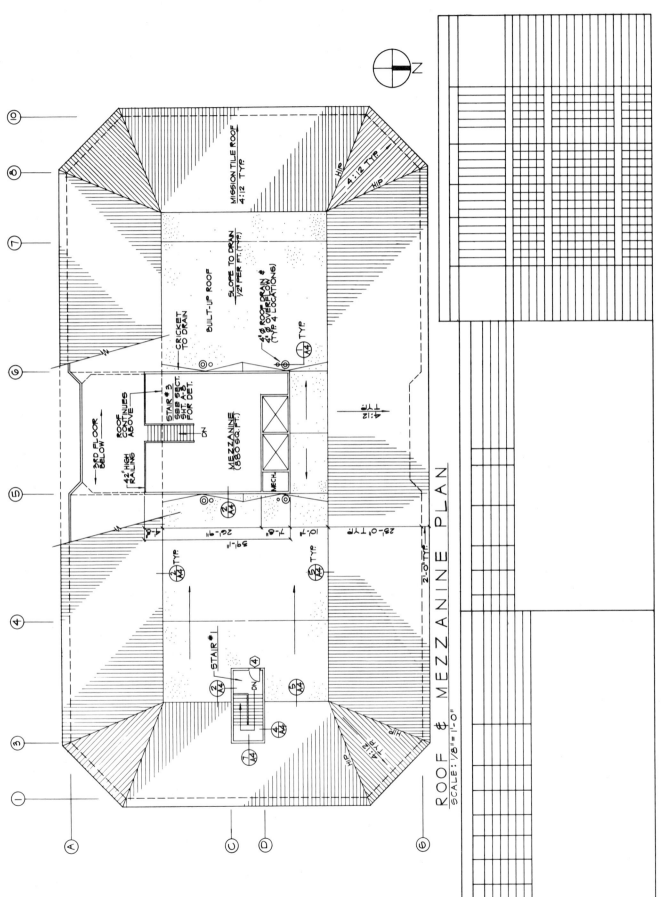

Figure 18.70 Roof plan—Stage II.

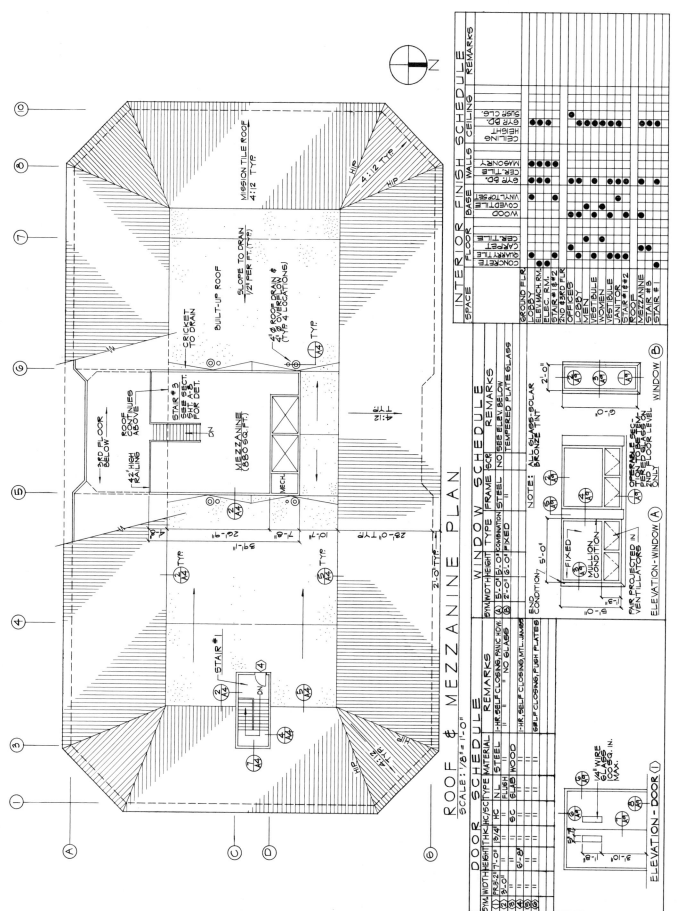

Figure 18.71 Roof plan—Stage III.

Second Floor Framing Plan

Stage I

Since this is the framing plan for the second floor, the ground floor plan is used. First a reproducible (a mylar or sepia print) and a diazo print were made of the ground floor plan at an early stage, without dimensions or notes. The diazo print was then sent to the structural engineer for structural information (column and beam locations, etc.). See Figure 18.72.

Stage II

The engineer returned the daizo print with his sketches. From these sketches the final details were drafted on the reproducible. See Figure 18.73.

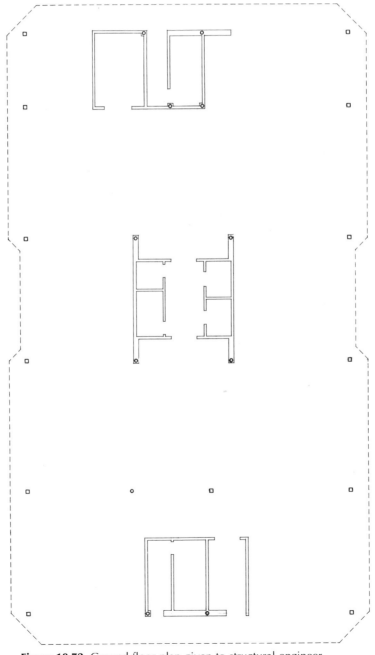

Figure 18.72 Ground floor plan given to structural engineer.

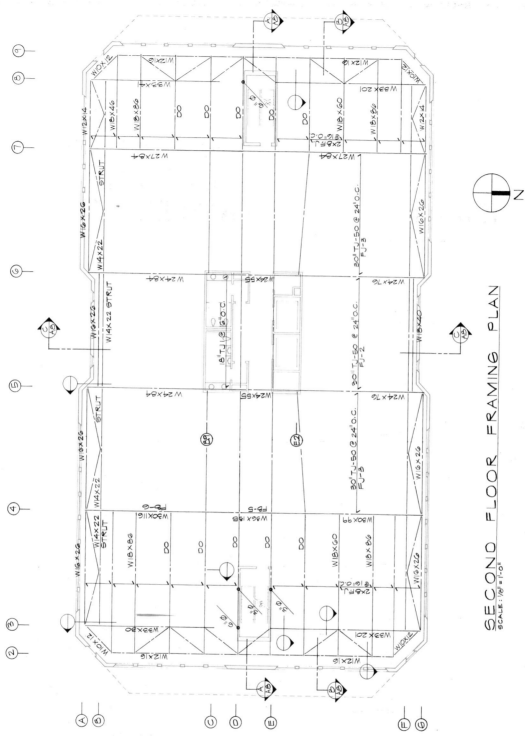

Figure 18.73 Second floor framing plan.

APPENDIX 1

A SURVEY OF REGIONAL DIFFERENCES

This appendix presents the results of a nationwide survey that collected information about regional differences in code requirements, materials used, climatic and geological concerns, and recommended construction techniques.

Table 1 Distribution of cities in survey.

ALASKA   HAWAII

Table 2 Cities responding to survey.

Alabama	Tallahassee	*Maryland*	*New Jersey*	*South Dakota*
Mobile	Tampa	Annapolis	Camden	Aberdeen
Montgomery		Hagerstown	Newark	Rapid City
Tuscaloosa	*Georgia*		Patterson	
	Atlanta	*Massachusetts*		*Tennessee*
Alaska	Columbus	Cambridge	*New Mexico*	Jackson
Anchorage	Macon	Leominster	Albuquerque	Knoxville
Fairbanks	Rome	New Bedford	Carlsbad	Nashville
Kodiak	Savannah	Springfield	Las Cruces	
			Santa Fe	*Texas*
Arizona	*Hawaii*	*Michigan*		Austin
Page	Hilo	Kalamazoo	*New York*	Dallas
Phoenix	Honolulu	Lansing	Buffalo	Fort Worth
Scottsdale		Midland	Ogdensburg	San Antonio
Tucson	*Idaho*	Mt. Pleasant	Syracuse	
Yuma	Boise	Saginaw		*Utah*
	Coeur D'Alene		*North Carolina*	Coalville
Arkansas	Moscow	*Minnesota*	Charlotte	Logan
Fort Smith	Nampa	Albert Lea	Greensboro	Ogden
Little Rock		Anoka		Provo City
N. Little Rock	*Illinois*	Fairmont	*North Dakota*	Salt Lake City
	Decatur	Grand Rapids	Bismarck	
California	Rock Island	Plymouth	Fargo	*Virginia*
Anaheim	Springfield	St. Paul	Grand Forks	Danville
Eureka		Two Harbors	Jamestown	Roanoke
Glendale	*Indiana*			
Los Angeles	Evansville	*Mississippi*	*Ohio*	*Vermont*
Sacramento	Fort Wayne	Gulfport	Akron	Burlington
San Diego	South Bend	Jackson	Cincinnati	Rutland
		Natchez	Dayton	
Colorado	*Iowa*			*Washington*
Boulder	Altoona	*Missouri*		Aberdeen
Brighton	Cedar Rapids	Columbia	*Oklahoma*	Bellevue
Brush	Des Moines	Jefferson City	Bartlesville	Des Moines
Colorado Springs	Fort Madison	Kansas City	Lawton	East Wenatchee
Craig	Indianola	Springfield	Oklahoma City	Ephrata
Denver	Mason City			Seattle
Durango	Sioux City	*Montana*		Spokane
Englewood	Waterloo	Billings	*Oregon*	Tacoma
Fort Collins		Bozeman	Astoria	Walla Walla
Golden		Great Falls	Corvallis	
Littleton	*Kansas*	Helena	Grants Pass	*West Virginia*
Louisville	Abilene	Missoula	Portland	Bluefield
Salida	El Dorado		Salem	Charleston
Woodland Park	Garden City	*Nebraska*	Sweet Home	Morganstown
	Wichita	Holdridge		Parkersburg
		Lincoln		
Connecticut	*Kentucky*	Seward	*Pennsylvania*	*Wisconsin*
Hartford	Ashland		Philadelphia	Eau Claire
New Britain	Frankfort		Pittsburgh	Green Bay
Wethersfield	Paducah	*Nevada*	York	Madison
		Carson City		Milwaukee
		Henderson		Woodland
Delaware	*Louisiana*	Las Vegas	*Rhode Island*	
Laurel	Monroe	Reno	Providence	
Newark	New Orleans			*Wyoming*
		New Hampshire		Casper
Florida	*Maine*	Claremont	*South Carolina*	Cheyenne
Daytona Beach	Auburn	Manchester	Charleston	Cody
Miami	Portland	Rochester	Columbia	
Pensacola	Waterville			

Table 3 States using uniform building codes.

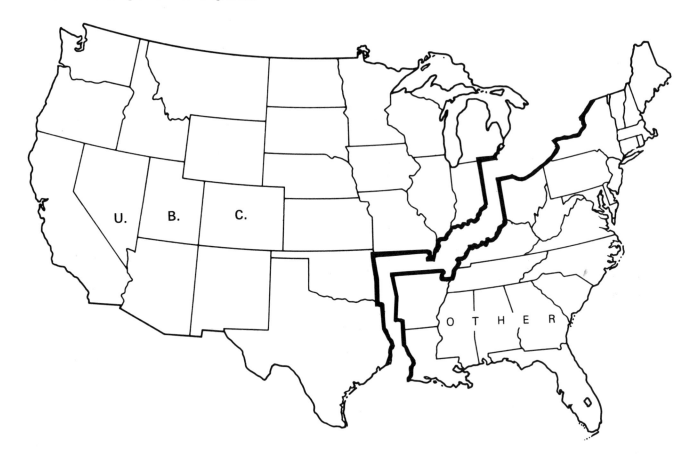

Table 4 Use of wood in residential structures based on questionnaire.

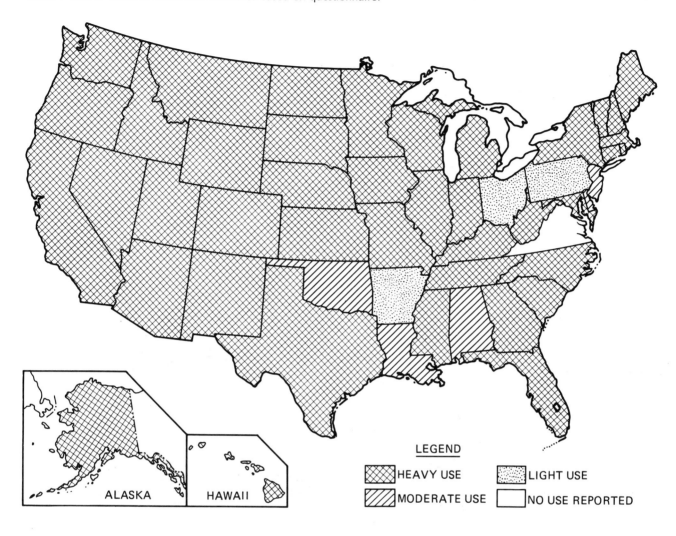

Table 5 Use of masonry in residential structures based on questionnaire

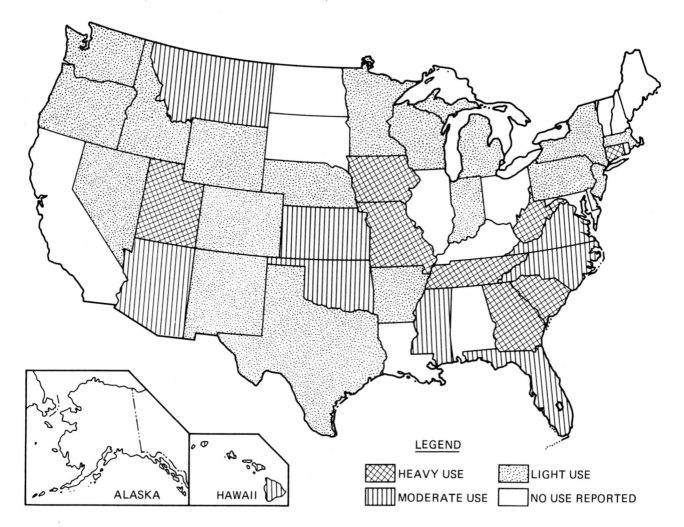

Table 6 Use of masonry in commercial structures based on questionnaire.

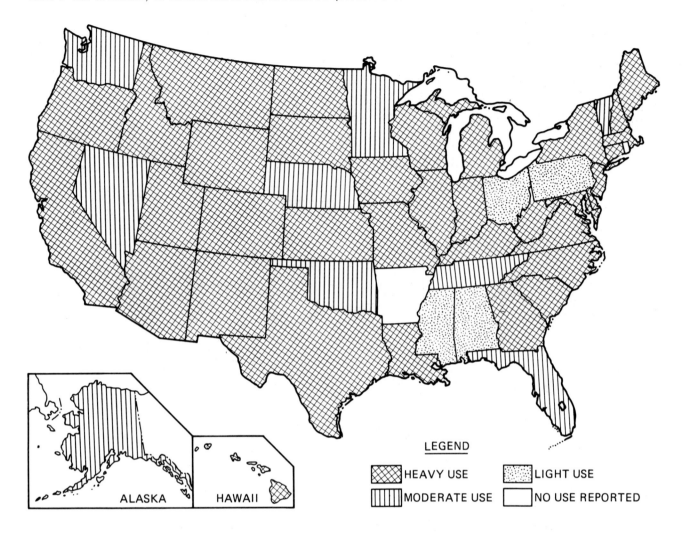

LEGEND

HEAVY USE   LIGHT USE

MODERATE USE   NO USE REPORTED

ALASKA   HAWAII

Table 7 Use of steel in commercial structures based on questionnaire.

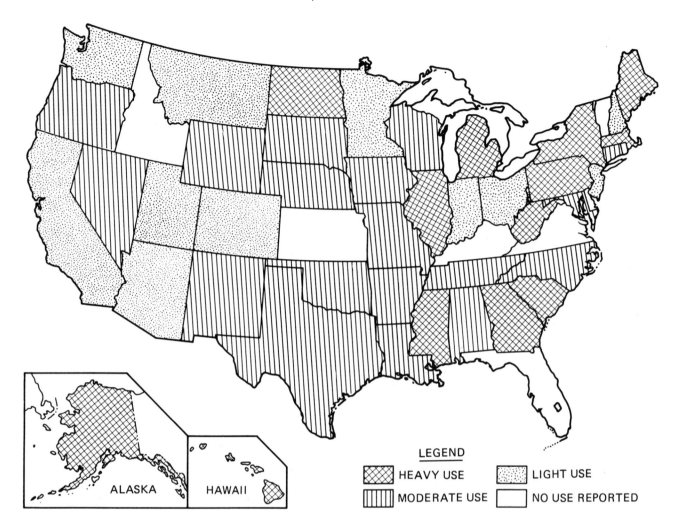

Table 8 Use of wood in commercial structures based on questionnaire.

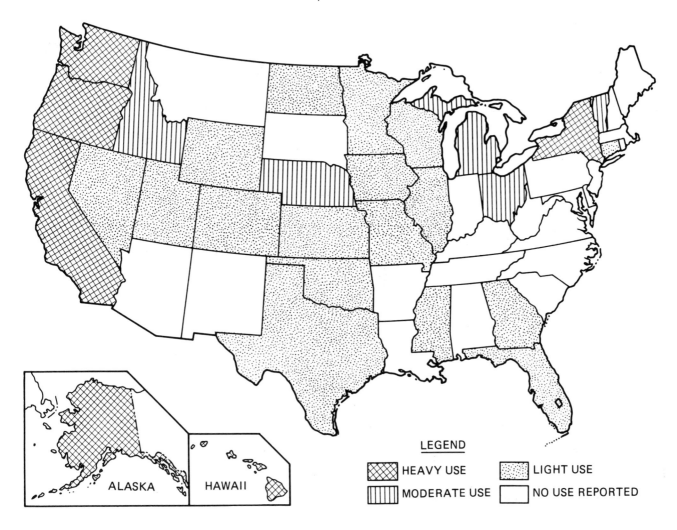

LEGEND

HEAVY USE	LIGHT USE
MODERATE USE	NO USE REPORTED

Table 9 Use of concrete in commercial structures based on questionnaire.

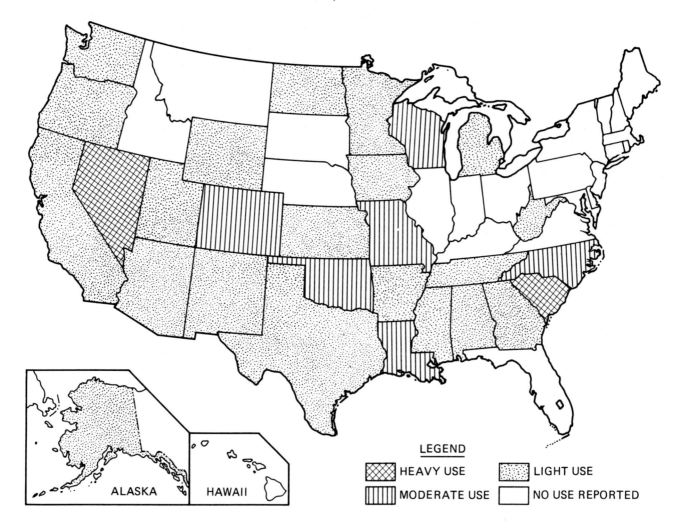

Table 10 Use of steel in industrial structures based on questionnaire.

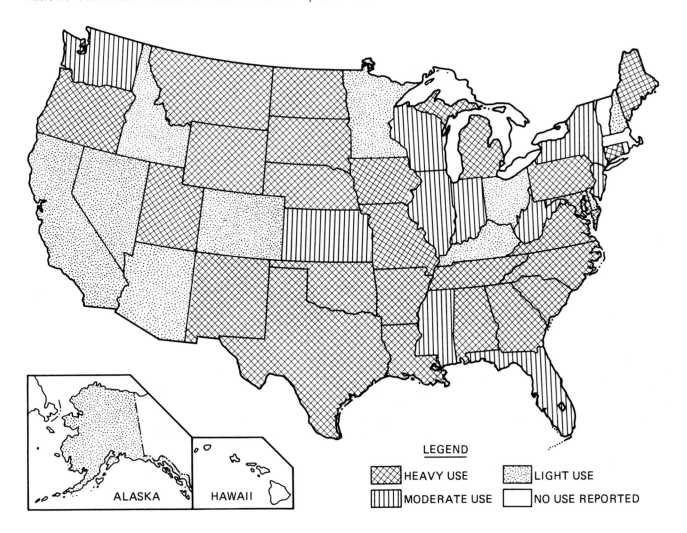

Table 11 Use of masonry in industrial structures based on questionnaire.

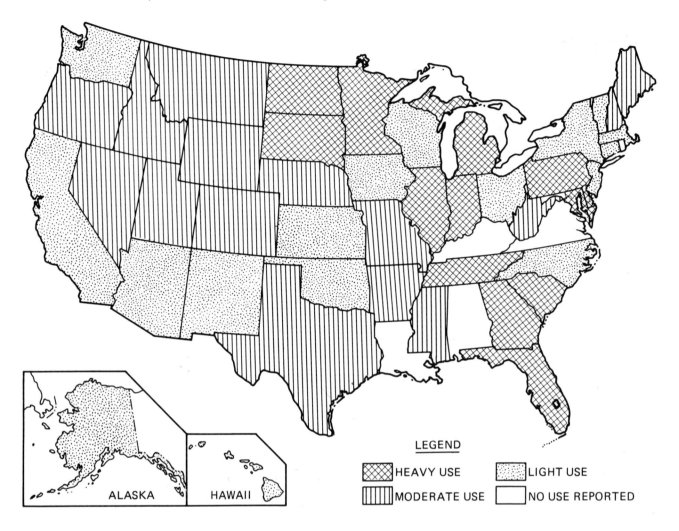

Table 12 Use of concrete in industrial structures based on questionnaire.

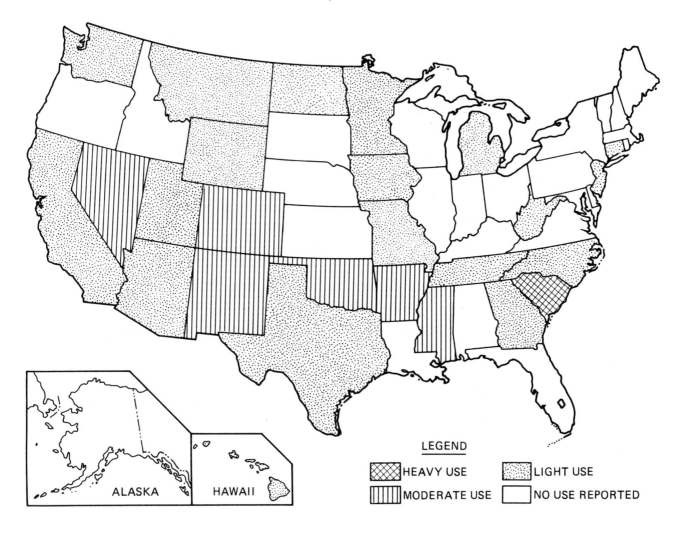

Table 13 Special concerns of the states by building departments.

	Wind	Snow	Seismic	Fire	Energy	Found. Desi	Flooding	Live/Dead Loads	Struc. Desi.	Frost Depth	Hurricane	Insulation	Handicapped	Water Table	Flr/Roof Loads	Temperature	Rain	Frost	Ext. Fin.	Vert. Load
Alabama	●					●		●	●		●									
Alaska	90 ● 100	40 ●	●		●	●														
Arizona	●	●	●	●								●					●			
Arkansas					●															
California	●		●	●	●	●													●	
Colorado	●	25 ● 175	●			●		●		●		●		●						
Connecticut	●	●								●										
Delaware	●		●																	
Florida	●		●								●									
Georgia	●					●	●				●									
Hawaii	●		●								●									
Idaho	●	25 ● 40	●			●				●										
Illinois	25 ●	30 ●		●		●														
Indiana	●	●					●		●	●				●						
Iowa	●	30 ● 40		●	●					●			●		●					
Louisiana	●					●		●												
Kansas	●	●	●					●												
Kentucky	●		●				●	●											●	
Maine		●																		●
Maryland																				
Massachussetts		●	●		●		●	●	●			●	●							
Michigan	●	●		●	●					●			●	●			●			
Minnesota	●	●			●	●		●	●	●			●		●					●
Mississippi	●					●				●										●
Missouri	●	●		●			●	●		●		●								

Table 13 (continued)

	Wind	Snow	Seismic	Fire	Energy	Found. Des.	Flooding	Live/Dead Loads	Struct. Des.	Frost Depth	Hurricane	Insulation	Handicapped	Water Table	Flr/Roof Loads	Temperature	Rain	Frost	Ext. Fin.	Drainage	Vert. Load
Montana	●	●	●			●			●	●				●							
Nebraska	●	30 ●	●													●					
Nevada	●	●	●				●									●					
New Hampshire		●	●	●	●																
New Jersey						●															
New Mexico	30 ●	●	●						●							●		●			
New York		●		●	●				●												
No. Carolina	●	●		●			●														
No. Dakota	●	30 ●				●															
Ohio		●		●	●	●															
Oklahoma	15 ●	25 ●	●				●														
Oregon	15 ● 20	25 ●	●	●	●	●	●		●			●	●				●				
Pennsylvania						●															
Rhode Island				●					●						●						
South Carolina	●		●				●														
South Dakota	●	●							●												
Tennessee	●	20 ●							●	●					●						
Texas	●	●				●	●	●	●		●										
Utah		20 ● 100	●																		
Vermont		●																	●		
Virginia						●	●														
Washington	●	30 ●	●	●		●						●	●			●	●	●			
W. Virginia	●	●		●		●															
Wisconsin		●		●																	
Wyoming	●	●		●																	

Table 14 Recommended construction techniques.

Question: What construction techniques do you recommend in your region?

ALABAMA	
Montgomery	No special recommendation—we only code check plans that are submitted.
Tuscaloosa	Platform framing, monolithic conc. slab on grade, brick veneer.
ALASKA	
Anchorage	Very little masonry veneer. Use reinforced masonry, tilt-up concrete panel, steel frame hi-rise, insulated curtain wall, triple glazing.
	Nationally recognized techniques accepted.
Fairbanks	Energy conservation techniques, designs utilizing scenic advantages and/or sunlight.
Kodiak	Recommended construction techniques should be IAW UBC standards, and the architects design to these standards with registered Alaska number and seal.
ARIZONA	
Phoenix	Construction techniques are initiated by the manufacturer . . . fabrication being controlled at the factory.
	Drywall—with consideration for fire stop, separations, rated wall divisions, and performance documentation of engineer analysis or test.
Scottsdale	Conventional 8″ conc. masonry units for commercial and residential.
Tucson	"Territorial" type construction with flat roofs which require the use of ledger boards. The method of attaching the ledgers to masonry and wood frame walls presents several headaches weekly.
	Western framing rather than balloon recommended; however, balloon is more popular.
Yuma	We recommend wood frame with as much insulation as can be practically installed and a stucco surface to withstand the heat and sun.
ARKANSAS	
Fort Smith	Wood, metal, concrete framing; brick, stucco, wood veneer, asphalt, wood, but mopped roofs.
CALIFORNIA	
Anahein	Plate splices and continuity, dragstruts connection, horizontal diaphragm sheating and nailing schedule, vertical diaphragm sheating and nailing schedule, horizontal shear bolting and uplift hold downs of vertical shear walls—grade beam construction; regular framing lay out. (Irregular shapes create many construction problems.)

Glendale	Western.
Los Angeles	Any technique that complies with code requirements is designed using sound judgment and conforms to good engineering principles.
Sacramento	Platform stud wall construction, masonry, concrete.
San Diego	Any method of construction that satisfies the performance standards contained in the UBC.
COLORADO	
Boulder	Elimination of basements, criteria for detailed hillside site plans, engineered foundation systems.
Colorado Springs	Residential is predominantly wood frame/balloon, but not limited to it. We have some veneer. We only check for structural integrity—the techniques choice is theirs.
Craig	Frame.
Denver	Platform (Western) framing, Cast-in-place concrete, prestressed and precast concrete, masonry (reinforced), structural steel.
Durango	Log const.—wood framing pumice block laid to Colorado Code.
Englewood	Caissons under foundation walls.
Fort Collins	Platform framing and post and beams.
Golden	All types of construction.
Littleton	Framing—masonry.
Louisville	Any techniques approved by UBC.
Salida	Platform framing (conventional).
Woodland Park	UBC.
CONNECTICUT	
New Britain	Our code is not a specification code. We have *performance* standards and do not discriminate against any material.
Wethersfield	Lightweight, and cont., and to meet energy conservation requirements; also revamp the handicapped code and make it workable.
DELAWARE	
Laurel	No recommendations as to techniques; code requirements only.
Newark	Brick veneer primary design for residential and lite commercial.
FLORIDA	
Miami	Special considerations to be made of wind loads. Use of various devices designed for high wind loads conditions.
Pensacola	All types designed for wind load as per code.

Table 14 (*continued*)

Tallahassee	Don't recommend. Follow or design under Table 400 standard building code.
Tampa	Reinforced masonry, P.T. wood frames.
GEORGIA	
Atlanta	Wood truss roof design; reinforced masonry; reinforced concrete precast, prestressed post-tensioned concrete construction, slip form.
Columbus	Modern braced framing, primarily brick veneer.
Rome	Enforcement of the Southern Standard Building Code.
Savannah	Stick built construction—wood frame, brick veneer mostly 1 and 2 story.
HAWAII	
Hilo	No specific recommendation; however, more of the platform frame construction techniques are practiced.
IDAHO	
Boise	Any approved method or any satisfactory innovative new method.
Coeur D'Alene	Fire separations. Set back proper classification of type of buildings when nonrated.
Moscow	Platform construction, exterior covering optional but mostly wood.
Nampa	We go strictly on the framing that is allowed in the Uniform Building Code.
ILLINOIS	
Decatur	Residential—wood frame—brick veneer. Commercial—masonry—steel frame.
Springfield	We do not recommend; only that they comply with the UBC as per occupancy requirement.
INDIANA	
Evansville	Architect/engineer option.
Fort Wayne	Chapter 23 and 29, UBC.
South Bend	Grade beams, masonry, steel bar joint.
IOWA	
Altoona	Wood frame—16 and 24 o.c.
Cedar Rapids	Fire-blocked wood framing; masonry veneer, architectural concrete.
Des Moines	Platform framing used exclusively in wood construction. Concrete or steel frame with precast or masonry veneer; metal buildings; pole type buildings; standard masonry construction.
Indianola	Wood and masonry veneer, proper insulation to conserve energy.
Mason City	Type I Fire resistive building: steel, iron, concrete, or masonry. Type II Fire resistive buildings: steel, iron, concrete, or masonry. Types III and IV buildings: III, 1 hour buildings shall be 1 hour fire-resistive construction throughout; and IV, heavy timber construction. Type V: any material allowed by UBC.
Sioux City	Precast Ts, steel studs, soundproofing, insulated cast panels.
Waterloo	Frame.
KANSAS	
Abilene	In the inspection field, we rely on engineering field.
El Dorado	As per uniform code.
Wichita	Platform framing and brick veneer (residential). Reinforced concrete and masonry (commercial).
KENTUCKY	
Ashland	Masonry veneer.
Paducah	Earthquake provisions, balloon framing.
LOUISIANA	
New Orleans	Frame
MAINE	
Portland	Masonry bearing.
Waterville	Masonry veneer for commercial; wood for residential.
MARYLAND	
Annapolis	See NBC 1976 edition.
Hagerstown	Masonry veneer.
MASSACHUSETTS	
Cambridge	Platform construction for frame structures, allow "lift-slab" construction.
Leominster	Reference EPS *Sweets Catalog File* 7.14(d)/So and 7.15(d)/So.
New Bedford	Residential—box frame; commercial and industrial—masonry and steel.
MICHIGAN	
Lansing	Residential—wood frame. Commercial—masonry, noncombustible.
Midland	We do not recommend any construction technique over another. We orient toward performance; any technique that meets those requirements is acceptable.
Mt. Pleasant	Platform framing, poured concrete basement, floor truss system.
MINNESOTA	
Brooklyn Park	Platform framing common in our area, very little single wall construction as allowed by code.
Fairmont	Any type construction allowed in the Building Code.
Plymouth	Use of available materials in their intended manner and not an unproven modification.

Table 14 (*continued*)

St. Paul	We do not recommend; code performance standards are used rather than construction techniques.		Code—low opinion of balloon framing and unprotected noncombustible.
Two Harbors	Platform framing.	Manchester	Balloon framing out of use. (Western frame prevalent.) Brick veneer on some frame buildings. Light gauge steel framing. Rigid frame structures also popular.
MISSISSIPPI		Rochester	Platform.
Gulfport	Western or platform is most popular. SBC Chapter XVII does not prohibit balloon framing or brace framing.	NEW MEXICO	
		Carlsbad	Steel frame masonry.
Jackson	Wood, brick veneer, preengineered metal and masonry.	Las Cruces	Platform frame, stucco exterior, masonry veneer, adobe.
Matchez	Masonry veneer and well insulated. Balloon alternate framing—masonry or panel board veneer (asbestos siding alternate), aluminum siding, etc., alternate roof orientation to sun and overhang protection.	Sante Fe	Residential: braced framing, platform framing, and adobe. Commercial: precast concrete and structured steel. Industrial: precast concrete "T"'s, panels and structure.
			Wood frame and adobe for residential. Masonry and metal for commercial.
MISSOURI			
Columbia	As long as it meets the code. Recommend insulation R-values be well exceeded.	NEW YORK	
		Ogdenburg	2 × 4 or 6 stud framing with firestopping wood truss rafters, no less than 4″ × 12″ pitch—all types siding.
Jefferson City	Platform framing, rigid frame steel, reinforced cast-in-place concrete.		
Kansas City	It is the opinion of this office that techniques of construction should be left to the discretion of the architect.	Syracuse	We follow the N.Y. State Building Code for most new construction.
Springfield	All types.	NORTH CAROLINA	
		Greensboro	Platform construction in residential construction.
MONTANA			
Billings	Glu-lam beam, truss-joist, 2″ deck roof systems; steel frame, masonry, or insulated metal walls. Manufactured homes, or factory built units and panels.	NORTH DAKOTA	
		Bismarck	Not partial as long as the intent of the code is met.
Bozeman	Conventional framing.	Fargo	Platform framing. Conventional construction practices.
Great Falls	Conventional framing, using dimension lumber of manufactured trusses for residences.	Grand Forks	Western framing and masonry veneer.
Helena	We accept any type of construction that can comply with the UBC.	OHIO	
		Akron	Platform framing—24″ o.c. construction. Masonry bearing walls.
Missoula	Western framing, wood trusses, Glu-lam beams, wood foundations (residential).	Cincinnati	Runs the gamut.
NEBRASKA		OKLAHOMA	
Seward	Standard 2 × 4, 2 × 6 framing, composition shingles, veneer or wood or comp. siding.	Bartlesville	Masonry and steel.
		Lawton	Platform framing masonry veneer for residential. Tilt-up concrete panels for commercial.
NEVADA			
Carson City	All standard techniques. Conventional framing; concrete foundations, per Seismic Zone #3.	Oklahoma City	Steel, single story construction. We also have "erection manual" on how to erect steel buildings.
Henderson	Masonry—steel and framing with stucco finish.	OREGON	
Las Vegas	Any which meet code requirements.	Astoria	Balloon framing, cedar or shake siding.
Reno	Western or platform framing is required. Wood foundation o.k.		Every foundation must be engineered, basic balloon framing.
NEW HAMPSHIRE		Corvallis	UBC—platform or Western framing, some balloon. Reinforced concrete block masonry (8″ × 8″ × 16″). High insulation
Claremont	Close adherence to table 214 of BOCA		

Table 14 (*continued*)

	requirements as required by state for energy conservation in all types of buildings.		(may include wood trusses). Brick veneer or other approved exterior.
	Wood framing—Western or platform framing. Balloon framing is not recommended.		Masonry veneer, structural concrete load bearing. Structural steel.
Portland	All acceptable UBC techniques—depends on building use and type—recommend reinforcing in concrete/masonry construction.		Platform framing (with hurricane strapping in Gulf Coast and some areas of the Panhandle) and masonry veneer are extremely widespread for residence.
	We do not recommend to the industry, but we do see mainly prestressed post-stressed, concrete, hi-lift masonry.	Dallas	Western platform framing.
		Fort Worth	Western framing.
Salem	Mostly Western platform-type wood framing, tilt-up concrete, preengineered metal buildings, lightweight concrete masonry units.	**UTAH**	
		Coalville	Masonry veneer or 6″ framing (wood).
		Logan	Just follow the requirements of the UBC.
	Double wall construction—fire stopping—utilization of automatic sprinklers wherever possible.	Ogden	The type of construction is totally governed on the Uniform Building Code. We do not recomment any specific type of construction.
	Building officials do not recommend techniques, but there is great need for information on energy conservation construction.	Provo City	Platform framing most common form of local construction.
		Salt Lake City	Masonry veneer.
Sweet Home	Primarily Western platform.		Earthquake-proof masonry veneer precast concrete structural frames in commercial buildings. High-life grout masonry.
PENNSYLVANIA			
Philadelphia	Wood frame construction is prohibited in the greatest portion of the city. Ordinary construction or better is thus generally required.		
		VERMONT	
York	As much noncombustible materials as possible.	Burlington	It is not within the scope of the job to truly recommend but point out where code is not being complied with.
RHODE ISLAND			
Providence	Department does not recommend a technique but prefers to see masonry or noncombustible stair enclosures in most buildings because of problems in fire rating wood frame.	**VIRGINIA**	
		Danville	No recommendations are made relative to how construction work is done so long as it meets the codes.
		Roanoke	Type of construction open but we rigidly enforce code requirements.
SOUTH DAKOTA			
Aberdeen	Stick built, recommend 2 × 6 walls with 6″ insulation due to cold.	**WASHINGTON**	
		Aberdeen	Wood framing techniques.
Rapid City	We cannot recommend a specific construction technique. Most residential contractors use the platform method of framing. Balloon framing in new construction has never been used in this particular area. Less than 20 percent of the dwellings built have a masonry veneer, usually of brick.	Bellevue	Standard frame, residential; tilt-up concrete, precast concrete, giant brick stucco for commercial.
		Des Moines	Reinforced concrete below grade; CMU and wood framing above grade.
		East Wenatchee	I feel strongly that builders should use 24″ framing, build their houses in multiples of 4′, etc., to achieve labor and material savings.
TENNESSEE			
Jackson and Knoxville	Masonry, veneer, etc.	Ephrata	UBC.
Nashville	Platform framing—residential construction. Steel frame/masonry units—commercial, industrial construction.	Spokane	Platform framing, truss roofs (residential), reinforced CMU, and concrete tilt-ups with Glu-lam roof systems (commercial/industrial).
		Tacoma	We do not recommend. We only approve based on the code requirements.
TEXAS			
Austin	Residential: conventional wood framing	Walla Walla	Anything that is above minimum code.

Table 14 (*continued*)

WEST VIRGINIA		Madison	All covered in codes.
Bluefield	Position of headers and size. Framing and spans of lumber.	Milwaukee	Very little balloon and framing. Masonry veneer used extensively on one and two story buildings; steel and poured concrete or steel and masonry used on buildings over two stories.
Charleston	Techniques are dependent on the choice of the structural design engineer. All techniques must conform to BOCA Code.		
Parkersburg	All plans and drawings are examined by our Plans Examiner.	Woodland	More attention to details—metal windows cause condensation, leak air.
WISCONSIN		WYOMING	
Eau Claire	All wood frame buildings are constructed using the platform method.	Cheyenne	All types as per minimum standards of the Uniform Building Code.
Green Bay	Western framing and masonry veneer.		

Table 15 Recommended foundation design.

Question: What foundation design do you recommend for your region?

ALABAMA			composition) or engineered foundations in an engineered fill.
Mobile	Recommendations only after review of soil reports.	Yuma	Monolithic footings since "frost line" is not a factor in Yuma. We enforce the specs in Table 29-A, UBC.
Montgomery	Minimum footing 12″ below grade with two #5 rebars.		
Tuscaloosa	8″ × 16″ for wood siding, 8″ × 20″ for veneer with top of footing 8″ below grade.	ARKANSAS	
		Fort Smith	16- to 18-inch frost line. We recommend a 16- to 24-inch wide footing by 8-inch minimum thickness poured below frost line with 2 pieces ½″ reinforcing steel installed horizontally. This footing to be used for 8 × 16 inch concrete block foundation wall.
ALASKA			
Anchorage	Standard foundation design; all footings 42″ or more below grade.		
Fairbanks	42″ minimum depth (frost line)—soils investigation prior to foundation design.		
Kodiak	36″ depth with width, compaction, drainage, and fill material for a very wet and high drainage situation.	Little Rock	Our standard footing is 9″ × 18″ in a 12″ deep trench.
		N. Little Rock	Frost line—12″.
ARIZONA		CALIFORNIA	
Page	Frost line at 24″ minimum.		
Phoenix	(Maricopa) County has no frost line—minimum footing per code per loads per soils.	Anaheim	Residential: Grade beam, design for garage door, shear walls, proper dowelings between first and second pour of footings and slabs.
	Our rules and regulations require that supports shall bear no greater load than 8,000 pounds and have a minimum vertical concentrated load failure rating of 14,000 pounds.		Commercial and Industrial: Eccentric design of footings at property lines.
	Small projects—18″ below grade.	Eureka	We have very little expansive soil and no frost penetration to speak of. We are in a seismically active area. Perimeter foundations with steel (minimum two #4 bars).
Scottsdale	No frost line problems; 16″ wide × 18″ below natural grade, concrete footings, with stem, and monolithic slab and interior-bearing footings.		
		Glendale	Grade beams and otm in condo/apts.
Tucson	No frost line problems—spread footing and stem wall (foundation wall). Some caissons used on beam-column construction.	Sacramento	Continuous concrete foundations per Chapter 29 of the Uniform Building Code designed to 1,000 psf soil bearing, or furnish soil report. No frost problem.
	No frost line. Foundations must be 12″ minimum into existing undisturbed soil (this is minimum level for reliable soil	San Diego	Any material having durability equivalent to concrete or masonry and so designed to support the structure without differential settlement or distortion.

Table 15 (continued)

COLORADO

Boulder	Caisson—grade beam in areas of expansive soils and on hillsides. 30 PCF equivalent pressure for basement walls.
Brighton	As designed by engineer (soil test), frost line is 30".
Brush	16" × 18" footers must be below frost line—8". Foundation walls—horizontal and vertical steel bar.
Colorado Springs	Below 30" frost depth—though groundwater is not a problem. Expansive soil conditions—balanced footing or caisson foundation.
Craig	Frost line—concrete.
Denver	Not less than 3 feet below finish grade.
	Frost line; in Denver metro area—expansive soils demand soil test and engineered foundation.
Englewood	Caissons and footings—voids for soil expansion—frost line.
Fort Collins	Frost line in the Fort Collins area is 30" below grade.
Golden	Frost line varies due to expansive soils. Engineered designs and soil testing required.
Littleton	36" depth—soils test necessary; 80% of footings are caissons.
Louisville	Bottom of spread footers 30" below finished grade.
Salida	8" × 16" footing with a 8" × 24" stem wall.
Woodland Park	30" below finished grade.

CONNECTICUT

New Britain	Below frost line (42") of any approved material designed to carry load.

DELAWARE

Laurel	Foundation footings below frost line approximately 18" to top of footing; foundation design according to load.
Newark	Our area is minimum 32" below finish grade.

FLORIDA

Daytona Beach	Residential—8" × 20" continuous footing with two #5 bars; no frost line.
Miami	Flood criteria considerations. Much soil conditions common in area.
Pensacola	12" below existing grade.
Tallahassee	6" below frost line.
Tampa	Reinforced concrete on sandy soil prevalent to this area.

GEORGIA

Atlanta	Wood concrete, metal piles; all foundations below frost line.
Columbus	Frost line 4" depth. Average soil bearing 2000 psi.
Macon	Footing depth 12" and design for soil conditions and load.
Rome	Require all footings be below frost line.
Savannah	No frost line foundation problems. Foundations may require piling on multistory or heavy industrial piling.

IDAHO

Boise	Footings and stem walls 2 feet below frost line.
	Engineered or standard design. Wood or masonry IAW, UBC.
Coeur D'Alene	Our frost line is 18" but does not always play a big part, although we feel it should.
Moscow	30" minimum frost line depth, maximum allowance soil pressure 1500#.
Nampa	Our frost line in this valley is 24" below grade. We don't use reinforcing steel in dwelling footings, except when it is too wet or an overdug. All commercial has to be designed to support the load.

ILLINOIS

Decatur	Concrete footings—frost line 36 inches plus; masonry or concrete walls.
Rock Island	As per code, using a minimum depth of 42" below finished grade.
Springfield	UBC on wall thickness—minimum of 30" to bottom of footings.

INDIANA

Evansville	Minimum specified in code.
Fort Wayne	Chapter 23 and 29, UBC.
South Bend	Prd. footing/foundation (36" depth minimum).

IOWA

Altoona	Footing 8" × 16" and below frost line.
Cedar Rapids	Footings to or below 42-inch frost line. Diversion of surface and groundwater to storm sewer.
Des Moines	Required footing depth = 42". Minimum footing for light buildings consists of 8" × 16" pad (continuous). All others must be engineered.
Fort Madison	36" below grade for footing; 8" walls poured or block.
Indianola	Frost line for this area 42".
Mason City	Footings and foundations, unless otherwise specifically provided, shall be constructed of masonry or concrete, and in all cases extend below the frost line.
Sioux City	Continuous pour concrete, auger, cast-in (prepack) place piling, frost line 42".
Waterloo	8" block, 6" poured, frost line 42".

KANSAS

Abilene	In the inspection field, we rely on engineering field.
El Dorado	Must extend below frost line (24").

Table 15 *(continued)*

Garden City	32 inches below finish grade (frost line). For pad mount structure a 6″ wide 24″ deep frost ledge required between pads.	Brooklyn Park	Concrete block primarily, some poured concrete.
Wichita	Continuous spread footings—concrete foundation walls, 24″ frost line.	Fairmont	42″ in the south and 60″ in the northern part of the state.
		Grand Rapids	5′0″ below grade.
KENTUCKY		Plymouth	Size of footing versus soils allowable loads. Frost depths 42″+.
Ashland	Frame 1 story 20″ × 10″—1½ or 2 story frame or masonry veneer 24″ × 16″, unless plans by registered architect—frost line 18″	St. Paul	42″ frost line.
		Two Harbors	5′ frost protection—finished grade to bottom of footing.
Frankfort	12″ below frost line.	**MISSISSIPPI**	
Paducah	24″ frost line.	Gulfport	Frost line is 12″ on Mississippi Gulf Coast; monolithic and conventional slab and foundation design is used. Soil condition may effect design in some cases.
LOUISIANA			
New Orleans	Pilings. Slab elevation above federal 100 yard flood level.	Jackson	Sand clay fill or cast-in-place piling.
Monroe	Frost line.	Natchez	6″ frost line, foundations minimum 12″ deep, with three rods #4 minimum perim. res. (Miss.). 6 × 6 × 10/10 WWF in slab. (LA. requires four #5 rods and 6 × 6 × 6/6 WWF in slab.)
MAINE			
Auburn	Concrete preferred poured. Frost line 4′0″, plus footing with frost wall.		
Portland	Minimum 10″ foundation walls. Minimum 4′0″ depth of footings.	**MISSOURI**	
Waterville	Frost line at least 4½′ below ground.	Columbia	As long as it meets the code; 30″ frost line.
MARYLAND		Jefferson City	Frost line 30″ minimum, footing 8″ × 16″ minimum, 8″ foundation wall minimum, #4 ∅ rerod 2″ o.c. both ways.
Annapolis	NBC, 1976 edition.		
Hagerstown	Soil and frost.	Kansas City	36″ frost line; also vertical and lateral bearing pressures consistent with clay soils.
MASSACHUSETTS			
Cambridge	All types, spread footings, piles, footings under foundations, "Franki-Piles," wood, etc. Frost line is 4 feet.	Springfield	36″ frost line.
		MONTANA	
Leominster	Reference EPS *Sweets Catalog File* 7.14(d)/So and 7.15(d)/So.	Billings	Concrete foundations with bottom of footings at 36″ to 42″ below finish grade. Treated wood or concrete block in rural areas.
New Bedford	Minimum depth foundation 4 feet below grade.		
Springfield	Depends on what section of the counrty the design is for.	Bozeman	While our frost depth can get as deep as 6′, we recommend a minimum 3′ depth of footings. (We have had no trouble in the past 20 years.)
MICHIGAN			
Kalamazoo	None recommended; frost line for foundations is 32″ to 36″.	Great Falls	Frost line recommended no less than 3′0″—42″ to 48″ is more realistic—many requests received for monolithic slabs. Very few block foundations are in use.
Lansing	Wood and masonry foundations system acceptable. 42″ minimum depth.		
Midland	Foundations must extend below the frost line (42″) and must be designed to carry the loads with the soil-bearing condition available.	Helena	Below frost line normally 3 to 4 feet deep.
		Missoula	Frost line 36″, reinforcing steel for seismic zone, clay soils conditions and groundwater.
Mt. Pleasant	8″ × 16″, 42″ deep, 1 story. 12″ × 18″, 42″ deep, two #4 rerod, 2 story.		
Saginaw	Frost line and subsoil drainage, also consideration for lateral resistance to soil loads.	**NEBRASKA**	
		Holdridge and Lincoln	3′ frost line.
		Seward	Must be at least 36″ below finish grade.
MINNESOTA		**NEVADA**	
Albert Lea	Frost line 42″ deep.	Carson City	Concrete spread footings—occasionally piles; frost line 30″ in north to 0 in south.
Anoka	Frost line is 42″.		

Table 15 (continued)

	Foundation and footing to include steel rebar, frost line a must at 24".
Henderson	We have no frost line in this area.
Las Vegas	12" minimum below grade, UBC minimums, or recommedations of soils engineer.
Reno	24" minimum frost line—wood foundation o.k.

NEW HAMPSHIRE

Claremont	Subbase prep, frost 4'–5', reinforce waterproof, and drain to ACA recommendation.
Manchester	Frost line depth 4'-0", footings placed on undisturbed soil of suitable br'g. or controlled fill.
Rochester	Frost line.

NEW JERSEY

Camden	Frost line 36'.
Newark and Patterson	Frost line 3'.

NEW MEXICO

Albuquerque	Frost line—16" below grade.
Carlsbad	Depending on the soils and fills.
Las Cruces	Monolithic slab and footings or stem wall. Some unstable soil requirements in valley lands near river.
Santa Fe	Regional frost lines, footing, widths based on soil compressive strengths.
	24" below frost line in northern part of state and 18" in southern part of state.

NEW YORK

Buffalo	Required minimum depth 4'0" below grade; construction allowed—concrete masonry or piles of all types.
Ogdensburg	Footer and foundation wall 5' below grade, waterproofing and dampproofing—insulation—structural design.
Syracuse	We follow the N.Y. State Building Code for most new construction.

NORTH CAROLINA

Greensboro	Typical foundation below frost line on residential and small commercial buildings.

NORTH DAKOTA

Bismarck	Foundations must go to frost depth or not less than 4' into the ground and normally is of reinforced concrete.
Fargo	Frost depth 60"—soil bearing 2000 psi.
	Depth of foundation at least 5' below grade.
Grand Forks	Concrete block with concrete footings, 5' below grade.
Jamestown	Frost line, unstable soils, changes in water table depths.

OHIO

Akron	Below frost line—soil evaluations—water conditions.
Cincinnati	Runs the gamut.
Dayton	30" minimum depth—16" wide spread footing for residential—other as designed by A/E.

OKLAHOMA

Bartlesville	Pier and footing, 18" to 24" frost line.
Lawton	Monolithic waffle slab and beam design and pier—grade beam.

OREGON

Astoria	Ground freezing is not a factor; however, concrete foundations and insulation of the under floor area techniques are practiced.
	Engineered and stamped by a professional engineer.
Corvallis	UBC—1 story single: 12" minimum below grade. Family dwelling: 12" minimum width footing.
Grants Pass	Standard spread footings normally used.
Portland	12" frost depth—foundation design depends on area/building—soils recommendations vary from 2000 psf to 6000 psf on native soils.
	Chapter 29 and 70 UBC, extend below frost line, engineered if in soils hazard area.
Salem	18" frost line, 2000 psf soil bearing (and greater). Expansive problems in soil not dominant in this area. Some problems in slope stability as construction extends into hill areas.
	See UBC, Chapter 29—frost line may be a problem to 24" in eastern Oregon. Some parts of state have expansive soils.
Sweet Home	Minimum one story—12 inches below grade; two story—18 inches.

PENNSYLVANIA

Philadelphia	Concrete footings minimum of 2'6" below grade (frost line) or piles or caissons.
Pittsburgh	Except when erected on hard pan or solid rock, foundations shall be at least 3 feet below grade.
York	Frost line 36" with the footer and 10" concrete blocks for foundation.

RHODE ISLAND

Providence	4' below grade for all foundations, engineering calculations required and test borings.

SOUTH CAROLINA

Charleston	We require foundations to be designed in accordance with section 1302 and 1303 of Standard Building Code.

Table 15 (continued)

SOUTH DAKOTA

Aberdeen — 4' frost line requires minimum depth of 4 for footing.

Rapid City — Minimum footing depth for bearing walls or columns is 42 inches below grade. Grade beams with piers are sometimes used and also below frost.

TENNESSEE

Jackson — Frost line—13".

Knoxville — Frost line—adaptation to various soils.

Nashville — Soils have excellent load bearing for light construction, limestone rock foundation for heavier construction, 12" frost line acceptable.

TEXAS

Austin — Foundations over fill or clay soil; drilled and underframed piers. Other: slab foundation with drop footings 12" pier. Minimum penetration of footings into undisturbed soil.

No frost line problem—recommend conventional flat slab and beam or engineered foundation.

Steel reinforced slab foundations with four #4 or #5 rebars in perimeter beams are widely used around the state. Vapor barriers are required in all except more arid areas.

Dallas — Continuous beam and piers or slab with perimeter beam.

Fort Worth — 12" frost line.

San Antonio — Floating slab or piers; for small houses, cedar posts acceptable.

UTAH

Coalville — 30" to 36" frost line. All wood foundations are starting to catch on.

Logan — Maintain footing 2' below grade to top of footing and maintain 6" from mud sill to grade.

Ogden — Ogden has a minimum frost depth of 30 inches. All other foundation design is based on the soils condition.

Provo City — Frost protection—minimum 30". Hillsides have unstable soils and slopes; flatlands have high water table.

Salt Lake City — In our climate, we would desire a minimum of 36" deep foundation. (30" average frost line in Utah.)

Frost line 30". Hillside development with open front face—retaining wall characteristics in the rear.

VERMONT

Burlington — Foundation shall always be built below frost; proper drainage, compaction, and load bearing.

Rutland — Concrete to below frost line.

VIRGINIA

Danville — Require 12" frost line depth to bottom of footing.

WASHINGTON

Aberdeen — Foundation designs for different types of soil conditions.

Bellevue — 12" frost line; concrete.

Des Moines — Frost line and soil bearing pressure.

East Wenatchee — Frost line—18" below finish grade; rebar for seismic zone 2.

Ephrate — UBC.

Seattle — Frost line 12".

Spokane — Continuous footing/foundation wall frost line depth—spread piers.

Tacoma — Table 29-A, UBC or as loads and soil conditions require.

Walla Walla — The conditions dictate design and size.

WEST VIRGINIA

Bluefield — Footer design and placement of reinforcing rods and depth.

Charleston — Any foundation that will carry the load and copes with our 14-inch frost line. Wood foundations are permitted.

Morgantown — Frost line.

Parkersburg — Frost line 18"; foundation design must be in accordance with the Southern Building Code.

WISCONSIN

Eau Claire — All buildings are required to have footings below frost line (48") except those designed for slab.

Green Bay — Full basement of concrete reinforced.

Madison — All footings must be at least 42" below grade.

Milwaukee — Below frost line.

Woodland — Steel reinforcing with all concrete foundations.

WYOMING

Casper — Engineering foundations from soils analysis.

Cheyenne — Minimum as required by the Uniform Building Code with a minimum of 28 inches for frost line.

Cody — Frost depth 48".

Table 16 Additional requirements and recommendations unique to your region.

Question: Are there any requirements or recommendations unique to your region?

ALABAMA

Mobile — Local requirements—hurricane loads and flooding and wave action.

Montgomery — Prairie soild requires floating-type slab or special critical soil design.

Tuscaloosa — All buildings that are heated or cooled must comply with energy "J" of Standard Building Code.

ALASKA

Anchorage — Strict regulations of urethane applications, i.e., 15-minute thermal barrier required on interior surfaces.

Energy conservation by ordinance for *all* structures, based on ASHRAE 90-75, using 10,760 degree day.

Fairbanks — Location of utilities (problems with freeze-ups).

Kodiak — There are none that are particularly unique to Kodiak; we follow the National Standard.

ARIZONA

Page — Energy savings and foundation drainage for split level and basement construction.

Phoenix — Heat of the summer is short, but year dryness presents roof leaks.

Low humidity and extreme temperature variation—poor experience with adhered veneer on exterior.

Tucson — A renewed interest is being shown in unburned clay (mud) adobe construction in this area.

Water drainage problems; "dry rot" potential.

Yuma — We have made no significant alterations to the Building Code.

ARKANSAS

Fort Smith — Due to a high water table, high infestation of insects and unstable soil conditions; we require the soil below concrete floors to be sprayed with insecticide and the concrete to have a waterproofing membrane and reinforced with 6 × 6— 12 Ga. wire mesh.

N. Little Rock — Extensive flood plain area.

CALIFORNIA

Anaheim — Recommendations: Providing decent "general notes" showing all types of materials used and their allowable stresses. Proper use of tables and charts that applies to the material used in construction and design.

Eureka — Most of our jobs get rain during construction. If construction proceeds, much moisture is trapped in areas that are now airtight under energy laws. I feel that, when the exterior is weather-proof, the interior should be dried before adding insulation and closing up.

Glendale — Energy and solar.

Los Angeles — Not necessarily unique, but should emphasize that all plans must be complete, including plot plan, floor plan, foundation plan, structural framing plans, elevations, construction sections, grading details, structural details, and comprehensive structural computations.

Sacramento — California energy standards. Most buildings are up to 3 stories.

COLORADO

Boulder — Mobile home tie-downs.

Brush — In those areas of the city designated as 100 year flood plain areas, we do require prior assurance of adequate elevations.

Colorado Springs — Low water table entices people to use below grade space—most of the time successfully—sometimes not. Backfilling around structures seems to be a common cause of water troubles in these areas.

Denver — Soil report required. Special study for wind pressures when building is over 300' in height.

New state law establishes Energy Conservation Performance Standards. Colorado has no state building code, except for factory-built homes, hotels, motels, and multi-family dwellings in jurisdictions with no codes.

Durango — Snow loads important; foundation also with frost lines and Colorado requirements all attached.

Englewood — Unstable soil problems.

Fort Collins —
a. Expansive soils.
b. Seasonal groundwater problems created by irrigation.
c. Problems with expansion and contraction on built-up roofs or low or flat pitch roofs created by extreme rapid temperature changes.
d. Condensation created by extreme rapid temperature changes.
e. Insulation (energy conservation).
f. Chinook winds—some clocked in excess of 100 mph.

Most of the above are unique to this area.

Golden — Flood plains, geological hazards, and engineered requirements.

Salida — These items are not unique to this area but items that are most often overlooked:
1. Fire protection separation in garage from living area.
2. Fire stops.

Table 16 (continued)

	3. Egress windows in bedrooms. 4. Stair construction (rise and run). 5. Fireplace construction.	**ILLINOIS** Rock Island	Soil slippage on bluff areas along Mississippi River—these areas may require soil test and special designed foundations.
Woodland Park	Special grounding, electrical system, lighting protection.	Springfield	Not unique; however, very strong for fire alarms.
CONNECTICUT Hartford	Connecticut codes adapted from 1978 BOCA has exaggerated wind provision.	**INDIANA** Evansville	Very little that is really unique in any area. Most requirements apply universally.
New Britain	Insulation and snow load consideration is required by our code.	Fort Wayne	All hollow masonry that is to be used below grade shall be filled solid because of soil conditions.
Wethersfield	Upgrade fire ratings in all types of structures.	South Bend	Snow load-increased dead load requirements (NE of Lake Michigan in line of prevailing winter winds).
DELAWARE Laurel	Height limitation in beach areas and various towns.	**IOWA** Altoona	Snow load—30 pounds per square foot, wind load.
FLORIDA Daytona Beach	Rust protection—windows, frame, etc.	Cedar Rapids	Care in designing and placing concrete; care in designing and placing insulation; control of groundwater and infiltration into sanitary sewers.
Miami	Energy conservation requirements, handicapped regulations.		
Pensacola	Flood-proof designs for low lying coastal areas.	Indianola	Soil shift causing many replacement foundations; recommendation—bond beams in blocks as minimum due to these conditions.
Tallahassee	Soil conditions, pipe clay (plastic).		
Tampa	P.T. wood for termites, flood plain alterations, and commercial fire limits.		
GEORGIA Columbus	Occasional high winds (not a coastal region, 200 miles inland).	Mason City	A site plan with setbacks is required before a building permit is issued. Sewer is required for each new structure. Stable soil conditions predominately loam, shale, and limestone rock.
Rome	Must comply with the following ordinances: zoning, flood plain, energy conservation.		
Savannah	This county is subject to 100 year flood plain regulations.	Sioux City	River causes downtown area to be pitted. Shallow basements, waterproofing problems.
HAWAII Hilo	Tsunami hazards—must be considered for building along certain parts of the shoreline.	**KANSAS** Abilene	Our region, I feel, does not have any unique areas; area consists of sandy clay, silty clay, and clay.
Honolulu	Single-wall wood frame construction. However, this is giving way to typical double-wall construction.	Garden City	The following requirements are suggested in the code as supplementations: studding, girders, ventilation, insulation, roofing, concrete.
IDAHO Boise	We have no additional requirements other than those outlined in the UBC. Energy-saving methods/materials, solar heating, data of fire resistance construction, properly designed exiting.	Wichita	Foundation drains required for below grade floors.
		KENTUCKY Ashland	Fire code requirements on buildings, within the fire limits.
Coeur D'Alene	Lumber tables for spans and length are the most easy way for everyone to understand. A 2 × 8 will span so many feet, etc.	Paducah	Humidity is very high.
		LOUISIANA New Orleans	Pile foundations, wind loads, 100 year flood plain, high-rise code, state foam plastic insulation standards.
Moscow	Adequate foundation drainage due to unusual soil condition.		
Nampa	The subwater has a high level in some areas within the city; therefore, basements can't be constructed.	**MAINE** Auburn	Snow loads, wind loads, to be large

Table 16 (continued)

	enough for the unusual weather we have here.	MISSISSIPPI	
Portland	Snow load design requires 0–4 inch pitch to be 50 pounds per square foot, 5–12 requires 40 pounds per square foot.	Gulfport	On concrete block construction, we require ⅝" rods from slab vertical each side of window, door opening, and each corner to top poured beam bent and tied to two rods in top beam. On wood frame construction, hurricane clips and straps required on all rafters to stud-bottom plate bolted to "J" bolts on 5' center. Plywood corners and at each wall intersection.
Waterville	Proper drainage inside and outside of buildings; proper ground elevation of building for drainage.		
		Jackson	Energy conservation.
MARYLAND		Natchez	Emphasize ventilation and insulation, humidity control. Insulation, window selection—size and orientation. Building orientation—roof slope to solar, etc.
Hagerstown	Fire resistive construction.		
MASSACHUSETTS			
Cambridge	Flood hazards.		
Leominster	Reference EPS *Sweets Catalog File* and 7.14(d)/So and 7.15(d)/So.	MISSOURI	
		Columbia	Fire codes, firewalls, party walls, means of egress, major problem area to enforce—dangerous building and rental unit conservation law.
New Bedford	Pushing energy code—insulations.		
MICHIGAN			
Kalamazoo	Nothing unique to the particular region; Barrier Free State regulations are applicable.	Jefferson City	Water proofing foundation walls and drain tiles; energy conservation code.
		Kansas City	Equivalent fluid pressures on retaining walls.
Midland	The groundwater table is high and the foundation (basement) walls need to be protected from water infiltration and a good drainage system must be provided.	MONTANA	
		Billings	Flood plain regulations along Yellowstone River and its tributary creeks (main floor to be 2'–0"+ above 100 year flood plain—no basement recommended). Energy conservation—require insulation, double-glazing, weather-stripping, limited ventilation for 7000–7500 degree-day winters.
Mt. Pleasant	With the energy concern, we have had a great interest in underground homes.		
Saginaw	Vapor barrier considerations of exterior walls and cold ceilings.		
MINNESOTA			
Albert Lea	The State of Minnesota has adopted a statewide building code that is enforced in both urban and rural areas. Enclosed is a list of documents included in the code.	Bozeman	Footing and foundation (some areas have a high water table). Seismic loading for commercial construction (seismic zone 3).
		Great Falls	Almost all builders want to build to foundation minimums without regard to frost depth, using the expansive soils as an excuse; i.e., let the structure float. Lack of or improper code enforcement in the past has made this practice a tradition that is hard to break. Many requests for permits are accompanied by insufficient plans or lack of plans altogether. To hold back costs of construction, builders have taken to drawing their own designs or have contracted draftsmen who design structures with little regard for designing loading and support provisions. As this practice is "allowed" by our city code (exemption of residences from architect or engineer design requirement), it places my department in a position to catch poor structural design as a part of our plan check procedure. Also, little regard is given to designing a structure so that utilities may be installed without cutting into
Brooklyn Park	Energy compliance as mandated by State Energy Code; frost/wind/snow requirement varies due to different designated areas.		
Fairmont	Minnesota State Energy Conservation and handicapped requirements; all major construction projects other than 1 and 2 family require plans and specs designed and stamped by a Minnesota registered architect or engineer.		
Plymouth	Roof load design incorporating drift effect of snow, prestressed panel connections to structural steel.		
St. Paul	40# roof load, 20# wind load energy conservation requirements; i.e., insulation required maximum size of heating equipment, handicapped requirements, and building security requirements.		
Two Harbors	Some type of reinforcing in masonry or concrete foundation wall due to heavy clay soils in area.		

Table 16 (*continued*)

	the structural members. The present "cry" is for the reduction of "excessive" requirements which they (the builders) say increase the cost of construction by 20%. My problem is how to get this minimum of information without someone screaming "bureaucracy." Perhaps in your publication, some time should be spent on the engineering aspect of design.	Jamestown	Continual updates on solar energy wind generators and earth berm housing.
		OHIO	
		Cincinnati	Balconies and porches with riverview (high-density residential occupancy).
		Dayton	Fire districts, historical districts, Ohio requirements.
Missoula	Due to climate, try to avoid low sloped roofs. Weather conditions usually cause periods of thawing and freezing and ice build-up.	**OKLAHOMA**	
		Lawton	(1) Proper insulation; (2) major concern for quality workmanship; (3) proper selection of foundation design—followed up by proper execution of design; (4) solar systems and wind power system should be utilized in this area; (5) underground (or partial) homes and buildings should also be considered.
NEBRASKA			
Lincoln	Materials of construction used must recognize the wide variation we have in both temperature and humidity.		
Seward	Wind design; snow load.		
NEVADA			
Carson City	Heat in summer in south; cold and snow in winter in north; dryness throughout.	**OREGON**	
		Astoria	High winds of 100 mph are not uncommon with heavy rains. Flooding has been a problem but, through planning and development, the flood plain has been taken care of.
	Structural design of roofs for snow loads depending on elevation; wind loads of building over 30' in height.		
Henderson	In some areas of our city we require Type 5 concrete 6 bag mis.		Most of the present structures are many years old and are set on wood pilings.
Reno	Higher than normal wind load requires soils report, with special requirement for high-rise buildings (fire and life safety).	Corvallis	Prime agricultural land (lots of farm-type buildings), mostly on low level flatlands with very high water table. Severe drainage problems, large flood plains, poor bearing soil capacities in middle of Willamette Valley adjacent to Willamette River, which is a major tributary of Oregon. Sanitation problems with individual septic tanks and drainfields with private wells becoming polluted; some landslide hazards with the few hills that we do have. I would like to see easier to use span tables for wood and metal beams, something for the do-it-yourselfers that can be readily understood. Also, need more info for construction of retaining walls.
NEW HAMPSHIRE			
Claremont	Life safety and energy, and statewide barrier free requirements are also in public finishing.		
Manchester	Ground snow load 56 psf, minimum L.L. design. (Flat roof = 45 psf.) Varies with roof pitch.		
NEW JERSEY			
Camden	Normally standardized.		
NEW MEXICO			Expansive soil—requires soil report.
Albuquerque	Energy conservation code mandatory; 4300 degree days.	Portland	Long periods of damp weather—special attention to moisture problems. Also freezing rain and high winds in Gorge areas. Flooding in Columbia/Willamette Basin. Landslides in steep hill sites.
Sante Fe	Adoption of Chapter 53, Energy Conservation Code to the UBC for State of New Mexico in 1977.		
	Flat roof construction details.		Flood plain; hi-rise requirements, Chapter 18, UBC.
NORTH DAKOTA		Salem	Oregon has energy conservation codes which exceed the ASHRAE 90-75 for residential buildings.
Fargo	Use of drain tile where basements are provided.		
	We encourage the use of drain tile. If block is used for a basement wall, it must be at least 10".		Statewide uniform codes developed by State of Oregon, Department of Commerce, Building Codes Division, Room 401, Labor and Industry Building, Salem, OR 97310 for further information.
Grand Forks	Yellow clay with 30" to 36" black loam top soil.		

Table 16 (*continued*)

	Special fire detection requirements for institutional facilities, special area requirements of open plan schools, copies of applicable sections attached.	Provo City	We are one of the few Utah cities that rigorously enforces code requirements and are still fighting the ''good old boy'' and ''village'' attitudes.
Sweet Home	Moisture control, treated wood, ventilation vapor barriers.	Salt Lake City	Utah is Seismic Zone 3. Masonry chimnies are common; however, they are not being built earthquake-proof. The codes, since printed in California, are not specific enough on basement construction. 95% of all homes in Utah have basements. They are being built without inspection, since the code is vague.
PENNSYLVANIA			
York	Enforcing the building, electrical, plumbing, city, and zoning codes would be the most unique to our region.		
RHODE ISLAND		**VERMONT**	
Providence	Statewide building code has been modified to take frost depth, soil bearing, floor loads, energy provision, etc., into account for this area of the country.	Burlington	Architectural design does not often enough take into account the fire requirements due to total building square footage and horizontal separation.
SOUTH CAROLINA		**VIRGINIA**	
Charleston	Flood zone requirement contains seven methods of flood proofing.	Danville	We do not have any unique requirements that require additional design over and above those required by the codes.
SOUTH DAKOTA		Roanoke	Energy requirements rigidly enforced. Handicapped requirements rigidly enforced.
Aberdeen	Recommend high insulation factor, since we are blessed with extreme cold temperature.		
		WASHINGTON	
		Aberdeen	Proper weather protection in areas of high wind and rain, insulation and requirements.
TENNESSEE			
Knoxville	Design for multi-use.	Ephrata	Foundation depth and vertical sizing (plumbing) largely due to frost build-up.
Nashville	Stable soils—12″ frost line—winter weather below freezing—0 seismic zone—four distinct weather seasons: spring, summer, etc.,—moderate winds—light average snow fall—moderate winter.	Seattle	Special fire and life safety requirements and concepts for high-rise buildings. Rehabilitation. More performance-oriented regulations. Seismic zone, soils (slide areas), wind on high rise.
TEXAS			
Austin	Avoidance of unburned clay masonry; more job supervision by responsible designer. The frost line ranges from 15″ to 18″ in the north to negligible in the south (10″ to 12″).	Spokane	Insulation requirements as per State of Washington; architectural barrier requirements for State of Washington.
Dallas	Orientation of structures and long roof over-hang.	Tacoma	Nothing unique but rather all loading conditions can be critical.
San Antonio	Insulation, safety glazing, and termite protection.	**WEST VIRGINIA**	
		Bluefield	Insulation.
UTAH		Charleston	Plenty of reinforcing bars in the footers to accommodate the constant movement of our hillside building sites.
Coalville	Because of heavy snow, we do not like to allow flat roof homes.	Parkersburg	All commercial buildings must be wired in conduit. All new construction must submit drawing to our office for construction codes and zoning.
Logan	Maintain 30″—put elevation on plan to get correct grading for run off.		
Ogden	Residential construction (R-1 and R-3) typically has a basement constructed of concrete. Reinforcing requirements are less than Uniform Building Code in this type of occupancy.	**WISCONSIN**	
		Eau Claire	Thermal performance requirements are included in both codes.
		Woodland	Entire area is old river bottom sand.

APPENDIX 2

PROFESSIONAL AND TRADE ASSOCIATIONS

The following is a listing of professional societies and construction industry organizations of interest to architects:

Acoustical and Insulating Materials Association
215 W. Touhy Ave., Park Ridge, IL 60068

Acoustical Society of America
335 E. 45th St., New York, NY 10017

Adhesive & Sealant Council
1410 Higgins Rd., Park Ridge, IL 60068

Adhesives Manufacturers Association of America
441 Lexington Ave., New York, NY 10017

Air-Conditioning & Refrigeration Institute
1815 N. Fort Myer Dr., Arlington, VA 22209

Air Pollution Control Association
4400 5th Ave., Pittsburgh, PA 15213

Aluminum Association
750 3rd Ave., New York, NY 10017

American Association of Nurserymen
Suite 835, Southern Bldg., Washington, DC 20005

American Bureau of Metal Statistics
420 Lexington Ave., New York, NY 10017

American Concrete Institute
P.O. Box 4754, Redford Station, Detroit, MI 48219

American Concrete Paving Association
1211 West 22nd Street, Suite 727, Oak Brook, IL 60523

American Concrete Pipe Association
8320 Old Courthouse Rd., Vienna, VA 22180

American Concrete Pumping Association
606 North Larchmont Blvd., Suite 4A, Los Angeles, CA 90004

American Hardboard Association
Suite 2236, 20 N. Wacker Dr., Chicago, IL 60606

American Hardware Association
20 N. Wacker Dr., Chicago, IL 60606

American Hardware Manufacturers Association
2130 Keith Bldg., Cleveland, OH 44115

American Home Lighting Institute
230 N. Michigan Ave., Chicago, IL 60601

American Institute of Architects
1735 New York Avenue, NW, Washington, DC 20006

American Institute of Interior Designers
730 5th Ave., New York, NY 10019

American Institute of Kitchen Dealers
199 Main St., Hackettstown, NJ 07840

American Institute of Landscape Architects
501 E. San Juan Ave., Phoenix, AZ 85012

American Institute of Planners
917 15th St., NW, Rm. 800, Washington, DC 20005

American Institute of Steel Construction, Inc.
101 Park Ave., New York, NY 10017

American Institute of Timber Construction
333 W. Hampden Ave., Englewood, CO 80110

American Iron & Steel Institute
150 E. 42nd St., New York, NY 10017

American National Standards Institute, Inc.
1430 Broadway, New York, NY 10018

American Pipe Fittings Association
60 E. 42nd St., New York, NY 10017

American Plywood Association
1119 A St., Tacoma, WA 98401

American Public Health Association
1015 18th St., NW, Washington, DC 20036

American Public Power Association
2600 Virginia Ave., NW, Washington, DC 20037

American Savings & Loan Institute
111 E. Wacker Dr., Chicago, IL 60601

American Society of Architectural Hardware Consultants
P.O. Box 599, Mill Valley, CA 94941

American Society of Civil Engineers
345 E. 47th St., New York, NY 10017

American Society of Concrete Constructors
2510 Dempster St., Des Plaines, IL 60016

American Society of Heating, Refrigerating and Airconditioning Engineers, Inc.
345 E. 47th St., New York, NY 10017

American Society of Landscape Architects

1750 Old Meadow Rd., McLean, VA 22101

American Society of Mechanical Engineers, Inc.
345 E. 47th St., New York, NY 10017

American Society of Planning Officials
1313 E. 60th St., Chicago, IL 60637

American Society of Real Estate Counselors
155 E. Superior St., Chicago, IL 60611

American Society for Testing and Materials
1916 Race St., Philadelphia, PA 19103

American Society of Sanitary Engineering
960 Illuminating Bldg., Cleveland, OH 44113

American Subcontractors Association
402 Shoreham Bldg., NW, Washington, DC 20005

American Walnut Manufacturers' Association
Room 1729, 666 N. Lake Shore Dr., Chicago, IL 60611

American Welding Society, Inc.
2501 N.W. Seventh St., Miami, FL 33125

American Wood Council
5454 Wisconsin Ave., Chevy Chase, MD 20015

American Wood Preservers Institute
2600 Virginia Ave., NW, Washington, DC 20037

Architectural Aluminum Manufacturers Association
1 E. Wacker Dr., Chicago, IL 60601

Architectural Precast Association
825 East 64th St., Indianapolis, IN 46220

Architectural Woodwork Institute
5055 S. Chesterfield Rd., Arlington, VA 22206

Asbestos-Cement Products Association
521 5th Ave., Rm. 2000, New York, NY 10017

Asphalt & Vinyl Asbestos Tile Institute
101 Park Ave., New York, NY 10017

Asphalt Roofing Manufacturers Association
757 3rd Ave., New York, NY 10017

Associated Builders & Contractors, Inc.
P.O. Box 698, Glen Burnie, MD 21061

Associated General Contractors of America
1957 E St., NW, Washington, DC 20006

Associated Schools of Construction
Department of Building Construction
Kansas State University, Manhattan, KS 66502

Association of Collegiate Schools of Architecture
1735 New York Ave., NW, Washington, DC 20006

Association of Women in Architecture
P.O. Box 1, Clayton, MO 63105

Brick Institute of America
1750 Old Meadow Road, McLean, VA 22101

Builders Hardware Manufacturers Association
60 E. 42nd St., New York, NY 10017

Building Congress & Exchange
2301 N. Charles St., Baltimore, MD 21218

Building Materials Research Institute, Inc.
15 E. 40th St., New York, NY 10016

Building Officials & Code Administrators International, Inc.
1313 E. 60th St., Chicago, IL 60637

Building Research Advisory Board

2101 Constitution Ave., NW, Washington, DC 20418

Building Research Institute
2101 Constitution Ave., NW, Washington, DC 20418

Building Waterproofers Association
60 E. 42nd St., New York, NY 10017

California Redwood Association
617 Montgomery St., San Francisco, CA 94111

Carpet & Rug Institute
P.O. Box 2048 Holiday Dr., Dalton, GA 30720

Carpet Wool Council, Inc.
919 3rd Ave., New York, NY 10022

Cast Iron Pipe Research Association
1301 W. 22nd St., Suite 509, Oak Brook, IL 60521

Cast Iron Soil Pipe Institute
2029 K St., NW, Washington, DC 20006

Cellular Concrete Association
715 Boylston Street, Boston, Mass. 02116

Ceramic Tile Institute
3415 W. 8th St., Los Angeles, CA 90005

Color Marketing Group
1000 Vermont Ave., NW, Washington, DC 20005

Concrete Pipe Association, Inc.
1501 Wilson Blvd., Arlington, VA 22209

Concrete Reinforcing Steel Institute
228 N. LaSalle St., Chicago, IL 60601

Concrete Sawing and Drilling Association
606 North Larchmont Blvd., Los Angeles, CA 90004

Construction Industry Foundation
211 E. 51st St., New York, NY 10022

Construction Specifications Institute
1150 17th St., NW, Washington, DC 20036

Continuously Reinforced Pavement Group
180 North LaSalle Street, Chicago, IL 60601

Copper Development Association, Inc.
405 Lexington Ave., 57th Fl., New York, NY 10017

Edison Electric Institute
750 3rd Ave., New York, NY 10017

Electric Heating Association, Inc
437 Madison Ave., New York, NY 10022

Expanded Shale, Clay & Slate Institute
1041 National Press Bldg., Washington, DC 20004

Expansion Anchor Manufacturers Institute, Inc.
331 Madison Ave., New York, NY 10017

Facing Tile Institute
500 12th St., SW, Suite 810, Washington, DC 20024

Federal Housing Administration
451 Seventh St., SW, Washington, DC 20411

Fine Hardwoods Association
666 N. Lake Shore Dr., Chicago, IL 60611

Flat Glass Marketing Association
3310 Harrison Bldg., Topeka, KS 66611

Gas Appliance Manufacturers Association
1901 N. Fort Myer Dr., Arlington, VA 22209

Gypsum Association
201 N. Wells St., Chicago, IL 60606

Hardwood Plywood Manufacturers Association
2310 S. Walter Reed Dr., Arlington, VA 22206

Home Ventilating Institute
230 N. Michigan Ave., Chicago, IL 60601

Illuminating Engineering Society
345 E. 47th St., New York, NY 10017

Indiana Limestone Institute of America, Inc.
Suite 400, Stone City National Bank Bldg.
Bedford, IN 47421

Industrial Designers Society of America, Inc.
60 W. 57th St., New York, NY 10019

Institute of Electrical & Electronic Engineers, Inc.
345 E. 47th St., New York, NY 10017

Institute of Heating and Air-Conditioning Industries
5107 W. 1st St., Los Angeles, CA 90004

Institute of Masonry Research
9013 Old Harford Rd., Baltimore, MD 21234

International Association of Wall & Ceiling Contractors
20 E. St., NW, Washington, DC 20001

International Conference of Building Officials
50 S. Los Robles, Pasadena, CA 91101

International Grooving and Grinding Association
1270 Avenue of the Americas, Suite 2810
New York, NY 10020

International Masonry Institute
825 15th St., NW, Washington, DC 20005

Interprofessional Commission on Environmental Design
917 15th St., NW, Washington, DC 20005

Inter-Society Color Council, Inc.
Rensselaer Polytechnic Institute, Troy, NY 12181

Lightning Protection Institute
2 N. Riverside Plaza, Chicago, IL 60606

Lightweight Aggregate Producers Association
546 Hamilton Street, Allentown, PA 18105

Manufacturing Chemists Association, Inc.
1825 Connecticut Ave., NW, Washington, DC 20009

Maple Flooring Manufacturers Association
424 Washington Ave., Oshkosh, WI 54901

Marble Institute of America
425 13th St., NW, Washington, DC 20004

Mason Contractors Association of America, Inc.
208 S. La Salle St., Chicago, IL 60604

Masonry Institute of America
2550 Beverly Blvd., Los Angeles, CA 90057

Mechanical Contractors Association of America, Inc.
5530 Wisconsin Ave., Chevy Chase, MD 20015

Metal Building Manufacturers Association
Keith Bldg., Cleveland, OH 44115

Metal Lath Association
221 N. LaSalle St., Chicago, IL 60601

National Architectural Accrediting Board
1735 New York Ave., NW, Washington, DC 20006

National Ash Association, Inc.
Federal Bar Building West
1819 H Street, NW, Suite 650

Washington, DC 20006

National Association of Architectural Metal Manufacturers
228 N. LaSalle St., Chicago, IL 60601

National Association of Building Manufacturers
1701 18th St., NW, Washington, DC 20009

National Association of Decorative Architectural Finishes
112 N. Alfred St., Alexandria, VA 22314

National Association of Home Builders
1625 L St., NW, Washington, DC 20036

National Association of Home Manufacturers
1619 Massachusetts Ave., NW, Washington, DC 20036

National Association of Housing & Redevelopment Officials
2600 Virginia Ave., NW, Washington, DC 20037

National Association of Plumbing, Heating,
& Cooling Contractors
1016 20th St., NW, Washington, DC 20036

National Association of Realtors
430 N. Michigan Ave., Chicago, IL 60611

National Association of Reinforcing Steel Contractors
P.O. Box 225, 10533 Main St., Fairfax, VA 22030

National Automatic Sprinkler & Fire Control Association
2 Holland Ave., White Plains, NY 10603

National Builders Hardware Association
1290 Avenue of the Americas, New York, NY 10019

National Building Products Association
120-44 Queens Blvd., Kew Gardens, NY 11415

National Bureau for Lathing & Plastering
938 K St., NW, Washington, DC 20001

National Bureau of Standards
Building Technology, Gaithersburg, MD 20234

National Ceramic Manufacturing Association
53 E. Main St., Moorestown, NJ 20277

National Clay Pipe Institute
1130 17th St., NW, Washington, DC 20036

National Concrete Masonry Association
1800 N. Kent St., Arlington, VA 22209

National Constructors Association
1012 14th St., NW, Washington, DC 20005

National Council of Acoustical Consultants
484 E. Main St., East Aurora, NY 14052

National Crushed Stone Association
1415 Elliot Pl., NW, Washington, DC 20007

National Electrical Contractors Association, Inc.
1730 Rhode Island Ave., NW, Washington, DC 20036

National Electrical Manufacturers Association
155 E. 44th St., New York, NY 10017

National Fire Protection Association
60 Batterymarch St., Boston, MA 02110

National Forest Products Association
1619 Massachusetts Ave., NW, Washington, DC 20036

National Hardware Lumber Association
59 E. Van Buren St., Chicago, IL 60605

National Hardwood Lumber Association
332 Michigan Ave., Chicago, IL 60604

National Home Improvement Council, Inc.

11 E. 44th St., Room 1105, New York, NY 10017

National Housing Conference
1250 Connecticut Ave., NW, Washington, DC 20036

National Housing Producers Association
900 Peachtree St., NE, Atlanta, GA 30309

National Institute for Architectural Education
20 W. 40th St., New York, NY 10018

National Kitchen Cabinet Association
334 E. Broadway, Suite 248, Louisville, KY 40202

National Limestone Institute, Inc.
1315 16th St., NW, Washington, DC 20036

National Lumber and Building Material Dealers Association
1990 M St., NW, Washington, DC 20036

National Lumber Manufacturers Association
1619 Massachusetts Ave., NW, Washington, DC 20036

National Mineral Wool Insulation Association
382 Springfield Ave., Summit, NY 07901

National Oak Flooring Manufacturers Association
814 Sterick Bldg., Memphis, TN 38103

National Ornamental Metal Manufacturers Association
724 Ingleside Shore, Ingleside, IL 60041

National Paint, Varnish & Lacquer Association
1500 Rhode Island Ave., NW, Washington, DC 20005

National Parking Association
1101 17th St., NW, Washington, DC 20036

National Particleboard Association
2306 Perkins Pl., Silver Spring, MD 20910

National Pest Control Association
8150 Leesburg Pike, Suite 1100, Vienna, VA 22180

National Planning Association
1606 New Hampshire Ave., NW, Washington, DC 20009

National Precast Concrete Association
2201 E. 46th St., Indianapolis, IN 46205

National Ready Mixed Concrete Association
900 Spring St., Silver Spring, MD 20910

National Recreation & Park Association
1700 Pennsylvania Ave., NW, Washington, DC 20006

National Retail Hardware Association
964 N. Pennsylvania St., Indianapolis, IN 46204

National Roofing Contractors Association
1515 N. Harlem Ave., Oak Park, IL 60302

National Safety Council
425 N. Michigan Ave., Chicago, IL 60611

National Sand and Gravel Association
900 Spring St., Silver Spring, MD 20910

National Sash & Door Jobbers Association
20 N. Wacker Dr., Chicago, IL 60606

National Slag Association
300 S. Washington St., Alexandria, VA 22314

National Slate Association
455 W. 23rd St., New York, NY 10011

National Society of Interior Designers
315 E. 62nd St., New York, NY 10021

National Society of Professional Engineers
2029 K St., NW, Washington, DC 20006

National Terrazzo & Mosaic Association
716 Church St., Alexandria, VA 22314

National Woodwork Manufacturers Association, Inc.
400 W. Madison Ave., Chicago, IL 60606

Nonprofit Housing Center
2100 M St., NW, Washington, DC 20037

Northeastern Lumber Manufacturers Association
13 South St., Glens Falls, NY 12801

Painting and Decorating Contractors of America
7223 Lee Highway, Falls Church, VA 22046

Perlite Institute, Inc.
45 W. 45th St., New York, NY 10036

Plastics in Construction Council
250 Park Ave., New York, NY 10017

Plastics Pipe Institute
250 Park Ave., New York, NY 10017

Plumbing-Heating-Cooling Information Bureau
35 E. Wacker Dr., Chicago, IL 60601

Porcelain Enamel Institute, Inc.
1900 L St., NW, Washington, DC 20036

Portland Cement Association
Old Orchard Rd., Skokie, IL 60076

Prestressed Concrete Institute
205 W. Wacker Dr., Chicago, IL 60606

Producer's Council, Inc.
1717 Massachusetts Ave., NW, Washington, DC 20036

Red Cedar Shingle & Handsplit Shake Bureau
5510 White Bldg., Seattle, WA 98101

Reinforced Concrete Research Council
5420 Old Orchard Rd., Skokie, IL 60076

Resilient Flooring & Carpet Association Inc.
P.O. Box 11082, Oakland, CA 94611

Scaffolding and Shoring Institute
2130 Keith Building, Cleveland, OH 44115

Society of American Registered Architects
180 N. Michigan Ave., Suite 1710, Chicago, IL 60601

Society of American Wood Preservers, Inc.
1501 Wilson Blvd., Suite 1004, Arlington, VA 22209

Society of Real Estate Appraisers
7 South Dearborn St., Chicago, IL 60603

Society of the Plastics Industry
355 Lexington Ave., New York, NY 10017

Southern Building Code Congress
1116 Brown Marks Bldg., Birmingham, AL 35203

Southern Cypress Manufacturers Association
805 Sterick Bldg., Memphis, TN 38103

Southern Forest Products Association
P.O. Box 52468, New Orleans, LA 70152

Soutern Hardwood Lumber Manufacturers Association
805 Sterick Bldg., Memphis, TN 38103

Southern Pine Inspection Bureau
Box 846, Pensacola, FL 32594

Stained Glass Association of America
3600 University Dr., Fairfax, VA 22030

Steel Deck Institute

9836 W. Roosevelt Rd., Westchester, IL 60153

Steel Door Institute
% A.P. Wherry & Assoc., Inc.
712 Lakewood Center N., Cleveland OH 44107

Steel Joist Institute
2001 Jefferson Davis Highway, Arlington, VA 22202

Steel Window Institute
2130 Keith Bldg., Cleveland, OH 44115

Structural Clay Products Institute
1750 Old Meadow Rd., McLean, VA 22101

Stucco Manufacturers Association
15926 Kittridge St., Van Nuys, CA 91406

Superintendent of Documents
U.S. Government Printing Office, Washington, DC 20402

Tile Contractors' Association of America
112 N. Alfred, Alexandria, VA 22314

Tile Council of America, Inc.
360 Lexington Ave., New York, NY 10017

Timber Products Manufacturers
951 E. 3rd Ave., Spokane, WA 99202

Underwriters' Laboratories, Inc.
207 E. Ohio St., Chicago, IL 60611

Urban Institute
2100 M St., NW, Washington, DC 20037

Urban Land Institute
1200 18th St., NW, Washington, DC 20036

Vermiculite Institute
Board of Trade Bldg., Chicago, IL 60604

Water Quality Association
477 E. Butterfield Rd., Lombard, IL 60148

West Coast Lumber Inspector Bureau
P.O. Box 23145, Portland, OR 97223

Western Red & Northern White Cedar
Association
P.O. Box 2786, New Brighton, MN 55112

Western Red Cedar Lumber Association
700 Yeon Bldg., Portland, OR 97204

Western Wood Products Association
1500 Yeon Bldg., Portland, OR 97204

Wire Reinforcement Institute
7900 West Park Dr., Suite 714, McLean, VA 22101

Wood & Synthetic Flooring Institute
1441 Shermer Rd., Northbrook, IL 60062

GLOSSARY

Adjustable Triangle A triangle made with a movable portion that is calibrated to produce a variety of angular lines.

Anchor Bolts Metal rods, varying in diameter, to join and secure one material to another.

Appliques A transparent or translucent adhesive film used primarily for notes and details.

Axial Load A weight that is distributed symmetrically to a supporting member, such as a column.

Axial Reference Plane The dimensional reference system produces a series of planes. The planes are collectively called the axial reference plane.

Back Hoe A mechanical device used to dig a trench of a specific width and for any length. Used primarily in foundation work or in trenching for underground service such as utility lines, etc.

Balloon Framing A system in wood framing in which the studs are continuous without an intermediate plate for the support of second-floor joists.

Baluster A vertical member that supports handrails or guardrails.

Balustrades A horizontal rail held up by a series of balusters.

Bar Chart A calendar that graphically illustrates a projected time allotment to achieve a specific function.

Base A trim or moulding piece found at the interior intersection of the floor and the wall.

Beam A weight-supporting horizontal member.

Blocking The use of internal members to provide rigidity in floor and wall systems. Also used for fire draft stops.

Blueprint A print with white lines and a blue background.

Break Line A line used to indicate that an object has been forshortened. Two break lines are used to indicate a portion of an object has been removed.

Brick Pavers A term used to describe special brick to be used on the floor surface.

Buck A frame found around doors.

Building Section A cross section through any portion of a building that illustrates a system and structural members for the erection of that portion.

Caisson A below-grade concrete column for the support of beams or columns.

Cantilever A structural condition where a member extends beyond a support, such as a roof overhang.

Cement Plaster Plaster that is comprised of cement rather than gypsum.

Checklist List of items used to check drawings.

Check Print A copy used to review for corrections, errors, or changes.

Column A vertical weight-supporting member.

Column Pad An area of concrete in the foundation for the support of weight distributed into a column.

Composite Drafting The process of making a single drawing by combining a variety of drawings. Usually done by photography.

Computer-Aided Drafting (C.A.D.) The process of programming a computer to draft.

Concrete Block A rectangular concrete form with cells in them.

Construction Documents A set of legal contract documents of drawings and specifications that graphically and verbally describe what is required for a specific construction project.

Contour Line A line that represents the change in level from a given datum point.

Coving The curving of the floor material against the wall to eliminate the open seam between floor and wall.

Cross Section A slice through a portion of a building or member that depicts the various internal conditions of that area.

Cul-de-Sac A curved turnaround with the radius determined by the traffic load, located at the end of a street.

Datum Point Reference point.

Details An enlarged drawing to show a structural aspect, an aesthetic consideration, a solution to an environmental condition, or to express the relationship among materials or building components.

Diazo The process of producing a print using light-sensitive chemicals on bond paper and an ammonia developer.

Dimensions Numerical values used to indicate size and distance.

Dimensional Reference System A system based on a three-dimensional axis. This system produces a three-dimensional matrix to which the plan, section, or elevation can be drafted.

Direct Projection   A drafting term used to describe the process of transferring measurements from a source directly—for example, projecting the width of an elevation directly from the floor plan.

Dowel   A metal or wood cylindrical member used for the joining and strengthening of structural elements.

Drafting Machine   Drafting instrument constructed very much like a human arm on which scales are mounted to draft horizontal, vertical, and angular lines.

Duct   Usually sheet metal forms used for the distribution of cool or warm air throughout a structure.

Easement   The right or privilege to have access to or through another piece of property such as a utility easement.

Eave   That portion of the roof that extends beyond the outside wall.

Egress   A place to exit. The act of exiting a building.

Elevation   The front, side, or back view of a structure.

Eraser Drafting   See **Reproduction Drafting.**

Face of Stud (F.O.S.)   Outside surface of the stud. Term used most often in dimensioning or as a point of reference.

Fascia   A horizontal member located at the edge of a roof overhang.

Finish Grade   The soil elevation in its final state upon completion of construction.

Fire Draft Stop   A member of varying materials placed in walls, floors, and ceilings to prevent a rapid spread of fire.

Flashing   Sheet metal to make a construction joint weathertight.

Floor Joist   Structural member for the support of floor loads.

Floor Plan   A horizontal section taken at approximately eye level.

Flush   Even, level, or aligned.

Flush Overlay   Term frequently found in cabinet making to denote a door that covers the frame of the cabinet itself.

Footing   The concrete base of a building foundation that distributes the weight of the structure on a required area of earth.

Foundation Plan   A drawing that graphically illustrates the location of various foundation members and conditions that are required for the support of a specific structure.

Framing Connectors   Metal devices, varying in size and shape, for the purpose of joining wood framing members together.

Frieze   A decoration or ornament shaped to form a band around a structure.

Frost Line   The depth at which frost penetrates the soil.

Furred Ceiling   The construction for a separate surface beyond the main ceiling or wall that provides a desired air space and modifies interior dimensional conditions.

Generic   Grouping or class. In drafting, used to denote items without using brand names.

Girder   A horizontal structural beam for the support of secondary members such as floor joists.

Glue-Laminated Beams   A beam comprised of a series of wood members glued together.

Guidelines   Light lines used for preliminary layout of a series of drafted lines. Also used for lettering.

Head   The top of a window or door frame.

Header   A horizontal structural member spanning over openings, such as doors and windows, for the support of weight above the openings.

Header Line   Line used to which the typical underside of the header is measured.

Hidden Lines   Dotted lines drafted with long dashes with spaces between them. Used to represent lines that exist but cannot be seen.

Hip Rafter   A rafter that bisects a corner and extends from the top plate to the ridge.

Interior Elevation   A straight-on view of the surface of the interior walls of a structure.

Isometric Drawing   A form of a pictorial drawing in which main lines are equal in dimension. Normally drawn using 30°, 90° angle.

Jamb   The side portion of a door, window, or any opening.

Jog   Offset

Joist Hanger   A metal connector for the end support of floor and ceiling joist.

Key Plan   A plan reduced in scale used for orientation purposes.

Leader Line   Line used from the beginning or end of phrases to point out objects.

Masonry   The construction term for materials such as brick, concrete block, or stone.

Masonry Opening   The actual distance between masonry units where an opening occurs. Does not include the wood or steel framing around the opening.

Masonry Veneer   A layer of masonry units that are bonded to a frame or masonry wall.

Material Designation Lines   Lines used to represent different types of material.

Modules   A system based on a single unit of measure.

Monolithic One-Pour System   A method of poured-in-place concrete construction that is without joints.

Mortar   The mixture of cement, sand, lime, and water that provides a bond for the joining of masonry units.

Nailer   A wood member attached to a steel, concrete, or masonry element for the purpose of connecting other materials with the use of nails.

Net Size   The actual size of an item.

Nominal Size   The call-out size. May not be the actual size of the item.

Office Standards   Standards subscribed to by a single office.

Offset   A jog in a wall.

Overlay Drafting   The process of overlaying a series of drawings on others to produce a finished product. See also **Reprodrafting.**

Pad   Term used for isolated concrete piers.

Parapet   A low wall extending above the roof level.

Paste-up Drafting   See **Reprodrafting.**

Photo-Drafting   The use of photography to produce a base onto which drafting can be done.

Pier   A concrete or masonry pillar for the purpose of a structural support.

Pilaster   A rectangular pier integral with a wall for the purpose of strengthening the wall and supporting axial loads.

Pin Drafting   See **Reprodrafting.**

Pivot Point   The point at which the end of one plane adjoins another.

Planes   Any two-dimensional surface.

Planking   A term for wood members having a minimum rectangular section of 1½″ to 3½″ in thickness. Used for floor and roof systems.

Plan Template   Plastic sheet with various forms in plan view punched out to aid in drafting.

Plan View   A top view.

Plate Height   The distance between the floor and the top of the two top plates above the studs.

Plate Map   A drawing of a surveyed piece of land illustrating boundaries, bearings, dimensions, and location.

Plenum   A predetermined air space for the use of mechanical systems such as heating and air conditioning.

Post-Holddown   A metal connector partially embedded in concrete for the purpose of anchoring down a wood post.

Pouché   To darken areas between lines on a drawing to make them stand out.

Profiling   Darkening the outline of an object to emphasize a specific shape.

Proportional Divider   Device used to transfer measurements from one scale to another.

Purlin   A horizontal beam spanning between trusses or columns for the purpose of supporting roof-framing members.

Rafter   The uppermost structural member found in a roof.

Reference Bubble   Symbol used to coordinate details to their origin.

Reprodrafting   Using reproduction methods as a means to produce drafted documents. Also called eraser drafting, paste-up drafting, photo-drafting, overlay drafting, system drafting, pin drafting, and scissors drafting.

Reproduction Drafting   The process of using any form of reproduction (such as photography) to aid in the drafting process.

Ridge   The topmost point on which two sloping roof planes meet.

Riser   The vertical portion of a stair.

Roof   The top portion of a structure.

Rough Opening   An unfinished opening in preparation for finished frames of doors, windows, and other assemblies.

Schedule   A chart with reference symbols and related information such as that used for windows and door schedules.

Schematic Drawings   Initial drawings usually drawn freehand for relationship studies.

Scissors Drafting   A method which existing drawings are spliced together to form another drawing, or a procedure in which existing drawings are pasted together and photographed. See also **Reprodrafting.**

Screen Drafting   A method of producing a secondary original that has different shades of gray on which new information can be drafted. The new information will stand out because of the contrast.

Scupper   An opening to allow the flow of water from a roof or deck on a structure.

Section   A drawing representing a slice through part of a structure depicting the internal conditions at that location.

Seismic   Pertaining to earthquake forces.

Sepia   Process of producing a print on tracing paper that is coated with light-sensitive chemicals and developed by ammonia.

Setback   A measurement locating the positioning of a building or other structure from a given property line.

Shear Wall   A wall designed to resist lateral forces such as wind or earthquakes.

Sheathing   Individual boards covering interior or exterior framing members, such as roof rafters or wall studs.

Shoe   Usually a small piece of wood found at the intersection of the wall and the floor.

Sight Line   Direction in which one views an object.

Sill   The horizontal member located at the lower portion of a window or a door.

Site Plan   A drawing that graphically illustrates a plot of ground, dimensioned building location, and other construction information required for the site development.

Soffit   The finished underside of a horizontal surface such as a boxed-in eave or floor overhang.

Specifications   That part of the construction documents that verbally identifies the materials and equipment to be installed in a structure.

Stair Tread   The horizontal surfaces of a stair run.

Steel-Reinforcing Bars   Round, deformed steel rods, varying in diameter sizes, for the purpose of strengthening concrete.

Stud   Vertical wood members in a wall.

Stud Line   Surface of the stud, usually the outside surface.

Subfloor   A flooring of unfinished boards or plywood on which a finished floor is to be applied.

System Drafting   See **Reprodrafting.**

Tongue and Groove   Continuous edge of a board that has been milled with a groove on one edge and a tongue on the other for a tight joining.

Topography   A detailed description or a graphic representation of the physical characteristics of a piece of land.

Top Plate   The uppermost horizontal piece in a stud wall.

Topset   A decorative member found on the interior of a structure at the intersection of the floor and the wall.

Tract Drafter   Instrument mounted on a horizontal and vertical track used to draft horizontal, vertical, and angular lines. The pencil is pressed against the instrument and moved with it. This is called tracking.

Transparent and Translucent Film   Film created with light-sensitive chemicals. Can be purchased with an adhesive backing.

Tread   The horizontal portion of a stair.

Tributary Area   An accumulated area directed to a specific point, such as the weight of a floor area directed to a specific supporting column.

Trimmer   Members found around windows, doors, or any openings parallel to the studs, joists, or rafters.

Truss   A framework of members used to support vertical loads over large spans.

Two-Pour System   Term used in concrete construction in which concrete is poured in two extended time periods.

Vellum   Special grade of paper on which working drawings are drafted.

Wainscot   A lining placed over interior walls for protection of the vertical surface and normally less than the full height of the wall.

Western (Platform) Framing   A method of wood framing in which the studs are terminated at each level by two horizontal plates for the support of floor framing at the next level.

Word Processing   The process of typing information into a computer for ease of correction, storage, and recall.

INDEX